The Metaphysics of Practice

The Metaphysics of Practice

Writings on Action, Community, and Obligation

WILFRID SELLARS

Edited by
KYLE FERGUSON
JEREMY RANDEL KOONS

Great Clarendon Street, Oxford, OX2 6DP,
United Kingdom

Oxford University Press is a department of the University of Oxford.
It furthers the University's objective of excellence in research, scholarship,
and education by publishing worldwide. Oxford is a registered trade mark of
Oxford University Press in the UK and in certain other countries

© Kyle Ferguson and Jeremy Randel Koons 2023

The moral rights of the authors have been asserted

All rights reserved. No part of this publication may be reproduced, stored in
a retrieval system, or transmitted, in any form or by any means, without the
prior permission in writing of Oxford University Press, or as expressly permitted
by law, by licence or under terms agreed with the appropriate reprographics
rights organization. Enquiries concerning reproduction outside the scope of the
above should be sent to the Rights Department, Oxford University Press, at the
address above

You must not circulate this work in any other form
and you must impose this same condition on any acquirer

Published in the United States of America by Oxford University Press
198 Madison Avenue, New York, NY 10016, United States of America

British Library Cataloguing in Publication Data
Data available

Library of Congress Control Number: 2022951295

ISBN 978–0–19–286682–0

DOI: 10.1093/oso/9780192866820.001.0001

Printed and bound in the UK by
Clays Ltd, Elcograf S.p.A.

Links to third party websites are provided by Oxford in good faith and
for information only. Oxford disclaims any responsibility for the materials
contained in any third party website referenced in this work.

Kyle dedicates this book to David Rosenthal

Jeremy dedicates this book to Bill deVries

Table of Contents

Editorial Notes ix
Acknowledgments xiii
List of Abbreviations xv
Note on Sources xix

    Editors' Introduction   1

PART 1. THE MORAL POINT OF VIEW

1. Mind, Meaning, and Behavior   61
2. Obligation and Motivation   73
3. "Ought" and Moral Principles   80
4. Science and Ethics   97
5. Reason and the Art of Living in Plato   116
6. Objectivity, Intersubjectivity and the Moral Point of View   138

PART 2. AGENCY AND MORAL PSYCHOLOGY: INTENTIONS AND VOLITIONS

7. Thought and Action   191
8. Metaphysics and the Concept of a Person   220
9. Actions and Events   248
10. Volitions Re-Affirmed   270

PART 3. FREE WILL AND *AKRASIA*

11. Fatalism and Determinism   293
12. Reply to Alan Donagan   319
13. On Knowing the Better and Doing the Worse   351

PART 4. DEONTIC LOGIC, PRACTICAL REASON, AND THE LOGIC OF INTENTIONS

14. Imperatives, Intentions, and the Logic of "Ought"   367
15. Reflections on Contrary-to-Duty Imperatives   421
16. On Reasoning about Values   465
17. Conditional Promises and Conditional Intentions   511

PART 5. MANUSCRIPTS AND CORRESPONDENCE

18. Practical Reasoning	537
19. Practical Reasoning Again	542
20. The Hare–Sellars Correspondence, 1953–1980	570
21. The Binkley–Sellars Correspondence, 1956–1959	615
22. The Castañeda–Sellars Correspondence, 1956–1967	636
23. The Aune–Sellars Correspondence, 1961–1979	659
24. Sellars to Solomon, 28 June 1976	732
Index	737

Editorial Notes

Inclusions and Omissions

Our wish was for this volume to include all of Wilfrid Sellars's major works in practical philosophy, including related correspondence and major unpublished manuscripts. We have done our best to accomplish this, and we have included (in addition to published works) previously unpublished materials from the Wilfrid S. Sellars Papers housed in the Archives of Scientific Philosophy at the University of Pittsburgh, as well as correspondence held in other archives and in private hands. To avoid redundancy, we have made some strategic omissions: We omitted Sellars's letter to Judith Jarvis Thomson (6 June 1979) as virtually all of it appears verbatim in "Conditional Promises and Conditional Intentions" (CPCI). We also omitted "Form and Content in Ethical Theory" (FCET) as most of it appears verbatim in "Objectivity, Intersubjectivity and the Moral Point of View" (OIM). The essay "...this I or he or it (the thing) which thinks..." (I) would merit inclusion, but it appears in Scharp and Brandom's *In the Space of Reasons: Selected Essays of Wilfrid Sellars*. Similarly, "Language, Rules and Behavior" (LRB) might merit inclusion, but it will appear in the companion volume to this one—*Fraught with Ought: Writings from Wilfrid Sellars on Mind, Meaning, and Metaphysics*, edited by James O'Shea, Mahdi Ranaee, and Luz Christopher Seiberth. We did not include essays written during Sellars's graduate or undergraduate career (although many of these are available at the archives).

We only included correspondence on ethical theory where there was a substantial exchange between Sellars and his interlocutor. Thus, the archive contains letters on Sellars's ethical theory from various correspondents (including Kurt Baier and J.J.C. Smart), but as this is intended to be an anthology of writings *by* Sellars (not to or about Sellars), we did not include letters from correspondents to whom Sellars wrote no reply. Further, we omitted much irrelevant correspondence—for example, Sellars and Aune carried on a substantial exchange on the philosophy of mind during the 1960s; this, naturally, falls outside the scope of the present work. Similarly, Sellars and Castañeda's correspondence on "Empiricism and the Philosophy of Mind" (EPM), while extremely valuable, does not find a home in the volume. We also omitted letters that were primarily social (rather than philosophical) in terms of their content.

Standard Paragraph Referencing

In consultation with O'Shea, Ranaee, and Seiberth, we agreed that a standard referencing system would simplify Sellars scholarship. In many cases, Sellars has numbered the paragraphs or sections of his essays, and we use these numbers when citing the article. When Sellars provided no such numbers, we have inserted in brackets (e.g., [5]) the paragraph numbers employed by Jeffrey Sicha, whose Ridgeview Publishing Company editions made Sellars's major works available to generations of scholars. These Sicha numbers are taken from the various Ridgeview editions and from the InteLex Past Masters series. In all cases, we refer to individual sections/paragraphs within an article using the "§" symbol (e.g., AAE §5). We also generally refer to Sellars's articles by their standard abbreviations (see "List of Abbreviations"). Sicha's numbers sometimes deviate from the paragraphs in previously published versions, and we will not be flagging those deviations. For example, the reader will occasionally encounter a paragraph that is not numbered. This happens when Sicha did not number a paragraph, or treated it as continuous with the previous paragraph. For citation purposes, such paragraphs should be treated as part of the preceding paragraph.

Quotation Marks

Sellars is not consistent in his use of single vs. double quotation marks. As Scharp and Brandom note in the introduction to *In the Space of Reasons*, "Sellars sometimes uses single, and sometimes double, quotes, to mention terms" (p. xxv). Following Scharp and Brandom, we have not standardized quotation marks across the various texts or made any changes (except, on occasion, to add missing quotation marks—e.g., when Sellars neglected to insert a closing quotation mark; see "Corrections to the Text" below). Nor did we standardize the placement of punctuation in respect to quotation marks (e.g., by moving periods inside of quotation marks).

Logical Notation

Again, following Scharp and Brandom, we have not modified or standardized the logical notation used by Sellars across the various texts. Very occasionally, Sellars will use periods or colons (instead of or in addition to parentheses or brackets) as scope indicators in logical formulas. None of the formulas in which these appear are very complex, and the interpretation is generally fairly intuitive. For example, in §63 of CDI we see

$$p \bullet p \rightarrow q : \rightarrow q$$

which clearly should be read as

$$(p \bullet p \rightarrow q) \rightarrow q$$

Marginalia

Much of the correspondence contains handwritten marginalia—mostly from Sellars, but also sometimes from his correspondents. The marginalia is often philosophically significant, and we have included all of it in our editorial notes. Sellars's handwriting often borders on the illegible, but we are confident that we were able to decipher all these marginal notes, and if any minor infelicities remain, they do not affect the sense of the text.

Corrections to the Text

Following Scharp and Brandom, we have not attempted to correct or standardize some of Sellars's idiosyncratic or inconsistent writing practices. For example, Sellars had a freewheeling or even libertine attitude toward punctuation, particularly in passages with indented words and phrases. We did not attempt to correct these. Sellars also sometimes employs British (rather than American) spellings and conventions; we have not changed these or tried to impose consistency across different texts. The following are the categories of corrections we did make:

Typos and other minor errors

In this, we have followed the guidance of the *Chicago Manual of Style*[1] and have silently corrected obvious misspellings, minor grammatical errors (such as missing apostrophes), and the like.

More significant errors

We have corrected more significant errors and used footnotes to indicate our corrections. For example, in §37 of "Reason and the Art of Living in Plato" (RAL), the published version reads "eternal"; it is clear, given the context, that Sellars means "external." We have corrected the word and noted the change in a footnote.

---

[1] "Obvious typographical errors and inadvertent grammatical slips may be silently corrected." *The Chicago Manual of Style*, 17th edition, §2.44 ("Compiling a Manuscript from Previously Published Material: Permissible changes to previously published material").

To offer another example, the formal proofs in "Reflections on Contrary-to-Duty Imperatives" (CDI) contain a number of errors (such as incorrect variables, justification lines that refer to the wrong proof line, etc.). We have corrected these and have noted our corrections and indicated what the original text was.

Typesetting and copying errors

The guiding principle for our editorial maxims was loyalty. We aimed for fidelity to the published versions of the texts this volume brings together. However, in some cases, past publication processes produced infelicities: Some errors were introduced into Sellars's publications during the typesetting process or when a revised typescript was being retyped. Some of these errors are significant, involving the omission of parts of sentences and, in the case of "On Reasoning about Values" (ORAV), a sentence and a half plus an entire footnote. We have compared Sellars's published works with the typescripts at the archives, and we have made (and noted) such corrections. In many cases, Sellars's typescripts have guided our correction of the errors discussed in the previous section ("More significant errors"). Trying to infer what Sellars intended to publish based on the extant typescripts is somewhat risky since, in many cases, the archives do not contain the final typescript from which the published article was produced. Thus, we have only made corrections from the typescript when it is obvious that a typesetting error was made (e.g., when the published sentence is incoherent and the typescript makes clear what verbiage was dropped during the typesetting process).

Acknowledgments

The production of this volume has been an immense project spanning many years, and we would not have been able to complete the work without the material support of a number of individuals. First, we would like to thank Robert Brandom, who offered not only encouragement but also unwavering advocacy without which this volume would not be a reality. We must also thank James O'Shea for his pivotal suggestion for this book's creation and brilliant recommendation for its title. We are also grateful to Carole Sargent for her generosity and guidance, which helped us navigate tricky territory on this journey. We also thank Peter Momtchiloff, our editor at Oxford University Press, for giving us the opportunity to produce what we hope will be a valuable contribution to Sellars scholarship.

We would also like to thank Haider Ahmar, our longest-tenured Georgetown University in Qatar work-study student, who assisted with formatting and proofing a number of manuscripts and who also did the initial transcriptions of "Practical Reasoning" and "Practical Reasoning Again." Zain Assaf also transcribed some correspondence we added midway through the project.

Our goal with this volume was fidelity to the published versions of the texts, and we could not have achieved this goal to such an exacting degree were it not for Karen Ingebretsen at Publications Professionals LLC, who did the final comparison proof, ensuring that the essays match the originals in every jot and tittle. We are immensely grateful to her for her tireless work and attention to detail.

Much of the content of this volume comes from the Wilfrid S. Sellars Papers housed in the Archives of Scientific Philosophy, Archives and Special Collections, University of Pittsburgh Library System. We are grateful to many individuals who work at the archives for the gracious assistance they provided both of us over the years. In particular, we would like to thank David Grinnell, Lance Lugar, and Jason Rampelt for their hospitality and their willingness to answer questions and aid us in our search for material for this volume. Jaimie George and Lance Lugar have done a tremendous service to philosophy by processing this collection.

A number of people were generous in corresponding with us, answering our questions, and providing us with documents for inclusion in this volume. These individuals include Bruce Aune, Willem deVries, John Hare, James O'Shea, Jeffrey Sicha, and Jim Stockton. Lionel Shapiro—with his superb knowledge of the Sellars archives—directed us to valuable resources we might otherwise have overlooked and assisted us with interpretive questions and with deciphering some of Sellars's marginalia from the correspondence. We are grateful to Stefanie Dach and Willem deVries for helpful feedback on the chapter summaries in our introduction;

Stefanie also corresponded with us during the revisions process, generously sharing her time and expertise. Nancy Sherman offered us valuable help in translating and interpreting the Greek in one of R. M. Hare's letters to Sellars.

Finally, we thank the Advanced Research Collaborative at The Graduate Center, City University of New York, and Georgetown University in Qatar, both of which provided financial support (in the form of a Knickerbocker Archival Research Grant in American Studies and a series of Faculty Research Grants, respectively) that underwrote much of the work on this anthology (including travel to the archives, the hiring of work-study students, and the hiring of professional editors to double-check our own comparison proofs of the chapters).

Kyle is deeply grateful to Bob Brandom for sponsoring his year as Visiting Scholar in the Department of Philosophy at the University of Pittsburgh in 2016. That was a life-changing year, the most philosophically stimulating of his life, and it allowed the completion of archival work he had begun years before. Kyle would also like to express his appreciation for David Rosenthal, who introduced him to Sellars's work in his legendary seminar, "Quine and Sellars on Thought and Language," and for Stefan Bernard Baumrin, who steered him toward ethics and applied philosophy. Kyle owes a great deal of thanks to Jesse Prinz for supervising his dissertation on Sellars, "Metaethical Intentionalism and the Intersubjectivity of Morals," and to Steve Ross and Catherine Wilson for serving on his committee. Finally, Kyle is endlessly indebted to his parents, Ed and Karen; his brothers, Alan and Daniel; and his most valuable discovery in Pittsburgh, Minyoung Jenny Park. Without their care, concern, and commitment, very little would ever get done and even less would be worth the while.

Jeremy would like to express his gratitude to Bill deVries, without whom Jeremy would not have embarked on this new journey in Sellarsian ethics. In 2015, at a conference on Wilfrid Sellars at Kent State University (where Jeremy presented a paper on Sellars's ethical theory), Bill invited Jeremy to submit a prospectus to Routledge Studies in American Philosophy, the series Bill co-edited. That prospectus turned into *The Ethics of Wilfrid Sellars* (2019), the first in-depth exploration of Sellars's ethical theory, and it set Jeremy's research on a new and fruitful path—one that has led, ultimately, to his collaboration in the publication of this volume. Finally, Jeremy owes his deepest gratitude to his wife, Lucy, who has supported him in every way during the years-long labor that produced this anthology. From transcribing letters, to holding down the fort while Jeremy was doing research at the archives, to her daily willingness to serve as a sounding board, Lucy's unwavering love and support have been Jeremy's greatest source of strength and encouragement during this project.

List of Abbreviations

Books

EPH: *Essays in Philosophy and Its History.* Dordrecht: D. Reidel, 1974.
KTM: *Kant's Transcendental Metaphysics: Sellars's Cassirer Lectures Notes and Other Essays,* edited by Jeffrey F. Sicha. Atascadero, CA: Ridgeview, 2002.
NAO: *Naturalism and Ontology.* Atascadero, CA: Ridgeview, 1980.
PPHP: *Philosophical Perspectives: History of Philosophy.* Atascadero, CA: Ridgeview, 1977.
PPME: *Philosophical Perspectives: Metaphysics and Epistemology.* Atascadero, CA: Ridgeview, 1977.
PPPW: *Pure Pragmatics and Possible Worlds: The Early Essays of Wilfrid Sellars,* edited by Jeffrey F. Sicha. Atascadero, CA: Ridgeview, 1980.
SM: *Science and Metaphysics: Variations on Kantian Themes.* The John Locke Lectures for 1965–66. London: Routledge & Kegan Paul; New York: Humanities Press, 1968. Reprinted, Atascadero, CA: Ridgeview, 1992.
SPR: *Science, Perception and Reality.* London: Routledge & Kegan Paul; New York: Humanities Press, 1963. Reprinted, Atascadero, CA: Ridgeview, 1991.

Articles

AAE: "Actions and Events." *Noûs* 7, no. 2 (May 1973): 179–202. Reprinted in EPH, 189–213.
AR: "Autobiographical Reflections." In *Action, Knowledge, and Reality: Critical Studies in Honor of Wilfrid Sellars,* edited by Hector-Neri Castañeda, 277–93. Indianapolis: Bobbs-Merrill, 1975.
CIL: "Concepts as Involving Laws and Inconceivable Without Them." *Philosophy of Science* 15, no. 4 (October 1948): 287–315. Reprinted in PPPW, 95–123.
CDCM: "Counterfactuals, Dispositions, and the Causal Modalities." In *Minnesota Studies in Philosophy of Science, Vol. 2: Concepts, Theories, and the Mind-Body Problem,* edited by Herbert Feigl, Michael Scriven, and Grover Maxwell, 225–308. Minneapolis: University of Minnesota Press, 1958.
CDI: "Reflections on Contrary-to-Duty Imperatives." *Noûs* 1, no. 4 (December 1967): 303–44.
CPCI: "Conditional Promises and Conditional Intentions (Including a Reply to Castañeda)." In *Agent, Language, and the Structure of the World: Essays Presented to Hector-Neri Castañeda, with His Replies,* edited by James E. Tomberlin, 195–221. Indianapolis: Hackett, 1983.
EPM: "Empiricism and the Philosophy of Mind." In SPR, 127–96.

xvi LIST OF ABBREVIATIONS

FCET: "Form and Content in Ethical Theory." The Lindley Lecture delivered at University of Kansas, Lawrence, KS, 17 April 1967.
FD: "Fatalism and Determinism." In *Freedom and Determinism*, edited by Keith Lehrer, 141–74. New York: Random House, 1966.
FDR: "Fatalism and Determinism." Revised unpublished version of FD. Document 31735062218957, Box 30, Folders 2–4, Wilfrid S. Sellars Papers, 1899–1990, ASP.1991.01, Archives of Scientific Philosophy, Archives & Special Collections, University of Pittsburgh Library System.
I: "... this I or he or it (the thing) that thinks..." *Proceedings and Addresses of the American Philosophical Association* 44 (1970–71): 5–31.
IIO: "Imperatives, Intentions, and the Logic of 'Ought'." *Methodos* 8, no. 32 (1956): 227–68.
IIOR: "Imperatives, Intentions, and the Logic of 'Ought'." In *Morality and the Language of Conduct*, edited by Hector-Neri Castañeda and George Nakhnikian, 159–218. Detroit: Wayne State University Press, 1963.
IM: "Inference and Meaning." *Mind* 64, no. 247 (July 1953): 313–38.
IV: "Induction as Vindication." *Philosophy of Science* 31, no. 3 (July 1964): 197–231.
KBDW: "On Knowing the Better and Doing the Worse." *International Philosophical Quarterly* 10, no. 1 (March 1970): 5–19. The 1969 Suarez Philosophy Lecture delivered at Fordham University. Reprinted in EPH, 27–43.
LRB: "Language, Rules and Behavior." In *John Dewey: Philosopher of Science and Freedom*, edited by Sidney Hook, 289–315. New York: The Dial Press, 1950. Reprinted in PPPW, 129–55.
MMB: "Mind, Meaning, and Behavior." *Philosophical Studies* 3, no. 6 (December 1952): 83–95.
MP: "Metaphysics and the Concept of a Person." In *The Logical Way of Doing Things*, edited by Karel Lambert, 219–52. New Haven: Yale University Press, 1969. Reprinted in EPH, 214–41.
OAFP: "On Accepting First Principles." In *Philosophical Perspectives, Vol. 2: Epistemology*, edited by James E. Tomberlin, 301–14. Atascadero, CA: Ridgeview, 1988.
OIM: "Objectivity, Intersubjectivity and the Moral Point of View." Chapter 7 of SM, 175–229.
OM: "Obligation and Motivation." *Philosophical Studies* 2, no. 2 (February 1951): 21–5.
OMP: "'Ought' and Moral Principles." Unpublished manuscript based on a lecture given at the University of Pittsburgh on 14 February, 1966. Document 31735062220516, Box 36, Folder 8, Wilfrid S. Sellars Papers, 1899–1990, ASP.1991.01, Archives of Scientific Philosophy, Archives & Special Collections, University of Pittsburgh Library System.
OMR: "Obligation and Motivation." In *Readings in Ethical Theory*, edited by Wilfrid Sellars and John Hospers, 511–7. New York: Appleton-Century-Crofts, 1952. A revised and expanded version of OM.
ORAV: "On Reasoning about Values." *American Philosophical Quarterly* 17, no. 2 (April 1980): 81–101.
P: "Particulars." *Philosophy and Phenomenological Research* 13, no. 2 (1952): 184–99. Reprinted in SPR, 60–105.

LIST OF ABBREVIATIONS   xvii

PH: "Phenomenalism." In *Intentionality, Minds and Perception: Discussions on Contemporary Philosophy*, edited by Hector-Neri Castañeda, 215–74. Detroit: Wayne State University Press, 1967. Reprinted in SPR, 60–105.

PR: "Practical Reasoning." Unpublished manuscript. Document 31735062214733, Box 16, Folder 8, Wilfrid S. Sellars Papers, 1899–1990, ASP.1991.01, Archives of Scientific Philosophy, Archives & Special Collections, University of Pittsburgh Library System.

PRA: "Practical Reasoning Again." Unpublished manuscript. Document 31735062222140, Box 43, Folders 1–3, Wilfrid S. Sellars Papers, 1899–1990, ASP.1991.01, Archives of Scientific Philosophy, Archives & Special Collections, University of Pittsburgh Library System.

PRE: "Presupposing." *Philosophical Review* 63, no. 2 (April 1954): 197–215.

PSIM: "Philosophy and the Scientific Image of Man." In *Frontiers of Science and Philosophy*, edited by Robert G. Colodny, 35–78. Pittsburgh: University of Pittsburgh Press, 1962. Reprinted in SPR, 1–40.

RAL: "Reason and the Art of Living in Plato." In *Phenomenology and Natural Existence: Essays in Honor of Marvin Farber*, edited by Dale Riepe, 353–77. New York: The State University of New York Press, 1973. Reprinted in EPH, 3–26.

RD: "Reply to Alan Donagan." *Philosophical Studies* 27, no. 3 (March 1975): 149–84.

SE: "Science and Ethics." In *Philosophical Perspectives*, 389–412. Springfield, IL: Charles C. Thomas, 1967. Reprinted in PPME, 209–32.

SRLG: "Some Reflections on Language Games." *Philosophy of Science* 21, no. 3 (July 1951): 204–28. Reprinted in SPR, 321–58.

SSMB: "A Semantical Solution of the Mind-Body Problem." *Methodos* 5 (1953): 45–82. Reprinted in PPPW, 219–56.

TA: "Thought and Action." In *Freedom and Determinism*, edited by Keith Lehrer, 105–39. New York: Random House, 1966.

TTC: "Toward a Theory of the Categories." In *Experience and Theory*, edited by Lawrence Foster and J. W. Swanson, 55–78. Amherst: University of Massachusetts Press, 1970. Reprinted in EPH, 318–39, and in KTM, 321–40.

VR: "Volitions Re-Affirmed." In *Action Theory: Proceedings of the Winnipeg Conference on Human Action, Held at Winnipeg, Manitoba, Canada, 9–11 May 1975*, edited by Myles Brand and Douglas Walton, 47–66. Dordrecht: D. Reidel, 1976.

Correspondence

CSBA: Correspondence between Wilfrid Sellars and Bruce Aune, 1961–1979. Box 158, Folders 4–5, Wilfrid S. Sellars Papers, 1899–1990, ASP1991.01, Archives of Scientific Philosophy, Archives & Special Collections, University of Pittsburgh Library System.

CSRB: Correspondence between Wilfrid Sellars and Robert Binkley, 1956–1959. Box 158, Folder 13, Wilfrid S. Sellars Papers, 1899–1990, ASP1991.01, Archives of Scientific Philosophy, Archives & Special Collections, University of Pittsburgh Library System.

CSCA: Correspondence between Wilfrid Sellars and Hector-Neri Castañeda, 1956–1967. Box 31, Folders 3–6; Box 159, Folders 2–3, Wilfrid S. Sellars Papers, 1899–1990, ASP1991.01, Archives of Scientific Philosophy, Archives & Special Collections, University of Pittsburgh Library System.

CSRH: Correspondence between Wilfrid Sellars and R.M. Hare, 1953–1980. Box 160, Folder 7, Wilfrid S. Sellars Papers, 1899–1990, ASP1991.01, Archives of Scientific Philosophy, Archives & Special Collections, University of Pittsburgh Library System.

CSDS: Letter to David Solomon, 28 June 1976. Box 166, Folder 3, Wilfrid S. Sellars Papers, 1899–1990, ASP1991.01, Archives of Scientific Philosophy, Archives & Special Collections, University of Pittsburgh Library System.

Note on Sources

1. "Mind, Meaning, and Behavior." *Philosophical Studies* 3, no. 6 (December 1952): 83–95.
2. "Obligation and Motivation." In *Readings in Ethical Theory*, edited by Wilfrid Sellars and John Hospers, 511–7. New York: Appleton-Century-Crofts, 1952.
3. "'Ought' and Moral Principles." Unpublished manuscript based on a lecture given at the University of Pittsburgh on 14 February, 1966. Document 31735062220516, Box 36, Folder 8, Wilfrid S. Sellars Papers, 1899–1990, ASP.1991.01, Archives of Scientific Philosophy, Archives & Special Collections, University of Pittsburgh Library System.
4. "Science and Ethics." In *Philosophical Perspectives*, 389–412. Springfield, IL: Charles C. Thomas, 1967. Reprinted in PPME, 209–32. First delivered as "Ethics and Philosophy" at Old Lyme, CT, 1960.
5. "Reason and the Art of Living in Plato." In *Phenomenology and Natural Existence: Essays in Honor of Marvin Farber*, edited by Dale Riepe, 353–77. New York: The State University of New York Press, 1973. Reprinted in EPH, 3–26.
6. "Objectivity, Intersubjectivity and the Moral Point of View." Chapter 7 of *Science Metaphysics: Variations on Kantian Themes*. The John Locke Lectures for 1965–66. London: Routledge & Kegan Paul; New York: Humanities Press, 1968. Reprinted, Atascadero, CA: Ridgeview, 1992.
7. "Thought and Action." In *Freedom and Determinism*, edited by Keith Lehrer, 105–39. New York: Random House, 1966.
8. "Metaphysics and the Concept of a Person." In *The Logical Way of Doing Things*, edited by Karel Lambert, 219–52. New Haven: Yale University Press, 1969. Reprinted in EPH, 214–41.
9. "Actions and Events." *Noûs* 7, no. 2 (May 1973): 179–202. Reprinted in EPH, 189–213.
10. "Volitions Re-Affirmed." In *Action Theory: Proceedings of the Winnipeg Conference on Human Action, Held at Winnipeg, Manitoba, Canada, 9–11 May 1975*, edited by Myles Brand and Douglas Walton, 47–66. Dordrecht: D. Reidel, 1976.
11. "Fatalism and Determinism." In *Freedom and Determinism*, edited by Keith Lehrer, 141–74. New York: Random House, 1966.
12. "Reply to Alan Donagan." *Philosophical Studies* 27, no. 3 (March 1975): 149–84.
13. "On Knowing the Better and Doing the Worse." *International Philosophical Quarterly* 10, no. 1 (March 1970): 5–19. The 1969 Suarez Philosophy Lecture delivered at Fordham University. Reprinted in EPH, 27–43.
14. "Imperatives, Intentions, and the Logic of 'Ought'." In *Morality and the Language of Conduct*, edited by Hector-Neri Castañeda and George Nakhnikian, 159–218. Detroit: Wayne State University Press, 1963. A revised and expanded version of IIO.
15. "Reflections on Contrary-to-Duty Imperatives." *Noûs* 1, no. 4 (December 1967): 303–44.
16. "On Reasoning about Values." *American Philosophical Quarterly* 17, no. 2 (April 1980): 81–101.

17. "Conditional Promises and Conditional Intentions (Including a Reply to Castañeda)." In *Agent, Language, and the Structure of the World: Essays Presented to Hector-Neri Castañeda, with His Replies*, edited by James E. Tomberlin, 195–221. Indianapolis: Hackett, 1983.
18. "Practical Reasoning." Document 31735062214733, Box 16, Folder 8, Wilfrid S. Sellars Papers, 1899–1990, ASP.1991.01, Archives of Scientific Philosophy, Archives & Special Collections, University of Pittsburgh Library System.
19. "Practical Reasoning Again." Document 31735062222140, Box 43, Folders 1–3, Wilfrid S. Sellars Papers, 1899–1990, ASP.1991.01, Archives of Scientific Philosophy, Archives & Special Collections, University of Pittsburgh Library System.
20. The Hare–Sellars Correspondence, 1953–1980. Box 160, Folder 7, Wilfrid S. Sellars Papers, 1899–1990, ASP1991.01, Archives of Scientific Philosophy, Archives & Special Collections, University of Pittsburgh Library System.
21. The Binkley–Sellars Correspondence, 1956–1959. Box 158, Folder 13, Wilfrid S. Sellars Papers, 1899–1990, ASP1991.01, Archives of Scientific Philosophy, Archives & Special Collections, University of Pittsburgh Library System.
22. The Castañeda–Sellars Correspondence, 1956–1967. Box 31, Folders 3–6; Box 159, Folders 2–3, Wilfrid S. Sellars Papers, 1899–1990, ASP1991.01, Archives of Scientific Philosophy, Archives & Special Collections, University of Pittsburgh Library System.
23. The Aune–Sellars Correspondence, 1961–1979. Box 158, Folders 4–5, Wilfrid S. Sellars Papers, 1899–1990, ASP1991.01, Archives of Scientific Philosophy, Archives & Special Collections, University of Pittsburgh Library System.
24. Wilfrid Sellars to W. David Solomon, 28 June 1976. Box 166, Folder 3, Wilfrid S. Sellars Papers, 1899–1990, ASP1991.01, Archives of Scientific Philosophy, Archives & Special Collections, University of Pittsburgh Library System.

Editors' Introduction

I

Wilfrid Stalker Sellars (1912–1989) was one of the most profound and systematic American philosophers of the 20th century. His writings touched on virtually every branch of analytic philosophy—from metaphysics, to philosophy of mind and language, to philosophy of action and ethical theory. Given the breadth, depth, and complexity of Sellars's work, it is impossible to provide in this brief introduction a comprehensive overview of his philosophical system. Thankfully, there are two excellent books for those seeking systematic introductions: Willem A. deVries's *Wilfrid Sellars* and James R. O'Shea's *Wilfrid Sellars: Naturalism with a Normative Turn*. In addition, Kevin Scharp and Robert Brandom's edited volume, *In the Space of Reasons*, brings together "the papers most important for understanding the core of [Sellars's] synoptic philosophical vision" (2007: vii). The list of major critical studies—monographs, edited volumes, special issues of journals—continues to grow, especially over the past decade.[1] A companion volume—*Fraught with Ought: Writings from Wilfrid Sellars on Mind, Meaning, and Metaphysics*, edited by James O'Shea, Mahdi Ranaee, and Luz Christopher Seiberth—is set to appear in the near future. Ours is a time of renaissance for Sellars studies, and we are just beginning to see the depth of Sellars's impact and the durability of his legacy.

Notwithstanding the range of Sellars's philosophical projects, his philosophical vision was always motivated by a desire to situate persons *qua* practically rational, norm-governed animals within the world as described by an ideal science. Thus, Sellars's overarching philosophical project was to reconcile—via a thoroughgoing nominalism—normativity (and the manifest image of persons in the world more generally) with a science-based naturalistic worldview. This project places practical philosophy at the absolute center of Sellars's concern. In Sellars's magnum opus, *Science and Metaphysics*, he writes,

---

[1] Koons and Loeffler 2023; Seiberth 2021; Brandt and Breunig 2020; Koons 2019; Corti and Nunziante 2018; Garfield 2018; Pereplyotchik and Barnbaum 2017; O'Shea 2016; Olen 2016; Reider 2016; Brandom 2015; deVries, 2010; 2005; Coates 2007; Rosenberg 2007; Wolf and Lance 2007; deVries and Triplett 2000.

Unless and until the "scientific realist" can give an adequate explication of concepts pertaining to the recognition of norms and standards by rational beings his philosophy of mind must remain radically unfinished business. Chapter VII on objectivity and intersubjectivity in ethics is, consequently, the keystone of the argument, for the lectures have stressed at every turn the normative aspects of the concepts of meaning, existence and truth.

(*Science and Metaphysics* [SM], Preface, §§ix–x)

This volume, *The Metaphysics of Practice: Writings on Action, Community, and Obligation*, brings together for the first time the writings that are most important for understanding the core of Sellars's moral-philosophical vision. In his review of *In the Space of Reasons: Selected Essays of Wilfrid Sellars*, deVries wrote, "omitting Sellars's essays on ethics and values is a tremendous pity, for at the very core of Sellars's synoptic vision is the distinction between empirical description and normative prescription" (2008: 861). While we agree, the truth is that in order to do justice to Sellars's moral philosophy, a whole volume entirely focused on this domain of his work is required. Thus, this book makes good on those omissions.

Mastering Sellars's ethical theory is a demanding task, largely because of his systematicity. To encounter any one of Sellars's essays is to encounter many or even all of them. His positions in one sphere of philosophical inquiry intersect with and refract his positions in another. As Scharp and Brandom put the point,

> Rather than each paper functioning as an independent puzzle piece, one typically finds all of Sellars's work reflected in some way in each paper. Although each one focuses on a particular topic, Sellars's points invariably depend on claims and arguments presented elsewhere. In any given piece, arguments and doctrines that appear in detail in other papers often appear compressed almost to the point of unintelligibility. Thus, in a very real sense, one must read a great deal of Sellars's work to understand any one text.   (2007: viii)

Sellars's moral writings are no different in this regard. None is a self-contained, stand-alone essay. Any argument he develops about ethics can only be fully grasped when placed in the broader context of his views on practical reason and the philosophy of action, and these, in turn, only when placed in the broader context of his other work. Although this imposes major demands, the reader now has many tools to aid in this task: As noted earlier, there are comprehensive overviews (deVries 2005 and O'Shea 2007) as well as an in-depth overview and development of Sellars's ethical theory (Koons 2019). The present volume should contribute to making Sellars's practical philosophy—central as it was to his overall philosophical vision—more accessible.

We have three hopes for this book. First, we hope that it will stimulate study of Sellars's ethical theory among Sellars scholars, given its centrality in his overarching philosophical project. Second, we hope that it will stimulate study of Sellars's moral writings among philosophers working in ethics and metaethics. Sellars offers pioneering insights and original answers to a number of very difficult metaethical problems that arose in his time and continue to resist resolution. Many philosophers who work on these problems are unaware of Sellars's contributions to their fields. Third, we hope that this book will provide a service to both groups by collecting in one place and curating Sellars's writings in ethics, metaethics, practical reason, and the philosophy of action. In his review of *In the Space of Reasons*, Scott F. Aikin wrote, "Collections of Sellars's essays existed until now only as binders filled with photocopies from various journals and conference proceedings. Working on Sellars is hard enough philosophically and the paper-chase element was an unwelcome obstacle" (2008: 363). By compiling his moral writings in this volume, and by including with them previously unpublished correspondence from the archives, we aim to enhance philosophers' understanding of and appreciation for Sellars's moral philosophy.

We now turn to a brief rehearsal of the major themes that run through Sellars's moral writings. After introducing these themes in §II, we provide in §III sketches of each chapter this volume comprises.

II

Sellars tells a story about morality that is strikingly both familiar and new, a mixture of recollection and innovation. Sellars's story reminds us of two things we already know about morality before we begin philosophically reflecting on it. First, morality is about what we *do*. Its basic function is to provide practical guidance and standards for evaluating our actions, our lives, and our characters. That is, morality is essentially practical. Second, morality is about what *we* do. The moral "form of life" is livable and is lived only when individuals adopt a social or communal point of view. That is, morality is essentially communal. The moral point of view, as opposed to the private or personal point of view, requires one to think, to care, to act, and to conceive of oneself as "one of us." To be a moral agent is to recognize oneself as a member of the community and to be committed to and concerned about its good and the good of its members. The animating idea in Sellars's story is that morality is a *social practice*.

In *The Grapes of Wrath*, John Steinbeck's omniscient narrator tells us, "This is the beginning—from 'I' to 'we.'" A move from "I" to "we" is also the beginning in Sellars's story about morality. But Sellars's story is not just a story. It is a complex philosophical account, one that embeds the basic idea of morality as a social practice within a naturalistic framework and within his broader philosophical system. This system includes his inferential role semantics and a philosophical psychology containing detailed accounts of intentions, volitions, and practical reason. In the context of this theoretical richness and argumentative labor, Sellars's account of "ought" in thought and language is no mere story; it is a complex and innovative philosophical achievement.

Sellars's master stroke is his ingenious move to identify moral judgments as a species of intentions. According to this thesis, which we might call metaethical intentionalism, moral judgments, when conceived as mental states, are not beliefs or desires or emotions, but *intentions*. Furthermore, moral judgments, when conceived as linguistic behaviors, are verbal expressions of such intentions.[2] In Sellars's account, intentions are mental states that, like beliefs, have conceptual status or intentional content but, unlike beliefs, are action oriented. Paradigmatically, an intention is a practical commitment to do action A in circumstance C. Sellars uses the verb "shall" as a marker of intentions' expression. Thus, when one utters,

"I shall do A in C,"

one verbally expresses the intention to do A in C, which Sellars regiments using a "Shall" operator:

Shall [I do A in C].

Without getting caught up in the details, let us note two important features of Sellars's account of intentions. First, in addition to the paradigmatic shall-do intentions (intendings to), there are shall-be intentions (intendings that), which have the form

"It shall be the case that p,"

and which are regimented using a "Shall be" operator:

Shall be [p].

Second, intentions are uniquely and intimately related to action because of their potential to develop into volitions. A volition is an intention whose time has come. Under the right circumstances, the intention,

I shall do A in C,

can "ripen" into a corresponding volition,

---

[2] Or, at least, this is Sellars's early view. Stefanie Dach (2021) argues that while early Sellars treats ought-statements expressively, Sellars's later writings treat ought-statements metalinguistically.

I shall do A now.

And this volition is the proximate cause or initial stage of the doing of A. Because so many of Sellars's contemporaries rejected the very idea of volitions, it was important for him to distinguish volitions from other kinds of mental event associated with *doings*:

> Notice that volitions are not *tryings*. To try to do A is to do one or more things which one thinks likely in circumstances to constitute doing A. Nor are volitions *choosings*. One can will to do A without choosing to do A rather than something else—even refraining from doing A. Nor are volitions *decisions*: a volition need not be the *culmination of a process* of deliberation or practical reasoning.
> ("Fatalism and Determinism" [FD] §39)

By viewing moral judgments as intentions, Sellars creates an account according to which moral "ought"s are (1) just as meaningful as other kinds of thought that we recognize as meaningful and (2) just as intimately tied to action as other kinds of mental state that we recognize as conative, motivating, or moving. So, intentionalism gives us a moral "ought" that both means and moves.

To better understand the ingenuity and significance of Sellars's intentionalist move, consider the historical and dialectical space in which it was developed. From his earliest major works on ethical theory (e.g., "Imperatives, Intentions, and the Logic of 'Ought'," both the early 1956 version [IIO] and the revised 1965 version [IIOR]), Sellars sought to reconcile competing strands in metaethical thinking of his time. The emotivists, as represented by (for example) A. J. Ayer, recognized that there is an internal connection between moral judgment and motivation. Sellars writes, "to know that there are certain things that one ought to do *is* to have a sense of duty," a view that he claims "smacks of emotivism" (IIOR §2). The chief weakness of emotivism, according to Sellars, is that it denies that moral judgments are cognitive—indeed, it denies that they are really *judgments* at all: Sellars attributes to Ayer the view that "the so-called thought that one ought to do A here and now is not, strictly speaking, a thought at all, but rather a specific way of being moved to do A" (IIOR §5).

By contrast, the intuitionists, as represented by (for example) H. A. Prichard, recognized moral judgments as *cognitive*: Such judgments are capable of truth and falsity, can be involved in valid inferences, and so on. Thus, Sellars writes, "It was the signal merit of intuitionism, particularly of the deontological variety, to have insisted on the uniqueness of prescriptive discourse... and on the truly propositional character of prescriptive statements, as over and against the emotivist contention that ethical concepts are 'pseudo-concepts' and the logic of moral discourse a 'pseudo-logic'" (IIOR §6). The chief weakness of intuitionism is that it denies an internal connection between moral judgment and motivation: Sellars writes, "the epistemological and metaphysical commitments of ethical intuitionism, which precluded it from understanding the logical connection between 'thinking that one ought' and 'being moved to do,' thus forced it to make a mystery both of the conduct-guiding role of moral discourse, and of the uniqueness of prescriptive discourse which it had so happily emphasized" (IIOR §6). Sellars recognizes that what is needed is a theory that combines the strengths of emotivism and intuitionism: "The situation seems clearly to call for a theory which, without denying that ought-statements stand, as such, in logical relation to one another, makes the connection between moral thinking and doing *analytic*, a matter of strict logic" (IIOR §7).

Thus, Sellars carves out a *via media*, a third way that captures what is right about intuitionism and emotivism without committing the missteps of either. Sellars's engagement with these ideas stretches back to his days as a Rhodes scholar at Oriel College, Oxford, from 1934 to 1936. There, he came under the influence of intuitionists Prichard and W. D. Ross just as Ayer's (1936) *Language, Truth and Logic* was published. Decades later, in his "Autobiographical Reflections," Sellars wrote,

> When emotivism appeared on the scene, it struck me as wrongheaded in its early insistence on the pseudo-conceptual character of ethical terms, propositions, and reasonings. And yet I also felt, from the start, that it had located one of the missing ingredients of the solution. Somehow intuitionism and emotivism would have to be *aufgehoben* into a naturalistic framework which recognized ethical concepts as genuine concepts and found a place for intersubjectivity and truth.
> (AR p. 285)

Sellars's metaethical intentionalism, where "ought" is a special case of "shall," reconciles the cognitive aspects of moral judgments on the intuitionist view with the conative, motivating aspects of moral judgments on the emotivist view. Intentions, *qua* states that ripen into volitions, are internally connected to action. But (as later authors such as Michael Bratman have pointed out—see Bratman 1999) we can and do reason among intentions; and so intentions have at least one element needed to be seen as cognitive. Sellars argues that inference among intentions is parasitic on the corresponding indicative. Using "Shall" as an operator to indicate an expression (rather than an attribution) of an intention, Sellars endorses the following basic principle of reasoning among intentions:

If "p" implies "q" then "Shall (p)" implies "Shall (q)"[3]

---

[3] For much of his career, Sellars formulates this as a biconditional. And in ORAV, he writes, "This principle can be formulated as a biconditional, but I forbear to do so lest I open the door to misunderstandings, based on other things I have written, which there would be no time to alleviate"

Sellars makes a number of refinements to his logic of intentions (all the way until "On Reasoning About Values" [ORAV], published in 1980), but this principle (which Sellars calls "S-Imp") remains the fundamental rule governing inference among intentions. Thus, one can reason

> Shall (I make an omelet)
> "I make an omelet" implies "I break some eggs"
> Therefore, Shall (I break some eggs)

Categorizing moral judgments as intentions gives them their practical orientation and their conceptual status. But something else is needed to supply their *communal*, and ultimately *moral*, dimensions. What is needed is an account of the *intersubjectivity* of moral judgments. And this is where the move from "I" to "we"—and back again—is crucial.

Sellars assigns moral judgments the paradigmatic form of we-intentions:

> "We shall any of us do A in C."

Using his "Shall" operator, Sellars regiments the above we-intention as:

> Shall [We, any of us, do A in C]

We-intentions contain at least two dimensions of intersubjectivity. First, we-intentions have intersubjective *content* in the sense that they are universalizable. That is to say, what I ought to do is what any of us ought to do when similarly situated. Second, moral judgments exhibit intersubjective *form* in the sense that they are shareable. Just as two agents can think the same thought, they can agree in their moral judgments, which, in the final Sellarsian analysis, means that they can share the same intention. We-intentions' universalizable content is supplied by the "any of us"; their shareable form is supplied by the "We." This shareability is crucial for moral judgments being truth-evaluable despite their status as intentions. As deVries puts the point, "moral judgments are expressions of intention, but, because of their universality and subjectivity, the vocabulary of 'true' and 'false' is appropriate to them" (2005: 311, n. 8).

Individual intentions are not fully intersubjective: Two individuals cannot have the same intention, nor can two individual intentions contradict each other. If Smith and Jones express the following intentions,

---

(ORAV §47, n. 8). Sellars probably has in mind here, for example, some of the criticisms raised by Aune. See the criticism from Aune (1977) described in *S16* of the Aune-Sellars correspondence in this volume; see also *A17* and *A18*.

SMITH. Shall be (the nations remain at peace)
JONES. Shall be (the nations remain at peace),

then, Sellars argues, these intentions are at best "parallel," but not identical. Sellars's account of we-intentions solves this family of problems. Thus, if Smith and Jones intend as follows,

SMITH. Shall$_{we}$ be (the nations remain at peace)
JONES. Shall$_{we}$ be (the nations remain at peace),

then they are expressing not merely parallel, but *identical*, intentions.

This brings us to a third dimension of intersubjectivity: There is a decision procedure for moral judgments, and some moral judgments are *in fact* true. Because they are intentions, we-intentions are not capable of truth or falsity (which belong to the realm of theoretical reason). But the analog, in practical reason, of truth and falsity is *reasonableness*. Sellars argues that in morality, there is an intrinsically reasonable we-intention: "It shall$_{we}$ be the case that our general welfare is maximized" ("Obligation, Intersubjectivity and the Moral Point of View" [OIM] §120). (Sellars does not give a detailed argument for the intrinsic reasonableness of this we-intention, but he indicates [OIM §§144–5] how such an argument should be developed.) Given this intrinsically reasonable we-intention, S-Imp, and a variety of nomologicals connecting the general welfare to specific actions that will promote the general welfare, we can derive various categorical imperatives as follows (see OIM §§120–1):

It shall$_{we}$ be the case that our general welfare is maximized
"x so acts as to maximize the GW" implies "x does A_i if in C_i"
It shall$_{we}$ be the case that each of us does A_i if in C_i

The conclusion of this syllogism is, according to Sellars (OIM §121), equivalent to

Shall [We, any of us, do A_i in C_i].

We-intentions are fundamentally different from I-intentions such as

Shall [I do A in C].

But ultimately one's moral judgments must be reflected and expressed in one's own actions. That is, one must engage in practical reasoning that takes one from

Shall [We, any of us, do A in C]

to

Shall$_{we}$ [I do A in C].

The latter statement, because it is derived from the intrinsically reasonable we-intention, is therefore *categorically* (although not intrinsically) reasonable. Just as truth is preserved by valid theoretical reasoning, reasonableness is preserved by valid practical reasoning. Thus, there is a *decision procedure* for moral judgments; this secures a crucial final element for intersubjectivity. Sellars argues, therefore, that "categorical imperatives are *derivative general conditional intentions*" (OIM §69).[4]

Of course, just because one holds a moral judgment—even a true one—one is not bound to act accordingly. Intentions, including we-intentions, sometimes fail to ripen into volitions. We are sometimes torn between acting from the personal (Shall$_I$) or communal (Shall$_{we}$) point of view. In "On Knowing the Better and Doing the Worse" (KBDW), Sellars writes,

> One *can* know the better and do the worse; not just from *impulse*, but from self-love, all things considered for what they really are. It is for this reason that genuine moral conflict is imaginatively pictured as a conflict between two persons—one representing inter-personal commitment to one's community, the other, personal commitment to one's own happiness on the whole. At the moment of decision, one or the other of these candidates for an orientation of the self-in-action—each in its own way over-arching—predominates. The choice is, in an important sense, between incommensurables. Which choice one makes is a revelation of what one, at that moment, *is*. It is often surprising, sometimes exhilarating, or disconcerting, even devastating—but always a revelation.
>
> (KBDW §59)

Sellars took his ethical theory to be deeply Kantian. And indeed, in the closing pages of OIM, he writes that his ethical theory amounts to "a thoroughly Kantian metaphysics of morals," comprising:

---

[4] A final note on Sellars's notational devices: In the case of shall-do intentions with the form
   Shall$_{we}$ [I do A in C],
the subscript "we" signals the intention's inferential origin in a we-intention. In the case of shall-be we-intentions,
   It shall$_{we}$ be the case that *p*,
regimented as,
   Shall$_{we}$ be [*p*],
the subscript "we" signals that intention's status as a we-intention.

(a) The conception of a moral polity—Kant's Kingdom of Ends...

(b) the conception of moral principles as universalized maxims—

we would that *anyone* in C_i do A_i

(c) by virtue of the logical relation of 'any' to 'all', the conception of moral principles as implying

We would that *all persons always did* A_i in C_i
(Kant's 'law of nature' formulation)

(d) the conception that there is a common epistemic obligation to accept categorical imperatives

(For categorical imperatives are simply the transposition into the moral framework of scientific truths of the form

(s) (t) '*s* promotes the common good at *t*'
implies 'if *s* is in C_i at *t*, *s* does A_i at *t*'   (OIM §134)

Further, since Sellars thinks that "the concept of oneself as a rational being implies the concept of oneself as a member of an ethical community consisting of all rational beings" (OIM §144), this means that the we-intention to promote the general welfare is binding on one simply in virtue of one's rational agency. Thus, to act on this intrinsically reasonable we-intention is to act *autonomously*, in the Kantian sense: In doing so, "one acts from a premise which does not come into practical reason from without" (I p. 29/§81). Sellars also (FD, "Reply to Alan Donagan" [RD]) develops a fascinating and thoroughly Kantian account of free will, according to which we are from one perspective subject to determinism, but from another perspective free.

Despite these and many other variations on Kantian themes, Sellars's moral philosophy is not merely Kantianism naturalized. It is often difficult to know where Sellars's Kant exegesis ends and the expression of his own views begins. This is especially true in OIM, which was originally titled "Objectivity, Intersubjectivity and the Categorical Imperative." At various places in his moral writings, Sellars displays non-Kantian or even anti-Kantian streaks in his ethical views. In "Science and Ethics" (SE), for example, when considering the question of what justifies moral principles, Sellars writes,

> The only frame of mind which can provide *direct* support for moral commitment is what Josiah Royce called Loyalty, and what Christians call Love (Charity). *This is a commitment deeper than any commitment to abstract principle.* It is this commitment to the well-being of our fellow man which stands to the justification of moral principles as the purpose of acquiring the ability to explain and predict stands to the justification of scientific theories. This concern for others is a precious thing, the foundation for which is laid in early childhood, though it *can* come about, in adult years, through the little understood phenomena of conversion and psychotherapy.   (SE §63)

This suggests that the adoption of categorically reasonable we-intentions, in Sellars's view, might involve less Kantian rational discovery than having the right cares, concerns, attitudes, commitments, and dispositions that result from having had the right kind of upbringing or other psychologically transformative interventions. As Kantian as Sellars's ethical theory is, there are Humean and Aristotelian features to be found at key junctures. The parts of us that Kant excludes from his account of moral agency are, for Sellars, features of persons that lead them to endorse, share, and find justification for "categorically reasonable" intentions.

In yet another example, when Sellars reintroduces the concept of we-intentions in "Thought and Action" (TA), he credits not Kant but Hegel with providing the theme:

> The theme is an Hegelian one in modern dress, a transposition into another key of his concept of Objective Spirit. It concerns the relation of "we" to "I" and postulates a form of thought which is intending *as one of us*.... The point is *not* that groups can, in a legitimate sense, be said to intend. It is the more radical one that individuals can intend *sub specie communitatis*. (TA §§68–9)

Finally, Sellars's ethical theory is deeply integrated into his larger set of philosophical commitments. Crucially, Sellars sees nominalism as a way to avoid what Huw Price (2013, Chapter 1.2) calls "placement problems" with normative discourse. Famously, Sellars denies that (for example) meaning-talk is relational; his account of meaning-talk avoids ontological commitment to meanings, universals, and so on. His expressive treatment of moral judgments is similarly ontologically modest. But Sellars will always insist that to deny the descriptive nature of normative or semantic discourse is not to relegate it to second-class status:

> Once the tautology "The world is described by descriptive concepts" is freed from the idea that the business of all non-logical concepts is to describe, the way is clear to an *ungrudging* recognition that many expressions which empiricists have relegated to second-class citizenship in discourse, are not *inferior*, just *different*.
> ("Counterfactuals, Dispositions, and the Causal Modalities" [CDCM] §79)

Taken all together, Sellars's writings offers a rich and innovative moral theory that rewards detailed study. This book makes accessible the writings that express this theory. Rather than arranging them chronologically, we have curated Sellars's moral writings by organizing them into five constellations, which form the five parts of this volume. Part 1 contains Sellars's most general accounts and widest-scope visions of the moral point of view, culminating in Sellars's central work in ethical theory, OIM. Part 2 presents Sellars's detailed account of agency and moral psychology, which has at its core his theory of intentions and volitions. Part 3 comprises three chapters in which Sellars applies his views on intentions and agency to philosophical problems about the will—specifically, how to understand the compatibility of free will with determinism, and how to understand the possibility of *akrasia*, which concerns weakness of will or how agents can fail to do what they know or otherwise judge that they ought to do. Part 4 focuses on Sellars's repeated attempts to understand the logic of practical reason, the nature of practical inference, and thus, the nature of moral reasoning. Finally, Part 5 contains manuscripts and correspondence, some never before published, from Sellars and the interlocutors with whom he engaged in long-lasting discussions about these topics.

III

[*Unless otherwise noted, paragraph references (e.g., §15) are to the chapter under discussion.*]

Part 1 The Moral Point of View

1 "Mind, Meaning, and Behavior"

"Mind, Meaning, and Behavior" (MMB) is central to Sellars's naturalism, because here he outlines the exact sense in which the normative and the intentional are reducible to the natural. The central question in MMB is "the Mind-Body problem," viz., "the problem whether intentional concepts relating to minds can be reduced to nonintentional concepts" (§1.23). Sellars argues that the question is ambiguous, as there are two kinds of reducibility. The first is *logical reducibility*, the question of whether intentional expressions ("believes," "intends," etc.) are *definable* in terms of non-intentional descriptions of bodily states. The second is *causal reducibility*, which implies material equivalences (*not* identity statements) between intentional expressions and extensional descriptions of bodily states. (The causal reducibility of "ought" to "is" differs from—and depends on—the causal reducibility of the intentional, so we will return to this later.) An assumption common to ethical naturalists and nonnaturalists is that causal reducibility entails logical reducibility; Sellars's view is that the moral Ought is causally *reducible* but logically *irreducible* to Is. The goal of MMB is to work out the details of the claim that *intentional* vocabulary is causally reducible but logically irreducible, without embracing epiphenomenalist dualism;[5] we then can see what ramifications this conclusion has for ethical naturalism. Sellars approaches the question by asking the sense in which an intentional claim can be *equivalent to* a purely descriptive claim about bodily states. The challenge will be this: Purely descriptive statements about the body will be (as descriptive and hence extensional

---

[5] Sellars addresses this issue at greater length (but not necessarily with greater clarity) in SSMB.

claims) truth-functional. But intentional claims are not truth-functional—"Jones believes it is raining" is "compatible with both the truth and the falsity of 'It is raining'" (§3.12). So at best, we get *material equivalence* between the two, not *identity of sense*. Sellars introduces a hypothetical PM language (after *Principia Mathematica*), in which all base expressions are truth functions. Sellars proposes to grant that modal and other claims essential to descriptive discourse (e.g., "It is unusual that...") can be built up out of claims that are truth-functions. Now consider the following equivalence:

(A) m has A(O) ≡ φb

where "m" is a mind, "A" is a kind of mental act with "O" as its intentional object, "φ" is a PM function, and "b" is the body associated with mind m. This thesis—which Sellars calls Scientific Behaviorism—expresses the *causal reducibility* of the mental to the bodily. This is contrasted with Philosophical Behaviorism, which replaces the above equivalence (≡) with identity (=) and holds by contrast "that the mentalistic expressions of our language can be defined by PM techniques in terms of the basic PM resources of our language" (§3.31)—that is, that the intentional is *both* causally *and* logically reducible to the bodily.

The basic course of Sellars's argument is that—given the constraint that the right side of the equivalence must employ purely truth-functional language—there is no way to cash out "φb" such that it *says* the same thing as does the expression on the left side of the equivalence. As Sellars puts the point, the left-side expression *conveys* the psychological information on the right side—to say "Jones believes that it is raining" implies certain actual behaviors on the part of Jones—but it does not make a psychological *assertion*. Hence, the left- and right-hand expressions are materially (i.e., extensionally) equivalent, but they do not say the same thing. Thus, Scientific Behaviorism is vindicated: Naturalism can commit to causal—but not logical—reducibility of the intentional to the bodily.

For similar reasons, "ought" cannot be logically reduced to "is." As Sellars puts the point in "A Semantical Solution of the Mind-Body Problem" (SSMB), "Whatever users of normative discourse may be *conveying* about themselves and their community when they use normative discourse, what they are *saying* cannot be said without using normative discourse" (SSMB §66/p. 256); he adds in the closing paragraphs of MMB, "That which is *said* by 'Jones ought to pay his debt' could not be said in even an ideal PMese" (MMB §4.111).

The relation among normative vocabularies—and the structure of causal reducibility—should be emphasized here. Sellars is actually working with *two* separate notions of causal reducibility[6]—something he is explicit about in

---

[6] We owe this distinction between causal reducibility$_1$ and causal reducibility$_2$ to Lionel Shapiro, and are indebted to him for the discussion that follows.

SSMB, where he writes, "It would be not only false but self-frustrating to hold that 'believes', for example, occurs in causal explanations only in such contexts as 'Jones believes that he believes that it is raining'. It is clear, therefore, that if our solution of the mind-body problem is to take the form, *mentalistic expressions are causally reducible but logically irreducible to PMese*, we must define the relevant sense of causal reducibility along radically different lines" (SSMB §20/p. 230). Thus, we might call the causal reducibility of the intentional *causal reducibility$_1$*. Mental terms are causally reducible$_1$ in the sense that "every mental event can (in principle) be described in terms of expressions which are definable in terms of bodily states" (§3.6). Moral, epistemic, and other normativity is causally reducible$_2$ in the sense that "obligation enters into the causal order only as an element in the intentional object of a mental act" (§2.222)—for example, via sentences of the form "Jones thinks that he ought to pay his debt" (§2.22, emphasis removed); this is clearly different from causal reducibility$_1$. Thus, the intentional is causally reducible$_1$ to the bodily, and Ought is causally reducible$_2$ to the intentional. Supposing the transitivity of causal reducibility, Ought would then be indirectly causally reducible to "expressions which are definable in terms of bodily states" *via* the causal reducibility$_1$ of Ought.

2 "Obligation and Motivation"

This 1952 essay (a revised version of an article published the previous year in *Philosophical Studies*) represents an early attempt by Sellars to tackle a problem that has bedeviled 20th-century metaethics—namely, how to reconcile the cognitive and motivating aspects of moral judgment. Moral judgment's conceptual tie to action is something that contemporary rationalists failed adequately to account for (in Sellars's view)—and is a feature of moral judgment that motivated error-theoretic accounts such as emotivism (and later arguments such as J. L. Mackie's famous "queerness objection").

Sellars tackles the problem by arguing for a non-relational account of practical vocabulary such as "want" and "ought." The parallel with Sellars's theory of meaning is instructive: It is tempting to construe "'S' means P" as having a relational form: "A r B." But of course Sellars denies that meaning-claims are relational, and this denial is central to his nominalism. Similarly, Sellars denies we should analyze "X ought to do A" as asserting a relation between X and an action or an obligation. Sellars's analysis instead is:

I ought to do X in C =$_{Df}$ *tokens of "Everybody ought to do X in C, and I am in C" tend to evoke my doing X in C.* (§14)

Sellars's analysis is complicated and difficult, but it essentially focuses on different roles that "ought" plays in our moral lives. These roles can be illustrated with reference to the moral syllogism:

Everybody ought to do X in circumstance C
I am in circumstance C
Therefore, I ought to do X.

The first role played by "ought" (§16) is its intralinguistic or narrow conceptual role, as illustrated by its role in the syllogism above. Rationalists—keen to capture the cognitive nature of moral judgment—focused on this role of "ought." However, moral statements "would be empty husks" (§17) without an intrinsic tie to motivation. Thus, in its second role, language learners are trained to be moved by the moral syllogism, such that "ought"-thoughts acquire a conceptual tie to action via the *feeling* of obligation that is inculcated in us by our training in normative discourse.

Sellars offers two clarifications to his account. First, the moral syllogism appears to commit one not only to the existence of objective obligations—something difficult to square with Sellars's nominalism. The moral syllogism might also lead us to think that obligation-talk asserts a relation between a person and an action—indeed, between everyone and the relevant action-type. Sellars offers the suggestion early in the essay that this dual mistake "is essential to the *correct* use of the word 'ought'" (§12). However, Sellars has already offered a non-relational account of ought-talk and argued that we explain the practical element of such talk not by appeal to obligations as such, but rather by appeal to the feeling of obligation. Thus, if we keep in mind this (correct) analysis of ought-talk, we can see that "strictly speaking, it is not true to say that a mistake is involved in the correct use of the word 'ought'" (§21).

Second, Sellars considers that his account might be circular, in that his definition of "I ought" is given in terms of "everybody ought." Sellars points out that, however, the definition only mentions "ought" rather than uses it: It is the *thought* of "everybody ought" that is motivating for (properly trained) individuals. (Compare Sellars's claim from MMB that "obligation enters into the causal order only as an element in the intentional object of a mental act" [§2.222]).

3 "'Ought' and Moral Principles"[7]

In this unpublished essay (dating from 1966), Sellars outlines some themes that will reappear in OIM concerning the nature of the prudential "ought" and its relation to the moral "ought." As Sellars points out, if Jones wants A, and if the corresponding nomological "Bringing about A entails bringing about B" obtains,

---

[7] We have included in this anthology the widely circulated version of this lecture. We are grateful to Bill deVries for sending us a copy of his mimeograph. However, as with many of his works, Sellars continued to revise OMP: A copy with significant notes for revision is housed at the University of Pittsburgh archive (document 31735062220516, box 36, folder 8, Wilfrid S. Sellars Papers, 1899–1990, ASP.1991.01, Archives of Scientific Philosophy, Archives & Special Collections, University of Pittsburgh Library System). The revised version of OMP begins at page 20. We thank Stefanie Dach for directing us to this revision of OMP.

we may say, "Jones ought to do B." But this cannot be a moral "ought," for A might be an immoral goal (say, poisoning one's aunt), as might be the means thereto (administering prussic acid). The "ought" of means-end reasoning, Sellars argues, is the "ought" of logical consistency: One cannot consistently intend A but not intend B.

Sellars wishes to investigate whether the moral "ought" can also be an "ought" of coherence. (Compare this discussion to OIM, where Sellars wishes to construct the moral "ought" on the basis of what one wants to do, *all things considered*.) Sellars's first suggestion is that the moral point of view might also involve individual means-end reasoning, where the end in view is the altruistic desire to promote the general welfare. However—and this point also resurfaces in OIM—this cannot generate the moral point of view, because from the standpoint of individual means-end reasoning, coherence doesn't determine a single "ought." Rather, we are confronted with at least two coherent "oughts"—that of self-interest and that of altruism. Each seems to be of similar force, as it is grounded in our individual desires.

The solution, of course, is to locate the moral point of view not in individual means-end reasoning, but in reasoning *as one of us*—reasoning from the point of view of the "we." The moral "ought" can then be an "ought" of coherence because—given the end-in-view of the general welfare and given various nomologicals concerning the promotion of this welfare—disagreements as to how to promote this welfare are in principle resolvable.

Thus, when the moral point of view conflicts with the point of view of rational self-interest, "the tension is between two different *ways of valuing*, not simply between two values which we have from our own point of view" (§46). However, as Sellars suggests in the closing paragraphs, there might in fact be a closer coincidence between the two ways of valuing than first appears; he argues that "the ability to love others for their own sake is...essential to a full life" and therefore that "*really* intelligent and informed self-love supports the love of one's neighbor which...directly supports the moral point of view" (§48).

4 "Science and Ethics"

This wide-ranging essay has two overarching goals: First, it motivates Sellars's expressivism as a solution to the problem of accommodating normative ethical discourse within the framework of scientific realism. Second—and related to the first—in offering an alternative to the positivist-influenced theories of conceptual content, it hints at how such an expressivist theory could (unlike, say, A. J. Ayer's expressivist theory) offer an account of moral expressions as intersubjective and objective.

An important distinction in ethical theory is between the derivation of subsidiary moral maxims from first principles—which is itself merely a matter of consistency—and the justification of the first principles themselves. Sellars argues

(§§35–44) that rationalism—as represented by G. E. Moore—fails to offer a satisfactory account of the justification of first principles. Empiricism—as represented by Ayer—takes the tack of denying that moral terms express concepts or denote properties.

Expressivists like Ayer were on to something, in that moral judgment is inherently tied to *"being positively concerned about"* (§46) the object of judgment. But they were constrained by (among other things) a faulty view of concepts, which only accepted as genuine concepts admitting of empirical verification. By contrast, Sellars argues that "a word stands for a concept when there are good arguments in which it is essentially involved" (§52)—a criterion that can explain the conceptual content of logical connectives, moral judgments, and other non-empirical terms. Crucially, then, moral terms can express concepts even if those terms do not admit of ostensive definition or cannot otherwise be defined according to traditional empiricist criteria.

Earlier in the essay, Sellars has defined a "rational discipline" as "a field of inquiry in which good reasons can be offered for answers to questions belonging to the field" (§19). Crucially, not all rational disciplines are empirical—take mathematics, for example. A subset of non-empirical rational disciplines is formal disciplines—again, like mathematics—where *"truth is a matter of consistency"* (§22).

Putting the pieces together, moral judgments (as expressions of attitudes) express genuine concepts because good reasons can be brought to bear concerning such judgments. Further, these reasons allow us to *vindicate* moral first principles. (Compare John McDowell [1986] and David Wiggins [1990–91] on the notion of a "vindicatory explanation" in non-empirical disciplines like mathematics and morality.) Finally—and this is only implied in SE but is explicitly argued in "'Ought' and Moral Principles" (OMP) and OIM—such vindication involves an appeal to consistency. As Sellars argues in OMP, the moral "ought" is an "ought" of coherence. Thus, by uniting expressivism, an inferentialist theory of conceptual content, a theory of how non-empirical claims can be vindicated, and a theory of we-intentions, Sellars can assert—*pace* Ayer, but consistently with his own scientific realism—that moral claims can be both *objective* and *intersubjective*, while at the same time having an internal connection to action.

5 "Reason and the Art of Living in Plato"

This essay—ostensibly a historical commentary on the "craft" of citizenship in Plato—in fact argues for some central themes in Sellars's practical philosophy and offers some critical insights on his view. According to Sellars, many philosophers have taken theoretical reason as the paradigm of rational activity and have taken practical reasoning to be a derivative (and possibly dispensable) form of reasoning. Sellars's interpretation of Plato's thesis that "the form of the Good is the Form of Forms" is that it is only in light of some practical end that any sort of reasoning is intelligible at all—that rationality essentially includes practical rationality. (Sellars hints early on [§9] at the more radical thesis that rationality essentially entails embodiment, but he does not argue for this stronger pragmatist thesis.)

Sellars's argument starts with Plato's notion of a craft, which involves a "recipe" (possibly a complex one) for producing a product (such as a shoe or a house). Given a determinate description of the end of the craft (and the available ingredients), there are factual principles of the craft telling one how to go about producing this end. To the extent that a group of individuals (say, a guild) creates certain conventions enforced by sanctions, these conventions might guide the craftsman *qua* self-interested person, but only the principles of the craft can guide the individual *qua* craftsman.

Similarly, given an end (that of a satisfying life) and certain "ingredients" for such a life, there are objective principles as to how one ought to live—and these may diverge from positive law. Thus, Sellars will insist on a distinction between the principles of the good life and mere conventions: There are objective principles governing our practical lives *qua* citizens and rational beings; questions concerning how we ought to live are not (solely) a matter of convention.

Crucially, for Sellars, for the world to have an intelligible structure, not all reasoning can concern "instrumentalities"—that is, not all reasoning can involve hypothetical imperatives. There must be a "nonhypothetical practical intelligibility" (§64), one "which gives all instrumentalities their ultimate *raison d'etre*" (§56). Thus, Sellars's reading of Plato is that the Humean conception of reasoning must be false because non-instrumental value must stand at the top of the hierarchy of intelligibility and structure the whole. (Compare "On Accepting First Principles" [OAFP], "Induction as Vindication" [IV], and also §§56ff. of SE, where Sellars argues that the adoption of first principles—whether in theoretical or in practical reasoning—is always itself a *practical* decision.)

6 "Objectivity, Intersubjectivity and the Moral Point of View"
OIM is perhaps the central work articulating Sellars's metaethics. It is also the work that most deeply displays the Kantian roots of this view. It is the culminating chapter of *Science and Metaphysics*, which is itself an attempt to reconstruct the Kantian project of transcendental idealism within the framework of Sellars's nominalism—an attempt, that is, to "naturalize" Kantianism. That Sellars's Kantian "magnum opus" culminates with a chapter (the longest of the entire book) on ethics shows not merely the centrality Sellars assigns to practical philosophy within the Kantian system—it points to how central practical philosophy is to his own philosophical project. Because of the centrality of OIM to Sellars's metaethics (and also because of its intricacy), we will offer a more detailed presentation of its contents than we have for the other essays.

The central problematic of OIM is how to interpret "ought" in terms of "shall." A consistent commitment of Sellars's was that there is no reasoning among imperatives or other candidates for expressivist interpretations of moral discourse, but we can (and do) reason among intention-expressions; this represents a distinct advantage of Sellars's account over other forms of expressivism. Sellars writes that "ethical truths are the projections of 'matter-of-factual' truths... into the framework of intentions and purposes" (SM, Chapter 5, §3). And, of course, one of Sellars's earliest commitments is that inference among intentions is parasitic on inferential relations among their contents (just as inference among beliefs is parasitic on relations among belief-contents). Sellars sees practical reasoning as resting on various nomologicals that state the necessary conditions for an agent achieving an end in a given circumstance (Section VIII/§§49ff.).[8] Thus, valid reasoning among intentions is parasitic on valid reasoning with the corresponding nomologicals.

Sellars's view (that "ought" is a species of "shall"[9]) must overcome a number of related challenges. First, "ought" has both an internal and an external negation, giving us four possible "forms" of ought-judgments:

Jones ought to do A
It is not the case that Jones ought to do A
Jones ought not to do A
It is not the case that Jones ought not to do A. (OIM §26)

Expressions of intentions—"shall"-statements—are not strictly speaking true or false, and hence they have only an internal negation, not an external one. Thus, there are only two possible forms:

Shall [I will do A]
Shall [I will not do A]. (OIM §24)

Second, "ought" statements are intersubjective "in a tough sense"—two people can share the same ought judgment; two ought judgments can contradict each other; and so on. But intendings are egocentric in a way that seems to bar such intersubjectivity. As Sellars writes, "it follows from the absence of an external negation that no one can contradict a 'shall' statement, not even the person who

---

[8] This view of practical reasoning is almost certainly incorrect: As various commentators (e.g., Aune [1977]) have pointed out, practical reasoning more closely resembles figuring out *sufficient* (rather than necessary) conditions for the production of an end. More recent work on Sellars's practical philosophy (e.g., Koons [2019, esp. chapter 6]) aims to correct this defect in Sellars's account.
[9] We are here presenting the "standard reading" of Sellars, according to which moral judgments express a certain kind of intention. Recently, various authors have advocated a "metalinguistic reading" of Sellars's later works (including OIM), according to which "ought" judgments make metalinguistic claims about intentions, or about inferential relations among intentions. Heath White (2009) attributes this view to the Sellars of OIM; Dach (2021) argues at length that while early Sellars (say, of TA) treats "ought" statements expressively, Sellars's later writings treat "ought" statements metalinguistically.

makes it" (OIM §33). Further, two individuals cannot share the same intention. To borrow Sellars's example from ORAV, consider the following pair of intention expressions:

> Jones: Shall be [the nations remain at peace]
> Smith: Shall be [the nations remain at peace]. (ORAV §151)

Sellars writes that "the descriptive content [of these two intentions] is, in a tough sense, the same," but of the intentions themselves, the most we can say is that they are *parallel* (OIM §35).

Sellars begins his approach to truth via the subject of detachment. In investigating moral (i.e., categorical) imperatives, Sellars always begins by discussing hypothetical imperatives (see, e.g., ORAV)—first, because they provide clear examples of practical reasoning, but second because he ultimately (as we will see) wants to build his account of categorical imperatives out of his account of hypothetical imperatives (see §99). If we are confronted with the following hypothetical imperative:

> If I want to poison my aunt, then I ought to administer this packet of prussic acid,

it seems implausible in the extreme (argues Sellars) that the addition of the premise,

> I want to poison my aunt

should allow us to *detach* the consequent of the hypothetical imperative and conclude,

> I ought to administer this packet of prussic acid;

for surely I *ought* to do no such thing! Thus, Sellars interprets hypothetical imperatives as merely expressing implication relations among intentions:

> 'Shall [I poison my aunt]' implies 'Shall [I administer this packet of prussic acid]'

What would allow detachment of a practical "ought"? Sellars returns to the analogy with theoretical reasoning: We can detach the consequent of an implication between *propositions* such as

> 'p' implies 'q'

if the antecedent is *true*. Expressions of intentions are not (Sellars has already conceded) true or false; but is there perhaps an analog for intentions that would allow detachment? Sellars's ultimate answer will be that there is at least one *intrinsically reasonable* intention, and that this allows the derivation of other intentions (and ultimately the detachment of "ought"). But what is this intrinsically reasonable intention?

As is often the case in this dialectic (see, e.g., ORAV), Sellars begins by considering rational egoism, as represented by the candidate valuing

Would that I led a satisfying life. (§65; see also section X/§§66ff.)

In section X, Sellars has us consider Smith, who is guided by a team of scientists (the "Academy"), who teach Smith the various nomologicals related to leading a satisfying life, nomologicals of the form

If I want to lead a satisfying life, I ought to lead a life of kind L
If I want to lead a life of kind L, I ought to do such and such actions (A_i) in such and such kinds of circumstances (C_i) (§§66–7)

Thus, assuming the *intrinsic reasonableness* of the intention corresponding to our candidate valuing (Shall [I lead a satisfying life]), Smith is able to derive (and hence detach) various ought-statements:

I ought to do A_1 in C_1
I ought to do A_2 in C_2
...

just as Smith is able to detach factual consequents in theoretical reasoning, given the truth of the antecedents.

Here, Sellars introduces one of the key components of his theory: the notion that an imperative can be at the same time derivative and categorical. If the intention

Shall [I lead a satisfying life]

is intrinsically reasonable for all rational beings, and if we can derive from the above the following general intention:

(For any t) shall [if I am in C_i at t, I will do A_i at t] (§69)

then the latter is categorically reasonable (because it is derived from an intrinsically reasonable intention) but nevertheless derivative. Thus, Sellars writes, "categorical imperatives are *derivative general conditional intentions*" (§69), and he cautions us not to conflate intrinsic with categorical reasonableness. (See §105 for more on this point.)

Sellars argues (§§72-4) that the standpoint of rational egoism cannot (pace Plato) generate the moral "ought." Nor does it help to suggest that Smith might act from the motive of benevolence:[10] The moral "ought" commands unequivocally, but what one wants to do all things considered is not univocal if one intends *both* that one lead a satisfying life *and* that the general welfare of all people be promoted. Part of the problem seems to be that we cannot construct a univocal "ought" out of "shall" as long as the "shall" in question is an individual intention—a "Shall$_I$." For what I want to do all things considered *from an individual standpoint* will always involve a conflict between the standpoints of egoism and benevolence, and hence any "ought" constructed from this point of view will be equivocal.

All of the above challenges to interpreting the moral "ought" in terms of "shall" can be addressed if Sellars can establish a version of 'shall' that reflects the intersubjectivity of the moral point of view. Such "shall" statements must satisfy (at least) three requirements, which turn out to be related in complex ways:

1) They must apply to all rational agents.
2) They must be capable of something analogous to truth. This would enable different rational agents to entertain the same intention, for different intentions to contradict each other, etc.
3) There must be a decision procedure for deciding what—all things considered—one ought to do. That is, the moral "ought" must be univocal.

Sellars addresses the first requirement in Section XIII (§§81-5). This element is secured by Kant's formalism: "It is a conceptual truth that, to put it roughly, what *one* person ought to do in a situation of a given description, *anyone* ought to do in a situation thus described" (§81). The chief difficulty faced by the Kantian project is that "it is notoriously difficult to supplement this formal consideration with material content" (§81)—a problem Sellars will attempt to solve in Section XXI with his wedding of deontology and teleology. For now, he points out that we should *not* understand the formal requirement as concerning the consequences of "everybody behaving in a certain way in a certain kind of circumstance," but instead in terms of "anybody acting in a certain way in a certain kind of circumstance" (§85). This way of thinking represents an advance over Sellars's early theorizing: Compare "Obligation and Motivation" (OMR), where Sellars argues that essential to the moral point of view is the (mistaken)

---

[10] And of course Sellars will go on to claim that the "point of view of benevolence... is not the moral point of view" (§86) and that intending (from the *individual* standpoint) the general well-being would merely "be expressing a friendly sentiment" (§86).

inference that my doing X is a logical consequence of everyone doing X; Sellars's early view can't account for moral obligation in the case where not everyone does X.

Also relevant for the first requirement is Section XV (§§107–11). Sellars notes "that not all intentions are intentions *to do*. There are also intentions *that something be the case*" (§107). Sellars elsewhere discusses at some length the distinction between "shall-do" and "shall-be" (see, for example, ORAV). Shall-do's allow us to formulate *general hypothetical imperatives*; these, however, seem still essentially egocentric. Sellars points out that "if the existence of one state of affairs causally implies another, then the intention that one obtain causally implies the intention that the other obtain" (§108); this allows us to formulate *general practical implications* (in terms of "shall be the case"). The crucial point here, though, is that while "[general hypothetical imperatives] authorize *each* person to reason *about himself*... [general practical implications] authorize *each* person to reason about *anybody*, including, of course, himself" (§111).

Sellars turns next to the second requirement for intersubjectivity. Truth allows for detachment in theoretical reasoning. The analog of truth in practical reasoning—that which allows practical syllogisms to be not merely valid but "good" (i.e., sound)—is *categorical reasonableness*. But a categorically reasonable intention can be *intrinsically* or *derivatively* categorically reasonable. If

I shall maximize the general welfare

is intrinsically categorically reasonable, and if

"I maximize the general welfare" implies "I do A_i in C_i."

is a true nomological, then

I do A_i in C_i

is categorically—but derivatively—valid.

However, true theoretical propositions can be identical with each other and can contradict each other. But intentions such as "I shall maximize the general welfare" are still "irreducibly egocentric" (§116) and seem to lack this crucial marker of truth. Sellars's solution, of course, is to introduce we-intentions:

TOM: *we* shall do what we can to end the war
DICK: *we* shall do what we can to end the war. (§117)

Sellars argues that such intentions are "in the strongest sense the same... [T]he *intendings* are two in number, but the *content* of these intendings is the *same*"

(117), just as the content of two individuals' beliefs can be identical. Thus, we have the further element of truth-aptness—namely, the possibility of disagreement. Sellars introduces the notations "Shall$_{we}$" and "Shall$_I$" to distinguish between we-intentions and personal intentions.

The third element of intersubjectivity concerns the aforementioned univocity of the moral "ought." Sellars makes two moves to secure this univocity. First, he argues that there is an intrinsically reasonable we-intention, one whose "authority...is more than a mere matter of its being generally accepted" (§132). Rather than merely being accepted, it is (as he describes it) an "intersubjectively valid intention" (§132). The intention in question is

It shall$_{we}$ be the case that our general welfare is maximized.

The intrinsic reasonableness of this intention secures the univocity of the moral "ought" as follows: Given its intrinsic validity, and given various nomologicals of the form

(Our general welfare is maximized) implies (Each of us does A$_i$ in C$_i$)

we can derive (via S-Imp) categorical imperatives of the form

It shall$_{we}$ be the case that each of us does A$_i$ in C$_i$.

Second, Sellars argues that to intend as such is to intend *from the moral point of view*, and not from the personal point of view. Remember, Sellars's view (§§72–4) was that an "ought" constructed out of "Shall$_I$" would be equivocal, as it inherently involved a conflict between egoistic and benevolent intentions. But an "ought" constructed from "Shall$_{we}$" is not similarly equivocal. Thus, the moral point of view delivers a univocal "ought."

As Sellars argues (section XIX), his demonstration that morality satisfies the three requirements for intersubjectivity leads to a further conclusion: "I see no reason why this objectivity should not be said to legitimate the use of the concepts of truth and falsity with respect to ethical discourse" (§133). For the remainder of the section, he enumerates the ways in which the resulting picture amounts "to a thoroughly Kantian metaphysics of morals" (§134). We emphasized at the beginning of this introduction the deeply Kantian nature of this project, and Sellars repeatedly emphasizes this facet of his moral theory in the final sections of OIM. (Interested readers should see "...this I or he or it (the thing) which thinks..." (I) for a further elaboration of this element of Sellars's theory.)

In section XX, Sellars turns to a final hurdle—perhaps the most difficult—for his theory. He has argued for an intrinsically reasonable moral intention:

It shall$_{we}$ be the case that our general welfare is maximized.

But what is the scope of the "we"? Sellars admits that from the considerations he has so far offered, "it in no way follows... that the answer must be 'rational beings generally'" (§137). Thus, Sellars must at least gesture toward an argument that would establish the widest possible scope for the "we."

Here, a comparison with ORAV is useful. At the end of that essay, Sellars introduces the concept of what might be called a "founding intention": It is because various members of the Whooping Crane Society share the intention

> Shall [each of us WCS members promote the survival of whooping cranes] (ORAV §186)

that the society exists in the first place. Were a certain collection of people not to share this intention, there would be no such group as the WCS. Sellars seems to take a similar view of the community of rational beings: Sellars notes that "It is possible... for a rational being to think of himself as a member of [the community of rational beings] even though this community does not actually exist" (§143). But unless there is some sense in which rational beings generally share the intention

> It shall$_{we}$ be the case that our general welfare is maximized.

then the community of rational beings does not exist *qua* group.

In §144 Sellars lays out the major premises for an argument that would establish that all rational beings are rationally committed to endorsing this "founding intention"—the intrinsically reasonable moral intention—and therefore that the community of rational beings is a reality. This intention would be implied by the concept of a rational being as such. "To be sure, this implication need not be recognized" (§144), but as a conceptual matter, each rational being is committed to endorsing this intention. Sellars does not try to establish the truth of these premises, claiming that "it would take all the dialectical skill of a Socrates, a Hegel, or a Peirce to bring [the implication] to the surface" (§144), and he concludes that "the argument for the reality of an *ethical* community consisting of all rational beings... remains incomplete" (§145). Nevertheless, as Sellars makes clear in his later writings (see, particularly, "...this I or He or It (The thing) which thinks..."), he believes that the derivability of the intrinsically reasonable moral intention from the nature of rational agency establishes the Kantian principle that acting morally is acting autonomously, since the moral imperative comes to us from *within* reason.

Sellars concludes OIM with comments (section XXI) on how his model of derivative categorical validity "enables us to see how 'teleological' and 'deontological'

26 THE METAPHYSICS OF PRACTICE

themes are harmonized in Kant's ethics" (§147). The intrinsically reasonable moral intention—It shall$_{we}$ be the case that our general welfare is maximized—is established a priori. But this intention concerns the general welfare of rational beings, and empirical data is necessary for the derivation of particular categorical imperatives, since such imperatives are derived *via* nomologicals of the form "(Our general welfare is maximized) implies (Each of us does A_i in C_i)."

Part 2 Agency and Moral Psychology: Intentions and Volitions

7 "Thought and Action"

TA is one of the early pieces in which Sellars lays out some of the key elements in his theory of action, such as intentions and volitions. (See the summary of "Volitions Re-Affirmed" [VR] for a more detailed explanation of the relation between the two.) Sellars also introduces the notion of implication relative to an assumption, which will be of critical importance to his later work on conditional intentions. Also worth noting is note 4, where he responds to the objection that although he does not allow logical operators outside of the scope of the "Shall" operator, he nevertheless allows sentences of the form "Shall [P] implies Shall [Q]." Sellars's reply is that "the latter, involving the *relation word* 'implies' which is not a truth-functional *connective*, is in the metalanguage, and *mentions* rather than *uses* the shall-sentences" (TA, n. 4, §18).

Much of TA is taken up with an analysis of desire. Sellars wishes to reconcile two features of desire: On the one hand, they are like intentions in that they are conceptually connected to action. On the other hand, they are unlike intentions in that they are conceptually connected to enjoyment or pleasure. Sellars resolves this dilemma by positing the assumption that "there is a conceptual connection between doing (not doing) and enjoying (disenjoying)" (§37); this allows him to derive an account of desire with both features.

The concluding sections (V–VI) are quite packed. In them, Sellars touches on a number of issues: He clarifies the relation of intention to belief; he explains the linguistic role of the "Shall" operator; he argues for a relation between intention and enjoyment that further resolves the puzzle about desire; he clarifies the stages of deliberation (involving intentions),[11] he examines what is involved in acting on

---

[11] A note of guidance here might assist the reader. It might seem that in this particular discussion in section VI, Sellars has committed an elementary logical error, since he claims that

$\sim(\sim E \bullet M_2 \bullet A_2)$

is logically equivalent to

$(\sim\sim E) \bullet \sim M_2 \bullet \sim A_2$

whereas it is instead equivalent to

$(\sim\sim E) \vee \sim M_2 \vee \sim A_2$.

a policy;[12] and he concludes with what he calls some "Hegelian" themes regarding we-intentions and their relation to I-intentions.

8 "Metaphysics and the Concept of a Person"

In this essay, Sellars wants to argue that the *concept* of personhood should be understood along Kantian lines, in that it is neutral as to the underlying substance constituting the experiencing subject. But he wants to reconcile this with an Aristotelian *metaphysics* of the person, according to which the physically embodied person is also the being who thinks. Thus, "it is the same thing,...a *person*, which both thinks and runs." Because of the trenchant critique of traditional agent causation, and the dualism often associated with this view, MP also contributes to Sellars's dialectic on free will (along with FD and RD, the latter of which cites MP and Donagan's response to MP).

Sellars's construal of the Kantian concept of personhood is that "the concept of the 'I' is the concept of that which thinks...and concepts pertaining to mental acts are 'functional'" in a way that "leaves open the question" as to what concretely embodies the "I" (§49). On Sellars's reading, Kant is agnostic about what constitutes—metaphysically—the thinking subject. Kant defends this agnosticism by refuting arguments against various possibilities for the constitution of the "I," showing that these are genuine possibilities and hence that we should withhold judgment. Sellars writes,

> Kant argues, *per contra*, that for all we know, the subject or representer might be:
> (a) an attribute of something more basic
> (b) a system (composite)
> (c) a series.

However, we must recall that in the context of Sellars's example, we are choosing between two options, and each option involves rejecting every conjunct of the other option. Thus, either we choose to do A_1 to bring about E (which also brings about M_1), thus:

Σ_1: E • A_1 • M_1

or we choose to do A_2 to bring about ~E (which also brings about M_2), thus:

Σ_2: ~E • A_2 • M_2.

Since *each* conjunct in Σ_1 individually entails the negation of *each* corresponding conjunction in Σ_2, Sellars is correct in asserting that rejecting Σ_2 in favor of Σ_1 yields:

(~~E) • ~M_2 • ~A_2.

Unfortunately, he doesn't render the above line of reasoning very perspicuously.

[12] In TA, he argues that "the intendings which manifest a policy are *underivative* intendings" (§63). This may conflict with his later view (OIM, chapter 6 of this volume), where Sellars argues that an intention can be *categorically* but *derivatively* valid. If so, this would not be the only claim from TA that Sellars had cause to revisit: In VR, he explicitly repudiates his argument from TA (§18) that there is no valid inference from "Shall [A], Shall [B]" to "Shall [A • B]."

Much of the middle part of MP is devoted to a careful reconstruction of the Kantian arguments showing that each of these is, in fact, a live possibility; this shores up the Kantian position that we must define personhood functionally and not in terms of the underlying material or substance.

Alongside the Kantian concept of personhood, Sellars defends the metaphysical thesis that persons are revealed to us (by modern postulational science) as constituted by swarms of microparticles. This swarm constitutes the being "which both thinks and runs," per Sellars's Aristotelian metaphysics. Sellars's view is that this is entirely consistent with the Kantian insight: As he writes in "Phenomenalism," "The idea that persons 'really are' such multiplicities does not require that concepts pertaining to persons be analysable into concepts pertaining to sets of logical subjects. Persons may 'really be' bundles, but the concept of a person is not the concept of a bundle" (PH §95/p. 101).

Sellars's defense of the Aristotelian view requires defending a certain construal of action- and intentional-attributions. There is perhaps a temptation to read claims such as:

Tom has a feeling

and

Tom dances a waltz

as asserting a relation between a person (*qua* substance) and a separate entity (a thought or an action). But Sellars argues that this conclusion mistakenly takes *event-talk* as basic—it takes the verb ("has," "dances") as asserting a relation between two items—when clearly event-talk is parasitic on talk about substances and what they are doing. Thus, claims of the form

X does V

are parasitic on claims of the form

X Vs

and so the above claims are merely different ways of asserting:

Tom feels

and

Tom waltzes.

Thus, we arrive at the Aristotelian view that it is the same person who both thinks/feels and dances, because these acts are modifications of the underlying "bundle" which constitutes the physical person. (Sellars does qualify his view by saying that this may only be true of "minimal actions"; non-minimal actions may perspicuously be represented as involving a causal relation between a person and an action.)

9 "Actions and Events"

On the face of it, "Actions and Events" (AAE) is a contribution to the debate over whether reasons can be causes. We can also understand AAE as articulating Sellars's view on the connection between practical judgment and action—including the connection between moral judgment and action. To use Ernest Nagel's example (§18), in the case of a person who believes A, who believes that A implies B, and believes B on the grounds that A, the belief that-A is both the *reason for* and the *cause of* the belief that-B. Sellars wishes to articulate a position according to which (contra Nagel) the connection between the two beliefs ("the causal sequence") is not merely logically contingent (even though in fact one can believe A, believe that A entails B, and yet fail to believe B).

First, all language transitions—whether language-entry, language-language, or language-exist—are for Sellars "cases of association," learned (as Sellars puts the point in "Language, Rules, and Behavior" [LRB]) "in a way which is essentially identical with that in which the dog learns to sit up when I snap my fingers" (LRB §15/p. 137). What distinguishes inference (and, in general, rational norm-guided behavior) from mere association is that rational animals can *reason* about these transitions in a metalanguage. It is because I can reason:

A
A implies B
Therefore, B

that the thought that-A is not merely the *associative cause* of the thought that-B, but is also (in rational animals such as myself) the *reason* for the thought that-B. This is the sense in which reasons can be causes. (The idea that the "superstructure" of metalinguistic activity sits atop our associative behavior and meshes in with it, transforming its character, is developed by Sellars in a number of other writings, mostly notably LRB and "Some Reflections on Language Games" [SRLG].)

Key to Sellars's meshing of the normative and the causal here is his claim that "when we characterize a person's utterance by using a quotation, we are implying that the utterance is an instance of a certain way of functioning" (§29). To characterize something functionally is to imply a range of normative claims—there is a right and a wrong way for it to behave—but it also implies certain regularities in its behavior. (This relates to what James O'Shea [2007, p. 138] calls the "norm-nature metaprinciple.") "For example," Sellars writes, "it would be absurd to say:

> Tom said (as contrasted with *uttered the noises*) 'It is not raining' but has no propensity to avoid saying 'it is raining and it is not raining.'"

These themes relate to practical reasoning because just as there is a conceptual connection between thinking that-A and thinking that-B (when one also thinks that A implies B), there is a conceptual connection between intending and action. As Sellars puts the point (§§44–6), we cannot treat a child's making of the sound "shall" as a *saying* until the child has required a propensity to perform the corresponding action. There is, to be sure, only a contingent connection between the *sound* "shall" and any given action. But, as Sellars writes, "When redescribed, however, as a *saying* of 'I shall now raise my hand,' the connection becomes a conceptual one, for it is a conceptual truth that *ceteris paribus* a saying or proximate propensity to say 'I shall *now* raise my hand' is followed by a raising of one's hand" (§45). As moral judgments are expressions of intentions, there is then a conceptual connection between moral judgment and action. This is, of course, how Sellars preserves the key insight of the emotivists—that moral judgment is internally or conceptually connected to action.

Sellars concludes AAE by arguing that "events are a species of proposition" (§58)—that all claims about events can be reconstructed in terms of "that"-clauses asserting that a particular proposition is true. This move is necessary for Sellars to defend his claim—made in the opening sections of AAE—that "causal connection is a species of logical implication or entailment" (§2); a defense of this theory requires that we be able to reconstruct event-talk in terms of propositions, which can then be placed in relations of logical implication (expressed by material rules of inference).

10 "Volitions Re-Affirmed"

In this relatively late piece (it was presented at a conference in 1975 and published in 1976), Sellars seeks to clarify the concept of a volition as it appears in his practical philosophy and also to resolve some obscurities concerning practical reasoning (particularly involving conditional intentions). Volitions are for Sellars a variety of intention—he writes, "volitions are...but one variety of occurrent intention (state), as perceptual takings are but one variety of occurrent belief (state)" (§29). In modern terminology, we would say that volitions are *intentions in action*, whereas Sellarsian intentions that have not yet "ripened" into volitions would be *prior intentions*.

Sellars emphasizes certain key features of volitions. First, volitions are essentially involved in practical reasoning. Second, although volitions are not a part of an action (but instead are the cause of actions), there is nevertheless a conceptual tie between volition and action. (McDowell will later take Sellars to task for thinking that action involves a language exit—that is, for thinking that volitions cause actions, but also conceiving "of actions as exits from the sphere of the conceptual" [McDowell 2011, p. 121].) This is, in a sense, the converse of McDowell's criticism of Sellars as thinking that perception involves a move from the non-conceptual to the conceptual.)

Most of the article involves clarification of Sellars's view regarding several aspects of practical reasoning. For example, Sellars reiterates the important connection between "shall be" and "shall do," which reflects his distinction between "ought to bes" and "ought to dos." He also formally introduces the rule "So-be-it," which allows states of affairs that are not up to one to enter the scope of the "Shall" operator and hence be taken up in one's practical reasoning. In addition, he develops a bit further his notion of a conditional intention (e.g., "If p, I shall do A"). This is a topic on which he and Castañeda corresponded,[13] and the last paragraphs of section III involve a concession to Castañeda and an attempt to revise his own account to avoid an objection raised by Castañeda.[14] Sellars concludes by specifying the sense in which reasons can (on his account) be causes of action, an issue Sellars tackled before in AAE.

Part 3 Free Will and *Akrasia*

11 "Fatalism and Determinism"[15]

Sellars wishes to defend a reconciliationist compatibilism, in the spirit of Hume and Mill, from the incompatibilist challenge. While sympathizing with the traditional argument that the incompatibilist conflates causation with compulsion, Sellars argues that this classical compatibilist move "simply won't do as it stands" (§2). Crucial to our understanding of human action is the distinction (from "Philosophy and the Scientific Image of Man" [PSIM]) between the scientific image and the manifest image. It is in the manifest image that we encounter the behavior of rational agents as intelligible, and it is intelligible through the framework of intentions and volitions. Crucially, although determinism is a presupposition of the scientific image, "the manifest image is not able, out of its own resources, to generate a deterministic picture" (§16).

---

[13] See the Sellars–Castañeda Correspondence, particularly letter C3.
[14] Sellars does not cite the source of the objection, but it can be found in Section II of Castañeda (1975).
[15] Sellars continued to revise FD after its publication, working on it at least until 1971. Two (apparently identical) copies of the latest revision are housed in the University of Pittsburgh archive: documents 31735062218957 and 31735062219013, Box 30, Folders 2–4, Wilfrid S. Sellars Papers, 1899–1990, ASP.1991.01, Archives of Scientific Philosophy, Archives & Special Collections, University of Pittsburgh Library System.

Sellars constructs a set of formal definitions of manifest-image action concepts such as "prevents," "has the ability," and "is able to," and argues that determinism is compatible with one's ability to do otherwise in roughly the following sense: If x does A at t, x was able to do A′ at t iff x had the ability to do A′ at t and nothing prevented x from doing A′ at t. "Prevent" is defined in terms of whether x would have done A′ if she had willed to do A′ at t; and so this naturally invites the question of whether x could have willed otherwise. "Willing otherwise" cannot be defined in terms of "able" and "ability," because volitions are not actions, on Sellars's account: There is, for example, no such thing as "willing to will." Nevertheless, Sellars thinks there is a perfectly coherent sense of "could have willed otherwise" that can be fleshed out in terms of the manifest image notion of *capability*, analogous to saying that "This car is going 5mph but it is *capable* of going 10mph."

At this point, the incompatibilist will argue that this talk of capabilities is irrelevant; and that given the total state of the universe (S) prior to t, it was *necessary* that x will to do A at t and physically impossible for x to will to do A′ at t. But—anticipating arguments like Christian List's (2019)—Sellars argues that S is a "pseudo-circumstance" that cannot be appealed to, to explain x's action. What he means is that in appealing to S, we have left the manifest image framework of intentions and volitions, which is the only framework within which human action is *rationally* intelligible, and have tried to appeal to a complex scientific cause to explain an action. This is illicit and is not a way of making someone's action intelligible. We can only understand and explain human action from within this manifest image framework.

12 "Reply to Alan Donagan"
In "Determinism and Freedom: Sellars and the Reconciliationist Theory," Donagan raises a number of objections to Sellars's views on free will and volition—chiefly to the views elaborated in FD, but also to those articulated in MP. Donagan offers a sympathetic reconstruction of Sellars's view and agrees that Sellars demonstrates that determinism is compatible with the ability to do otherwise than one actually does; but argues that (as Sellars recognizes), the crux of the issue is whether (if determinism is true) one can will otherwise than one actually does. He argues that Sellars's specific account of ability to will otherwise fails, but he concedes that "it seems to me highly probable that, following [Sellars's] general strategy of analyzing ability to will in terms of the absence of conditions preventing willing, he can find an analysis of conditions preventing willing that will do what he wants" (Donagan, p. 71). However, Donagan goes on to question the very foundations of Sellars's theory of free will, asserting that it is based on "Sellars' conviction that only one who in one way or another confounded causation with compulsion would imagine free will to be incompatible with determinism" (Donagan, pp. 71–2)—a conflation philosophers have not been guilty of for

some time. Donagan then turns to an elaboration of contemporary "agent causation" accounts of free will, such as that offered by C. D. Broad. Sellars has been critical of the notion of agent causation, arguing that Broad's "non-occurrent causation" obscures rather than explains what it is for a person to act. Sellars argues, "Nobody would think of dancing a waltz as causing a waltz" (MP §40/ p. 242; quoted in Donagan, p. 76), insisting that the waltz just is the performance of the dance and there is no separate agent *causing* the dance. Donagan disagrees: "[Richard] Taylor and myself, at least, *do* think of dancing a waltz as causing a waltz" (Donagan, p. 77). Donagan concludes his piece with some critical reflections on Sellars's notion of the manifest image, noting that a person's image of himself in the world in "ordinary life" often has a spiritual dimension. "What could be more natural than that a man whose image of himself is orthodox Christian—an immaterial soul informing a living body—should investigate the implications of that image with respect to a deterministic conception of the physical world?" (Donagan, pp. 79–80)

Sellars begins by denying that he accuses his opponent of conflating causation with compulsion; the conflation is instead between compulsion (which is in a sense still compatible with the ability to do otherwise) and circumstances that make one unable to do otherwise in the strong sense that they make one a "patient rather than an agent" (§47), one who *suffers* rather than one who *does*, as when one "go[es] out the window propelled by a team of wrestlers" (§47). He elaborates on this with reference to his example from FD—"x hears an explosion at t"— where x is subsequently rendered unable to do certain things (e.g., feel unafraid). Donagan takes Sellars "tacitly to accept [this counterexample] as decisive" (Donagan, p. 70). Sellars demurs, referring again to the notion of a capacity, noting that even in the SI there is a notion of substances having and losing capacities, as when "elastic substances require a recovery time before they regain their capacity to respond again to tension and release" (§10). Thus, we must distinguish between antecedent states which result in a failure of x to will A, and those states which cause x to *lose the capacity* to will A—as always, being careful not to confuse circumstances with pseudo-circumstances. We must also not follow the "vulgar determinist" in assimilating "caused" with "predictable," or assimilating action as an expression of character with "habit" or "addiction."

Sellars turns to Broad's well-known analysis of free will and Broad's claim that free action must satisfy both a negative condition ("that it is not causally predetermined" [§28]) and a positive condition (that it is caused by the self or agent). The libertarian's construal of the negative condition is based on a misconception that "scientific determinism is incompatible with the claim that the agent could have acted (or willed) otherwise" (§51), and Sellars reiterates the point (from FD) that the manifest image lacks the resources to construct a deterministic model of human action. Turning to the libertarian's positive condition, Sellars finds agent causation mysterious, arguing it is unclear how the mere existence of an agent at time t could explain the existence of a particular volition. Sellars concedes Donagan's point that there is a sense in which we can talk about someone causing his dancing, but he argues that this doesn't illuminate the libertarian's notion of agent causation, arguing that "when the dust has settled it will turn out that 'agent causation' *as construed by the libertarians* amounts to nothing more than an unilluminating reparsing of the fact that people will and act" (§39). Sellars has "no ... objection to speaking of a person as 'the cause' of his volitions, provided that it is recognized that such a concept would be built on that of occurrent causation" (§44). There is a sensible construal of the positive condition (which Sellars illustrates with the example of an agent being manipulated by a brain probe), where such talk is consistent with Sellars's compatibilist model of free will. On Sellars's understanding, agents can be the "immanent causes" of the actions where the proximate cause of the action lies within the agent. Further, Sellars emphasizes that his notion of "could have done otherwise" is absolute, not conditional (i.e., should not be read "could have done, if ... "). Sellars concludes this section by noting that in response to the libertarian claim that the remote past requires certain actions, if determinism is true, "the determinist is certain to reply that the rest of history of the world must fit around our lives as we fit into it. In this abstract sense, at least, we are autonomous" (§61). Sellars then reiterates the point that for him, the crux of the issue surrounding free will is that of reasons vs. causes. If reasons and causes turn out to be radically discontinuous, then compatibilist accounts of free will must fail. But "if explanations of action in terms of *reasons* is a *special case of* explanation in terms of (occurrent) *causes*, then the concept of agent causation can be given a positive analysis in terms of immanent causation along the lines I have suggested" (§63). Thus, Sellars emphasizes (as always) the importance of integrating the normative into the natural/causal order.

Sellars concludes by responding to Donagan's critical commentary on Sellars's notion of the manifest image. Sellars denies, for example, that various religious claims belong either in the scientific image or in the manifest image. He also denies that free will is a principle belonging in the manifest image, arguing instead that "it is a *higher order* principle concerning the limits of the derivability of events from prior events" (§67).

13 "On Knowing the Better and Doing the Worse"

Sellars frames this perennial problem in terms of an inconsistent trilemma:

(1) People know the better yet deliberately do the worse.

(A_2) To *know* (rather than merely believe) that course A is, all relevant things considered for what they really are, better than course B is to have a *conclusive* reason for following A rather than B.

(B_2) If a person has a conclusive reason for following course A rather than course B he will (impulse aside) follow A rather than B.

Sellars doesn't use the language of "justifying reasons" versus "motivating reasons"—he distinguishes between, on the one hand, motives, and justifications (which are equivalent, respectively, to justifying reasons and *good* justifying reasons) and, on the other hand, "motives in the occurrent sense," which are motivating reasons. His initial attempt at resolving the trilemma is to diagnose it as resting on a confusion of two different senses of "having a reason": A_2 employs the phrase in the sense of "having a conclusively *good* reason" (i.e., justification), whereas B_2 employs it in the sense of "having a necessarily *prevailing* reason" (i.e., an occurrent motive or motivating reason). This solution is not satisfactory, for the extreme internalist (as Sellars calls his dialectical opponent) will argue that "if a reason is conclusively *good*, then, when known, it is, of necessity, conclusively *powerful*."

Through a discussion of Plato (during which Sellars previews a number of themes that will reappear in "Reason and the Art of Living in Plato" [RAL]), Sellars diagnoses the problem as arising from the view that there is one standpoint from which to judge "what one ought to do, *all things considered as they really are*"—and that is the personal standpoint. If there is a single standpoint, it seems as though all reasons can be weighed and compared from within this point of view, giving us a univocal answer to the question of what *conclusively good* reasons one has to act. It is but a short step to the extreme internalist conclusion that knowledge of this conclusively good reason should entail (conceptually) that one is moved to act in accordance with this reason.

But Sellars argues that there are in fact two separate standpoints, corresponding to two separate motives:

(1) the interpersonal standpoint of the community, where we intend as 'one of us', and promote the welfare of the community
(2) the personal standpoint, where one intends individually, and promotes one's own happiness or well-being.

This model, argues Sellars, "would be a form of 'internalism,' but not of that 'extreme internalism' which equates 'conclusively *good* reason' with 'conclusively *powerful* reason.'" For one can have a conclusively good reason (as dictated by the interpersonal standpoint) but act instead from the motive of one's personal welfare. Hence, weakness of the will is acting from the personal point of view when the interpersonal (moral) point of view dictates a contrary course of action. This theme of practical reason as involving two distinct and, to some extent, incommensurable points of view—the moral point of view, and the point of view of "Self-Love," as Sellars calls it—is a theme that repeatedly resurfaces in his writings on ethical theory (see SE, OIM, ORAV).

Part 4 Deontic Logic, Practical Reason, and the Logic of Intentions

14 "Imperatives, Intentions, and the Logic of 'Ought'"

IIOR is (along with IIO, the essay on which it is based) Sellars's earliest sustained treatment of ethical theory (aside from OM and OMR) and his first published discussion of the logic of intentions, and it is here that he lays out fundamental commitments that will structure his discussion of the subject for the remainder of his career. Broadly speaking, in Sellars's day (as in ours), battle lines in ethical theory were drawn as follows: Intuitionists (like W. D. Ross) held that obligation is intersubjective, but they denied that there is an analytic connection between moral judgment and moral motivation; emotivists (like A. J. Ayer) conversely held that there is an analytic connection between moral judgment and moral motivation but denied that such judgments are intersubjective. After canvassing (and rejecting) a few possible solutions (including R. M. Hare's), Sellars notes that expressions of intentions are analytically connected to action. Furthermore, although there is no reasoning among promises or imperatives, there is reasoning among intentions, so one dimension of intersubjectivity is secured. (Sellars elaborates on this argument concerning the difference between promises, imperatives, and intentions in the Appendix.) Using "Shall" as an operator to denote the expression of an intention, Sellars introduces the inferential principle which will remain central to his logic of intentions:

(P) implies (Q)
So, (Shall [P]) implies (Shall [Q]) (§28),

a principle he subsequently names "S-Imp" (see, e.g., ORAV §47). As an initial formulation, Sellars suggests "Would that everybody universally did A in C!" as our central moral principle, where "'Would that X did B!' [has] the force of 'X shall do B'" (§38).

A difficulty with the attempt to interpret "ought" in terms of "shall" is that different oughts can logically contradict each other, but conflicting expressions of intention are not logically incompatible (although perhaps "they cannot both be realized" [§65]). Sellars, of course, introduces "we-intentions" to solve this problem, which gives Sellars the other element of intersubjectivity he was seeking.

The precise contours of Sellars's solution (which he lays out in §§71–75) can be difficult to discern, perhaps in part because Sellars himself has not worked out the details as well as in later works (e.g., OIM). Sellars introduces the notion of an *autobiographical counterpart* of an "ought" statement; he argues in §73 that the autobiographical counterpart of "I ought to do A" is "We intend to do A," where "we intend" seems both to express and ascribe an intention. It seems (and again, it is not entirely clear) that we-intentions can contradict each other because they can ascribe incompatible intentions. (Sellars is much clearer on this in his later writings: In OIM, for example, he argues directly that different people can express we-intentions that are "in a tough sense" the same, or that can conflict with each other in the sense we care about for intersubjectivity.) At any rate, Sellars concludes that because we can make sense of the intersubjectivity of we-intentions, we can therefore interpret "ought" in terms of "shall": "*I suggest that ought, as an expression of intention, is a special case of shall$_w$.*" (§75).[16]

IIOR also contains a subtle discussion of what it is to act on a principle. Sellars begins in §§8–9 by initially rejecting the compatibility of consequentialist accounts with the notion of acting on principle, writing, "I shall just assume for the time being, that there is no sense in thinking that having the principle *Everybody ought to do A in C* is a matter of wishing that everybody did A in C *for the sake of the consequence of such action*" (§41). Sellars revisits this claim in §84, imagining something like the following argument:

Would that people generally were happy!
(People generally being happy) implies (People generally doing A in C, A' in C', etc.)
So, would that people generally did A in C, A' in C', etc.
(People generally doing A in C, A' in C', etc.) implies (People generally espousing $P_1, P_2, \ldots P_n$)
So, would that people generally espoused $P_1, P_2, \ldots P_n$!
So, would that I espoused $P_1, P_2, \ldots P_n$!

The principles themselves ($P_1, P_2, \ldots P_n$) demand certain actions in certain circumstances; our reasoning in such circumstances can be represented as follows:

Doing this would be a case of a person's doing A in C (or A' in C', etc.)
So, I shall do it. (§82)

Sellars notes that this reasoning fully represents our intention in a given case. So while our "efforts to acquire (and maintain) these dispositions have the purpose of doing that which is conducive to the well-being of men generally" (§82), our intention in acting is to realize the principle—that is, to do A in C. Thus, in a move that foreshadows Sellars's claim from OIM to have "harmonized... 'teleological' and 'deontological' themes... in Kant's ethics" (OIM §147/p. 226)—and which echoes the distinction between justification of an institution and justification of an action within an institution from John Rawls's "Two Concepts of Rules"—Sellars argues that acting on principle is consistent with a moral system that has an ultimately consequentialist element.

---

[16] We are grateful to Stefanie Dach for helpful conversations regarding the interpretation of these difficult passages.

A problem with the argument sketched in §84 is that it seems to founder on the recognition that not all people will do A in C, A' in C', etc. Sellars responds by interpreting "men generally" as "most men." But this leaves open the option that the agent, who no doubt possesses at least a modicum of self-love in addition to whatever benevolence she possesses, interprets the principle as "Most men but not I." Sellars claims there is a sense of benevolence that precludes the above compromise. This sense of benevolence is the "simple recognition of people generally as *we*" (§86). Thus, the consistent "Most men but not I" is replaced by the incoherent "*We* but not I." He concludes that "the only frame of mind which can provide direct support for moral commitment is what Royce called Loyalty, and what Christians call Love of Neighbor (*caritas*)" (§92).

15 "Reflections on Contrary-to-Duty Imperatives"
"Reflections on Contrary-to-Duty Imperatives" (CDI) is Sellars's response to Roderick Chisholm's famous paradox of deontic logic (Chisholm 1963). Deontic logic, if interpreted along the lines of standard propositional or modal logics, generates various paradoxical conclusions; modern forms of this challenge are (for example) the Paradox of the Gentle Murder (Forrester 1984).[17] We can generate the paradox as follows, where "O" represents "is obligated," "k" represents "kill," and "g" represents "kill gently":

(1) $O(\sim k)$ Premise
(2) k Premise
(3) $O(k \rightarrow g)$ Premise
(4) $O(g)$ (2), (3) modus ponens

Sellars's first move is to distinguish between two ways of understanding conditional obligation:

CO1: $O(s \rightarrow b')$
CO2: $O(s \rightarrow b)'$

The prime symbol (') indicates the "target" of the obligation. Thus, in the first case, only "b" is the target of the obligation. Thus, if you steal, then you are obligated (to pay reparations). Given the first interpretation, we can infer according to the following principle of deontic inference:

---

[17] Chisholm's paradox, with which Sellars begins his discussion, involves the derivation of a contradiction using principles of deontic logic. The Paradox of the Gentle Murder involves the derivation not of a contradiction, but merely of a counterintuitive conclusion. However, Sellars discusses both types of problematic derivations in CDI; we are illustrating his solution with an example of the latter sort.

Ia: If O(p → q′) and p, then O(q)

Understanding conditional obligation in terms of CO1 allows for *factual detachment*—an indicative statement can be used to "detach" the conclusion of the deontic conditional, giving us the paradoxical conclusion above. However, in CO2, the entire conditional is the target of the obligation: You are obligated to bring it about that (if stealing, then paying reparations). CO2, then, only supports *deontic detachment*:

Ib: If O(p → q)′ and O(p), then O(q)

Sellars ultimately endorses a version of Ib (namely, principle P_2) precisely to avoid factual detachment and the resulting paradoxes.

This move may not in itself be sufficient to avoid paradox, however, given other inferential principles Sellars endorses. Thus, I might have the following commitments:

Shall$_{we}$ (If I kill Smith, I kill him gently)
I kill Smith

By an operation of So-be-it—the principle Sellars introduces later in ORAV—"I kill Smith" can be moved inside the "Shall"-operator so we have "Shall$_{we}$ (I kill Smith *and* if I kill Smith, I kill him gently)," and, by a single operation of modus ponens, we then get "Shall$_{we}$ (I kill Smith gently)."

Sellars can avoid this unwelcome conclusion, however, because of two qualifications he notes. First, Sellars notes that an obligation to do s (or ~s) is always conditional on a "total circumstance": This is "a maximum set of compatible [normatively relevant] circumstance factors" (§41). Second, he introduces a restriction on the deployment of conditional obligation. In deploying a principle like Ib, we must require "that the assumption on which the implication rests be normatively cotenable with the ground [i.e., the total circumstance] of [O(p)]" (§63). Thus, consider again our formalization of the gentle murder argument—formalized this time in terms of the "Shall"-operator, not in terms of the deontic logic operators of CDI; "C_1" represents the total circumstance that grounds the obligation not to kill Smith:

(1) C_1 — Premise
(2) Shall$_{we}$ (I do not kill Smith) /C_1 — Premise
(3) Shall$_{we}$ (If I kill Smith, I kill him gently) — Premise
(4) I kill Smith — Premise
(5) C_1 and I kill Smith — 1, 4, CI
(6) Shall$_{we}$ (I kill Smith *and* if I kill Smith, I kill him gently) — 3, 4, So-be-it
(7) Shall$_{we}$ (I kill Smith gently) — 3, 4, MP

This argument violates the restrictions Sellars places on conditional obligation and hence is unsound. The implication (premise [3]) that supposedly generates the contradiction rests on the assumption "I kill Smith." But then, as we see, the total circumstance in which I find myself (and hence the total circumstances that purportedly ground the obligation not to kill Smith) is not C_1, but rather C_1 *and* I kill Smith. While my killing Smith might be compatible with an obligation not to do so, Sellars argues that the *ground* of my obligation not to do so cannot include my killing (or not killing) Smith (cf. §65). Thus, we have incompatible commitments—one to C_1 being the total relevant description of the circumstances, the other to C_1 *and* I kill Smith being the total relevant description (cf. §67).

16 "On Reasoning about Values"

ORAV represents the final and most mature statement of Sellars's theory of reasoning among intentions. After noting the various ways in which different categories of words contribute to the meaning of sentences pertaining to matters of fact, Sellars turns to sentences concerned with values (as opposed to facts) and argues that practical language is primarily expressive in function. He focuses in particular on locutions that express intentions, as these have the most immediate tie to action. Using, again, "Shall" as an operator to denote the expression of an intention, Sellars introduces a number of principles and restrictions governing reasoning among intentions. First is the familiar rule S-Imp, which is that if "P" implies "Q," then "Shall[P]" implies "Shall[Q]." Sellars is keen to emphasize, however, that "expressions of intention do not occur within the scope of logical constants and quantifiers" (§56). This means, for example, that "Shall[P] and Shall [Q]" is not well formed. It also means that "Shall" has no external negation. So "Not-Shall[P]" is not well formed—indeed, Sellars argues that this is "conceptually incoherent" (§57)—but "Shall[not-P]" is well formed. Thus, reasoning with intentions involves moving all elements of reasoning *inside* the scope of the "Shall"-operator, and Sellars introduces a number of rules—such as Conjunction Introduction and So-be-it—for doing so. (He also introduces a rule—simplification—for moving from "Shall[P and Q]" to "Shall[P]," but he seems to assume this as the simple converse of CI and doesn't formally introduce this principle as he does with the others.) All of this shows that there is genuine reasoning from an intention to a subsidiary intention—that is, it shows that there is "rational elaboration" of intentions. But is a choice *among* incompatible intentions rational? Roughly: Is there only means-end reasoning, or can we also reason about our ends?

Anticipating arguments by later authors such as Jean Hampton and Christine Korsgaard, Sellars argues that if the only kind of practical rationality we have is means-end rationality, then there is no practical normativity *per se*. A properly derived intention can be reasonable *relative* to the intention from which it was derived, but we can only conclude that you *should* or *ought* to do A (i.e., we can only detach the consequent of a bit of practical reasoning) if this conclusion was derived from an *intrinsically reasonable* intention. Sellars first considers the maxim of Rational Egoism as a candidate for the intrinsically reasonable intention, relative to which other intentions are reasonable. He argues it is psychologically possible to act contrary to Rational Egoism, all things considered, but sets this intention aside to explore the possibility of a moral maxim.

Sellars begins by rehearsing considerations, familiar from IIOR, regarding how ordinary expressions of intentions are egocentric and cannot contradict each other. However, expressions of we-intentions do have this intersubjective element. Furthermore, certain groups are constituted *as* groups by the fact that they share a specific intention. Thus, it is by virtue of the fact that members of the Whooping Crane Society (WCS) share the intention:

Shall [each of us WCS members promote the survival of whooping cranes]

that the WCS exists in the first place; the intention *constitutes* the group. Is there an analogous intention that both (a) is intrinsically reasonable and (b) constitutes the moral community in the same way that the above intention constitutes the WCS? Sellars suggests the following candidate:

Shall be [each and every one of us leads a satisfying life, all relevant things considered].

Sellars suggests that membership in the "us" is determined by who is capable of sharing the above intention, and he explicitly ties this to his discussion in OIM (XVII–XXI/§§119–54), emphasizing again the conceptual connection between rational agency and membership in the moral community.

ORAV may also mark an evolution in Sellars's account of what it is that makes we-intentions intersubjective. Dach (2023), for example, argues that Sellars's early view (from IIOR) was akin to what Schweikard and Schmid (2021) call a "mode" account—we-intentions are a special kind of attitude or psychological state. However, Dach argues that by ORAV, Sellars has adopted more of a content account—we-intentions are intersubjective by virtue of their inferential structure. Thus, on this account, if I begin with the intention "Shall [Each of us members of the Whooping Crane Society do what we can to promote the welfare of the whooping crane]" and infer "Shall [I, *qua member of the Whooping Crane Society*, do what I can to promote the welfare of the whooping crane]," the latter is a we-intention by virtue of its derivation from the former.

17 "Conditional Promises and Conditional Intentions"
This very late essay (published in 1983) grew out of a letter (dated 6 June 1979) that Sellars wrote to Judith Jarvis Thomson. (We have not included that letter in

this volume since virtually all of that letter was incorporated, verbatim, into the present essay.) Sellars begins with a brief discussion of conditional promises. Sellars long held that there was no "logic" of promising—something he and Castañeda disagreed about (see the Castañeda-Sellars correspondence, this volume, Chapter 22). Here, Sellars reiterates that while there are not valid arguments involving *expressions* of promises, for example,

I promise to do A, if p
p
Therefore, I promise to do A

there are valid arguments involving *reports* or *ascriptions* of promises, for example

I have promised to do A, if p
p
Therefore, I have promised to do A.

However, Sellars's chief goal in this essay is to respond to an objection raised by Castañeda regarding Sellars's view on conditional intentions. Consider the conditional intention, "I shall visit Bruce Aune at time t', if I finish my essay at time t," which we can (according to Castañeda) represent as follows:

1) Shall [I finish my essay at time t → I visit Bruce Aune at time t']

Since the logic of intentions is parasitic on the logic of their contents, it would seem that we can take the contrapositive of the conditional within the brackets and generate the following, logically equivalent, intention:

2) Shall [I do not visit Bruce Aune at time t' → I do not finish my essay at time t]

While the former seems like a perfectly good expression of a conditional intention, the latter does not; the antecedent is not a condition on the performance of action stated in the consequent.

Sellars acknowledges the force of Castañeda's objection, and he offers the following refinement of his account of the logic of intentions. Sellars distinguishes between elements of an intention which are introduced via So-be-it (see "Practical Reasoning Again" [PRA], ORAV)—and so are considered as given, or not up to the agent—and those that are taken to be up to the agent. In conditional intentions, the condition is introduced via So-be-it. He suggests in §106 that "In the written expression of an intention, those constituents of the scenario which [are believed to be the case or about to be the case] might be underlined, and those which [are considered by the agent to be 'up to me'] might be marked with an asterisk." Thus, we can more perspicuously write our above conditional intention as:

1′) Shall [I finish my essay at time t → I visit Bruce Aune at time t′*]

If we were to rewrite 2 as a conditional intention, we would write it as follows:

2′) Shall [I do not visit Bruce Aune at time t′ → I do not finish my essay at time t*]

But we can now see, argues Sellars, that these are not in fact equivalent intentions, and the difference is secured by "the *propositional* character of the antecedent and the *resolutive* character of the consequent in the... expression of the conditional intention" (§118). Thus, argues Sellars, we can make sense of two intentions having "logically equivalent contents [while not being] equivalent with respect to their logical powers" (§63).

One reason this essay is important concerns Sellars's development of the notion of dependent implication or implication relative to a hypothesis (a topic on which Sellars had lengthy correspondence with both Aune and Castañeda). This is important because, as Sellars notes, "Obligations are essentially tied to grounds" (§89). Thus, obligations must be stated as conditional upon a "circumstance of action," that is: "Shall [if I am in C, I will do A]" (OIM §14). Given the various restrictions Sellars has placed on applying logical operators to "Shall," it is crucial to reconstruct how one can "detach" an obligation which is stated in conditional form.

Part 5 Manuscripts and Correspondence

18 Practical Reasoning

This essay fragment is likely related to TA, as it covers many of the same themes. One issue discussed in detail (more so than in TA) is implication relative to an assumption. Here, Sellars discusses it under the heading of "derivable intentions" and employs the formal notation he uses in CDI. Given

Shall [P] implies Shall [Q]

'Shall [Q]' "expresses a derivable intention, a derivable intention relative to the assumption 'Shall [P]'" (§12/p. 23 in original). He connects this with the notion of acting on a policy (an issue also discussed in TA), writing, "Let us call a derivable general conditional intention a policy for realizing the goal or end in view" (§12/p. 24 in original).

Another issue discussed at length is self-love (which occurs in the context of an analysis of the aims of desire, another topic from TA). Self-love is, of course, a

44 THE METAPHYSICS OF PRACTICE

central issue for Sellars's practical philosophy: In many of his essays (e.g., KBDW, OMP, OIM), the competitors for the intrinsically reasonable intention—that which can confer categorical (but derivative) validity on other human intentions—are (a) self-love and (b) the moral point of view.

19 Practical Reasoning Again

This is a transitional essay between TA and VR; many elements in it appear in the latter essay (and also in ORAV). For example, Sellars begins by endorsing conjunction introduction, that is, the rule that from "Shall [P]" and "Shall [Q]" you may infer "Shall [P and Q]"—a principle he denied ("for a very bad reason," he writes) in TA. Also, this essay is where Sellars first introduces the So-be-it principle, which allows us to introduce the agent's factual beliefs into the scope of the "Shall"-operator so that they may be taken up in practical reasoning.

There are, however, some unique elements in this essay that appear nowhere else. First, Sellars denied in TA (§14) that implications of the form "Shall [P] implies Shall [Q]" have a contrapositive, on the grounds that "shall" has no external negation. In PRA, Sellars realizes his mistake, and he realizes that the contrapositive can be formed without external negation, writing,

> It should be remembered that the contrapositive of
>   'Shall [P]' implies 'Shall [Q]'
> is
>   'Shall [not-Q]' implies 'Shall [not-P]'
> for the latter, like the former, is parasitical upon its indicative counterpart. I emphasize, once again, that 'shall'-statements are not subject to external negation. (§16 note 6/p. 10 in original)

(Curiously, though, Sellars does not mention his denial of this point in TA; nor is it clear where we are supposed to "remember" this from, given his earlier denial.)

A second unique point occurs in the context of a lengthy discussion of So-be-it and conditional implication. The two are intimately related; since the "Shall"-operator may not appear within the scope of logical operators, "If a, then Shall [P]" is not well-formed. Thus, we must push the antecedent inside the "Shall"-operator, such as: "Shall [If it rains, I will study]"; and the consequent can be inferred only by using So-be-it to push the relevant factual belief inside the "Shall"-operator, as well: "Shall [If it rains, I will study *and* it is raining]; therefore, Shall [I will study]."

It is within this context that Sellars discusses apparently valid examples of practical reasoning that issue in intentions (e.g., "Shall [It does not rain]") whose contents are entirely not up to the agent—a seeming absurdity (as well as a contradiction to the explicit principle Sellars later asserts in ORAV §79). Sellars's solution to this conundrum is to argue that such reasonings are always implicitly "bracketed by the rubric 'if such and such were up to me'," and further, that such reasonings are "a way of making explicit the implications of one's preferences, in abstraction from what is up to one" (PRA §47/p. 30 in original).

20 The Hare–Sellars Correspondence

The Hare–Sellars correspondence chiefly concerns Sellars's early attempts to develop a viable theory of moral expressivism (in IIO). Hare, like Sellars, was trying to bridge the gap between cognitivism and non-cognitivism by offering a theory according to which the moral "ought" is subject to rules of inference but also tied to action. The first substantive entry in the correspondence is from Sellars. Sellars is trying to articulate a position different from either the intuitionist (cognitivist) or the emotivist (non-cognitivist). For Sellars, the moral "ought" has a conceptual tie to action. The intuitionist, of course, denies this; but the emotivist misconstrues the connection, understanding it as merely causal, where the moral "judgment" acts as a "prick or a goad" rather than being internally conceptually connected to the resultant action. Sellars goes on to criticize the solution Hare offers in *The Language of Morals*. Sellars objects to Hare's claim that "ought" statements entail imperatives, arguing "it is my conviction that ethical discourse has motivational force which is not borrowed from non-ethical discourse" (S2 §8), and concluding that if he were to follow Hare in offering an imperatival analysis of moral language, he "would claim that 'I ought to do A' *is* (rather than *entails*) an imperative" (S2 §8). Nevertheless, Sellars dissents from what he takes to be Hare's presupposition, that only imperatives are tied to action.

Hare replies that ought-sentences (like imperatives) have a *conceptual* tie to action in that to know the meaning of an ought-sentence is to know that one is to do something. But Hare cautions that we must distinguish between what the sentence means and the effect it is supposed to have on the listener; thus, one can understand the meaning of an "ought"-statement (and its conceptual tie to action), but will only do A if one *really thinks* that one ought to do A (where one's doing A is a necessary, but not sufficient, condition of really thinking that one ought to do A. One is reminded here of Hare's distinction between genuine moral judgments and "inverted comma moral judgments"). Thus, Hare thinks he can do justice to the emotivist's intuition, while holding that the tie between moral judgment and action is more than a mere causal one.

Hare reiterates his view that connection between prescriptives and motivation is logical, rather than psychological. He ends *H3* by offering a somewhat lengthy defense of the claim that prescriptives are not, but (conditionally) entail, imperatives: For any possible action one does, "a command to do it can be framed *ex post facto*"; and so any prescriptive sentence of any kind entails an imperative in this strictly logical sense. This doesn't mean (contrary to Sellars's charge in S2) that imperatives somehow have a "monopoly" on action-explanation.

Sellars objects (S4) that Hare has too far divorced the normative and the causal. While Sellars has rejected the naïve causal connection of the emotivist (S1), nevertheless there is some sense in talking about causal connections between imperatives and prescriptives and action, just as there is some sense in talking about a causal connection between observation reports and the states of affairs that evoke them—although of course the relation isn't *merely* causal/psychological. Thus, Sellars rejects the intuitionist's view that one could really think that one ought to do A in C "without ever doing or being to any degree moved to do A in C." Much of the early part of S4 concerns spelling out the proper connection between moral judgment and motivation; the reader should be reminded of the internalism he endorses in KBDW (which he contrasts with extreme or radical internalism).

In pushing back against Hare's imperativism, Sellars outlines a number of his commitments regarding "ought"-statements. Singular "ought"-statements (such as "Jones ought to do A in C") are genuinely singular, but they conceptually presuppose universal "ought"-statements (i.e., "Everyone ought to do A in C"); such "ought"-statements guide the conduct of the person who sincerely asserts them; and such action-guidance is itself dependent upon the agent's subscribing also to the universal "ought"-statement. (One can see here a connection with Sellars's reasoning in OMR.) *Both* "ought"-statements *and* imperatives are prescriptives "in the primary sense"—contrary to the view Sellars attributes to Hare, who (in his view) holds that only imperatives are "primary prescriptives," and that any other action-guiding discourse is only derivatively so. Sellars continues to push back forcefully on Hare's claim that "ought"-statements entail imperatives in more than the trivial sense that "ought"-statements (sincerely uttered) imply doings, which themselves can logically be stated as the fulfillment of an imperative. If a more robust sense of entailment is meant by Hare—wherein acting on an "ought"-statement is acting on an imperative, or something along those lines—Sellars finds this undermotivated. Sellars concludes S4 by replying to comments Hare supplied on "Inference and Meaning" (IM).

In S5 Sellars clarifies for Hare his conception of "motive." It is easy to read Sellars as making the (now-familiar) distinction between justifying and motivating reasons; but this doesn't seem to be what Sellars has in mind. "Motive," for Sellars, does indeed seem to be akin to motivating reason; it is, he says, "that part of the envisaged scenario of his action the thought of which moves him to act. It is, so to speak, the *effective* part of the *intention*, more accurately, of the set of things he would admit to having brought about intentionally." Such motives are involved in causal explanations (we are explaining why the agent acted in such-and-such a way), but in causal explanations that essentially invoke the agent's reasons for acting—thus, such motives are invoked in *rational* explanations, explanations that place agents within the space of reasons. Sellars is concerned about this question in connection with his investigation of "the relation of *ought* to 'motivation.'" However, the other conception of "motive" is invoked when we are explaining a person's conduct not in terms of reasons, but purely in terms of causes; for example, "The sound *you-ought-to-do-A* impinging on his ears initiated a chain of stimulus-response connections which resulted in a rapid to-and-fro motion of his right index finger."

Along with S5, Sellars had sent Hare a copy of IIO; and the item of substantive interest included with H6 is Hare's lengthy commentary in this paper. Unlike in some of his earlier correspondence, Hare provides little in the way of detailed point-by-point criticism. Rather, he makes an overall strategic suggestion for expressivists such as Sellars and himself. Hare begins by noting that (despite the accusations of some critics) he never equated moral judgments with imperatives; and in any case, his sense of "imperative" is largely a stipulative one, understood on analogy with our ordinary language conception of imperatives but not identical to this conception. However, in a significant break from *The Language of Morals*, Hare suggests that instead of a two-step analysis (which connects moral judgments to imperatives, and then imperatives to action), we ought instead to analyze moral judgments (and other action-guiding judgments) directly in terms of their connection to action. Thus, quoting from the *Nicomachean Ethics*, Hare asserts that if you assent both to "All sweet things must be tasted" and "Yonder thing is sweet" and yet don't act, then you "*must* (logically) have either misunderstood or been insincere." He recommends a similar approach to Sellars, arguing that Sellars should similarly abandon "resolutives" as a "brick" in his analysis of action-guiding language.

Sellars seems to have sent Hare a revised version of IIO, on which Hare provides some brief commentary in H7. Sellars argued in IIO that while there are no valid inferences involving expressions of promises, there are valid inferences involving reporting of promises. Thus, if Jones promises to call Smith if it rains, then Smith can validly reason as follows:

He promis*ed* to call me, if it rained
It is raining
So he promis*ed* to call me (IIO §15/p. 234)

Hare pushes back on this, arguing that "with a valid inference, if the premisses are true, one can do the inference and affirm the conclusion, and forget about the premisses. But with this inference, one cannot do this. For it just isn't the case that, even given that the premisses are true, [Jones] promised to call [Smith], period."

Sellars, while not convinced by Hare's objection, admits that it "hit home" (*S10*), and he includes a lengthy suggested revision to the manuscript. Sellars reiterates some familiar points—that there are no inferences among promises *qua* performances, but there are inferences among reports about promises. He suggests some principles that would govern such inferences; such principles would allow (contrary to Hare's suggestion) the assertion of an unconditioned promise in the case that someone makes a conditional promise and the condition is satisfied. Sellars concludes, however, that he is "very uneasy about all this"; and indeed, the specific language of this letter does not make it into IIOR (although some of the ideas do, such as the idea that we can infer among reports of promises, but not among promises *qua* performances).

Part of Sellars's reply to Hare hinges on what a person says and what a person does by so saying. Thus, if Jones promises to do A, if p; and if p obtains; then we can infer that Jones has promised to do A; but we cannot infer "Jones said, 'I promise to do A.'" Hare finds this restriction on allowable inferences troubling, and he charges in *H11* that "some of your later arguments depend on the validity of inferences of the type under dispute." Hare might have in mind here inferences in IIO such as the following:

He told me he would call me, if it rained
It is raining
So he told me he would call (IIO §19/p. 237)

While in IIO Sellars claims that such inferences are valid, they may be of the type Sellars disavows in note 13a of letter *S10*; it depends on whether you construe "he told" as operating analogously to "Jones said." At any rate, the relevant section (with these example inferences) was omitted from IIOR, so it is possible that Hare convinced Sellars on this point. What remains in IIOR is the claim that while there is no valid inference among tellings-to *qua* performances, there are valid inferences among *reports* of tellings-to, that is:

X tells Y (to do A if *p*)
p
So, X tells Y (to do A) (IIOR §5)

But again, if we are to understand Sellars as holding to the principle asserted in 13a of *S10*, the conclusion of such an inference does not report what X *said*, but rather what speech act X *performed* (i.e., a telling-Y-to-do-A).

21 The Binkley–Sellars Correspondence

The Binkley–Sellars correspondence dates from 1956 to 1959, and it primarily concerns themes from the early (*Methodos*) version of IIO. Many of the ideas and suggestions from Binkley foreshadow future developments in Sellars's own thinking, and one can only suspect that Sellars's association with Binkley was influential on the development of Sellars's later ethical theory. One key theme both wrestle with concerns how the *universalization* constraint places a rational requirement of moral behavior on the individual. As Binkley notes (*B1*), believing (for example) that a good society requires that most people subscribe to a principle doesn't rationally require that *I* subscribe to it. Considerations like this no doubt push Sellars to deny that moral reasoning involves reasoning from the individual point of view in the first place, as such reasoning can never (in Sellars's view) answer objections such as this.

Relatedly, we see Sellars in this early correspondence still working out how best to analyze the *universality* of moral statements. In OMR, he argues that "I ought to do X" is the conclusion of an argument, the major premise of which is "*All agents in circumstances C do X*"—a premise which is, of course, false. However, this premise serves to motivate the agent, as well as providing an element of universality: "When I truly say 'I *ought* to do X in circumstances C,' it is the thought of *myself doing X* (*in circumstances C*) as an instance of *everybody doing X* (*in circumstances C*) which tends to evoke the doing of X in circumstances believed to be C" (OMR §9). In his more mature writings, Sellars wants to avoid forms of universalization that entail such commitments—including analyses that "require that there is such a thing as intending that everybody keep promises, knowing that in many cases people don't" (S4 §9). His proposed solution is that moral claims issue "inference tickets" of the form,

"P is a person in C" implies "Shall [P doing A]"

This move (from OMR to the present correspondence) perhaps foreshadows his line of thinking in OIM, where he argues, "Moral principles are not to be derived from considerations pertaining to the consequences of *everybody* behaving in a certain way in a certain kind of circumstance...Moral principles primarily concern the consequences of *anybody* acting in a certain way in a certain kind of circumstance" (OIM §85).

Another key issue discussed by Sellars and Binkley is reasoning among intentions. Sellars denies (S2) that the "Shall"-operator (and the indicative on which it operates) should be understood using the neustic/phrastic model (where the indicative phrase is the phrastic and the "Shall"-operator is the neustic). Although Sellars argues in IIO that one can reason among intention-expressions, he does not there formally introduce "Shall" as an operator that takes indicative sentences as its object; Sellars develops this device between IIO and IIOR (where the "Shall"-operator first makes its formal appearance). Binkley himself (inspired both by Sellars's early ruminations on the issue and by Castañeda's published work, which he references in B6) suggests his own "Shall"-operator, as well as some adjunct operators and rules for relating them (B5 and B6).

22 The Castañeda–Sellars Correspondence

The first three letters in the Castañeda–Sellars correspondence concern IIO, several copies of which Sellars apparently sent to Castañeda for sharing with the

Duke University Philosophy Department. Castañeda eventually develops his own version of prescriptivism that deviates in important ways from Sellars's—Castañeda's *The Structure of Morality* argues that practical discourse consists of a variety of acts and attitudes, including not only imperatives but also commands, promises, and so on; and that there is valid reasoning involving these different varieties. And of course Sellars is also responding to prescriptivists such as Hare. In IIO, Sellars argues forcefully that while there are genuine inferences among imperatives, there is no such thing as inference among commands, promises, etc.; and so the prescriptivist cannot build an account of practical discourse on any of the latter.

In these early letters, Castañeda pushes back against Sellars's line of thought here, arguing (largely through example and by appeal to intuition) that there are valid examples of inferences involving promising, commanding, etc. Sellars substantially revises IIO, no doubt at least partially because of his correspondence with Castañeda—see, in particular, sections 3–5 of IIOR, where he is discussing prescriptive inference—but never backs down from his claim that while there are valid inferences among imperatives, there are not among promises, commands, etc.

(Incidentally, Sellars's view in IIO seems to be that promises, commands, etc., only validly appear in inferences when they are being reported, not when they are being expressed. Thus, there is no such valid reasoning as:

Take all the boxes to the station!
This is one of the boxes
So take this to the station! (IIO §21/p. 239)

However, one *can* validly reason as follows:

He told us to take all the boxes to the station
This is one of the boxes
So he told us to take this to the station (IIO §21/ p. 239)

And, indeed, one who failed to be able to reason along the latter lines "would have convincingly shown that he did not understand one or the other of [the premises]" (IIO §22/p. 240).)

Nor is Castañeda convinced by Sellars; in his final letter from this early period (C3) he pushes back against some of the central claims from IIO. In that essay, Sellars argued that there is no such thing as imperative inference, en route to offering his own account of inference among intentions. Castañeda challenges Sellars on both of these points. First, Castañeda argues that there are legitimate reasonings involving imperatives. He offers examples such as "open the window, *because* he needs some fresh air" and "He is very sick, *so* call a doctor," and he argues that "so," "for," "because," and other logical connectives work here precisely as they do when connecting indicative sentences (e.g., "He is sick for his X-ray shows it").

Castañeda is also critical of Sellars's account of intentional inference. For Castañeda, inferences of the form "If p, then I shall do A; p; So, I shall do A" are legitimate as is. But from his earliest writings, Sellars denied that "shall" can appear within the scope of logical operators, and so must reconstruct reasoning like the above; and he reconstructs such inferences in a way that foreshadows his introduction of S-Imp in later writings. Castañeda complains that this needlessly complicates an inference that is, on the face of it, perfectly valid. Thus, Sellars holds that "shall"-statements cannot embed within logical operators—and so there are no first-order relations of logical implication among "shall"-statements, or between "shall"-statements and factual statements; any such relations are metalinguistic and mention rather than use the "shall"-statements. Logical relations among "shall"-statements are, of course, parasitic on logical relations among their contents. Castañeda, on the other hand, seems to want to argue that ordinary usage indicates the contrary. He thinks that arguments such as the following ought to be read straightforwardly as asserting "I shall do A" as a logical consequence of p (which is not allowable in Sellars's logic of intentions):

I shall do A, if p.
p.
So, I shall do A. (Castañeda, C3)

C4 and S5 deal with "Form and Content in Ethical Theory" (FCET), most of which was incorporated into OIM. Castañeda is mostly concerned with what he sees as some ambiguities in Sellars's exposition of his logic of intentions, such as whether Sellars's notion of "reasonableness" is a semantic or pragmatic value, why the "Shall"-operator cannot embed, whether Sellars is consistent in his projection of nomologicals into the practical realm, and so on. Castañeda's letter reveals that although, by his own account, his view and Sellars's have become "much closer than ever before," there are nevertheless some fairly basic disagreements between the two (e.g., on the question of whether the "Shall"-operator can embed). Sellars's reply to Castañeda is relatively brief; he indicates agreement on a number of points but is generally unmoved by the criticisms from C4. OIM appeared with the sections from FCET largely unrevised; since SM was published in 1967, Castañeda's comments would no doubt have come too late to be taken into account, although it is unclear what, if any, changes Sellars would have made. Sellars did, of course, continue to develop and refine his account of the logic of intentions, culminating in ORAV in 1980.

23 The Aune–Sellars Correspondence

Sellars and Bruce Aune carried out a wide-ranging correspondence that lasted almost 20 years. We have included here the 20 letters that bear directly on ethical theory and Sellars's philosophy of action.

The first three letters deal with Sellars's theory of free will. In *S1*, Sellars lays out a number of considerations that will reappear in FD (chiefly in Section IV [§§51–61]). Given the definitions Sellars gives for the various practical modal predicates (such as "CAN"), Sellars wants to argue that the *relative impossibility* of performing minimal action Am at *t* does not entail that one is not able to perform Am at *t*; when unpacked, these two statements have forms that do not contradict each other.

Aune (*A2*) is largely sympathetic to Sellars's analysis, although he suggests that Sellars revise the role of the circumstance-clause in his analysis of ability, since it seems to make ability contingent on being in the right circumstances—and, as Aune puts it, "it would be odd if one could gain and lose a number of abilities merely by undergoing the change in circumstances involved in walking round the block!" Sellars (*S3*) seems sympathetic to Aune's suggestion, and he offers various refinements to his treatment of circumstances—in particular, to how circumstances are implicated in ability.

Aune and Sellars's correspondence turned to other topics during the 1960s; it returned to practical philosophy in late 1969 with a long exchange (*A4–A11*) about the adequacy of Sellars's principles governing the logic of intentions. Aune raises a number of concerns about Sellars's notion of dependent implication and his treatment of conditional intentions (i.e., "Shall [I will do A, if p]"), as well as for his principle (which he eventually names "S-Imp") that "Shall-p" implies "Shall-q" iff "p" implies "q." (See our summary of "Conditional Promises and Conditional Intentions" [CPCI] for an explanation of why an account of dependent implication or implication relative to a hypothesis is crucial for Sellars's practical philosophy.) Aune is concerned, for example, that Sellars doesn't relativize S-Imp to what the agent believes to be the case (*A5*); that the propositional logic underlying the logic of intentions is too strong, and this leads to counterintuitive results (see, e.g., *A7*); and that some of Sellars's inferential principles are insufficiently justified (or even false—see *A4* and *A5*). Sellars offers detailed replies to Aune's objections. For example, he argues (*S6*) that although Aune's criticisms would be accurate if "implies," as it appears in the context of practical reasoning, "has the sense of 'strictly implies' or 'logically implies,'" but this is not the notion of implication meant by Sellars. As to the point that the logic of intentions must be relativized to the agent's beliefs, Sellars argues (*S6*) that this point is easily addressed by making a move in practical reasoning analogous to the move, in theoretical reasoning, of "distinguish[ing] not only between the validity of an argument and its goodness (i.e. its being valid and having true premises) but between these and the reasonableness of a given person offering it." Despite Sellars's arguments (and his further elaboration of his notion of dependent implication, especially in *S8* and *S10*), he fails to convince Aune; this series of letters ends with Aune writing, "I decided to write up a little paper putting all my doubts about your views on practical reasoning together" (*A11*)—an effort that culminated in Aune (1975).

The Aune-Sellars correspondence returns to practical philosophy with letters from Aune (*A12* and *A13*) in 1973. Aune has by this point been formally working on Sellars's practical reasoning for some time (having apparently already completed the final version of Aune [1975]), and he has concluded that many of his earlier criticisms of Sellars's theory were mistaken—or, at least, that Sellars's theory can avoid the most serious problems if Sellars will adopt some friendly amendments suggested by Aune (such as treating S-Imp as a "meta-theorem," and importing some logical machinery from Castañeda to deal with conditional intentions).

In *A14*, Aune reports having received a copy of VR and says he is dissatisfied with the theory of practical reasoning outlined there, writing, "I like your earlier, simpler theory better." Among other criticisms, Aune denies that there is a strong logical difference between intentions to do vs. intentions that-p; nor is he convinced that an intention that p be the case *entails* an intention to do something. Nor (Aune argues), when we reason about future actions, is there a logical difference between "actions to be done" and "actions it is hypothesized that I will do."

In his reply (*S15*), Sellars argues that even if there is no logical difference between two statements, there might be a practical or causal—and hence even a *conceptual*—difference between the two. In *S15*, Sellars offers a lengthy elaboration of how this crucial difference underlies the distinctions he makes in TA.

In *S16*, Sellars responds to a criticism from Aune (1977):

You claim that my principle
  P1. 'S(α)' implies 'S(β)' $\equiv$ 'α' implies 'β'
generates such relative implications as
  (p $\supset$ q) $\vdash^{S(p)}$ q

Aune thinks (1977, p. 5) this is a problematic consequence because it makes Sellars's theory of practical reasoning subject to what Joel Feinberg calls the "accordion effect":

We can, if we wish, inflate our conception of an action to include one of its effects, and more often than not our language obliges us by providing a relatively complex word for the purpose. Instead of saying that Peter did *A* (a relatively simple act) and thereby caused *X* in *Y*, we might say something of the form "Peter *X*-ed *Y*"; instead of "Peter opened the door causing Paul to be startled," "Peter startled Paul." (Feinberg 1970, p. 134)

We thus, it seems, become responsible for all of the causal consequences of anything we intend—and indeed that these consequences are something that we *do*.

Sellars denies that relative implication works this way on his account of practical reasoning. "After all," he argues,

> whereas I hold that
> 'S(P)' implies 'S(Q)' ≡ 'P' implies 'Q'
> in which indicatives and resolutives appear symmetrically, I also hold that
> 'S(P)' implies 'S(Q)' *because* 'P' implies 'Q'
> in which they do not. It is the *explanatory primacy* of indicative implication which underlies my theory of practical reasoning. (*S16*)

Aune's criticism does not respect this explanatory primacy. (It is perhaps because of Aune's criticism that Sellars formulates S-Imp not as a biconditional in ORAV, but as an implication— if '*P*' implies '*Q*,' then "It shall be the case that-*P*" implies "It shall be the case that-*Q*"—and adds a footnote reading, "This principle can be formulated as a biconditional, but I forbear to do so lest I open the door to misunderstandings, based on other things I have written, which there would be no time to alleviate" [ORAV §47, n. 8].)

Aune pushes back in *A17*, noting that on Sellars's view,

> we may move from
> (1) p ⊃ q implies q (relative to p)
> to
> (2) S(p ⊃ q) implies S(q) (relative to p). (*A17*)

Aune argues that since these two implication statements are equivalent on Sellars's view, we may (by the Interchange of Equivalents principle) move either from (1) to (2) or from (2) to (1). Thus, Aune argues that his objection (from Aune 1977), which Sellars discusses in *S16*, has not been refuted. Aune further develops his argument in *A18* by offering what he takes to be some counterexamples to Sellars's principle of dependent implication. Although Sellars offers (*S19*) a length defense of his theory of dependent implication—denying, for example, that he is relying on a principle of Interchange of Equivalents—Aune (*A20*) is still not entirely convinced of the viability of Sellars's theory of practical reasoning, arguing that given Sellars's basic principles, one can still (for example) derive a contradiction or derive other counterintuitive results.

24 Sellars to Solomon, 1976

This short letter from Sellars to Solomon might be of particular interest in the debate over whether Sellars held an individualist or a collectivist view of we-intentions.[18] Sellars is clear that we can *ascribe* both intentions and actions to

---

[18] For an individualist interpretation of we-intentions, see Ferguson 2023.

groups, but neither ascription formally entails the corresponding intention or action for any particular member of that group. Similarly, if I *express* a group intention ("We shall disperse"), this doesn't formally entail "I shall disperse"; but it

will have *some* implications (*which* will depend on the circumstances) of the form
'I shall do A.'
Thus, at the very minimum, it implies
'I shall not impede the dispersal.' (§7)

Sellars stresses to Solomon a theme he consistently held since IIOR—that a we-intention "need not...be 'chorused'" (§9). The point is not that a we-intention is *in fact* shared—the point is that it *can be* shared; the logically intersubjective form of these intentions "*permits* different people to have, in a strong sense, the *same* intention" (§8).

Sellars concludes by arguing that there is a "fundamental intention characterizing the moral point of view," namely,

'We shall any of *us* do that which (in his/her circumstances) promotes (maximizes) *our* common good.' (§15)

It is this intention that defines the moral point of view (in contrast to the personal point of view—see §18), and this intention is categorically valid "because sharing such an intention defines what it is to be members of a community" (§16).

Works Cited

Aikin, Scott F. 2008. "Review of *In the Space of Reasons: Selected Essays of Wilfrid Sellars*." *Transactions of the Charles S. Peirce Society* 44:2 (Spring): 363–367.

Aune, Bruce. 1975. "Sellars on Practical Reason." In Hector-Neri Castañeda (ed.), *Action, Knowledge, and Reality: Critical Studies in Honor of Wilfrid Sellars*. Indianapolis, Indiana: The Bobbs-Merrill Company, Inc., 1–26.

Aune, Bruce. 1977. *Reason and Action*. Dordrecht: D. Reidel Publishing Company.

Ayer, A. J. 1936. *Language, Truth and Logic*. London: Victor Gollancz.

Brandom, Robert B. 2015. *From Empiricism to Expressivism: Brandom Reads Sellars*. Cambridge, MA: Harvard University Press.

Brandt, Stefan, and Anke Breunig (eds.). 2020. *Wilfrid Sellars and Twentieth-Century Philosophy*. New York: Routledge.

Bratman, Michael E. 1999. *Intentions, Plans, and Practical Reason*. Stanford: CSLI Publications.

Castañeda, Hector-Neri. 1974. *The Structure of Morality*. Springfield, Illinois: Charles C. Thomas.

Castañeda, Hector-Neri. 1975. "Some Reflections on Wilfrid Sellars's Theory of Intentions." In Hector-Neri Castañeda (ed.), *Action, Knowledge, and Reality: Critical Studies in Honor of Wilfrid Sellars*. Indianapolis, Indiana: The Bobbs-Merrill Company, Inc., 27–54.

Chisholm, Roderick M. 1963. "Contrary-to-Duty Imperatives and Deontic Logic." *Analysis* 24:2 (December): 33–36.

Coates, Paul. 2007. *The Metaphysics of Perception: Wilfrid Sellars, Perceptual Consciousness and Critical Realism*. New York: Routledge.

Corti, Luca, and Antonio M. Nunziante. 2018. *Sellars and the History of Modern Philosophy*. New York: Routledge.

Dach, Stefanie. 2021. "Sellars, We-Intentions, and Ought-Statements," *Synthese* 198: 4415–4439.

Dach, Stefanie. 2023. "Sellars on the Intersubjectivity of 'We-Intentions.'" In Jeremy Randel Koons and Ronald Loeffler (eds.), *Ethics, Practical Reasoning, Agency: Wilfrid Sellars's Practical Philosophy*. New York: Routledge.

deVries, Willem A., and Timm Triplett. 2000. *Knowledge, Mind, and the Given: Reading Wilfrid Sellars's "Empiricism and the Philosophy of Mind," Including the Complete Text of Sellars's Essay*. Indianapolis: Hackett Publishing Company.

deVries, Willem A. 2005. *Wilfrid Sellars*. Chesham, UK: Acumen Publishing.

deVries, Willem A. 2008. "Review of *In the Space of Reasons: Selected Essays of Wilfrid Sellars*." *The Review of Metaphysics* 61:4 (June): 860–862.

deVries, Willem A. (ed.). 2010. *Empiricism, Perceptual Knowledge, Normativity, and Realism: Essays on Wilfrid Sellars*. Oxford: Oxford University Press.

Donagan, Alan. 1975. "Determinism and Freedom: Sellars and the Reconciliationist Theory." In Hector-Neri Castañeda (ed.), *Action, Knowledge, and Reality: Critical Studies in Honor of Wilfrid Sellars*. Indianapolis, Indiana: The Bobbs-Merrill Company, Inc., 55–81.

Feinberg, Joel. 1970. "Action and Responsibility," in Joel Feinberg, *Doing and Deserving: Essays in the Theory of Responsibility* (Princeton: Princeton University Press): 119–151.

Ferguson, Kyle. 2023. "We-Intentions and How One Reports Them." In Jeremy Randel Koons and Ronald Loeffler (eds.) *Ethics, Practical Reasoning, Agency: Wilfrid Sellars's Practical Philosophy*. New York: Routledge, 37–61.

Forrester, James William. 1984. "Gentle Murder, or the Adverbial Samaritan." *The Journal of Philosophy* 81:4 (April): 193–197.

Garfield, Jay L. 2018. *Wilfrid Sellars and Buddhist Philosophy: Freedom from Foundations*. New York: Routledge.

Hare, R. M. 1952. *The Language of Morals*. Oxford: Oxford University Press.

Koons, Jeremy Randel. 2019. *The Ethics of Wilfrid Sellars*. New York: Routledge.

Koons, Jeremy Randel, and Ronald Loeffler (eds.). 2023. *Ethics, Practical Reasoning, Agency: Wilfrid Sellars's Practical Philosophy*. New York: Routledge.

List, Christian. 2019. "What's Wrong with the Consequence Argument," *Proceedings of the Aristotelian Society* 119:3 (October): 253–274.

McDowell, John. 1986. "Critical Notice of *Ethics and the Limits of Philosophy*, by Bernard Williams," *Mind* 95:379 (1986): 377–386.

McDowell, John. 2011. "Pragmatism and Intention-in-Action." In Rosa Maria Calcaterra (ed.), *New Perspectives on Pragmatism and Analytic Philosophy*. Amsterdam: Rodopi, 119–128.

Olen, Peter. 2016. *Wilfrid Sellars and the Foundations of Normativity*. London: Palgrave Macmillan.

O'Shea, James R. 2007. *Wilfrid Sellars: Naturalism with a Normative Turn*. Cambridge, UK: Polity Press.

O'Shea, James R. (ed.). 2016. *Wilfrid Sellars and His Legacy*. Oxford: Oxford University Press.

O'Shea, James R. Mahdi Ranaee, and Luz C. Seiberth (eds), forthcoming. *Fraught with Ought: Writings from Wilfrid Sellars on Mind, Meaning, and Metaphysics*. Oxford: Oxford University Press.

Pereplyotchik, David, and Deborah R. Barnbaum (eds.). 2017. *Sellars and Contemporary Philosophy*. New York: Routledge.

Price, Huw, with Simon Blackburn, Robert Brandom, Paul Horwich, and Michael Williams. 2013. *Expressivism, Pragmatism and Representationalism*. Cambridge: Cambridge University Press.

Reider, Patrick J. (ed.). 2016. *Wilfrid Sellars, Idealism, and Realism: Understanding Psychological Nominalism*. London: Bloomsbury.

Rosenberg, Jay F. 2007. *Wilfrid Sellars: Fusing the Images*. Oxford: Oxford University Press.

Scharp, Kevin, and Robert B. Brandom (eds.). 2007. *In the Space of Reasons: Selected Essays of Wilfrid Sellars*. Cambridge, MA: Harvard University Press.

Schweikard, David P., and Hans Bernhard Schmid. 2021. "Collective Intentionality," *The Stanford Encyclopedia of Philosophy* (Fall 2021 edition), Edward N. Zalta (ed.), URL = <https://plato.stanford.edu/archives/fall2021/entries/collective-intentionality/>.

Seiberth, Luz Christopher. 2021. *Intentionality in Sellars: A Transcendental Account of Finite Knowledge*. New York: Routledge.

White, Heath. 2009. "'Ought': The Correct Intention Account," *Philosophical Explorations* 12:3 (September): 297–317.

Wiggins, David. 1990–1991. "Moral Cognitivism, Moral Relativism and Motivating Moral Beliefs," *Proceedings of the Aristotelian Society*, New Series vol. 91(1): 61–85.

Wolf, Michael P., and Mark Norris Lance (eds.). 2007. *The Self-Correcting Enterprise: Essays on Wilfrid Sellars*. Poznan Studies in the Philosophy of the Sciences and the Humanities 92. Amsterdam: Rodopi.

PART 1
THE MORAL POINT OF VIEW

1
Mind, Meaning, and Behavior*

1. In one sense of "exist" it is beyond question that both minds and bodies exist; in another the question whether both minds and bodies or either or neither exist is the crux of a legitimate and intricate philosophical puzzle—the Mind-Body problem. 1.1 Accordingly, the philosopher, after agreeing with common sense that there are both minds and bodies, mental events and physical events, goes on to ask whether mental facts are "reducible" to physical facts, or vice versa, or whether both are "reducible" to facts which are neither. 1.11 Where the reduction in question is taken to be explicit definition (in that broad sense which includes the *Principia* definition of the number Two in terms of logical primitives, not to mention the definition of Oxford University in terms of its colleges), we find philosophers exploring such alternatives as these: (a) neither mentalistic nor physicalistic concepts are definable in terms of the other, nor both in terms of a third type of concept; (b) mentalistic concepts can be defined in terms of physicalistic concepts, or vice versa; (c) both mentalistic and physicalistic concepts are definable in terms of a third type of concept.

1.12 Materialism and Neutral Monism have in common the claim that mentalistic concepts can be defined in terms of non-mentalistic concepts. Neutral Monism, however, claims that concepts relating to physical objects can be explicitly defined in terms of concepts relating to sense data. The materialist denies this. 1.121 The most widespread form of Neutral Monism today is Phenomenalism. Neutral Monisms differ according to their account of the logical form to be given definitions of mentalistic and physicalistic concepts in terms of concepts relating to sense data. 1.1211 Only if these concepts relating to sense data are non-mentalistic can Neutral Monism hope to realize its program of reducing mentalistic and physicalistic concepts to concepts which are neither.

1.2 But before we can decide whether concepts relating to sense-data are or are not mentalistic, we must first determine how the class of mentalistic concepts is to be delimited. 1.21 I shall without further ado state my agreement with the classical thesis (represented, among others, by Descartes and Brentano) that the distinguishing feature of mental facts is *intentionality* or *aboutness*. Thus, some typical mentalistic concepts are *believes, doubts, desires, fears, expects*, etc. 1.22 The question as to the status of concepts relating to sense-data thus turns out to be

---

* AUTHOR'S NOTE. This is a revised version of a paper read at the Ann Arbor meeting of the American Philosophical Association, May 1952.

Wilfrid Sellars, *The Metaphysics of Practice: Writings on Action, Community, and Obligation*. Edited by: Kyle Ferguson and Jeremy Randel Koons, Oxford University Press. © Kyle Ferguson and Jeremy Randel Koons 2023.
DOI: 10.1093/oso/9780192866820.003.0002

the question as to the role of intentionality, if any, in such concepts. 1.221 It is immediately clear that the concepts of the sense qualities red, sweet, C#, etc. are not concepts of intentional acts.

1.2211 The phrase "concepts relating to sense data" is ambiguous. For while the concepts of the sense-qualities are not mentalistic concepts, it may well be the case that the concept of the givenness of sense-data, of their datumness, so to speak, *is* a mentalistic concept. 1.2212 Thus, when Neutral Monism claims that mentalistic and physicalistic concepts are definable in terms of concepts relating to sense data, it must be using the phrase "concept relating to sense-data" in the sense of "concept definable in terms of sense qualities (and relations)" unless it is prepared to hold that the datumness of sense-data is a nonintentional fact. 1.2213 Furthermore, since it is not plausible to claim that sense qualities can be defined in physicalistic terms, Materialism must be interpreted as the claim that mentalistic concepts can be defined in terms of physicalistic concepts together with concepts of sense qualities, neither of these latter two types being definable in terms of the other.

1.23 Thus, the Mind-Body problem is, at bottom, the problem whether intentional concepts relating to minds can be reduced to nonintentional concepts, whether concepts of sense qualities, or physicalistic concepts, or both, and if so, in exactly what sense of "reduced."

2. It is often wise to draw back *pour mieux sauter*. We shall be following this advice if we glance at the dialectics of a familiar problem in moral philosophy; the familiar one of the relation of Ought to Is. 2.1 Let us notice two similarities between the Ought-Is problem and the Mind-Body problem. (a) In both cases one asks about the reducibility of one type of concept to another. (b) In both cases sentences employing a concept whose reducibility is in question characteristically have two verbs. 2.11 Just as "Jones desires to go downtown" has the two verbs "desires" and "to go," so "Jones ought to pay his debt" has the two verbs "ought" and "to pay." 2.12 Just as "Smith believes it is raining" is not a truth function of "It is raining," so "Jones ought to pay his debt" is not a truth function of "Jones pays his debt."

2.2 If we suppose that to ask whether Ought is reducible to Is is to ask whether Ought is (contextually) definable in descriptive terms, we find a clash between Ethical Naturalism which claims that it is, and Ethical Non-naturalism ("Intuitionism") which claims that it is not. 2.21 Let us put this by saying that for the former Ought is *logically* reducible to Is, while for the latter it is not.

2.22 Consider now a position according to which, while Ought is not logically reducible to Is, nevertheless the only way in which moral obligation enters into the causal explanation of human history is via facts of the form *Jones thinks that he ought to pay his debt*. 2.221 "Ought," in other words, enters into the antecedent or consequent of causal laws only as a subordinate element in a mentalistic context—as, e.g., "entails" occurs in "Jones believes that responsibility entails indeterminism." 2.222 In traditional terminology, obligation enters into the causal order only as an element in the intentional object of a mental act. 2.223 If, as seems proper, we so use "ethical assertion" that while "Jones ought to pay his debt" is, of course, an ethical assertion, "Jones thinks he ought to pay his debt" is not, then the above claim can be rephrased as the claim that although the normative is not logically reducible to the descriptive, one can nevertheless explain the history of moral agents without making ethical assertions. 2.224 Let us agree to put this by saying that although Ought is not *logically* reducible to Is, Ought is *causally* reducible to Is.

2.3 Traditional moral philosophers, however, Naturalists and Non-naturalists alike, have tended to assume that Ought can be *causally* reducible to Is only if Ought is *logically* reducible to Is. 2.31 Thus, Ethical Naturalists have tended to assume that it can only be possible (which they think it to be) to explain the history of moral agents without making ethical assertions in characteristically ethical language, on condition that Ought is logically reducible to Is. 2.32 While Ethical Non-naturalists have tended to assume that it is reasonable to deny (as they do) that Ought is logically reducible to Is, only if one is prepared to deny that Ought is causally reducible to Is. This latter, of course, they are prepared to do, since they characteristically insist that the existence of moral concepts and beliefs in the human mind cannot be accounted for in purely descriptive terms. Human thinking on ethical matters is, as they see it, ultimately grounded in and controlled by objective values and obligations.

2.33 The moral philosophy we have been adumbrating combines a thesis characteristic of Ethical Naturalism with a thesis characteristic of Ethical Non-naturalism; the causal reducibility of Ought with the logical irreducibility of Ought. Is it a form of Naturalism? of Non-naturalism? 2.331 Would we not dodge these alternatives, and point out that the value of a system of classification is threatened when one of its presuppositions is abandoned?

3. Let us return to the Mind-Body problem. But first some general considerations. 3.1 Let us now speak of *terms* rather than *concepts*. Thus, let us discuss the logical properties of "…believes…" rather than the status of the concept of Belief. 3.11 Among the expressions of our language we find some which, in their primary use, appear in sentences which have sentences or quasi-sentences as component parts. By a quasi-sentence I mean an expression (containing a verb) which becomes a sentence when the mood of the verb is changed. Thus "It is necessary that all giants be tall" contains the quasi-sentence "all giants be tall." 3.111 Let us call such expressions "connectives." Both "believes" and "and" are connectives. Thus, "It is raining" is a component part of both "It is raining *and* the temperature is low" and "Jones believes that it is raining." 3.12 Some connectives are, in a familiar sense, truth functions. Others are not. The truth of "Jones believes that it is raining" is compatible with both the truth and the falsity of "It is raining." The falsity of "It is unusual that Jones has come to the meeting" is compatible with both the truth and the falsity of "Jones has come to the meeting."

3.2 The connectives which belong to the primitive expressions of the language form developed in *Principia Mathematica* are all truth functions. Let us call a language built on the pattern laid down in *Principia Mathematica* with a certain set of primitive descriptive predicates, a PM language. 3.21 In addition to its primitive expressions, a PM language will include expressions definable in terms of its primitive expressions. 3.22 A recurring question in philosophy A. P. (after *Principia*) has been "Can the language we speak be 'reconstructed' as a PM language?" 3.221 An obvious stumbling block in the way of such a "reconstruction" is the presence in ordinary discourse of connectives which are not truth functions. To this category belong, as we have noticed, certain expressions characteristic of normative, modal, and mentalistic discourse. 3.222 That it is not absurd to hope that this goal may be achieved is suggested by the fact that "It is unusual that Jones has come to the meeting" can plausibly be regarded as identical in meaning (vagueness aside) with "Jones has come to the meeting and Jones was absent from 75% of the preceding meetings," a sentence of a kind which *Principia Mathematica* was designed to "reconstruct." 3.2221 Might not the same be true of "It is necessary that Jones has come to the meeting," "It is fitting that Jones has come to the meeting," and "It is believed that Jones has come to the meeting"?

3.3 Can our language insofar as it contains mentalistic expressions be "reconstructed" in PMese? 3.31 Let us call "Philosophical Behaviorism" the thesis that the mentalistic expressions of our language can be defined by PM techniques in terms of the basic PM resources of our language. 3.311 By "basic PM resources of our language" I mean those expressions which can reasonably be reconstructed as expressions belonging to the basic syntactical categories of PM. 3.312 No connective which is not a truth function, and hence no mentalistic expression, belongs to the basic PM resources of our language.

3.313 Caution would require that the following qualification be added to the definition of "Philosophical Behaviorism" (3.31) after "... the basic PM resources of our language," namely: with the possible addition of modal expressions, should these be regarded as indispensable, and as incapable of definition in PMese. 3.3131 Fortunately, to explore the question at hand it is not necessary to commit ourselves on the issue whether an adequate language of science must contain modal connectives (in particular, the causal modalities) so regarded. In the remainder of this paper, therefore, I shall assume that the requirements of scientific discourse (including the formulation of subjunctive conditionals and the definition of disposition terms) can be met by an extensional logic. In short, I shall assume that the major part of the "extensionalist" program can be carried out, and concentrate attention on that part of the program which concerns the Mind-Body problem.

3.32 Let us use the term "(Mind-Body) Dualist" to refer to philosophers who reject Philosophical Behaviorism and insist that at least one mentalistic expression in our language must be construed as a primitive connective. 3.321 Is one committed to Dualism if one rejects Philosophical Behaviorism? (Assuming, of course, that Mentalism is out of the question.)

3.322 Before we attempt to answer this question, let us note that our rejection of Ethical Naturalism did not entail an acceptance of Ethical Non-naturalism—for we saw that both are complex theses involving a *logical* claim and a *causal* claim. We rejected the logical claim of Ethical Naturalism, but accepted its causal claim; we rejected the *causal* claim of Non-naturalism, but accepted its *logical* claim. 3.3221 The common presupposition of Naturalist and Non-naturalist is causal reducibility implies logical reducibility. We rejected this presupposition.

3.323 Notice the parallel provided by the Mind-Body problem. 3.3231 Dualists buttress the denial that mentalistic expressions are logically reducible to PMese with the claim that a causal account of the world must make use of mentalistic expressions. 3.32311 This is, of course, true even of the Epiphenomenalistic variety of Dualism—though it ceases to be so if "physical world" is substituted for "world." 3.3232 On the other hand Philosophical Behaviorists buttress the assertion that the world is causally explainable in PMese, with the claim that mentalistic expressions are logically reducible to PMese.

3.33 May it not, however, be possible to hold that while mentalistic expressions are not logically reducible to PMese, nevertheless a causal account of the world (including psychological phenomena) can, in principle, be given in PMese?

3.331 Let us use the function "m has A(O)" to say that in mind m there occurs a mental act of kind A of which the intentional object is O. Thus, A might (for the moment) be illustrated by *believes* and O by *it is raining*, so that "m has A(O)"* says of mind m that it believes that it is raining.

3.332 Now Behaviorism as a substantive thesis is the claim that in an ideally complete psychology it would turn out that to each mentalistic function "m has A(O)" there corresponded a PM function "ϕb" such that

(A) m has A(O) $\equiv \phi b$

where the values of "m" and "b" are pairs of minds and bodies which "belong" to each other. It follows that for every law involving a mentalistic function there would be an equivalent law in PMese. 3.3321 Let us refer to this claim as the thesis of Scientific Behaviorism. It must by no means be confused with the thesis of Philosophical Behaviorism. The latter differs in two respects: (1) It is a stronger thesis. For the '$\equiv$' of schema A it substitutes the '=' appropriate to statements of analysis. (2) It is not prospective. It claims that what we *now* say by using mentalistic expressions we can *now* say by using PM expressions. To be sure, it adds "in principle." The reference, however, is not to future developments or

---

* [Eds.—In the published version, this close quotation mark is at the end of the sentence (after "it is raining"); we have moved it to where it seems to belong.]

to an ideal knowledge, but to the disjunctive complexity of the appropriate PM expressions. Mention is also made of "open texture."

3.3322 We shall also refer to Scientific Behaviorism as the thesis of the *causal* reducibility of mental events to bodily events, where causal reducibility does not preclude logical reducibility (cf. Burks).

3.333 In the argument to follow, I shall be assuming that the thesis of Scientific Behaviorism is true. I shall attempt neither to establish its truth, nor even to make it plausible. To those readers who are disinclined to accept it, I can only say that they may find the following pages interesting as a philosophical counterpart of "If Napoleon had won the battle of Waterloo..." 3.3331 If Scientific Behaviorism *were* true, what would follow for the Mind-Body problem? 3.3332 If one *were* to assert

$$m \text{ has } A(O) \equiv \phi b$$

and yet deny the logical reducibility of "m has A(O)" to "ϕb" would one not be committed to Dualism in its epiphenomenalistic form?

3.33321 Can the joint thesis of the causal reducibility but logical irreducibility of the mental to the bodily be held otherwise than as Epiphenomenalism?

3.4 As our first step toward answering this question, let us examine that crude form of Scientific Behaviorism according to which the PM functions correlated with mentalistic functions concern the linguistic utterances of the body and their role in its economy. 3.41 Consider, for example, the claim that the following equivalence obtains

(B)   m believes it is raining $\equiv$ b tends to utter "es regnet"

3.411 What is the import of such a statement as "b tends to utter 'es regnet'"? Clearly the utterance "es regnet" is not being considered here as a mere sequence of squeaks and whistles such as a parrot might emit. It is conceived to be a *meaningful* sequence of sounds. 3.412 The natural way of making this fact explicit is by reformulating (B) to read

(B′)   m believes it is raining $\equiv$ b tends to utter "es regnet" and
        "es regnet" means *it is raining*

3.4121 If we explore the right-hand side of (B′), the first thing we note is that the second clause ("'es regnet' means *it is raining*") contains the connective "means" which is clearly not a truth function. 3.4122 Next we note that to say of an utterance that it "means it is raining" clearly *conveys information* about how the utterance is being used. 3.41221 Thus,

(B′-R)   b tends to utter "es regnet" and "es regnet" means *it is raining asserts* that b tends to utter "es regnet" and *conveys* psychological information about b's use of "es regnet."

3.41222 But granted that (B'-R) *conveys* psychological information about b's use of "es regnet," does it follow that (B'-R) makes a psychological *assertion* about b's use of "es regnet"? 3.4123 Let us agree, for the moment, to make this inference. In other words, let us agree that "b's utterances of 'es regnet' mean *it is raining*" makes a *psychological assertion* about b's utterances of "es regnet." 3.41231 If we continue along the lines of the analysis above, we note that Scientific Behaviorism is committed to an equivalence of the form

"Es regnet" uttered by b means *it is raining* $\equiv \psi$("es regnet," b)

where the right-hand side says of b that it has certain habits with respect to utterances of "es regnet." 3.41232 Consider now the case of a Frenchman who utters "Il pleut." We are in any case authorized by our assumptions to write down the equivalence

"Il pleut" uttered by b means *it is raining* $\equiv \Theta$("il pleut," b)

But clearly the Scientific Behaviorist is committed to the thesis that if "es regnet" uttered by Germans has the same meaning as "il pleut" uttered by Frenchmen, then the habits of the latter with respect to "il pleut" share a common generic feature with the habits of Germans with respect to "es regnet." Let us represent this common feature by "K('...,' b) ." Then we can write down the equivalences

"Es regnet" uttered by b means *it is raining* $\equiv$ K("es regnet," b)

"Il pleut" uttered by b means *it is raining* $\equiv$ K("il pleut," b)

or generally,

"..." uttered by b means *it is raining* $\equiv$ K("...," b)

3.41233 Notice, therefore, that

"It is raining" uttered by b means *it is raining* $\equiv$ K("It is raining," b)

3.412331 Now, when I say

Jones' utterances of "es regnet" mean *it is raining*

I am *mentioning* "es regnet" and *using* "It is raining" to convey what is meant by "es regnet" as uttered by Jones. According to Scientific Behaviorism, if what I say of Jones' utterance is true, then the utterance "It is raining" which I *use* is the manifestation of habits generically identical with Jones' habits with respect to "es regnet." 3.4123311 Notice that since utterances convey information about language habits by virtue of being manifestations of these habits, an utterance may (potentially) convey more information than is appreciated (actually conveyed) at a given stage of human knowledge. Thus (to exaggerate), "'Es regnet' uttered by Jones means *it is raining*" might today convey only that Jones has the 'same' habits with respect to "es regnet" as the speaker has with respect to "it is raining," but might convey in the future that Jones has habits of (specific) kind and with respect to "es regnet."

3.412332 And when the Scientific Behaviorist is in a position to propose specific equivalences of the form

"..." uttered by b means *** ≡ F("...," b)

they will be subject to the condition that they can only be true if they are "pragmatically consistent," that is, if the "***" used on the left-hand side is a *manifestation* of the kind of habit *mentioned* on the right-hand side. By virtue of this fact they will be more than "mere" material equivalences. 3.412333 Yet they are neither laws of nature nor, in any usual sense of the term, logical equivalences. They are validated not by showing that the left-hand side can be constructed out of the same (PM) primitives as the righthand side, but rather by knowing the circumstances in which it is correct to use the left-hand side. 3.4123331 As an illuminating parallel it can be pointed out that although "x is here" said by Smith who is at s is, in a strong sense, equivalent to "x is at s," nevertheless it is not, in any ordinary sense, logically equivalent to it.

3.4124 Now the truth of the matter, of course, is that while

(C) b's utterances of "es regnet" mean *it is raining*

conveys psychological information about b's utterances, it does not make a psychological *assertion* about b's utterances. We must abandon the inference momentarily sanctioned in 3.4123. 3.41241 Semantical assertions, such as (C), *convey* psychological information about language users, but they are not psychological *assertions*.[1] They do this by virtue of the feature of their use pointed out above (3.412331). 3.41242 When Jones says to me

---

[1] It is my hope that this distinction between what is asserted, and what is conveyed but not asserted, by semantical statements in ordinary usage throws some light on what I was trying to say in Section IV of my "Realism and the New Way of Words," *Philosophy and Phenomenological Research*, vol. 8 (1948), (reprinted in *Readings in Philosophical Analysis*, edited by Herbert Feigl and Wilfrid Sellars, and published by Appleton-Century-Crofts, New York, 1949).

Smith's utterances of "es regnet" mean *it is raining*

I can *infer* that Smith uses "es regnet" as I use "It is raining," even though Jones is not making an assertion about the way in which Smith uses "es regnet."
3.41243 It should now be pointed out that it is not only linguistic events in the narrow sense of the use of conventional languages that are correctly said to "mean such and such." If we use the term "symbol" for items which are correctly said to mean such and such (whereas "sign" means *symptom* of such and such, and is not a semantical expression), then the class of symbol events is radically more inclusive than that of linguistic events in the narrower sense. It is only if "language" is taken in the broader sense of the use of symbols, that it is plausible to identify thought with the use of language.[2]
3.5 Before we can put the results given above to good use, we must take another look at mentalistic discourse. 3.51 It is a familiar fact that many mentalistic expressions are definable in terms of other mentalistic expressions. Indeed, a scrutiny of the psychological (and philosophical) literature devoted to the descriptive phenomenology of the mental suggests that an adequate basis for the definition of all mentalistic terms can be found in "act of thought" (which we shall abbreviate as "thought") and "about," together with non-mentalistic expressions. 3.511 Thus, "x is a thought about O" would be the form of a basic sentence of mentalistic discourse. A thought in this sense is a mental *episode*. Furthermore, to say of x that it is a thought is not to ascribe any dispositional features to x.
3.5111 Yet it may be the case that in order to be correctly characterized as a thought, x must be a complex state of affairs with dispositional as well as purely episodic components. Compare our remarks in 3.4124 above on semantical statements. To say of certain grunts and groans that they mean *it is raining* is not to ascribe any dispositional feature to these grunts and groans, although it is only if they are the manifestation of certain habits that it is correct to say of them that they mean *it is raining*. 3.512 Mentalistic verbs relating to motivation ("desires," "chooses," "hates," etc.) would be defined in terms of the tendency of thoughts about conduct to bring about conduct.
3.52 As a matter of fact, further reflection suggests that our list of two mentalistic primitives is redundant, and that the single term "about" would suffice. It would be absurd to speak of a thought which was not about something. Can we not therefore define an act of thought as an event which is correctly said to be about something? 3.521 And a mind as a continuant which has thoughts?

---

[2] Implicit in this paragraph together with 3.41231–3.41232 and 3.41241 is the *semantical* (not psychological) distinction between linguistic *types* (linguistic functions) and *token-classes* which I have developed in several papers, most recently in "Quotation Marks, Sentences and Propositions," *Philosophy and Phenomenological Research*, vol. 10 (1950); and "The Identity of Linguistic Expressions and the Paradox of Analysis," *Philosophical Studies*, vol. 1 (1950).

3.522 But what is *aboutness* but *meaning*? Thus (3.4124) to say of an event e that it is *about* something (and hence that it is a mental event) is not to make a psychological assertion about e, even though it is to convey psychological information about e. 3.5221 To say of an event e that it is *about* something is not to describe e. In general, to make semantical assertions about psychological events is not to describe these events, though it is to *convey* information the *assertion* of which would describe them.[3]

3.5222 But if in saying of an event that it is *about* something we are not describing the event, it follows that to say of an event that it is mental is not to describe it in a way which precludes a correct description of the event in bodily terms. In other words, "x is mental" does not stand to "x is ϕ" (where "ϕ" is definable in terms of bodily states) as "x is green" to "x is red."

3.5223 Indeed, it follows that every mental event must (in principle) be describable in non-mentalistic terms. 3.5224 And while, of course, it does not follow from the above alone that mental events must (in principle) be describable in terms of bodily states (for they might be describable in terms which were neither mentalistic nor definable in terms of bodily states), this does follow from the above together with the thesis of Scientific Behaviorism.

3.5225 Notice, of course, that if Scientific Behaviorism is to be plausible, we must include in the class of bodily states such activities as seeing colors, hearing sounds, tasting tastes, and having images. 3.52251 Prichard has correctly pointed out that seeing a color is not *cognizing* a color. Ducasse's insight that tasting a taste is like waltzing a waltz was vitiated only by his failure to appreciate that tasting a taste is not cognizing a taste. 3.52252 To see colors, hear sounds, etc., is, in one sense of this everyday term, to be conscious, but not *cognitively* conscious. The latter involves *aboutness*, the former does not. Seeing a color is not a *mental* activity. 3.522521 The epistemological notion of the givenness of colors, sounds, etc., must not be confused with the notions of seeing colors, hearing sounds, etc. Givenness is a form of cognitive consciousness and requires mention of *aboutness* in its analysis.

3.52253 Seeing a color cannot be defined in physico-chemical terms, or, for that matter, in terms of overt behavior. But it is a mistake to suppose that "bodily state" (in ordinary usage) *means* state definable in either of these ways. 3.52254 Since sensory states do not occur apart from what would readily be called bodily states, and since they are not mental states, the decision to use "bodily state" to include them would not be absurd. 3.52255 If, on the other hand, one decided to exclude them from bodily states, then Scientific Behaviorism would have to be

---

[3] This paragraph, together with 3.4243 and 3.522521 is a restatement of the thesis, argued in "Realism and the New Way of Words," that the *semantical* (as opposed to psychological) concept of a *token* is the central concept of an epistemology which is to avoid both forms of psychologism distinguished in that paper (see *Readings*, p. 430, notes 2 and 3).

reformulated in terms of "states of the body" and "states of the sensorium," as something like the latter would have to be the continuant language for sensory events.[4]

3.6 To sum up our results: If Scientific Behaviorism is correct, and if our account of sentences of the form "...means ___" or "...is about ___" is correct, then every mental event can (in principle) be described in terms of expressions which are definable in terms of bodily states. 3.61 We have thus shown how it is possible to accept Scientific Behaviorism, that is (3.3322) the thesis of the causal reducibility of the mental, yet deny the logical reducibility of the mental, without being committed to Epiphenomenalism (cf. 3.33321). And we have shown how it is possible to reject Philosophical Behaviorism without being committed to Dualism (cf. 3.321).

4. The logical irreducibility of mentalistic discourse to Behaviorese, insisted on by traditional dualisms, turns out, if the argument above is sound, to be exactly the logical irreducibility of semantical metalanguages to PMese.

4.1 Now, while we often use semantical statements to *convey* information which could (in principle) be formulated in PMese, and while this use constitutes the *application* of the semantical language form, it must not be inferred that what is *said* by semantical discourse could, in principle, be said in PMese. 4.11 Just as from the fact that the use of normative discourse *conveys* a great deal of information about the speaker and his community, and from the fact that the normative form of discourse gains *application* through functioning in motivation,[5] it must not be inferred that what is said by normative discourse can be said in psychological and socio-psychological discourse about motivation. 4.111 That which is *said* by "Jones ought to pay his debt" could not be said in even an ideal PMese. 4.12 That which is said by "'It is raining' is true if and only if *it is raining*" or even by "'It is raining' means *it is raining*" could not be said in even an ideal PMese.

4.2 It is indeed important to see that (in principle) the world, including human behavior, could be *described* and *predicted* without using semantical discourse. But the proper way to interpret this fact is not by propounding an "extensionalist thesis" according to which *everything can be said* without using semantical discourse, but rather offering a careful account of the interrelationships which would obtain between semantical discourse and an ideal behaviorese. 4.21 In general, the task of the philosopher is to explore without prejudice the syntactical and pragmatical relationships which obtain between the various forms of

---

[4] It may not be out of place to point out that the account of the Mind-Body problem given in Section IX of "Realism and the New Way of Words" (see also the second paragraph of note 22 to page 455 of *Readings*) differs from that of the present paper only in its greater obscurity. Its primary flaw was to suppose (p. 453 of *Readings*) that a dualism of sense qualities and brain events *qua* describable in physicalistic terms, would be a *mind*-body dualism.

[5] See my "Obligation and Motivation" in *Readings in Ethical Theory*, edited by Wilfrid Sellars and John Hospers (New York: Appleton-Century-Crofts, 1952), p. 516. [Eds.—OMR is Ch. 2 of this volume.]

discourse, descriptive, semantical, normative, modal, etc. 4.211 Surely the hankering to give bad marks and a pseudo-conceptual status to other forms of discourse merely because they are discerned not to be descriptive discourse belongs with other left-wing deviations in the Madame Tussaud's Wax Work Museum of the analytic movement.

2
Obligation and Motivation

I

[1] The following paragraphs will be devoted to a somewhat schematic discussion of the significance of the word "ought" in such distinctively ethical sentences as "I ought to do X (in circumstances C)" and "One ought to do X (in circumstances C)." The frame is provided by the thesis, formulated here without spit and polish, that to be aware of a property is to have "in one's mind" a token of an expression which designates that property. If the expression is a simple one, in that it is not compounded out of other expressions, then the awareness is a simple or unstructured awareness; otherwise a complex or structured awareness.

[2] Thus, one can be aware of circularity by tokening the simple expression "circle" or by tokening the complex expression "closed plane curve with a constant degree of curvature." The former would constitute a simple awareness of what, after all, is a complex property. The latter would be a structured awareness of this same property, though the complexity of the awareness would be far from doing justice to the complexity of the property. Now, an unstructured awareness of a complex property may be mistaken, by philosophers, for the awareness of a simple property. This can occur even where the expression tokened by the simple awareness is paired in ordinary usage with a complex expression as neatly as "circularity" might be supposed to be paired with "closed plane curve..." Here the philosopher speaks of supervening Gestalt properties, e.g., of an unanalyzable *circularity* which rides piggy-back on *closed-plane-curve-with-constant-degree-of-curvaturehood*. The mistake, however, is much more likely to be made where common usage contains no such unambiguous correlation.

[3] Before applying these tools to "I ought to do X," let us try them out on "I want to do X." (For the sake of brevity, the phrase "in circumstances C" will be omitted but understood.) Consider Jones who is tokening this sentence "in his mind" and who therefore has an unstructured awareness of whatever it is that is meant by "want (to do)." Now if Jones has been sufficiently corrupted by philosophy, it is not beyond the bounds of probability that he would reply to the question "What kind of situation is described by the above sentence?" by saying, "It asserts an ultimate and unanalyzable relation of *want* to obtain between *myself* and *the doing of X by me*." From here he might go on to wonder how there could be a relation between himself and an action which might remain a mere possibility. This might lead him to interesting metaphysical discoveries.

[4] Let us refrain, however, from following Jones along this path. As a matter of fact we took French leave at the beginning of his remarks with an unexpressed comment to the effect that Jones was misled by a superficial grammatical resemblance between "(I) (want) (to do X)" and "(I) (eat) (apples)." If we were challenged to show that this resemblance is indeed superficial, and that Jones was indeed misled, we should surely reply by offering an *analysis* of sentences of the form "Y wants to do X." As a first attempt we might suggest "Y finds the thought of doing X attractive," following this with "Y's thought of doing X tends to evoke the doing of X." Though these are drastic oversimplifications, they do indicate the essential features of a successful analysis.

[5] As our next step we might claim that the sentence "Y's thought of doing X tends to evoke the doing of X" is to be understood in terms of a tendency of tokens "in Y's mind" of the expression "Y doing X" to evoke the doing of X by Y. I suspect, however, that we should hesitate to speak of this step as an analysis. But would such a hesitation be, after all, warranted? The term "analysis," having as its core the notion of explicit definition (usually definition in *usu*) seems clearly to cover the following gamut of cases: (1) The definition reflects an antecedent mutual substitutability in ordinary usage of expressions having a clear-cut and unambiguous sense. (2) The definition would reflect such a mutual substitutability only if ordinary usage were focused and fixed. (3) The definition would reflect such a mutual substitutability only if ordinary usage were enriched by a new set of expressions.

[6] To this last category belongs the analysis of material objects in terms of the micro-particles of modern physics. Analyses of both the latter two types are actually proposals for reform. The second urges a better use of materials already at hand; the third requests the introduction of new materials together with a demotion of words already in current use from the status, in effect, of primitive terms to that of defined terms. A basement is proposed for an already existing house. Where in this scale do the above analyses of "Y wants to do X" belong? It is reasonably certain that none of them belongs in the immediate neighborhood of (1). The two analyses in terms of "the thought of doing X" would seem to belong in the neighborhood of (2); as for the analysis in terms of tokens of the expression "Y doing X," its place in the scale could be determined only after a far more protracted discussion.

[7] In an earlier paragraph we pointed out that insofar as he tokens "in his mind" the simple expression "want (to do)," Jones has an unstructured awareness of whatever it is that is meant by this term. Let us now agree to say that "want (to do)" means that which would be mentioned by a successful analysis of "Y wants to do X." Assuming, then, that the above analyses are in the right direction, the term in question means a dispositional complex, and we can say that Jones has an unstructured awareness of a dispositional complex involving the thought of his

OBLIGATION AND MOTIVATION 75

doing an action, and the doing of the action. On the whole, philosophers have been fairly successful in avoiding the mistake of treating *wanting (to do)* as a simple relation obtaining between agents and actions. The materials for a successful analysis have been sufficiently close at hand to keep all but a determined few from falling into this trap.

[8] Let us now suppose that Jones has a token "in his mind" of the sentence "I ought to do X," and, therefore, has an unstructured awareness of whatever it is that is meant by "ought." This time we should by no means be surprised to find Jones claiming that this sentence asserts an ultimate and unanalyzable relation of *ought* to obtain between *himself* and *his doing of X*. Nor would we be surprised to find him modifying and refining the metaphysics of oughtness as new perplexities occurred to him. Now it is my intention to defend an analysis of "ought (to do)" which has a fundamental kinship with the account above of "want (to do)." The parallel is easily stated. "Ought" as used in "I ought to do X" refers to a type of motivation, to a dispositional complex involving the thought of doing X and the doing of X. Yet it is the differences that must be stressed, for our moral consciousness finds all the difference in the world between merely wanting to do something and being morally obligated to do it.

[9] Let me begin by putting my finger on the heart of the matter, though this involves an oversimplification which must later be made good. In wanting to do X (in circumstances C) it is the thought of *oneself doing X (in circumstances C)* which tends to evoke the doing of X in circumstances believed to be C. On the other hand, when I truly say "I *ought* to do X in circumstances C," it is the thought of *myself doing X (in circumstances C)* as an instance of *everybody doing X (in circumstances C)* which tends to evoke the doing of X in circumstances believed to be C. Let us call the content of the thought which tends to evoke action, the *logos* or "formula" of the motive-tendency. (To simplify our account, we shall suppose that any restriction on the class of agents in the formula of an ought is included in the "circumstances.") Then, the formula in the case of *want (to do)* concerns only the agent, the action, and the circumstances, whereas in the case of *I ought (to do)* the formula has a major premise which concerns the doing of X by all agents in circumstances C.

[10] Impartiality has often (e.g. by Westermark) been found to constitute the essence of moral attitudes and motivations. However, it has almost as often been sadly misconstrued. According to the usual account, if Jones responds with approval to all situations of kind S regardless of who participates in S, his approval is *ipso facto* to be called impartial. Impartiality is thus conceived to be an "external" property of a feeling of approval, a matter of its being an instance of a uniformity. According to our account, on the other hand, the impartiality of an attitude, emotion or motive is a matter of the logical structure of its *logos*, and is therefore "intrinsic." The distinction between these two conceptions of

impartiality corresponds to Kant's distinction between action *in accordance with* a rule, and action *because of* a rule.[1]

[11] It will be noticed that I have gone out of my way to emphasize the autobiographical form "I ought to do X." I have done this deliberately as I wish to claim that this is the form through which alone "ought" can be understood. "You ought..." is not related to "I ought..." as "You eat..." is to "I eat..." (Or shall we say it is not *merely* related to it in this manner? The following remarks will explain this hesitation.) Note that in the analysans given above for "I ought to do X," the word "ought" does not occur in the statement of the formula of the motive-tendency. We conceived its major premise (and our account of ethical motivation will shortly become even more Aristotelian[2]) to be *All agents in circumstances C do X, not... ought to do X!* Instead of being a mere application of "Everybody ought to do X," "I ought to do X" is the *fons et origo* of "Everybody ought to do X." It is because "Everybody doing X (in circumstances C)" plays a motivational role in my conduct that there is such a significant sentence as "Everybody ought to do X." In other words, "I *ought* to do X" rests on "Everybody *doing* X," and "*Everybody* ought to do X" rests on "*I* ought to do X."

[12] Yet we must hasten to add that in another sense, "I ought to do X" rests on "Everybody ought to do X." It is, indeed, an oversimplification to say that "I ought to do X" is an autobiographical sentence attributing to myself a tendency to be moved to action by a syllogism whose major premise has the form *Everybody does do X in circumstances C.* For the truth of the matter is that the word "ought," which as far as our analysis has gone stands for the motivational force of a syllogistic formula whose major premise is of this form, has stolen a syntactical disguise which can be said to embody the mistake of thinking of *ought* not only as a unique relation between myself and an action, but one which is objective and independent of me in that it holds between *me* and *my doing X* because it holds

---

[1] For a discussion of this and related topics, see my "Language, Rules and Behavior," in *John Dewey: Philosopher of Science and Freedom*, a volume of essays edited by Sidney Hook, and published by the Dial Press, New York, 1950.

[2] "The one opinion is universal, the other is concerned with the particular facts, and here we come to something within the sphere of perception; when a single opinion results from the two, the soul must in one type of case [Translator's note: i.e. in scientific reasoning] affirm the conclusion, while in the case of opinions concerned with production it must immediately act (e.g. if 'everything sweet ought to be tasted,' and 'this is sweet,' in the sense of being one of the particular sweet things, the man who can act and is not prevented must at the same time actually act accordingly). When, then, the universal opinion is present in us forbidding us to taste, and there is also the opinion that 'everything sweet is pleasant,' and that 'this is sweet' (now this is the opinion that is active [Translator's note: i.e. determines action]), and when appetite happens to be present in us, the one opinion bids us avoid the subject, but appetite leads us towards it (for it can move each of our bodily parts); so that it turns out that a man behaves incontinently under the influence (in a sense) of a rule and an opinion, and of one not contrary in itself, but only incidentally—for the appetite is contrary, not the opinion—to the right rule." Aristotle, *Nicomachean Ethics*, Bk. VII; Ch. 3, 1147a25–1147b2, translated by Sir David Ross and quoted from *The Basic Works of Aristotle*, edited by Richard McKeon, and published by Random House, New York, 1941. I have emphasized the kinship of my analysis with Kant's moral philosophy in "Language, Rules and Behavior," printed in *John Dewey: Philosopher of Science and Freedom*, cited in footnote 1 above.

between *everybody* and *their doing X*. To assume this disguise, which is an essential condition of moral consciousness, the word "ought" worms its way into the expression of the formula of the motive, and the formula becomes the familiar moral syllogism *Everybody ought to do X in C, I am in C, therefore I ought to do X*. To put the matter in a paradox: the *mistake* of thinking of *ought* as a *sui generis* relation is essential to the *correct* use of the word "ought."

II

[13] We are now in a position to reformulate our thesis in a somewhat more systematic manner. Our basic line of thought was that "I ought" resembles "I want" in being the vehicle of our consciousness of a certain mode of motivation. This led to the suggestion that "ought" is to be analysed (in some sense of "analysis") in terms of a tendency to be moved by a syllogistic *logos*. Yet when we attempted to give a plausible analysis along these lines, we soon ran into a serious difficulty. For we saw that to be the *logos* of ethical motivation, the major premise of the *logos* must contain a term with the force of "ought." Can this appearance of circularity be overcome?

[14] In discussing this point, let me begin by pointing out that whereas the definiendum of our proposed analysis of *I ought to do X in C* contains the word "ought," the definiens contains the expression "...the thought of...ought..." If we put this in terms of linguistic tokens rather than thoughts, we notice that whereas the definiendum *uses* the word "ought," the definiens *mentions* it. *I ought to do X in C* $=_{Df}$ *tokens of "Everybody ought to do X in C, and I am in C" tend to evoke my doing X in C*.

[15] But does this really enable us to escape the charge of circularity? Clearly it does so only if we find it possible to characterize the tokens of "...ought..." *mentioned* by the definiens, without *using* the word "ought," at least in the sense in which it is used in the definiendum. This, I believe, can be done. The point is bound up with our previous claim that there is a sense in which "Everybody ought to do X in C" is prior to "I ought to do X in C," even though in another sense "Everybody ought..." would be completely lacking in significance unless I were able honestly to say "I ought..."

[16] The fact of the matter is that the word "ought" plays at least four intimately related roles. In its minimal and, as such, incomplete role, it is the central term in the "language of norms," a mode of discourse which presupposes, but is irreducible to, the "language of fact." The term "ought" has a characteristic syntax by which it is related to other normative expressions, as well as to logical and descriptive categories. It is this role of "ought" which Prichard, Ross and other "'deontological intuitionists" have ferreted out and made the core of their theory of morals. Their mistake, almost inevitable in view of their rationalistic

background, was to suppose that it is merely by grasping the conceptual logic of the "language of norms" that we become conscious of having obligations.

[17] Now, "I ought to do X in C" illustrates this minimal role of the word "ought." It is a statement in the normative mode of discourse, and *as such* is incapable of analysis in terms of factual discourse. Yet, if the only significance possessed by "I ought to do X in C" were that which it derives from being an application of "Everybody ought to do X in C," both these statements would be empty husks, interesting only because of their unique logical grammar. The crucial fact is that while we are learning to use the word "ought" in accordance with its grammar, we are also acquiring tendencies to be moved to act by moral syllogisms in which this term appears. It is by virtue of this involvement in motivation that the "language of norms" gains "application." This involvement may be compared to the way in which factual language gains application through the process misdescribed as "ostensive definition." This is the *second* of the four roles mentioned above.

[18] Now, if we can honestly say "I ought to do X in C," and are not "mistaken," then we must have the tendency to be moved by the corresponding moral syllogism. Furthermore, if we made use of the familiar distinction between a *symptom* or *expression* of a state of mind, and a *mention* of a state of mind, we can safely say that "I ought to do X in C" is normally the *expression* of a motivational tendency. This is its *third* role.

[19] But "I ought to do X in C" is also a *mention* of the motivational tendency in question. As such it is capable of analysis (though in which sense of "analysis" it is by no means easy to say) in descriptive terms along the lines we have suggested. This is the *fourth* role.

[20] It should be noticed that of the four roles distinguished in this paper only the first and fourth concern the conceptual meaning of "ought." Notice also that by virtue of these two roles, the word "ought" in "I ought to do X in C" has *two* logical grammars. Indeed, this one word embodies two distinguishable concepts which differ in their degrees of clarity and articulation. The first is the concept of *obligation*; the second might be called, in the light of the idiom, "I feel obligated to...," the concept of *feeling obligated*.

[21] At the end of the first section of this paper, I was moved to put its thesis in the form of a paradox, namely, "the mistake of thinking of *ought* as a *sui generis* relation is essential to the correct use of the word 'ought.'" It should be clear by now that to think of *obligation* is indeed to think of a *sui generis* connection between acts and agents. Thus, strictly speaking, it is not true to say that a mistake is involved in the correct use of the word "ought." It is, however, a mistake to assume that because there is such a thing as *thinking of a sui generis connection between acts and agents* (which thinking is just the use of the "language of norms"), there must be a subclass of facts called obligations, so that a description of the world would be incomplete unless it mentioned *obligations*. It is rather the

concept of *feeling obligated* that is required by a complete description of the world, and this is an analysable concept of empirical psychology. Now, it may be argued that the above mistake is a philosopher's mistake, and not a mistake of the plain man. I am strongly inclined to think, however, that the mistake is part and parcel of common-sense moral consciousness, and that the intuitionist does little more than dress it up in technical language. If so, this would justify the paradox on which we have been commenting. But I do not wish to press the point.

[22] I shall conclude with three brief remarks. (1) If the main contention of this paper is sound, we can run with the "naturalists" (the psychology of *feeling obligated* can be developed in purely descriptive terms), while hunting with the "intuitionists" (in a perfectly legitimate sense, the concept of *obligation* is ultimate and irreducible). (2) The four roles of "ought" distinguished in the course of the argument are not intended to constitute an exhaustive list. For a perceptive treatment of additional roles played by the "language of norms," as well as of practical discourse in general, the reader is referred to C. L. Stevenson's *Ethics and Language*.* (3) The normative mode of discourse has as its characteristic sentence not "If anybody is in C, then he ought to do X" (which would raise questions as to the nature of the implicative relation), but rather a sentence of a unique type which we may perhaps represent by the form "Ought(anyone, X, C)." For this reason one is tempted to speak of *ought* as a 'category' or a 'modality.' But to explore the pros and cons of either classification would take us to the growing edge of metaphysics.

---

* [See also his paper on "The Emotive Meaning of Ethical Terms," reprinted in this volume.] [Eds.— Sellars is referring to the volume *Readings in Ethical Theory*, eds. Wilfrid Sellars and John Hospers (New York: Appleton-Century-Crofts, 1952).]

3
"Ought" and Moral Principles*

1. My aim this evening is to explore a central issue—indeed *the* central issue—in moral philosophy; the relation of scientific knowledge to moral principles. By 'scientific knowledge' I mean science in so far as it tells us what *is* the case. For even if there is a sense in which science tells us what ought to be the case—and there is such a sense[†]—we can distinguish, as we shall see, between science *qua* telling us which is the case and science in its role of telling us what ought to be the case. The original question could indeed be reformulated in terms of the relationship between these two roles.

2. The Sciences I have in mind include everything from logic and mathematics on one end of the spectrum to psychology and the social sciences on the other. And, since the issue I have in mind is a conceptual one which does not hinge on the current status of any of these sciences, I shall not hesitate to make thought experiments which amount to philosophical fiction about science.

3. Before I get the substantive part of my argument under way, I must introduce some terms and draw some distinctions. The terms will be used[‡] in a technical sense, though I hope that they will group together in a perspicuous way things which can be seen to belong together from the high altitude of abstraction in which our problem exists.

4. First a few words about moral principles. At this stage it will be useful to give what might be called the standard account. Whether or not or to what extent the features of this account apply to anything in our experience will be left open for the time being. In philosophy one rarely begins by being absolutely clear about one piece of a conceptual puzzle and unclear about the rest. Philosophical perplexities tend to spread and often the things which seem obvious when one begins become even more puzzling than the initial problem.

---

* [Eds—As noted in the volume introduction, we have republished here the most widely circulated version of this manuscript. However, the archive contains a copy with significant handwritten revision notes. We have not attempted to reconstruct the manuscript as indicated by these notes. However, in his revision notes, Sellars corrects a number of typographical errors contained in the text; we have followed these notes in making corrections to the present essay. The essay with notes for revision is document 31735062220516, box 36, folder 8, Wilfrid S. Sellars Papers, 1899–1990, ASP.1991.01, Archives of Scientific Philosophy, Archives & Special Collections, University of Pittsburgh Library System. The revised version of OMP begins at page 20. We thank Stefanie Dach for directing us to this revision of OMP.]

† [Eds.—This reads "science" in the original manuscript; Sellars corrects this in his revision notes.]

‡ [Eds.—This reads "based" in the original manuscript; Sellars corrects this in his revision notes.]

Wilfrid Sellars, *The Metaphysics of Practice: Writings on Action, Community, and Obligation*. Edited by: Kyle Ferguson and Jeremy Randel Koons, Oxford University Press. © Kyle Ferguson and Jeremy Randel Koons 2023.
DOI: 10.1093/oso/9780192866820.003.0004

5. According to the standard account, a moral principle is a statement which says what people ought to do in a certain kind of circumstance. It is added that to be a *moral* principle the people in question must be all of us, and to be a *principle* in the sense of first principle it must not be an application of a more general principle in the way in which, for example,

everybody ought to keep his *written* promises

follows from

everybody ought to keep his promises

or in which, with the additive premise

measles is a distress
everybody ought to help people with measles

follows from

everybody ought to help people in distress

6. Two* other features belong to the standard account, at least in its more sophisticated form

(a) Since† principles of the kind I have formulated can conflict, they must be regarded as abstractions from more complicated principles which specify what ought to be done in *combinations* of the kinds of circumstances mentioned in these simpler principles. This qualification has the consequence that principles, properly speaking, are far more complicated than the sort of thing we usually give as examples—for these, on reflection, always carry the rider "other things being equal"—which they rarely are. Indeed, it commits us to the idea that a moral principle, properly speaking, specifies the circumstances in which a certain kind of action ought to be performed in a *very* complex way. Yet they remain *principles* in that they apply to anybody in that kind of circumstance.
(b) It has the further consequence that instead of moral principles (unlike copybook maxims) being already at hand, our task being merely to apply them, serious moral thinking starts from the complexities of the actual case and arrives at a conclusion concerning the principle which applies

---

* [Eds.—This reads "That" in the original manuscript; Sellars corrects this in his revision notes.]
† [Eds.—This reads "science" in the original manuscript; Sellars corrects this in his revision notes.]

82   THE METAPHYSICS OF PRACTICE

(i.e. concerning what *anybody* ought to do in that kind of case in the very process of arriving at a conclusion concerning what *I* ought to do in that case).

7. Yet we can abstract, for the moment, from this latter feature and suppose that however difficult it may be to arrive at them, they are in some sense "there" to be arrived at. This brings me to another feature of the standard account. Moral principles, however complex, are *objective* in the sense that there is truth and falsity with respect to them—that thinking doesn't make them so—that there are false beliefs about moral principles just as there are false beliefs about scientific laws.

8. Of course, if moral principles *were* scientific laws, or if they were uniquely determined by scientific laws, there would be nothing paradoxical about *this*, nor about the difficulty of discovering what we ought to do. Moral truth would be either a special case of scientific truth—or—consequence of scientific truth.

9. But against this it is argued that science tells us what is the case and moral principles what ought to be the case and one can't get from 'is' to 'ought'.

10. Finally, according to the standard account, not only can we be mistaken about what we ought to do; even when we are quite confident that we know what we ought to do, we may well fail to do so. Duty may fall before inclination.

II

11. But before we beard the venerable problem of the relation of 'is' to 'ought'— which is simply a restatement of our original topic, more distinctions are in order. Let me first introduce the expression 'to value' as in the context

   x (a certain person) values y

when y is a state of affairs e.g. x's having a substantial income—or, perhaps, the Washington Senators winning the pennant. The latter example is intended to bring out the fact that the state of affairs valued need not exist, nor need it include the person who does the valuing. Indeed, I shall use the expression that the state of affairs valued is always in the future, for we are concerned with action and it seems unlikely that action can influence the past.

12. The states of affairs a person 'values' in this technical sense can be very complex. Indeed, what people value is clearly a function of its context and implications, and that valuing involves preferring some states of affairs to others.

But there is, I believe, no need to spend time in botanizing the complications which any attempt to classify valuings would involve. Such distinctions as I will draw arise naturally, I hope, out of the broader requirements of our problem.

13. As a final preposition, let me call attention to the difference between the *expression* of a valuing by someone and the ascription of a valuing to someone. Suppose that Jones values the Senators winning the pennant this year. The statement in our terminology which ascribes this valuing to Jones is simply:

Jones values the Senators winning this year.

Other statements in more ordinary speech which ascribe valuings of various kinds to Jones would be

Jones wishes that...
Jones aims at...
Jones intends that...
Jones has such and such a goal.

14. Anybody with the relevant information, including Jones himself, can ascribe a valuing to Jones. On the other hand, only Jones himself can *express* his valuings. This he may do, for example, by saying

Would that the Senators won this year's pennant!*

There are many ways of giving expression to valuings, and, indeed, different valuings call for different sentences to express them. But the pattern of my argument as a whole will stand out more clearly if we rise above detail and use the above as our standard sentence for the expression of a valuing. Thus even the valuing of an action a person is about to perform will be supposed to have as its expression

Would that I shortly do A!

15. I pointed out that anybody, including Jones himself, can ascribe a valuing to Jones. Thus Jones can say

I wish that the Senators would win this year

---

* [Eds.—Following a pattern laid out in IIOR and followed (more or less) consistently through ORAV, Sellars here uses an exclamation point at the end of "Would that...!" statements which express desires, wishes, or valuings. However, in what follows, Sellars is inconsistent about including the exclamation point at the end of "Would that...!" expressions; we have added them when missing.]

or, in our straightjacket,

I value that the Senators win this year

Notice that this *self-ascription* can serve as a secondary *expression* of the valuing. For

Would that... but I don't value that...

is as conceptually odd as

It is raining, but I don't think that it is

16. Two final points: (a) to value something is to be disposed to think thoughts properly expressed by

Would that...

(b) to value, all things considered, an action which one can do right here and now is to do the action (or at least try to do it).

III

17. Let us now introduce a team of scientists on the scene. First, let them be quite ordinary and let them do something simple. They see Jones near a heavy object (O), a long rod (R) and a stone. They mobilize their science and agree that

A necessary condition of Jones raising the stone is his using the rod as a lever

They then rephrase this as

Jones raising O implies Jones using R as lever.

So far so good. Then we suddenly find them saying:

If Jones wants to raise O (values raising O), he ought to use the rod as lever.

Here the word 'ought' has crept in—and yet seems to belong in a tough-minded, scientific way. Suppose they now hear Jones say

Would that I raised O!

They infer, naturally enough, that* he values the state of affairs of his raising O. He wants to raise O. Can they conclude

Jones ought to use the rod as lever?

i.e. can they determine what Jones ought to do? The answer seems clearly 'no.' Consider its parallel case where they pool their scientific knowledge and decide

If Jones wants to poison his Aunt quickly, he ought to give her prussic acid

and they hear him say

Would that I poisoned my Aunt quickly!

Suppose they come to Jones and say

If, other things being equal, you value poisoning your Aunt quickly, then the same things being equal you ought to give her prussic acid.

There seems to be no absurdity in their adding (or anybody who shares their scientific knowledge asserting) "but, of course, you ought not to give your Aunt prussic acid!" The 'ought' does not seem to be a moral 'ought.'
18. The point is a familiar one, but its exact nature must be spelled out—for after a few turns and twists it will enable us to clarify and, finally, solve our problem.
19. Clearly the scientific information could have been directly communicated to Jones before it was put in terms of 'ought.' In that case, if he was convinced of its truth, he too could have made the move to the 'ought,' thus

If, other things being equal, I want to poison my Aunt quickly, I ought (the same things being equal) to give her prussic acid.

and it is clear that what this amounts to is that the valuing expressed by

Would that I poisoned my Aunt quickly!

is logically tied to the valuing expressed by

Would that I gave her prussic acid!

by virtue of the scientific facts of the case.

* [Eds.—Correction of "then" in original version.]

20. In general terms

> If x wants A, he ought to bring about B

tells us that if x were to think

> Would that A but would that I not bring about B!

his valuings would be inconsistent.

21. Of course people often hold inconsistent values; and even when they are persuaded that these valuings are inconsistent they do not always change their mind and substitute consistent valuings. Thus, suppose our scientists approach Jones and persuade him that

> Bringing about A implies bringing about B

He may move with alacrity to the thought

> If (other things being equal) I value bringing about A, then I ought (the same things being equal) to bring about B.

And yet continue to think both

> Would that I brought about A!
> Would that I not bring about B!

22. The situation, thus, is the same with respect to our valuings as with respect to our beliefs. We may well continue to hold inconsistent beliefs even after we have been shown that they are inconsistent.

23. Yet logic has *some* grip on our minds and if, for our present purposes, we exaggerate, we may say that a person who is convinced that

> Bringing about A implies bringing about B

and hence, that

> (*ceteris paribus*) if I value bringing about A, then I ought to bring about B

will abandon either

> Would that I brought about A!

or

Would that I not bring about B!

24. We can sum up the apparent moral of our discussion to date by saying that although the 'ought' of

If X wants A, he ought to do B

looks as though it concerned the propriety of *doing B* on a certain hypothesis, it actually concerns the logical propriety or impropriety of certain complex valuings. To offer advice of the form

If you want A, you ought to do B

is not to offer *substantive* advice as does

You ought to do X

It is to give *logical* advice.

IV

25. We seem to have shown that the 'ought' which our team of scientists can generate is not the 'ought' which tells us what to do, but rather an 'ought' which pertains to the coherence of our valuings. Since the 'ought' of moral principles *does* tell us what to do, it would seem that the 'ought' which scientists generate is not the ought of morals.

26. Yet is this so clear? After all, even if the 'oughts' which our team of scientists have come up with do in a sense pertain to the coherence of Jones' valuings, they are formulated in such a way that they take actions as their objects

If X wants A, he ought *to do* B

Thus the mere fact that moral ought tells us what we ought *to do* is no decisive argument against the idea that they too pertain to the coherence of our valuings. Let me develop this thought.

27. It will not have gone unnoticed that I have been careful to sprinkle my story to date with such phrases as '*ceteris paribus*' and "other things being equal." But is not

If, all things considered, I value A, then I ought to do B

closer to what we want? Perhaps. Yet what does "all things considered" mean?

28. Without attempting a direct answer, let me sketch a classical theory—essentially Plato's in modern dress—which can be called the "informed or enlightened self-interest model." It conceives of a ground floor of human valuations, which arise naturally out of bodily, mental or social need. These specific valuings need not be ego-centered. Only the tough-minded like Hobbes thought that the valuing expressed by

Would that he not be suffering!

is really what would be candidly expressed by

Would that I not be in his shoes!

But whatever the character of these ground-floor or specific valuings, they are dominated by an over-arching ego-directed valuing expressed, in our terminology by

Would that I led a happy life!

To the extent that people are logical, this valuing, combined with beliefs about the world and the propensities of our fellow men, and also what constitutes a happy life, generates a life plan valuing which allots subordinate places to ground-floor valuings, and is carried out in action. Most people lead blurred and fluctuating lives because of their changing beliefs, the faltering grips of logic and the breaking in of impulse.

29. Let us re-introduce our team of scientists. Let us now* idealize them and suppose that they really know what things and persons are like. They turn their attention to a budding young genius (Jones, again) and say among themselves.

If Jones wants to lead a happy life, he ought to lead a life of kind L

(The neo-Freudian-Pavlovians among them, we suppose, have conclusively shown that for budding geniuses L is the happy life.) They go to Jones and say

If you want to lead a happy life, you ought to lead a life of kind L.

And when he questions it, they then persuade him to come to the Academy of Sciences. After several years study Jones says "I see!" and proceeds to think along the following lines:

If I want to lead a happy life, I ought to lead a life of kind L.

---

* [Eds.—This reads "not" in the original manuscript; Sellars corrects this in his revision notes.]

Ex hypothesi he has built unto him the valuing

> Would that I led a happy life!

Being logical he now derives from* this the valuing

> Would that I led a life of kind L!

Drawing on additional knowledge he has gained in the Academy he continues

> If I want to lead a life of kind L, I ought to do such and such things in such and such circumstances

Always logical, he adds to his battery of valuations

> Would that I do such and such things in such and such circumstances!

where the policies he has in mind take account of all the subtle ways in which circumstances can vary, yet seem on casual inspection to be the same.
Confronted with a particular circumstance C, he reasons

> If I want† to do A whenever I am in C, I ought to do A now, for C now obtains

As before his valuings remain coherent and he adds the valuing

> Would that I now do A!

which, since it constitutes his being favorably disposed to doing A generates the action in question.

30. Plato's basic analogy here, is that of an art or craft. He develops in a number of dialogues the concept of an art of living which he conceives of as the art of achieving happiness. Assuming that a shoemaker values, for whatever reason, the making of shoes, and that no other values become relevant during shoemaking hours, that he knows what the various stages of making a shoe require him to do to the leather and that he knows how to do it, then he will turn and make a good shoe within the limitations of his material. So, too, a man in possession of the art of living will turn to and create a happy life within the limits of his opportunities.

---

* [Eds.—This reads "conjoins with" in the original manuscript; in his revision notes, Sellars changes this to "derives from," which makes more sense in the present context.]
† [Eds.—In his revision notes, Sellars has changed "If I want" to "If I ought."]

31. But what, it will be asked, guarantees that our genius, Jones, however meticulously he plans his life and carries out his plans will behave in the ways we think of as moral? In other words what guarantees that the rules of the art of living coincide in their content with the content of the principles of morality? Mightn't the rules include such items as

> Would that whenever I wear a ring which makes me invisible, I take all available loose cash to spend on research!

Not to mention more exotic pursuits?

32. Plato has a lengthy argument designed to prove that the rules of the art of living coincide in content with what we think of as sound moral principles. The argument has more bite to it than is usually allowed, but this is because Plato tacitly introduces some themes from the next and concluding section of my lecture. Even if he were successful in showing this coincidence, however, he would not have succeeded in showing that the conclusion of the reasoning

> Since* I want to lead a happy life
> .
> .
> .
> .
> I ought to do such and such in such and such circumstances

is identical in sense with the statement

> I morally ought to do those things in those circumstances

We find it quite meaningful to say

> I morally ought to do such and such actions in such and such circumstances even if it would result in my unhappiness and other courses of action would make me happy.

V

33. Yet we still have not shown that the 'ought' of moral principles is not what we have called the 'ought' of coherence; when the principles of coherence are supplied by logic and the other sciences. For the trouble may not be with the pattern of

---

* [Eds.—This reads "Sure" in the original manuscript; Sellars corrects this in his revision notes.]

Plato's theory, but with the valuing which he postulates as the unbuilt motor of the well-lived life. In particular, the trouble may be with the egoistic or self-centered nature of this valuing. An altruistic goal might, it would seem, do the job.

34. Our team of scientists returns and this time, we suppose, say with good reason

> If Jones wants to promote the general welfare, he ought to do such and such things in such and such circumstances.

And they now allow that a person can seek to promote the general welfare for its own sake; as before they come to Jones and say

> If and to the extent that you want to promote the general welfare, you ought to do such and such things in such and such circumstances

and take him to the Academy. He returns to the world convinced and reasons

> If (and to the extent that) I want to promote the general welfare, I ought to do such and such actions in such and such circumstances

He is convinced, in other words of the coherence of

> Would that I promoted the general welfare!
> Would that I do such and such, etc.!

and the incoherence of

> Would that I promoted the general welfare!
> Would that I not do such and such, etc.!

and, other things being equal, he values promoting the general welfare. This certainly has a more moral ring to it. Yet it is not completely satisfying. And when we see why, we will have the answer to our problems.

35. Our team of scientists might equally have pointed out that

> If, and to the extent that, Jones wants to promote the welfare of hummingbirds, he ought to do such and such in such and such circumstances.

A coherent system of valuings along these lines is not egoistic. Yet it does not have the ring of morality. Even if we replace it by

> If Jones wants (*ceteris paribus*) to promote the general welfare of language-using featherless bipeds

which comes a bit closer, we can picture Jones, who, other things being equal, also values his own happiness, confronted by *two* coherent sub-systems of valuings, thus

If I want (*ceteris paribus*) to be happy, I ought to pursue such and such policies	If I want (*ceteris paribus*) to promote the general welfare, I ought to pursue such and such other policies

And it is not clear how these can be resolved into one embracing coherent system of valuings so that the 'ceteris paribus' could be dropped and a *single* 'ought' remains.

36. We feel that moral 'ought' is *in principle* embracing and unequivocal, i.e. that if we had ideal knowledge, what we ought to do would be uniquely determined. Egoism plus ideal knowledge did uniquely determine an 'ought'—but not the 'ought' of moral reasoning. While if we recognize a duality of basic valuings, the moral pattern seems closer, but the uniqueness disappears.

37. Is there any way in which the uniqueness desired can be restored while retaining the idea that the moral 'ought' is the 'ought' of coherence? The first of the above objections gives the clue. People are not hummingbirds—not even language-using featherless bipeds. They are *us*; or, to come to the point, the moral point of view is not that in which we do good to the language-using featherless bipeds which surround us. It is that in which each of us seeks, as one of us, the common good of all of *us*.

38. There is a sense in which we all understand this, but how is it to be understood in the abstract categories of philosophy? The terminology developed at the beginning will prove, I believe, invaluable. It will be remembered that I distinguished between the sentence which expresses a valuing

would that...

and the sentence which ascribes a valuing to someone:

Jones values--------

Now in the examples I have been considering, it has been tacitly* assumed that Jones values X, so to speak, "as himself" or "from a personal point of view". Let me, therefore, use a device, lurking in but not highlighted by ordinary language, to bring this out in the very expression of the valuing.

---

* [Eds.—This reads "tautly" in the original manuscript; Sellars corrects this in his revision notes.]

I would that X were the case!

The corresponding ascription would be

Jones, from a personal point of view, values X

where "from a personal point of view" doesn't mean selfishly (nor does it preclude it).

39. What are we to contrast with this? (The very terminology should give a clue.) I spoke above of valuing as *being a member* of one's community. And since I am concerned with the moral point of view, I have in mind the most embracing community to which we belong; those who are in the biblical sense of the term our brothers. To value in this way is to think in terms of *we*, in the embracing sense, thus

We would that X were the case!

Notice that it is still the individual who is valuing. The corresponding ascriptive sentence is

Jones values X *as one of us*

indeed

...from a moral point of view

valuing has, if I may so put it, a subjective form as well as a content.

40. Let me emphasize that from the fact that *Jones* values X as one of us it doesn't follow that

we value X

We may well—indeed often do—differ in what we value as members of the community. Yet *in principle* there would be agreement.

41. Let me give a parallel from our discussion of self-interest. The specific things Smith values may differ from time to time as his beliefs about human nature and the world change. But in relation to valuing of a happy life on the whole, then *in principle* i.e. if he had had at all times the knowledge provided by our team of scientists, he would have agreed with himself at all times about the valuings consistent with this overarching aim. There is *in principle* agreement between, so to speak, Smith at t_1, Smith at t_2, etc. His disagreements with himself at different times are *in principle* resolvable.

42. The same is true of the members of a community in so far as they aim at the common good. Thus, if our team of scientists considers the community, they can, we suppose, by virtue of their knowledge of individuals and groups, come up with something of the following form:

> If the members of the community value promoting the common good, they ought to support such and such (intricate) practices

and, addressing themselves to the group:

> If we value promoting the common good as members of the community, you ought to support such and such practices

and, convinced, let us suppose, by scientific arguments, each member of the community, e.g. Jones, will reason:

> If I value as one of us the common good, I ought to support doing such and such things in such and such (intricately specified) circumstances

which tells him that the valuings

> We would that the common good was promoted!

and

> We would that the practice of doing such and such things in such and such circumstances was supported!

cohere. Thus, from the moral point of view they are confronted by the logical 'ought'

> Since I value (as one of us) the promotion of our common good, I *ought* to support the practice of doing such and such in such and such circumstances

and since the same considerations would confront each member, and they share the same primary valuing with which their other valuings are to cohere, they would share valuings of the form

> We would that if any of us is in C, he does A!

which is, I submit, the valuational content of a moral principle, the 'ought' in the more familiar formulation expressing the coherence of this valuing with the valuing of our common good in the light of the relevant facts about men and the world.

43. These valuings are, though valuings by individuals, universal in *three* dimensions

   (a) in their *content*
   ...that if *any* of us is in C, he do A
   (b) in their subjective form
   We would that...
   (c) in their acceptance, i.e., in the fact that all *agree* in so valuing

44. Alas! The ideal knowledge of our philosophical fiction is not shared by all, nor is it even at hand. Thus the ideal (if I may use the word) consensus sketched above is only in principle "there", and reasoning in the moral point of view proceeds in a context of disagreement and diversity of opinion.

45. Yet the question

   What ought I to do in these circumstances (from the moral point of view)?

is at heart the question

   What would we that I do in these circumstances?

and to answer the question is to answer the question

   What would we that any of us do in these circumstances?

and this again

   On what valuings of the form "we would that any of us did such and such in these circumstances"
   Would we agree if we had ideal knowledge?

and this again

   What practices would we agree to be conducive to our common good—if we had Ideal Knowledge?

Yet, since the one who asks the question lacks the ideal knowledge, he must make the best of such knowledge as he has (though we know more than we think about human nature, its propensities and needs).

46. If my argument is sound, the moral 'ought' is the 'ought' of coherence once again—but this time in the moral point of view. Thus, where inclination—whether selfish or sympathetic—points in one direction and moral valuation in another, the tension is between two different *ways of valuing*, not simply between two values which we have from our own point of view.

Yet we are, more frequently than we are willing to allow, confronted by a choice between actions one of which is called for by one way of thought, the other by the other. It is notorious that the outcome does not always have its source in the moral point of view.

47. Does our argument not commit us to the idea that the moral point of view and the personal point of view are unrelated alternatives? Two alternatives which *simply* present an either-or? The either-or aspect is not to be ignored, yet at the level our argument has reached we can see how there might be a harmony between the two points of view, a harmony more basic than the slipshod attempt to fit self-interest and sympathy into a coherent framework of valuings from the personal point of view, and call the result morality.

48. Most people live on second-hand moral thinking, and the momentum of childhood training. Suppose such a person were to meditate as follows:

> Granted then I and my fellows have been brought up to have such and such commitments as to what one is to do in various kinds of circumstances. Why shouldn't I let these commitments wither away and encourage self-regarding attitudes? Is there any reason why I should nourish my commitment to the moral point of view?

What could we say? In effect we have seen that the only frame of mind which is the living source of moral commitment is what Josiah Royce called Loyalty, and what Christians call Love (Charity). *This is a commitment deeper than any commitment to abstract principle.* It is this commitment to the well-being of our fellows which stands to the justification of moral principles as the purpose of acquiring the ability to explain and predict stands to the justification of scientific theories. This concern for others is a precious thing, the foundation for which is laid in early childhood, though it *can* come about, in adult years, through the little understood phenomena of conversion and psycho-therapy.

I will close with the remarks that recent psychological studies make clear what has in a sense been known all along, that the ability to love others for their own sake is as essential to a full life as the need to feel ourselves loved and appreciated for our own sakes—unconditionally, and not as something turned on or off depending on what we do. This fact provides, for those who acknowledge it, a connection which can justify a course of action designed to strengthen our ability to respond to the needs of others. Thus *really* intelligent and informed self-love supports the love of one's neighbor which alone directly supports the moral point of view when, as the Eighteenth century British divine, Bishop Butler, put it, we sit down in a cool hour and ask why we should do our duty.

4
Science and Ethics[1]

[1] The fundamental data of ethics are the concrete moral judgments and evaluations which we and other peoples make on particular occasions. They include the general maxims and principles which are formulated in reflective moments and which play a central role in passing our way of life on to the next generation.[2]

[2] These same data are also data for the anthropologist. This generates the question, "What is the difference between the approach of the anthropologist and the approach of the philosopher?" One possible answer is that the anthropologist is concerned with a question of *fact*. He is concerned to discover what moral principles are in fact *espoused* by various cultures (including his own), whereas the philosopher is concerned to determine which set of moral principles is *true*. This answer is not without merit, but it is a radical oversimplification.

[3] Let us begin by exploring the situation as it appears to the anthropologist. He attempts to structure the moral consciousness of the culture in terms of some such distinction as

1. The spontaneous evaluations of particular acts and situations made by members of the culture. These are his fundamental data.
2. What I shall call intermediate principles or maxims.
3. The "first principles" which express the most basic and general evaluations in terms of which the former would be justified.

[4] Let me explain these distinctions by means of a simple analogy.

1. Particular evaluations: The Smiths are coming tonight. We ought to buy playing cards.
2. Maxim: When the Smiths come, we play bridge.
3. First principle: When one has guests, one ought to do what the guests like.

---

[1] A revised version of a paper read to the Phoebe Griffin Noyes Library Association, Old Lyme, Connecticut, on January 26, 1960. [Eds.—The 1960 paper was titled "Ethics and Philosophy."]

[2] It is always dangerous to take copybook maxims at their face value, for to be a realistic expression of our fundamental moral convictions, they would have to be accompanied by a complicated set of qualifications which specify exceptions, make clear what kind of context is presupposed, and stipulate an order of priority for those situations in which different maxims would call for opposite plans of conduct.

The maxim is derivable from the principle together with the fact that the Smiths like to play bridge. The same "first" principle together with the fact that the Joneses like to dance generates the maxim, "When the Joneses come we dance."

Another example: A nomadic tribe amid hostile tribes.

1. Particular evaluation: It's time to put Mom and Dad away. (They can't keep up with the tribe.)
2. Maxim: When people can't keep up with the tribe, they should be put away.
3. First principle: People who endanger the safety of the tribe should be put away.

[5] Sophisticated cultures abound in abstract formulations of maxims and "first" principles, though, as was pointed out above,[3] what people formulate as general moral propositions are not necessarily adequate expressions of the way they actually think on moral matters. The formulated maxims and principles are almost always oversimplified to a high degree.

[6] The best way of finding out what people's attitudes really are is to watch what they do and say in concrete situations and, by using the "hypothetico-deductive method," determine what small number of abstract principles would lead to the concrete evaluations actually made and acted on in the culture in question, if these principles were espoused by the culture and applied in terms of what it believes about the world and about the consequences of actions. If these hypothesized principles coincide with what is actually said, so much the better; but what is said should never be taken at its face value. The fundamental moral attitudes of the culture need never have received explicit formulation.

[7] Suppose, then, that an anthropologist studies a number of cultures and looks for the "first principles" of their moral frameworks. It is obvious that the intermediate principles or maxims he finds will differ, often drastically, from culture to culture. The maxims of an agricultural community are notoriously different from those of hunting communities. But this difference at the intermediate level is compatible with agreement at the level of first principles. Would the anthropologist find such agreement? This question enables us to explore one sense of the phrase "cultural relativism." This sense concerns a matter of fact.

[8] Thus, suppose he found agreement; that all disagreement at the level of maxims and concrete judgments could be accounted for in terms of the different circumstances of the cultures and their different beliefs about nature and about the consequences of their action. Would this agreement show that the principles in question were true or correct or valid? How does one show a first principle to be not only *held* but *rightly held*? Can one?

---

[3] Footnote 2.

[9] Suppose, on the other hand, that he found different cultures to have different first principles. Would it make sense to ask which is correct or true? Could the different cultures not only in point of fact have different first principles, but rightly or justifiably have them?

The claim that they have different principles would be cultural relativism as a *scientific* or *factual* thesis.

The claim that each *rightly* has its own first principles would be cultural relativism as an *ethical* or *evaluative* thesis.

[10] Is it, perhaps, the task of the anthropologist not only to discover what principles are espoused by a culture, but whether the principles are rightly espoused? If the latter, on what grounds would he argue? Consider a culture in which a high degree of aggressive behavior is sanctioned among young men. Dueling is encouraged. And suppose that this aggressive behavior is sanctioned, so to speak, as an end in itself and not a means of training men for the rigors of war. The anthropologist might see that if the culture persists in this policy, its stock will deteriorate and the culture will be in danger of perishing. Can he argue as anthropologist that the policy is bad or incorrect? Or take the case of a culture which adopts a policy of celibacy and continence as a way of life. In both cases, the anthropologist can say

If these principles are maintained, the culture will be in danger of disappearing.

And obviously he can conclude that the policy is wrong or incorrect if he assumes that the disappearance of the culture is a bad thing.

[11] Another example: A culture has a system of practices which result in an ant-like way of life, monotonous, conforming, but warm and comfortable. He can argue that if its members changed their way of life, they would have more ups and downs and perhaps less comfort and more anxiety, but would, on the other hand, have a richer esthetic and intellectual life. Can he argue as anthropologist that the culture ought to change its way of life? Or ought not?

[12] Obviously, at this point, the anthropologist must take into account his own principles; the fundamental attitudes in terms of which he and his fellows approach problems of living. Anthropologist, know thyself! And if he does a bit of auto-anthropology and discovers what his first principles are, can he say that his principles are the *correct* ones and mean anything more by this than they are *his*?

[13] We can now distinguish between three dimensions of ethical theory:

1. Descriptive or anthropological ethics (including auto-anthropology).
2. Normative ethics. Its aim is to discover the true first principles of conduct and evaluation; if there are such things as true moral principles and a method of discovering them.

3. Criteriological ethics. Its concern is with how one can settle a dispute about which (if any) moral principles are true—by rational means (as opposed to brute force or propaganda). Criteriological ethics is concerned with the very possibility of normative ethics as a rational discipline.

[14] These three branches of ethics are paralleled in the field of scientific knowledge by the distinction between

1. The history and anthropology of science. What beliefs do such and such people *have* about the workings of the world and how did they come to have them?
2. Science. What beliefs about nature are *true*?
3. Scientific methodology (or criteriology). What are the criteria of a good scientific theory; what constitutes a *good reason* for accepting a scientific hypothesis?

[15] The philosopher is particularly concerned with criteriological questions. Thus he wishes to know whether it makes sense to say of a set of moral first principles that they are not only accepted, but correct or true, and how one would go about defending by rational means the assertion that they are true. In short, he wants to know *whether* moral principles can be rationally justified and, if so, how.

[16] With the above distinctions under our belt, let us try to get an overall picture of what philosophers have had to say on the subject. We have seen that particular moral judgments are justified by subsuming them under intermediate principles or maxims, and that intermediate principles are justified by subsuming them under more general principles and, ultimately, first principles. This kind of justification is purely logical. Its forms are illustrated by

I ought to help Jones because Jones is hungry and penniless, and one ought to help people who are hungry and penniless.

One ought to assist people who are hungry and penniless because people who are hungry and penniless are in distress, and one ought to help people who are in distress.

This mode of justification appeals to logical consistency. There would be a logical inconsistency in holding the general principle and yet, granting that Jones is hungry and penniless or that people who are hungry and penniless are in distress, rejecting the specific application.

[17] But mere logic cannot commit us to the principles themselves. The denial of a moral principle is never absurd in the way in which a contradiction is absurd. Logic by itself can discover relations of consistency and inconsistency between our principles. It can classify them according to their degrees of generality. It can show

that one principle follows from another. But when it comes to the most abstract and general principles—first principles—of a moral code, logic by itself is powerless to decide whether they are *worthy* of acceptance.

[18] (It is worth pausing to note that the language by which we classify actions often reflects a commitment to principles: e.g., "murderer" means, roughly, unjustified homicide. Thus, there is indeed a sense in which it is "flying in the face of reason" to deny that murder is wrong. It is equally, and for similar reasons, flying in the face of reason to deny that a *Euclidian* straight line is the shortest distance between two points. It is only when these commitments are peeled away from the formulation of the principles that the powerlessness of logic to certify them becomes apparent.)

[19] Is there any way in which a rational choice can be made between competing first principles? To this question philosophers have traditionally given three answers: rationalism, empiricism, and skepticism. In order to explain these three positions, let me introduce the notion of a "rational discipline." By this phrase, I shall mean a field of inquiry in which good reasons can be offered for answers to questions belonging to the field. The empirical sciences are clearly rational disciplines in this sense. The physicist knows when he has good reasons for answering a question in one way rather than another. So does the biologist and the historian. The mathematical sciences are also rational disciplines in the sense that mathematicians, by and large, agree on when there are good reasons for accepting a certain mathematical proposition as true.

[20] If we leave aside the historical sciences which are concerned with particular matters of fact and concentrate our attention on those disciplines which seek to establish laws and principles, we see that they fall into two groups, according to whether or not they make use of empirical or observational evidence. Thus, a physical theory, however abstract its principles, must ultimately stand or fall on the evidence provided by observation and experiment. The "first principles" of the theory are justified by the ability of the theory as a whole to do its job, which is to enable us to understand the general course of experience.

[21] Again, pure mathematics is a rational discipline. It is not, however, an empirical science. Mathematicians use pencil and paper, not, of course, to make experiments, but simply because thinking on paper is more reliable (and capable of being checked and rechecked) than thinking in one's head. Pure mathematics is, so to speak, an armchair science. In philosophical terminology, it is *a priori*.

[22] Pure mathematics is not only an *a priori* discipline in the sense that it doesn't appeal to observation and experiment (a negative point). It is also, speaking positively, a *formal* discipline. Within a mathematical system more specific principles can be justified by deriving them logically from more general principles. The same is true of an empirical science. But when we ask how the more general principles—the first principles—are justified, the answer is quite different from that appropriate to the empirical sciences. It is simply that to deny

these principles leads to contradiction. Not only the *coherence* of a mathematical system, but its very *truth* is a matter of consistency.

[23] Pure mathematics tells us nothing about the specific properties of things. Its truths hold of any consistently thinkable world, however strange and uncouth. The proposition that two plus two equals four tells us that it would be inconsistent to say

There are two plus two apples on this table, but three altogether (or five or more)

—inconsistent, however, in a more complicated way than is

This table top is both round and square.

The mathematically formulated hypotheses of physics tell us something specific about the world, not by virtue of being mathematical, but by virtue of being mathematically formulated empirical hypotheses. In this respect, they resemble

This table is eight feet long,

which is not a mathematical statement, although it uses the mathematical concept of *eight*. If mathematics is a formal discipline, the same is clearly not true of physics, chemistry, and biology. Worlds are consistently thinkable which obey laws quite different from those of the actual world. Let us say that a rational discipline makes a *commitment* about the world if it makes claims which go beyond the demands of mere consistency—if it makes statements about the world in which we live which would not be true of all consistently thinkable worlds. Mathematics makes no commitment in this sense; physics and the empirical sciences do.

[24] Notice that we have drawn two contrasts:

1. between rational disciplines *based on observation* and those which are *not*,
2. between rational disciplines which *make a commitment* and those which do *not*.

How do these two contrasts correlate? Are they, perhaps, two ways of drawing the same distinction? This question is the crux of classical philosophy.

[25] The issue can be put as follows:

Are there any rational disciplines—bodies of knowledge with objective criteria for evaluating answers to questions falling within their purview—which are *a priori* like mathematics but which, unlike mathematics, make a *commitment* about the world?

Philosophers who answer in the affirmative are called rationalists; for they hold that important truths about the world and man can be established by mere reflection, by a method other than the experimental method characteristic of the empirical sciences. Among the candidates proposed for such bodies of truth are (1) philosophy itself, (2) rational theology, and (3) normative ethics.

[26] Empiricists, traditionally, are philosophers who argue that all rational disciplines which commit us beyond the limits of mere consistency belong to the empirical sciences. It follows from their position that, if a commitment is not a testable empirical hypothesis, it falls outside the realm of rational discussion.

[27] This opposition between rationalism and empiricism is expressed in ethics as the opposition between the claim that the first principles of morals are known *a priori* and the claim that they are empirical hypotheses which it is the responsibility of science (in particular, biology, psychology, and sociology) to test and confirm or refine.

[28] It has become clear that neither of these positions is satisfactory. Not rationalism, for once it is granted that no contradiction or inconsistency is involved in denying a moral principle, what reasons could mere armchair thinking have for preferring it to its alternatives? *Ex hypothesi* it is a *first* principle and cannot be derived from a higher one. If it could, the same question would arise concerning the latter. The rationalist falls back on *intuition*. Pure thought simply *sees* certain moral principles to be true, but has no way of supporting its intuition with reason. This view plays into the hands of skepticism, for it is notorious that in different cultures and in different persons in the same culture, "pure reason" makes contradictory deliverances. And according to intuitionism there is no way of arbitrating between contrary intuitions. There would seem to be no significant difference between an intuition which cannot be supported by reasons, and a basic commitment which we *make* without being able to *justify*.

[29] Nor does empiricism fare much better. For while observation and experiment and scientific method do provide good reasons for general commitments about the world, these commitments concern what *is* the case rather than what *ought to be* the case. Thus even the anthropological study of what things people value, what they approve and disapprove, and of the circumstances in which people tend to value one thing rather than another, gives us knowledge about what is *valued* or *prized*, but not about what is *valuable* in the sense of *worthy* of being valued. Certainly a scientific knowledge of the needs and abilities of men would play a determining role in shaping the actions and policies of one who already has a moral perspective. But mere knowledge of things as valued or prized does not present them to the knower as *values* (i.e., as things which, other things being equal, *ought* to be brought about or realized).

[30] The failure of both rationalism and empiricism seems at first sight to leave us no alternative but skepticism, the view that moral principles are commitments which we find ourselves having, indeed, which we have been brought up to have, but which are incapable of rational justification. Curiously enough, in order to escape from this dilemma, we must first plumb the depths of the skeptical point of

view. And to set the stage for this we must look at a different dimension of what we have called "criteriological" ethics. We have been stressing the question "Can ethical first principles be given a rational justification? And if so, how?" Or, to put it somewhat differently, "Can a good reason be given for committing oneself to a set of ethical first principles without contradicting their status *as* first principles?" But recent criteriological ethics has stressed rather the questions "What exactly are we saying of a state of affairs when we say that it is intrinsically *good*, worth having for its own sake?" and "What exactly are we saying of an action when we say that it ought to be done?" Recent philosophy has rightly paid a great deal of attention to problems pertaining to meaning and the clarification of meaning. In ethics, this emphasis led for a time to an almost exclusive concern with "the meaning of ethical terms."

[31] It would seem evident that there is an intimate connection between concepts pertaining to the intrinsic value of states of affairs and concepts pertaining to what people ought to do. Reflection on this fact has often generated the idea that one of these two groups of concepts can be explicated or defined in terms of the other. Thus, according to one group of philosophers, the concepts of duty, right, and wrong, which pertain to action, are to be explicated in terms of the concept of the intrinsic value of the consequences of action. Roughly,

x ought to do A $=_{df}$ the consequences of A could be intrinsically better than the consequences of any alternative action open to x.

[32] Other philosophers have found it more plausible to orient the explication in the opposite direction and have proposed definitions of the following types:

States of affairs of kind S are intrinsically good $=_{df}$ in so far as an action open to one would bring about a state of affairs of kind S one ought to do it

or

States of affairs of kind S_1 are intrinsically better than states of affairs of kind S_2 $=_{df}$ if of two actions open to x, one would bring about S_1 while the other would bring about S_2, then, in so far forth, x ought to do the former

[33] The issues we are concerned with now, however, are sufficiently general not to depend on a decision between these two points of view. For, whether the first principles of ethics are principles concerning what actions one ought to do or principles concerning what states of affairs are intrinsically good, the problem

remains: "What new meanings, if any, are involved when we move from simply describing how things are or might be—with no use of distinctively ethical terms—to saying of a state of affairs that it is or it would be *good,* or of an action that it *ought to be done*? As a matter of historical fact, the basic distinctions were thrashed out in connection with the meaning of the term "good," since it was, on the whole, taken for granted by British and American philosophers in the early years of this century that "good" was a more basic notion than "ought."

[34] The argument developed as follows: (1) we must obviously distinguish between a good thing or state of affairs (in short a good) and its goodness (i.e., the property by virtue of which it is good). More accurately, since, as we shall see, there are two senses in which a property might be that "by virtue of which" something was good, we must distinguish between the good thing and that property the having of which *constitutes* its being good. (2) Even when people agree as to what items are good, they may disagree in the accounts they give of the property the having of which constitutes their being good. Not only philosophers, but people generally can agree in the *application* of a term (roughly its denotation) but disagree in their account of what the term *means* (i.e., its "sense" or "intension"). A notorious example is the term "cause." People agree, by and large, about *what* causes *what.* But if asked to explain what it means to say that something, *x,* *causes* something else, *y,* the accounts are almost as many as the people who give them. (3) It is important to see that the fact that different philosophers have offered different accounts of causation does not imply that these philosophers used the word "cause" in different senses in their non-philosophical discourse. The meanings of words (including their ambiguities) are public, intersubjective facts, and, while a person may use a word in a *stipulated* sense, stipulated senses presuppose a vocabulary with non-stipulated senses which has the public status of a custom or practice or institution. Words do not mean what the user thinks they mean. It is possible to use a word meaningfully and correctly but give, when asked, a mistaken account of its meaning. If merely by virtue of being able to use a word correctly a person had the ability to give a clear and distinct explanation of its meaning, one of the most difficult tasks of philosophy—explaining the meaning of these abstract terms which crystalize the symbolic forms of human discourse—would be a task for children.

[35] Now as Moore[4] saw it, there were three possibilities:

1. The adjective "good" stands for a property which is also signified by an expression belonging to a vocabulary other than that of ethical discourse, that is to the vocabulary of one of the disciplines which is concerned with what *is* or *is not* the case, as contrasted with what *ought* to be the case.

---

[4] G. E. Moore, *Principia Ethica,* Chapter I.

Representative views of this kind are those in which "good" stands for a biological property (e.g., "conducive to survival") or a psychological property (e.g., "pleasant," "approved of by the speaker,") or a sociological property (e.g., "approved of by one's social peers"). These alternatives barely scratch the surface of this type of approach to the concept of intrinsic value.

2. The adjective "good" stands for a property which is uniquely ethical and can neither be equated with nor defined in terms of any property with which sciences of what is the case are directly concerned.[5]

3. The word "good" does not stand for a property at all. Moore himself, in his early writings, seems to have assumed that since "good" is an adjective, it either stands for a property as "circular" stands for circularity or else is a *flatus vocis*.

[36] Regarding the latter alternative as absurd, he dismissed (3) and focused his attention on the problem of choosing between (1) and (2). As is well-known, he decided in favor of (2) and defended his decision by interesting and important arguments about which it may be worth while to say a few words.

[37] The first line of thought can be summed up as follows: Suppose it is claimed that two predicative expressions, each of which may be either simple or complex, have the same sense. Represent these two predicate expressions by "P_1" and "P_2," respectively, and let "x" refer to a subject to which these predicates are appropriately (though not necessarily truly) applied. Now form the question

Is x, granted that it is P_2, P_1?

For example

Is x, granted that it is bounded by three straight lines, triangular? Is x, granted that it is a featherless biped, human? Is x, granted that it is approved of by me, good?

Moore points out that if such a question, in spite of the concessive clauses, is *open*, then it cannot be true that the two predicate expressions have the same sense. He proceeds to test representative views of type (1) each of which claims that "good" has the same sense as a predicate expression in a vocabulary which is used when one's concern is simply to state what is or is not the case in a certain domain of fact, without any commitment as to what ought or ought not to be the case. He claims that if one constructs for each such claimed identity of the form

---

[5] The psychologist and the sociologist are, of course, concerned with the predicate "believed to be good" and with such facts as that John believes x to be good. But it would obviously be absurd to define the predicate "good" in terms of the predicate "believed to be good."

"P_1" has the same sense as "P_2"

a corresponding question of the above form, the latter is readily seen to be an open question. He contends that every such claimed identity is false, and that the only identities which are not clearly ruled out by this test are those in which both predicate expressions are patently ethical, e.g.,

"good" has the same sense as "ought to be desired"
"good" has the same sense as "worthy or worth having for its own sake."

[38] Moore also argued[6] that any adequate account of the property *good* must preserve the *prima facie* contradictoriness illustrated by the dialogue

Mr. A: x is good
Mr. B: x is not good

whether A and B are different members of the same cultural group or members of different cultural groups. He argues (and this is a recurring pattern of argument in his philosophy) that it is more probable that a philosophical view which rejects this *prima facie* (but by no means superficial) contradictoriness is based on a mistake than that the contradictoriness is an illusion. This argument provides an additional ground for rejecting views of the type illustrated by

x is good = I like x
x is good = my culture approves of x

[39] These and other considerations led Moore to the following theses:

1. Goodness is a simple property.
2. Goodness is a uniquely ethical property. It does not fall within the province of the empirical sciences.[7]
3. Goodness is a "resultant quality." If anything has the property of being good, it must have it by virtue of being of a certain sort or kind. An example might be
    x is good *because* (and in so far as) it is a feeling of pleasure
   which corresponds to the principle
    if anything is a feeling of pleasure, then it is (in so far forth) good.

---

[6] *Ethics*, Chapter III.
[7] The property of being *believed to be good*, of course, does belong in the province of the empirical sciences. But, of course, a parallel distinction can be drawn in the case of *divisible by two* and *believed to be divisible by two*. The sense in which *P* is a constituent of *believed to be P* calls for careful analysis.

The properties which, though they are not identical with goodness, are the grounds of goodness might be called, with C. D. Broad,[8] "good-making properties." According to Moore, there are a number of "good-making properties," thus, among others, the properties of being a consciousness of pleasure, of being a state of knowledge, and of being an affectionate and loving frame of mind.

4. True principles of the form

P_1 is a good-making property

are "synthetic necessary truths" and our knowledge of them is neither deductive nor inductive. They are first principles whose evidence must be self-evidence. Moore's position is, therefore, a clear cut and straightforward example of the *rationalistic* type of criteriological ethics.

[40] There are many interesting features of Moore's position which would have to be taken into account if our purpose was to present it as a reasonably lifelike representation of moral experience. To put some flesh on the above bare bones, we would have to discuss his views on such topics as the commensurability of values, the relation of intermediate principles to first principles, and, which for Moore is a special case of this, the relation of principles of obligation to principles of value, etc. For our purposes, however, the bare bones of Moore's argument suffice, for in terms of them we can explain the distinctive trait of ethical skepticism in the early post-Moore period.

[41] In his later writings, Moore supplemented his earlier and essentially negative characterization of the property for which the predicate "good" stands as a "non-natural" property with a no less negative, but potentially far more illuminating characterization of it as a "non-descriptive" property. By thus distinguishing "descriptive" properties (e.g., circularity), the ascription of which to an object describes it (as circular), and "non-descriptive" properties (e.g., goodness), the ascription of which to an object does not describe it, he raised the question, "What is one doing with respect to an item when one ascribes goodness to it, if one is not *describing* it?" It was not long before the general lines of an answer were forthcoming. But the initial formulations were so inadequate, so burdened with positivistic commitments, that the insight they contained had a difficult time surviving.

[42] I shall take a brief look at these initial formulations in a moment. But it will be instructive to develop Moore's distinction between "descriptive" and "non-descriptive" properties in a way which joins more directly with the best contemporary thinking on the subject. To come to the point directly, suppose we were to

---

[8] "Some of the Main Problems of Ethics," *Philosophy*, 21, 1946. (Reprinted in Feigl and Sellars [eds.]: *Readings in Philosophical Analysis*, New York, 1949).

say that goodness is a normative property,[9] what would this (intuitively) imply? Surely that goodness is a resultant property by virtue of which that which possesses it has a claim on our conduct and on the attitudes and choices which manifest themselves in our conduct. The term "claim" is not, of itself, particularly illuminating. It does, however, serve to convey the essential truth that a norm or standard in the desired sense is something which, when the individual recognizes it as such, has a unique resonance in his affective life. It is somehow an essential fact about that which we believe to be good that we *care* about it, are *concerned* about it. Roughly speaking, goodness is a property which is such that, *in the absence of contrary aims and desires*, to believe that a certain state of affairs would be good is to be disposed to act in such a way as to bring it about.

[43] Now if one is not content to postulate the existence of such a property and attempts to explain its possibility, one is confronted by the fact that the properties which modern empirically and scientifically-minded philosophers have taken as "paradigm cases" of properties are without exception such that

1. If anybody believes that x is φ, he tends to approve of x

is always synthetic. This is obviously true in the case of such a property as circularity. But even when "φ" stands for the property of being approved of by the person in question, the statement is still logically synthetic. In the absence of a reassessment of the structure and scope of the "space" of *properties* which succeeds in demonstrating that in the case of goodness the statement corresponding to (1) is logically analytic, a phenomenologically adequate account of goodness must claim that (1) is true *ex vi terminorum*, and, if it sees no grounds for expecting that such a demonstration might someday be forthcoming, that it is a synthetic necessary truth. As is well-known, those who, under the influence of Moore, took goodness to be a unique, resultant, and normative property took the latter course. We thus see that the sophisticated, ethical rationalist invokes the concept of synthetic necessary truth at two crucial junctures in his theory:

1. The first principles of value or obligation are synthetic necessary truths
2. The connection between goodness or obligation and approval is a synthetic necessary truth.

[44] Let me end this part of my argument by pointing out that according to a position which accepts (2) there would be no *contradiction* in the idea of a community which intellectually knows what sorts of things are intrinsically good (or what kinds of actions ought to be done in various kinds of

---

[9] There is no intention here to imply that "descriptive" and "normative" exhaust the varieties of property.

circumstances) and yet has no concern or (in the broad sense) feeling about these items *qua* being good or *qua* what ought to be done. If the idea of such a community is nevertheless held by these philosophers to be absurd, they must trace the absurdity to *a priori* insight, to intuitive *evidence*, in short, to synthetic *a priori* knowledge.

[45] Now recent ethical skepticism, under the name "emotivism" or "non-cognitivism," developed within the framework of Moore's analysis, but adopted the alternative, which Moore was unable to take seriously, that "good" does not stand for a property at all—unique or non-unique, natural or non-natural, descriptive or non-descriptive. Thus, to choose one of the earlier and less sophisticated formulations of emotivism, Ayer, in his *Language, Truth and Logic*, after agreeing that the views Moore criticizes will not do and acknowledging that, if one of these was the only alternative, Moore's position with its unique, non-natural, non-empirical, non-descriptive resultant property of goodness, and its synthetic necessary first principles of value, would carry the day—a result which would conflict painfully with the epistemology developed in earlier chapters of the book—announces to us that the dilemma is to be overcome by escaping between the horns. In spite of the fact that "good" functions grammatically as an adjective, its job is quite other than that of standing for a property, even though standing for a property is what adjectives usually do. He calls attention to the difference between "expressing" or "evincing" an emotion and describing oneself as having the emotion. "I am angry" is the first person present tense counter part of "he was angry", and is either true or false. A person, however, can *express* his current anger (but no one else's anger, or his own past or future anger) by using an expletive, or speaking in an angry tone of voice. Sentences of the form "x is good," although they grammatically resemble sentences which are used to ascribe properties, have as their primary function to give expression to the speaker's attitude. They ape sentences which are used to ascribe properties and by doing so give objective and rational protective coloring to the business of expressing one's attitudes. But, in their primary use, they do not ascribe properties or assert propositions and are neither true nor false. The *prima facie* contrariety between

x is good

and

x is bad

which Moore had emphasized, is interpreted by Ayer and his disciples as the expression of a "disagreement in attitude," where a clash between attitudes is to be understood in terms of the incompatibility of the states of affairs which would result from implementing them.

[46] Now emotivism was on to *something*. The best way to see this is to notice that it makes analytic the connection between *believing something, x, to be good* and *being positively concerned about x*, which for the ethical rationalism sketched above is synthetic *a priori*. It does so, however, by trivializing the connection into a tautology, for it turns believing *x* to be good into "believing" *x* to be good and simply *equates* the latter with approving of *x*.

[47] Indeed, early emotivism assimilated ethical judgments "so-called" to the non-rational, non-conceptual order by a liberal use of non-rational, non-conceptual models. Thus, an examination of Ayer's discussion shows that he compares ethical statements (1) to symptoms of feeling in the narrow sense illustrated by pain, thus "bad" to "ouch," and (2) to *stimuli* which arouse or provoke other people into action in a manner reminiscent of the conditioned responses exhibited by a trained soldier being put through the manual of arms by a barking sergeant. But even though words of command can *become* response-evokers, commands, and, more obviously, requests, belong to the conceptual order and so do the forms of words which we use to express our appraisals and evaluations.

[48] It is by now a familiar story that *crude* emotivism failed to distinguish between emotions and attitudes. Attitudes are settled ways of viewing the world. They are commitments which manifest themselves in a variety of ways. In different circumstances, radically different ways of behaving, thinking, and feeling can be expressions of the *same* attitudes. Thus, an attitude of superiority to a certain group can find its expression in one situation in an outburst of anger, and in another by a cool withdrawal. Attitudes can be compared to long-range policies. Emotions, on the other hand, are short-run outbursts highly colored by visceral sensations and incipient activity. It is possible to regard ethical statements as expressions of *attitudes*, but not to compare them in their capacity as ethical statements to shrieks of joy or cries of anger.

[49] Crude emotivism failed equally to distinguish between emotions and feelings in the narrower sense in which pain is a feeling. When a person feels pain and says "ouch," the "ouch" is a symptom of pain. It belongs to the sub-rational level of human behavior. One must not confuse between "is an expression of" and "is a symptom of." It is as rational beings that we feel emotions, and while expressions of emotion are neither true nor false, nevertheless the devices by which emotions are expressed are as much a part and parcel of the inter-subjective symbolic forms of human discourse as the vocabulary of description and explanation which philosophers, with few exceptions, have placed at the center of their interest.

[50] As a result of these two confusions, emotivism overlooked the fact that attitudes and the expression of attitudes belong to the *rational* order—which is not, of course, to say that there are no *ir*rational attitudes, but rather no *non*-rational ones. It is as a rational being that a man has attitudes. All commitments, scientific as well as ethical, are attitudes, and in no case is an attitude a sensation or feeling which accompanies a "pure thought."

[51] Before I attempt to characterize the distinctive traits of the attitudes we call moral or ethical, I want to return to the topic, central to the controversy between Moore and the emotivists, as to when a word stands for a *concept*. For central to the emotivist's contention that

"good" is "cognitively meaningless" and *merely* expresses an emotion, etc.

is a theory as to when words belong to the conceptual order. Crude emotivism was developed by philosophers (e.g., Ayer) who held that if a word is not (1) a logico-mathematical word expressing a *formal* concept or (2) definable in terms of perceptible (or introspectable) states of affairs with the aid of logico-mathematical words and expressing an *empirical* concept, it does not belong to the conceptual order at all and merely apes words which do. It belongs rather, with "ouch" and "hup." Concept empiricists were dominated by the ostensive training aspect of learning how to use words: the formation of habits of responding to *things* with *words*. But it is obvious that we learn the use of many words where such a correlation does not even make sense. This is surely the case with *logical* words and reflection shows it to be equally true of such words as "was," "will be," "this," and, to move closer to practical discourse, such words as "shall," as in "I shall do A."

[52] I shall not press this point, but rather proceed directly to formulate a different criterion as to when a word stands for a concept or, more accurately, belongs to the conceptual order. The criterion I wish to recommend has two virtues as over and against concept empiricism:

1. It explains why both formal and empirical words belong to the conceptual order
2. It permits—indeed requires—the recognition that other words belong to the conceptual order.

The criterion I propose is that a word stands for a concept when there are good arguments in which it is essentially involved. Consider the following three arguments:

1. This is *red*
   therefore, it is *extended* and *not green*
2. Tomorrow *will be* Tuesday
   therefore, yesterday *was* Sunday
3. I *shall* get to Hartford by 8 *PM*
   therefore, I *shall* leave New Haven before 6 *PM*.

[53] Once such a humble word as "shall" is seen to belong to the conceptual order, the way is clear to recognizing that "good" and "ought" belong there too. Indeed,

I would argue that the meaning of "ought" is related to that of "shall" and is indicated, roughly, by the context

We shall all always (other things being equal) do A in C

(i.e., "ought" statements express [presumptively] shared *intentions,* where "intention" is used in an extended sense to cover moral attitudes and where the scope of "we" includes everybody that we recognize as one of *us*).

[54] But before I carry this further, I must pick up a theme from an earlier stage of the argument. It concerns the possible parallel between the empirical sciences as rational disciplines and a putative rational discipline of normative ethics. If we turn our attention to the former, we find that we must distinguish between three ways in which statements belonging to an empirical science of an advanced type (e.g., chemistry or physics) are capable of rational justification. The first of these, which raises serious problems which transcend the scope of this essay, concerns the move from statements reporting the results of experiment or controlled observation to the acceptance of a generalization applying to all cases in which the same conditions are realized. The problem of the rational warrant for moves of this kind is the classical problem of induction and will not concern us here.

[55] More germane to our purpose is the structure of reasoning at the level of theoretical explanation. The distinction I had in mind is that between the logical derivation of statement from statement *within* the framework of the theory and the reasoning by which we justify the decision to adopt the framework. Reflection on the former type of move readily generates a distinction between the more general principles of the theory and the implications they have for a wide variety of specific conditions and circumstances which can be formulated in terms of the theory. And if, by a certain idealization, we construe the theory as a deductive system, we are led to a distinction between the first principles or fundamental postulates of the theory and the derivative principles or theorems which follow from them in accordance with logical procedures.

[56] Our rational warrant for accepting the first principles of the theory clearly cannot consist in the fact that they have been logically derived from other statements of the theory. If this were the case, it would simply mean that they were misdescribed as the *first* principles of the theory. On the other hand, the decision to accept the theory of which these principles are the first principles can be given a rational defense. Let us follow a terminological suggestion by Herbert Feigl and say that a set of theoretical first principles is *vindicated* by giving a successful rational defense of the decision to espouse it.

[57] The rational defense of a decision is a piece of practical reasoning and, in the type of case with which we are now concerned, involves the relationship of means to end. Thus we are concerned with reasoning of the form

I shall do that which is conducive to E.
Doing A is conducive to E.
So I shall do A.

Notice that the major premise of this reasoning is a statement of intention. The reasoning relates a specific course of action to this intention.

[58] If this distinction between the logical derivation of statement from statement within a theory and the vindication of the first principles of the theory is to be of assistance in understanding the rational status of normative ethics, we must presumably be able to put our finger on sound arguments of the form

I shall do that which is conducive to E.
Doing Action$_1$ in Circumstance$_1$, Action$_2$ in Circumstance$_2$, etc., is conducive to E
Therefore: (1) I shall do Action$_1$ in Circumstance$_1$, etc.
  (2) I shall espouse the principles: "Anybody shall do Action$_1$ in Circumstance$_1$," etc.
  (3) I shall support the general practice of doing Action$_1$ in Circumstance$_1$, etc.

[59] But what could be the end, E, in terms of which the espousal of moral first principles is to be rationally defended? In the case of scientific theory, the end is presumably the goal of providing scientific understanding, the ability to explain and predict phenomena falling under the scope of the theory.

[60] To answer this question, or at least indicate the lines along which an answer might be found, let me return to the basic line of argument. It will be remembered that we have emphasized the distinction between statements which, as expressing attitudes, belong to the conceptual order, and mere symptoms of feeling ("ouch," etc.) which, though socially conditioned, do not belong to the conceptual order. What, we must now ask, is the distinctive character of those attitudes which we call moral? One essential trait, emphasized by the German philosopher Kant, but illustrated also by the Golden Rule, is that they are attitudes in which we view ourselves *impersonally*, and approve or disapprove of *our* doing something in certain circumstances because we would approve or disapprove of *anyone* behaving in that way under similar circumstances. Moral attitudes are in this sense impartial. They are also, I have suggested, inter-personal or shared attitudes in the sense that their proper expression involves not simply "I intend, approve, etc.," but rather "we intend, approve, etc." They are subjectively universal (inter-personal) as well as objectively universal (impartial).

[61] Let us suppose then that ethical principles express *impersonal* attitudes towards life and conduct in the sense just defined. What becomes of the problem of justifying ethical principles? It becomes the following:

Granted that I and my fellow man have been brought up to have such and such impersonal commitments concerning what is to be done in various kinds of circumstances, is there any reason why I should not let these commitments wither away and encourage self-regarding attitudes, attitudes which, in the vernacular, look out for Number One?

It is reasonable to suppose that it is to each of our advantages to have other people have moral attitudes. A society in which everyone was guided by intelligent self-interest might work if people were intelligent and knowledgeable enough. But a moment's reflection makes clear how very intelligent and knowledgeable and cool-headed they would have to be. Thus, as things stand, it is clearly to each of our advantages that *other* people have the moral point of view.

[62] But is there any reason why we should nourish our own commitment to a system of moral principles? Self-interest, certainly as ordinarily construed, cannot do it, for, while it can lead us to do for the most part the actions which morality enjoins, it does so only as a means of gaining rewards and avoiding penalties, and has no tendency to take us to, or support, the impersonal point of view.

[63] The only frame of mind which can provide *direct* support for moral commitment is what Josiah Royce called Loyalty, and what Christians call Love (Charity). *This is a commitment deeper than any commitment to abstract principle.* It is this commitment to the well-being of our fellow man which stands to the justification of moral principles as the purpose of acquiring the ability to explain and predict stands to the justification of scientific theories. This concern for others is a precious thing, the foundation for which is laid in early childhood, though it *can* come about, in adult years, through the little understood phenomena of conversion and psychotherapy.

[64] I said above that a society based on intelligent self-love might survive if its citizens were intelligent and knowledgeable enough. I will close this essay by adding that recent psychological studies make clear what has in a sense been known all along, that the ability to love others for their own sake is as essential to a full life as the need to feel ourselves loved and appreciated for our own sakes— unconditionally, and not as something turned on or off depending on what we do. This fact provides, for those who acknowledge it, a means-end relationship around which can be built practical reasoning which justifies a course of action designed to strengthen our ability to respond to the needs of others. Thus *really* intelligent and informed self-love supports the love of one's neighbor, which alone directly supports the moral point of view when, as the eighteenth century British divine, Bishop Butler, put it, we sit down in a cool hour and ask why we should do our duty.

5
Reason and the Art of Living in Plato*

I

[1] In Book VI of the *Republic*, Plato begins his exploration of the principles in accordance with which the city must be governed if it is to be an enduring and autonomous embodiment of the various forms of excellence of which men, individually and collectively, are (at least in approximation) capable. These principles have a two-fold status. In the first place, they must, if the city is to endure, be 'objective' in the sense that the distinction between truth and falsity is relevant to them and in the second place, they must be capable of being known, where 'knowledge' contrasts with that mere 'belief or 'opinion' which, however true it may be, is, as lacking the support of rational insight, at the mercy of sophistical argument and the persuasive techniques of the orator.

[2] The knowledge of these objective principles, must be present in the city as the possession of its rulers if the city is to endure. This knowledge must also be acquired by Socrates and his companions if the city they are constructing is to be more than a play of the imagination which expresses the happenstances of their political experience.

[3] These points can be paralleled at the level of the individual, for it is a central theme in the *Republic* that the city is the individual "writ large." Just as the excellent city must contain the knowledge of what makes a city excellent, so the excellent man must know what makes for excellence in the individual.[†]

[4] The above paragraphs contain several expressions which can be expected to arouse the spirit of controversy in any one concerned with how life is to be lived. Indeed, I have woven into its fabric four words which, taken one, two, three, even four at a time, in various permutations, define the subject-matter of this essay: 'principle,' 'objectivity,' 'knowledge,' and 'excellence.' Now 'subject-matter' is, in Aristotelian terms, a special case of matter for form: and to indicate the form I am

---

* Presented in a conference of Greece: The Critical Spirit, 450–350 B.C. held at Ohio State University, April 5 and 6, 1968. A discussion of closely related issues is to be found in my essays "The Soul as Craftsman" in *Philosophical Perspectives* (Springfield, Illinois, 1967).

† [Eds.—In the published version, this sentence reads, "Just as the excellent city must contain the knowledge of what makes for excellence in the individual." We have inserted the original language (from Sellars's typescript) which was apparently garbled during the typesetting process. The relevant typescript is document 31735062220946, Box 38, Folder 6, Wilfrid S. Sellars Papers, 1899–1990, ASP.1991.01, Archives of Scientific Philosophy, Archives & Special Collections, University of Pittsburgh Library System.

striving to realize in this subject matter, it will suffice to remind the reader that according to Plato, beyond the excellences of individual and community, beyond the knowledge of these excellences, indeed (Plato tells us in a tantalizingly obscure passage[1]) beyond all knowledge and beyond all being is the Form of the Good. It is this which I propose to discuss, and everything I say will be directed to this end. The fact that, as I hope to show, these two ways of describing the subject matter of this essay ('Plato's conception of the objectivity and knowability of the principles of excellence' and 'the key role in Plato's philosophy of the Form of the Good') ultimately coincide, both illuminates Plato's thought and makes possible an appreciation of the profound truth it contains.

II

[5] If one asks a metaphysician to say which sweeping classification of the things (in the broadest possible sense of the term) which confront our minds and bodies he finds most illuminating one gets such answers as 'atoms and the void,' 'matter and form,' 'substance and power,' 'appearance and reality,' 'the mental and the physical'—not to mention more recent answers of great subtlety and sophistication. It is notoriously difficult to see what these answers have in common, or, even, in what sense they are answers to the same question. But, then, the most difficult task of philosophy has always been to define itself in meaningful ways. Fortunately my initial aim in this essay is historical rather than systematic, and it is with a sense of relief that I turn from the impossible to the improbable, from the evaluation of philosophical categories to the task of exhibiting, as closely as possible in his own terms, the fundamental structure of Plato's metaphysical thought.

[6] What, then, are Plato's basic metaphysical categories? A formula trips readily off the tongue. The mature Plato distinguishes between

(1) the unchanging realm of Ideas or Forms—the proper objects of mind or intelligence;
(2) the changeable realm of physical things—the objects of the senses in perception;
(3) the mediating realm of souls or minds, which animate bodies and, distinct from both Forms and physical things (though more akin to the former), have the task of shaping and controlling changeable things in the light of their degree of insight into the Forms.[2]

---

[1] *Republic*, VI, 508.
[2] He distinguishes a fourth level of being, Space (or Place), the receptable and, as it were, the womb of physical becoming. But nothing I shall have to say hinges on its distinctive role.

[7] These three categories of 'what there is' are mutually irreducible, yet so related that each 'makes sense' only in relation to the other. Thus, the Forms are essentially *intelligibles*, which means that one cannot understand what it is to be a Form without grasping it as something which is capable of being understood by an intelligent being or mind. Again, a mind is, at heart, something which is capable of grasping, more or less adequately, intelligible connections—connections which are independent of its fancies, and are such that thinking does *not* make them so.

[8] The role of mind or soul as the mediator between the intelligible realm of Forms and the visible world of the physical is rooted in the fact that thinking is, in its own way, a process, an activity which has its goals, its means and ends, its standards and principles. Others (e.g. Aristotle) may conceive of thinking at its best as an act of contemplation, an actuality which endures without change, as does the continued hearing of a single musical note, and is an unchanging vision of unchanging Forms. Those who share this conception are tempted to think that a universe which consisted of unchanging intelligibles and unchanging intellects would be a coherent one; indeed, that such a universe would be not only coherent, but ideal. Plato, himself, may have flirted (e.g. in the *Phaedo* and the *Phaedrus*) with the idea that an unchanging contemplation of truth could exist in abstraction from the internal dialogue of question and answer which is thinking to some purpose. But I think it reasonable to say that to the mature Plato, the Plato, for example, of the *Sophist*, the concept of contemplation makes sense only in relation to that of the discursive thinking of which it is the culmination, and the concept of a mind which is capable of nothing but contemplation is incoherent.

[9] If there is mind, then, there must be becoming, change, goal directed activity. But why *physical* becoming? Why could not the Universe consist of disembodied spirits exploring intelligible connections between eternal Forms? If it were conceptually necessary that minds be embodied, or if it were conceptually necessary that the realm of Forms include Forms pertaining to physical becoming, then it would be an intelligible fact that the changeable world includes bodies as well as minds, physical becoming as well as thought. Yet the existence of such conceptual necessities has not yet been demonstrated to the general satisfaction of the philosophical public. There may be answers to the above questions but Plato does not face them directly, and we seem to be left with the brute fact that there is physical becoming, and Form pertaining to physical becoming. On the other hand, perhaps Plato's implicit answer is that among the pre-eminent Forms are those of Courage, Temperance and Justice, and that these would not 'make sense' unless there were bodily hurts, and scarce means* of satisfying bodily hungers.

---

* [Eds.—Published version reads "as men" rather than "means"; we have substituted the language from Sellars's typescript.]

III

[10] As Plato's thought developed, he became more and more concerned with the overall structure of the realm of Forms, and came to conceive of philosophy as an exploration of this structure in a continuing and disciplined dialogue in which, as Hegel reminds us, the 'evident' continually generates the 'absurd' and only reasserts itself, chastened and modified, when the dialogue reaches out to new horizons. In that stretch of the dialogue which took place within his soul, Plato came to see that Forms are related to each other in many ways none of which can be ignored without distorting the other. Some of these ways are of particular interest to formal logicians, and to those metaphysicians whose concerns make abstraction from the distinctive features of ethical and political Ideas. But this abstraction, legitimate as a moment in the larger dialogue, is fatal if it becomes settled policy. It might, indeed, seem that ethical and political Forms are simply that subset of the total domain which is important to us, confronted, as we are, with the problem of how to live our lives; but that they have no pre-eminent role in the intelligibility which, as we have seen, pertains to the very essence of the Forms. Yet it is clear that, at the time of composing the *Republic*, Plato was convinced that the very *intelligibility* of the Forms involves the *distinctive* traits of ethical and political Forms. The form of the Good is the Form of Forms, and to grasp it clearly is the culmination of the philosophical enterprise. There are many who believe that this elusive conception was a vision* which Plato was never able to reproduce in concrete, or even meaningful, terms, an unsupported conviction that values are not incidental to the Universe, but somehow the ground of both its existence and its intelligibility.

[11] In recent years, philosophers, particularly in the Anglo-American tradition, have been prone to take as their paradigm of intelligibility, the intelligibilities of logic and mathematics or, to the extent that they find these 'empty,' the intelligibilities of the results and methods of the natural sciences. The latter indeed, have advanced so rapidly in recent years as to make moral and political thinking appear static, if not retrograde, and to deal with intelligibilities neither in method nor in results.

[12] The dimensions of intelligibility on which recent Anglo-American philosophy has focused its attention are, in the traditional sense of the term, 'theoretical.' They contrast with 'practical' intelligibility, i.e., that intelligibility which pertains to ends and means, to instruments and their uses, and to rules, conventions and principles of conduct. Usually the contrast between these two modes of intelligibility is no sooner drawn than dismissed as sound but insignificant. It is argued that the intelligible connections involved in 'practice' (in that broad sense in which all purposive behavior is practice) are simply the intelligible

---

* [Eds.—Published version reads "version" rather than "vision"; we have substituted the language from Sellars's typescript.]

connections of logic, mathematics and science, used as a framework which, given our circumstances, can connect our desires and appetites, into a compatible, i.e. jointly realizable, system. That some practical intelligibilities are, in this way, derivative is non-controversial. Whether *all* the intelligibilities of practice are, in this way, derivative is, perhaps, *the* key issue in the philosophy of practice, thus, in ethical theory. Plato's thesis in the *Republic* to the effect that the Form of the Good is the Form of Forms, the ground of all the Forms and of the intelligibility which is essential to them, would seem, however, to be an outright rejection of the idea that all intelligibility pertaining to practice is theoretical intelligibility (causal and logical) at' the service of appetites and desires, in other words, as Hume put it, the slave of the passions.

IV

[13] To interpret Plato correctly on this point we must begin, as he does, with familiar examples of practical intelligibility. Only after small scale distinctions have been drawn, can we hope to understand the Form of the Good as the supreme principle of the realm of Forms.

[14] As might be expected, the distinction which provides us with our initial insight into the characteristic features of practical intelligibility is the familiar means-end relationship between actions and outcomes. Perhaps the most obvious point—the importance of which, however, is often overlooked—is that reference to actions is correlative with reference to the circumstances in which they are done. A circumstance is roughly a standing[3] condition in which a given action may or may not be done.

[15] In the simplest case, causal truths of the form

Bringing about E implies doing A, if the circumstances are C

appear in practical guise in the form

If one wants E, then if one is in C, one 'must do' (or 'ought' to do) A

This is the simple means-end intelligibility which Kant (misleadingly) baptized with the phrase 'hypothetical imperative.' The words 'ought' and 'must' express practical concepts which carve up and transpose into the 'practical mode' the causal connections which exist between doing A, being in C and bringing about E.

---

[3] Needless to say, a standing condition need not be static—the term 'standing' simply reinforces the contrast between the circumstance, and that which may or may not be done by an agent in that circumstance.

In the case we have considered, E is an event or happening, the bringing about of which, if one is in C, requires and is fulfilled by doing A. Typically, the same outcome (or what counts as the same outcome) will eventuate, even if the circumstances are different, if one compensates by doing a correspondingly different action. This generates the more complex schema

If one wants E, then if in C_i, one ought to do A_j

where 'C_i' indicates a range of circumstances and 'A_j' the corresponding range of actions which would eventuate in E.

[16] The preceding remarks do little more than rehearse familiar distinctions. It is now time to introduce a related family of concepts, central to Plato's thought, which pertains to that kind of practice which is *making* something (a product, e.g., a shoe), as contrasted with bringing about an event (e.g., an explosion). One might try to assimilate the two cases by referring to the making of the shoe as the bringing about of the event of a shoe's coming into existence. But the assimilation is superficial and obscures important distinctions.

[17] The product of a craft (or art—the Greek term is *techne*) is, typically, an instrumentality which is used (or, to extend a familiar term, 'consumed') in a certain way. Thus, to consider two out of many possible examples, the product may serve as part of the raw material for the product of another craft—as a nail is ingredient in shoes—or, to take an example from the other end of the spectrum, it may serve to provide enjoyable experiences.

[18] In considering the structure of a craft as a form of practice, we are led to distinguish the following categories: (baking a cake provides a particularly useful example)

Ingredients:
  Materials: flour, cups of; butter, tablespoons of; etc.
  Objects: eggs (these might be compared to products of another craft—the producing of eggs by hens)
Recipe:
  Number and proportion of ingredients combined
  Program of action:
    (If one wants) to bake a cake: if ingredients are in state C_i, one ought to do A_j.

The concept of 'making' can be extended to include (a) contributing to making (as where a number of craftsmen must cooperate); and, in another direction, to cover (b) maintaining (and repairing) products to keep them in something like their optimum state.

[19] If we simplify our schema of the practice of a craft to read

(If one wants) to make an O, then: in C_i one ought to do A_j

we can characterize the family of statements of the form

In C_i one ought to do A_j

as the action-principles of the craft. It can hardly be stressed too much that such principles may be extremely complex and numerous. Anyone who has done such a 'simple' thing as successfully bake a cake will recognize this fact. It will be important to bear this in mind as more interesting cases are considered. For our present purposes, however, the important point is that statements which purport to formulate the action principle of a craft are subject to rational debate and that the distinction between truth and falsity applies to them. They are matters of 'objective fact' and belong to the rational order. Furthermore, there is an important sense in which they exist 'by nature,' if the latter term is so used as to contrast with 'convention.' But this remark is but the opening shot in a long campaign.

[20] We distinguished above between an artifact and its use or 'consumption.' If we call the use or consumption for which an artifact is designed its *external* purpose, we can say that whether or not an artifact serves this external purpose is, in general, also a matter for rational discussion, and that the distinction between truth and falsity is relevant. On the other hand, whether the *ultimate* ends served by artifacts are themselves subject to rational discussion and to the distinction between the true and the false (or, to put it differently, whether these ultimate ends are in any interesting sense 'objective'), has at least the appearance of being a question of quite a different kind. That the crafting of instrumentalities belongs, as practice, to the intelligible order, is not surprising. On the other hand, if one could show that the *ultimate* ends served by instrumentalities have in their own way a practical intelligibility akin to that of the crafting of instrumentalities, one would be well on the way to illuminating the *objectivity* of ultimate ends.

V

[21] The above account of the structure of craftmanship, schematic though it may be, gives us a powerful tool for analyzing the contrast between 'nature' (*physis*) and 'convention' (*nomos*) the validity of which is the central issue between Plato and the Sophists. The word 'nature' should not mislead, for that which exists 'by nature' and is contrasted with convention is as it is, regardless of what we think it to be. It is characterized by objectivity, and is discoverable, if at all, by rational methods. Conventions, on the other hand, exist as *ways of thinking*, in that broad sense of 'thinking' which includes attitudes. That a certain mode of practice is a convention, is itself, of course, an objective fact. Yet this objective fact is a fact

about the existence, in the community, of a certain way of thinking which might well have been otherwise. Philosophers, almost from the beginning, have given the term, 'convention' and its approximate equivalents in other languages—e.g., the Greek *'nomos'*—technical senses which so extended and modify their original meaning, that it is a philological task of the first magnitude to trace the family trees of the uses to which they have been put. For our purposes, it will be helpful to construe conventions as general imperatives which have come to be accepted and enforced in a community, either by deliberate initiative on the part of specific individuals, or by the slow process which is the coming to be of tradition.

[22] The conventions in which we are interested are those which correspond, in ways to be defined, to the principles of a craft. For, as I hope to show, an understanding of how this distinction works in simple cases provides the essential clue to the contrast between positive law and political principle which Plato seeks to defend against the attacks of the Sophists.

[23] The first point to be made is that statements which purport to formulate *principles* are not, as such, in the imperative mood. In this respect they are like any matter-of-factual statement, e.g., "The sky is blue." But although statements of principles are not general imperatives, to each statement of principle there corresponds, in a straightforward sense, a sentence in the imperative mood. Statements of principle are either true or false; imperatives, as such, are neither. Imperatives are used to tell people to do something, and are capable of being enforced, i.e., accomplished* by the threat (or promise) of sanctions.

[24] The distinction I have in mind can be illustrated in simple terms by the contrast between

If it is raining, John ought to use an umbrella

which we may suppose to be a true proposition resting on the tacit premise that John wants to keep dry, and the corresponding imperative

If it is raining, John, use an umbrella!

Notice that although a person who uses the imperative sentence to tell John to use an umbrella, if it rains, might offer as *his* reason for doing so "because you, John want to keep dry and using an umbrella is the way to do it," he may neither *have* this reason, nor *offer* it. He may *have* quite another reason, and yet *offer* the above reason; or, perhaps, have no reason at all. Yet whatever his reason, if he has any, by using this sentence he has genuinely told John to carry an umbrella, if it rains; and may undertake to treat John in friendly or unfriendly ways depending on whether or not he does as he is told.

---

* [Eds.—In Sellars's typescript the word here is "accompanied," not "accomplished."]

[25] On the other hand, the statement

If it is raining, John *ought* to use an umbrella

is no mere 'say so' independent of reasons. There is no difficulty in supposing it to be an objectively true statement which is grounded in the fact that John wants to keep dry, along with familiar scientific facts about umbrellas and rain.

[26] That we often use 'ought'-statements in such a way that they enable us to achieve results which we could obtain by using imperative sentences, must not blind us to the difference between 'ought' statements and imperatives. After all, I can use the non-imperative

There is a spider on your head.

to get someone to slap his head, where the imperative

Slap your head!

might be met by a hostile stare.

[27] Let us apply these distinctions to the case of the builder's craft. In the interest of simplicity, let us suppose that the purpose of a house is to provide shelter, and that there is only one type of house which satisfactorily serves this purpose. Consider the family of practical statements.

If one wants to build a house, then if the circumstances
  (including the state of the raw materials) are C_i, one ought to do A_j

or, equivalently,

The principles of house building are:
  If in C_i, one ought to do A_j.

It is readily seen that the statements making up this family are either true or false and, if true, are true by virtue of (a) the 'nature' of the materials and (b) the design of a satisfactory house.

[28] Let us now suppose that our builders form a guild. Some of its members are experienced builders; others mere apprentices. Even experienced builders will differ in their skills and in the extent of their insight into the principles of the craft. They may even have different beliefs concerning these principles. Let us, therefore, suppose that, formally or informally, the guild adopts a 'builders' code,' a system of enforced imperatives, thus

In building a house:
   If in C_i, do A_j!

[29] We can conceive that, if pressed for reasons for this 'legislation,' they might offer something like the following:

...because these are the things it is necessary to do to build a house, and by enforcing this legislation we will insure that this is what builders do.

In other words, the builders' establishment might believe that in the absence of this code, many builders would follow false principles even though their sincere purpose was to build satisfactory houses. Or the builders' establishment might believe that many builders are not so much ignorant as corrupt, and that in the absence of the code they might deliberately build defective houses to line their pockets. We might call both types of reason for adopting and enforcing a code, *craft-oriented reasons*.

[30] There is always the possibility, of course, that the builder's establishment has as its reason for adopting and enforcing a certain code, not that it embodies what they believe to be the true principle of the craft, but rather (though they would be understandably reluctant to publicize the fact) that action in accordance with the code would be to their advantage, in that, for example, the establishment has privileged access to certain kinds of material. This type of reason for adopting and enforcing a code might be called an *external reason*.

[31] Now it is clear that individual builders will tend to regard the codes as a guide to what a builder ought to do, *qua* builder, only to the extent that they believe the collective wisdom of the establishment to be a more reliable guide to the objective principles of the craft than is their own unaided judgment. They would regard it as silly to say that something is a principle of the craft simply by virtue of being a promulgated and enforced imperative, i.e., a convention.

[32] Of course, since the code is enforced by fines and other sanctions, each builder *qua* person will have a reason for conforming to the code. But this reason, in its turn, can be called an external reason. Thus, supposing a builder to be convinced that one of the principles of the craft is

In C_i one ought to do A_j*

whereas the enforced code says

---

* [Eds.—In the published version, this principle reads, "In C_i one ought to do A_k"; but in Sellars's typescript, it reads, "In C_i one ought to do A_j". We have substituted the version from Sellars's typescript here, as we think what Sellars means to discuss here is a case of conflict between the principles of a craft and an enforced imperative relating to the craft.]

In C_i, do A_k!

He will regard this latter enforced imperative as throwing no light on what he ought to do *qua* builder, but as by no means irrelevant to what he ought to do *qua* having hungry mouths to feed.

VI

[33] Now it is a familiar fact that Plato's moral and critical philosophy makes use of structures of ideas fundamentally akin to those involved in the [above*] analysis of the builder's craft. The early dialogues make constant use of analogies with features of craftsmanship to throw light on specific philosophical puzzles. The pattern recurs in the more systematic philosophy of the later dialogues. The most obvious case is the *Timaeus* where Plato makes use of the concept of a Divine Craftsman who builds the world, as a device for explicating the general categories in terms of which the world is to be understood. Even where the use of analogies with craftsmanship is not explicit, it is often present to the discerning eye, and provides essential clues to the understanding of his thought.

[34] Plato regards the study of humble crafts as philosophically illuminating, because he sees them as the lesser members of a hierarchy which culminates in two crafts of intrinsic concern to the philosopher: (a) the craft of the statesman or, as I shall put it, of the citizen; (b) the craft of shaping one's life as an individual.

[35] Our primary conception of craftsmanship is the production of instrumentalities. We are therefore not surprised to find Plato speaking of statesmanship as a craft, for we are fully prepared to think of the well-ordered city as an instrumentality for the general welfare, and, therefore, to find the analogy between statesmanship and familiar crafts as illuminating. (It would be tempting to turn our attention to other crafts, e.g., medicine, in order to highlight other analogies, but the fundamental points can be made with reference to the builder's art as I have described it.)

[36] The product, then, of the stateman's craft is a city ordered to the wellbeing of its citizens, and its proximate raw material involves, in addition to physical instrumentalities, persons with diverse characters and talents. Now, in the case of some crafts (e.g., cooking and building) it seems reasonable to say that consumers 'know' how the products are to be used and can transmit their 'knowledge' to the craftsman. It is less plausible to suppose that 'consumers' of cities 'know' how they are to be used, i.e., in what the well-being of the community consists. Compare the case of the physician's art. Plato, however, thinks that 'tradition' embodies

---

* [Eds.—The word "above" appears in Sellars's typescript, but not in the published version.]

substantial insights into these matters; it is, to use his metaphor, an 'image' or 'likeness' of the truth. But he also thinks that in the Athens of his day, the insights of tradition are at the mercy of sophistry and the rhetorical skills of ignorant men.

[37] If we postpone questions concerning the specific character of wellbeing or 'happiness,' and make what philosophers call a purely 'formal' or 'placeholding' use of the term 'general welfare' we can continue our exploration of the craft of the citizen along the following lines. We have already referred to the 'external*' aim of the craft (the general welfare), and to its proximate raw materials. It remains to explore the political counterpart of the principles or programs of action in accordance with which a craftsman shapes his materials to make the finished product. Analogy suggests the following general schema

If a citizen wants to contribute to making and/or maintaining a city ordered to the general welfare, then
If a citizen is in C_i, he ought to do A_j.

(It must be borne in mind that the simplicity of this schema conceals the number and complexity of the principles it represents.) As in the case of the builder's art, these statements of principle will be 'objective' in the sense that the distinction between truth and falsity is relevant to them. They express belief about the impact of various kinds of action in various kinds of circumstance on the life of a community. It is clear that the question whether they are true or false presupposes a specific conception of the welfare which is to result from the use of the instrumentality which is the so-ordered city. But given such a specific concept, that a specific plan of action is required to order a city to welfare, thus conceived, is an objective matter for rational determination.

[38] If we continue to draw on analogies between statesmanship and the builder's art, we arrive at the following account of the distinction between *nomos* (convention) and *physis* (nature: in other words principle and truth) in the political context. The principles of the craft of the citizen are, no more than those of the builder's art, to be confused with enforced imperatives, whether the latter exist as traditions informally enforced or as positive law enforced by specific agencies, themselves created by law. The conceptual distinction between *principles* and *conventions* is as sharp as it was in the case of the builder's craft, and the relations between principles and conventions in politics are at bottom, the same as those which were sketched in our parable of the builder's guild.

[39] We contrasted builders engaging in their craft, without being organized in a guild which adopts and enforces general imperatives pertaining to building-type

---

* [Eds.—Correction of "eternal" in published version; cf. Sellars's discussion of the "external purpose" of a craft in §20.]

activity, with* builders so organized. We can similarly draw a contrast, in principle, between a number of citizens engaging in the citizen's craft, without being subject to enforced general imperatives pertaining to citizen-like activity, with citizens so organized as to exist in an ambience of enforced conventions.

[40] If we assume that our citizens are organized into a guild (i.e., city) and subject to positive law, and refer to those who have the power to adopt and enforce general imperatives as the 'establishment' of the city, we can transpose our parable of the builder's guild into the political context along the following lines. Assuming that the establishment has reasonably true opinions or opinions as to what constitutes the general welfare of the city, and assuming that the legislative and administrative activity of the establishment is, as we put it, craft-oriented in its motivation, we would expect the resulting conventions to correspond in rough approximation to the principles which specify the program of action by which individual citizens can make their contribution to ordering the city as an effective instrument for the general welfare.

[41] As in the case of the builder's guild, a citizen who has the well-ordered city as his end-in-view will not, unless confused, regard the fact that a course of action is prescribed by an enforced imperative as making that course of action what he ought to do *qua* citizen. Principles specify what he *ought* to do, conventions tell him to do certain things under certain penalties. Even if these conventions are *formulated* in terms of 'ought' they do not *as conventions*†, bring it about that, as citizen, he *ought* to act in the manner prescribed. As in the case of the builder's guild, a citizen may regard the fact that a course of action is prescribed by enforced legislation as a good, though not conclusive reason, for supposing that the course of action *does* correspond to a principle.

[42] Again, as in the case of the builder's guild, a person who views himself on a particular occasion, not as citizen but, say, as one who has his own interests at heart, may find the penalty attached to the law to constitute a compelling reason for conforming to the law, whether or not, as citizen, he concedes that the law tells him to do what in fact he ought to do.

[43] So far the parallel works out smoothly. It is now time to note a complication which can generate confusion. The raw materials relevant to making a shoe are, for example, rubber, nails, etc., and the program of action of the shoemaker concerns the shaping and arranging of such raw materials. In the case of the art of the citizen, however, the materials with which he is concerned include, in addition to what we have already mentioned, such things as

---

* [Eds.—Published version reads "upon" rather than "with"; we have substituted the language from Sellars's typescript.]

† [Eds.—Correction of "convection" in original printing.]

(a) current beliefs about the principles of the citizen's craft as well as beliefs about the specific nature of the general welfare to which the city is to be ordered as an instrument.
(b) currently enforced general imperatives.

The second special feature of the circumstances in which the citizen must act involves an interpenetration of principles and conventions which, misinterpreted, can lead to a confusion of the two categories, a failure to find the distinction between principles and conventions, in the political context, meaningful.

[44] Suppose that one of the principles of the art of the citizen is

In C_i one ought to do A_j

and suppose that there is *no* enforced imperative to a contrary effect, for example

In C_i, do A_k!

On these assumptions, what one ought to do *qua* citizen, if one is in C_i is A_j. But suppose, now, that the latter imperative comes to be promulgated and enforced. Then, although an adequate account of the implications of this fact would require a more sophisticated apparatus, the following gives the gist of the matter. There now cease to be circumstances of the kind originally referred to as C_i—for these were defined in terms of the *absence* of this legislation. The closest counterpart of such situations now become those which are like C_i but involve the additional element of the existence of the enforced imperative

In C_i do A_k!   ($L_{i,k}$) where 'L' stands for 'law'

Let us represent such situations by

$C_i [+ L_{i,k}]$

We now note that it could very well be the case that the promotion of the general welfare requires that in *such* situations a citizen does A_k; that it be a *matter of principles* that

In $C_i [+ L_{i,k}]$, one ought to do A_k

It is along these lines that a convention

In C_i, do A_k!

could, *in a sense*, generate a principle

In C_i [+ $L_{i,\ k}$], one ought to do A_k*

which one might be tempted to represent as

In C_i, one ought to do A_k

and confuse with the corresponding convention.

[45] On reflection, however, it is clear that although this provides a sense in which convention (enforced imperatives) determines what a person exercising the craft of the citizen ought to do, it nevertheless determines it *not qua convention*, but *qua* just another factor in the circumstances in which a citizen must act. Like other circumstance-factors it contributes to determine, along with the nature of the instrumentality to be produced or maintained, the manifold principles of the craft. And, as in the case of any craft, these principles, however complicated, have an objective status which distinguishes them from conventions, even though they take account of and even refer to convention.

[46] To sum up, Plato—and I have simply been representing the structure of his thought—argues that what one ought to do *qua* exercising the art of the citizen is *never*, except in the above derivative sense, a matter of convention.

[47] Before proceeding to the next stage of the argument, some terminological points will be helpful. The principles of the art of the citizen, or, to put it in superficially different terms, the principles of the statesman's craft, are what we would be tempted to call 'principles of political obligation.' It must, however, be borne in mind that the line between the ethical and the political is difficult to draw, and it will be conducive† to clarity to conceive of the principles in question as simply those principles which relate to our obligations to others in so far as the relevant instrumentality is the well-ordered city as a whole, as contrasted, for example, with those principles pertaining to the family as an instrumentality for the well-being of a more limited community. The relationship of the citizen's craft to the craft of the household is a subtle one, for like all crafts, that of the household has its own relative autonomy and generates its own 'oughts' or principles. Yet, since families are among the ingredients to be shaped into the well-ordered city, which is the proximate instrumentality for the *general* welfare, the principles of the craft of the household are subject to overriding principles pertaining to the craft of the citizen.

---

* [Eds.—Correction of "A_i" in original printing.]

† [Eds.—Published version reads "conductive" rather than "conducive"; we have substituted the language from Sellars's typescript.]

[48] But what does 'overriding' mean in this context? Here we must remember that although the principles of a craft are *objective*, they are relative to two ends: (a) one immanent to the craft, the end of making and/or maintaining a certain instrumentality (i.e., an automobile); (b) the external end which is defined by the characteristic use to which the instrumentality produced by the craft is put. To say that a person is acting, during a certain period, *qua* practitioner of a certain craft, is to say that whatever the larger framework of purpose he has in mind, he has committed himself, during this period to the immanent end of the craft, i.e., to seeking to contribute to the making and/or maintaining of the relevant instrumentality. If, then, a person, during a certain period, has making this contribution as his proximate end or purpose, then the principles of the craft *objectively* specify what he ought to do, given his circumstances (the raw material, so to speak, which he must shape) to make this contribution. Thus, although the principles are *objective*, they are, in a familiar sense hypothetical. They tell him what he ought to do in given circumstances if he proposes to make his contribution to the existence of the product. Thus the principles of the shoemaker's craft specify the steps a person must take if he is to make good shoes out of available raw material. If he has no interest in making shoes, he will, so to speak, simply look the *objectivity* of the principles in the eye and move on. Again, one who has only the interests of his family at heart and is consequently engaged in the craft of the household, may acknowledge the objectivity of the overriding principles of the craft of the citizen yet, unless he is committed to the overriding end of the latter craft, will look the objectivity of these principles in the eye, but limit himself to the practice of the family craft.

[49] This conception of the subordination, coordination and relative autonomy of the various crafts is the key to Plato's thought. It is now time to show how he puts this concept to use in defending the objectivity of 'justice'—in the sense of our obligations *qua* citizen to our fellow man—against the attacks of the Sophists.

[50] The first point to emphasize is that it is not too difficult for Plato (in the person of Socrates) to get his opponents to admit that abstractly considered there are many crafts, ranging from shoemaking to the crafting of a city ordered to the well-being of its citizens. There is, of course, much controversy about such philosophical issues as 'what is objectivity' 'how is it to be determined which principles are objectively true?'—in short the omnipresent issues embodied in the skeptic's challenge. Yet the philosophical skeptic can be led to admit that in whatever sense there is a craft of shoemaking with objective principles, there are other crafts which pertain more closely to living, and perhaps, even, a craft of so ordering a city as to promote the happiness of its citizens. Needless to say, any such formal admission leaves room for argument concerning what constitutes happiness or, to introduce a familiar phrase, 'the good for man.'

[51] Thus it is worth noting that among the Sophists Protagoras is closest to Socrates in his general outlook on how life is to be lived. Plato was convinced that

the traditions of Athens embody confused but substantially true opinions about the principles of the art of the citizen. (In Platonic terms, confused but substantially true opinions about justice, i.e., the principles of just action.) To the extent, and it is a large one, that Protagoras is an effective representative of these traditions, Plato looks on him with a sympathetic and even admiring eye. What Plato attacks in Protagoras is his failure to appreciate the objectivity of principles, the relevance of rational argument to deciding what they are, and, above all, his failure, in the case of the political art, to appreciate the distinction between principles and conventions. Protagoras' failure, in these respects, combined with his talents as a persuader, prepare the way for the influence of persuaders less friendly to tradition and the images of truth it embodies.

[52] How are we to construe the controversy between Socrates and Thrasymachus in the First Book of the *Republic*? Is it possible for the latter to grant that there is a craft of the citizen (or statesman) along the lines we have defined, and yet disagree with Socrates in an interesting way about its status? The answer is yes. Thrasymachus makes two central contentions:

(1) What point is there in recognizing the existence of a craft of shaping the city to serve the general welfare, if no one in any genuine sense *engages* in this craft? He, Thrasymachus, can perhaps be led to admit that by 'justice' we mean the principle of such a craft, but if no one commits himself to the end in terms of which this craft is defined, these principles, however *objective*, are as irrelevant to life as the principles of the craft of building ladders to the clouds.

(2) Thus, even if it is granted that our conception of justice involves the conception of a craft of a citizen along the lines we have defined, and that this concept is, in a sense, the core of its meanings, the hard fact of the matter is that as far as the *usage* of "the term 'justice' is concerned" ("what is called justice"), it is employed by the establishment to describe the political imperatives they promulgate and enforce. Furthermore, the purpose of the political establishment in enforcing this legislation is not the 'internal' purpose of embodying their beliefs about the true principles of the craft of the citizen in effective conventions, but rather the external purpose of shaping conventions to serve their private interests.

With respect to the first point, it is as though no one who shaped pieces of leather did so with the settled purpose of making shoes, but only, for example, with immediate personal interests in view. In this case, it would be, so to speak, an accident that he ever finished a shoe.

[53] With respect to the second point, it is as though (a possibility we have already glanced at) the builder's establishment called its enforced imperatives concerning the manipulation of housing materials 'principles of building,' even

though it was moved to adopt and enforce these imperatives not to facilitate the making of houses well-ordered to the shelter of those who live in them, but rather to promote the economic interests of the builders themselves.

[54] Clearly, to reply to these contentions, Plato must make some points like the following:

(1) He must convince us that people generally do, as a matter of fact, have a settled interest in the well-ordering of the city for the welfare of its citizens. We would expect him to add, however, that this settled interest largely rests, not on insight, but on tradition and upbringing, and is correspondingly vulnerable to sophistical arguments and the techniques of persuasion. Since it is clear that, according to Thrasymachus the only *settled* interest people have is in their own well-being, Plato must show not only that this is in point of fact false, but that a settled and at least relatively autonomous interest in the general welfare has a justifiable place in a well-conceived life.[4]

(2) Plato must show that, in point of fact, the establishment does not legislate solely with a view to its own interest, *as contrasted with* interests of citizens generally. More positively put, he must show that the imperatives enforced by the establishment are (to a greater or lesser extent) designed to embody its beliefs concerning how to shape the city for the common good. He will grant, as before, that the fact that the establishment is so disposed is rooted in tradition and upbringing, and is consequently vulnerable to temptations and sophistry. At a deeper level, however, he must show that it is a part of a well-conceived life that those in a position to legislate seek to embody in their legislation their convictions concerning the principles of the craft of the citizen, the art of statesmanship.

[55] I pointed out at the beginning of the section that Plato conceives of arts or crafts as constituting a hierarchy which culminates in two supreme crafts: (a) the craft of the statesman or citizen; (b) the craft of shaping one's life as an individual. It is to the latter that I now turn, for the conception of such a craft or art of living is, as I hope to show, the keystone of Plato's thought.

[56] The first thing to notice is that references to an art or craft of living are at their most explicit in the controversies with Callicles in the Gorgias, and with Protagoras in the final stages of the dialogue of that name. The conception of such an art or craft becomes less explicit (though evident to the discerning eye) in his constructive account of how life is to be lived in the *Republic*, and, particularly, in the *Philebus*. The reason is not far to seek. Craftsmanship in the literal sense is

---

[4] That, for Plato, the ultimate court of appeal of the life of reason is self-interest adequately conceived is a theme to be explored on a subsequent occasion.

concerned with instrumentalities. Even the craft of a statesman has as its immanent end the shaping of an instrumentality, a city ordered to the well-being of its citizens. On the other hand, the central issues pertaining to the life of the individual concern not instrumentalities, but that which gives all instrumentalities their ultimate *raison d'etre*.

[57] Nevertheless, although the satisfactory life is not an instrumentality, the program of action by which it can be realized has, in all other respects, the structure of craftsmanship. In this case, however, the internal and external ends of the craft are so intimately related that they seem almost to coincide. Roughly speaking the instrumentality is a system of abilities ordered to form a character, while the 'use' or 'consumption' of the instrumentality is the actualization of this character in satisfying activity. The crafting is done by those who shape and maintain the character, not the least important of whom is the individual himself.

[58] The word 'character' is perhaps too Aristotelian to use in the context of the *Philebus*. Aristotle, in discussing the satisfying life lays great stress on habits and dispositions. Plato lays equal stress in the *Republic* on habits of feeling, thought and action when discussing the happiness available to men of silver and bronze. In the *Philebus*, however, where he is discussing life at its best, the stress is less on habits and dispositions than on insight into the nature of soul and its relation to other dimensions of reality.

[59] The instrumentality crafted by the art of living is knowledge of the nature of the satisfying life, and it is crafted by dialectic, i.e., well-ordered philosophical thought. Yet the true product of the art of living is not this instrumentality, nor is this knowledge itself *merely* an instrumentality. The ingredients which are shaped to achieve the purpose of the craft are shaped not into an instrumentality, but into a pattern of enjoyed activities. These ingredients can be classified under two headings: 'knowledges' and 'pleasures.'

> Socrates: Then here, we may say, we have at hand the ingredients, intelligence and pleasure, ready to be mixed, and the materials in which, or out of which, we, as builders, are to build our structure: that would not be a bad metaphor.
> (*Philebus*, 59DE)

The lists of ingredients must not be misunderstood. Early in the dialogue the life of pleasure unmixed with any form of knowledge *and* the life of "intelligence, thought, knowledge and complete memory of everything without any pleasure" are contrasted with a 'mixed' life which includes pleasure, on the one hand, and reason with intelligence on the other. We are told that neither of the unmixed lives "is sufficient and desirable for any human being or any living thing (21DE)." In 33B, the unmixed "life of reason and intelligence" with "no experiencing of pleasure, great or small," is reintroduced, and Socrates tells us that "perhaps it is not a wild surmise that this of all lives is the most godlike." To which Protarchus adds "it is not to be supposed that the gods feel either pleasure or its opposite."

Socrates: No, of course it is not; it would be unseemly for either feeling to arise in them.

From this latter exchange it has often been concluded that the godlike life is devoid of pleasure, and that only the ideal life *for man* involves pleasure as well as knowledge. But this is surely a misunderstanding, as Socrates hints, when he adds to the sentence quoted above "but to that question we will give further consideration later on if it should be relevant." For implicit in the subsequent discussion is a distinction between those feelings of pleasure which arise out of the satisfaction of needs, where the needs either may be painful (as in the case of thirst) or, as in the case of "the pleasures which attach to colors which we call beautiful, to figures, to most odors, to sounds," imperceptible and painless, but their fulfillment 'perceptible and pleasant," (50E), and of those enjoyed activities which would not usually be called pleasures.

[60] Thus when it is said that "it is not to be supposed that the gods feel... pleasure," this must not be taken to mean that a divine life is without enjoyment. For in 60BC we are told that

A creature which possesses [the Good] permanently, completely and absolutely has never any need of anything else; its *satisfaction* is complete.

and in the account of the recipe of the satisfying life which concludes the dialogue, reference is made to "the pure pleasures of the soul itself, some of them attaching to knowledge, others to sensations." (66C)

VII

[61] Before I began my exploration of the conceptual structure of craftsmanship, I was engaged in pointing out that Plato conceives of the realm of Forms as a realm of intelligibilities. I then pointed out that whereas recent British and American philosophy has tended to take as its paradigm of intelligibility the intelligibilities of logic, mathematics, and the natural sciences, there is *prima facie*, a domain of intelligibility, not unrelated to the former, which can be called the domain of practical intelligibilities.

[62] In exploring the intelligibilities of craftsmanship, I pointed out that these intelligibilities involve such mathematical intelligibilities as numbers, ratios, and such other intelligibilities as pertain to the causal properties of the materials to be shaped by the craft. Yet these theoretical intelligibilities are, insofar as they

contribute to the practical intelligibilities of the craft, subordinated to that organizing intelligibility which is the *recipe* of the product. We might put this by saying that the Form of the practical intelligibilities of a craft is the Form 'recipe for making something to some purpose.'

[63] When Plato tells us that the Form of Forms is 'the Form of the Good,' is he not telling us that although there are many varieties of structure which relate Forms to other Forms, the most illuminating way of conceiving of the realm of intelligibilities is a complex system of recipes for crafting a world which includes not only instrumentalities, but satisfying lives? The second book of the *Republic* begins with a classification of goods into:

(a) those which we desire for their own sake
(b) those which we desire both for their own sake and for their consequences
(c) those which we desire only for their consequences.

To say that the Form of the realm of Forms is the Form of a complex system of recipes is to imply that it contains not only recipes for instrumental goods (e.g., the Form Bed) but also for goods which are not instrumentalities, and that the latter Forms are the recipes for different levels of satisfying life, divine and human.

[64] We have seen that the practical intelligibilities involved in the instrumental crafts are hypothetical. They specify what must be done if one wants to make or maintain an instrument. Is there such a thing as a nonhypothetical practical intelligibility? A practical intelligibility which is not of the above form? Plato surely thinks that there is, for he tells us on a number of occasions that statements of the form

S wants to lead a satisfying life

or, as he puts it,

S wills the good

are final answers to the question 'why does S do what he does?' Such answers are formal in that S's specific beliefs about what kind of life would in point of fact be satisfying may well be mistaken. But that the question 'what kind of life would really satisfy me?' is, *in principle*, capable of a reasoned answer, though it involves a self-knowledge which has passed through all the stages of disciplined reflection on the source* of things, is Plato's abiding faith as a philosopher.

---

* [Eds.—Sellars's typescript reads "nature" rather than "source."]

[65] It is surely along these lines that the supposedly mysterious passage in Book VI of the *Republic* in which Plato describes the 'place of honor' of the Good in the system of Forms is to be understood.

> Glaucon: you are giving it a position of extraordinary splendor, if it is the source of knowledge and truth and itself surpasses them in worth. You surely cannot mean that it is pleasure.
>
> Socrates: Heaven forbid, I exclaimed. But I want to follow up our analogies still further. You will agree that the sun not only makes the things we see visible, but also brings them into existence and gives them growth and nourishment; yet it is not the same thing as existence; and so with the objects of knowledge: these derive from the Good not only their power of being known, but their very being and reality; and goodness is not the same thing as being, but even beyond being, surpassing it in dignity and power.

If my account of Plato's thought is correct, this passage paints no picture of an abstract essence which has no intelligible connection with what we ordinarily mean by 'good,' but simply sums up in compendious, if dramatic, form the conception of the realm of Forms as constituting a complex of recipes for building an intelligible world, the intelligibility of which is *practical* intelligibility, the intelligibility of the satisfying life, whether human or divine.

6
Objectivity, Intersubjectivity and the Moral Point of View*

I

1. Practical reasoning, in a broad sense, brings particular matters of fact, empirical generalizations, scientific laws and logical principles to bear on our values. Even the most casual attempt to botanize values confronts one with the fact that they can be classified in many ways: with respect to their material content, their logical form, their factual presuppositions, their place in various hierarchies, their status as derivative or not derivative, the distinction between values pertaining to objects, values pertaining to thoughts about objects, to thoughts about thoughts about objects, etc., etc. A full theory of practical reasoning would bring out, for example, its involvement in scientific reasoning, where the values involved are epistemic. It would also recognize the inseparability, yet distinguishability, of theoretical and practical reason in all dimensions of human life.

2. Theoretical reason is, I have argued in Chapter V [of *Science and Metaphysics*—Eds.], a structure of many levels. Each level has, as its basic skeleton, the statement forms and sequences of statement forms of truth functional and quantificational logic; yet, as I have indicated, these structures exist in an ambience of rules of criticism, which themselves belong to the domain of practical reason, *qua* concerned with epistemic values. A critique of pure practical reason must obviously concern itself with the way in which it contains the skeletal forms of deductive logic, and by an interesting symmetry, which robs such slogans as 'the priority of practical reason' and 'the priority of theoretical reason' of unconditional truth, a critique of pure theoretical reason must concern itself with the essential involvement of practical reason in theoretical reason. As usual, there are different dimensions of priority. The philosophical landscape is not only not a desert, it is not even a flat-land.

3. But my aim in this chapter is not to botanize values, nor to explore the epistemic values which are the rationale of the scientific enterprise. It is rather to

---

* [Eds.—OIM initially appeared as the final chapter of Sellars's John Locke lectures, *Science and Metaphysics*. Much of the material from OIM is taken verbatim from Sellars's Lindley Lecture, FCET. In the original printed version, the first footnote on each page was note number 1, the second was 2, etc. In Sicha's Intelex edition, all notes in the entire book are numbered sequentially; the notes in Chapter 7 begin with 50. We have elected to number all notes sequentially starting with number 1.]

explore the fundamental principles of a metaphysics of practice, with particular reference to the values in terms of which we lead not just one compartment of our lives but our lives *sans phrase*. I have said enough, however, to indicate that in my opinion the metaphysics of morals is but a fragment of a broader critique of practical reason. A philosophical interpretation of 'ought to be' and 'ought to do' with respect to everyday living must ultimately cohere with an account of theoretical reason which makes intelligible the truth and intersubjectivity of epistemic evaluation.

4. And, indeed, a theory of practical reasoning in morals which denies the *in principle* intersubjectivity and truth of the ought-to-be's and ought-to-do's of everyday life must face the challenge of the ought-to-be's and ought-to-do's of theoretical reason. This challenge has largely been ignored. But though I think, with Charles Sanders Peirce, that the facing of this challenge is the culmination of the philosophical enterprise, I shall say nothing more about it; for my task concerns the foundations, and the keystone is nowhere at hand. Yet if the outcome of my argument is to make intelligible the intersubjectivity and truth of moral *oughts*, the argument will be in the spirit, at least, of this more embracing enterprise.

II

5. Practical reasoning is often many times removed from practice. Yet without a conceptual tie to practice, however indirect, it would not be practical reasoning. The parallel with reasoning in the empirical sciences is obvious. The latter is often many times removed from singular descriptive statements and, in particular, from those singular descriptive statements which formulate observations. Yet without its conceptual tie to such singular descriptive statements it would not be empirical science.

6. Thus, first in the order of business must be a provisional account of the coming together of practical reasoning and practice.[1] This coming together is found in volition which, as I have put it, is the point at which the conceptual order evokes its image in the real order, as, in observation and self-knowledge, the real order evokes its image in the conceptual order.

7. Volitions are conceptual episodes which we conceive on the analogy of such candid thinkings-out-loud as

I shall *now* do a

---

[1] For an elaboration of the framework sketched below the reader is referred to my 'Thought and Action', in *Freedom and Determinism*, Keith Lehrer (ed.), New York, 1966, pp. 104–39. [Eds.—Chapter 7 of this volume.]

Thus in one sense of 'manifest' a volition is the sort of episode which is manifested in candid overt speech by saying

I shall *now* do A (e.g. raise my hand)

In another sense, however, a volition is the sort of episode which is manifested, *ceteris paribus* (thus in the absence of paralysis and in the presence of favorable circumstances), by a doing of A, e.g. a raising of the hand.

8. We could put this by saying that, *ceteris paribus*, volitions cause actions of the kinds involved in the description of these volitions—in a broad sense of cause which must not be confused with the idea that volitions cause us, in the ordinary sense of cause, to do the action. In action 'of one's own free will' one is not caused to do what one does, and when one is caused to do something the cause is not a volition but, for example, a threat or a promise on the part of someone who, if one complies, can subsequently be said to have caused one to do what he did.

9. A child who has not acquired the propensity, for example, to raise his hand on saying

Now I shall raise my hand

has not learned 'shall'-talk, and until he has acquired this propensity he cannot be said to understand the full meaning of any practical term, for all practical terms owe their connection with action to the conceptually necessary tie between

Now I shall (action)

in the first place, as candid willings-out-loud, and, in the second place, as the conceptual representings which find overt expression in willings-out-loud, and performances (*ceteris paribus*) of the actions willed.

10. I have emphasized that volitions are not *actions* but acts in the Aristotelian sense of actualities. It does not make sense to speak of willing to will to do A, any more than it makes sense to speak of willing to feel sympathy for someone. (In each case, however, there is such a thing as willing to do something which one conceives likely to influence one's mental propensities in the desired direction.) Nor are volitions *tryings*. Trying to do A is, roughly, doing one or more things which one thinks likely in the circumstances to grow into a doing of A. Nor are volitions *choosings*. One may will to do A without choosing to do A rather than B, even where B is refraining from doing A. Nor are volitions *decisions*. A volition need not be the culmination of a process of deliberation or practical reasoning.

11. Since my purpose in this chapter is to explore the conceptual framework of practice, I shall no longer highlight the problem of the status of mental acts and their relation to propensities and dispositions pertaining to candid overt speech.

I shall speak of practical 'statements' or 'assertions' in the non-performatory sense in which these terms are used in logic; and of practical 'reasonings',[2] leaving open the question as to the exact status of these practical episodes.

12. The simplest connection of an intention with a volition is illustrated by the example of Smith, who has formed the intention of raising his hand in ten minutes. He *thinks*

I shall raise my hand in ten minutes

and, if we suppose that the intention continues as an occurrent, rather than lapsing into dispositional status, which, however, would leave the example untouched in relevant respects, and if we suppose that nothing leads him to consider an alternative course of action, we may picture him as thinking

I shall raise my hand in ten minutes

.
.
.

I shall raise my hand in six minutes

.
.
.

I shall raise my hand *now*

the last of which, if Smith is not paralysed nor, unbeknownst to him, in a strait-jacket, becomes a raising of his hand. That one's 'place' in time is constantly and systematically changing is an essential feature of our conceptual framework, one which is reflected in and, indeed, constituted by, a systematic change in the content of thought with respect to tense, temporal connectives and the like.

13. In addition to the 'chronologic', which transforms intentions of an appropriate form into volitions, there are other logical features of intention which find expression in the culminating stages of practical reasoning proper. These can, in the first instance, be summed up by the general principle:

'It is the case that-P' implies   ↔   'It shall be the case that-P' implies
'it is the case that-Q'   'it shall be the case that-Q'

---

[2] The term 'argument' is perhaps too fraught with performatory overtones (as something which one 'gives' to one's public) to be completely satisfactory as a term in logical theory, in that narrower sense in which it can be contrasted with 'dialectics', the theory of rational discussion.

14. The following comments bring out the force and significance of this principle:

(*a*) I am reconstructing English usage pertaining to 'shall' in such a way that, in candid speech, it always expresses an intention on the part of the speaker with respect to a certain state of affairs. In other words, I shall use 'shall' and 'will' in such a way that 'shall' always expresses an intention, whereas 'will' is always a simple future.

(*b*) I am so using 'implies' that '"p" implies "q"' is equivalent to '"q" may be inferred from "p"'. Implication statements, for our purposes, can be regarded as meta-linguistic in a sense which is unencumbered by the refinements introduced in our discussion of abstract singular terms. Thus,

that-p implies that-q

will be construed as

'p' implies 'q'

It must not be confused with 'if p then q' which is, at heart, the '$p \rightarrow q$' of truth functional logic.

(*c*) I shall reconstruct 'shall' to be an operator which turns indicative statements into statements of intention. Thus,

I shall do A

becomes

Shall [I will do A]

(*d*) All basic practical reasoning pertaining to intentions can be reconstructed as a sequence of shall-statements, each of which follows from that which precedes it in accordance with the above principle or, more accurately, since this principle belongs to the third level of practical discourse, in accordance with a second-level principle which accords with it. Thus, according to this principle,

'Shall [P and Q]' implies 'shall [P]'

follows from

'P and Q' implies 'P'

and hence the following piece of first-level practical reasoning

Shall [P and Q]
Therefore, shall [P]

is valid.

(*e*) For the purposes of my argument it will be useful to construe empirical laws as implications or principles of inference. Thus, one state of affairs will be said to imply physically or causally another state of affairs, where others might prefer to say that the former logically implies the latter on the assumption of a true general premise. This interpretation of law-like statements as principles of inference, which, in any case, I think to be the true one, will make more intuitive the relation of causal implications to moral principles. I shall use 'implies' without qualification to mean causally or physically implies, where the context makes it clear that this is what is involved.

(f) A careful distinction must be drawn between 'shall' as an operator which operates on action verbs and 'shall' in the sense, roughly, of 'shall be the case' which operates on statements. The context will make it clear, in particular cases, which is involved. I mention the point, however, because many careful distinctions are necessary here to avoid the paradoxes which are familiar in deontic logic, but which also arise, unless care is taken, in the logic of practical discourse generally.[3]

(g) I shall reconstruct

If it is raining, then I shall come in

as

Shall [if it is raining, I will come in]

Here the action verb governed by 'shall' is 'will come in'. I shall call intentions of this form 'conditional intentions'. The 'if..., then - - -' is not 'implies' but the '→' of truth functional logic.

(h) Consider the practical syllogism

Shall [if it is raining, [I will come in]
It is raining
Therefore, Shall [I will come in]

Introducing the concept of 'implication relative to an hypothesis or assumption', we can say that

'If it is raining, then I will come in'

implies

'I will come in'

relatively to the assumption 'it is raining'. Thus, relatively to the hypothesis that it is raining,

'Shall [if it is raining, I will come in]'

implies

'Shall [I will come in]'

---

[3] For an exploration of the logic of action discourse which articulates these distinctions see my 'Reflections on Contrary-to-Duty Imperatives', *Nous*, 4, 1967. [Eds.—Chapter 15 of this volume].

Since it makes use of this dependent implication, the reasoning

Shall [if it is raining, I will come in]
Therefore, shall [I will come in]

can be said to be dependently valid. I shall make constant use of dependent implication. The context will make it clear on what hypothesis the implication depends.

(*i*) The preceding example is a further illustration of the point that all of the implications involved in practical reasoning can be established in the first instances as implications pertaining to matters of fact. There is, therefore, no need for a special 'logic of intentions' other than that formulated by the third-level principle on which I am commenting together with certain conceptual truths about the function of 'shall'. Having made this point, I shall not hesitate to use mixed practical syllogism, thus

Shall [if p, then I will do A]
p
Therefore, shall [I will do A]

(*j*) Finally, the conditional intentions with which we will be concerned are those in which the antecedent can be construed as a 'circumstance of action', and can, therefore, be represented by the schema

Shall [if I am in C, I will do A]

III

15. Intentions imply intentions just as beliefs imply beliefs. This point must be carefully made. We must distinguish between intentions as *states of intending* and intentions as *what is intended*, just as we distinguish between *states of believing* and *what is believed*, the so-called 'content' of the believing. In the latter case we distinguish between the implications of the *content* of a belief and the implications of the state of having a belief with that content. Thus the belief which would be expressed by the conjunction of Peano's postulates (P) implies the belief which would be expressed by any arithmetical theorem (T), however recondite, in the sense that the one belief content implies the other. Yet, obviously, the existence of *this* implication does not carry with it the idea that

Jones believes P implies Jones believes T

16. Corresponding distinctions obtain in the case of intentions. Thus, when I speak, as I shall, of one intention I_1 implying another intention

I_2, I shall be speaking about an implication between two intention-*contents*. That in *this* sense an intention I_1 implies an intention I_2 does not carry with it the idea that

Jones intends I_1 implies Jones intends I_2

An ideally rational being would intend the implications of his intentions, just as he would believe the implications of his beliefs.[4]

17. Philosophers analyse the logical relations of belief-contents by determining the logical relations of the factual statements which express them. In this chapter I shall explore the logical relations of intention-contents by exploring the implications of the practical statements which express them.

18. If 'P' implies 'Q', then it is *unreasonable* to believe that P is the case without believing that Q is the case. (Though, as noted above, in point of fact one may well believe the former without believing the latter.) Similarly if

'It shall be the case that P' implies 'It shall be the case that Q'

It is *unreasonable* to intend that P be the case without intending that Q be the case. (Though, again, in point of fact one may very well intend the former without intending the latter and may even intend that the latter *not* be the case.)

IV

19. Intentions are not limited to intentions *to do*, whether now, or later, or on the condition that a certain circumstance obtains. There are also intentions *that something be the case*. The latter, however, are *intentions*, practical commitments, only by virtue of their conceptual tie with intentions *to do*. Roughly

It shall be the case that-*p*

has the sense, when made explicit, of

(*Ceteris paribus*) I shall do that which is necessary to make it the case that-*p*.

---

[4] It is, however, a familiar fact that when we become aware of the implications of our beliefs we often change our mind. It is equally true that when we become aware of the implications of our intentions we often, shall I say, change our heart.

20. It is important to see that I can not only intend to do something myself, I can also intend that someone else do something, i.e. that it be the case that he does it. Intentions pertaining to the actions of others are not 'intentions to do' in the primary sense in which

> I shall do A

is an intention to do. Thus, in spite of their superficial similarity,

> Tom shall do A

and

> I shall do A

do not have the same conceptual structure. The former has the form

> (*Ceteris paribus*) I shall do that which is necessary to make it the case that Tom does A

whereas the latter cannot, without the absurdity of an infinite regress, be supposed to have the form

> (*Ceteris paribus*) I shall do that which is necessary to make it the case that I do A[5]

21. These considerations highlight the fact that the intention expressed by a 'shall' statement is invariably the speaker's intention. Thus,

> Tom shall do A

expresses the speaker's intention that Tom do A. This 'first person' feature of intentions consists in part in their relation to the

> I shall do

which can become the commitment to do something *here* and *now* which is volition.

---

[5] This is not to say, however, that

> It shall be the case that Tom does A

has no first person parallel which would be subsumable with it under common practical principles. It is merely to emphasize the conceptual primacy of intentions to do even in the case of intentions that someone do.

22. Now it is clearly important to distinguish between the *expression* of an intention and the *ascription* of an intention. Thus,

Shall [I will do A]

expresses, in candid speech, an intention to do A. On the other hand,

S intends to do A

ascribes to S an intention which he would express by using the former sentence.
23. In the case of autobiographical self-ascriptions, thus

I intend to do A

one ascribes to oneself an intention to do A and 'implies' the shall-statement

Shall [I will do A]

as made by the speaker, in much the same sense of 'implies' as the autobiographical belief ascription

I believe that it is raining

'implies' the statement

It is raining

as made by the speaker.
24. This familiar point enables me to highlight the first logical challenge to the idea that practical reasoning is reasoning in a proper or full-blooded sense of the term. For whereas ascriptions of intention have proper negations, shall-statements do not.[6] Thus, in the case of ascriptions of intention, there are the four forms

S intends to do A
It is not the case that S intends to do A
S intends not to do A
It is not the case that S intends not to do A

---

[6] For an exploration of the place of negation in practical statements see my 'Imperatives, Intentions and the Logic of "Ought"', *Methodos*, 8, 1956 [reprinted with substantial alterations in *Morality and the Language of Conduct*, edited by H. N. Castañeda and George Nakhnikian, Detroit, 1963]. [Eds.—The latter appears as chapter 14 of this volume.]

But at the level of the corresponding shall-statements, there are only the statements

Shall [I will do A]
Shall [I will not do A]

25. Of course, a person need not commit himself to either of these statements, just as a person need not commit himself to either 'It is raining' or 'It is not raining'. And we must recognize the interrogative

Shall I do A? = Shall [I will do A]?

just as we recognize the interrogative

Is it raining?

26. The absence of what I shall call external negation in the case of shall-statements is in sharp contrast not only with its presence in the case of ascriptions of intention but, also, and with this we begin to touch directly on the issues I wish to discuss, its presence in the case of obligation statements. Thus, statements of all of the following forms seem to be appropriate:

Jones ought to do A
It is not the case that Jones ought to do A
Jones ought not to do A
It is not the case that Jones ought not to do A

27. This radical difference between 'shall' and 'ought', together with the fact that ought-to-do's seem to be as legitimately the subject matter of practical reasoning as shall-do's, presents us with our initial problem. What is the relation of 'ought' to 'shall'?

V

28. It might be thought that 'ought' differs from 'shall' in that 'ought' is used to tell someone to do something. This is a mistake. We can think and, if I am right, think truly and even know, that we ought to do a certain action. There need be no performance of telling anyone—even ourselves—to do anything. We can, and do on occasion, tell ourselves to do something, but deciding what to do is no more telling ourselves what to do than deciding what is the case is telling ourselves what is the case.

29. Of course, moral obligations rest on states of affairs, many of which are actions or the results of actions. Interesting cases are provided by promises, demands, legislation, verdicts, sentences, etc., etc. But these grounds of *prima facie* obligation must be distinguished from the practical premises and reasonings which take them into account, and the latter is essentially non-performatory and can, without changing its character, go on *in foro interno*.

30. The actions we and others have performed (including illocutionary acts) are relevant to our practical reasoning as part of the circumstances in which we must act, and even deliberating *in foro interno* about what to do is a course of action which can itself be deliberately undertaken. But neither 'shall' thoughts nor 'ought' thoughts are themselves actions, and when practical reasoning is done out loud it is, as such, the sort of thing which is *overheard*—which means that we are abstracting from the rights and duties which might arise from the fact that it is heard.

31. Moreover, the idea that the job of 'ought' statements is to tell someone to do something would not, by itself, throw any light on the fact that 'ought' statements, unlike 'shall' statements, have an external negation. For we can also use 'shall' statements to tell people to do something.

32. For all these reasons it can be doubted that the contrast between mere thinking-out-loud and illocutionary performance throws any light on the difference between 'shall' and 'ought'.

VI

33. 'Shall' statements are, as such, neither true nor false (which indicates, again, that an extended use is being made of the term 'statement'), though the descriptive statements embedded in them are either true or false. Furthermore, it follows from the absence of an external negation that *no one* can contradict a 'shall' statement, not even the person who makes it. This raises the question of the intersubjectivity of 'shall' statements. In what sense can two people have the same intention?

(1) There is the sense of 'same intention' which parallels that in which two people in different places say the same thing if they say 'the book is *here*'. In this sense two people who intend to visit the Taj Mahal can be said to have the same intention.

(2) Yet two people can have the same intention in a tougher sense, thus that a certain state of affairs obtain—e.g. that a certain child be happy. Of course, the derivative intentions to do that which might bring this happiness about are no longer in the tough sense the same.

(3) I can intend that someone else do A (intend him to do A), and he can intend to do A, and the verbal expression of the two intentions may be similar, thus,

He shall do A
I will do A

and even more similar if 'shall' is used in our technical sense. There is, nevertheless, an asymmetry. For, obviously, only *his* intention can grow directly into *his* volition and *his* action. My intention with respect to his action can grow into a volition only if practical reasoning draws a conclusion from it concerning some influence I can bring to bear.

34. This latter consideration highlights the obvious fact that even where the descriptive content of two people's intentions is in the strongest sense the same not only are the intendings numerically different, which is true even in the case of belief, but the total content of the intendings involves a special mode of egocentricity (expressed by the word 'shall') which is, in practical discourse, the counterpart of the egocentricity of demonstratives. The latter is the egocentricity involved in the impact of the world on discourse, the former is the egocentricity involved in the impact of discourse on the world in volition.

35. If, therefore, we distinguish between the descriptive element in the content of an intending, and that element which is expressed by the operator 'shall', we can say that where the descriptive content is, in a tough sense, the same—as in the case of the child's happiness—the two intentions are 'parallel'. Traditional emotivism would speak here of an 'agreement in attitude'.

36. The egocentricity (in the practical mode) of 'shall', and the absence of an external negation, pose the problem of the relevance of the concepts of intersubjectivity and truth to practical discourse.

VII

37. From these initial considerations concerning the conceptual grammar of 'shall' let us turn our attention to 'ought'. We have emphasized that 'ought' has an external as well as internal negation. This fact gives rise to a strong feeling that there is truth and falsity with respect to 'ought', for it seems absurd (and in the last analysis is absurd) to admit the form

$\sim Op$

as well as

$O \sim p$

without accepting

It is true that O*p*
It is false that O*p*

Indeed, to read

~O*p*

as

It is not the case that O*p*

is tantamount to admitting that there is truth and falsity with respect to obligation, for

It is not the case that O*p*

has the same sense as

It is false that O*p*

Of course, we can pitchfork Nature out of the door by insisting on reading

~O*p*

as

Not O*p*

refusing to use the locution

It is not the case that O*p*

but it may well return by the window.

38. However it may be with truth, there remains the question of intersubjectivity. In how tough a sense of 'same' can two people make the same ought statement?

39. Let me begin with a simple and familiar model, the story of one Smith who moves through the world accompanied by a team of ideal scientists. Among them are physicists, geologists, historians, neuro-physiologists, logicians, even students of the gods. They are masters of what have been called the 'positive' sciences. Yet we shall grant them knowledge (in whatever sense it *is* knowledge) of the ought-to-do's and ought-to-be's pertaining to epistemic activities—without staying to analyze the authority of epistemic norms. Let us refer to this team as the Academy.

40. Smith is near a heavy object (O), a long steel rod (R) and a stone (S). The members of the Academy consult among themselves and agree that

> The necessary and sufficient condition of Smith's raising the heavy object is his using the rod as a lever and the stone as a fulcrum

They rephrase this as

> Smith raises O implies and is implied by Smith using R as lever on O with S as fulcrum

So far, so good. Then we find them saying

> If Jones wants to raise O, he ought[7] to etc.

At this point they hear Smith say

> I shall raise O

and, since he seems to be speaking candidly and not deceiving himself, they conclude that Smith intends—or, for our present purposes, wants—to raise O. We might expect them to continue by reasoning as follows,

> If Smith wants to raise O, he ought to use R, etc.
> Smith wants to raise O
> Therefore, Smith ought to use R, etc.

Yet, particularly when we reflect on other examples, we are perplexed by the idea that the 'ought' statement can be derived by *modus ponens*. To use a familiar type of example, suppose they see Smith's aunt coming and hear him say

> I shall poison my aunt this afternoon

After surveying the environs and finding that a small packet of prussic acid is the only poison available, they agree that

> A necessary and sufficient condition of Smith's poisoning his aunt this afternoon is his administering this packet of prussic acid

---

[7] Cf. 'If Jones is going to raise O, he must use R, etc.'

They even say

If Smith wants to poison his aunt, then he ought to administer, etc.

Can they proceed by *modus ponens* to infer

Smith *ought* to administer, etc.?

41. It does not seem so, and it is essential to see *exactly* why. Hare[8] has given us the beginning of the thread, yet it remains to follow it to the end of the labyrinth. Put in our terms, separated, that is, from the 'logic' of imperative performances in which it is embedded, his point is that the schema

If S wants to bring about X, he ought to do Y

which is the schema of what are technically (but misleadingly) called hypothetical imperatives, has the sense of

'Shall [S brings about X]' implies 'Shall [S does Y]'

which implication concerning shall-statements is grounded in the implication

'S brings about X' implies 'S does Y'

in accordance with our third-level principle discussed above.

42. To appreciate the soundness of this analysis of the hypothetical imperative and its importance for our problem, it is enough to see that

'S wants to bring about X'

has the sense of

'S intends to bring about X'

Since to say that a person intends to bring about X is to ascribe to him a propensity to represent 'I shall bring about X', the fact that the reconstruction offered above mentions the relevant shall- statement counts in its favour. And since the hypothetical imperative is clearly grounded on the causal implication

---

[8] R. M. Hare, *The Language of Morals*, Oxford, 1952, pp. 33 ff.

'S brings about X' implies 'S does Y'

the overall form of the reconstruction seems appropriate.

43. If, now, returning to the original example, we take into account the fact that the intending in question is Smith's intending we notice that to capture the sense of the hypothetical imperative, the implication has the peculiar feature that *only one person, i.e. Smith, can draw an inference in accordance with this implication*. To make this fact explicit, let us reformulate the implication as

'Shall [I poison, etc.]' implies (*quoad* Smith) 'shall [I administer, etc.]'

44. Thus, Smith, but no one else, is authorized by *this* implication to reason

Shall [I poison my aunt]
Therefore, shall [I administer, etc.]

45. Of course, if Roberts and his aunt come on to the scene the Academy could have arrived at the conclusion

If Roberts wants, etc., he ought, etc.

which would mean

'Shall [I poison, etc.]' implies (*quoad* Roberts) 'shall [I administer, etc.]'

But this implication authorizes no one but Roberts to reason in the parallel way.

46. Even if our scientists saw pairs of men and their aunts galore approaching, and accepted as relevant the general theoretical implication

For all values of '*s*' '*s* poisons his aunt here this afternoon' implies '*s* administers, etc.'

which transposes into the general practical implication

For all *s*, 'shall [I poison, etc.]' implies (*quoad s*) 'shall [I administer, etc.]'

47. Notice that the second implication involves a double use of quantification, for it is equivalent to

For all values of 'I' and for all *s*, 'Shall [I will poison my aunt, etc.]' implies (*quoad s*) 'shall [I will administer, etc.]'

OBJECTIVITY, INTERSUBJECTIVITY AND THE MORAL POINT OF VIEW   155

The fact that the range of values of 'I' coincides with the range of values of '*s*' should not obscure this important difference. The modification of 'I' by '(*quoad s*)' is required by what we have called the special egocentricity of 'shall'.

48. Thus the general practical implication becomes an implication proper which governs possible inference only when specified with respect to particular values of '*s*', thus,

'Shall [I will poison my aunt, etc.]' implies (*quoad* Tom) 'shall [I will administer, etc.]'

which authorizes Tom to reason

Shall [I will cause my aunt, etc.]
So, shall [I will administer, etc.]

VIII

49. Hypothetical imperatives typically rest on causal connections, and, like most singular causal statements in everyday life, they are rarely if ever the direct application of a general causal law. Thus,

If Jones wants a drink, he ought to go to the next corner

is not the application of a supposed general law to the effect that

If anyone is to get a drink, he must go to the next corner

50. We have already noted that hypothetical imperatives typically presuppose that the person in question is in a certain circumstance. This point must now be elaborated. The first step is to bring this presupposition into the content of the imperatives, thus,

(Since S is in C)
If S wants to bring about E, he ought to do A

becomes

If S wants to bring about E, he ought to do A, if he is in C *and* S is in C

Let us focus our attention on the complex if statement, and neglect the conjoined assertion.

51. There are many ways in which general law-like statements can be idealized. Thus it is often required that a 'genuine' law-like statement contain no reference to particular objects, times or places. Whether or not ideal science would give us such, it's clear that we often have to settle for less. Now the nomologicals with which we are concerned are those which can generate general hypothetical imperatives. These nomologicals concern the causally necessary conditions for bringing about a certain kind of state of affairs in a certain kind of circumstance.[9] They have the form

Doing A_i if C_j is causally necessary to the realization of E_k

Or, putting it in terms of causal implication, we have the family of implications

'x brings about E_k' implies 'x does A_i if in C_j'

These implications, which for obvious reasons can be called 'instrumental implications', are 'binding on all rational beings' in the sense that as empirical generalizations their inductive soundness is independent of the desires and inclinations or cultural ties of specific individuals or groups. Transposed into practical discourse as a general hypothetical imperative, they become

'I shall bring about E_k' implies 'I shall do A_i, if in C_j'

Even after this transposition the implications remain binding on all rational beings. Any restriction belongs in the circumstance clause. Thus to restrict it to WASPs is to include the characteristic of being a WASP in C_j. For if being a WASP is irrelevant to bringing about E_k by doing A_i in C_j, then there is no point in including it anywhere; while if it is relevant, the relevance is a causal one and belongs in the content of the implication and not as a limitation on those for whom it holds.

52. Thus a limitation of the general hypothetical imperative to WASPs will not take the form

'I shall bring about E_k' implies (for all WASPs) 'I shall do A_i in C_j'

but

---

[9] The complexity of the instrumental nomologicals which are relevant to the bringing about in social contexts of any but the most trivial ends must constantly be borne in mind. The simplicity of the schematic letters 'A', 'C' and 'E' should not blind us to this fact. We must take into account the effects of our action on the actions of others as well as the effect of the actions of others on the outcomes of our own.

'I shall bring about E_k' implies 'I shall do A_i in $C_{j\Diamond}$'

where '$C_{j\Diamond}$' differs from 'C_j' by including the additional characteristic of being a WASP. In this sense general hypothetical imperatives can be said to hold 'for all rational beings'. They are simply the transposition into practical discourse of empirical instrumental generalizations.

53. Notice, however, that although general hypothetical imperatives hold for all rational beings, there is an important sense in which each such imperative formulates not one single implication but a family of implications, one for each rational being. This complication reflects the fact that 'I' is a systematically ambiguous term. A general hypothetical imperative asserts that each rational being can *validly* argue

> I (Tom) shall bring about E_k
> So I (Tom) shall do A_i if in C_j
> I (Dick) shall bring about E_k
> So I (Dick) shall do A_i if in C_j
> etc.

54. There is an obvious temptation to use *modus ponens* to detach the *ought* from the hypothetical imperative, thus,

> If S wants to bring about X, he ought to do Y
> S wants to bring about X
> So, S ought to do Y

On the above analysis the premises become, respectively,

> 'I shall bring about X' implies (*quoad* S) 'I shall do Y'

and

> S accepts 'I shall bring about X'

From these premises the only thing of any interest that we can infer seems to be

> 'I shall do Y' is implied (*quoad* S) by an intention S accepts

55. This *suggests* an analysis of

> S ought to do Y

as

'I shall do Y' is implied (*quoad* S) by an intention S accepts

Such an analysis, however, clearly won't do as it stands. For even in the first person there is something odd about the reasoning

If I want to poison my aunt, I ought to administer, etc.
I want to poison my aunt
Therefore, I ought to administer, etc.

and hence about the idea that it is equivalent, as the analysis claims, to the reasoning

'Shall [I will bring about X]' implies (*quoad* me) 'shall [I will do Y]'
I accept 'shall [I will bring about X]'
Therefore, 'shall [I will do Y]' is implied by an intention I have

56. Notice that in the case of purely theoretical reasoning an implication statement generates a corresponding pair of reasonings, thus,

'*p*' implies '*q*'

governs the inference

p
Therefore, *q*

and serves as a premise in the inference

'*p*' implies '*q*'
I accept *p*
Therefore, '*q*' is implied by a proposition I accept

57. Even more important, for future reference, is the fact that

'*p*' implies '*q*'

presupposes the truth of '*p*' and must be distinguished from

'*p*' (if true) would imply '*q*'

Thus the following is, in an important sense, complete:

'*p*' implies '*q*'
Therefore, '*q*' is implied by a true proposition

If, therefore, there were a concept pertaining to intentions paralleling that of truth (call it, perhaps, 'validity') then

'Shall [*p*]' implies 'shall [*q*]'

as opposed to

'Shall [*p*]' (if valid) would imply 'shall [*q*]'

would presuppose the *validity* of the antecedent.

58. For the moment, however, we have only the concept of an intention which one *has* or *accepts* to hold the place of this concept of validity.

59. It is clearly one thing to reason

Shall [I will bring about X]
Therefore, shall [I will do Y]

where the major premise may be an impulse, or where the principle in accordance with which it is made is not itself explicitly considered, and quite another to be at the reflective level of the hypothetical imperative. Thus, if

I ought to do Y

did have the sense of

'I shall do Y' is implied by an intention I have

it would be because of some special feature of this level of practical reasoning.

IX

60. But is the first person use of *modus ponens* to get

I ought to do Y

so absurd? Surely, it might be said, the fact that this reasoning occurs at the second level of discourse about intentions enables it to have the force of

'Shall [I will do Y]' is implied (*quoad* me) by an intention which I have *all things considered*

61. The phrase 'all things considered' is scarcely sufficient, in and of itself, to render the suggestion plausible. The best it can do is to make possible a willing suspension of disbelief during which further exploration can take place. The first attempt to be considered is almost as old as philosophy itself. It rests on the concept of 'informed' or 'enlightened' self-interest. It conceives of 'intentions' as generated by reasoning in which factual premises are combined with valuational premises which, though not themselves intentions, are the sort of thing which when combined with factual information about what a person is or will be in a position to, lead to conclusions which are intentions.

62. We have been using 'shall' as our intention operator. Let us use 'would' as our valuation operator.[10] The pattern I have in mind for generating 'shall's out of 'would's goes somewhat as follows:

Would that-p were the case
'That-p is the case' implies and is implied by 's does A'
It is possible for s to do A

    Shall be the case [that-p]
    Shall [s does A]

Needless to say, this schema requires a commentary in which it is pointed out that when a person considers only the state of affairs that-p he may be prepared to say

Would it were the case that-p

but, when he considers it along with the state of affairs that-q, be prepared to say, rather,

Would it were not the case that-($p \cdot q$)

---

[10] It is common to use it in connection with that-clauses, thus
    Would that such and such were the case
But it is important to see that it can—and must, if our analysis is correct—occur in first level discourse, thus
    Would he were here
as contrasted with
    Would it were the case that he was here

More generally, in addition to the above schema, an account of valuational preference is required. I shall assume that such an account is available, for the special problems it raises are not at issue.

63. Now the classical theory I have in mind postulates a ground floor of dispositions and propensities to have thoughts of the form

Would that-*p*

(where that-*p* may be relatively simple or very complex), which need not remain the same and which, indeed, may well differ from person to person. These specific valuings are shaped in many ways and can be shaped by self-training. Yet it is also true to say that they arise out of the individual's bodily, mental and social needs, and are initially shaped by a social training which, of course, continues to play a more or less subtle and more or less dominant role.

64. These specific valuings need not be ego-centred. Only the crudest form of the theory takes the valuing expressed by

Would that he not be suffering

is really the valuing candidly expressed by

Would that I not be in his shoes

65. But whatever the character of these ground-floor valuings, the theory holds that they are dominated by an over-arching ego-directed valuing expressed, in our terminology, by

Would that I led a satisfying life

To the extent that a person is logical, this valuing, combined with beliefs about the world, about the propensities of his fellow man, about the character of his ground-floor valuings and about available sources of satisfaction, generates a life-plan valuing which organizes ground-floor valuings into a coherent system. As circumstances develop, the application of this plan generates intentions which are carried out in action. Most people lead blurred and fluctuating lives because of their doubts, their ignorance and the faltering grip of logic and the breaking in of impulse.

X

66. Let us reintroduce Smith, who is a budding genius, and the Academy. After studying him they consult among themselves and agree

If Smith wants to lead a satisfying life, he ought to lead a life of kind L

They go to him and tell him this. When he challenges this, they persuade him, after a little Socratic deflation, to come to the Academy as a Junior Fellow. After several years of study he cries 'I see!' and proceeds to think along the following lines

If I want to lead a satisfying life, I ought to lead a life of kind L

Ex hypothesi he has built into him the over-arching valuing

Would I led a satisfying life

In accordance with the previous analysis, he concludes

'Would that I led a life of kind L' is implied (*quoad* me) by a value which, all things considered, I accept

[Perhaps, on the egoistic assumption, he is entitled even to say

'Would that I led a life of kind L' is implied (*quoad* me) by a *valid* value, indeed, the primarily valid value]

However this may be, according to the theory, the above is equivalent to

I ought to lead a life of kind L

67. Drawing on additional knowledge of scientific principles, laws, empirical generalizations, the probable outcomes of actions of various kinds in various kinds of circumstance described with a subtlety of a casuist, he continues

If I want to lead a life of kind L, I ought to do such and such actions (A_i) in such and such kinds of circumstance (C_i)

where these policies take into account all the subtle ways in which circumstances may vary and yet seem, on casual inspection, to be the same. These policies, therefore, are not to be interpreted as rules of thumb. Smith has available all the general knowledge which is even *in principle* relevant to his conduct. His policies are general in the logical sense in which a fantastically complex lawlike statement is general, even though it happens to apply to but one instance. *Indeed, his policies are the practical counterparts of just such law-like statements.*

68. Assuming the premise of possibility necessary to turn 'would's into 'shall's, he draws two families of conclusions

(a) Shall [I will do A_i on any occasion in which the circumstances are C_i]

(b) 'Shall [I will do A_i on any occasion in which the circumstances are C_i]' is implied (*quoad* me) by an intention which, all things considered, I accept (or, perhaps, by a valid intention)

69. The latter is considered by the theory to be equivalent to

(For any *t*) I ought to do A_i at *t*, if I am in C_i at *t*

The theory thus claims that a categorical ought statement asserts that one is committed to a general intention of the form

(For any *t*) shall [if I am in C_i at *t*, I will do A_i at *t*]

by virtue of its being implied by the life-plan valuing. Roughly, categorical imperatives are *derivative general conditional intentions.*

70. Confronted by a particular circumstance, Smith surveys his scheme of classification, classifies the circumstance as C_j, sees that the relevant action is of kind A_i and infers

'Shall [I will do A_i]' is implied (*quoad* me) by my life plan intention

which, according to the theory, has the sense of

I ought to do A_i

In harmony with all this machinery he draws the first-level practical conclusion

Shall [I will do A_i]

which, if the relevant time is *now,* is a volition. In the absence of paralysis, not to mention overwhelming intellectual fatigue, this volition grows into a doing of A_i.

71. The core of the above practical reasoning, given the factual information, can be telescoped as follows:

Shall [I will lead a satisfying life]
Therefore, shall [I will do A_i at *t*]

At the second level we have

'Shall [I will lead a satisfying life]' implies (*quoad* me) 'shall [I will do A_i at t]'

which is regarded by the theory as equivalent to

If I want to lead a satisfying life, I ought to do A_i at t

interpreted as

'Shall [I will do A_i at t]' is implied by my life-plan intention

which, according to the theory, authorizes

I ought to do A_i at t

XI

72. Is this view plausible? It is, as Prichard[11] saw, one strand in Plato's thought. The latter develops, in a number of dialogues, the concept of an art of living which he conceives of as the art of achieving, in so far as possible, a satisfying life. Assuming that a shoemaker values, for whatever reason, the making of shoes, and that no other values become relevant during shoemaking hours, that he knows what the various stages of making a shoe require him to do to the leather, and how to do it, then he will turn to and make the shoe—within the limits of his material. So, too, a man in possession of the art of living will turn to and create a satisfying life within the limits of his opportunities.

73. 'But,' the question naturally arises, as Plato saw, 'what guarantees that Smith, however meticulously he plans his life and carries out his policies, will behave in the ways we think of as moral?' In other words, what guarantees that the intricate policies of his art of living coincide in content with the content of moral principles? Might not his policies include such items as

(At any time t) shall [if I have a ring which makes me invisible at t, I will wear it at t and take all available loose cash to buy research equipment with]

not to mention more exotic policies?

---

[11] See his Inaugural Lecture, *Duty and Interest*, Oxford, 1928.

74. Plato, of course, offers a lengthy argument to prove that the policies of the art of living, i.e. of achieving a satisfying life, coincide with sound moral principles; and there is more than a little to his argument. Yet, as Prichard points out, even if Plato had been successful in establishing this *coincidence*, he would not have established the conceptual identity of moral reasoning with the reasoning we have been illustrating; nor that the 'ought' of

If I want to lead a satisfying life, I ought to do A_i

can yield, by *modus ponens*, given the over-arching aim of leading a satisfying life, the unqualified assertion

I ought to do A_i

There seems to be no conceptual absurdity in either

Doing A_i would be conducive to a satisfying life, but I ought not to do A_i

or

Doing B would not be conducive to a satisfying life, but I ought to do B

XII

75. It might be thought that the trouble is easy to locate. It consists, it might be said, in the fact that the 'all things considered' of our story is ego-centred. Well, let us postulate, then, that Smith is a benevolent man not only at the level of specific valuations but that, in addition to valuing his own happiness for its own sake, he values the welfare of people generally (including himself) for its own sake.

76. He returns to the Academy and further study convinces him that

In the case of anyone, if he wants to promote the general welfare, he ought to do A_j whenever the circumstances are C_j

where, as before, his classificatory framework for actions and circumstances is ideally fine-grained, yet the reference to actions and circumstances is logically general. He applies this general hypothetical imperative to himself, thus,

If I want to promote the general welfare, I ought to do A_j whenever C_j

77. On the other hand, he still has available the hypothetical imperatives pertaining to the art of achieving a satisfying life for himself which were explored in the previous sections. And are there not available such hypothetical imperatives as

In the case of anyone, if he wants to promote the welfare of hummingbirds, he ought to do A_k whenever C_k

which he can also apply to himself?

78. It begins to look as though with the abandonment of psychological egoism the general approach we have been considering conceptually permits the use of *modus ponens*, given relevant information, to conclude

I ought to do A_i

or

I ought not to do A_i

depending on what one wants, *all things considered*, whether it is one's own happiness, the welfare of people generally or the welfare of hummingbirds. Yet we feel that the moral ought is, *in principle*, unequivocal, i.e. that if, like Smith, we had ideal knowledge, what we ought to do would be uniquely determined.

79. It will have been noticed that I have just introduced the phrase 'the moral ought'. This, it might be thought, gives us the answer. The moral ought is to be *defined* in terms of the schema

I morally ought to do A   ↔   'Would [I will do A]' is implied by a valuation I accept all things *pertaining to the general welfare* considered

80. But this is too easy. It still leaves us with the puzzling idea that *unqualified* 'ought' is a matter of what we *want*, all things considered.

XIII

81. Yet what is the alternative? Perhaps the whole attempt to construe 'ought' in terms of the hypothetical imperative is a mistake. Perhaps we should concentrate on the clue that it is a conceptual truth that, to put it roughly, what *one* person ought to do in a situation of a given description, *anyone* ought to do in a situation

thus described.[12] Yet it is notoriously difficult to supplement this formal consideration with material content, and to do so in a way which has an equally clear conceptual tie with the concept of obligation. I know of no successful theory along these lines, though interesting attempts, in different directions, have been made by Marcus Singer and R. M. Hare.

82. Singer's attempt involves, as I see it, a failure to grasp the significance of the distinction between 'ought to be' and 'ought to do'. In other words, it fails fully to take into account the difference between

It ought to be the case that everyone, if in C, *does* A

and

In the case of everyone, he ought, if in C, *to do* A

and, by so doing, fails to appreciate a logic of the concept of a 'circumstance' in a principle of action.[13] It is the latter of the above statement forms which expresses principle concerning what people ought to do.

83. Singer's argument, when spelled out, looks as follows:

(1) Ought-to-be (not-[(x) x is in C $\rightarrow$ x does A])
(2) Ought-to-be ((Ex) x is in C • x *does* not-A)
(3) (Ex) ought-to-be (x is in C • x *does* not-A)
(4) (Ex) ought-to-be (x is in C $\rightarrow$ x *does* not-A)
(5) (Ex) ought (x is in C $\rightarrow$ x *to do* not-A)
(6) (*Ceteris paribus*): (x) ought (x is in C $\rightarrow$ x *to do* not-A)

Unfortunately, the *ceteris paribus* move from 'somebody ought to do' (5) to 'everybody ought to do' (6), which appeals to the 'generalization principle'—roughly, what's right for one is right for all, *in the same circumstances*—cannot discount the fact that the 'circumstances' referred to in (1) are, from the standpoint of the relevant principle of action, an incomplete description, for from the latter point of view the circumstances proper include *everybody else doing A*.

84. When formulated in such a way as to bring this out, the argument becomes

(1) Ought-to-be (not-[(x) x is in C $\rightarrow$ x does A])
(2') (y) ought (y is in {C • (z) $z \neq y$ • z is in C $\rightarrow$ z does A} $\rightarrow$ y *to do* not-A)

---

[12] This conceptual truth, it will be noticed, is embodied, *in a certain sense*, in the accounts we have been considering, whatever their shortcomings.

[13] For an exploration of this concept see my 'Reflections on Contrary-to-duty Imperatives', *Noûs*, 4, 1967. [Eds.—Chapter 15 of this volume.]

and the relation between (2') and

(6') (*Ceteris paribus*): (*y*) ought (*y* is in C → *y to do* not-A)

becomes either trivial (i.e. 'ceteris paribus' amounts to 'provided that everybody else in a circumstance which includes C, *does* A') or a *non-sequitur*, since the relevance of the other circumstance factors must be empirically determined on their own merits.

85. Moral principles are not to be derived from considerations pertaining to the consequences of *everybody* behaving in a certain way in a certain kind of circumstance, whether it be a matter of the consequences being undesirable (as in negative utilitarianism) or desirable (as in traditional utilitarianism). Moral principles primarily concern the consequences of *anybody* acting in a certain way in a certain kind of circumstance, and it is only because of the subtle involvement of what others do in the relevant description of an agent's circumstances that it is a conceptual truth that if the consequences of *anyone* doing A in a certain fine-grained kind of circumstance are good, the consequences of *everyone* doing A in *precisely that kind of circumstance* must also be good. With these careful qualifications, the move is simply that from 'any' to 'all'.

XIV

86. The point of view of benevolence described above is not the moral point of view, though, as Kant saw, it is easily confused with it. Even generalized and embracing benevolence is, so to speak, an external point of view. If I were to say, in all candour,

Would that language-using featherless bipeds generally led satisfying lives

I would be expressing a friendly sentiment, which might be very strong indeed, with respect to language-using featherless bipeds. What, then, is the moral point of view? If anyone has captured its essence it is surely Kant. And in the following argument I shall lean heavily on his views, though I shall not hesitate to restructure them, where necessary, to bring them into touch with the current state of the problem.

87. The central theme of Kant's ethical theory is, in our terminology, the *reasonableness* of intentions. In what sense or senses, if any, can *intentions* be said to be reasonable, i.e. have a *claim* on the assent of a rational being? Kant clearly construes this task as parallel to the task of defining in what sense or senses, if any, *beliefs* can be said to be reasonable, i.e. have a *claim* on the assent of a rational being. As in his epistemology, Kant sides with the rationalists against both

the empiricist and the sceptic—but gives rationalism that twist which makes all the difference. In both areas his insights were so revolutionary that they are even now just beginning to be absorbed.

88. The primary distinction Kant draws, with respect to the reasonableness of intentions, is that between 'hypothetical' (or, as I prefer to put it, 'relative') and 'categorical' reasonableness. The simplest examples of intentions whose reasonableness is purely 'relative' are provided by what Kant calls 'hypothetical imperatives'.

89. In the terminology suggested above, the hypothetical imperative asserts that (since S is in C) the intention which he would express by saying

I shall do A

is reasonable *relative to* the intention which he would express by saying

I shall bring about E

90. One merit of using the term 'relative' to characterize the reasonableness of the above intention is that it enables us to avoid confusing the reasonableness (for S) of the intention to do A relative to the intention to bring about E, with a supposed reasonableness (for S) of the intention to do A *on the hypothesis that he intends to bring about E*.[14] This confusion generates the mistaken idea that the hypothetical imperative authorizes S (since he is in C) to reason

I intend to bring about E
So, I shall do A[15]

whereas the hypothetical imperative actually says that (given that S is in C) a reasoning on his part to the effect that

I shall bring about E
So, I shall do A

would be valid, in that the premise does (given that S is in C) imply the conclusion.

---

[14] This mistake is a consequence of the failure to bear in mind the distinction between what is implied by an intention-content and what is implied by the state of having an intention with that content.

[15] This argument clearly presupposes, for its validity, the principle that it is reasonable to do whatever is implied by the content of an intention we happen to have. Explicitly formulated, this principle would read

If x has an intention of content I, and I implies (for x) 'I shall do A', then x ought to do A

and this can be readily seen to be a false categorical imperative.

91. Thus the reasonableness invoked by a hypothetical imperative is the reasonableness of a conclusion intention relative to the premise intention in a (possible) piece of practical reasoning. It does not commit itself concerning the reasonableness of either the premise intention or the conclusion intention *per se*.

92. Let me prepare the way for the next stage of the argument by reminding you of the distinction between the *validity* and the *goodness* of arguments in the domain of theoretical reasoning. An argument can be valid, but fail to be good, by having a false premise. To say that it is *valid* is, in our terminology, to say that its conclusion is reasonable *relative to* its premise. To say that it is *good* is to add that its premise is reasonable—for, I shall assume, truth is a special case of reasonableness. A true proposition is one which has a certain claim to be assented to by a rational being. Just how this claim is to be analyzed is the problem of truth, which was explored, if not resolved in Chapters IV and V [of SM—Eds.].

93. One would expect, then, that a good practical argument is one in which the conclusion intention is not only implied by the premise intention, so that it is reasonable *relative to* the premise, as in the case of arguments authorized by hypothetical imperatives, but also one in which the premise intention is reasonable *per se*. And, indeed, Kant is clearly looking for a property of intentions which corresponds to *truth*. In short, he is attempting to discover what might make practical arguments *good* as opposed to merely *valid*. My purpose in this chapter is to show that he took us to the very threshold of success.

94. Let us now make a preliminary attempt to understand what it might mean to say of an intention that it is 'categorically reasonable' or 'categorically valid'.

95. Let us suppose that in the circumstance in which I now find myself I ought to do a certain kind of action A. The following *categorical* ought statement we shall suppose is true.

I ought to do A

Standing behind this categorical statement, however, is a condition of the form *since* (or *because*) I am in 'C', we are thus led to the *conditional* ought statement

If I am in C, I ought to do A

This in turn points in the direction of

Anybody ought to do A, if he is in C

but before attempting to understand the logical status of the reference to *anybody*, let us dwell for a moment on the first person conditional.

OBJECTIVITY, INTERSUBJECTIVITY AND THE MORAL POINT OF VIEW   171

96. The first point to be made is that the antecedent of this conditional refers to a circumstance, rather than, as in the case of

If I want to bring about E, I ought to do A

to an intention. Thus, if the ought statement tells us that the intention to do A is reasonable, it does not tell us, at least explicitly, that it is reasonable relative to *another intention*. Its explicit message is that the intention to do A is reasonable relative to *the condition of being in C*. On the other hand, if we accept, as we have, the principle that intentions can only be derived from other intentions, this reasonableness points to the argument

I shall do A, if I am in C
I am in C
So, I shall do A

in other words, *implicitly* the reasonableness of 'I shall do A' is relative not only to the circumstance, but also to the *conditional* intention

I shall do A, if I am in C

It is, therefore, *this* intention which must be categorically reasonable, if the original ought statement is to express a categorical imperative.

97. We are thus led to the idea that

I ought to do A, if I am in C

is equivalent to

'I shall do A, if I am in C' is categorically reasonable

Note that in this statement categorical reasonableness is predicated of a *conditional* intention. 'Categorical' in the sense which applies to reasonableness must not be confused with 'categorical' as a classification of propositional forms.

98. But what are we to make of the idea that an intention of the form

I shall do A, if I am in C

can be categorically reasonable? Obviously the reasonableness does not consist in the logical form of the intention. Intentions of this form do not show themselves to be sound, for example, by unpacking into tautological intentions such as

I shall stay or go, if I am threatened

or unsound by unpacking into contradictory intentions such as

I shall stay and go, if I am threatened.

99. But how can the specific subject matter of an intention be involved in its reasonableness without turning the latter into a disguised form of the relative reasonableness asserted by a hypothetical imperative? Curiously enough, the key to the answer is found by seeing how close we can come to capturing the distinctively *categorical* reasonableness of morally sound intentions by construing it as a special case of the relative reasonableness ascribed to intentions by hypothetical imperatives.

100. Now the hypothetical imperative which comes closest to capturing the moral point of view is that of impartial benevolence. Granted that it fails, how is this failure to be understood? One is tempted to say that the actions it prescribes coincide with the prescriptions of morality. If this is indeed the case, then it is difficult to see how the hypothetical imperatives of impartial benevolence and the categorical imperatives of morality could be as radically different in form as they are commonly taken to be. Granted that their difference is one of conceptual form rather than content, are there not other dimensions of conceptual form than the superficial ones which meet the eye?

101. Thus notice that the hypothetical imperative

If S wants to maximize the general welfare (GW), S ought to do A_i if S is in C_i

combines the two modes of conditionality, expressed, respectively, by 'if S wants' and 'if S is in C'. According to our analysis, this hypothetical imperative tells us that

'I shall maximize GW' implies (for S) 'I shall do A if I am in C'

The implication is, as we have seen, one of our special kind we have called 'instrumental'. And if the implication holds for S it holds for any rational being, for we are supposing, as before, that the hypothetical imperative is simply the transposition into practical discourse of an inductively established empirical generalization.

102. This complex hypothetical imperative *as such* asserts the reasonableness of the conditional intention

I shall do A, if I am in C

relative to the intention

I shall maximize GW

We can now point out that *if* the antecedent intention was itself *categorically reasonable*, and *if*, as we have been assuming, categorical reasonableness is the practical counterpart of truth, *it would follow that the consequent intention was itself categorically reasonable.*

103. It has been easy to assume that relative and categorical reasonableness are incompatible: that an intention can have one or the other, but not both.[16] This assumption is simply false.

104. To bring out the implications of this point, remember that a good theoretical argument is one in which (*a*) the conclusion is reasonable relative to the premise, and (*b*) the premise itself is categorically reasonable, i.e. true. Implication preserves truth in theoretical arguments. We should explore the possibility that it preserves categorical reasonableness in practical arguments. If so, then, an intention can be categorically reasonable, and yet *derivative* from another intention—provided, of course, that the latter in turn is categorically reasonable.

105. *Categorical* reasonableness must not be confused with *intrinsic* reasonableness. The confusion between these two has been even more damaging to Kant exegesis than the tendency to suppose that a categorically reasonable intention cannot be conditional in its logical form. On the other hand, even if categorical reasonableness is not the same as intrinsic reasonableness, we are faced with the fact that if there are to be *derivative* categorically reasonable intentions there must be one or more intentions whose categorical reasonableness is non-derivative or intrinsic. Are any to be found?

106. What of the antecedent of the above complex hypothetical imperative

I shall maximize the GW ?

It is a worthy intention, one that we should encourage people to have—though not, as Kant emphasizes, at the expense of the sense of duty. Yet it does not seem to have any feature which calls for the predicate 'intrinsically and categorically reasonable'.

XV

107. Let us continue to beat about in the neighbouring bushes. The first thing to note is that the instrumental nomologicals on which the above complex

---

[16] Of course, if an intention is *merely* relatively or hypothetically reasonable it cannot be categorically reasonable as well.

hypothetical imperatives rest generate not only hypothetical imperatives but other practical implications which, though closely related, are not in the strict Kantian sense hypothetical imperatives. For not all statements to the effect that one intention implies another can be put in the form of a hypothetical imperative, at least if we tie this term to Kant's paradigms.

108. To develop this point, we must remember that not all intentions are intentions *to do*. There are also intentions *that something be the case*. And if the existence of one state of affairs causally implies the existence of another, then the intention that the one obtain causally implies the intention that the other obtain.

109. Thus the instrumental nomologicals which generate the general hypothetical imperatives

'I shall maximize GW' implies (for each rational being) 'I shall do A_i, if I am in C_i'

also generates, for example,

'It shall be the case that Tom (Dick, Harry) maximize GW' implies (for each rational being) 'It shall be the case that Tom (Dick, Harry) does A_i, if he is in C_i'

and, indeed, the doubly general practical implication

For all values of 'x', 'it shall be the case that x maximize GW' implies *(for each rational being)* 'it shall be the case that x does A_i if x is in C_i'[17]

110. Here the 'shall's are 'shall be the case's and though the egocentric 'I' has *apparently* dropped out, it is still present by virtue of the conceptual relationships between 'it shall be the case...' and 'I shall do...'

111. The difference between the general hypothetical imperatives and the general practical implications schematized in §109 lies in the fact that whereas the former authorize *each* person to reason *about himself*, thus,

I shall maximize GW
So, I shall do A_i if in C_i

---

[17] The implications which are formulated in ordinary language as hypothetical imperatives are formulated as 'ought to do's because the consequent intentions are intentions to do

If one wants..., then one ought to do...

On the other hand, the implications with which we are now concerned are intentions that something be the case. They appear in the material mode of speech as hypothetical 'ought to be's, thus,

If one wants X to be the case, Y ought to be the case

e.g.

If one wants a good crop, the soil ought to be moist

the latter authorize *each* person to reason about *anybody*, including, of course, himself. It authorizes Tom to reason about himself, thus,

It shall be the case that Tom maximizes GW
So it shall be the case that Tom does A_i, if in C_i

and also about Dick, thus,

It shall be the case that Dick maximize GW
So, it shall be the case that Dick does A_i, if in C_i

XVI

112. We are now ready for the thirty-two-dollar question. We have been grooming categorical reasonableness to be the practical counterpart of truth. But in theoretical reasoning truth, and hence the *goodness* of arguments, is *intersubjective*.

113. Consider the argument offered by Tom,

There was lightning at t p
So, there was thunder at $t + \Delta t$ so, q

This is, we shall assume, not only *valid* given the familiar law of nature but *good*, i.e. it is true that there was lightning at t.

114. If so, then Dick's argument

There was no thunder at $t + \Delta t$ $\sim q$
So, there was no lightning at t so, $\sim p$

though equally valid, can't also be *good*. This is because Tom and Dick are contradicting one another, when Tom says 'p' and Dick says '$\sim p$'.

115. Tom's practical reasoning,

It shall be the case that Dick maximizes GW
So, it shall be the case that Dick does A_i if in C_i

although it is *valid*, as being in accordance with an implication which is binding on each rational being, it is essentially *private*. In spite of the fact that Tom is reasoning validly about Dick, and that he would be reasoning with equal validity if he reasoned in the same way about *anybody*, including himself, his argument does not have the *intersubjective* status which would make possible a logical clash of his argument with Dick's equally valid argument

It shall *not* be the case that Dick does A_i if in C_i
So, it shall *not* be the case that Dick maximizes GW.

Dick's

It shall not be the case that Dick maximizes GW

does not stand to Tom's

It shall be the case that Dick maximizes GW

as Dick's

It is not the case that there was lightning at t

stands to Tom's

It is the case that there was lightning at t

116. Two people can affirm the same proposition in a strong sense of 'same'. But as far as the intentions we have so far considered are concerned, intentions can at best be parallel. They are irreducibly egocentric, even when this egocentricity is latent as in

Tom: it shall be the case that the war ends
Dick: it shall be the case that the war ends

This dialogue provides an excellent example of 'agreement in attitude'. But if the depth form of these statements is

Tom: (*Ceteris paribus*) I (Tom) shall do what I can to end the war
Dick: (*Ceteris paribus*) I (Dick) shall do what I can to end the war

the agreement in attitude is not an identity of intention.[18]

117. What of

Tom: *we* shall do what we can to end the war

---

[18] It might be thought that since two people can use egocentric referring expressions and yet 'make the same statement', the same might be true in the case of intentions. But egocentric referring expressions can be counterparts and hence used by different people to make the same statement (e.g. 'Jones is here by me' : 'Jones is there by you'), because they gear in with an intersubjective framework of relative location. If there were intersubjective intentions..., but then this is exactly the problem.

Dick: *we* shall do what we can to end the war

These statements in the first person *plural* have the interesting properties that (*a*) they express the speakers' intention, yet (*b*) the intentions expressed are in the strongest sense the same. Put in terms of the distinctions I drew in my opening remarks, the *intendings* are two in number, but the *content* of these intendings is the *same*, in as strong a sense as the content of the two believings expressed by

Tom: There was lightning at *t*
Dick: There was lightning at *t*

is the same. I shall put this by saying that the *intendings* expressed by

We shall do...

have an intersubjective form.

118. This intersubjective form stands out when it is a matter of intendings to do. When, however, it is a matter of intendings that something be the case, the distinction is likely to be lost, unless we index the 'shall' to indicate the form of the intending *to do* which the intendings imply.[19] Thus the intersubjective intention expressed by

It shall$_{we}$ be the case that the war end

would contrast in form, for example, with the personal intention

It shall$_I$ be the case that the roses be planted

XVII

119. We have answered the thirty-two-dollar question by finding the necessary dimension of intersubjectivity. There remains, however, the sixty-four-dollar question of categorical reasonableness. Some paragraphs back, when we were beating about in the neighbouring bushes, I asked if the antecedent of a certain complex hypothetical

---

[19] In the case of wishes as contrasted with intentions we have the locution
   We would that...
to contrast with
   I would that...
Here the 'we' and 'I' express the form of the wish. In the case of intentions, however, it is only intentions to do which exhibit this distinction. The functions of the indices is [sic] performed in ordinary language by the contrast between 'from a personal point of view' and 'from the point of view of the group' or, of more interest, 'from a moral point of view'.

178 THE METAPHYSICS OF PRACTICE

imperative could be construed as categorically reasonably valid, pointing out that if so, its categorical reasonableness would be transmitted to that which it instrumentally implied. Since that time we have (*a*) taken into account intentions that something be the case, and (*b*) brought into the picture intentions which have intersubjective form. Have these additional resources brought us closer to our goal? I believe they have.

120. Consider* the intersubjective intention

It shall$_{we}$ be the case that our welfare is maximized

If this intention were intrinsically categorically reasonable, or valid, then, by virtue of the relation of 'shall be the case' to 'I shall do', so also would

We shall each of us so act as to maximize our welfare

121. We now take into account the vast number of complicated instrumental nomologicals which we suppose to have been established (in principle) by the physical and behavioural sciences, and are represented by the schema

'*x* so acts as to maximize GW' implies '*x* does A_i if in C_i'

Given these implications, the categorical validity of the above intention entails the categorical validity of the family of intersubjective intentions

It shall$_{we}$ be the case that each of us does A_i in C_i

which, on our analysis, is equivalent to the family of ought statements

If any of us is in C_i he ought to do A_i

122. Notice that although the validity which these ought statements ascribe to the intersubjective intentions with respect to any of us that he do A_i in C_i is a *derivative* validity, it is nevertheless a *categorical* validity. The 'ought' itself can properly be characterized as categorical, and contrasted with the 'relative' ought of the hypothetical imperative.

XVIII

123. We ascribe a valuing to Smith by saying

---

* [Eds.—Correction of "Cerid" in original printing.]

Smith values...

In the argument to date, we have taken the appropriate sentence which Smith might use to express his valuing to be

Would that...

Now when the valuing is, as I put it, from a personal point of view, let us suppose that it is properly expressed by the sentence

I would that...

e.g.

I would that I were in England
I would that Tom was well

Corresponding to these, there would be ascriptive sentences having the form

Smith values, from a personal point of view, ...

124. What are we to contrast with this? What is to be the expressive counterpart of the ascription

Smith values, *from a moral point of view*, ...

The answer suggests itself

We would that...

Roughly, to value from a moral point of view is to value *as a member of the relevant community*, which as far as the present argument is concerned, I shall assume to be mankind generally.[20]

125. Notice that the above sentence, which *expresses* a valuing, must not be confused with the plural value *ascription*

---

[20] Thus, interesting points remain to be made about the tribocentricity of moral judgments in the not too remote past, and on what it would be to change from speaking of a being as 'it' to speaking of it as one of 'them' in a sense which radically contrasts with 'one of us', and from there to speaking of the being as a member of the encompassing community within which we draw relative distinctions between 'we' and 'they'. Perhaps the most interesting point is that to discuss with another person what ought to be done *presupposes* (shall I say dialectically?) that you and he are members of one community.

We value...

It is still an individual who is valuing, but he is valuing in terms of *we*. Let us suppose that Smith and ourselves belong to the same community (as on the above assumption we do), then the corresponding value ascription would be

Smith values as *one of us*...

126. Valuing, in other words, has a *subjective form* as well as a *content*. The subjective form we have hereto taken into account is the 'personal point of view'. Moral philosophers have emphasized the universality of the *content* of a moral evaluation, thus,

Would that anyone in C_i did A_i

I wish to emphasize the universality of the subjective form of moral evaluation

We would that anyone in C_i did A_i

127. Let me emphasize that from the fact that Smith values something, X, as one of us, it doesn't follow that

We value X

We may well—indeed, often do—differ in what we value as members of the community. Yet *in principle* there could be agreement. 'We would that...' lacks the logical privacy of 'I would that...'

128. Let me give a parallel from our earlier exploration of classical theories. Our ego-centred Smith might well value things differently at different times, as his beliefs about himself and the world change. Thus at noon he might say

I shall not cross the Rubicon tomorrow

and at evening

I shall cross the Rubicon tomorrow

But although his 'shall' is egocentric, it is *abidingly* egocentric. He is, in a tough sense, asking the *same* question when he asks at different times

Shall I cross the Rubicon on such and such a date?

129. Furthermore, given his over-arching aim of a satisfying life, he would be, *in principle*, at all times in agreement with himself about his values; that is to say, if he had at all times the knowledge available in his ideal Academy he would have agreed with himself at all times about the values implied by this over-arching aim. There would be, *in principle*, agreement between, so to speak, Smith-at-t_1, Smith-at-t_2, etc. His categorical oughts at one time can contradict those of another time. Yet these contradictions are, in principle, resolvable.

130. The parallel logical point holds with respect to the members of our community, in so far as they value the general welfare not from a personal point of view—external benevolence—but *as one of us*.

131. I pointed out above that if the intersubjective intention

It shall$_{we}$ be the case that our welfare is maximized

were intrinsically categorically reasonable, the family of intersubjective intentions

It shall$_{we}$ be the case that each of us does A_i in C_i

would also be categorically reasonable, though derivatively so.

132. Let us now remove the 'if', for the intention

It shall$_{we}$ be the case that our welfare is maximized

does seem to have an authority which is more than a mere matter of its being generally accepted. It is a conceptual fact that people constitute a community, a *we*, by virtue of thinking of each other as *one of us*, and by willing the common good *not* under the species of benevolence—but by willing it as one of us, or from a moral point of view. Thus, the autobiographical

An intention which I accept

is replaced by '... is an intersubjectively valid intention'.

XIX

133. If my argument is correct, the valuings which are expressed by ethical statements are universal in *three* dimensions.

(a) in their content
   ... if any of us is in C_i he do A_i

182 THE METAPHYSICS OF PRACTICE

(b) in their subjective form (their logical intersubjectivity)
We would that...
(c) in their objectivity (in that there is, in principle, a decision procedure with respect to specific ethical statements)

I see no reason why this objectivity should not be said to legitimate the use of the concepts of truth and falsity with respect to ethical discourse.

134. These considerations pertaining to the conceptual structure of the moral point of view amount to a thoroughly Kantian metaphysic of morals. Thus, they amount to:

(a) The conception of a moral polity—Kant's Kingdom of Ends

(It is this conceptual feature of the moral point of view which implies the Kantian principle that everyone shall be treated as an end in itself and not as a means only. For to treat someone as a means only is, in effect, to consider his place with respect to our conduct not from the point of view

We would that...

but from a point of view which singles him out, by virtue of some special relation to ourselves, as an exception. It is to consider him from the point of view

I would that...

or, at least, from the point of view of a sub-community to which I belong.)

(b) the conception of moral principles as universalized maxims—
we would that *anyone* in C_i do A_i
(c) by virtue of the logical relation of 'any' to 'all', the conception of moral principles as implying
We would that *all persons always did* A_i in C_i
(Kant's 'law of nature' formulation)
(d) the conception that there is a common epistemic obligation to accept categorical imperatives

(For categorical imperatives are simply the transposition into the moral framework of scientific truths of the form

(s) (t) 's promotes the common good at t'
implies 'if s is in C_i at t, s does A_i at t')

OBJECTIVITY, INTERSUBJECTIVITY AND THE MORAL POINT OF VIEW 183

135. Alas, the ideal knowledge of our philosophical fiction is not even close at hand. Thus, the ideal 'consensus' of those who share the moral point of view is only 'in principle' there, and reasoning from the moral point of view proceeds in a context of ignorance and diversity of opinion. But, then, the same is true of consensus on matters of fact, scientific laws and theoretical principles. There, as here, the philosophical task must be to exhibit the conceptual structure within which this ignorance and this difference of opinion exist, and which, by making rational inquiry possible, provides the means by which (in principle, alas!) they can be overcome.

XX

136. Kant believed himself to have established that the 'we' of the moral point of view is *rational beings generally*. At first sight, however, this seems to be a mistake, a confusion between the class of those for whom instrumental *implications* are binding, which does, indeed, consist of rational beings generally, and the class of those for whom categorically valid intersubjective *intentions* are binding.

137. The distinction involved can best be made by returning to the general hypothetical imperatives of benevolence

'I shall maximize the GW' implies 'I shall do A_i, if in C_i'

We pointed out that the scope of the 'I' consists of rational beings generally, since the implications are simply the transposition into practical discourse of inductively established nomologicals. We failed, however, to emphasize that the welfare to be maximized is the welfare *of a group to which a particular 'I' belongs*, thus,

'I shall maximize the GW of my group' implies (for each rational being) 'I shall do A_i if in C_i'

And if we ask which group is that, we see that it by no means follows from the above that the answer must be 'rational beings generally'. We must draw at least a conceptual distinction between the class of those on whom the implications are binding, and the class of those the promotion of whose welfare is the object of the benevolent intention of a particular 'I'.

138. The distinction remains when we transpose the instrumental implication into the realm of intersubjective intentions.

'It shall$_{we}$ be the case that each of us so acts as to maximize our welfare' implies 'It shall$_{we}$ be the case that each of us does A_i if in C_i'

As before, the 'implies' can be glossed with 'for each rational being'. But, as before, it by no means follows that the group whose welfare is 'our' welfare consists of rational beings generally.

139. It might, however, be argued that only if the 'we' of 'our welfare' is the 'we' of 'we rational beings generally' is an intersubjective intention of this form categorically valid. This *might*, as we shall see, be true if the welfare in question is what might be called epistemic welfare, but not if we take into account, as we must, needs and desires generally.

140. Now, we saw that the categorical validity of an intersubjective intention of the form

It shall$_{we}$ be the case that our welfare is maximized

would seem to consist in the fact that it is by virtue of such an intention that a group or community *is* a group or community. Roughly, a community consists of individuals who intend *sub specie* such an intention, the scope of 'we' being the members of the community.

141. This is not to say, of course, that there will be agreement as to just what is instrumentally implied by this intention, or that on particular occasions the implications a person believes it to have will prevail against an alternative arrived at by practical reasoning 'from a personal point of view'.

142. Can we say that rational beings generally constitute a community? They would do so if they shared the intersubjective intention

It shall$_{we}$ be the case that each of us rational beings so acts as to promote our welfare

143. Now, since an individual can have an intention of intersubjective form even if no one else in point of fact shares it, an individual rational being could have an intention of the above form even though few, if any, other rational beings had such an intention. To have this intention is to *think* of oneself as a member of a community consisting of all rational being. It is possible, therefore, for a rational being to think of himself as a member of such community, even though this community does not actually exist.

144. If, however, the following two premises were established, this community could be shown to be a reality:

(*a*) To think of oneself as rational being is (implicitly) to think of oneself as subject to epistemic oughts binding on rational beings generally

(b) The intersubjective intention to promote *epistemic* welfare implies the intersubjective intention to promote welfare *sans phrase*

These premises would entail that the concept of oneself as a rational being implies the concept of oneself as a member of an ethical community consisting of all rational being. To be sure, this implication need not be recognized. Indeed, it would take all the dialectical skill of a Socrates, a Hegel or a Peirce to bring it to the surface. Yet if the above premises were true, all rational beings would 'implicitly' think of themselves as members of an ethical community consisting of all rational beings. But since a community exists if the relevant individuals think of themselves as its members, the ethical community of rational being would have an 'implicit' existence.

145. The first of the above premises is not implausible. If we accept it we can conclude that 'implicitly' all rational being constitute an *epistemic* community. The second premise, despite Peirce's valiant efforts, remains problematic, and without it the argument for the reality of an *ethical* community consisting of all rational beings, the major premise of which is the 'fact of reason', remains incomplete.

XXI

146. I shall conclude by drawing the implications of the above analysis for certain traditional puzzles pertaining to Kant's ethical theory. For this purpose the most significant feature of this analysis is the point that the categorical validity of an intention can be derivative.

147. It is this fact which enables us to see how 'teleological' and 'deontological' themes are harmonized in Kant's ethics. Thus specific moral principles are categorical oughts, but the categorical validity of the intersubjective intentions, that any rational being in a certain kind of circumstance do a certain kind of action,[21] is derivative from the categorical validity of the intersubjective intentions that our welfare be maximized. Thus, when Kant speaks in the *Metaphysical Elements of Ethics* of the happiness of others as a categorical end,[22] what he says is

---

[21] "...this 'I ought' (*Sollen*) is properly an 'I would' (*Wollen*) valid for every rational being, provided only that reason determined his actions without any hindrance" (Abbott, p. 68). [Eds.—This and subsequent references to "Abbott" are to: Immanuel Kant, *Kant's Critique of Practical Reason and Other Works on the Theory of Ethics*, trans. Thomas Kingsmill Abbott. London: Longmans, Green, and Co., 1889.]

[22] Abbott, p. 303.

in no way inconsistent with his claim that the ought of moral principles is categorical rather than the hypothetical ought which pertains to the relation of means to ends.

148. Again, when Kant stresses intentions, he is not disregarding consequences. It is because doing A_i in C_i maximizes the general welfare that the intention to do A_i in C_i is categorically valid. Of course we may be, and often are, mistaken about what kind of action in what kind of circumstance will promote the general welfare, but what we ought to do hinges on what would actually happen. On the other hand, the moral character of our motive is a function of what we *think* will happen as a result of our action, though not of this alone.

149. When Kant insists that we ought to act from a sense of duty he is not making the absurd mistakes which have often been attributed to him.[23] He is simply repeating the point with which he opens the argument of the *Fundamental Principles of the Metaphysics of Morals*, that the only unconditional good is a good will. By this he means that the only state of a person which is unconditionally good from a moral point of view is the disposition to act from a sense of duty. He has two points in mind: (*a*) Whereas action from *any* motive can have bad results, the sense of duty alone is such that only *by virtue of ignorance* does it have bad results. Action from other motives even where ignorance is absent can lead to bad results. Thus the sense of duty is the only motive which has a direct conceptual tie to the categorically valid end of moral conduct. In this sense a good will is a categorical ought-to-be. (*b*) Although the general welfare is also an end in itself, a categorical ought-to-be, the ought-to-be of the happiness of any *given* individual is, Kant believes, conditional on his having a good will.

150. As Broad has pointed out, Kant is not always clear about the respective status of specific categorical imperatives (categorically valid maxims) and higher order principles about what distinguishes categorically valid maxims from those which are not. Thus, when he writes in *The Critique of Practical Reason*,

> 'The principle of happiness may, indeed, furnish maxims, but never such as would be competent to be laws of the will even if *universal* happiness were made the object. For since the knowledge of this rests on mere empirical data ... it can supply only *general* rules, not *universal*'.[24]

he confuses the *sound* point that the intersubjective *validity* of the intention to maximize universal happiness cannot be explicated in terms of benevolence, with the *unsound* idea that empirical data are not relevant to determining the validity of specific categorical imperatives (general conditional intentions or maxims). The meta-ethical principle that those intentions of the form

---

[23] E.g. by Sir David Ross in *The Right and the Good*, p. 5.   [24] Abbott, p. 125.

OBJECTIVITY, INTERSUBJECTIVITY AND THE MORAL POINT OF VIEW   187

We would that anyone did A_i if in C_i

are categorically valid, which would be the legislation of an organized community of ideally rational beings *qua* motivated by the categorically valid intention to maximize the common good, does not absolve us from the necessity to use empirical data in our attempt to determine what ought to be done in particular kinds of circumstance. *Any* legislator, motivated by the common good, must ask questions of the form: What kind of action in this kind of circumstance would promote the common good? Only an omniscient legislator would not have to hedge his answers with 'probably' and 'for the most part'.

151. Kant is insisting that the principles in terms of which the concept of a categorically valid intention is to be explicated are not empirical principles. They are *a priori*, and can, in principle, be known by a 'mere analysis of the conceptions of morality'.[25] The fallibility of moral philosophy is not the fallibility of empirical induction.

152. The various so-called formulations of 'the categorical imperative' are meta-ethical principles which locate categorical imperatives (in the sense of specific categorically valid maxims) in the total structure of categorically valid intentions to which they belong. Thus the formulation in terms of legislation appropriate to a 'Kingdom of Ends', though it comes last, actually points to the derivability of categorically valid maxims from the intrinsically categorical intention that 'all ends [be] combined in a systematic whole (including both rational beings as ends in themselves, and also the special ends which each may propose to himself)'.[26]

153. The formulation: 'act on maxims which can at the same time have for their objects themselves as universal laws of Nature'[27] reflects the logical relation between *any* and *all*. The intention—from the moral point of view or, as Kant would say, from the point of view of a rational being as such—with respect to *anybody* that he do A_i in C_i doesn't entail the *intention* that everybody do A_i in C_i (for we don't intend the impossible). Thus, a state of affairs in which everybody conforms to categorically valid maxims is itself a categorical ought-to-be, and the wish that it be the case a categorically valid wish.

154. Finally, the principle that '... each [rational being] must treat itself and all others never merely as means, but in every case at the same time as ends in themselves'[28] reflects the fact that the intrinsically valid intention which is the prime mover of the domain of categorically valid intentions is the intersubjectively valid intention that each of us rational beings promote our common good. This state of affairs is an end-in-itself in which particular individuals appear symmetrically as *agents* and *patients* in an ethical community.

---

[25] ibid., p. 59.   [26] Abbott, p. 51.   [27] Abbott, p. 56.   [28] Abbott, p. 52.

PART 2

AGENCY AND MORAL PSYCHOLOGY: INTENTIONS AND VOLITIONS

7
Thought and Action

I. Intentions

[1] My aim in this essay is to explore the interconnection of a number of concepts which are of particular interest to the philosophical psychology of action. The interconnection of these concepts concerns their respective roles in the concept of practical reasoning, and it is with some reflections on the latter that this essay will begin and end. By "practical reasoning" I understand reasoning which, if carried to its conclusion, ends in a practical assertion in one's heart and, possibly, on one's tongue. By a practical assertion, I mean in the first instance an assertion which is of the form

such and such shall[1] be the case.

I use the very uninformative place-holder "such and such"—which amounts to a variable for states of affairs—because part of my task is to determine what sort of expressions can appropriately replace it, i.e. what sort of states of affairs are appropriately referred to by a practical assertion.

[2] The above stipulation involves many promissory notes, not the least of which concerns the fact that the phrase "practical reasoning" is normally construed to cover not only such reasonings as that expressed by

I shall drive this nail,
Therefore, I shall get my hammer,

but also reasonings which culminate, not in practical assertions of the narrow kind described above, but rather in assertions to the effect that such and such an action *ought* to be done, or that such and such an object or state of affairs is or would be *good*. And, indeed, I would agree that such reasonings are cases of practical reasoning. It will therefore come as no surprise when I propose the thesis that, in their primary use, "ought" and "good" are special cases of "shall." If I am right, the above definition of practical reasoning is not as narrow as it looks, and an

---

[1] Let me remind the reader that in this and other essays I use "shall" in such a way that it always (as it does not in ordinary English) expresses an intention—in a suitably broad sense to be characterized below—of the speaker.

exploration of the structure of reasonings which culminate in explicit "shalls" is capable of throwing light on reasoning which pertains to obligations and values. But, for the moment, this more general application must remain a promissory note.

[3] It is clear that the above line of thought is akin to the imperativist interpretation of practical reasoning developed by, among others, R. M. Hare and Hector Castañeda. It differs from them primarily in stressing that practical reasoning, like theoretical reasoning (in the classical sense in which it is contrasted with practical reasoning), need not be addressed to an audience. It can, and usually does, "go on in one's head." An imperative is essentially something that is addressed to somebody, telling him or her to do something. Thinking is, I believe, fruitfully conceived as "inner speech," though it would be a mistake to construe all "inner speech" as "talking to or addressing oneself." I *may* address myself in inner speech—as when I think "Watch out, Sellars, you nearly split an infinitive." Thus, while we *can* address imperatives to ourselves in inner speech— tell oneself to do something—the thought expressed by

I shall drive this nail

should not be construed as though it would be more perspicuously expressed by

Myself, drive this nail!

[4] Yet, for all this, there is much in common between the fundamental position I am taking and that of the imperativists. They conceive of a practical statement as either an imperative or a statement which entails an imperative. I conceive of a practical statement as either a shall-statement or a statement which entails a shall-statement.

[5] Shall-statements express intentions. To explain exactly what this means, let me introduce some notions from the Philosophy of Mind. First of all, let us distinguish between a thought and its overt expression in language. By "a thought" I mean a mental episode, something that occurs in a mind at a certain moment.[2] Thoughts, as I am using the term, are examples of "mental acts." But the term "act" is misleading, as we shall see, for it is easily confused with *action*. Thoughts are characterized by reference to the utterances in which they would eventuate if the thinker were in a thinking-out-loud frame of mind. If, now, we draw on the familiar distinction between an episode and a disposition or propensity, we can characterize a *belief* as a disposition to have thoughts of a certain kind. Thus, to believe that LBJ is President is to be disposed to have (in appropriate contexts) thoughts of the "LBJ is President" kind.

---

[2] The word thought is also used in the sense of *what* is thought. In the latter sense a thought is, for example, a proposition which can be thought by many minds or by the same mind at different times.

[6] Similarly we must distinguish between three meanings of "intention."

1. The *what is intended*: in scholastic terms, the *species* to which the mental act or disposition belongs e.g. The "I shall go downtown at 3 p.m." kind of intention;
2. The *act* of intending: an episode which is an instance of one of these species;
3. The *disposition* to have acts falling under one of these species.

Thus, a certain person may be thinking

I shall go downtown at 3 p.m.

or, though not actually thinking this, he may be disposed to have such thoughts. Just as a person can be said to believe something throughout a certain period of time, even though he is not constantly thinking the relevant thought (indeed, it may not occur to him), so a person may be said to intend something throughout a period of time, even though the appropriate shall-thought does not occur to him. The classical doctrine that actions are typically initiated by volitions has recently come in for some hard knocks. I have defended this thesis, and shown, to my own satisfaction, at least, that the major types of objection to it are based either on category mistakes or on too narrow a conception of empirical meaningfulness. According to the account I there offered, we acquire what rational psychology calls the "faculty of volition" in the course of learning the language of intention or "shall-talk."

[7] There is an important similarity between learning to make the language-entry transition[3] of responding to presented red objects by saying "This is red," and learning the language-departure transition, which joins the *saying* of

I shall *now* do A

and, consequently, the thought

I shall *now* do A

with a doing of A. Until a child has acquired this connection, he has not learned the meaning of "I shall *now* do A," and until he has learned this, he cannot learn the full meaning of "shall," for all other uses of "shall" owe *their* connection with action to their connection with this use of "shall."

---

[3] Wilfrid Sellars, *Science, Perception and Reality* (London, 1963), pp. 328ff. [Eds.—Sellars is referring to SRLG.]

[8] According to the proposed model, a volition is a thought of the form

> I shall *now* bring about X (or avert Z) by Y-ing,

where Y-ing is something, as we say, within the agent's voluntary control, and where, in the limiting case of minimal actions done for their own sake, "bring about X (or avert Z) by Y-ing" collapses into "do Y." The above formula is designed to avoid the mistake of supposing that the content willed is limited to actions that are under the agent's voluntary control. But though not limited to them, volitions must *include* them. Somewhat more artificially, we can represent a volition as having the form

> I shall *now* do A in order to bring about (or avert) B,

noting that its contents may even be more complicated, thus

> I shall *now* do A in order to bring about (or avert) B in spite of bringing about or preventing C.

What differentiates a volition from an act of intending, is (a) its *now* character, and (b) the fact that the central place in what is intended is something (putatively) doable here and now.

[9] A simple case of the relation of intending to volition can be illustrated by considering Jones, who has formed the intention of raising his hand in ten minutes. Suppose that no alternative course of action recommends itself to him. Then we may picture the situation as follows:

> I shall raise my hand in *ten* minutes
>
> .
> .
>
> .
>
> I shall raise my hand in *nine* minutes
>
> .
> .
>
> .
>
> I shall raise my hand *now*
> (which culminates in action, if Jones happens not to be paralyzed).

Intentions, like beliefs pertaining to particular matters of fact, involve an apperceptive framework of orientation in a spatio-temporal world. That one's "place" in time is constantly and systematically changing is, of course, an essential feature of this framework; one that is reflected in—indeed constituted by—a systematic change in the content of thought with respect to tense, temporal connectives and the like.

[10] But the fact that certain shall-thoughts are such that, in the absence of paralysis, they culminate in action, is only one, if an essential, feature of the framework of shall-thoughts or intentions. Two other major features remain to be noted. They concern, roughly, the existence of *underivative* intentions, and the mode of derivation of one intention from another. The latter topic is cousin to the familiar topic of imperative inference, which concerns the conditions under which an imperative sentence may be validly derived from a given set of sentences. In our framework, it is the problem of the circumstances under which a shall-conclusion can be validly arrived at from a given set of premises.

[11] The first principle is easy. It parallels Poincaré's principle that no imperative conclusion can be drawn from premises which do not include an imperative. Once this has been agreed upon, however, it has proved easy to get bogged down in controversy concerning what the other principles should be. Fortunately for our purposes, it turns out that only one principle is needed. It goes

If P implies Q, then Shall [P] implies Shall [Q].

The one word that causes trouble, of course, is the little word "implies." I have in mind the ordinary sense in which implication is the relation which authorizes inference. I shall assume that we know our way around in this ordinary sense of "implies," and that it involves no paradoxes. I shall further suppose that there are at least two species of implication in the ordinary sense: (a) logical, and (b) physical or natural; finally, that there is such a thing as derivative implication, where something implies something else, *relatively to a given assumption*.

[12] Notice that according to the above principle a shall-implication has the form

Shall [P] implies Shall [Q];

and it is true if and only if P implies Q. If so, then, all steps in practical reasoning would have to be, as reconstructed in this framework, derivations of one Shall from another. There would be no mixed derivations, such as:

Shall [if it is raining, I will come in]
It is raining
Therefore, Shall [I will come in].

Fortunately, it can be shown that this pattern of argument can be reduced to our paradigmatic form. For, *relatively* to the assumption that it is raining,

I will come in, if it rains implies I will come in,

just as *relatively* to the assumption that Socrates is a man

All men are mortal implies Socrates is mortal.

Thus, relatively to the proposition that it is raining,

Shall [I will come in if it rains] implies Shall [I will come in].

In short we admit as valid those practical reasonings the premises of which combine an intention with factual information, provided that, *relatively to the factual information*, the content of the premise-intention implies the content of the conclusion-intention.

[13] Notice that no meaning has been given to "not shall [P]", as contrasted with "Shall [not-P]." Shall-sentences, unlike ought sentences, do not have contradictories. It is particularly important, in this connection, to distinguish first-person present-tense statements, of the form "I intend to do A," or "I intend that S shall be P," from simple expressions of intention. Of these two statement forms, the latter (and, less perspicuously, the former) stands to the simple expression of intention "S shall be P" ("I shall do A"), much as "I believe that S is P" stands to "S is P." Unlike shall-sentences, sentences of the form "X intends that S shall be P" have two negations:

X intends that S shall not be P

and

X does not intend that S shall be P.

[14] These considerations throw additional light on the principle which relates "P implies Q" to "Shall [P] implies Shall [Q]," for they commit us to the position that the latter implication does not have a contrapositive. If it is countered that an implication which has no contrapositive is not an implication, the answer is that this simply reflects the extent to which the theory of implication has been dominated by the study of reasoning concerned with mathematical relationships and empirical matters of fact.

[15] The analogy drawn above between

X intends that S shall be P

and

X believes that S is P

calls to mind the problem of the "logic" (which might better be called the "axiomatics") of belief, and raises the corresponding problem of the logic of intention—where this means *not* the logic of shall-sentences, but rather the logic of intention-sentences. The latter is a richer topic, the study of which is scarcely under way. Two remarks will be helpful in connection with later stages of the argument: (1) We must distinguish between

I. P implies Q → Shall [P] implies Shall [Q]

and

II. P implies Q → (X intends that Shall [P]) implies (X intends that Shall [Q]).

The latter principle is, as stated, false. Only if radical restrictions are placed on the way in which P implies Q, as by limiting it to the case where seeing that P implies Q is a necessary condition for understanding these propositions, can it be true. (2) If such a restriction is introduced, II becomes a special case of principle

III. X thinks that P implies Q → (X intends that Shall [P]) implies (X intends that Shall [Q]);

or, equivalently,

IIIa. X thinks that P implies Q → (X does not intend that Shall [Q]) implies (X does not intend that Shall [P]).

II. Preference

[16] Before I turn to the central part of this essay, which concerns the relations between intention, desire, enjoyment and action, a *further* group of distinctions is necessary. The first concept to be defined is that of *preference*. The concept, as I introduce it, is a thin one, for it makes no reference to enjoyment or satisfaction, but is defined solely in terms of intendings or shall-thoughts. A preference is a disposition pertaining to such thoughts. Roughly,

X prefers A to B

implies that where A and B are thought to be relevant, but incompatible (not jointly realizable), X on asking himself,

198   THE METAPHYSICS OF PRACTICE

Shall [A • ~B]?   Shall [B • ~A]?

will intend

Shall [A • ~B].

[17] It should, of course, be noted that

X prefers A to B

is compatible with

X prefers B • C to A • C,

which tells us that, in relevant circumstances, X will intend

Shall [B • C • ~A]

rather than

Shall [A • C • ~B].

A more complete expression of this intention, given that the answer to the previous questions is as above, would be

Shall [B • C in spite of ~A].

[18] Here is the place to supplement our previous remarks on the logic of shall-sentences by noting that there is no logical move from

Shall [A],   Shall [B]

to

Shall [A • B],

let alone

Shall [A] • Shall [B].

No sense has been given to the latter, nor, if an attempt is made to appeal to the peculiar sense ("conjunction introduction") in which

P, Q

'implies'

P • Q

has any sense been given to "Shall [P, Q]".[4]

[19] We can introduce the concept of indifference to a kind of state of affairs with respect to another kind as follows:

X is indifferent to G with respect to K

has the sense of

X prefers neither G • K to ~G • K nor ~G • K to G • K.

[20] Finally, we can say that

X is favorably disposed to L

has the sense of

X prefers L to ~L,

which tells us that X will intend

Shall [L • ~~L], i.e. Shall [L]*

rather than

Shall [~L • ~L], i.e. Shall [~L].

[21] It is important to note that not all choices are expressions of preference, a fact which requires a refinement of the above definition. The point is an important one in moral psychology, although to elaborate it would take us beyond the scope of

---

[4] It might be claimed that I am inconsistent in denying sense to '~ Shall [P],' and 'Shall [P] • Shall [Q]' while admitting 'Shall [P] implies Shall [Q]'. But the latter, involving the *relation word* 'implies' which is not a truth-functional *connective*, is in the metalanguage, and *mentions* rather than *uses* the shall-sentences. [Eds.—So, the latter should read "'Shall [P]' implies 'Shall [Q]'."—Note that in later writings, Sellars backtracks on his rejection of Conjunction Introduction, writing, "In 'Thought and Action' I rejected the principle that 'Shall [p] and shall [q] imply 'shall [p and q]'. It is not clear why I did so" (VR §39); and he introduces Conjunction Introduction as a rule for making precisely this move. See also ORAV (Chapter 16 of this volume).]

* [Eds.—Correction of "Shall [L • ~L], i.e. Shall [L]" in original printing.]

the present paper, because it brings out into the open a widespread confusion between *character* and *nature*. Thus, if a person queries

Shall it be the case that X • ~Y? Shall it be the case that Y • ~X?

and answers

It shall be the case that X • ~Y,

it is presumably true of S at that time that, if he were to query thus, he would answer thus—from which, together with the above definition, it would follow that all choice is an expression of preference.

[22] But preferences and traits of character in general are not *just* true hypotheticals about intendings. They are hypotheticals defined in the vocabulary of practice or conduct, which are such that the *primary* mode of establishing them is induction within this conceptual framework.[5] Thus, even if invisible cerebroscopes and a knowledge of psychophysical connections enable invisible Martian interlopers to formulate true hypotheticals about which of two alternatives a person would choose, if he were to deliberate, they would not have discovered, *ipso facto*, a preference or character trait. All choice may, in a suitable sense, be the expression of the *nature* of a language-using animal. But it is certain that not all choice is an expression of *character*. Choices form character as well as express them.

[23] Just how the above definition of preference should be amended to meet this point is hard to say. Perhaps something along the following lines would do the job:

S prefers X to Y   = df   If S were to query 'Shall it be the case that X • ~Y?'
during period P   'Shall it be the case that Y • ~X?' on a number of
                            occasions during P, he would answer (most if not
                            all of the time) 'It shall be the case that X • ~Y.'

III. Desire: A Statement of the Problem

[24] Given that intentions can be derived from other intentions along the lines explored at the end of part I, what is the status of *underived* intentions? In other words what is the status of intentions that have not been reasoned from other

---

[5] This does not mean that a preference for X over Y must be inferred only from past choices of X as against Y. That a person prefers X to Y may reasonably be inferred from his physiological make-up or childhood training.

intentions? Roughly, what is it to desire something for its own sake? I say *roughly*, because the word "desire" has in ordinary usage a more specific meaning than the technical usage I have in mind. Yet a provisional explication of this technical usage will help us build the framework in terms of which the more general concept can be understood. This strategy is supported by the fact that, since the time of Plato, philosophers have tended to use the term "desire" in something like the technical sense that I have in mind.

[25] It might be thought that the interesting question about desires is "how do desires get us to act?"—which they obviously do. Do desires *cause* volitions? Actually this question is the *least* interesting of the questions we can ask about desire; for, on the account which I shall give, the connection between desire and volition is a *logical* one. This follows from the fact that desires are relatively long-term dispositional intentions. Thus their relation to action is a matter of the fact that, relatively to acquired information intentions imply and can be seen to imply other intentions, and indeed, on those occasions in which practical reasoning reaches its proper conclusion, intentions pertaining to action, and hence, where the time of action is *hic et nunc*, volitions.

[26] But to say that the desire that-p is a disposition to have thoughts of the form

Shall [that-p]

or, perhaps, that to desire a state of affairs is to be favorably disposed toward it, in the sense defined above, leaves unexplained the fact that, in addition to having something to do with action, desires also have something to do with pleasure or satisfaction. I believe that the best model for understanding this relationship is to construe desires as mental needs on the model of bodily needs. The key theme here is the fact that the "filling"—to use Plato's metaphor—of a need brings with it (*ceteris paribus*) pleasure.[6] Thus, if "X desires that-p" could be explicated as "X needs to believe that-p," the connection between desires and "pleasure" would be a special case of the connection between needs and "pleasure"; and is it not plausible to say that "X desires to be loved" implies "X needs to believe that he is loved" and "X would be pleased if he believed himself to be loved"?

[27] But even if we ultimately conclude that desires are of the nature of needs to believe, the perspective of the preceding paragraphs precludes any quick move in this direction, for we have construed them as dispositional intentions. It may, however, be the case that a closer examination of this construction will narrow the

---

[6] A bodily need, such as that for calcium, requires, of course, no awareness that anything is lacking. Mental needs, on the other hand, clearly involve awareness in one way or another—just how, remains to be seen. Yet they have this in common with bodily needs, that we can have them without knowing that we do.

gap between "disposition to intend" and "need to believe." Desires clearly resemble intentions in the sense that they are capable of being realized. Realization in this sense is a concept akin to truth. Intentions—and volitions in particular—are realized if and only if the state of affairs intended comes to exist. Similarly, a desire is realized if and only if the state of affairs desired comes to exist. And just as a judgment can be true without being known to be true, so, in this technical sense, an intention or a desire can be realized without being known to be realized.

[28] But for a desire to be *realized* in this sense is obviously not the same thing as for it to be *satisfied*. Desires seem to have a logical connection with enjoyment or satisfaction, which is not accounted for by anything we have said so far about intentions and their realization.

[29] We seem to be confronted by a dilemma. If we define a desire as a dispositional intention, we acknowledge a logical tie between desire and action, but seem to leave no place for a logical tie between desire and enjoyment or satisfaction. If, on the other hand, we define desire in such a way as to establish a logical tie between desire and satisfaction (along lines hinted at above), we seem to leave no place for a logical tie between desire and action. Yet *prima facie* desire is logically tied to both satisfaction and action.

[30] In order to clarify the problem, we must explore the concept of the satisfaction of a desire. As has already been indicated, this requires a discussion of the concept of enjoyment, i.e. of the context

X enjoys Y-ing.

The first point to be made is a familiar one. To enjoy Y-ing is not to do *two* things—i.e. to Y and "feel pleasure." This phenomenological point was appreciated by Aristotle, and misused by Berkeley. The misuse is instructive. Berkeley argued that a loud noise is a pain and drew the conclusion that, since pain is a mental state, loud noises must be mental states, and hence (by considerations of continuity) all noises must be mental states. The argument is, of course, a bad one. The major premise should have been *not* "a loud noise is a pain" but "hearing a loud noise is a pain, i.e. painful." And from this the desired conclusion does not follow. Yet Berkeley had, like Aristotle, seen that the painful character of the hearing of a loud noise is not a matter of doing two things, hearing and feeling, but rather doing one thing in a certain manner, i.e. hearing painfully.[7]

---

[7] This phenomenological fruit of conceptual analysis, which emphasizes the *adverbial* character of painfulness and enjoyment is, needless to say, compatible with a non-phenomenological, *theoretical*, account of these verb-adverb situations, which interprets them as psychophysical fields, the describing of which involves the use of neither verbs nor adverbs. It is the feeling that some such account must *ultimately* be given which has often led to the conviction that enjoyment and unenjoyment are to be *analyzed* as composites of non-hedonic and hedonic states.

[31] Taking the contexts

X enjoys Y-ing
X disenjoys Y-ing

as phenomenologically ultimate, and limiting ourselves, for simplicity's sake, to the former, we turn next to the distinction between conceptual and non-conceptual enjoyments. Obviously thoughts can be enjoyed as well as muscle movements. Yet to draw the distinction is to recognize that, since distinctively human activities involve conceptual as well as non-conceptual components, the extent of purely non-conceptual enjoyments is less than might initially be thought. Indeed, in so far as Y-ing is not a minimal action, but extends beyond a bodily or mental motion, and is a bringing about of something that is not in our immediate voluntary control, to enjoy Y-ing is to enjoy the thought that one is Y-ing.

[32] Now the satisfaction of a desire obviously has *something* to do with the belief on the part of the person who is doing the desiring that the desired state of affairs obtains. This suggests that

X desires that S be P

has a strong conceptual tie with

X is disposed to enjoy the thought of S being P.

It will be remembered that in *Principia Ethica*, G. E. Moore finds an intimate connection between the idea of a certain state of affairs being a pleasant idea and the desire that the state of affairs obtain. Moore interprets the connection, however, as a causal one, a link in a longer chain which can be represented (with the necessary qualifications) by the schema

(i) X finds the idea of a certain state of affairs pleasant
(ii) X desires the state of affairs in question
(iii) X (thinking that doing A would bring about this state of affairs) wills to do A

This picture presents the relations between desire and enjoyment, on the one hand, and desire and action, on the other, as causal. Our problem is to see whether we can so reconstruct the situation that both relations are logical or conceptual.

[33] If we were to define desire in a broad sense (which includes, for example, wishes) as a disposition to enjoy the idea of a certain state of affairs obtaining (and, perhaps, to disenjoy the idea of its not obtaining), then we would have a strategy for explaining the conceptual connection between desire (in that narrow sense in

which it is contrasted with wishing) and enjoyment. Here the enjoyed idea of a state of affairs obtaining would be an enjoyed belief that the state of affairs obtains. To speak of a desire in this sense as *satisfied* may well imply that it is also *realized*[8] and hence that the belief enjoyed is true. But it would at least imply that the relevant belief was enjoyed—if only for a moment.[9]

[34] But such a definition destroys, at least in appearance, the logical connection we feel to exist between desire and action, a feeling which found expression in our previous definition. We would seem to be forced to construe the connection between desire and volition as, in a broad sense, a causal one. The other horn of the dilemma, it will be remembered, was that to define the desire that p be the case as some form of disposition to intend that p be the case would, even though it recognized the logical tie between desire and action, fail to account for the *prima facie* connection between desire and satisfaction.

IV. Doing and Enjoying

[35] Is there any way in which both connections can be accounted for, so as to give them at least an element of conceptual necessity? It could, of course, be done in a trifling way, by defining desire in terms of a simple conjunction, a disposition to enjoy thinking that p is the case and a disposition to intend that p be the case. But it is clear that what we are looking for is a logical connection between these two dispositions, by virtue of which they belong together and the conjunction is not arbitrary. Is there some mediating connection that we have overlooked?

[36] What about a possible connection between

X is disposed to enjoy Y-ing

and

X is disposed to Y?

---

[8] Otherwise one might say that the person merely thought that it was satisfied.
[9] Whether the person gets any *other* enjoyment if the desire is realized in fact, as well as in belief is, in many cases, a matter of the causal impact on him of the desired state of affairs. It is, of course, conceivable, in these cases, at least, that even if a person's desires were always realized, the world might be so arranged and his ignorance of causal relationships so profound that the *only* satisfaction he ever got was an ephemeral conceptual enjoyment of believing that the states of affairs desired were realized. Where on the other hand the object of desire is to engage in an immediately enjoyable activity, the connection between a desire's being realized and the existence of satisfactions other than that of believing the desired state of affairs to exist is considerably closer. It might be added that, at the very moment of coming to believe that the state of affairs in question obtains, one may see that it involves features to which one has a strong aversion, so that this belief is not even momentarily enjoyed. But we are speaking of propensities which are manifested only *ceteris paribus*.

That some such connection seems to exist is clear. Is it logical or causal? Is it a logical or a causal fact that, other things being equal, people do what they enjoy doing? Of course, given a certain description of what a person is doing, it may be true that he does not enjoy doing *that*. Thus a person may eat shredded wheat for breakfast and not enjoy what he is doing *quâ* eating shredded wheat.[10] But might it not be the case that there is another description of what the person is doing, which preserves the desired connection?[11]

[37] Now I am strongly inclined to think that there is a conceptual connection between doing (not doing) and enjoying (disenjoying). I do not have anything particularly helpful to say on this subject. It does, however, seem to me that, *if* there is such a connection, *then* the strategy to be employed in connection with the problem I have posed becomes clear.

[38] Thus, if we assume that the above principle is true, and apply it to the case where the *doings* in question are *thinkings*, we get the derivative principle

X is disposed to enjoy thinking 'it shall be the case that-p' implies that S is disposed (*ceteris paribus*) to think 'it shall be the case that-p.'

If, therefore, we can find a connection between

X is disposed (*ceteris paribus*) to enjoy thinking 'it *is the case* that p'

and

X is disposed (*ceteris paribus*) to enjoy thinking 'it *shall be the case* that p,'

we would have succeeded in finding a mediating link between

X is disposed (*ceteris paribus*) to *enjoy thinking* 'it is the case that-p'

and

X is disposed (*ceteris paribus*) to *think* 'it shall be the case that-p,'

---

[10] For the sake of completeness we must make at least a passing reference to disenjoyment. The corresponding question would concern the character of the connection between

X is disposed to disenjoy Y-ing

and

X is disposed not to Y.

[11] Notice that it is not being suggested that everything a person does falls under an action-description which specifies something he is (*ceteris paribus*) disposed to do. We have already seen that not every action is an expression of character.

and, therefore, between desire as the sort of thing that can be *satisfied*, and desire as the sort of thing which, *ceteris paribus*, finds its expression in action.[12]

[39] But what of the additional hypothesis, introduced in the previous paragraph, to the effect that there is a logical connection between

X is disposed (*ceteris paribus*) to enjoy thinking "it *is the case* that-p"

and

X is disposed to enjoy thinking "it *shall be the case* that-p"?

Notice that there is a subtle tense difference between the thinkings involved in the two dispositions. But if we suppose, for the sake of the argument, that tense as such is transparent to enjoyment, i.e. that, *ceteris paribus*, if, at t, X enjoys thinking "it *will be* the case that-p," then at the appropriate time $(t + \Delta t)$ X enjoys thinking "it is *now* the case that-p," and vice versa, then we can focus our attention on the connection between

X is disposed (*ceteris paribus*) to enjoy thinking 'it *will be* the case that-p'

and

X is disposed (*ceteris paribus*) to enjoy thinking 'it *shall be* the case that-p.'

But if *this* is the connection on which the argument hinges, then we are in the neighborhood of an old friend, the problem of the relation between *intention* in the ordinary sense and *belief*, the problem, in other words, of the relation between intending to do something and believing that one will do it.[13]

---

[12] Notice that, if the point made in §31 [Eds.—original reference reads "on p. 120"] is correct, then in addition to the above mediating connection between enjoying thinking that p is the case and intending that p be the case, there would be a direct connection between "S enjoys Y-ing" and "S enjoys thinking I am Y-ing," and hence, by virtue of the connection between "S enjoys Y-ing" and "S is disposed to Y," and between "S is disposed to Y" and "S is disposed to intend 'I shall Y,'" there would be the desired connection between "S is disposed to intend to Y" and "S is disposed to enjoy thinking 'I am Y-ing.'" If we replace the verb "to Y" with "to bring it about that p is the case," the connection becomes that between

X is disposed to think "I shall bring it about that p is the case"
and
X is disposed to enjoy thinking "I am bringing it about that p is the case."

This, however, would at best be a special case of the connection for which we are looking, for one can clearly desire to *bring it about* that p is the case while being indifferent to the idea of p's being the case as such.

[13] The problem is often formulated in terms of the relation between intending to do A and "predicting" that one will do A. But it is clear that predicting is a performance which can occur in the absence of belief, or, to put it in terms of our earlier discussion, to publicly predict that p will be the case is not as such a case of thinking-out-loud that p will be the case. It is, therefore, a mistaken model for thinking covertly that p will be the case.

[40] Now I think it would generally be agreed that intending to do A is *not the same thing* as believing that one will do A. If they *were* the same, then our question would already have been decided in the affirmative, and the argument could stop right here. On the other hand, granted that they are not identical, there is nevertheless a very close relationship between them. For intending to do A involves knowing that, unless one is paralyzed and unless unfavorable circumstances prevent one's minimal action from developing into a doing of A, one *will* do A—that is, of course, unless one changes one's mind before the time of action occurs. Thus, while intending to do A does not *consist in* believing that one will do A, it essentially *includes* it. How is this to be understood?

[41] Notice that coming to intend to do A neither requires a *prior* belief that one will do A, nor is it incompatible with the existence of such a belief. One may believe on inductive grounds[14] that one will, in all probability, do A and then ask oneself, "After all, shall I do A?" and deliberate whether or not to do it.[15]

V. Intending and Believing

[42] As I see it, the key to an understanding of the involvement of belief in intention is a rejection of Hare's neustic-phrastic analysis of the linguistic expression of intentions and beliefs. According to this type of analysis, it will be remembered, the expression of an intention (which Hare mistakenly models on imperative performances) has the form

S shortly being P, please.

Thus reconstructed, it has the phrastic "S being P" in common with the corresponding expression of belief, which joins to it a different neustic and is reconstructed as

---

[14] On the other hand, coming to intend to do A *is* logically incompatible with prior existence of such a belief, if that belief is described as grounded in the decision to do A.
[15] No metaphysics of scientific determinism can contradict the conceptual truth in the framework of persons and what I call the practical modalities—that one could always have done something other than what one did, and, hence, that one can always do something other than what it is highly probable that one will do.
The idea that scientific determinism entails fatalism rests, as I see it, on the confusion between

It could not have been the case, relative to the antecedent state of the universe, that S did A,

which involves the modality of scientific explanation, with

S could not have done (was unable to do) A, although he was neither paralyzed nor were the circumstances unfavorable,

which involves the practical modality "can do" (or "is able to do").

S shortly being P, yes.

[43] Now it is clear that to take this line is to remove the commitment to its being the case that S is shortly P from both intendings-out-loud and the covert mental episodes for which they are the model. As I see it, on the other hand, thinkings-out-loud that S is P are not to be analyzed as a matter of "S being P" plus an assertion sign or affirmative nod. Rather the participial phrase "S being P" is to be understood as a sterilized or "bracketed" form of "S is P," for use in larger contexts where the commitment to its being the case that S is P is to be suspended.

And, as I see it, the context provided by that in the verbal expression of intention which *makes* it an expression of intention *does not suspend this commitment*. If we take the word "shall" to be the specific sign of intention, then I suggest that if any reconstruction is to be done, we reconstruct

S shall be P,
I shall soon do A

as

Shall [S will be P],
Shall [I will soon do A]

—i.e. as involving *not* sterilized phrases such as "S going to be P" or "I doing A shortly," but the corresponding full-blooded indicatives. On this interpretation, an intending is *more than* but *includes* a thinking that something will be the case, just as being under the visual impression that S is P *includes* but is *more than* a thinking that S is P.

[44] But surely, it might be said, one could agree that

S thinks "I *shall* shortly do A"

entails

S thinks "I *will* shortly do A"

(not, of course, vice versa), or even, more generally, that

S thinks "it *shall be the case* that-p"

entails

S thinks "*it will be the case* that-p"

without granting that

S *enjoys* thinking "it will be the case that-p"

entails

S *enjoys* thinking "it shall be the case that-p";

or, to focus the issue decisively, and presupposing what we called the transparency of tenses to enjoyment, without granting that

S is disposed to enjoy thinking "it *is the case* that-p"

entails

S is disposed to enjoy thinking "it *shall be the case* that-p."

[45] The counter I must offer, if my thesis is to stand up, is that "shall" is also transparent to enjoyment. Is there any reason to suppose this? Certainly, if one makes a confusion between an *expression* of intention and the corresponding autobiographical statement which *ascribes* to oneself that intention, thus between

I shall shortly do A

and

I intend to do A shortly,[16]

then the thesis will seem to be false. Roughly, I may approve of doing A, but when the question is raised, I may well not approve of the fact that I so approve. Again, I may enjoy the thought of doing A, but may well not enjoy the thought that I enjoy this thought. This is a special case of the general point that where φ is a predicate applying to state of affairs Σ, it does not follow from the fact that someone enjoys thinking that Σ obtains, that he enjoys thinking that $\varphi(\Sigma)$ obtains. But to all this the proper rejoinder is that "shall" is not a predicate. It is a concept-word only in that broad sense in which words which play essential roles in reasonings can be said to express concepts. The logical "or" is also not a predicate,

---

[16] That this form of words can, and often does, serve the purpose of expressing the intention is granted.

yet it also expresses a concept. On the other hand, "or" and "shall" differ in this key respect: that, whereas the former pertains to the *content* of thought, and is essential to the logical space of predicates, "shall," in spite of its logical role, can be said to be a *manner* rather than a *content* of thought. This is the element of truth in the notion of "shall" as a neustic, and explains why, in spite of its logical role, it is most misleading to say that "shall" expresses a concept.

[46] The central role of "shall" in the rational reconstruction of practical reasoning, and in the logic of ends, means, policies and principles (topics which have been adumbrated in the first section of this essay and which will be further developed in the next section) is the guiding thread of the entire argument.[17] For the moment, however, I must limit myself to the bare assertion that when we enjoy thinking something, the enjoyment is a function of the conceptual content of the thought in the *narrower* sense of content into which "shall" does not enter. *If*, in this sense, "shall" is transparent to enjoyment, and *if* there is the postulated connection between enjoying thoughts and thinking them, then the thesis that desire, defined as a dispositional intention, has a logical connection with both satisfaction and action would be established.

[47] Let me emphasize once again that not all current uses of the term "desire" can be explicated along these lines. As far as I can see, the term is sometimes used in such a way that desires constitute a subspecies of the sort of thing I have been talking about, so that it would remain to spell out the differentia. Sometimes, on the other hand, the term is used to refer to what I would call "hungers" or "appetites"—i.e. dispositions not to intend, but to enjoy or disenjoy Y-ing. But the botanizing of mental states and dispositions is a task of great complexity which, at a sophisticated or critical level, remains largely to be done. Many attempts along these lines have failed because they were based on mistaken theories about the fundamental categories of mentalistic discourse, thus "philosophical behaviorism."

VI. Focal Point: The Practical Syllogism

[48] It will be useful to return to the topic of practical reasoning with an artificially simple case. Let us suppose a situation in which a certain end E can be realized by bringing about state of affairs M_1 which in turn can be brought about by

---

[17] In the above argument as elsewhere in this essay, I have attempted to apply to the practical aspects of mind the neo-classical framework developed in "Empiricism and the Philosophy of Mind" in Herbert Feigl and Michael Scriven, eds., *Minnesota Studies in the Philosophy of Science, Volume I* (Minneapolis: University of Minnesota Press, 1956). Initial steps were taken in this direction in "Imperatives, Intentions and the Logic of 'Ought'" in *Methodos* Vol. III (1956), 227–268; reprinted with substantial revisions in Hector-Neri Castañeda and George Nakhnikian, eds., *Morality and the Language of Conduct* (Detroit: Wayne State University Press, 1963). [Eds.—The latter, IIOR, is chapter 14 of this volume.]

performing minimal action A_1. Let us also suppose that there is only one available alternative course of action, initiated by minimal action A_2, which would prevent the occurrence of E, by bringing about M_2. Finally let us assume that, to the person doing the deliberating, everything but E is indifferent.

[49] From an analytical point of view, two stages can be distinguished in the deliberation. The first lays out the basic implications involved. Indeed we have, according to our assumptions, two pairs of equivalences:

E if and only if M_1 ~E if and only if M_2
M_1 if and only if A_1 M_2 if and only if A_2

Hovering in the background, we have the intention which finds its expression in

Shall [E].

The second stage of deliberation might be called the summative stage. In it the various features of two alternative courses of actions are brought together logically to be evaluated as wholes. Thus the above equivalences generate the two summative implications:

$A_1 \leftrightarrow E \cdot M_1 \cdot A_1$
$A_2 \leftrightarrow {\sim}E \cdot M_2 \cdot A_2$

[50] Given the assumption made above that everything mentioned but E is indifferent, it follows that our deliberator prefers Σ_1 to Σ_2 (where Σ_1 represents $E \cdot M_1 \cdot A_1$ and Σ_2 represents ${\sim}E \cdot M_2 \cdot A_2$)—i.e. that he is disposed to think

Shall [$\Sigma_1 \cdot {\sim}\Sigma_2$]

rather than

Shall [$\Sigma_2 \cdot {\sim}\Sigma_1$].

It should also be noted that relative to the equivalences specified in the first stage,

${\sim}\Sigma_2$, i.e. ${\sim}({\sim}E \cdot M_2 \cdot A_2)$

is necessarily equivalent to

$({\sim}{\sim}E) \cdot {\sim}M_2 \cdot {\sim}A_2$.

212   THE METAPHYSICS OF PRACTICE

Thus the next stage of the deliberation can be represented as the categorical intention

Shall [E • M_1 • A_1 • (~~E) • ~M_2 • ~A_2].

It is particularly important to note that it is the complex intention which has just been analyzed, rather than the simpler intention

Shall [E],

which serves as the major premise in the practical syllogism in which the deliberation culminates.

[51] The form of this syllogism is a simple one, which rests upon the fact that

'Shall [X • Y]' implies 'Shall [X]'.

Thus the "syllogism" is simply

Shall [E • M_1 • A_1 • (~~E) • ~M_2 • ~A_2]
Therefore, Shall [A_1].

[52] Although E can properly be said to be the end of the action in which this deliberation culminates, 'Shall [E]' is not the major premise of the relevant practical syllogism. The importance of this point stands out clearly in more complicated cases of deliberation. As our second example, let us consider a case which differs from the above in that M_1 and M_2 are not indifferent, but positively valued.

[53] The first stage of the deliberation remains as before, as does the summative stage. It is when preference turns one of the envisaged incompatible courses of action into an intention that the difference appears.

[54] Let us suppose that although E, M_1 and M_2 are all positively valued by the deliberator, he prefers

~E • M_2 • A_2

to

E • M_1 • A_1.

This means that, in the absence of any restructuring of the situation, the deliberation will culminate in a practical syllogism, of which the major premise is

Shall [~E • M_2 • A_2 • ~E • ~M_1 • ~A_1*],

and which has as its conclusion

Shall [A_2].

[55] If, to tie up our present discussion with our early remarks on volition, we suppose that this conclusion has, from the standpoint of a finer-grained analysis, the form

Shall [I will do A_2 in ten minutes],

then, *ceteris paribus*, this intention, which can be characterized as a *decision*, will, by virtue of meshing in with the agent's sense of temporal location, develop into the volition

Shall [I will *now* do A_2],

which volition is the initial stage of doing A_2.

[56] We have often been warned against thinking that the end (in the sense of end-in-view) of an action is that which comes last in its envisaged scenario. In avoiding this trap, one might make the opposite mistake of supposing that the end of the action is the state of affairs specified by what we have found to be the major premise of the practical reasoning which culminates in the action. This, however, would not correspond to the way in which we actually use the term "end." The latter seems rather to stand for the combination of states of affairs ingredient in the scenario which carries the burden of the preference.

[57] Thus the end (or purpose) of doing A_2 in the second example is *to bring about M_2*. If we add to the latter phrase the qualification "*in spite of* preventing E and M_1" we have what is often called the *intention* of the action, but "intention" in this sense must be distinguished from a broader (and technical) use, in which it refers as well to states of affairs to which the agent is indifferent, but which he believes to be involved in the relevant implications. In the latter sense, the intention of the agent can be described as that of bringing about ~ E • M_2 by doing A_2, rather than bringing about E • M_1 by doing A_1.

[58] The above analysis permits a brief aside on the logical relation of

X desires that-p

---

* [Eds.—Correction of
~A_2
in original printing.]

to action. It suggests that, whatever a more complete analysis would yield,

X desires that-p

logically implies

if X believes that he can bring about, in a way to which he is indifferent, M, to which he is indifferent, and which is the immediate necessary and sufficient condition of its being the case that-p, *and* X prefers no available alternative course of action, *then* X intends the realization of M.

[59] A third example adds relatively little that is new, but it is perhaps worth considering because it prepares the way for an exploration of more realistic cases. Suppose this time two "ends," E_1 and E_2, such that

$E_1 \leftrightarrow M_1$* $E_2 \leftrightarrow M_3$
$M_1 \leftrightarrow M_2$ $M_3 \leftrightarrow M_4$
$M_2 \leftrightarrow A_1$ $M_4 \leftrightarrow A_2$

where A_1 and A_2 are incompatible. The deliberation is sparked by the questions 'Shall [I will bring about E_1]?' 'Shall [I will bring about E_2]?' These questions are themselves generated by the thoughts 'Shall [E_1]?' and 'Shall [E_2]?', together with a recognition of the impossibility of realizing both of the states of affairs in question.

[60] This time the summative stage is represented by the questions

Shall [$E_1 \bullet M_1 \bullet M_2 \bullet A_1 \bullet \sim E_2 \bullet \sim M_3 \bullet \sim M_4 \bullet \sim A_2$]?
Shall [$E_2 \bullet M_3 \bullet M_4 \bullet A_2 \bullet \sim E_1 \bullet \sim M_1 \bullet \sim M_2 \bullet \sim A_1$]?

That is, schematically,

Shall [$\Sigma_1 \bullet \sim \Sigma_2$]?   Shall [$\Sigma_2 \bullet \sim \Sigma_1$]?

Suppose that the preference is Σ_1; then

Shall [$\Sigma_1 \bullet \sim \Sigma_2$]

becomes available to serve as a premise from which follows the conclusion

---

* [Eds.—Correction of
$E \leftrightarrow M$
in original printing.]

THOUGHT AND ACTION   215

Shall [A_1].

Since, in this context, the person deliberating thinks that E_2 implies A_2 and, indeed, that $\sim A_2$ implies $\sim E_2$, and since the major premise of the practical syllogism implies not only

Shall [A_1]

but

Shall [$\sim A_2$],

the reasoning

Shall [$\sim A_2$]
Therefore, Shall [$\sim E_2$]

is available. It is the immediate availability of this reasoning which supports principle IIIa (§15 above*). Needless to say, when the period of deliberation is over and the implications of E_2 are out of mind, 'Shall [E_2]' may well tend to reassert itself. We may then well desire *in abstracto* that which we have earlier decided to forgo in favor of an incompatible alternative.

[61] The next type of case I shall consider, but only by way of indicating broad lines of strategy, concerns action on policy. The fundamental point I wish to make is that it is essential not to assimilate action on policy to using means to achieve an end. Thus, one might think that, in action on policy, the fact that

On all C-occasions I will do A

logically implies

On this C-occasion I will do A

makes my doing A on this C-occasion a logically necessary means to the end of my doing A on every C-occasion. There is, indeed, such a thing as intending to bring about a series of like events. Thus, I might want to win every one of a series of games; to bring about *this* end, winning each game *is* a logically necessary means. But this is not an example of action on a policy.

---

* [Eds.—Original reference reads "p. 113 above."]

[62] As a first approximation, we can say that a person acts on the policy of doing A when he is in C, if, with respect to every situation which promises or threatens to be of kind C, he is disposed to think

Shall [if I am in C, I will do A].

Notice that the universality comes into the description of the agent's propensity rather than into the content of the particular intendings which it is his propensity to have.

[63] Notice, again, that the intendings which manifest a policy are *underivative* intendings. That is to say, the propensity in question is not that of coming to think

Shall [if I am in C, I will now do A]

as a conclusion from another intention.

[64] The implementation of policies involves practical reasoning, but the intention which expresses the policy is not itself the conclusion of practical reasoning. It is essential not to confuse the fact that

Shall [I will espouse policy P],

which expresses the intention to acquire a certain propensity, can well be the conclusion of a practical inference, with the mistaken idea that the intention which defines the policy must therefore be derivative. A means-end argument can justify

Shall [I will espouse policy P],

without requiring that the policy intention

Shall [If I am in C, I will do A]

be derivable from another intention in accordance with an implication of the form

(Shall [X]) implies (Shall [If I am in C, I will do A]).

[65] Thus the difference between an intending which constitutes a whim and one which expresses a policy is not that the former might *begin* with

Shall [If I am in C, I will do A],

as an underived intending, whereas the latter would begin with

Shall [All of my C-occasions will be occasions on which I do A]

and move thence to the conclusion

Shall [If I am in C, I will do A];

the difference is rather (at least in first approximation) that, although the intending is the same in each case, the whim intention does not manifest a general propensity to have underived intentions of this kind.

[66] A simple case of a conflict between achieving an end and carrying out a policy can thus be represented as follows:

    Shall [E]*   Shall [If I am in C, I will do A_2]

Relative to being in C: Relative to being in C:

    $E \to M$ (If I am in C, I will do A_2) $\leftrightarrow$ (I will do A_2)
    $M \to A_1$

I am in C   I am in C

    $E \leftrightarrow E \bullet M \bullet A_1$ (If I am in C, I will do A_2) $\leftrightarrow$ (I will do A_2)
    $\Sigma_1 = E \bullet M \bullet A_1$ $\Sigma_2 = $ (If C, then A_2) $\bullet A_2$

The summing-up stage can be represented as:

    Shall [$E \bullet M \bullet A_1 \bullet \sim$(if C, then A_2) $\bullet \sim A_2$]?
    Shall [(if C, then A_2) $\bullet A_2 \bullet \sim E \bullet \sim M \bullet \sim A_1$]?

[67] If the person in question does A_1, we would regard this as a good reason for saying that, when the chips were down and he was in C, he preferred bringing about E by bringing about M by doing A_1 to doing that which conforms to this policy in that kind of circumstance.

[68] We have arrived at the point where, to say anything more of interest, one would have to say a great deal. I have in mind the general topic of action on principle. While the latter grows naturally out of the topic of action on policy, it requires an exploration of the relation of the forms of thought in terms of which

---

* [Eds.—Correction of
Shall E
in original printing.]

individuals believe and intend, to the fact that they are members of a community. This is a large and difficult area which far transcends the limits of this essay. I have barely scratched the surface on another occasion,[18] and the following remarks are intended only to indicate the general character of the relevant distinctions as they relate to the problem at hand. The theme is an Hegelian one in modern dress, a transposition into another key of his concept of Objective Spirit. It concerns the relation of "we" to "I" and postulates a form of thought which is intending *as one of us* or, as I put it in the essay referred to above,

Shall$_{we}$ [X],

as contrasted with

Shall$_I$ [X]

[69] The point is *not* that groups can, in a legitimate sense, be said to intend. It is the more radical one that individuals can intend *sub specie communitatis*. Thus, an *individual* can have an intention of the form

Shall$_{we}$ [X].

And the members of a group can have common intentions not only by virtue of the fact that each thinks *sub specie individualitatis*

Shall$_I$ [——],

but by virtue of the fact that each thinks *sub specie communitatis*

Shall$_{we}$ [——].

[70] "I" and "we" come into the *form* as well as the *content* of intending. We need an expression that is related to "We intend that—" as "shall" is recognized to be related to "I intend that—."

[71] I shall not attempt to carry this through on the present occasion. The essential point is that after "we"-intentions have been botanized in terms of such notions as policy, means-end, etc., and the concept of practical reasoning has been expanded to include them, it turns out that the concept of preference must also be

---

[18] "Imperatives, Intentions and the Logic of 'Ought'," in Hector-Neri Castañeda and George Nakhnikian, eds., *Morality and the Language of Conduct* (Detroit: Wayne State University Press, 1963). [Eds.—See chapter 14 of this volume.]

expanded to include not only the dimension in which policies conflict with ends, but that in which a person's answer to the questions

Shall$_I$ [$\Sigma_i \bullet \sim\Sigma_j$]?
Shall$_I$ [$\Sigma_j \bullet \sim\Sigma_i$]?

breaks or coincides with

Shall$_{we}$ [$\Sigma_i \bullet \sim\Sigma_j$].

8
Metaphysics and the Concept of a Person

[I*]

[1] In the first edition "Paralogisms of Pure Reason" Kant suggests that "the substance which in relation to outer sense possesses extension" might be "in itself the possessor of thoughts and that these thoughts can by means of its own inner sense be consciously represented." On this hypothesis, which is a purely speculative one, "the thesis that only souls (as particular kinds of substances) think would have to be given up, and we should have to fall back on the common expression that *men* think, that is, that the very same being which, as outer appearance is extended is, in itself, internally a subject and is not composite, but is simple and thinks." (A359–60)

[2] Kant, of course, does not commit himself to this hypothesis. Indeed it is a part of his methodology to advance alternative hypotheses concerning things as they are in themselves, which hypotheses can be neither refuted nor established by speculative reason, as a means of keeping what he calls dogmatic metaphysics in check. Thus, another such speculative hypothesis would be a dualistic one to the effect that as things in themselves, persons consist of a real mind and a real body, the latter appearing in perception as a complex material thing. In the course of his critique of traditional metaphysical theories of mind and body, he suggests still other hypotheses that are of even greater interest, a theme to which I shall return.

[3] To set the stage for an appreciation of Kant's insights, both critical and constructive, let us take as our point of departure his reference to the "common expression" that *men* think, that is, "that the very same being which is...extended is...a subject...and thinks." This "common expression" is, of course, characteristic of the Aristotelian tradition, extending from antiquity to the Oxford Aristotelianism being reborn before our very eyes. According to this tradition it is the same thing, a *man* or, as we now say (since the equality of the sexes has moved into the higher levels of ideological superstructure), a *person*, which both thinks and runs.

---

* [Eds.—In the original published version, the section numbers are omitted. However, they are present in Sellars's typescript, and Sicha included the section numbers when he anthologized the essay in KTM. Thus, we have included the section numbers in brackets. The relevant typescript is document 31735062219898, Box 34, Folder 3, Wilfrid S. Sellars Papers, 1899–1990, ASP.1991.01, Archives of Scientific Philosophy, Archives & Special Collections, University of Pittsburgh Library System.

METAPHYSICS AND THE CONCEPT OF A PERSON   221

[4] Even a Cartesian dualist, of course, can acknowledge that it is one and the same thing, a person, which runs and thinks, for sameness is ubiquitous. Thus it is one and the same thing, a family, which gets and spends. But perhaps the family gets by the husband getting and spends by the wife spending. The Aristotelian counterpart would be the bachelor who does both the getting and the spending. The dualist thinks of the person as a family or team, a mind that thinks and a body that runs. The Aristotelian, on the other hand, construes reference to minds as reference to persons qua having those states and capacities which are distinctive of rational animals, and references to human bodies as references to persons qua having those states and capacities by virtue of which they belong to the larger family of corporeal substances. The Aristotelian can grant, then, that there are minds and bodies without being in any more interesting sense a dualist. References to minds and bodies are *façons de parler*. They have a derivative existence or "mode of being."

[5] It is worth pausing to note that since one must, as Aristotle himself emphasizes, be careful to distinguish between priority in the order of knowing or conception, and priority in the order of being, a dualist could grant that our primary concept of a person is Aristotelian, and yet insist that when we explore the behavior of the things to which we apply this concept, we discover facts that force us to postulate a dualism of minds and bodies. A useful parallel is provided by the development of microphysical theory. It is clear that in the order of knowing concepts pertaining to perceptual objects are primary. Yet, from the standpoint of Scientific Realism, perceptual objects are derivative and secondary—however these terms are to be construed—in the order of being.

[6] Considerations of many different types have been advanced to support dualism—ranging from the interpretation of dreams and religious experience to abstruse metaphysical arguments. In the modern period, the mechanistic revolution in physical science provided the chief motive power for mind-body dualism. If the body is a cloud of particles, must not the unitary thinking, feeling subject be a distinct existent—perhaps, as some have thought, like a captain in his ship; perhaps, as others thought, like a dog tied to a chariot.

[7] My aim here is to do some hard-core metaphysics. I shall therefore begin by taking the Aristotelian framework seriously and assume that persons are, in the toughest of senses, single logical subjects: that persons are in no sense systems of logical subjects. If it is objected that according to well-confirmed scientific theory persons are, at least in part, made up of molecules, and as such are systems of individual things, I shall take temporary refuge in the familiar line that such scientific objects are "conceptual fictions"—useful symbolic devices.

[8] As for such perceptible "parts" as arms, legs, etc., your true Aristotelian construes them as merely potential parts, much as the two sides of a uniformly colored expanse are potential parts—a line could be drawn dividing it in two. And just as statements can be made about the two sides of the expanse without presupposing that it is actually divided in two, so, on strict Aristotelian principles,

statements can be made about the arms or legs of a person without presupposing that they are distinct individual things in their own right. Of course, the arms or legs can be made really distinct from the person, by cutting them off; but then, as Aristotle points out, they would no longer be arms or legs in the primary sense—any more than a corpse is a man.

[9] A person, then, according to the Aristotelian analysis, is a single individual which does not have subordinate individuals as its parts. Its unity is not that of a system. A person is a complex individual, of course, but his complexity is a matter of the many predicates applying to that one individual who is the person.

[10] Identity or sameness is one of the least informative of concepts. As Bishop Butler pointed out long ago, "everything is what it is and not another thing." Thus, even if a person were a system he would be self-identical, for anything—even a system—is self-identical. Consider identity through time. Philosophers often attempt to distinguish between a "loose" and a "strict" sense of identity. The language is misguided, although the contrast they have in mind is sound. As far as I can see, to insist that a person is literally identical through time—as the Aristotelians do—is simply to insist that a person is not a system of successive "person-stages." On the other hand, even if a person were a series of person-stages, he would still be self-identical through time, for he would be the same series with respect to each moment of his existence.

[11] It has sometimes been argued that anything which endures through time must be a series. If this is presented not as revisionary metaphysics, but as an analysis of the conceptual framework we learned at our mother's knee, it is sheer confusion. One such argument, recently elaborated by Gustav Bergmann,[1] is interesting as an example of how mistaken a metaphysical argument can be even when buttressed by all the technical resources of the new logic. It has the form of a *reductio ad absurdum* and goes as follows:

(1) Suppose (contrary to fact) a Substance S—a logical subject of which the identity through time is *not* that of a series—and suppose that S becomes successively red and green.
(2) Then redness and greenness would both be true of S.
(3) But redness and greenness are incompatible.
(4) To be coherent, then, we must say that redness is true of S at one moment or period of time t_1 and that greenness is true of S at another moment or period of time t_2.
(5) Thus, to describe S coherently we must mention moments or periods of time.
(6) But [argues Bergmann] moments or periods of time are conceptual constructions and must not be mentioned in a list of ontological ultimates.

---

[1] 'Some Reflections on Time,' in *Meaning and Existence*, University of Wisconsin Press, Madison, 1960.

(7) Hence basic statements about the world must not mention moments or periods of time.
(8) But, according to the substance theory, this is exactly what basic statements about substances must do.
(9) Hence the theory of substance commits one to a false ontology and must be rejected.

Roughly, a substance ontology is committed to a "container" or "absolute" theory of time.

[12] The flaw in this argument is that, in its attempt to formulate a substance ontology within the tidy language of *Principia Mathematica*, it overlooks the role of tenses and temporal connectives in actual usage. Thus, to take account of the incompatibility of redness and greenness, a substance theorist is not forced to move directly to propositions of the form

S is red at t_1
S is green at t_2

let alone to such supposititious PMese counterparts as

Red (S, t_1)
Green (S, t_2).

The latter, indeed, are counter-intuitive, for they present colors as relations between substances and times, rather than as qualitative characteristics. If a substance theorist were forced to make this move, he would indeed be in trouble.

[13] If, on the other hand, we introduce the relational predicates 'red at' and 'green at', and write:

Red at (S, t_1)
Green at (S, t_2)

we see intuitively that these locutions presuppose the propriety of the nonrelational forms

Red (S)
Green (S).

But is this not to admit that the substance theorist cannot solve the incompatibility problem without countenancing times as ontological ultimates and doing violence to the intrinsic grammar of color predicates?

[14] The answer is "no," for he needs only point to the availability of such forms as

S is red
S will be green

which preserve the nonrelational character of color predicates.

[15] It might be objected to this that sentences containing the tensed verbs 'is,' 'was,' and 'will be' are covertly relational. Thus one might be tempted to construe

S is red

as

S be red *now*

where 'be' is a "tenseless" (or "pure") copula; and the latter, in turn, as

Red(S, *now*)

and as unfolding into

Red(S, t_1) and Simul(t_1, context of utterance).

Similarly, one might construe

S will be green

as

S be green after *now*

and as unfolding into

(Et) Green (S, t) and After(t, context of utterance).

But once one sees that the job done by sentences involving tokens of 'now' requires *not* that they *mention* a relation to the context of utterance, but rather that they *stand in* a relation to the situation they describe, it becomes clear that the same is true of the tensed verbs 'is,' 'was,' and 'will be.' The concept of a pure tenseless copula is a myth—at least as far as our ordinary conceptual framework is concerned.²

[16] Again, the substance theorist can point to the related forms

S was red before it was green
S is red and will be green
S will be green after it is red.

It is surely a mistake to assume that 'before,' 'while,' 'after,' and other temporal connectives³ are to be analysed in terms of a reference to moments or periods of time, as we saw it to be a mistake to assume that 'is,' 'was,' and 'will be' are to be analysed in terms of a tenseless copula and a reference to a relation.

[17] Thus it is open to the Aristotelian to agree with Bergmann that moments and periods of time are conceptual constructions, but to claim that they are constructible within the framework of a substance ontology in terms of such concepts as before, after, while—rather than in terms of relations between events, where "event" is taken to be the basic ontological category.

[18] Even more transparent is a closely related argument for the thesis that the identity of a person is the identity of a series. It involves a confusion between a person and his history. The history of a person is the sequence of events in which he is relevantly involved. There clearly are such things as events; and the events in which a person participates *do* constitute a series. But if we look at one such event, say,

the event of Caesar crossing the Rubicon

it becomes apparent that what can be said by referring to the event in which Caesar participated can also be put without such reference. Thus, instead of saying,

The event of Caesar crossing the Rubicon took place

we can simply say,

Caesar crossed the Rubicon.

---

² That there might be a use for such a copula in a contrived conceptual framework is argued in 'Time and the World Order,' in *Minnesota Studies in the Philosophy of Science*, University of Minnesota Press, Minneapolis, 1962, pp. 527–616*. For a discussion of the copula 'is' as a pseudotenseless copula equivalent to the 'be' introduced by the equivalence 'S be $P \equiv$ S was P or S is P or S will be P,' see p. 533. [*Eds.: In the original printing, the publication date is 1963, and the page range is indicated to be 577–93. We have corrected both. The final page reference—to p. 533—is correct in the original.]

³ I speak of them as connectives, for unlike relation words they are not contexts calling for abstract singular terms (e.g. that-clauses). A broad theory of temporal and other nonlogical connectives is urgently needed. See pp. 550–51 of the essay cited above.

[19] Indeed, it is clear that in ordinary discourse event-talk is in some sense derivative from substance-talk. If one did not understand the simple subject-predicate sentence

Socrates ran

one could not understand the more complex locution

(The event of) Socrates running took place.

The latter presupposes the former in a very straightforward sense. Indeed, it contains it, with a slight grammatical modification.

[20] To appreciate the sense in which the latter statement contains the former, as well as to understand how the two statements can be strongly equivalent without having the same sense, an analogy will help. Consider the pair of statements

Snow is white
It is true that snow is white.

These statements are strongly equivalent, but not identical in meaning. Furthermore, the second statement in some sense contains the former. (In a literal sense it contains the sign design of the former.)

[21] I have argued in a number of places[4] that '-ity,' '-hood,' '-ness,' and 'that' (as used to form propositional clauses) are to be regarded as quoting devices which (a) form sortal predicates which apply to expression tokens in any language or conceptual scheme which are doing in that language or conceptual scheme that which is done in our language by the design with which they are conjoined; (b) turn these sortal predicates into distributive singular terms. Thus "andness" is to be construed as 'the •and•' where '•and•' is the sortal predicate formed from the design *and*. On this analysis the singular term

that snow is white

becomes

the •snow is white•

and

That snow is white is true

---

[4] Most recently in *Science and Metaphysics*, London 1968, chapter 3.

becomes

The •snow is white• is true.

[22] Since statements which have distributive singular terms as subjects

The lion is tawny

can be "reduced" to statements which have the sortal predicate from which the singular term is constructed as their grammatical subjects,

Lions are tawny

the above analysis enables the reduction of

That snow is white is true

to

•snow is white•s are true

which tells us that in a relevant mode of correctness

•snow is white•s are correctly assertible

i.e. authorizes one, so to speak, to step down from one's metalinguistic stilts and *use* a •snow is white•, which is, in our language, to use a 'snow is white.' My generic term for such assertibility is "semantic assertibility" (abbreviated to "S-assertibility").[5]

[23] To focus these considerations on our original topic of events, notice first that there are a number of locutions which, used in appropriate contexts, are equivalent to the predicate 'true.' Thus:

That snow is white is the case.

Of particular interest are examples in which it seems appropriate to take seriously the prima facie tensed character of the copula in 'is the case.' Consider, for example, the statements

---

[5] For an elaboration of this account of truth see *Science and Metaphysics*, chapter 4.

That Socrates runs is the case (right now).
That Socrates runs was the case (yesterday at 2 PM).
That Socrates runs will be the case (tomorrow at 3 PM).

The suggestion I wish to make is that 'is taking place,' 'took place,' and 'will take place' are to be construed as specialized truth-predicates that are used in connection with statements in which the predicate is a verb standing for a kind of change, activity, or process. The most interesting case, as we shall see, is that of statements in which the predicate stands for a kind of action.

[24] To return to our example of event talk, the statement

(The event of) Socrates running took place

has, in the first place, the form

That Socrates runs was true

and, more penetratingly considered, the form

The •Socrates runs• was true.

A further step in the analysis (though by no means the final one) takes us to

The •Socrates runs• was S-assertible

and

•Socrates runs•s were S-assertible.

To develop this analysis into a full-fledged theory of event-talk would take us into problems pertaining to quantifying into statements containing abstract singular terms. My present purpose has been to sketch a strategy for explaining the sense in which event-talk is dependent on substance-talk, and the sense in which statements about events taking place can be strongly equivalent to statements about substances changing, without being synonymous with the latter. It may be possible, as I have indicated above, to construct a conceptual framework and a use of 'event' in which events are more basic than their counterparts in the substance framework of ordinary discourse. But to construct such a framework would not be to analyse the concept of event which we actually employ.[6]

---

[6] In the essay referred to in note 2, however, I failed to appreciate the kinship of event-expressions with abstract singular terms. With this exception, the argument of the essay and the distinctions it draws still seem to me to stand up reasonably well.

[II]

[25] Having taken the metaphysical bit into our teeth, let us turn to issues more directly related to the topic of persons. Consider, for example, the endless perplexities which have arisen about the ownership-relation between persons and their "experiences." The fundamental point to be made is of a piece with the considerations advanced above: Philosophers should be wary of verbal nouns. Failure to do so has generated about as much bad metaphysics as has been sponsored by 'is' and 'not.' Words like 'sensation,' 'feeling,' 'thought*,' and 'impression' in such contexts as

Jones has a sensation (feeling, etc.)

have mesmerized philosophers into wondering what Jones' mind is, as contrasted with his sensations, feelings, etc. If Jones qua mind is a haver of "experiences," then, since to be a haver is to have a relational property, must not the mind be a *mere* haver—in other words a "bare particular"? Are we not confronted by a choice between accepting bare particulars[7] with ontological piety, and avoiding them at the price of committing ourselves to a "bundle theory" of the self?

[26] Since the above dialectic is a special case of a more general dialectic pertaining to subject-predicate statements, we find philosophers pressing their brows in anguish over the dilemma of choosing between "things are havers (bare particulars)" and "things are bundles of what they are said to have." The fundamental mistake, of course, is that of construing subject-predicate statements as relational. It is that of construing, for example,

Tom is tall

as expressing a relation between two objects, Tom and tallness. The issues involved are complex, and I cannot do justice to them here.[8] I shall simply point out that if we consider the contexts listed at the beginning of this section, it is surely implausible to take such statements as

Tom has a feeling

---

* [Eds.—Correction of 'though' in original printing.]
[7] The term 'bare particular' has come to be ambiguous. Traditionally it was used in connection with the view that ordinary things (e.g. horses) are composites of a *this*-factor and a *such*-factor, where the *this* factor was conceived to be a pure substratum in the sense that it has no empirical character, but only the metaphysical character of standing in the *having* relation (or *nexus*) to a *such* factor. Neither the *this* nor the *such* factor would be the horse.
  Recently, however, the term has come to be used in connection with the view that particularity is an irreducible category, i.e. that particulars are not "complexes of universals." To accept bare particulars in the first sense is to accept them in the second, but not vice versa.
[8] I have examined it in some detail in chapter 7 of *Science, Perception and Reality*, London 1963. See also *Philosophical Perspectives*, Springfield, Ill., 1967, chapter 6.

to be anything but a derivative (but legitimate) way of saying what is said adequately and nonrelationally by such statements as

Tom feels...

Thus, in general,

Tom has a V-tion,

where 'V-tion' is a verbal noun for a kind of "experience," would be a derivative (but legitimate) way of saying what is said adequately and nonrelationally by

Tom Vs.

Clearly there is a strong equivalence between

Tom feels

and

Tom has a feeling

and, in general, between

Tom Vs (e.g. Tom senses)

and

Tom has a V-tion (e.g. Tom has a sensation),

but this is no more a sign of synonymy than is the strong equivalence between

Snow is white

and

It is true that snow is white.

Clearly, 'Snow is white' is, in a straightforward sense, more basic than 'It is true that snow is white.' The strategy employed above with respect to events suggests that the sense in which 'Tom Vs' is more basic than 'Tom has a V-tion' is essentially the same. According to such an analysis,

Tom has a sensation

would be reconstructed as

That he senses is true of Tom.

We have already construed *events* as a special kind of proposition, and *taking place* as a special form of truth. It is but a small step along this path to construe an object's *participating in* an event as a special case of an attribute being true of the object.

[27] Now it might be objected that what I have been advancing is interesting and possibly even true—but irrelevant. It might be conceded that the relational locution

Tom has a V-tion

can, in many cases, be "reduced" to the "more basic"

Tom Vs

but urged that the latter statement is itself—when made explicit—relational. In other words it might be urged that the basic thesis of the relational theory of "experiencing" concerns *not* the metaphysical relation of *having*, but the *empirical* relations of feeling, sensing, thinking, etc. For even if we turn our attention from

Tom has a V-tion (sensation)

to

Tom Vs (senses)

we see, on reflection, that the latter is equivalent to

Tom senses *something*

which, prima facie, has the form

(Ex) Senses(Tom,x).

[28] Here is where the so-called "adverbial" theory of the objects of sensation becomes relevant. For, joining in the move from

Tom has a sensation of a red triangle

to

Tom senses a red triangle

the adverbial theory denies that the latter has the form

(Ex) x is a red triangle and Tom senses x.

To take a more intuitive example, the adverbial theory denies that

Tom feels pain

has the form

Feels(Tom,pain)

but interprets it rather as

Tom feels-pain

and, thus, ascribes to it the form

Tom Vs.

The example is more intuitive because we are struck by the rough equivalence of 'Tom feels pain' to 'Tom hurts.'
[29] To make this move is to construe 'pain,' in the above context, as a special kind of adverb; one which modified 'feels' to form a verbal expression which stands to the latter as "determinate" to "determinable": roughly, as species to genus.
[30] If the verb in

Tom feels pain

is 'feels-pain' thus construed, then in the context

Tom has a feeling of pain

the 'of pain' must be construed as the corresponding adjective which makes a specific verbal noun out of the verbal noun root 'feeling.'
[31] The adverbial theory views such verbs as 'feels,' 'experiences,' 'senses'— and, as we shall see, 'thinks'—as generic verbs, and the expressions formed from

them by "adding a reference to the objects felt, experienced, etc." as specific verbs. It follows from this that in a perspicuous language, we would not use the generic verb in forming its species, but, instead, say

> Tom pains

rather than

> Tom feels pain

just as we say

> The book is rectangular

rather than

> The book is rectangularly shaped.

In this perspicuous language we would not say,

> Tom senses a red triangle

but

> Tom a-red-triangles

where the verb 'a-red-triangle' stands for that kind of sensing which is brought about in standard conditions, and in standard perceivers, by the presence of a literally red and triangular object.

[32] In the case of conceptual activity, on the assumption that thinking is to be construed as "inner speech,"[9] parallel considerations lead to parallel results. In the first place,

> S has the thought that snow is white

or

> The thought that snow is white occurs to S

---

[9] For a discussion of the concept of thinking as a quasi-theoretical concept modeled on the concept of meaningful verbal behavior, see chapter 5 of *Science, Perception and Reality*; also chapter 6 of *Science and Metaphysics*.

would be the higher-order equivalence of

 S thinks (i.e. is thinking) that snow is white.

And, in the second place, the latter statement would not have the form

 Thinks(S, that snow is white)

but rather

 S Vs.

For 'thinks that snow is white' would stand to 'thinks' as specific verb to generic verb. Here, again, we are to construe the expression following the verb as a special kind of adverb. And, as before, in a perspicuous language the verb root 'thinks' would drop out of the specific verbs. What would the perspicuous specific verb be? The answer lies in our previous account of abstract singular terms as classifying expressions. There we abstracted from the fact that the primary mode of being of language was nonparroting verbal activity by one who knows the language, and construed

 That snow is white

as

 The •snow is white•

where '•snow is white•' applies to any expression in any language which does the job done in ours by the design *snow is white*. But, as we must now realize, the primary mode of being of "expressions" is people speaking (writing, etc.). Thus what we are really classifying are linguistic activities. To take this into account, instead of saying

 'Schnee ist weiss's (in German) are •snow is white•s

we should say

 'Schnee ist weiss'ings (in G) are •snow is white•ings

and once we have these verbal nouns we are led to form the corresponding verbs. Thus when all the proper moves have been made,

Jones said that snow is white

becomes

Jones •snow is white•ed.

Parallel considerations lead to parallel results in the case of thinkings as inner speech. Thus,

The thought that snow is white occurred to Jones

which is doubly relational in appearance, turns out to have as its foundation the nonrelational state of affairs expressed by

Jones •snow is white•ed[10].

[33] The above considerations will play a crucial role in the argument to follow. As a preliminary means of grasping their significance, consider the following objection often raised against Descartes. It is argued that instead of claiming that

I think (*cogito*)

formulates a piece of primary knowledge, Descartes should have given this role to something like

This thought exists.

To get the existence of the "I," then, we would have to make the inferential move

This thought exists
So, a thinker (i.e. the thinker of this thought) exists.

"I" would then be identified as the thinker who 'has" the thought. To start down this path is obviously to raise the question: what would justify this inference?
[34] From the perspective we have reached we can see that this objection overlooks the fact that reference to thoughts is derivative from references to thinkers thinking. Thus the fundamental form of the mental is not

---

[10] The dot-quoted expressions in the context of inner speech are analogical counterparts of dot-quoted expressions in the context of speech proper. For an elaboration of this point see chapter 6 of *Science and Metaphysics*.

There are thoughts (or, more generally, representations)

but rather as Kant saw,

x thinks (represents),

of which a special case is

I think (represent).

[III]

[35] Before I turn my attention to Kant's treatment of the "I" and the relevance of this treatment to the views I have been developing, I must enlarge my canvass to take into account other features of the Aristotelian metaphysics of the person. The theme I have particularly in mind is that of causation.

[36] Off hand, one would be inclined to say that Richard Taylor belongs in the mainstream of the perennial tradition, and, indeed, his recent study of *Action and Purpose* contains much to warm the hearts of those who seek to defend classical insights against the dogmas of reductionist empiricism and naturalism. Yet in spite of the many positive virtues of his analysis, the total effect must be counted a failure, largely because of the inadequate account of causation on which it rests. Actually, this comment is a bit unfair, since Taylor has many interesting and perceptive things to say about causation. The trouble is that he overlooks the ambiguity of the term, the fact that it stands for a whole family of concepts. Once he commits himself to a paradigm it becomes the paradigm of all causality and blurs key distinctions.

[37] One familiar sense of "cause" is embodied in locutions of the form

X caused Y to Z by doing A

e.g.

Jones caused the match to light by striking it.

This concept of causation can be called "interventionist." In its primary form, as the illustration suggests, the cause *is* a person and a person causes something to happen by *doing* something. This concept, by a metaphorical extension, is applied to inanimate objects, thus

The stone caused the glass to shatter by striking it.

The extended use, as a frozen metaphor, is invaluable, but philosophers have often sensed in it the original life. This accounts for the traditional conviction that, strictly speaking, only persons can be causes.

[38] Now I take it as obvious that persons are or can be causes in this sense of "cause." Let us, therefore, explore it by means of examples, thus

Jones caused the pawn to move by pushing it.

This is an excellent example of personal causation, of a piece with many Taylor gives. But at a critical stage in his argument, we find him arguing that, on occasion at least, persons cause their actions. Thus, as he sees it, when Jones moves his finger, we can appropriately say

Jones caused his finger to move.

Now if we were to ask

By doing what?

which our original paradigm requires, the answer must surely be "nothing." For if we were to say, for example,

Jones caused his finger to move by pushing it

Taylor would, correctly, object that in this event the motion of the finger would not be an action, but the result of an action—the pushing. This indicates that something is wrong. Our previous concepts of a person as a cause is out of place in this context. The point must, however, be made carefully, for when we leave the context of "minimal actions," this concept of persons as causes *is* relevant. Thus the assertion that

Jones killed Smith

can be met with the question

By doing what?

that is

What did Jones do which caused Smith to die?

to which the answer,

238   THE METAPHYSICS OF PRACTICE

Jones caused Smith to die *by firing the gun at him*

is appropriate and falls under our canonical form. A minimal action is exactly one to which the question

By doing what?

is inappropriate. And for this reason the concept of persons as causes with which we have been working is inapplicable.

[39] Notice that to admit that in the context of nonminimal actions a person caused something to happen is not to admit that what the person caused is an action. Minimal actions are not the causes of nonminimal actions, they are rather the initial stages of nonminimal actions. (Of course, not every "initial stage" of an action is itself an action; consider nerve impulses or, more to the point, volitions.) Thus granting, for the moment, that crooking one's trigger finger is a minimal action, whereas the action of firing a gun is not, the relation of the former to the latter is not that of cause to effect, but that of an action to a larger action of which it is a part. To be sure, the crooking of the finger causes the firing of the gun in the sense of the gun's going off. But in *this* sense the firing of the gun is not an action, but a purely physical event. The relation of minimal actions to nonminimal actions should not be pictured *thusly*,*

but rather thusly,

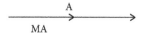

---

* [Eds.—Sellars's rendering of these images in his typescript more clearly portrays the relation of minimal actions to nonminimal actions; we reproduce his sketch below:

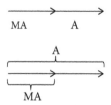

Sicha, in the Intelex Past Masters version of MP (https://www.nlx.com/collections/701), clarifies the relation by captioning 8.1, "MA [is followed by] A" and 8.2, "[MA is part of A]".]

[40] Now it might be said that by using the paradigm

X caused Y to Z by A-ing

to explore Taylor's idea that persons cause their actions, I am being seriously unfair. After all, it could be pointed out, Taylor explicitly contrasts "personal" causation with "natural" causation, whereas my comments amount to the idea that he fails to draw this distinction. There is some truth to this charge. I do claim that Taylor fails to draw this distinction; but as I see it this is because his concept of personal causation is vacuous. For, in effect, I have been arguing that the sense in which, according to Taylor, persons cause their actions amounts to no more than that they do them; indeed, in the last analysis, to no more than that persons act. Thus, as used by Taylor,

Jones caused action A

is a misleading way of saying

Jones did action A

which amounts to

Jones did an A-ing

and is, as I put it, the higher order equivalent of

Jones Ad.

Nobody would think of dancing a waltz as causing a waltz. Taylor may have been misled by the fact that we do speak, for example, of "making" a gesture, and "making" in some contexts is certainly "causing." But, surely,

Jones made a gesture

stands to

Jones gesticulated

as "Jones performed a waltz" stands to "Jones waltzed," and the appearance of causation is an illusion.

[41] I conclude that persons do not cause their actions, though, except in the case of minimal actions, by doing one thing they can cause something else to

happen, and can, therefore, be said to have done a correspondingly more complex action. Thus, by firing a gun and causing a death, one kills.

[42] If persons do not cause their actions, does anything else cause them? On occasion, yes. I can be caused to do something by someone else, as when I am caused by someone in authority to make amends. By a metaphorical extension of this usage, inanimate objects can also cause one to do something. Two points must, however, be made in this connection. In the first place, it is obvious that not every action is in *this* sense caused. And in the second, one must be careful to distinguish between those cases in which an action is caused, and those in which one is not, properly speaking, an agent at all, but rather a patient, as when one is overpowered by superior force.

[43] If, now, we turn to other senses of 'cause,' and take Aristotle as our guide, we find it quite sensible to say, that actions have causes indeed, in Aristotle's sense, *efficient* causes. For not all efficient causation is to be construed on the above model.

[44] Taylor's account of the teleological explanation of purposive behavior consists of two theses:

(1) A negative thesis to the effect that purposive behavior is not caused by anything other than the agent, i.e. he is not caused to do it;
(2) A positive thesis to the effect that purposive behavior is to be explained in terms of such locutions as 'X did Y in order to bring about Z.'

Unfortunately, he leaves the latter thesis unexplicated except in tautologous ways, thus 'X did Y with the aim of bringing about Z.'

[45] Taylor does consider the possibility that actions are caused by volitions. But this account of volitions and causation by volition is a caricature. The following points need to be made:

(1) Taylor assumes that volitions are actions in the practical sense, pieces of conduct (in this case mental conduct)—the sort of thing which, *if there were any*, could themselves be caused by volition. Thus he argues that according to the theory of volitions, in order to do one action (A) one must first do another (willing to do A). This, he points out, if taken seriously, would generate a vicious regress.

To this the answer is simple and straightforward. Volitions are not to be construed as pieces of conduct. They are "actions" only in that broadest sense in which anything expressed by a verb in the active voice (e.g. sleeping) is an action. They are actualities, indeed episodes, but not actions in any more interesting sense.[11]

---

[11] For a more complete account of this and other methods pertaining to volition, see *Science and Metaphysics*, chapter 7. [Eds.—OIM, Ch. 6 of this volume.]

(2) Taylor assumes that because playing a phrase on the piano consists of striking successive notes, the willing that causes the playing of the phrase must consist of a volition for each note.

To this, the obvious answer is that learning to play a piece of music, and, in general, learning to play the piano, involves the building of behavioral elements into patterns which can be intended as wholes. It is only the beginner who has to think out each step as he goes along. The point is familiar to anyone who has learned to ride a bicycle or to swim.

(3) Taylor agrees (with Melden) that since (with the necessary qualifications) there is no logical connection between cause and effect, and since there *is* a logical connection between the volition to raise one's arm and the raising of the arm, the volition cannot be the cause of the action.

To this the proper reply is that the so-called "logical" connection between the volition and the action is the "aboutness" relation between a thought and the state of affairs it represents, and not a putative relation of entailment between events. If Taylor's argument were correct, it would follow that a red book couldn't be the cause of the perceptual belief that one is confronted by a red book. Taylor, indeed, overlooks the point that volitions are to be construed as thoughts and have intensionality. It is obvious that when we act purposively we must be thinking of the state of affairs to be realized. This thinking can't be merely matter-of-factual thinking about the future. What generates action is not descriptive thinking to which has been added a nonconceptual impetus or push. It is practical thinking.

(4) Taylor ridicules volitions by arguing that all that can be said of the volition which causes one's finger to go up is that it is a "finger-raising volition."

This claim overlooks the complex logical and conceptual relations that can be traced between volitions and other modes of practical thinking.[12] For our present purposes, it is sufficient to note that Taylor's objection could also be raised against the concept of perceptual taking or belief. What is the perceptual taking (normally) caused by a red book in front of one? It is a red-book-in-front-of-one taking. Why not?

(5) Taylor argues that if volitions are the causes of our actions, they must cause us to do them.

---

[12] I have discussed these relations in some detail in 'Thought and Action,' in *Freedom and Determinism* (ed. by Keith Lehrer), Random House, New York, 1966. [Eds.—TA, Ch. 7 of this volume.]

This argument is a simple consequence of his assimilation of all senses of 'cause' to his paradigm. His conclusion that if volitions are the cause of actions then we are not free, but are caused or compelled to do what we do, is sheer confusion.

[46] Finally, it should be noted that just as motions are things moving, so volitions are persons willing. To suppose that in "personal" causation (or "agency") one is confronted by a mode of causation which can be schematized as

Person causes event

and contrasted with "natural" causation, the latter being schematized as

Event causes event

is to make a radical mistake. Even in the case of purely physical causation it is permissible to say, for example

The bomb caused the disaster

which has the form

Thing caused event.

Here, however, we recognize that although this form of statement is legitimate, the truth of such statements requires that of statements of the form

Event caused event

thus,

The explosion of the bomb caused the disaster.

It is, therefore, essential to see that exactly the same situation obtains in the case of personal causation. The truth of statements of the form

Jones brought about E

requires that of statements of the form

(In the circumstances) Jones' willing to bring about E' caused E

which also has the form

Event caused event.

That the causing event is a volition, i.e., a conceptual event of the kind which is central to practical thinking is what distinguishes 'actions' from 'mere events.' To construe the difference in terms of the contrast between 'person causes event' and 'event causes event' is sheer error.

[IV]

[47] I shall now return to the Kantian idea that "I think" or "I represent" is the basic and irreducible form of self-awareness with respect to distinctively human states of one's person. Traditional metaphysicians had argued that the subject of representations (the representer) is a simple, noncomposite substance which is "strictly" or, as it is sometimes put, "literally" identical through time—i.e. does not have the identity of a series. Kant argues, *per contra,* that for all we know the subject or representer might be:

(a) an attribute of something more basic
(b) a system (composite)
(c) a series.

[48] Of these possibilities, the first (although it has other overtones) amounts to the idea that from God's point of view a person's mind might be an Aristotelian unitary person qua having mental states and capacities, as contrasted with those states and capacities which are the real counterparts of bodily states and capacities. Kant defends this possibility by showing that a traditional argument to the contrary is a fallacy. His reconstruction of this fallacy or "paralogism" can be paraphrased as follows:

(1) The concept of the "I" (representer) is the concept of a subject of representations.
(2) The concept of the "I" is not the concept of a derivative or dependent logical subject.
(3) Therefore the concept of the "I" is the concept of a nonderivative subject.[13]

---

[13] To get an initial insight into the surface structure of the argument, consider the following:
We conceive of *x* as colored
We do not conceive of *x* as red
Therefore we conceive of *x* as nonred.

Kant concedes that the argument would not be a fallacy if we could add the premise that our concept of the "I" is the concept of a determinate kind of object, as the concept of a species of material thing is the concept of a determinate kind of object. For this premise would entail that the concept of the "I" is the concept of a specific type of logical subject; and from this, together with the premise that it is not the concept of a logical subject of specific type T, one could establish that it is the concept of a logical subject of specific type T',* if these were the only relevant alternatives.

[49] But the concept of the "I" is the concept of that which thinks (thus, as Kant uses the term 'I,' it is equivalent to 'mind'), and concepts pertaining to mental acts are "functional" in a way which leaves open the question as to the "qualitative" or, as I prefer to say, contentual character of the items that function in such a way as to be the kind of mental act they are. To use a well-worn analogy, one may distinguish between the contentual and the functional aspects of the activities involved in a game of chess. The contentual aspects concern the material out of which the pieces and the board are made, and the specific kinds of changes which are to count as the various moves. We can conceive of widely different contentual embodiments of chess, i.e. we can conceive of the functionings in ways which abstract from specific embodiments, though they lay down abstract requirements which any specific embodiments must satisfy. Notice that these abstractly conceived functionings could be embodied in different types of logical subject. Thus there could be a game of chess in which the pieces were simple substances, or composite substances, or persons qua bodies, or, in the case of mental chess, conceptual entities. This can be put by saying that these abstractly conceived functionings are "transcategorial" with respect to the type of logical subjects in which they might be embodied (e.g. simple, complex, person qua moveable).

[50] Now the peculiar feature of concepts pertaining to conceptual activity is that they are purely functional. To get purely functional concepts pertaining to chess, we start with concepts involving specific content and proceed by abstraction. Our concepts pertaining to conceptual activity, on the other hand, are purely functional *ab initio*. This lack of a specific contentual aspect is what lies behind the temptation to think of mental acts as "diaphanous." And Kant's point can be put by saying that conceptual acts are transcategorial with respect to the type of logical subject which might engage in them (e.g. simple, complex, person qua capable of conceptual activity).

[51] Thus, to represent the mind as a substance (as contrasted with a person qua capable of conceptual acts) is not to know that the mind is such a substance. For to know that latter we would have to have an adequate contentual concept of mental activity (i.e. we would have to know the mind "as a determinate object"),

---

* [Eds.—Correction of "T" in original printing. In the typescript, this reads as "T'", which makes more sense in the context of the sentence.]

METAPHYSICS AND THE CONCEPT OF A PERSON   245

and this we do not have. Thus, from the standpoint of knowledge "representing the mind as a substance" amounts to no more than "not representing it as a contentually specific dependent subject". Indeed, by parity of reasoning, "representing the mind as a dependent subject" would amount to no more than "not representing it as a contentually specific substance".

[52] To sum up, if we conceive of the "I" (or mind) determinately as a determinate object of knowledge, without conceiving of it as a dependent logical subject, we must be conceiving of it as an independent or nonderivative object of knowledge. Thus Kant traces the fallacy to a failure to note that the term 'I' (or 'mind') does not express the concept of a determinate kind of object. It is because of this that, even granted that we do not conceive of the "I" as a derivative subject, it does not follow that we are conceiving of it as a nonderivative subject, or substance.

[53] Kant finds a similar fallacy in the argument "rational psychologists" had used to prove the simplicity of the "I"—to prove that its identity is not that of a system or composite. His reconstruction of the argument can be paraphrased as follows:

(1) The concept of the "I" (representer) is the concept of one subject.
(2) The concept of the "I" is not the concept of a composite.

Therefore

(3) The concept of the "I" is the concept of a noncomposite entity. Its unity is not that of a system.

[54] As before, Kant concedes that if our concept of the "I," as a *one* subject, were the contentually determinate concept of a determinate object, then the conclusion would be established. If we are not conceiving of it as a system or composite, we must be conceiving of it as a determinate noncomposite or simple object of knowledge. But, again, our knowledge of the mind is the knowledge of that which acts in ways which we conceive of in purely functional terms. And since these functions could, in principle, be activities of either (a) a simple substance, (b) a composite substance, or (c) a substance (simple or composite) qua capable of conceptual activity, our knowledge does not determine to which of these types of logical subject the "I" belongs.

[55] In connection with this second Paralogism, Kant makes two points that show the subtlety of his thought. It is, he argues, indeed true that the subject of thoughts cannot be a *many* in the sense of *many subjects of thought*. To make the point in terms of a familiar type of example, if one thinker thinks 'Tom,' another thinks 'is,' and yet another thinks 'tall,' this does not entail that there is an "I" which thinks 'Tom is tall.' But, Kant points out, it does not follow that the "I" which thinks cannot be a plurality or system.

The subject of thoughts, the "I," is a plurality

is not the same as

The subject of thoughts is a plurality of "I"s.

[56] The third Paralogism concerns the claim that the identity of the "I" through its successive states is not the identity of a series. It has a similar form, and Kant's treatment of it is equally sound and illuminating. Here, too, it should be noted that the idea that the "I" is a series must not be confused with the idea that it is a series of "I"s.

[V]

[57] I have often characterized my metaphysical views as strongly Kantian in structure. Thus I have argued that the common-sense world, the world of the "manifest image" is, in the Kantian sense, phenomenal; the way in which things as they really are appear to minds endowed with a certain conceptual framework. The fact that this framework is a subtle one, particularly in those respects which concern action and practice, by no means guarantees that its ontology is an adequate representation of the way things are.

[58] In the manifest image, our concept of a person is not the concept of something of which the behavior can be assimilated to the triggering off of causal properties in the interaction of material things. Persons acquire second natures—in the literal sense, dispositions. But their *first* nature is not that of a system of causal properties—dispositions in the metaphorical sense—but rather that of a system of capacities pertaining to the various modes of thinking.

[59] In the Paralogisms Kant has kept the way clear for the view that in reality the "I" is a system, and, in particular for the view that it is a system of scientific objects, the true counterparts of Kant's things-in-themselves. Again he has kept the way clear for the view that thoughts and other representations are in reality complex states of a system and, in particular, of a neurophysiological system. Here again one must beware of assimilating scientific intelligibility to Taylor's paradigm of causation. Kant also kept the way clear for the view that in reality the identity of the "I" through its successive acts of representation is the identity of a series.

[60] Kant's fundamental error was to construe the phenomenal world in Cartesian terms. The Aristotelian–Strawsonian reconstruction is along sounder lines. But, as I see it, this (unavoidable) error was but one more symptom of his pre-evolutionary commitments. Correctly rejecting standard empiricism, he was forced into the platonic alternative of innate ideas. This led him to tie together in one bundle the diversity of concepts in terms of which we explain the course of

nature. Different levels of spatial and temporal concepts were identified and construed in terms of the Space and Time of Newtonian mechanics. The framework of emerging microphysics was assumed to be already in the mind awaiting its Socrates, as did geometry in the soul of Meno's slave.

[61] Today we are in a better position to distinguish between the conceptual framework of which nature was the cause, and the freely elaborate conceptual frameworks with which we now challenge nature. It is the greater explanatory power of the latter which stands behind the claim that things as they are in themselves are things as ideal science would find them to be. But the details of this neo-Peircean conception of truth and reality must be left to another occasion.[14]

---

[14] For an initial attempt see chapters 3–5 of my *Science and Metaphysics*.

9
Actions and Events*

I

1. In his essay, "Sovereign Reason," which gives its name to the book in which it is contained, Ernest Nagel attributes to Brand Blanshard the view that "serious consequences for morals and the life of reason follow from the denial that logical necessity is involved in causal relations" and describes him as arguing that "'unless necessity does play a part in the movement of inference, no argument will establish anything,' since on the hypothesis that no such necessity exists the distinction between being moved by reasons and being moved by causes is simply an illusion" ([3]: 290).

2. Now, as Nagel points out, a number of quite different considerations are blended together in this way of looking at 'the life of reason.' There is, in the first place, the thesis that causal connection is a species of logical implication or entailment. Nagel to the contrary, I believe that this is a respectable position provided that logical implication or entailment is not identified with the 'subject-matter neutral' implication which, until recently, has been the primary object of attention by professional logicians. Even extreme anti-Humeans have learned from Hume that causal laws are synthetic in the sense that no definitional transformation will exhibit them as instances of subject-matter neutral truths. But it is doubtful that anyone who has held an entailment theory of causality has thought that causal connections were, in the corresponding sense, analytic. And the mere fact that they have referred to causality as a form of *logical* implication should not be taken to carry this commitment, since the restriction of the adjective 'logical' to analytic implications is an expression of Humean commitment and reflects actual usage only to the extent that it is shaped by teachers of logic.

3. I take it, then, that there is nothing absurd (though much that is controversial) in entailment theories of causation. And, indeed, I have devoted considerable effort over the past twenty years to elaborating and defending such a theory (thus in CDCM and in IV). To engage in this, perhaps quixotic, enterprise is not my purpose on the present occasion, though I have thought it proper to warn the reader that it and related views are closely related to the topics I shall discuss.

---

* This paper was originally presented at a symposium on the topic at the University of North Carolina, November, 1969.

4. Next let me note that 'implies' and 'entails' are relation words taking abstract singular terms as their subjects in accordance with the schema:

That-p implies (or entails) that-q.

This is true whether the implication in question be causal, or logical in that narrower sense to which it has been professionally restricted and to which, for present purposes, I shall also restrict it.

5. Statements to the effect that one proposition logically implies another formulate principles of inference. And it is notoriously important to distinguish the principle of an inference from its premises. Thus, the *regimented* inference,

p
Therefore, q

has as its premise the proposition that-p, for its conclusion the proposition that-q, and as its principle the higher order proposition:

The proposition that-p implies the proposition that-q.

6. Notice that this schema leaves it open whether or not the principle of inference is a logical truth. Thus, for present purposes, the following schema would be more explicit:

Not both p and not-q
p
Therefore, q.

Here, the premises are the propositions that-(not both p and not-q) and that-p, the conclusion is the proposition that-q, and the principle of inference is the proposition:

that-(not both p and not-q) and that-p imply that-q,

or, if the premises are conjoined into one premise,

that-[(not both p and not-q) and p] implies that-q.

7. Having offered this finer grained example, however, we can return to the simpler schema, for it suffices for the philosophical points I wish to make.

8. First, a terminological point which is not merely terminological, but a bridge to the point at issue between Blanshard and Nagel. The implication statement

that-*p* implies that-*q*

can be rephrased as the necessity statement

that-*p* necessitates that-*q*.

In traditional terms, to say that one state of affairs implies another is to say that they are 'necessarily connected,' that the one 'necessitates' the other.

9. Notice that I have dropped the word 'proposition' in favor of 'state of affairs.' My reason for doing so has deep roots in the theory of abstract entities. 'Proposition', in actual usage, is a verbal noun based, I believe, on some such verb as 'propose' or 'propound.' Propositions in this sense are events—indeed they are actions. They have the form:

(Someone) proposing that-*p*.

The proposition that-*p*, in this sense, would not be what ontologists ordinarily have in mind by 'the proposition that-*p*', but would rather be an event- or action-type which 'involves', in a manner by no means easy to analyze, the proposition that-*p* in the technical sense of 'proposition' in which this term has come to be used.

10. Just how this technical usage is to be explicated involves reflection on the manifold of distinctions between:

1. A propounding;
2. A proposition in the sense of what is propounded;
3. A proposition in the sense of the physical product of a propounding—e.g., an ink inscription, a sound, or, more long lived, a trace on a tape recorder;
4. A proposition in the sense of *what is meant* by inscriptions and traces;

to which other distinctions can, I am sure, be added.

11. Yet, if I find the term 'proposition' a dangerous one, I am not altogether happy with the term 'state of affairs,' for two reasons: The first is that in ordinary usage states of affairs are temporal, and it would be awkward to rephrase the locution:

the proposition that 2 plus 2 equals 4

by:

the state of affairs that 2 plus 2 equals 4.

The second reason cuts a bit deeper, for the term 'state of affairs' in ordinary usage is connected *not* with that-clauses but with participial expressions, thus:

Tom's being home for the holidays was a happy state of affairs.

I shall have more to say on this topic later.

12. For something like these reasons many ontologists have been tempted to coin technical terms and to say, for example, that that-clauses refer to 'objectives.' I think that this is a useful term, but having called attention to its availability, and to the considerations which have led to its adoption, I shall continue, for the moment, with the above warnings, to use both 'proposition' and 'state of affairs' in something like the technical senses in which they have been used by ontologists. Needless to say, I do not regard these technical senses as 'clear and distinct.' They are, however, conveniences. We are thrown into philosophy as Heidegger was thrown into the world; the dialogue we continue, we did not begin, and a Whitehead can introduce a whole new vocabulary, and still be understood—as well as before.

II

13. But enough of this backing and filling. What does this logic chopping have to do with Blanshard's contention that "unless necessity does play a part in the movement of inference" the distinction between being moved by reasons and being moved by causes is simply an illusion?

14. Nagel points out correctly—though I rephrase what he says in terms of the above distinction—that from the fact that one state of affairs, that-p, entails another state of affairs, that-q, it does not follow that if the thought that-p occurs to a person, the thought that-q will occur to him. Thus, the necessity which relates to two states of affairs does not carry over into a relation of necessity between the thinking of the one and a subsequent thinking of the other.[1] He concludes that even where the relation between two states of affairs is necessary, the relation between the thought of the one and the thought of the other is contingent.

15. Now, this seems obviously to be the case when the thinker in question, as we say, doesn't *know* that the one state of affairs entails the other. And, clearly, there are many entailments which a given person does not know and many entailments

---

[1] I am quite aware that I am using thoroughly regimented examples of inference. A botanizing of the thought patterns which can appropriately be characterized as inferential would require the space of another essay. It should not be forgotten that the dialectics of the controversy has developed in connection with such regimented examples and, in my opinion, rightly so. As far as I can see (although this might not have been the case), no essential changes in the overall strategy of the argument would be involved in taking less tidy cases into account.

which nobody knows. What, then, if we add the premise that the thinker knows the entailment? Does this remove the contingency?

16. Is it a purely contingent fact that Jones, who knows the entailment between the two states of affairs, thinks of the second upon thinking of the first?[2] Nagel points out that we can readily think of cases where Jones thinks of the first state of affairs without thinking of the second. Does this suffice to make the relation between the occurrence of the two thoughts,[3] when they do both occur, a contingent one? I shall argue, to the contrary, that it can be a conceptual truth that, *other things being equal*, the one thought is followed by the other, even though on many occasions the one occurs without the other—indeed, even if, to push the matter to the edge of paradox, a Jonesean thought that-p is never followed by a Jonesean thought that-q.

17. If I am right, then the way is open to giving something like the 'classical' account of the idea that reasons can be causes. For this account insists that it is *because* that-p entails that-q that a thought that-p is, *ceteris paribus*, followed by a thought that-q.

18. It will be instructive to contrast this thesis with Nagel's account of the sense in which reasons can be causes:

A man who first notes a premise A, and then perceives that A logically implies B, is moved by reasons when he accepts B *on the evidence of* the premise, even if the causal sequence, the thought of A, the perception of the connection between A and B, the assertion of B is a logically contingent one. ([3]: 290; italics mine.)

Three comments are in order:

1. Nagel implies that to be moved to think B 'by reasons' involves the occurrence of the thought that A logically implies B. Yet, surely, it is only if A's implying B were functioning as a premise that a thought of it would be required; and if it must occur as a premise, then accepting a conclusion *for reasons* would involve an infinite regress. If it does not function as a premise, the most that is required is that the knowledge (or belief) that A implies B be available.
2. Nagel speaks of 'accepting B *on the evidence of* the premise.' But this is just the idea to be explicated. There is more to accepting B "on the evidence of A"

---

[2] Notice that his knowledge that the one entails the other should not be construed as the employment of an additional premise—for, as has often been pointed out, most brilliantly by Lewis Carroll, the principle of *this* inference would not be the original entailment but a more complicated one to the effect that, roughly,

that-(that-p is the case) and that-(that-p entails that-q) entail that-q.

[3] The regimented inferences with which we are dealing constitute only one of the many patterns of thought which are governed, in the sense to be clarified, by entailments.

than first thinking *A* and then thinking *B*. And this *more* is the heart of the matter. It won't do simply to sandwich in the thought that *A* logically implies *B*. For although accepting *B* on the evidence of *A* involves the presence, in some sense, to the mind of the fact that *A* logically implies *B*, what concerns us is *how* the entailment functions to make an accepting of *B following* an accepting of *A* an accepting of *B on the evidence of A*. It is the idea that the entailment *somehow* plays a causal role that is the source of the temptation to suppose that a thought of it must occur in the process itself.

3. By characterizing "the causal sequence, the thought of *A*, the perception of the connection between *A* and *B*, the assertion of *B*" as "logically contingent," Nagel implies that the concept of a world in which people invariably have thought sequences in accordance with the schema:

a thought of *A*,
a perception of the connection between *A* and *B*,
an assertion of not-*B*,

is a coherent one, which is surely not the case.

III

19. An important step in coming to understand how the existence of an entailment between that-*p* and that-*q* carries with it the idea that *ceteris paribus* a person is caused to think that-*q* by thinking that-*p*, is to ask what is the difference between thinking that-*q* upon thinking that-*p*, where one would characterize this as a mere case of association, and thinking that-*q* upon thinking that-*p*, where we are prepared to call this an inference? Note that if, as this question implies, we are prepared to say that inferences of our regimented type are cases of association in which certain additional conditions are satisfied, then we should be happy to say that the premise thought of such an inference causes the conclusion thought. For surely association of ideas is, as critics of Hume have long pointed out,[4] a paradigm case of causation, the causing of one mental event by another.

20. I am assuming, it will be noticed, that we are not taking as our paradigm of causation:

One thing (or a group of things) by changing in a certain way causing a different thing (or a group of things) to change in a certain way.

This interventionist model of causation is only one variety of a relation between events by virtue of which the occurrence of the one explains the occurrence of the

---

[4] Though the use they have made of this point can be criticized.

other. Clearly, we often explain why an object comes to be in one state or to change in a certain way by referring to an antecedent condition of *the same object*. And even a mechanical explanation need not have the interventionist form, as when, in dealing with a closed mechanical system, one explains its being in a certain state s' at t' with reference to its being in another state, s, at a preceding time, t.

21. Thus we must distinguish between the questions,

What caused Jones to associate B with A?

and

What caused Jones to think B?

The cause of the association may well be a fact about his environment. But *given that he has the association*, and that no countervailing factors are present, the cause of his thinking B is his thinking A. Furthermore, though his thinking B has a cause, he is not 'caused to think B' in the sense that a thing or person other than Jones himself caused him to think B. One could, if one wished, say that Jones was the cause of his thinking B. But unless this is just another way of saying that Jones thought B, it could only mean that, in the context, Jones' thinking A was the cause of his thinking B.

22. To explain the difference in our regimented cases between inference and mere association, and to understand *how*, in the case of inference, the causal relationship involves the *fact* that the premise entails the conclusion—or even the *belief* that the premise entails the conclusion—it will be useful to adopt a Rylean type position which I shall call Verbal Behaviorism.[5] According to this reconstruction, 'thinking that-p', where this means 'having the thought occur to one that-p,' has as its primary sense *saying* 'p', and it has a derivative sense in which it stands for a short term proximate disposition to say 'p'.

23. Notice that I am unabashedly treating that-clauses as quotations in spite of the fact that

Julius Caesar said that the die was cast

is not equivalent to

Julius Caesar said 'the die is cast.'

---

[5] For an elaboration of the strategy of using Verbal Behaviorism as a model to clarify issues in the philosophy of mind, see my LTC.

An adequate account of that-clauses as quotations would require reference to a mode of quotation which spans different languages, as familiar quotation spans the difference between written and spoken forms of the same language. (For an account of such quotations, see my AE; also SM, Chapter 3.)

24. Verbal Behaviorism, defined as above, is a radical oversimplification. Yet the proper method of rational reconstruction is by successive approximation, and Verbal Behaviorism provides a useful strategy for approaching key philosophical issues in the philosophy of mind; in particular, issues pertaining to perception, inference, and action. Before we can use it, however, we must guard against certain misconceptions which would render it worse than useless. Thus, it is essential to note that just as *thinking that-p*, in the sense of having the thought occur to one that-*p*, is not a mental performance, something that one does or could do voluntarily, so, in the Verbal Behaviorist model, *saying 'p'* is not to be construed as an illocutionary act. It is to be construed, as I have elsewhere put it (for example, in LTC), as candidly *thinking-out-loud that-p*, and it is not to be confused with 'asserting that-*p*,' 'telling someone that-*p*,' or any other of the verbal performances so lovingly collected by the late John Austin. Of course, in any ordinary sense, *saying 'p'* is a performance, because the phrase permits the utterance episode to which it applies to be either a spontaneous thinking-out-loud that-*p or a deliberate use of words to achieve a purpose*, malicious or benign. I, on the other hand, am using the expression "S says '*p*'" in a contrived sense in which these options are closed and the utterance specifically construed as a spontaneous or candid thinking-out-loud.

25. We can imagine a child to learn a rudimentary language in terms of which he can perceive, draw inferences, and act. In doing so, he begins by uttering noises which *sound like* words and sentences and ends by uttering noises which *are* words and sentences. We might use quoted words to describe what he is doing at both stages, but in the earlier stage we are classifying his utterances as *sounds* and only by courtesy and anticipation as *words*.

26. Only when the child has got the hang of how the sounds function in the language can he be properly characterized as saying 'this is a book,' or 'I shall raise my hand,' or 'it is not raining,' or 'lightning, so shortly thunder,' or 'you spanked me, so you don't love me.'

27. To say what a person *says* is to give a functional classification of his utterances. The Verbal Behaviorist agrees with Wittgenstein that the meaning of an utterance is its use, but, unlike Wittgenstein, he is careful to distinguish 'use' in the instrumental sense (in which utterances are construed as Austinian performances) from use as function. It is in this latter sense that the meaning, for example, of logical words is their use.

28. Some functional relationships are purely intra-linguistic (syntactical), and are correlated with formation and transformation rules. Others concern language as a response to sensory stimulation by environmental objects—thus, candidly

saying (or having the short term disposition to say) 'lo, this table is red'.[6] Still others concern the connection of practical thinking with behavior. All these dimensions of functioning recur at the metalinguistic level in the language in which we respond to verbal behavior, draw inferences about verbal behavior, and engage in practical thinking about verbal behavior—i.e., practical thinking about thinking.

29. From this point of view, the basic point I wish to make is a simple one. When we characterize a person's utterance by using a quotation, we are implying that the utterance is an instance of certain specific ways of functioning. For example, it would be absurd to say:

Tom said (as contrasted with *uttered the noises*) 'It is not raining' but has no propensity to avoid saying 'it is raining and it is not raining.'

Thus to characterize a person's utterances by quoting sentences containing logical words is to imply that the corresponding sounds function properly in the verbal behavior in question and to imply that the uniformities characteristic of these ways of functioning are present in his sayings and proximate dispositions to say.

30. But what, even in our simplified model, does all this have to do with the involvement of entailments in the causation of conclusion thoughts by premise thoughts in our regimented cases of inference? The answer is that statements of the form:

that-p implies that-q

are *normative* statements to the effect that, from a logical point of view, thinkings that-p ought not to be accompanied by thinkings that-not-q and that if a thinking that-p is epistemically sound, then it is properly accompanied by a thinking that-q. These ought-to-be[7] statements are essential to the practical thinking which shapes the language learning of the young and keeps entropy away from language once acquired.

31. The functioning which gives the utterances of one who has learned the language their meaning *can* exist merely at the level of uniformities. When Tom utters or is disposed to utter the sequence: 'p', 'q', where we would not classify his utterances as 'p' and 'q' unless the relevant functioning of these utterances was in

---

[6] I use the contrived operator 'lo' to indicate that the context is one in which the sentence which follows it is functioning as a perceptual response to an environmental object, and to indicate that this context is preserved in the retention of the sentence in the 'memory system' of the perceiver. In this respect, 'lo' functions in perceptual contexts much as 'shall' will be used to function in contexts pertaining to practical reasoning.

[7] For an exploration of the distinction between 'ought to be' and 'ought to do'—where the 'do' ranges over actions proper—see LTC.

his repertoire, we could say that *ceteris paribus* the former caused the latter and also that the fact that the former is followed by the latter is an instance of a uniformity *for which the entailment is responsible*—in the sense that persons who accept the entailment statement have followed the norm it formulates in teaching him the language. In this respect, the linguistic community plays a role importantly analogous to that of the natural environment when it causes association.

32. The child begins at the 'pattern governed'[8] level of verbal behavior but subsequently becomes a full-fledged member of the linguistic community and thinks thoughts (theoretical and practical) not only about *non-linguistic* items but also about *linguistic* items, i.e., from the Verbal Behaviorist point of view, first level thoughts. At this later stage, he can not only reason *in accordance with* entailments, he can reason *about* entailments. And since entailments are principles of criticism, he has now developed from being the object of training and criticism by others to the stage at which he can train and criticise himself and even develop new and more complicated standards in terms of which to guide his own development.[9]

33. Notice that Verbal Behaviorism permits us to say not only that, *ceteris paribus*, Jones' thinking that-p caused his thinking that-q (whether this be mere association or inference) but also to penetrate beneath the *functional description* classification of the utterances (and propensities to utter) by the use of quotation and the devices of indirect discourse, and describe for example, the child as acquiring the propensity to follow one utterance *phonemically* classified with another utterance *phonemically* classified. At the verbal level, we can penetrate beneath *functional* descriptions which, in the case of basic statements and inferences, carry with them causal commitments, to *non-functional* descriptions of the same utterances which, as non-functional, carry no such conceptual commitment. This is analogous, at a more complicated level, to retreating from:

The burn was caused by fire

to:

The blister was caused by fire.[10]

34. It is a most significant fact, as I have pointed out elsewhere,[11] that the classification of thoughts, construed as classical mental episodes, permits of no such easy retreat to a non-functional level. Roughly, our classification of thoughts,

---

[8] This term was introduced in an earlier attempt to understand how rules are causally involved in the generation of meaningful verbal behavior, SRLG, reprinted as the concluding chapter of SPR.

[9] For a theory of induction built around this interpretation of entailment see IV; see also SRLG.

[10] Compare [1].

[11] Most recently in MP. [Eds.—Chapter 8 of this volume.] For an early formulation, see EPM, especially sections XII–XIV.

construed as episodes which belong to a framework which *explains* the kaleidoscopic shifts of sayings and propensities to say, is almost purely functional. We have only the foggiest notion of what kinds of episodes, non-functionally described, perform the relevant functions, though philosophers of a scientific orientation are prepared to characterize them *generically* as 'neuro-physiological.' As a result, philosophers unaware of this alternative strategy have the illusion of an *ultimacy* of the conceptual functioning of thoughts which is responsible for continuing philosophical puzzles about how mental acts are to be fitted into a naturalistic picture of the world.

IV

35. Donald Davidson in his classic paper on "Actions, Reasons, and Causes" ([1]), opens by asking "what is the relation between a reason and an action when the reason explains the action by giving the agent's reason for doing what he did?" He gives the term 'rationalization' a new (and non-pejorative) use by saying that "we may call such explanations rationalizations and say that the reason rationalizes the action." He proceeds to defend "the ancient and common sense position that rationalization is a species of ordinary common sense explanation" ([1]: p. 685). It should be clear by now that I am in general sympathy with this thesis, though I have as yet not even touched on the topic of action.

36. My main uneasiness with Davidson's treatment is that although much of what he has to say is sound, and although he actually puts his finger on the nub of the matter, by failing to discuss the causal character of *inference*, he leaves a serious gap in his account of how reasons are causes.

37. Davidson puts his thesis in two parts:

C1. R is a primary reason why an agent performed the action A under the description d only if R consists of a pro attitude of the agent towards actions with a certain property and a belief of the agent that A, under the description d, has that property. ([1]: 687).

C2. The primary reason for an action is its cause. ([1]: 693).

38. Now the main source of my discomfort is the expression "pro attitude." Davidson is well aware that this is an omnibus term and lists, in the course of his discussion, some of the specific mental states to which this term applies. Yet he has little to say about this, and the total effect is that when it comes to the mental *episodes* involved in the causation of action, what he stresses are episodic *beliefs* about *matters of fact*.

39. He correctly notes that dispositions and propensities can come and go almost as rapidly as the happenings we take as paradigm cases of causally related events. Thus, he writes "states and dispositions are not events, but the onslaught [and presumably the flight: WS] of a state or disposition is" ([1]: 694). The Verbal Behaviorist would point out that the propensity to say "Damn, I just missed the bus" begins at a certain time in a familiar situation and ceases shortly afterwards, being replaced by somewhat less proximate dispositions to mutter about missing the bus.

40. I pointed out in paragraph 38 that what disturbs me about Davidson's account is that in his examples he tends to stress the onslaught of factual thoughts and leaves the relevant pro attitudes to be relatively long term dispositions which constitute the mental background of the functioning of reasons. Before I elaborate this point, however, let me quote a passage in which Davidson puts his finger on the *sort* of point I have been trying to make. He is criticizing Melden and, using one of Melden's examples, writes:

> A man driving an automobile raises his arm in order to signal. His intention, to signal, explains his action, raising his arm, by redescribing it as signaling. What is the pattern that explains the action? ... is the pattern this: the man is driving, he is approaching a turn; he knows he ought to signal; he knows how to signal, by raising his arm. And now, in this context, he raises his arm. Perhaps, as Melden suggests, he does signal. And the explanation would then be this: If under these conditions a man raises his arm, then he signals. The difficulty is, of course, that this explanation does not touch the question of why he raises his arm. He had a reason to raise his arm, but this has not been shown to be the reason why he did it. If the description 'signaling' explains his action by giving his reason, then the signal must be intentional; but on the account just given, it may not be. ([1]: 692–3).

Shortly afterward, Davidson pinpoints the issue by arguing that:

> In order to turn the first 'and' to 'because' in 'He exercised *and* he wanted to reduce and thought exercise would do it,' we must, as a basic rule, augment condition C1 with:
> C2. A primary reason for an action is its cause. ([1]: 693).

41. It is now time to notice that his discussion of the example of signalling quoted above suggests that Melden has in mind an alternative account of the pattern which explains the action, namely that:

> [it is] the familiar pattern of an action done for a reason.

He then makes the above point that, in this case,

> [the pattern] does, indeed, explain the action, but only because it assumes the relation of reason and action that we want to analyse.

Davidson, as I see it, is here making the same point against Melden that I made against Nagel by calling attention above, paragraph 18, to the fact that the locution "accepting *B on the evidence of* the premise" is exactly the one that needs to be explicated in order to cope with Blanshard's problem.

42. Yet Davidson's account, as I see it, is really not much better off, for although he argues, correctly, that causality is the key to a reason's being the reason for an action, he devotes his primary effort not to explicating the mode of causation involved but to defending the idea that the relation could be a causal one against the standard objections offered by philosophers of the Ryle-Melden-Peters stripe. His answers to these objections are sound and to the point. On the other hand, Davidson's constructive account remains undeveloped save insofar as he points out that the onslaught of a disposition is an event and hence that dispositions can serve as causes. Nevertheless, the onslaught he finds to be the key to the signaling example is the driver's noticing or thinking he has noticed his turn coming up. I quote:

> To dignify a driver's awareness that his turn has come by calling it an experience, much less a feeling, is no doubt exaggerated, but whether it deserves a name or not, it had better be the reason why he raises his arm. ([1]: 692).

This is immediately followed by a passage in which the role of the pro-attitude, which presumably is a proximate disposition of which the onslaught is equally relevant, is obscured:

> The intention with which the driver raises his arm is also not an event, for it is no thing at all, neither event, attitude, disposition, nor object. ([1]: 692).

I am sure that Davidson could have made the same point about the 'belief' in which the driver raises his arm. But although both objects of 'belief' and objects of 'intention' are queer objects which undoubtedly merit a Quinean regimentation, to treat 'belief' and 'intentions' differently in the present context is to muddy the waters.

43. The point I'm making will stand out more clearly if we consider, by contrast, the account which can be given by our Verbal Behaviorist. This account gives, in principle, the cash for the promissory notes[12] contained in Nagel's reference to

---

[12] The reader will, of course, be able to distinguish between such cash 'in principle' and a promissory note.

"accepting *B* on the evidence of the premise" and Davidson's reference to the essential role of causation in explaining an action in terms of the reason for which it was done.

44. Consider the child who is learning to use sentences which, as we say, formulate intentions; sentences involving an intention-expressing auxiliary verb—for simplicity, I shall suppose that it is always 'shall.' From the standpoint of non-functional description, it is a matter of learning how to use sentences involving the *sound* 'shall':

I shall *now* raise my hand.

Clearly, the child has not learned how to use this sound unless he acquires the propensity to raise his hand, *ceteris paribus*, upon uttering (or being disposed to utter) the sound 'I shall *now* raise my hand.' Given that this propensity has been acquired, a necessary condition has been met for *redescribing* his utterances of the sound '—shall—' as *sayings* of '—shall—.'

45. But by the same token, the utterance of the *sound* 'I shall now raise my hand' has become, in the relevant circumstances, "the" cause of his raising his hand. Thus described, the connection is conceptually contingent. When redescribed, however, as a *saying* of 'I shall now raise my hand,' the connection becomes a conceptual one, for it is a conceptual truth that *ceteris paribus* a saying or proximate propensity to say 'I shall *now* raise my hand' is followed by a raising of one's hand.

46. A further condition is that the child acquire the ability to draw practical inferences, that is, inferences which move from practical premises to practical conclusions; thus, and I continue to draw on regimented examples,

I shall do *A*, if *C*.
C.
So, I shall do *A*;

and, more directly related to the problem of reasons and causes,

I shall bring about *X*.
Bringing about *X* implies doing *Y* in ten minutes.
So, I shall do *Y* in ten minutes;

where, given that the child has acquired the ability to "tell time," to ascribe to him a candid saying or proximate disposition to say:

'I shall do *Y* in ten minutes'

is to imply that, *ceteris paribus*, this thought will be succeeded by:

I shall do Y in nine minutes.
I shall do Y in eight minutes.
.
.
.
I shall *now* do Y.

47. To put it bluntly, to say that Jones did Y *in order to* bring about X, is to say that he went through *something like* the above practical reasoning. It is in this sense that the 'reason':

to bring about X

is 'the' cause (and it is familiar fact how context-oriented the definite article is) of his doing Y.

48. In short, it is because practical premises can be *causes* of practical conclusions that reasons can be *causes* of actions. This is the connection between the dispute about inference between Blanshard and Nagel with which I began and the problem of how reasons can be the causes of *actions*.

49. Notice that from the standpoint of Verbal Behaviorism, saying (or having the short term proximate propensity to say) 'I shall *now* raise my hand' is a *willing* (volition) to raise one's hand. And conceptual connection between willing to raise one's hand and raising it turns out to be a special case of the conceptual connection of thoughts of certain forms with the context in which they occur. Another example, which has already been discussed, is the connection between having a red book present to one's senses and saying (or having the proximate propensity to say) 'Lo, here is a red book.'

50. Obviously, these conceptual connections are not to be confused with the semantical facts that:

'Lo, this is a red book' (said by S at t) is true ≡ there is a red book in a certain place at a certain time,

or that:

'I shall raise my hand' (said by S at t) is realized (i.e., its descriptive content is true) ≡ the person in question raises his hand at the relevant time.

The conceptual connection between the volition and the raising of the hand *pertains to* causality, yet it is not itself the causal connection; for what is conceptually true is *that there is* a causal connection between the volition non-functionally described and the raising of the hand; and, again, between the presence of the red book to one's senses and the saying 'Lo, here is a red book' *non-functionally described*.

51. A fuller account would explore the relations between the various mental states summed up under the *omnium gatherum* 'pro-attitude' and such immediate practical thoughts as 'I shall *now* do A.' Thus, desires are, roughly, relatively long term dispositions to have thoughts of the form:

(Other things being equal) I shall do A (or bring it about that-p),

where it is presupposed that doing A or contemplating the truth of 'p' is something one would enjoy. (I have explored some of the problems connected with the botanizing of 'pro-attitudes' in TA). A wish is like a desire, save that the possibility of doing A (or bringing it about that-p) is in doubt. Thinking that one ought to do something or bring about something is like a desire, save that, in a sense which requires careful analysis, the 'point of view' is impersonal. It is along the latter lines that one would defend Prichard's statement that desire and the sense of duty are coordinate species of motive.

V

52. I shall conclude this paper with some remarks on the logic of actions and 'mere' events. As this formulation implies, actions *are* events. They are events of which the subject, in a sense to be characterized, is a person and are *ceteris paribus* caused by the person's willing to do them. This implication is built into action words and is reasonably explicit in such locutions as 'bringing it about that...'. Actions have a non-action core which could, in principle, be formulated in ways which abstract from this implication. In addition to this implication of causation by volition, many action words imply a reference to the purpose for which it is typically done. It should be noted that in speaking of the 'non-action core' of an action concept, it is important not to use such phrases as 'one's hand going up.' Obviously, the subject of this expression is not the person but the hand. Thus to formulate the non-action core of the concept of raising one's hand properly, one would have to make it explicit that it is the *person* that is the logical subject of the event.

53. What is an event? 'Event' is a category expression, and to ask the question is to ask for the place of 'event' in a system of categories. Leaving aside such puzzling occurrences as claps of thunder and flashes of lightning, we notice that events are referred to by singular terms which have, to use a technical locution, 'propositional form' and, more specifically, both a logical subject (or subjects) and a corresponding verbal expression; thus:

Caesar's crossing the Rubicon.[13]

54. Event expressions, being propositional singular terms, remind us of that-clauses, which are also propositional singular terms, and it is tempting to assimilate the two. And, indeed, we say:

That Caesar crossed the Rubicon is true,

as well as:

Caesar's crossing the Rubicon took place.

Are these not intimately related? Each is a statement in which the subject is a singular term and the verb is in the third person singular, thus, 'is [true],' and 'took place'. Obviously, not all that-clauses correspond to event expressions (thus, 'that 2 plus 2 equals 4'). But can we not regard event expressions as a proper subset of that-clauses? I think the answer is yes; but in defending it, some explanation must be given of the fact that that-clauses contain tensed verbs, whereas event expressions contain participial expressions. Thus, in sentences to the effect that a certain event took place, typically the event expression itself contains a present participle but is followed by such full-fledged tensed verbs as 'is taking place,' 'took place,' and 'will take place,' as in the above example.

55. If we are to regard event expressions as that-clauses, then we must construe event expressions as they occur in the primary contexts we have been considering as that-clauses in which the main verb has the peculiar form illustrated by:

That Caesar crosses the Rubicon in 56 B.C.

Notice that we are prepared to say, somewhat wistfully,

That Nixon ends the war in 1970 will be true.

(One is struck by the appropriateness of the phrase 'narrative present.') On the other hand, we are less likely to say:

That Caesar *crosses* the Rubicon in 56 B.C. was true,

---

[13] Perhaps lightning flashes and claps of thunder can be included in the general category of singular terms having propositional form by taking into account those strange sentences which involve the pseudo-subject 'it,' which have intrigued many philosophers; thus:

It thundered,

to which would correspond the singular term 'it's thundering'. In the case of lightning, the candidates would be the sentence 'There was lightning' and the singular term 'there being lightning.'

preferring instead,

That Caesar *crossed* the Rubicon in 56 B.C. *is* true,

and, if we were forced to use the predicate '*was* true,' we would say:

That Caesar *crossed* the Rubicon in 56 B.C. *was* true.

56. Temporal that-clauses and event expressions play different roles, but, I suggest, they can fruitfully be assimilated, provided these differences are taken into account. My suggestion, then, is that we reconstruct:

Caesar's crossing the Rubicon in 56 B.C. took place

to read:

That Caesar crosses the Rubicon in 56 B.C. was true.

This account carries with it the idea that (and I continue to leave aside interlinguistic considerations) both formulations be construed as referring to past use-occasions of the English sentence:

Caesar crosses the Rubicon

and as characterizing these past use-occasions as true.

Nixon's ending the war in 1970 will take place

would, correspondingly, characterize future (1970) use-occasions of the sentence:

Nixon ends the war in 1970

as true. Hopefully by 1971 we will be in a position to say:

Nixon's ending the war in 1970 took place,

in which case we will be referring to then past use-occasions of the sentence:

Nixon ends the war in 1970,

and be saying of them that they *were* true.

57. In brief, this reconstruction gives us a unified grasp of apparently unrelated modes of discourse by assimilating event expressions to that-clauses, and the predicates 'is taking place,' 'will take place,' and 'took place' to the straightforwardly semantical predicates 'is true,' 'will be true,' and 'was true.' I realize, of course, that those who regard using a tensed copula with the predicate 'true' as a sin against the Holy Ghost will not be persuaded.

58. I might put my thesis by saying that events are a species of proposition. I am not unhappy about this way of putting it, provided we bear in mind the ambiguities of the term 'proposition' to which I alluded above, for, as we saw, propositions as *propoundings* or *proposings* are themselves a species of events.

59. The most frequent objection I encounter when defending the view that events are a species of proposition is that propositions are 'abstract' entities, whereas "what could be more *concrete* than an event!"[14] The proper answer is that what ontologists call 'abstract' entities are more properly called 'conceptual' entities. For although historically such things as triangularity and justice, which are in a straightforward sense abstract, have been taken to be paradigm cases of conceptual entities, not all conceptual entities conform to those paradigms. This stands out most clearly if, as I believe we must, we take *individual concepts* seriously. It would be paradoxical in the extreme to say that in the context:

Socrates is a substance,

where 'Socrates' stands for an individual concept (see TTC), *what* it stands for is an 'abstract entity.' Or, to use a somewhat less controversial example of a Fregean type, in the context:

Jones believes that Socrates was captious,

the word 'Socrates' stands for an individual concept—that is, in a suitable sense, a conceptual entity. But, again, it would be paradoxical to say that, even in this context, 'Socrates' stands for an abstract entity.

VI

60. The generic form of events, sentences, and, hence, of action sentences is:

$$S\text{'s } V\text{-ing} \begin{cases} \text{took place} \\ \text{is taking place} \\ \text{will take place} \end{cases}.$$

---

[14] Needless to say, in this context, events must be carefully distinguished from event types.

I have proposed that this generic form be reconstructed as:

$$\text{That } S \text{ } Vs \begin{Bmatrix} \text{was true} \\ \text{is true} \\ \text{will be true} \end{Bmatrix}.$$

As for the finer grained form of event sentences, the key, as I see it, has been given us by Professor Romane Clark, whose unpublished paper, "In Any Event: Davidson's Analysis of the Logical Form of Action Sentences," caused so many of the ideas with which I was groping to fall into place, that I rarely have read a paper with greater excitement.[15]

61. Clark correctly calls attention to the fact that to understand the logical form of statements involving event expressions, we must understand the logical form of those more basic statements which, without the use of event expressions, tell us that something has taken place. Thus, in my terms, to understand the form of:

S's V-ing took place,

we must understand the structure of:

S V-ed.

In terms of a by now classic example, to understand the structure of:

(The event of) Jones' buttering the toast in the bathroom at midnight for Smith, while the band was playing in honor of Georges Pompidou, took place,

we must understand the structure of the corresponding first level statement:

Jones buttered the toast in the bathroom at midnight for Smith while the band was playing in honor of Georges Pompidou.

62. I threw in the 'while'-clause, because I have long been groping for an account of the basic use of such words as 'while,' 'after,' 'before,' which does not treat them as relation words. For to treat them as such forces us into an event ontology. Thus, if in their basic use they are relation words, they require singular terms of which to be predicated, and these singular terms would be event expressions, construed as

---

[15] This paper has since been published as Section I of [2].—Editor's note. [Eds.—This is an original note from the editor of *Noûs*, not from the anthology editors.]

basic, for surely 'while,' 'during,' etc., must occur in ground floor descriptions of the world. (See, for example, TWO, esp. pp. 550-2, 567-77.*)

63. Leaving aside the 'while'-clause, why is not the remainder of the sentence to be construed as asserting a five term relation to hold between Jones, the toast, the bathroom, the time, and Smith? Clark, to my mind, uses the correct strategy—although his formal apparatus may need some reshaping—by construing 'in the bathroom,' 'at midnight,' and 'for Smith' as adverbial modifiers of the verb 'to butter.' Adverbial modifiers *of this kind* (though this does not seem to be true of all adverbs) make, in effect, big verbs out of little ones, just as logical connectives make big sentences out of little ones. Thus, the second sentence above, in spite of its complicated surface structure, would still have the form:

V-ed (Jones, the bread).

The 'bit' verb construed by the use of these modifiers remains a dyadic one, in spite of the involvement of the bathroom, the time, and Smith. Looking at it more closely,

Jones buttered the toast for Smith at midnight in the bathroom

can be reconstructed as:

[In the bathroom [at midnight [for Smith]]] buttered (Jones, the toast),

which, given carefully formulated rules (implicit in ordinary usage), entails:

Jones buttered the toast,
Jones buttered the toast for Smith,
Jones buttered the toast at midnight,
Jones buttered the toast in the bathroom,

not to mention various combinations of the same ingredients, all of which, properly regimented, begin,

Jones buttered the toast....

64. Clark's analysis, in my opinion, also provides the key to the problem of the identity of events and hence of actions. This problem, which any theory of events must face, is at the center of the stage—not only in action theory, but, for example,

* [Eds.—Sections XI, XVI, and XVII.]

in recent discussions of the mind-body problem. But that is, again, a story for another occasion.

References*

[1] Donald Davidson, "Actions, Reasons, and Causes", *Journal of Philosophy* 60 (1963): 685-700.
[2] Romane Clark, "Concerning the Logic of Predicate Modifiers", *Noûs*, 4(1970): 311-35.
[3] Ernest Nagel, *Sovereign Reason and Other Studies in the Philosophy of Science* (Glencoe, Illinois: Free Press, 1954).

---

 * [Eds.—We removed the bibliographic entries for Sellars's own works, and replaced the in-text citations with standard abbreviations, rather than references to the number of the bibliographic reference. The removed entries (referred to in the text) are to SRLG, EPM, CDCM, AE, SPR, TWO, IV, TA, SM, LTC, MP, and TTC.]

10
Volitions Re-Affirmed

I

1. What is a volition? It is a mental act, as conceptual a mental act as an occurrent believing.[1] Like the latter it is an event which finds overt expression—if one is in a thinking-out-loud frame of mind—in a sentential utterance, thus

   I will do *A* here and now.

In order that the trees not obscure the forest, it will be useful to regiment a little and adopt a philosophical idiolect in which it is 'shall' rather than 'will' which expresses intention. I will accordingly rewrite the above as

   I shall do *A* here and now

to bring it in line with

   The gardener shall mow the lawn.

2. As acts, volitions are episodes, as are occurrent believings. The basic grammar of 'volition' is

   Person wills to do *A* then and there.

3. The verb 'to will', so used, strikes many as not only contrived (which to a certain extent it is), but contrived to save a theory which urgently needs a verb to support the verbal noun 'volition'. But is it really a contraption? After all, it does occur in first person *expressions* of intention. As for second and third person *ascriptions* of occurrent here-now intentions to act, it must be confessed that the verb or its equivalent is more difficult to find. But how serious is this deficiency? In this respect the verb 'to will' and the verbal noun 'volition' are in the same boat. What we can say, and this is the heart of the matter, is that if the one is needed, so is the

---

[1] I use the phrase 'occurrent believing' in my dialectic, not because I think it is a particularly happy one, but because it implies the 'assertion' (not, of course, in the illocutionary sense) as contrasted with the 'entertaining' of a propositional content. I would be happier with 'occurrent thinking that'.

other. If the theory of volitions is a sound one, so is the theory that people will to do actions.

4. A parallel point can be made about occurrent beliefs. If the theory of occurrent belief is a sound one, there is a need for some such verb as 'to (occurrently) believe'. Now many philosophers believe (sometimes occurrently) in occurrent belief. Some of them seem to assume that ordinary language contains an expression for this concept, among the candidates being 'to suddenly think that-p' and 'to be struck by the thought that-p'. But the latter imply, as the desired locution does not, that the thinking in question is not the conclusion of a process of reasoning.

5. The key to the situation, surely, is that our ordinary interest in mental events is highly specific and concerned to differentiate cases and contexts. This is particularly true of those *on the spot* intentions which result in action. What concerns us is whether the agent acted on impulse or did not act impulsively, considered alternatives or did not consider alternatives, deliberated or did not deliberate. From the standpoint of volition theory, in all these cases action is caused by volition. But the volitions themselves came about in importantly different ways.

6. Volitions, of course, though acts are not actions, pieces of conduct. They are mental *actualities* in Aristotle's sense of the term (*energeiai*). The same is obviously true of occurrent beliefs. Since what one wills is always an action, it doesn't even make sense to speak of willing to will, any more than it makes sense to speak of willing to (occurrently) believe something.[2] One can, of course, will to do something now which one thinks makes it likely that at a certain time in the future one will will to do a certain action. Similarly, one can will to do something now which one thinks makes it likely that at a certain time in the future one will occurrently believe a certain proposition.

7. Consequently, volitions are not tryings, for trying to do A is acting in a way which one hopes will eventuate in a doing of A. (It should be noticed, however, that some philosophers who have flirted with volitions, while shying away from the term have given 'try' a technical use in which it comes close to standing for volition.)

8. Although volitions are acts, they should not be thought of as instantaneous. Here, again, we can draw on Aristotle, who distinguished between a continuing act and a change. One could sense-red for a minute (or contemplate an essence), without the sensing (or contemplation) being a process of change, even though it is accompanied, perhaps necessarily, by change. How long do volitions last? Long

---

[2] The very centrality of the concept of volition in the theory of action has tempted philosophers to claim that in the last analysis what agents *really* do is will. 'Volitions are the true actions.' I certainly do not wish to deny either the essential connection between volition and agency or the fact that in a broad sense of 'do' willing is a doing. The fact remains, however, that in the specific sense of 'do' which is involved in the practical question 'What shall I do?' volitions are not doings.

enough to do their job of getting actions going. It must be borne in mind that reference to volitions (and to mental acts generally) as well as to intentions, beliefs and propensities pertaining thereto, is part of our theory of persons, and they have the properties attributed to them by the theory—to the extent that, of course, the theory is a good one.[3]

9. Nor is it correct, I believe, to characterize volitions as parts of actions, the initial stages which bring the rest. Thus, when I move my finger and my finger moves because I will to move it, the initial stage of the moving is exactly that; the initial stage of the moving begins when the finger begins to move.

10. What makes it tempting to think that a volition is part of a willed action is that the *concept* of a volition is contained in—i.e. is a part of—the *concept* of an action. An action is essentially the sort of thing that is brought about by volition, though not necessarily the volition to do that action.

11. This implication is carried by action locutions (e.g. 'raising one's arm'), as contrasted with locutions which describe bodily occurrences which a person is (usually) able to bring about (e.g. 'one's arm going up'). Even if one takes the strong position that to ascribe an action to an agent is to imply the occurrence of a volition, it would be a mistake to conclude that the volition, though 'essential' to the occurrence of the action, is part of it. 'Part' is, indeed, said in many ways, and in many ways actions have 'parts'. However close the conceptual tie between volition and action, the decisive consideration remains that volitions are causes of actions, and it would, indeed, be a strange sense of 'part' in which a cause is part of its effect.

12. If volitions bring about actions, they do not always bring about the action which is willed. Indeed, no action at all may result. To explore these facts we must make use of the familiar concept of a minimal action, i.e. an action which one does not do by doing another action. Consider a volition which has the form,

I shall do [minimal action] in order to bring about X and thus do A

or

I shall do A by doing MA

for example,

I shall close my finger in order to cause the gun to go off and thus to fire it.
I shall fire the gun by closing my finger.

---

[3] That a Scientific Realist can take seriously the Aristotelian conception of continuing mental acts which are not changes and yet envisage their 'identification' with neurophysiological processes which are essentially changes (in which, however, certain spatio-temporal patterns are preserved) is grounded in his view of the essentially functional and contentually gappy character of mental acts as conceived in the Manifest Image.

Let us suppose that I am not paralyzed nor prevented from doing the minimal action. I do it, but instead of causing X, cause Y. As a result I do not do A, but rather B; thus, I dislodge the trigger—the gun being defective.

13. One does non-minimal actions by doing minimal actions which have certain results. Does this entail that one wills to do a non-minimal action by willing to do a minimal action *which one believes* will have a certain result? Here one must be careful, for this way of putting it implies that there occurs a separate volition to do the minimal action. The idea that this is in fact the case has proved tempting. I trace this temptation to a misuse of a (not unimportant) contrast between minimal and non-minimal action which is closely related to the conceptual distinction between them.

14. In addition to being actions which are not done *by* doing something else, minimal actions are as securely under our voluntary control as anything could be. Only abnormal states (e.g. paralysis) which deprive us of our very ability to do them remove them from our voluntary control. Even when physical restraint prevents us from doing one minimal action, we can resist by resorting to other minimal actions which we hope will have the same ultimate effect. In short there is a striking difference in the extent to which minimal and non-minimal actions involve the friendliness of circumstance.

15. It is this theme which makes possible the confusion. An analogy may be helpful. Suppose someone were to argue that perceptual 'takings' of physical objects are to be analyzed in terms of takings *proper* which are not of physical objects. One 'takes' there to be a red-topped table in front of one by virtue of *taking* there to be a red rectangular expanse, and 'accepting' the idea that the red rectangular expanse is a constituent of a near-by table top. And suppose that we were offered as a reason for this claim the fact that there is less epistemic risk in taking there to be a red rectangular expanse in front of one than there is in taking there to be a red-topped table in front of one. More can go wrong. Most of us, I believe, would reject the argument, even if embellished along familiar lines.

16. Unless circumstances are such as to make us wary, we simply take there to be a red-topped table over there. Similarly, unless the circumstances are such as to make us wary, we simply will *to open the window by pushing it*, where this does not mean that we will to push the window, believing that pushing it will cause it to become open.[4] In precisely this sense there is no separate volition to push. Volitions to do *A* by doing *MA* no more consist of volitions *proper* to do *MA* plus causal beliefs, than takings of tables consist of takings *proper* of expanses plus beliefs as to where these expanses make their home.

17. A related point is that if one wills to play a melody, there need be no volition, with respect to each note, to sound that note. It is those who are learning

---

[4] This is not, of course, to deny that there is a sense in which if Jones willed to open the window by pushing it, he willed to push the window.

to play the melody who are in this position, as was the fabled centipede who fell into confusion when he was asked how he walked.

18. There is, thus, an important place for the concept of an action being in one's voluntary control in the sense that if, just before doing it, one had willed not to do it, one would not have done it, a concept obviously akin to that of avoidable action as defined by Charles Stevenson.[5] Playing each note in a learned melody would be an action in one's voluntary control, even though playing the melody which is willed.

19. I shall conclude this initial stock-taking of volition theory with a bow and a wave of the hand to a question which raises central issues in metaphysics and the philosophy of mind, a serious treatment of which would take me far beyond the scope of this essay. How can a volition to raise one's finger have so close a conceptual tie with finger raising and yet be the cause of a finger raising? The crux of the answer must be that to specify the content of a mental act is analogous to saying what an expression means. In each case we classify by the use of a (usually) complex functional sortal built from expressions which have specifiable linguistic functions. The correct application of the sortal implies that the item is subject to pattern-governed uniformities which can be described without the use of intentional terms. Thus, to every explanation in mentalistic terms there corresponds *in principle* an explanation in non-mentalistic terms.[6] I say 'in principle' because, in even the simplest cases, the complexity of such an explanation would be unmanageable. Mentalistic explanations involve a cumulative wisdom which early researchers in artificial intelligence soon came to appreciate.[7]

II

20. I return to the task of locating volitions in the larger framework of mental activity. Once again it will be helpful, I believe, to take another joint look at volitions and perceptual takings. The latter, which can for our present purposes be construed as a variety of occurrent belief, are not, of course, actions. One acts, in perception, by opening one's eyes, looking, observing, focussing one's attention, etc. The point of all this action is to make possible a certain non-action, one's

---

[5] *Ethics and Language*, New Haven, 1944, p. 298.

[6] This is the positive side of the argument for the identity theory which Davidson rests on the 'anomalousness' of the mental. (Donald Davidson, 'Mental Events', in L. Foster and J. W. Swanson (eds.), *Experience and Theory*, Amherst, 1970.)

[7] The metaphysics and philosophy of mind adumbrated in this paragraph are developed in *Science and Metaphysics*, London, 1968. The essential points are made in 'Meaning as Functional Classification', in J. G. Troyer and S. C. Wheeler III (eds.), *Intentionality, Language and Translation*; *Synthese* 27 (1974), Dordrecht, Holland, and 'Language as Thought and as Communication', *Philosophy and Phenomenological Research* 30 (1969). (Reprinted in *Essays in Philosophy and Its History*, Dordrecht, Holland, 1974.)

being caused to have a perceptual occurrent belief. If circumstances are favorable, the belief is true. Its content is available to serve as a *premise* in our thinking about how things stand in the world around us.

21. In perceptual taking the world impinges on our mind. In volition the mind impinges on the world—indeed, in many cases, on itself, for the mind is part of the world, and while the concept of a mental act must be carefully distinguished from that of a mental action, there obviously are mental actions. If circumstances are favorable, and we have the relevant abilities, a volition to do A is the cause of one's doing A and is *realized* (a concept closely akin to that of truth) by the doing of A.

22. Furthermore, just as it is an essential part of the function of perceptual takings to provide *premises*—though they may occur without the content they provide actually serving as a premise—so it is an essential part of the function of volitions that their content serve as *conclusions* of practical reasonings—though, as in the case of impulsive action, they may occur without their content actually having served as a conclusion.

23. This is not the occasion on which to elaborate a theory of practical reasoning. I cannot, however, dispense with some reflections on the topic. I have touched on it in print on a number of occasions, though not always, I am afraid, either clearly or distinctly.[8] I do, however, think that I was on the right track, and that in spite of serious blemishes and, on occasion, downright mistakes, the general picture was true. According to that picture, practical reasoning is genuinely, *reasoning*, reasoning in a full blooded sense.

24. The fundamental thesis is that one intention can imply another intention in that sense of 'imply' in which implication authorizes inference, just as one belief can imply another belief. Here, of course, we must be careful. In the latter case we distinguish between belief as someone's state of believing, and belief as what is believed. We distinguish between what is implied by *what* Jones believes, thus p, and what is implied by the fact that he believes it. An ideally rational person would, of course, believe all the implications of what he believes. He would equally intend all the implications of what he intends. Neither, of course, is true of ordinary mortals.

25. I shall momentarily adopt a convention, which I shall not attempt to justify here,[9] according to which the content of a state of belief is represented by

---

[8] See, for example, 'Imperatives, Intentions and the Logic of "Ought"['], in H. N. Castañeda [and G. Nakhnikian] (ed[s].). *Morality and the Language of Conduct*, Detroit 1965, and 'Thought and Action' in Keith Lehrer (ed.), *Freedom and Determinism*, New York 1966. For an attempt to single out the distinctive features of practical reasoning in the context of the moral point of view, see Chapter 7 of *Science and Metaphysics*, London 1968, also 'On Knowing the Better and Doing the Worse' and "...this I or he or it (the thing) which thinks" in *Essays in Philosophy and Its History*, Dordrecht, Holland, 1974. [Eds.—See Chs. 6, 7, 13, and 14 of this volume.]

[9] But see Chapter 3 of *Science and Metaphysics*; for a brief presentation of meaning and intentionality which provides the metaphysical underpinning which the present essay obviously requires, see 'Meaning as Functional Classification', in *Intentionality, Language, and Translation*; Synthese 27 (1974), (ed. by J. G. Troyer and S. C. Wheeler III), Dordrecht, Holland.

dot-quoting the sentence in our language which would be the appropriate expression of that belief. We can think of the dot-quoted expressions as standing for propositions. Thus '·2 + 2 = 4·' stands for the proposition that 2 + 2 = 4. Suppose that Jones believes that he himself is wise. Then the content of his state of belief is the proposition ·I am wise· [Jones]* where the bracketed 'Jones' serves as an index which informs us that the English sentence used to formulate this content is construed as one which would appropriately express Jones' belief state, if he belonged to the English speaking community. I put the bracketed 'Jones' outside the quotes, because, as Castañeda has pointed out, Jones may not believe that he himself is Jones, which '·I (Jones) am wise·' would imply.

26. It is a familiar story that other indices are necessary to represent other features of propositional contents, those features traditionally called 'egocentric', but now appropriately called, following Pierce, 'indexical'. In what follows I shall abstract from these niceties. Indeed, I shall shortly fall back on the standard literary conventions by which authors represent what is going on in the minds of their characters.

27. But before taking a relaxed stance, I shall continue for a moment to regiment, for a parallel technical point needs to be made about intentions. Thus, if at t_1 Jones intends to do A at t_2, the content of his intention is represented by '·I shall do A at t_2·' (with appropriate indices). And if Jones at t_1 intends to do A there and then, the content of his intention is represented by '·I shall now do A·' with appropriate indices. This content itself, as contrasted with the intending of which it is the content, can be said to be an intention, as the content of a believing can be said to be a belief (proposition).

28. Using 'I_i' as a variable which ranges over intention-contents, as 'P' 'Q' ... range over propositions, we represent that one intention-content implies another intention-content by

I_i implies I_j

as we represent that one belief-content implies another belief-content by

P implies Q.

29. Volitions are, as I have emphasized, but one variety of occurrent intention (state), as perceptual takings are but one variety of occurrent belief (state).

* [Eds.—Correction of
·I am wise [Jones]
in the original printing. The corrected text matches Sellars's typescript. The relevant typescript is document 31735062222454, Box 44, Folder 9, Wilfrid S. Sellars Papers, 1899-1990, ASP.1991.01, Archives of Scientific Philosophy, Archives & Special Collections, University of Pittsburgh Library System.

Volitions, accordingly, can be subsumed under the general thesis that one occurrent intention can have relevantly the same content as another occurrent intention, and as a disposition or propensity to be in a certain occurrent intention (state), just as one occurrent belief can have relevantly the same content as another occurrent belief and as a disposition or propensity to be in a certain occurrent belief (state).

III

30. I now turn to a relatively informal treatment of some of the more important aspects of practical thinking to which the above distinctions are relevant.

31. I noted at the beginning that one kind of intention an agent can have is the intention that something come to be the case. In the kind of case we considered, the auxiliary 'shall' which expresses intention occurred within a grammatically simple sentence, directly modifying the main verb, thus

The gardener shall mow the lawn

With an eye to constructing expressions for intentions that complex (e.g. conjunctive) states of affairs be the case, it will be useful to adopt the phrase 'it shall be the case that...' which has the desired flexibility.[10] As a notational convenience, let us rewrite

It shall be the case that-p

as

Shall be [p]

Using the same general style, intentions of the shall-do kind, thus

I shall do A at t

can be rewritten as

Shall [I to do A at t]

---

[10] It has the drawback, from the standpoint of metaphysics, of involving the use of a that- clause, and, hence, of explicitly introducing propositions. The reader should reflect on the reading 'it is not the case that p and q' for 'not (p and q)'. This suggests that what is wanted is a 'shall' operator which has '...' as its scope without climbing the ontological (indeed, semantic) ladder.

32. We clearly need a principle to relate 'shall be' to 'shall do'. In the absence of further distinctions which would be necessary to spell it out, I propose to rely on the intuitive (to me, at least) equivalence of

It shall be the case that-p

with

I shall do what I can to make it the case that-p[11]

which I shall rewrite as

Shall make [p].

33. Another principle is to the effect that

Shall make [I will A at t]

implies

Shall [I to do A at t]

These principles connect intentions that something be the case with intentions to act.

34. Still another principle, the correct formulation of which would involve a return to the topic of indices, is to the effect that if at t one intends

Shall be [p is the case ten minutes from now]

then, if one minute later one intends

Shall be [p is the case nine minutes from now],

in an important sense one has not changed one's mind. This connects the 'logic' of intentions with their 'chronologic'.

35. I now come to a key topic, my views on which have led Castañeda[12] to say that according to my theory practical reasoning is not reasoning 'in the full

---

[11] It should be borne in mind that intentions (as contrasted with hopes, wishes, etc.) carry with them the presupposition that what is intended is (in considerably more than the purely logical sense) possible. (From this point on I let the ontological chips fall where they may.)

[12] In an unpublished manuscript.

blooded sense'. I have steadfastly denied that expressions of intention belong in the scope of either truth functional connectives or quantifiers.

36. Thus, while I regard

Shall be [p and q]

as well formed, I do not so regard

Shall be [p] and shall be [q]

Similarly, although I regard

Shall be [not-p]

as well formed, I do not so regard

Not (shall be [p]).

37. In my early writings on practical reasoning,[13] I claimed that it is governed by only one basic principle concerning implications pertaining to intentions. I formulated it thus

'Shall [p]' implies 'shall [q]' ↔ 'p' implies 'q'

I still think that this was not wrongheaded, but have come to see that it must be carefully embedded in a far more complicated framework than I then realized.[14]

38. To begin with, I made too crude an assimilation of

I shall do A

to

Shall be [I will do A]

for, although contrary indications were not lacking in my actual formulations, I tended to view the constituents of all intentions as future indicatives, thus overlooking, for example, the fact that my own future actions can enter into my

---

[13] E.g. The initial version of 'Imperatives, Intentions and the Logic of "Ought"', *Methodos* 8 (1956).
[14] The many shortcomings in my published discussions of practical reasoning have been pointed out by patient and friendly critics—in particular Hector Castañeda and Bruce Aune, from both of whom I have learned a great deal. [Eds.—For Sellars's correspondence with Castañeda and Aune, see Chs. 22 and 23 of this volume.]

280 THE METAPHYSICS OF PRACTICE

reasonings *sometimes* as actions to be done and *sometimes* as actions which it is hypothesized that I will actually do.[15]

39. Before I end this breast beating and begin to accentuate the positive, one more confession is essential. In 'Thought and Action' I rejected the principle that

'Shall [p]' and 'shall [q]' imply 'shall [p and q]'

I am not clear why I did so, since it was clearly required by my basic principle together with Conjunction Introduction for propositions. I have long recognized and regretted this mistake—which, however, I tacitly circumvented in my treatment of what I called the "summative stage" of deliberation.[16]

40. Getting back to fundamentals, my strategy was to picture practical reasoning as presenting the agent with alternative scenarios between which a choice could be made. I regarded these alternative scenarios as having the form

Shall be [p_i and p_j...and...I will do A_i at t_j...]

with appropriate sprinklings of negation to generate a family of intendible possible futures. Logical and causal implications between states of affairs served to enrich intendible futures with their implications, and to eliminate intendible futures with inconsistent constituents.

41. Thus I thought of a choice between scenarios as having the form of a set of questions.

Shall be [scenario$_1$]?
Shall be [scenario$_2$]?
.
.
.
.
Shall be [scenario$_n$]?

42. If the chosen scenario included as a conjunct the agent's doing A_i at t_j, then by simplification one would get

Shall be [I will do A_i at t_j]

and, hence, in my idiolect,

---

[15] See paragraphs 66–7 below.   [16] *Op. cit.*, pp. 131ff.

I shall do A_i at t_j.

43. How do states of affairs get into a scenario? The obvious, but unilluminating, answer is that they are thought to be relevant. This points to a concept of preference. Here one must be careful to distinguish an *expression* of preference from an autobiographical *ascription* of a preference to oneself. The former is the expression of a choice, and can be schematized in terms of the questions,

Shall [X and not-Y]? Shall [not-X and Y]?

and an outcome,

Shall [X and not-Y]

the sequence representing a choice of X as over and against Y. A person's preference of X over Y can be viewed as a disposition to make such a choice. Preference of an object of one kind to an object of another kind can be viewed as a preference concerning appropriate states of affairs involving such objects—thus, eating an apple as contrasted with eating an orange.

44. In general, preference is relative to an assumed context, α. Thus,

Shall [α and X and not-Y]?
Shall [α and not-X and Y]?
Shall [α and X and not-Y]

Clearly, given a different context, β, one might choose Y instead of X.

45. A concept of indifference is also needed, but I am concerned to sketch rather than map. It is essential to note, however, that the concept of preference I have been sketching has made no appeal to such concepts as desire, aversion, satisfaction, enjoyment, and disenjoyment.

46. Notice also that choice has been described in a way which involves no reference on the agent's part to his preferences. I do not, of course, deny that references to one's preferences—or, for that matter, intentions, desires and aversions—can occur in the scenarios between which one chooses. But such references are at a higher rung on the semantic ladder than first-level practical thoughts, and one should be clear about the latter before starting to climb.

47. It is as much a mistake to think of choice as essentially involving a reference to one's preferences, as it is to take as a paradigm of practical reasoning, an argument which has as its major premise

I intend to bring about X.

If one is looking for a simple paradigm, neatly regimented into syllogistic form, one would do better to choose

I shall bring about X
[Bringing about X implies doing A at t]
So, I shall do A at t.

48. Notice that the account I have been giving implies that what is represented in the preceding paragraph by a syllogism can be expanded—for the purpose of getting insight into its depth structure—into a choice between two scenarios,

Shall be [α and I will bring about X and I will do A at t]?
Shall be [α and I will not bring about X and I will not do A at t]?
Shall be [α and I will bring about X and I will do A at t]

(where 'α' represents that common part of the scenarios which is not in question at the time of the choice—i.e. has in some sense already been decided), an inferential move to

Shall be [I will do A at t]

and, from there to

Shall [I to do A at t]
i.e. I shall A at t.

49. The syllogism, however, implies, as the expanded version does not, that the *ground* of the preference for scenario$_1$ lies in the bringing about of X, rather than in the doing of A.

IV

50. Let us now take a closer look at constituents of scenarios other than actions by the agent. My concern is with the distinction between those which are up to the agent and those which are not. My linguistic intuitions tell me that we so use 'up to the agent' that a state of affairs, that p, is up to the agent if and only if

Agent is able to bring it about that p and also able to bring about that not-p

i.e. it is up to the agent whether or not p. It might be thought that the 'not-p' is redundant, but it seems clear that an agent might be able to bring it about that p, without being able to bring it about that not-p. I may be able to bring it about that Jones dies at t by shooting him, but not able to bring it about that Jones lives at t (since another gunman may shoot him just in case I don't).

51. Since most actions involve bringing about states of affairs by consisting in doing something which brings these states of affairs about, it is important to see that the above does not conflict with the fundamental principle that if an agent is able to do A he is also able to do not-A. For

Jones is able to bring it about that p, but not able to bring it about that not-p

is compatible with

Jones is able to bring it about that p, and able not to bring it about that p.

52. In view of these considerations, the basic distinction we need is between those constituents of a scenario which the agent conceives to be in his power, including certain actions on his part, and those which he conceives not to be in his power.

53. All this, however, is rather crude, and needs to be refined and articulated. Unfortunately there is only time to sketch the essentials. I shall focus my attention on those constituents of a scenario which are common to a set of competing scenarios which practical reasoning has presented for a choice.

54. Suppose that an agent has decided that a certain state of affairs obtains. As I see it, we need a principle—which I have called the So-be-it principle,[17] but which might also be called the Reality principle, if the latter phrase had not already been pre-empted, to the effect that

'p' and 'shall be [α]' imply 'shall be [p and α]'

The phrase 'so be it' is misleading; it implies a fatalistic attitude which has nothing to do with the principle. Indeed, there is an important class of cases where the agent's reason for deciding that p will be the case, is that p is in his power and he has decided to bring it about.

55. To swallow this principle, one must bear in mind that to intend

Shall be [p and α]

a person need not *desire* that p be the case nor even *like* the idea of p's being the case. The point of the principle is simply that the state of affairs gets into the logical framework of practical thinking.

---

[17] 'Notes for a Revision of "Thought and Action"' (1971), an unpublished manuscript on which I have drawn heavily for this lecture. [Eds.—PRA, Ch. 19 of this volume.]

56. By virtue of So-be-it, an agent who has the intention that α be the case,

Shall be [α]

and has decided that p is (or will be) the case, is, if he is rational, confronted by the alternatives,

Shall be [p and α]?
Shall be [p and not-α]?

We can represent constituents which the agent has decided to be the case by 'F' (for 'Fact'). Thus,

Shall be [F and I bring about X and I will do A]

It is by virtue of this principle that practical reasoning presents a family of alternative scenarios which have 'F' as a common constituent, thus

Shall be [F and ...]?
Shall be [F and —]?

.
.
.
.

57. Needless to say there are many things which an agent has decided to be the case which don't get into the scenarios he actually considers, because they are taken to be irrelevant. But the same is true in the case of theoretical reasoning. The role of Conjunction Introduction is always subject to considerations of relevance, otherwise premises would proliferate to absurdity. I shall not pause to explore relevance, however, because the topic is in good hands.

58. The 'reality' principle throws light on a topic about which I, at least, have been confused. Thus consider

If it rains, I shall study.

I have been torn in different directions. In the *first* place I have been committed to the view that, when properly regimented, expressions of intention do not occur in the scope of truth functional connectives. This kept me from representing the above conditional intention by

$p \rightarrow$ shall [I will study].

59. In the *second* place, my conception of practical reasoning as culminating in a choice between intention scenarios which contain all the states of affairs believed to be relevant, led me to think of the scope of 'shall' in the above conditional intention as the entire hypothetical, thus

Shall [If it rains, I will study]

60. In the *third* place I had convinced myself that the premise from which an intention to act is derived is best construed—by an (I hope) rational reconstruction—as a single, if complex, premise which has the form of an intention.

61. In the *fourth* place, I was committed to the view that logical connectives within the scope of 'shall' connect sentences in the indicative mood. This pointed to

Shall [It is raining at $t \rightarrow$ I will study at t].

62. As I now see it, none of these considerations was wrongheaded. They were, however, embedded in an inadequate framework of principles and distinctions, the result being paradox.

63. What led me up the garden path was a too simple minded equation of the 'if, then' involved in conditional intention with material implication, a mistake which at the time was not entirely idiosyncratic. I was so hypnotized by the idea that the 'if, then' does *not* represent even a weak entailment-like relation between 'It will rain' and 'Shall [I will study]' that I leaped from that frying pan into the fire of taking it to represent material implication, with the above results.

64. But, as Austin has made us emphatically aware, there are cases in which 'if, then', represents neither material implication nor entailment. I by no means agree with all the uses to which he put this insight. It did, however, open my eyes to possibilities I had ignored. Of direct concern to us are those cases in which

If p, q

contextually implies that there is a valid argument which, perhaps with additional premises, would justify, given p, the conclusion that q; schematically,

p
$[r, s, t]$
.
.
.
―――
So, q.

Taking this as a cue, I found[18] it plausible to construe

If p, I shall do A

as a commitment to the idea that there is a valid form of practical reasoning, all of the constituents of which, save p, have already been decided; i.e. are such that either I have decided on factual grounds that they are the case, or I have decided to make them the case. What I am waiting on is only my decision (if I should so decide) that p is (or will be) the case.

65. The point I wish to make is that if I decide that p is the case, and do not change my mind in other respects, the relevant reasoning does not have the form

If p, I shall do A
p
───────────
So, I shall do A

but rather,

1. p	premise
2. Shall $[\alpha$ and $(p \to$ I will do $A)]$	premise
3. Shall $[p$ and α and $(p \to$ I will do $A)]$	1,2, So-be-it
4. So, shall be [I will do A]	MP (shall)[19]
I shall do A	

Notice that the conditional intention implies not only that I believe that doing A is up to me, but that I have not already decided that it is unconditionally the case that I will do it.

66. Castañeda has argued* that according to my original analysis, the following sentences

I. If I don't press button B, I shall press button A
II. If I don't press button A, I shall press button B

express logically equivalent intentions, although it is clear, after a moment's reflection, that they don't. He is right. In my original account they both transform into

───────────

[18] In the MS referred to in the previous note.
[19] I write 'MP (shall)' since, by virtue of the principle relating intention-implications to propositional implications, 3 implies 4.
* [Eds.—In "Some Reflections on Wilfrid Sellars' Theory of Intention," in H. N. Castañeda (ed.) *Action, Knowledge and Reality* (Indianapolis, 1975), pp. 27–54; at pp. 40–1.]

Shall [either I will press *B* or I will press *A*]

67. On the present account, the first expression, I, treats my not pressing *B* as something which is to be decided to be the case, my pressing button *A*, on the other hand, as something to be decided to do—the reverse holding in the case of II.

68. Accordingly, the first conditional intention points to the validity of

1. I did not press *B*	premise
2. Shall be [α and (I did not press *B* → I will press *A*)]	premise
3. Shall be [α and I did not press *B* and (I did not press *B* → I will press *A*)]	1,2, So-be-it
4. So, shall be [I will press *A*] I shall press *A*	3, MP (shall)[20]

The second conditional intention points to the validity of a similar argument with an interchange of buttons *A* and *B*.

V*

69. I have argued above (and elsewhere) that there are occurrent intentions, and that in the sense in which an occurrent belief can be said to be the conclusion of a process of reasoning from certain premises, an occurrent intention can be said to be the conclusion of a process of practical reasoning.

70. I have argued elsewhere[21] that it is proper to think of the fact that a person has certain beliefs and/or intentions which serve as *premises* in his drawing of a *conclusion*, as the *cause* of his accepting the conclusion. Given his frame of mind, they are an essential part of the explanation of how he came to accept the conclusion.

71. It follows from these considerations that *reasons* can be *causes* of actions. For practical premises can be causes of practical conclusions, and practical conclusions, in the form of volitions, cause actions.

72. However, not every constituent in a premise of practical reasoning can be said to be part of the reason why the agent acted as he did. Thus, in the text book type of case which is regimented by the form

I shall bring about *X*
[Bringing about *X* implies doing *A*]
I shall now do *A*

---

[20] See previous note. * [Eds.—Mistakenly numbered 'IV' in original.]
[21] 'Actions and Events', *Noûs* 7 (1973), reprinted in *Essays in Philosophy and its History*, Dordrecht, Holland, 1974. [Eds.—See Ch. 9 of this volume.]

it is implied that the constituent of the alternative scenarios the agent has been considering which accounts for the preference

Shall be [α and I will bring about X and I will do A]

is the bringing about of X. The agent is 'favorably disposed' toward the bringing about of X.

73. Shall we say that the agent *wants* or *desires* to bring about X? He clearly *intends* to bring about X. He clearly *prefers* bringing about X and doing A to not bringing about X and not doing A.

74. According to the account of preference sketched in Paragraphs 43ff. above, to be favorably disposed towards X is to be disposed to answer the questions

Shall be [X]?
Shall be [not-X]?

by

Shall be [X]

as contrasted with answering

Shall be [not-X]

or shrugging one's shoulders.

75. What is the relation between this, so to speak, purely conceptual sense of being favorably disposed, to the richer notion of desire? An intention is *realized* if the intended state of affairs comes to obtain. But desires can not only be *realized*, they can also be *satisfied*. How is this to be understood?[22] It seems to me that desiring that X be the case implies something like being disposed to enjoy the thought of X being the case. This, however, does not quite hit the mark. We must take seriously the fact that philosophers have traditionally connected desire with the will.

76. To connect desire with the will is, in our framework, to place it in the domain of intentions (and such cousins as hopes and wishes). This suggests that, in first approximation, to desire that X be the case is to be disposed to enjoy thinking 'it *shall* be the case that X,' i.e. 'I shall do what I can to make it the case that X'. One must bear in mind, of course, that one can enjoy thinking 'It shall be the case that X' without enjoying thinking 'It shall be the case that X and Y.'

---

[22] My initial wrestling with this problem in Section III of 'Thought and Action' was not without its insights, but got bogged down in inessentials.

77. It is a plausible psychological principle that if one is disposed to *enjoy* thinking 'It shall be the case that X' then one will have a propensity (other things being equal) to *think* 'It shall be the case that X.'[23]

78. Thus, in some cases at least, we can explain the fact that a person acts from a certain scenario in terms of his desires and aversions. I have been careful, however, not to imply that all dispositions to choose X and not-Y rather than not-X and Y are cases in which one desires X more than Y or has a greater aversion to Y than to X.

---

[23] I would hate to have to fill out the *ceteris paribus* clause. The topics of how one comes to have preferences between conceptually entertained states of affairs, and how one comes to enjoy (or disenjoy) contemplating the realization of certain states of affairs, as well as the role of conceptual connections in building up complex preferences and in transmitting 'hedonic tone', take one to the heart of nascent psychological theory ('The Law of Effect and the Higher Processes'). It is to be hoped that philosophers will play a constructive part in this enterprise as they have in other areas of scientific theorizing. Keeping the theory which is embedded in our practice clear of conceptual confusions (e.g. psychological hedonism) is the least they can do.

PART 3
FREE WILL AND *AKRASIA*

11
Fatalism and Determinism

I. Some Traditional Considerations

[1] It will be useful to begin our discussion of the reconcilability of the concept of "action of one's own free will" with scientific determinism by a discussion of the so-called Hume–Mill solution. In this tradition, it will be remembered, the problem appears as one concerning the compatibility of personal responsibility with the principle that every event has a cause. The fundamental move is to distinguish between causation and compulsion, and to argue that, while action of one's own free will is, of course, incompatible with compulsion, it is thought by Libertarians to be incompatible with causation because they have taken causation to be a form of or to involve compulsion. Action of one's own free will is no more to be equated with uncaused action than causation is with compulsion. As the Hume–Mill tradition sees it, two pairs of opposites, "free"–"compelled," "uncaused"–"caused" are collapsed by the Libertarian into one.

[2] Now there is certainly something of value in this way of approaching the problem, but it simply won't do as it stands. A series of comments, most of which are recognized, either explicitly or implicitly, by the tradition, will set the stage for a discussion of the problem as it exists today.

[3] The first thing to be noted is that the term "cause," as it appears in this argument, has a technical meaning, which by no means corresponds to that which it has in everyday life. The point is a familiar one, but it should at least be mentioned because it is a paradigm example of the role of ambiguity in the free-will issue.

[4] As Collingwood and others have pointed out, causation in the ordinary sense is the idea of the intervention of an agent in a system, thereby bringing about changes which would not otherwise have occurred. The root metaphor, to use Pepper's invaluable expression, is that of a person bringing it about that another person or a group of persons does something which the first person wishes to have done. It is worth noting, therefore, that this root metaphor is essentially that of compulsion. That this root metaphor is by no means completely "frozen" undoubtedly accounts, at least in part, for the fact that many philosophers find it simply "absurd" that an action which was caused could be done of the agent's own free will. It might also be added that, in this sense of causation, it is simply not the case that every episode has a cause. The king who causes a prisoner to be brought before him is not himself caused to make this move.

[5] The practical sense of causation in its application to nature was gradually "depersonalized" into the analogical concept of a non-person—a merely material thing—intervening in a system of non-persons—other merely material things—bringing about changes which would not otherwise have occurred. Familiar examples are to be found in the areas of mechanics and electrodynamics: the cue ball in a break; a thermostat in a heating system. Notice, however, as Collingwood has emphasized, that persons hover in the background of even this ostensibly depersonalized sense of the term. The cause may not be a person, but it is conceived of as manipulable by a person, at least in principle, and the objects involved are cut up, from this point of view, into that which intervenes and the remainder which constitute the system under intervention. This fact, as I see it, is essential to understanding what is ordinarily meant by a causal explanation. Not even in this extended sense is it true that every event has a cause. Furthermore, an event which is not in this sense caused need not therefore be a brute matter of fact, an unintelligible happenstance. Common sense and science alike make constant use of the concept of a system which changes in intelligible ways in the absence of external intervention.

[6] We shall have more to say at a later stage in the argument about the intelligibility of episodes which do not have intervening causes. Our next move must be to give a more adequate formulation of the Hume–Mill approach against the background of the above distinctions. In this reformulation, the intelligibility of episodes becomes their *predictability*, and determinism, although still couched in terms of "cause," becomes the thesis that all episodes are in principle predictable.

[7] It is often thought that universal predictability is an incoherent notion. The problem arises at two levels: (a) the level defined by the common sense framework of persons; (b) the level defined by the framework of microphysical theory. I shall be concerned with the place of predictability in the framework of persons shortly. As for (b), and abstracting from scientific issues pertaining to quantum mechanics, conceptual difficulties do arise about universal predictability if we fail to distinguish between what I shall call *epistemic* predictability and *logical* predictability. By epistemic predictability, I mean predictability by a predictor *in the system*. The concept of universal epistemic predictability does seem to be bound up with difficulties of the type explored by Gödel. By logical predictability, on the other hand, is meant that property of the process laws governing a physical system which involves the derivability of a description of the state of the system at a later time from a description of its state at an earlier time, without stipulating that the latter description be obtained by operations within the system. It can be argued, I believe, with considerable force, that the latter is a misuse of the term "predictability," but it does seem to me that this is what philosophers concerned with the free will and determinism issue have had in mind, and it simply muddies up the waters to harass these philosophers with Gödel problems about epistemic predictability.

[8] Returning now to the Hume-Mill gambit, we see that the point is well taken that, if causality is construed in terms of predictability rather than intervention, then the fact that an action is caused does not imply that it is compelled. On the other hand, the overtones of the ordinary use of the word "cause," pointed out above, make it unlikely that the Libertarian will be persuaded by one who puts the matter in this way.

[9] There is, as we have seen, a tension between the idea of "acting out of one's own free will" and "being caused to do something." It is therefore important to note that there may be a sense of "cause" which is stronger than that of mere predictability, and in which it is true to say that *actions are caused,* but not *that persons are caused to do them.* I shall be arguing shortly that there is such a sense, and that in this new sense volitions are, at least on occasion, the causes of actions. That causation in this further sense does not imply compulsion is indicated by its departure in grammar from the form "thing (or person) impinging on things (or persons) bringing about a change, etc."

But the Hume–Mill substitution of predictability for causation raises problems of its own, problems which in one way or another will be with us throughout the remainder of this paper. The crucial issue concerns the conceptual framework in which (or, as it used to be put, the level of explanation at which) the predictability is supposed to obtain. I have distinguished in a number of papers between what I call the "manifest image" and the "scientific image" of man-in-the-world.[1] Roughly, the manifest image corresponds to the world as conceived by P. F. Strawson—*roughly* it is the world as we know it to be in ordinary experience, supplemented by such inductive procedures as remain within the framework. The manifest image is, in particular, a framework in which the distinctive features of persons are conceptually irreducible to features of nonpersons, e.g. animals and merely material things.

[10] The scientific image, on the other hand, is man-in-the-world as we anticipate he would be conceived by a unified scientific account, which makes use of the familiar techniques of theory construction. The scientific image, although methodologically rooted in the manifest image, freely transcends the conceptual framework of the latter, introducing new concepts, as it is said, by "postulation," rather than by explicit definition, however widely construed. To articulate the philosophical tensions aroused by "scientific determinism," let us suppose that the scientific image contains a picture of man as part and parcel of a deterministic order. To make our thought experiment as forceful as possible, let us suppose that, sooner or later, quantum phenomena will be found to have a

---

[1] See, in particular, "Philosophy and the Scientific Image of Man," in Robert Colodny, ed., *Frontiers of Science and Philosophy* (Pittsburgh, 1962), reprinted as Chapter 1 in *Science, Perception and Reality* (London, 1963).

deterministic substructure. Only by pressing this assumption can the *irrelevance* of quantum indeterminacy to the problem of free will be made manifest.

[11] An indefinite amount of time could be spent in giving these two images of man-in-the-world a higher polish. I think, however, that the above remarks suffice to mobilize a useful conception of the contrast I have in mind. The question I want to raise concerns the force of the term "predictable" in these two radically different conceptual frameworks. Thus we have supposed it to be a framework principle of the scientific image that every episode, including the scientific counterparts of human thoughts and actions, is predictable. Is it, correspondingly, a framework principle of the manifest image that all human actions be predictable? Could it perhaps be a framework principle of the manifest image that not all actions are predictable, although the very same actions that are "manifestly" unpredictable are, as projected in the scientific image, in principle predictable? And, if so, would we have to say that one or the other image, no matter which, gives a false account of what there really is?

[12] If we now turn our attention to the manifest image, and examine the use of the term "predictable" in connection with persons and what they do, a number of points stand out quite clearly—provided, that is, that we are careful to avoid mixing in elements from the scientific image. To say of a person that his actions are predictable is not always a compliment. Even a person who can be counted on to do what is right is marked down a little when it is said that one can predict *exactly* what he will do. For to say this implies that he meets situations in routine ways, never thinking things through afresh or gaining new insight.

[13] To be predictable, in this image, means that a person's actions are habitual, inferable by inductive reasoning based on observation of his past behavior. For an action to be predictable is for it to be an expression of character. It is therefore essential to note that, however predictable a person may become, not all of his actions can be expressions of character. Actions form character as well as express it, and the idea that actions which, in one respect, *form* character must, in another respect, he *expressions* of character can be traced to a confusion of the concept of the *nature* of a person (which concept belongs to the scientific image) with the concept of *character*.

[14] Even within the manifest image, of course, things have natures. The natures of material things are their abilities and predictabilities. The "realm of nature" consists traditionally of those things the observable behavior of which is either predictable, even if only "for the most part," or unintelligible because random. Their intelligibility is a matter of dispositions and propensities working themselves out and being called into play.[2]

---

[2] When one thing acts on another it changes not only its state but also its short-term dispositions and propensities. Thus, when falling temperature causes water to freeze, it changes its propensities with respect to location and the transmission of light. This seems to be the sort of thing Kant has in mind when he speaks [A444, B472] of nature as the realm in which the causality of the cause is caused.

FATALISM AND DETERMINISM 297

[15] In the post-renaissance period, there began that blurring of the distinction between the manifest and the incipient scientific image that has been, ever since, a source of philosophical confusion. The combination of the failure to draw a clear distinction between inductive generalization and theory construction with an increasing appreciation of the power of scientific thought, led to an exaggerated conception of the place of predictability within the manifest framework of perceptible things. And since, whatever else persons may be, they are perceptible things, the modern form of the problem of free will began to take shape.

[16] It is therefore important to realize that, even with respect to merely material things, the manifest image is not able, out of its own resources, to generate a deterministic picture. A deterministic picture arises at best indirectly, by the correlation of perceptible things with systems of imperceptible scientific objects, which are metaphorically said to be "in" them.

[17] To explain what an observable thing does by reference to theoretical processes that are taking place 'within' it is a radically different sort of thing from explaining the same behavior in terms of observable antecedent states.

[18] A parallel, I believe, can be drawn between the above two modes of explanation and two modes of explaining the observable behavior of persons: (a) in terms of other observable behavior; (b) in terms of inner mental states. From this point of view, the explanation of behavior in terms of character would be analogous to explaining the observable behavior of material things by means of inductive generalizations. And when what a *person* does is not in this sense predictable—i.e. not an expression of "second nature" or character—it would nevertheless not be an "unintelligible" episode, as would be true if it were the behavior of a merely material thing, which could not have been predicted without appealing to theoretical considerations. The role of inner episodes in the manifest image can be compared to that of theoretical entities in the scientific image. They are, however, elements of an *autonomous* framework—not a speculative extension of microphysics—which carries the imprint of the specifically human observable behavior they are designed to explain.[3]

[19] Thus, whereas the inductively unexplainable behavior of a merely material thing would be said to be unintelligible, a matter of chance, an inductively unexplainable action of a *person*—i.e. one which could not be explained in terms of character—can be intelligible in terms of being capable of explanation with reference to the practical reasoning and, ultimately, the volition of which it is the expression.[4] Needless to say, character defined in terms of dispositions and

---

[3] For an elaboration of this interpretation of "mental acts" as commonsense theoretical episodes, the model for which is overt speech, see *Science, Perception and Reality*, pp. 181ff. (also in "Empiricism and the Philosophy of Mind," Vol. I of *Minnesota Studies in the Philosophy of Science*, pp. 311ff.). See also "Intentionality and the Mental" (with Roderick Chisholm) in Vol. II of the same *Minnesota Studies*, pp. 507–39.
[4] As, of course, are actions which are expressions of character or "second nature."

propensities pertaining to overt behavior will have its counterpart in the framework of mental episodes, just as causal properties operationally defined in the observation framework have their counterparts in the theoretical framework which explains them.

[20] Suppose it is granted that, in the manifest image, actions which are not intelligible in terms of character can nevertheless be intelligible in terms of the practical reasoning which is its cause.[5] But what, it may be asked, of this reasoning itself? Must not the occurrence of those inner episodes that explain the behavior of a rational being have a kind of *intelligibility?* And must not this intelligibility be a matter of *predictability?* The answer to the first question is, of course, yes. But to the second it is no! The intelligibility of thoughts is no more a matter of predictability than is the intelligibility of moves in games of chess—and for essentially the same reason.

[21] I have been arguing that, in the manifest image, not everything that even a routine person does is predictable in the sense of being an expression of character, and that its intelligibility does not require predictability in this sense. I want now to make the stronger point that when, in ordinary discourse, we speak of predicting what a person will do, we have in mind what I referred to above (§7*) as *epistemic* predictability. I want therefore to point out that, *given that this is the sense of predictability involved,* it is indeed a framework principle of the manifest image that the behavior of rational beings cannot be supposed to be universally predictable. This point transcends the more elementary one that acquiring a character presupposes actions which are not themselves expressions of character. For to be a rational being is to be a being who is capable of action that is not in character, and hence cannot be predicted within the framework of the manifest image.

[22] But might not all human action be predictable if no holds are barred—if, that is, we take into account its projection in the scientific image? And if so, would *this* predictability be compatible with any genuine sense of individual responsibility? (That the predictability in question would have to be *logical* rather than *epistemic* is clear.) But, before we take up these questions, it will be helpful to introduce some concepts pertaining to voluntary action and put them to use in defining additional dimensions of the problem of free will.

---

[5] The sense of "cause" involved is that in which theoretical episodes are said to be the cause of the observable behavior of material things.

* [Eds.—Original reference is to page 143 of the published version; we have replaced this with the specific paragraph referenced in the typescript. The relevant typescript (which is clearly not the typescript from which the published version was produced, but seems to be the closest one to the published version deposited in the archive) is document 31735062218940, Box 30, Folders 2–4, Wilfrid S. Sellars Papers, 1899–1990, ASP.1991.01, Archives of Scientific Philosophy, Archives & Special Collections, University of Pittsburgh Library System.

II. Volition

[23] The central concept pertaining to practical reason is that of volition. A volition is an inner episode, a mental act, which is, in the absence of paralysis and granted the existence of favorable circumstances, the cause of the corresponding action. Thus, in the absence of paralysis or constraint, the volition to raise one's right arm causes a raising of that arm. Before key issues in the free will-determinism syndrome can be properly formulated and resolved, it will be necessary to justify this concept.

[24] Volitions are a subclass of *thoughts*, which can be initially characterized as mental episodes having a propositional form. As I have argued in "Empiricism and the Philosophy of Mind" (and Peter Geach has also so argued in *Mental Acts*), the concept of the propositional form of a thought is to be construed as an analogical extension of the concept of propositional form as it applies to meaningful overt speech.

[25] The relation of a thought-episode to *what* is thought is correspondingly analogous to the relation of a meaningful utterance to *what* is said. Here the key is that to say of an utterance U that

U says that-p

is to classify the utterance as a 'that-p' utterance, in terms of its role in the language to which it belongs. 'That-p' is a class term, formed from the expression, in the language in which the classification is made, which plays the same role. Thus statements about what expressions mean *classify* rather than *relate:* a token which means that-p is a 'that-p' token.[6] It is often said that it is people rather than utterances which mean. But utterances are people uttering; the claim in question is true only in the trivial sense in which certain movements are a waltz only in so far as a person moving in certain ways is a person waltzing.

[26] By analogy, to say of a thought-episode that it is a thought that-p is to classify the episode as a 'that-p' episode. The framework of thoughts is to be construed as an explanatory framework of entities postulated by a commonsense theory, and the analogical character of thoughts is to be compared to the analogical character of the conceptual framework postulated by, say, microthermodynamics.

[27] The model for this commonsense theory is what I shall call "thinking-out-loud."[7] Here it is essential to distinguish between *thinking-out-loud* and *verbal*

---

[6] These points are developed in "Abstract Entities," *Review of Metaphysics*, XVI (1963), 627–671. See also "Notes on Intentionality," *Journal of Philosophy*, LXI (1964), pp. 655–65.

[7] This technical use of "thinking-out-loud" does not have the sense illustrated by "I was merely thinking out loud."

performances or *actions*. Telling someone something, or telling him to do something, are actions; thinking-out-loud is not. Imagine a person who wonders, observes, reasons, deliberates, decides, and initiates action "out loud." That thinkings-out-loud are not actions, in the sense of pieces of conduct, follows from the simple but basic fact that they are not the sort of thing that is voluntarily brought about. There are, indeed, actions which are initiated by utterances; these, *if they were spontaneously or candidly made*, would be thinkings-out-loud. Thus, telling someone that there is a snake in the grass might be *phonetically* identical with thinking-out-loud that there is a snake in the grass. But to classify it as a *telling* is to characterize it as the sort of thing that could be initiated by deciding-out-loud to do it. And an utterance thus initiated is, just for this reason, *not* a thinking-out-loud.

[28] One must be careful here, for there *are* actions pertaining to thinking-out-loud. But these actions are not such items as thinking-out-loud that-p, but rather such items as

thinking-out-loud about whether $39 \times 7 = 273$

or

deliberating-out-loud whether to go to a movie.

[29] Thus, consider the person who notices-out-loud that the table is green. His utterance

Lo, the table is green!

would not be a noticing-out-loud, unless it were a spontaneous reaction to the visual stimulus. An utterance like it in other respects, but which was brought about in the manner

"I shall utter 'Lo, the table is green,'
so, lo, the table is green"

would not be a thinking-out-loud, nor would

"...therefore, it will rain,"

if its context was

"I shall utter 'therefore, it will rain';
so, therefore, it will rain,"

as contrasted with

"It is cloudy;
therefore, it will rain."

[30] Thinkings-out-loud can, of course, be indirectly brought about through self-training. But then the actions involved are not these thinkings-out-loud themselves, but rather the bringing about of propensities to think-out-loud in these ways in specified kinds of circumstance.

[31] To sum up, then, thoughts-out-loud are not actions, where "action" is understood to mean the sort of thing that one can appropriately be said to decide to do. The same is true of covert thoughts. They are "acts," *not* in the conduct sense in which "action" was just used, but only in the sense that they are *actualities*. The same is true of such nonconceptual "inner episodes" as sensations, feelings and sense-impressions. These are "doings," only in that broad sense in which any verb in the active voice that stands for an episode expresses a doing. This is not to say that there are no such things as covert mental actions in the conduct sense. But, as in the case of actions pertaining to thinking-out-loud, these actions are not such items as thinking that Tom is tall, but rather such items as working on a mathematical problem, or deliberating about whether to go to a movie.

[32] Thoughts, then, are, in the first instance, theoretical episodes designed to explain how people can behave intelligently, not only when their behavior is permeated by thinking-out-loud, but when they are silent.[8] That covert thoughts are to be reconstructed, in the first instance, as theoretical entities, carries with it the consequence that what determines the frequency and rapidity with which thoughts can legitimately be said to occur is the character of the overt phenomena which they are designed to explain. Roughly, we have reason to suppose that people do that amount and kind of thinking in a given time-span that is necessary to account for such of their behavior as could be imagined to be thought-through-out-loud. But if thoughts are in the *first* instance "theoretical," they are in the second instance accessible to direct self-knowledge. We have acquired the ability (within limits) to monitor our thoughts—i.e. to respond to them, and set ourselves to respond, with second-level thoughts which are true of them in a way analogous to that in which, in perception, we respond, and, in observation, set ourselves to respond, to perceptible things with true first-level thoughts. This monitoring makes it possible for our thought processes to be under our voluntary control, to the extent that they are in mental action proper. But I have, I hope, said

---

[8] A mediating link in this explanation is the fact that, though the persons in question are silent, there is reason to believe that they *would* think-out-loud in relevant ways, if certain circumstances were to obtain.

enough to make it clear that unmonitored thinking is thinking in a straightforward sense. The important distinction here is the depth-psychological one, between thinkings which we are able to monitor (preconscious) and thinkings we are *not* (unconscious).

[33] Notice that there are two senses in which an utterance can be said to "express" a thought. (a) In the first sense, by "thought" (cf. *"Gedanke"*) is meant a proposition, and the utterance expresses *what* it says.[9] (b) There is the radically different sense in which one characterizes an utterance as the "expression" of an inner episode, i.e. as the spontaneous culmination of a process initiated by the inner episode. (That the episode itself is classified as, for example, a thought (i.e. thinking) that-p, tempts unwary philosophers to run the two senses of "thought" and "expression" together.) That an utterance expresses *in the first sense* a certain thought (i.e. proposition) is a semantical fact. That it expresses *in the second sense* a certain thought-episode is a psychological fact which explains its occurrence. These two senses of "express" can be distinguished, respectively, as the logical or semantical, on the one hand, and the psychological or causal, on the other.

[34] So far we have been discussing the status of episodes of thinking that-p. The concept of believing that-p can be explicated as a related disposition. Very roughly, to believe that-p is to be disposed to have thoughts that-p, rather than thoughts whether-p, let alone thoughts that-not-p.

[35] All of the above distinctions apply to intentions. In the first place, we must distinguish between episodes of intending (a species of thought-episode) and the corresponding dispositions. Dispositional intentions are the counterparts of believings. Intendings are, in the classical sense, practical thoughts, and the reasonings in which they occur are practical reasonings. Again, we must distinguish between intention as *what* is intended—the counterpart of a proposition—and intention as an act of intending or a disposition to intend.

[36] The model for covert intendings is thinkings-out-loud of the kind illustrated by:

I shall raise my hand in ten minutes.
The victim shall be avenged.

The variety of intendings-out-loud is comparable to the variety of thinkings-out-loud that something is the case. I shall not, however, attempt to botanize them, save by implication. The "practical" character of intendings is a matter of their logical relation to action. In terms of intendings-out-loud, this can be put by saying that intentions of the form

---

[9] It was pointed out above, §25, that to say *what* an utterance says is to classify it. [Eds.—Reference in published version is to pp. 150–1; we have replaced this with the specific paragraph referenced in the typescript.]

"I shall *now* do A"

grow, in the absence of paralysis or hindrance or unfavorable circumstances, into doings of A. Intentions of other forms have a more or less indirect logical relation to action, by virtue of their logical relation to intentions that have a more direct logical relation to action. Intendings-out-loud of the form

"I shall *now* do A"

can be called willings-out-loud. They are the model for volitions. Thus, covert volitions are the inner episodes which find expression (in the psychological sense) in candid resolutive utterances, pertaining to action here and now.

[37] But volitions are not only expressed in the psychological sense by overt speech (if one is in a thinking-out-loud frame of mind); they also find expression in a different, but equally psychological sense in action. Thus, *ceteris paribus*, the volition "I shall now raise my hand" finds its expression, in *one* sense, in the overt resolutive

"I shall now raise my hand,"

and its expression in *another* sense in the action of raising my hand.

[38] Shall we say that the volition is the *cause* of the action? I see no harm in doing so, if one is sufficiently sensitive to the variety of relationships that can be called causal, and avoids construing this case in terms of a paradigm that would lead one to say that the volition *causes the person* to do the action. In voluntary action, we are not caused to act.

[39] Notice that volitions are not *tryings*. To try to do A is to do one or more things which one thinks likely in the circumstances to constitute doing A. Nor are volitions *choosings*. One can will to do A without choosing to do A rather than something else—even refraining from doing A. Nor are volitions *decisions*: a volition need not be the *culmination of a process* of deliberation or practical reasoning.

[40] The idea that there are such things as volitions—mental episodes that cause actions—has recently been under severe attack. Thus it has, in the first place, been subjected to the general attack on the idea of mental episodes proper—i.e. episodes that are not short-term dispositions pertaining to overt behavior. It has become increasingly clear, however, that this attack was based on the overly narrow interpretation of the limits of concept-formation and rational belief, which takes as its paradigms ostensive teaching and induction by simple enumeration. To follow this road with single-minded conviction is to end in absurdity.

[41] In the second place, there is the objection that, if volitions are episodes, they must be *actions*—that is, the sort of thing which can be done voluntarily.

The conclusion is drawn that a vicious regress is involved in explaining voluntary action in terms of volitions. But the premise of this argument is simply false. Thus, feelings of warmth are episodes, but they are not actions. Furthermore, we have already seen that thoughts *that* something is the case are not actions. It is a logical fact about thoughts that they are not directly brought about.[10] It is equally a logical fact about our intendings-at-the-moment that they are not under our voluntary control, just as it is a logical truth that our noticings-at-the-moment are not under our voluntary control.[11] I have no doubt that some philosophers have thought of volitions as actions, indeed as what we *really* do. Prichard's curious notion that what we *directly* do is "set ourselves to bring something about" is a conflation—grounded in the thesis that we can be said to *do*, strictly speaking, only what we *know* that we can do—of the concept of volition as causing an action, with that of the *minimal* action by doing which, in the circumstances, we bring it about that we are doing such complex actions as shooting a person or paying a debt.

[42] Finally, there is the objection that there would be a logical connection between these supposed episodes of willing to do A and the actual doing of A, which would be inconsistent* with the Humean principle that it is logically possible for anything to cause anything. Could a willing to raise one's hand cause a wiggling of the ears? The objection is a naive one, which overlooks the distinctive features of the level at which the causality obtains. The point stands out most clearly if we turn our attention to thinkings-out-loud, the primary mode of conceptual activity. Thus, to think out loud,

"I shall now do A"

is not simply to utter noises. One hasn't learned to think-out-loud in this mode—i.e. to use resolutive sentences—unless one has acquired a disposition to do A on saying "I shall now do A." In the absence of this propensity, such utterances could simply not be said to express an intention or volition. The logical connection between "I shall now do A" and the doing of A is a presupposition of the parental training which results in the propensity. Thus, the characterizing of the utterance as a willing-out-loud logically implies the propensity. A willing-out-loud is the sort of thing that plays a specific role in language-guided behavior. In the absence

---

[10] This fact does not however, preclude that we can, as a matter of empirical fact, bring about changes in our propensities to have specific kinds of thoughts.

[11] We can, however, train ourselves to have propensities to notice one kind of thing rather than another. Similarly we can train ourselves to have different propensities pertaining to intending. This point is involved in the clarification of Sir David Ross' claim that it is a mistake to say that we ought to do A *from a motive*.

* [Eds.—Correction of "consistent" in original printing.]

of the conceptual commitments involved in classifying an utterance as a willing-out-loud, there would, of course, be no reason why

"I shall now raise my hand"

should be connected with hand-raisings rather than ear wigglings, or, indeed, with any particular form of behavior.

[43] The same point stands out in the context of perception. Someone might argue: How can a green object in standard conditions be said to cause a person to be under the visual impression that he is confronted by a green object in standard conditions? Why shouldn't green objects in standard conditions cause persons to be under the impression that a brass band is playing the Star-Spangled Banner? The answer, once again, stands out clearly at the level of thinking-out-loud. To learn how to perceive-out-loud involves learning to respond with such utterances as

"See: this is a green object in daylight"

or, schematically,

"Lo: this is a φ object in perceptual circumstance C"

to green objects in daylight or to φ objects in perceptual circumstance C. Furthermore, to learn to use perceptual predicates in the full way in which people who see use color words involves learning to use them in some such rubric.

[44] Much more, of course, would have to be said in order to give even an elementary account of perceiving-out-loud, but for our present purposes the important thing to note is that the existence of these response propensities is a necessary condition of being able to perceive-out-loud. Notice that the logical connection with which we are concerned does not consist in the fact that 'S perceives-out-loud that-p' implies 'It is true that-p'. For the connection in which we are interested is one which permits of error. This corresponds to the fact that, if a person is unwittingly paralyzed, no amount of his willing to raise his hand will cause his hand to rise.

[45] It is perhaps worth noting here that both in the framework of thinking-out-loud and in that of covert thought, it makes sense to suppose that training (e.g. learning to play a composition for the piano) is able to link behavior into complex patterns which can be conceptualized and performed thinkingly *as units*, without each component being separately conceptualized and performed thinkingly as such. Thus, if I seem to be picturing waking life as threaded on a steady stream of thoughts—in particular, volitions—this proliferation of mental acts must not be taken to imply that every motion that is under our voluntary control springs from a separate volition.

III. Voluntary Action and Compulsion

[46] In the primary sense of the phrase, a "voluntary action" is one that is caused by an act of will. In a derivative sense, it is equivalent to the phrase "action under the agent's voluntary control." To say of an action, A, that it is under the agent's voluntary control is to say that if, just before doing A, the agent had willed not to do A, he would not have done A.

[47] If an action is not voluntary, at least in the latter sense, then it is not really an action, but rather behavior of a sort which *would* be an action if it *were* voluntary. An involuntary wink is not a wink at all, but rather a blink. Even a compelled action must be voluntary in the sense defined. To go out the window propelled by a team of professional wrestlers is not to *do* but to *suffer*, to be a patient rather than an agent. Thus we can distinguish a narrower sense of "voluntary," in which it means "voluntary in the previous sense *and not compelled.*"

[48] The concept of compulsion is closely related to that of excuse. To say of a person that he was compelled to do something is to imply that the degree of duress to which he was submitted was sufficient to constitute an excuse for doing what he did. It is a familiar fact that the degree of duress which would be sufficient to excuse a civilian, for having performed or not having performed a certain act (thus betraying a secret), would not excuse a soldier.

[49] Compulsion being a paradigm case of excusable circumstance, the term has naturally been extended to other cases of excusable behavior. Thus, for example, we find the term "inner compulsion" used when it is a question of excusing the behavior of mentally disturbed persons. The extensions are instructive, because they focus our attention on the relative thinness of the concept of voluntary action, as defined above. Consider, for example, the case of the narcotics addict who succumbs to clear and present temptation. If we say that the action was not under his voluntary control, the concept of compulsion is misapplied, and we should rather say that the addict didn't *do* anything but rather, so to speak, blinked or twitched. If, on the other hand, we say that the action was under his voluntary control, in the sense that if he had willed to refrain he would have refrained, we are struck by the question "*Could* he have willed to refrain?" It occurs to us that there is a striking difference between those cases of compulsion in which it is true nevertheless that a person could have willed to do otherwise, and those in which it is not. In the latter case, action seems to be excusable in what one is tempted to call an "absolute" rather than a "relative" sense. Indeed, as we shall see, it is just because determinism *seems* to imply that no one *could have willed* to do what he did not will to do, that it seems to give everybody an absolute excuse for *all* his wrongdoing, however relatively inexcusable he may be, as well as to strip him of all genuine merit, however relatively meritorious his actions may have been.

[50] One often gets the impression that philosophers influenced by psychoanalytic theory have two models for human behavior, and believe there to be little

behavior, indeed, which fails to conform to one or the other of these models. The first is the model of addiction. Its promiscuous use implies that psychoanalytic theory provides us with reasons for supposing that we are *often* unable to will other than we do. The other model is that of unavoidable ignorance, and, in particular, unavoidable ignorance of our preferences and desires. The primary value of John Wisdom's thought-experiment,[12] concerning a person the strength of whose desires is fixed by the Devil, is that it makes us see that to be a free and responsible agent is to be able to bring it about (indirectly, by a program of self-training) that one's desires are different or of different strengths. And it is indeed true that if one is unavoidably ignorant of what these desires and preferences are, one can scarcely be held responsible for not undertaking to change them. But under what circumstances are people thus unavoidably ignorant? It is of the utmost importance to keep metaphysical issues from confusing this scientific question.

IV. Could One Have Done Otherwise?

[51] If microdeterminism is true, then, when X does A at t, this means that there was an antecedent partial cross-section of the universe such that, relatively to that cross-section, it is physically necessary that X do A at t; or, equivalently, such that it is physically impossible, relatively to that cross-section, that X do something other than A at t—i.e. something which he did not in point of fact do.

[52] It has seemed to many to follow from determinism, thus understood, that X could not at t have acted differently—that he was *unable* at t to do anything but A.

[53] If it does have this consequence, then microdeterminism is, indeed, incompatible with our framework conceptions pertaining to action, for in that framework the following implications obtain:

X did A at t → X was able to do A at t
X was able to do A at t → X was able to do something else at t
X did A at t → X was able to do something else at t

These implications can be spelled out in more detail as follows:

(1) X did A at t → A was under X's voluntary control at t
(2) X did A at t → there is some action A' incompatible with A, such that *if* X had willed to do A' he would have done A' rather than A at t
(3) X did A at t → X was able to do something other than A at t

---

[12] *Mind and Matter*, pp. 116ff.

[54] The first two steps, (1) and (2), are justified [in §§46ff*] above. The crucial step is (3). Where does it come from? The answer is to be found by exploring what it means to say of a person that he is able to do a certain action. I shall first discuss the problem in a highly oversimplified context, and then introduce the complications necessary to give it a reasonably realistic flavor and to bring out its full relevance to the problem of free will.

[55] I shall first introduce some familiar concepts and distinctions pertaining to the physical or "causal" modalities. Since at no time will I be concerned with the logical modalities, I shall use familiar symbols from modal logic without any subscript to indicate that it is the physical modalities which are in question. Thus I shall use "N" for physically necessary, and "M" for physically possible. By means of this symbolism, I shall draw the familiar distinctions between absolute, hypothetical and relative modalities as follows:

(a) *Absolute or intrinsic*: an absolutely or intrinsically necessary state of affairs is one the necessity of which depends only on the conceptual content of the state of affairs as formulated. Thus (to use crude, but indicative examples):
It is physically necessary that whenever there is lightning, it thunders.
$N[(t) L(t) \to T(t + \Delta t)]$
It is physically possible that lightning occur at t_1
$M[L(t_1)]$

(b) *Hypothetical*: a state of affairs q is necessary on the hypothesis that-p, if the proposition p → q is absolutely or intrinsically necessary. Thus:
That thunder occur at t_1 is necessary on the hypothesis that lightning occur at $t_1 - \Delta t$
$N[T(t_1)] / L(t_1 - \Delta t)$

(c) *Relative*: a state of affairs q is necessary relative to the *fact* that p, if q is necessary on the hypothesis that-p, and it is the case that-p. The basic form for representing relative necessity will be the same as that for hypothetical necessity, except that an exclamation mark is added at the end to indicate that the state of affairs to which the necessity is relative actually obtains; thus:
$N[T(t_1)] / L(t - \Delta t)!$

It is also useful to introduce quantified forms for hypothetical and relative necessity, thus

(Ep) N[q]/p   or, simply,   NH[q]

and

---

* [Eds.—Original reference reads "on pp. 159-160"; we have replaced this with the specific paragraphs referenced in the typescript.]

FATALISM AND DETERMINISM 309

(Ep) N[q]/p!   or, more simply,   NR[q]

[56] In putting these concepts to use, the first simplification I shall make, which, in one form or another, will persist throughout the paper, is a limitation of the problem to the case of "minimal actions"—actions, that is, that do not have other actions as parts.[13] At least some minimal actions can be characterized as "bodily changes under direct voluntary control." That the concept of action is being simplified in other useful ways will come out as the argument progresses. I shall use the following symbolism for statements pertaining to minimal actions (A):

'A(x, t),' for 'x does A at t'
'$V_A(x, t)$' for 'x wills at t to do A'
't'' for '$t - \Delta t$'
'ABLE[A(x, t)]' for 'x is able to do A at t'[14]

[57] I shall next put these resources to use in presenting an oversimplified but essentially sound account of the compatibility between determinism and "could have done otherwise." The key to this account is the following definition:

$$ABLE[A(x,t)] =_{df} N[V_A(x,t') \rightarrow A(x,t)]$$

i.e. x is able to do a certain minimal action at time t if, *were* he to will at t' to do A, he *would* do A at t—i.e. willing to do A at t' physically implies doing A at t.

[58] Notice that while

ABLE[A(x, t)]

entails

M[A(x, t)]

i.e. that x's doing of A at t is intrinsically or absolutely possible (thus A is not the action of drawing a square circle in the air or completely rotating one's head) it does *not* entail

(p) M[A(x, t)]/p!

---

[13] Roughly, an action has another action as a part if one can be said to have done the former by doing the latter in those circumstances.

[14] Actually it would be more perspicuous to introduce the compound predicate 'able-to-do-A' or 'A-ABLE' and the sentence forms 'able-to-do-A(x, t)' or 'A-ABLE(x, t)' which would predicate abilities of persons at times. I use the above form, however, in which 'ABLE' is made to look like a modality, so that my symbolism will be able to *picture* a key confusion in most discussions of our problem.

where 'p' is a variable ranging over states of affairs assumed to be logically compossible with x's doing A at t. If we represent this statement of relative possibility by

$MR[A(x, t)]$

we see that

$ABLE[A(x, t)]$

entails

$M[A(x, t)]$

but not

$MR[A(x, t)]$.

[59] Now, if determinism is true,

$\sim A(x, t)$

entails

(EK) $K(x, t') \cdot N[K(x, t') \rightarrow \sim A(x, t)]$

i.e. that there is a kind of state, K,* such that the universe was in that state just prior to t, and that it is absolutely physically necessary that, if the universe is in that state at a certain time t', then x does not do A at t. If now we use 'α' to represent the state which satisfies this quantified formula we see that if determinism is true, from

$\sim A(x, t)$

we can infer

$\sim M[\alpha(x, t') \cdot A(x, t)]$
$\sim M[A(x, t)]/\alpha(x, t')!$
$\sim MR[A(x, t)]$.

[60] The last of the preceding formulas, although it asserts the relative impossibility of a doing, turns out, when unpacked, to assert the absolute impossibility of

---

* [Eds.—"K" does not appear in the published version, but Sellars has handwritten it into a preprint, which is document 31735062218981, Box 30, Folders 2-4, Wilfrid S. Sellars Papers, 1899-1990, ASP.1991.01, Archives of Scientific Philosophy, Archives & Special Collections, University of Pittsburgh Library System. The correction is on page 165 of the preprint.]

FATALISM AND DETERMINISM 311

a complex state of affairs, of which x's doing A is one conjunct. It does not assert that x was *unable* to do A at t, for

$$\sim MR[A(x,t)]$$

does not entail

$$\sim ABLE[A(x,t)]$$

Thus, although "it was (relatively) impossible that x do A at t" and "x was unable to do A at t" look deceptively alike in the above representation, which pictures a classic confusion, the former has the form

$$\varphi(x,t') \cdot N[\varphi(x,t') \to \sim A(x,t)],$$

while the latter has the form

$$\sim N[\varphi(x,t') \to A(x,t)].$$

The former denies the possibility of A(x, t) relative to (and, hence, on the hypothesis of) α(x, t'), whereas the latter asserts the possibility of ~A(x, t) on the hypothesis V_A(x, t').

[61] To put it somewhat differently, both determinism and the statement that x could have done otherwise tell us that something is hypothetically necessary, the former that

$$(Ep)N[\sim A(x,t)]/p \qquad p = \alpha(x,t'),$$

the latter that

$$(Ep)N[A(x,t)]/p \qquad p = V_A(x,t'),$$

where A is the action that was not done. It is clear that these statements are in no way incompatible.

V. A More Realistic Account

[62] I pointed out above that the above discussion would be oversimplified in a number of respects. The complexity I shall now take into account involves the concepts of "circumstance," "being in a position to do something," "having the ability to do something," and "being able to do something at a certain time." Let us add the following symbols to our previous lists:

'Γ' for kinds of circumstance
'A'' for a kind of action incompatible with A

'Π' as a variable for periods of time
't' for moments of time (in a vague sense of 'moment');

thus one speaks of *during* Π and *at t*.
[63] As sentence forms we have:

'Γ'(x, Π) for "x is in Γ throughout Π"
'A(x, t)' for "x does A at t"
'V_A(x, t)' for "x wills at t to do A"
'A(x, Π)' for "x does A at some time during Π"
'V_A(x, Π)' for "x wills to do A at some time during Π," (or, where appropriate, "x wills to do A at any time during Π")
'P ◊ Q' for "P is physically compossible with Q."

[64] In terms of these, we introduce the following definitions:

1. PVT (read 'prevents')
PVT[Γ, A(x, Π)] $=_{df}$ [Γ(x, Π) ◊ V_A(x, Π)] • N[Γ(x, Π) → ~A(x, Π)]
2. POSIT (read 'is in a position to')
POSIT[A(x, Π)] $=_{df}$ ~(EΓ) PVT[Γ, A(x, Π)]
POSIT[A(x, t)] $=_{df}$ (EΠ) t ∈ Π • POSIT[A(x, Π)]
3. CAN (read, alternatively, as "has the ability")
CAN[A(x, Π)] $=_{df}$ POSIT[A(x, Π)] → N[V_A(x, Π) → A(x, Π)]
CAN[A(x, t)] $=_{df}$ (EΠ) t ∈ Π • CAN[A(x, Π)]
4. ABLE (read "is able during Π (or at t)...")
ABLE[A(x, Π)] $=_{df}$ POSIT[A(x, Π)] • CAN[A(x, Π)]
ABLE[A(x, t)] $=_{df}$ (EΠ) t ∈ Π • ABLE[A(x, Π)]

[65] In terms of these definitions, we can now set down the following action framework principles:

PA-0 $A(x, t) \to ABLE[A, (x, t)]$
PA-I $A(x, t) \to (EA') ABLE[A'(x, t)]$,

of which the latter is the more important for our purposes. From it follow:

PA-II $A(x, t) \to (EA') POSIT[A'(x, t)] \cdot CAN[A'(x, t)]$
PA-III $A(x, t) \to (EA') N[V_{A'}, (x, t') \to A'(x, t)]$.

Since

$A(x, t) \to \sim A'(x, t)$,

we have, using PA-I, the consequence that

$$A(x, t) \to (EA') \sim A'(x, t) \bullet ABLE[A'(x, t)]$$

[66] Let us return, this time in a more complex framework, to the question of the compatibility of determinism with the conceptual framework of action. The thesis of determinism applied to actions can be formulated as the principle:

PD-I $\quad A(x, t) \to \alpha(x, t') \bullet N[\alpha(x, t') \to A(x, t)]$

where '$\alpha(x, t')$' expresses the unspecified antecedent state of the universe relevant to x's doing A at t. To build up the picture which generates the puzzle I am trying to clarify, let us transpose α, as a function of x with respect to t', into a function γ which holds x with respect to t. We then have

PD-II $\quad A(x, t) \to \gamma(x, t) \bullet N[\gamma(x, t) \to A(x, t)]$

In accordance with our conventions, this can be reformulated along the lines:

$$A(x, t) \to N[A(x, t)]/\gamma(x, t)!$$
$$\to \sim M[\sim A(x, t)]/\gamma(x, t)!$$
$$\to (A') \sim M[A'(x, t)]/\gamma(x, t)!,$$

so that we have as our third formulation of the principle of determinism

PD-III $\quad A(x, t) \to \sim(EA') M[A'(x, t)]/\gamma(x, t)!$

[67] Let us now compare the consequent of PD-III

$$\sim(EA') M[A'(x, t)]/\gamma(x, t)!$$

with the consequent of PA-I

$$(EA') ABLE[A'(x, t)].$$

If we put these in words along the following lines:

> It is not the case that there is an alternative action which it was possible [relative to $\gamma(x, t)$] that x do at t,
> There is an alternative action which x was able to do at t,

they might look like contradictories. If we reformulate the latter to read:

> There is an alternative action which it was possible *for x to do* at t,

it might be thought that the consequent of PD-III differs from the straight contradictory of the consequent of PA-I, by mentioning in addition the *ground* on which the possibility of x doing A is denied. The consequent of PD-III is then interpreted as:

It is not the case that there is an alternative action which it was possible *for x to do* at *t*—because γ(x, t).

Notice, however, the shift from

...which it was possible *that* x do at *t*

to

...which it was possible *for x to do* at t.

This shift is a telltale symptom of the confusion which is being made.

[68] The solution of the puzzle is essentially the same as that which was given above in the simpler framework, as becomes clearer when we turn our attention to PA-III:

$$A(x, t) \to (EA') N[V_{A'}, (x, t'^*) \to A'(x, t)]$$

[69] It might be thought that by virtue of the fact that, from PD-II it follows that

PD-IV $\quad A(x, t) \to (A') \gamma(x, t) \cdot N[\gamma(x,t) \to \sim A'(x, t)],$

it also follows that alternative actions are *prevented*, for one is tempted to rewrite PD-IV as

$$A(x, t) \to (A')(E\Gamma) N[\Gamma(x, t) \to \sim A'(x, t)]$$

and to use the definition of 'PVT' to get

$$A(x, t) \to (A') PVT[A'(x, t)].$$

I am certain that something like this move has been the source of many misconceptions. This line of thought amounts to construing the antecedent state of the universe which makes A(x, t) relatively necessary, as a *circumstance* in which A is done! When it is put thus baldly, it is intuitively evident that this is a mistake.

[70] The mistake is highlighted by two features of the definition of 'PVT' which the above move violates: (a) that which concerns the role of a *period* of time in the concept defined; (b) the neglected requirement that, in order to prevent an action, a circumstance must be compatible with *willing* the action. The requirement imposed by (a) can be only verbally satisfied by the antecedent state of the

---

* [Eds.—Prime marker (′) missing in original.]

universe. Thus, if an object y is φ at a certain time t, we can not only introduce a new predicate 'φ'* which applies to things *at* a time such that

$$\phi'(y, t + \Delta t) =_{df} \phi(y, t),$$

it being true *at* $t + \Delta t$ that y *was* φ at t; we can also introduce the predicate φ" which applies to things *during periods* such that

$$\phi''(y, \Pi) =_{df} (Et) \, t \in \Pi \bullet \phi(y, t).$$

The former was the move which took us in our discussion of PD-I from α(x, t') to 'γ(x, t)'. The latter is a similar move to satisfy a stronger requirement.

[71] The second feature (b) of the concept "*prevents*," which precludes the possibility that the antecedent state of the universe envisaged by scientific determinism should prevent the agent from doing anything other than he did, concerns the requirement that a preventing circumstance be physically compatible with willing to do the prevented action. This requirement is incompatible with the fatalistic use of the principle of determinism; for, given that x did not will to do A', then it is physically impossible, relative to the antecedent state of the universe, that x have willed to do A'.[15]

VI. Could One Have Willed Otherwise?

[72] This brings me to the final section of my argument. Someone might grant that determinism is compatible with

PA-I   A(x, t) → (EA') ABLE[A'(x, t)],

which tells us that having done A at t implies having been *able to do* something else instead, but yet he might argue that this is a superficial truth. If one cuts deeper, one finds—so he claims—that determinism is incompatible with the idea that one could have *willed to do* anything other than what one did. And if so, is there not a *deeper sense* in which, if determinism is true, one could not have done anything other than one actually did?

---

* [Eds.—From this point onwards in the published version, Sellars begins using the upper-case phi (Φ) instead of the lower-case phi (φ) which he has been using. It is not clear if this is intentional, or if it is a typesetting error. In the typescript, he uses the lower-case phi throughout; the new symbol he introduces is distinguished only in virtue of the presence of the prime marker ('), and in the definition that follows, φ' is defined in terms of φ.]

[15] The only way in which, given that x did A, it could have been the case that x willed to do A', would be if he actually willed to do A' but, through some switching of circuits, his willing to do A' resulted in his doing A—e.g., Jones wills to raise his right hand, but his left hand goes up.

[73] We noted above (§§31 and 41*) that, although to will to do something is a "doing," in the broad sense in which any episode expressed by a verb in the active voice is a doing, it is not a doing *in the conduct sense*. And, since "willing" is always "willing to do" something in the conduct sense of "do," it follows that

x wills to will to do A

makes sense only as elliptical for something like

x willed to develop a frame of mind conducive to his willing to do A.

[74] Now it might be claimed that our concept of *ability to do* is too narrow, since according to it *ability* applies only to doings in the conduct sense (actions), and not for example, to volitions. Is there not, indeed, a broader sense of "able," in which persons are able to *will* as well as to *act*? And, if this is recognized, is not the way open for an argument to the effect that determinism is incompatible with the idea that a person could have *willed* to do something other than, in point of fact, he did will to do? Surely, it might be added, there is a correspondingly broad sense of "prevent" in which people can be prevented from *willing*. Does not determinism imply that, in *this* sense, people are *prevented from willing* to do what they did not will to do, and, hence, in a deeper sense than previously examined, from *doing* what they did not do?

[75] I have already tipped my hand by pushing this line of thought to the conclusion that the antecedent state of the universe is the sort of thing that can *prevent* one from willing to do something. The absurdity, however, doesn't stand out so clearly if we focus our attention on expressions such as

x was able to will to do A′
it was possible for x to will A′.

Once again the temptation is present to confuse

it is *not possible that* x at *t* willed to do A′ [*because*, according to the principle of determinism, etc.]

with

x *was not able* at *t* to will to do A′.

---

* [Eds.—Original reference reads "pp. 153 and 156-7"; we have replaced this with the specific paragraphs referenced in the typescript.]

[76] The confusion is so radical that it appears in the context of purely material things, as well as persons. The problem: does it make sense to say:

x at t is able to will to do A and also able to will to do A'[16]

is paralleled by the problem: does it make sense to say, using a familiar type of example:

x at t is able to go five mph and able to go ten mph?

[77] What we want to say, roughly, is that circumstances do not prevent in the one case the *willings*, in the other the *goings*. But what is to count as a circumstance? The familiar phrase "standing conditions"[17] gives the clue. The concept of being in a circumstance is, as already pointed out, a *period* concept. We can introduce this broader sense of "able" for which we are looking, as follows, representing it by 'CAP':

$$CAP[\phi(x, \Pi)] =_{df} \sim(E\Gamma)\, \Gamma(x, \Pi) \bullet N[\Gamma(x, \Pi) \to \sim\phi(x, \Pi)].$$

As before, ability *at a time* is derivative from ability *over a period*.

[78] Is determinism compatible with

$$\sim\phi(x, t) \bullet CAP[\phi(x, t)]?$$

Well, if determinism is true,

$$\sim\phi(x, t) \to (E\gamma)\, \gamma(x, t) \bullet N[\gamma(x, t) \to \sim\phi(x, t)],$$

and it might look as though we could treat the consequent as a substitution instance of

$$(E\Gamma)\, \Gamma(x, t) \bullet N[\Gamma(x, t) \to \sim\phi(x, t)],$$

and conclude that, according to determinism,

$$\sim\phi(x, t) \to \sim CAP\phi(x, t)],$$

which *is* compatible with

$$\sim\phi(x, t) \bullet CAP\phi(x, t)].$$

[79] Well, why not? What is the objection to taking

---

[16] Which must not, of course, be confused with x at t is able to [will to do A and will to do A'].
[17] It is equally familiar that standing conditions, of course, need not be *stationary*.

x's having participated in an antecedent state of the universe which physically implies that x is not ϕ at t

as a circumstance which holds of x during a period to which t belongs? After all, it might be said,

x's having heard an explosion at t

defines a physically relevant circumstance which obtains with respect to x during a subsequent period of time. There are various things which he may not be capable of during that period—e.g. feeling peaceful and unafraid.

[80] But surely this very example brings out the essential difference between deterministic pseudo-circumstances and genuine circumstances. For the law which relates hearing explosions at t to not being in certain states during the subsequent period is a *specific* law of nature, an "historical law" which is paralleled at the physical level by historical laws pertaining, for example, to elastic substances. It is with reference to "real" circumstances that abilities and hindrances are defined.

[81] Thus, as I see it, we are often prevented by real circumstances from willing as we did not will. But the "metaphysical" circumstances implied by determinism do not render us *unable to will to do* what we did not do, and therefore do not, indirectly, render us *unable to do* what we did not do.

12
Reply to Alan Donagan*

I

[1] Donagan sets the stage for an examination in depth of my views on 'determinism and freedom' by sketching the general philosophy of mind which underlies them, and by contrasting it, in relevant respects, with those of certain other philosophers (e.g. G. E. Moore and John Austin), whose contributions to the topic have become contemporary classics. After correctly describing my views on 'free will' as reconciliationist in the Hume–Mill tradition, he carefully reformulates in more perspicious terms the technical apparatus which I used in an attempt to make more precise the distinctive features of my analysis. There is little if anything in his restatement of my definitions and principles with which I would wish to quarrel. Indeed, I am most grateful for the clarity of his translations. It is, as one might expect, with the philosophical commentary which follows that issues begin to arise. It is to these that I now turn.

[2] Donagan claims that my "argument...has combined...two classical reconciliationist themes. They are that anti-determinists (1) have misunderstood what human freedom of action is, and (2) have confounded causal necessity with some form of compulsion." (p. 66.) He is quite right about (1). I did argue that anti-determinists have offered a mistaken analysis of ordinary concepts pertaining to freedom of action. He is, however, quite wrong about (2). Indeed, in the second paragraph of my essay I expressed the conviction that although the Hume-Mill charge that libertarianism rests on the confusion between causation and compulsion contains "something of value" it "simply won't do as it stands." (pp. 141–2 [§2].) Nevertheless, I did point out (p. 142 [§4]) that the theme of compulsion lurks as a frozen metaphor in our ordinary use of 'cause' and implied that this theme has played an important role in tempting both anti-reconciliationistic determinists and anti-determinists alike to think that action which admits (in principle) of causal explanation cannot be action 'of the agent's own free will', and is rather action for which the agent has a (metaphysical) excuse, and lacks 'real' or 'ultimate' responsibility. The distinctive feature of my argument began to emerge, when I warned against confusing 'compulsion' with the kind of circumstance which, rather than

---

* [Eds.—This is a reply to Alan Donagan, "Determinism and Freedom: Sellars and the Reconciliationist Thesis," in *Action, Knowledge and Reality: Critical Studies in Honor of Wilfrid Sellars*, ed. Hector-Neri Castañeda (Indianapolis: Bobbs-Merrill, 1975), 55–81.

compelling one to *do*, rather than *refrain from doing*, a certain action, precludes, rather, the possibility of *either* doing *or* refraining from doing that action. I pointed out that "to go out the window propelled by a team of professional wrestlers is not to *do* but to *suffer*, to be a patient rather than an agent." (p. 166 [§47].) Indeed, I not only made, rather clumsily, the point that there is a broad sense in which "even a compelled action must be voluntary,"[1] (p. 160 [§47]) I also clearly intended the following principle, which I offered as a conceptual truth (p. 152*), to the effect that

X did A at $t \to x$ was able to do something other than A at t,

to apply to compelled action. Thus

X was compelled to do A at $t \to x$ was able to do something other than A at t.

[3] It is the above example of *non-agency* which lays the ground work for the formal argument of the paper, according to which the *primary* confusion involved in the free will controversy is between the concept of

a *circumstance* which precludes the possibility that a person does A

which applies, as in the case of the wrestlers, to states of affairs which entail that a person is not, in the relevant sense, an agent at all, and that concept

a *state of affairs* which precludes the possibility that a person does A

which applies, according to deterministic principles, to those relevant antecedent states of affairs which are followed by a person's not doing A. It is the former concept which I generalize into the concept of a *preventing circumstance*, which is clearly intended to be *toto caelo* different from that of a circumstance which *compels* one to refrain from doing A.

[4] Thus the central argument of my paper in no way hinges on accusing the libertarian of a confusion between causation and compulsion. For the confusion on which I centered my attention leads to the conclusion that if an action has (in principle) a causal explanation, then *it is not really an action*; whereas, by itself, the confusion between causation and compulsion would lead only to the weaker conclusion that an action which has (in principle) a causal explanation is, as compelled, an action for which the agent has an excuse and for which 'something else' is *really* responsible.

---

[1] Though in a narrower (and more usual) sense an action is voluntary only if, in addition to being voluntary in the broad sense, it is not compelled.

* [Eds.—This reference is to §§28-9, which is not obviously correct. Sellars may have intended reference to §46, which appears on p. 159 of the published version.]

[5] It is nevertheless worth noting that if, in addition to this primary confusion, one is not clear about the concept of compulsion, nor, in particular, about the sense in which, by compelling someone to do something, one 'precludes the possibility' that he does otherwise (i.e. insures that he acts as desired), the "confusion between causation and compulsion" which was pitchforked out the door *may* return by the window. Thus, although, like most contemporary reconciliationists, I concentrate on showing that scientific determinism is compatible with 'could have done otherwise,' I nevertheless do believe that in one way or another much libertarian literature makes a smooth and easy transition from 'Jones's action has (in principle) a causal explanation' to 'Jones was caused to do what he did,' to 'Jones was not responsible for his action.' Only if the libertarian explicitly says (as, of course, the best ones do) that if determinism is true then *there are no actions*, would I absolve him of a direct or indirect running together of causation and compulsion.

[6] Donagan is, of course, well aware of the fact that my primary charge against the libertarian is that he is confused about the relationship between the forms

x was able to do otherwise at t
x was able to will otherwise at t

and the thesis of scientific determinism. He also sees that in an effort to make this charge stick, I attempted to analyze these forms and argued that if my analysis is correct, then both

x was able to do otherwise at t

and

x was able to will otherwise at t

are compatible with scientific determinism. He correctly points out that I explicate the concept of being able to do (or will) otherwise in terms of the concept of not being *prevented* by *circumstances* from doing (or willing) otherwise. But as I have pointed out he errs in assuming that the latter concept, as I have explicated it, has anything to do with compulsion.

II

[7] It still seems to me that if my analysis of

x was able to (will) otherwise,

is correct, anyone who thinks that scientific determinism *entails* that no one was ever able to do (or will) otherwise than he did must be somehow thinking of the antecedent state of the universe as a *circumstance* in which we act. He must, at some level, be thinking that if determinism is true, then the *circumstances* at which we act are physically incompatible with our doing or willing otherwise than we do.[2] This confusion (for surely it is a confusion) can, of course, play its role without generating for scrutiny an explicit proposition to the effect that 'antecedent conditions are part of the circumstances in which we act, so that if determinism is true, the circumstances in which we act are physically incompatible with, hence prevent, our doing (or willing) otherwise than we do.'

[8] This brings me to Donagan's commentary on my claim that the character of 'having been involved in a certain antecedent state S of the universe a short time before t' is a 'pseudo-' rather than a genuine circumstance of action by x at t. Obviously, if I were to grant it to be a *genuine* circumstance, the fact that if determinism were true, the circumstances in which x acts would always be physically incompatible with his willing otherwise than he does at t, would entail, given my analysis, that x is always prevented from willing otherwise than he does at t.

[9] Donagan notes that I consider the following objection:

> After all, it might be said, "x's having heard an explosion at t" defines a physically relevant circumstance which obtains with respect to x during a subsequent period of time. There are various things which he may not be capable of doing during the period—e.g. feeling peaceful and unafraid. (p. 174 [§79])

He finds in this "a very strong counter-example to the thesis that *all* states of affairs that obtain before the period in which x is able to will A, but does not, are pseudo-circumstances of his not willing A, and hence cannot be circumstances preventing him from willing A." (p. 70.) As he sees it, I "tacitly accept it as decisive," because I proceed to give "an altogether new argument for writing off prior states of the universe as 'pseudo-circumstances'." (p. 70.) Nothing could be further from the truth. What I *did* do was point out that "the law which relates hearing explosions at t to not being in certain states during a subsequent period is a specific law of nature, an 'historical law', which is paralleled at the physical level by historical laws pertaining, for example, to elastic substances." To which I added that "it is with respect to 'real' circumstances that abilities and hindrances are to be explained." (p. 174 [§80].) Donagan neglects the phrase "historical law" and treats the passage as though the phrase "specific law"—I should have written 'specific *kind* of law'—carried the burden of the argument. He then objects, quite rightly, that if scientific determinism is true, every failure by x to will A is covered by a

---

[2] It is surely no news that philosophers have not always paid adequate attention to the specific character of the *practical* concept of a 'circumstance of action'.

specific law (better 'complex of laws') relating this failure to antecedent conditions, and that if I were to include *every* such case as one in which the antecedent condition constitutes a 'real' circumstance, then x would always be prevented from willing anything he fails to will.

[10] But the operative phrase was "historical law," and the context should have made it clear that what I had in mind was that, whether or not we are in a position to give a *theoretical* explanation of the fact, it is a matter of inductive fact at the empirical level that hearing an explosion affects the abilities of people to act and will for a certain period of time, and hence 'having heard an explosion at t' satisfies the criteria for being a circumstance of action during the subsequent period. Presumably this fact has a neurophysiological counterpart in the ideal scientific image, just as the fact that elastic substances require a recovery time before they regain their capacity to respond again to tension and release has an explanation at the micro-physical level. But though the empirical law relating the circumstance of hearing an explosion to the absence of certain *abilities* presumably requires, from the theoretical point of view, that x, who has heard an explosion at t, is, as a result, for a certain time in states which are physically incompatible with willing A, it would be a mistake to assume that every physical state of x which is physically incompatible with willing A is a theoretical *circumstance* of his will which implies the absence of an ability to will A, let alone that it is the result of a circumstance which implies this absence. To make this assumption is to discount the specific meanings of 'circumstance of action' and 'ability to act (will)' which distinguish them from the generic notions of 'state of affairs' and 'physical possibility.'

[11] Even at the micro-physical level there is a place for capacity concepts. Thus it makes sense to say of a micro-physical system that during a certain period it was able to φ and able not to φ, and to say that even though the system did not φ at t, and even though not-φing* was necessary relative to the state of the system at $t - dt$, it did not, by virtue of this antecedent state, lose the ability to φ during the period from $t - dt$ to t. It is part of the logical grammar of capacity concepts that systems (macro- or micro-) do not lose at t their ability to φ simply by virtue of the fact that at t they are not φing. An automobile does not lose its capacity to go ten miles per hour when it is going one hundred miles per hour, however necessary the latter speed may be, relative to the antecedent state of the universe. In other words, we distinguish between those happenings by virtue of which a system fails to φ at t *without losing its capacity to φ*, and those other happenings by virtue of which it fails to φ at t *by being caused to lose, for a longer or shorter time, its capacity to φ*.

[12] At the manifest level, hearing an explosion at t is physically incompatible with the occurrence of certain mental states during the subsequent period by virtue of causing a loss of capacity to be in these states. If the identity theory is correct, the core of the scientific counterpart of a person's having the capacity to

---

* [Eds.—Correction of "not-ψing" in original printing.]

will A, B,... is a neurophysiological sub-system S, which is capable of being in states α, β.... And here also we would wish to distinguish between those antecedent states of the person, scientifically considered, which result in the failure of S to be in state α (the correlate of willing A) *without causing S to lose its capacity to be in this state*, and those conditions which result in the failure of the sub-system S to be in state α, by causing it to lose, for a time, its capacity to be in that state.

[13] Presumably, then, when the hearing of an explosion causes a person to lose the capacity to deliberate, or the seeing of an available batch of heroin causes an addict to be unable to will to refrain from grabbing it, the counterpart in the scientific image would involve a process which results in the temporary loss by the neurophysiological sub-system, S, of the capacity to be in those states which correspond to the relevant volitions.

[14] However all this might best be spelled out—and the task of explaining the various ways in which capacities can be nested and botanized is not an easy one—it is some such distinctions I had in mind when I characterized "the law which relates hearing explosions at t to not being in a certain state during the subsequent period" as "a *specific* law of nature, an 'historical law' which is paralleled by... historical laws pertaining, for example, to elastic substances." Thus I meant by a *real* circumstance, which *prevents* one from willing otherwise, one which is by virtue of *specific* laws (which need not be historical) physically incompatible with *having the ability to will otherwise*: whereas the 'pseudo-circumstance' defined by my hypothetical libertarian consists in having participated in a prior state of the universe which is nomologically incompatible with willing otherwise—a definition which tacitly identifies the concept of a state of affairs which is nomologically incompatible with willing otherwise, with that of a state of affairs which is incompatible with having the capacity to will otherwise.

[15] Donagan apparently senses that something like the above is hidden in my obscure remarks, for after claiming, not unfairly, that I have "not... succeeded in providing an analysis of ability to will, according to which determinism is compatible with ability to will otherwise than one wills," he admits that it "seems... highly probable that, following his general strategy of analyzing ability to will in terms of the absence of conditions preventing willing, he can provide an analysis of conditions preventing willing that will do what he wants." He puts the point nicely by writing

> The concept of a condition preventing the willing of A is restricted, I am strongly inclined to think, in a way in which the concept of the condition under which the willing of A is physically impossible is not. And if that is so, then ability to will otherwise than one does (understood as the absence of conditions preventing it) is compatible with determinism. (p. 71)

III

[16] I have argued above that, unlike traditional compatibilists, I do not build my strategy on the charge that libertarians confuse causation with compulsion. Thus I am prepared to grant negative answers to Donagan's rhetorical questions

> Is it true, as a matter of historical fact, that competent philosophers have, in the last hundred years, confused causation with compulsion?... Did Thomas Reid in the 18th century, or Henry Sidgwick in the 19th century, imagine that if a man's acts of will are causally determined, they must be compelled? Do C. D. Broad, or Richard Taylor, or R. M. Chisholm now imagine it? (p. 72)

This clears the way for a discussion of the considerations which, according to Donagan, the above listed philosophers offer in support of the claim that determinism is incompatible with the concept of man as, in any meaningful sense, an autonomous and responsible agent. "Consider Sidgwick," writes Donagan. An excellent suggestion. Donagan quotes Sidgwick as follows:

> ...When I have a distinct consciousness of choosing between alternatives of conduct, one of which I conceive as right or reasonable, I find it impossible not to think that I can now choose to do what I so conceive—supposing that there is no obstacle to my doing it other than the condition of my desires and voluntary habits,—however strong may be my inclination to act unreasonably, and however uniformly I may have yielded to such inclinations in the past.
> (Sidgwick [1], 65*)

I reply that there is absolutely nothing in scientific determinism which is incompatible with this datum of consciousness. The 'determinism' against which this passage is a protest is a vulgar determinism formulated in terms of the concepts and categories of common sense psychological explanation. As has often been pointed out, if 'strong' stands for 'felt strength', then there is no empirical law which says that having an inclination of a certain felt strength is incompatible with willing to do what, all things considered, one thinks one ought to do. After all, one's sense of duty is not as neatly associated with a cluster of sensations and feelings, as is, for example, the inclination to eat when hungry.[3] It is often the contemplation of the results of frustrating inclination in accordance with reason

---

* [Eds.—The reference is to Henry Sidgwick, *The Methods of Ethics* (seventh edition; London: Macmillan, 1907). The quote is from page 72 of Donagan.]

[3] This is not to say that there are no characteristic states of feeling and emotion which, on occasion, accompany the contemplation of doing one's duty. But it would be a serious mistake to suppose that when we do our duty, it is because such feelings occurred.

which generates states of feelings—and these unpleasant states are part of what one has in mind when one speaks of the felt strength of the inclination.

[17] At most vulgar determinism is entitled to the weaker claim that, other things being equal, the greater the felt strength of the inclination, the greater the likelihood that it will find expression in action. But this is because a *strongly felt* inclination is likely to be *strong* in the sense discussed in the next paragraph. After all, an inclination need not be 'felt'—it is had; nor a strong inclination, 'strongly felt'. But such wishy washy, *ceteris paribus* likelihoods would scarcely satisfy your true ideological determinist.

[18] If on the other hand, 'strength' is taken to mean 'great likelihood of prevailing over the voice of reason', it follows analytically that strong inclination need not prevail. And if 'great likelihood' is replaced by 'certain to prevail', it would, indeed, follow that it is not possible that one act against strong inclination, but nothing in scientific determinism requires that *there are* in this sense any strong inclinations. If such there are, it is a matter of empirical fact and is not to be known by armchair reasoning about the freedom of the will.

[19] So much for the clause "... however strong may be my inclination to act unreasonably." What about "... and however uniformly I may have yielded to such inclinations in the past", which is supposed to formulate a (not unrelated) deterministic thesis? It should be clear that once again Sidgwick has as his target— not scientific determinism—but that vulgar determinism which blurs the distinction between habits and causal properties. Doing A in C can become habitual, but no matter how habitual it becomes it remains possible to A in C in a manner which removes it from the category of habitual action (e.g. by deliberating anew about the point of doing A in C), or, even to do B instead. No such distinction holds in the case, for example, of the propensity of hydrochloric acid to dissolve iron filings. Nothing in scientific determinism requires that if a person has acquired the habit of doing A in C by doing it ever so often, he has lost the ability to do B in C instead of A, let alone to do A in C in a non-habitual manner.

[20] The vulgar determinist supposes, by a confusion of categories, that if every action admits of a (in principle) causal explanation and is, say, the manifestation of a causal property of the agent as a system of scientific objects, then it must be an 'expression of character', thus assimilating predictability in principle to the inductive predictability of habitual action.[4] But, of course, scientific determinism by no means implies the absurdity that all action is habitual. Add to this the tendency of vulgar determinism to conflate 'habit' with 'addiction', and no wonder the libertarian is up in arms. On the other hand, it must be granted that people are, to a large extent, 'creatures of habit,' that inductive reasoning based on what people have done in the past gives us a clue to their habits, and that people are likely to do

---

[4] See my 'Fatalism and Determinism', in Keith Lehrer (ed.), *Freedom and Determinism*, Random House, New York, 1966, p. 146 [Eds.—Ch. 11 of this volume, §§12–3], hereinafter referred to as *FD*.

what they habitually do. These truisms, however, no libertarian will deny, and only if scientific determinism had the above consequences would Sidgwick be entitled to his appeal to the deliverances of consciousness.

[21] At this point Donagan muddies the waters by offering the following as a summary of Sidgwick's appeal:

> In short, he simply found it impossible not to conceive himself as having the power to make choices that were not psychologically predetermined. (p. 72)

The phrase "psychologically predetermined" is not semantically luminous. 'Predetermined', in ordinary language, has a cluster of uses, most if not all of which carry with them (as do 'compelled', and 'unavoidable') an implication of a high degree of excusability or absence of responsibility. Thus one might say to a football coach: 'What happened was predetermined. Regardless of what plays you sent in, the team would have lost because of the prior decision of players x, y and z to throw the game.' A vulgar determinist, looking at habitual action, might say that it is 'predetermined', meaning that it is the expression of a habit formed by prior decisions. This seems to be the point of the modifier 'psychologically'. But 'all events, including actions, are predetermined' may also be used as a metaphorical—and hence, for the unwary, dangerous—way of saying that every event, including action is, under a certain redescription, in principle predictable, given an ideal deterministic theory, from antecedent conditions. Thus Donagan's summary of the passage he has just quoted from Sidgwick obscures the fact that instead of making a valid point against *scientific* determinism, Sidgwick's appeal is relevant only as a counter to the confused claims of the vulgar or ideological determinist who is snared in the confusions from which, according to Donagan, the sophisticated libertarian has long been free.

[22] Vulgar determinism argues:

X's action was the necessary consequence of antecedent conditions
X's action was (in principle) predictable from antecedent conditions
X's action was 'caused' by these conditions
X was 'caused' by his circumstances to do the action
X was unable to do (or will) anything else in the circumstances...compelled... prevented...predictable...predetermined...
So, X was not responsible for his action

[23] Vulgar libertarianism argues:

X was responsible for his action
X was not caused by circumstances to do the action

X was able to do (will) some other action in the circumstances...not compelled...not prevented...not predictable...not predetermined...
X's action was not caused by antecedent conditions
X's action was not (even in principle) predictable from antecedent conditions
So, X's action was not the necessary consequence of antecedent conditions

[24] After obscuring the force of his first quotation from Sidgwick, Donagan introduces his second quotation of claiming that Sidgwick "did not begin by expounding a conception of free will, and then, by means of some middle term (e.g. not compelled) try to show that free will, so conceived, excludes determinism; rather it was not until he confronted determinism that he clarified his conception of free will." (p. 72.) The end of this introduction is speculative intellectual biography, and, though not without interest, does not, as such, illuminate Sidgwick's argument. However, the opening clause, though it, too, has a biographical ring, makes the negative claim that Sidgwick's argument does *not* have the form

If there is free-will, then p.
If p, then not-q (e.g. our actions are not compelled).
[If determinism is true, then q.]
So, if there is free will, determinism is false.

Now, in a sense, Donagan is right, for a careful scrutiny of the passage he proceeds to quote discloses the following argument, which is of quite a different form:

> The concept of action implies that if on a certain occasion I act contrary to my rational judgement, then I have free choice with respect to that action, i.e. it is not predetermined that (by being so constituted and in such circumstances) I do that action.
>
> Therefore, if determinism is true, and it is predetermined that (by being so constituted and in such circumstances) I 'act' in a way which is contrary to my rational judgement, i.e. do not have free choice, then the concept expressed by 'I act' must be fundamentally different (and incompatible with) that which I find it to express when I speak of myself as an agent performing actions.

[25] Notice that I have separated this from the concomitant theme of auto-predictability to which it owes at least part of its appeal. The latter attributes to determinism the thesis that in principle a person could predict that he himself will do that which is contrary to his own rational judgement, an idea which naturally evokes the response that a person who infers with scientifically warranted conviction that, as a result of antecedent conditions, he will 'do A' must be using a

concept other than, and incompatible with, the concept ordinarily expressed by 'doing A'. But, of course, it is no part of scientific determinism that such auto-prediction is possible. Thus, to make the argument effective, we must interpret it as appealing not to auto-predictability, but to the 'predictability' which is simply a matter of the nomological connection between antecedent and consequent states of affairs in a deterministic system.

[26] Not even the most extreme libertarian would deny that much of what we do is predictable. We would all, of course, (rightly) deny that *everything* we do is predictable where the predictability in question rests on knowledge formulated in the categories of ordinary psychological explanation—though most of us could readily be lead to admit that *more* of our actions were predictable than we had previously realized. And who would dispute that if someone else, even someone who knew our weak spots and settled habits, would claim to our face that we will do a certain action in ten minutes, we would not only *feel* but *know* that we could refrain from doing it, if we thought it worth our while to do so. Only by confusion generated by the careless use of metaphors could one suppose that if scientific determinism were true all our actions would belong in the same bag with the actions of compulsive neurotics and addicts.[5] Does this not explain why a philosopher who misconstrues determinism along the above lines might believe that he could not accept determinism "without at the same time conceiving of [his] whole concept of what [he now calls 'his'] action fundamentally altered"? If, on the other hand, we leave aside the chimaera of auto-prediction, it is difficult to understand why Sidgwick should have thought that *x does A* entails *x's doing A is not the consequence of his 'constitution' and his 'circumstances'*.

[27] Above all, why, in the passage quoted, does Sidgwick tacitly *equate* the idea of free choice with the idea that a person's action is not (pre-) determined by the antecedent state of himself and his environment? Some light is thrown upon this question by the fact that although the *primary* thrust of the passage we have been examining concerns the connection between 'determinism' and the concept of action and takes the form of the argument presented above, it nevertheless *also* contains an argument of the very form Donagan denies to be present. Made fully explicit this argument has the following structure:

[Freely chosen action $=_{df}$ action not pre-determined]
[Actions *in the strict sense* are 'actions' which are not predetermined]

---

[5] It is worth noting that on reflection we tend to become uneasy about saying that the 'actions' of compulsive neurotics and addicts are *actions* in the full blooded sense—which does not mean that we are tempted to think of them as 'mere bodily motions'. For a discussion of this and related points see FD, pp. 160–1 [Eds.—§49], and below p. 132. [Eds.—The reference is to page 132 of the author's proof, which is paginated differently from the published version of RD. Sellars seems to intend reference to §§52–3, which appear on p. 174 of the published version. The author's proof is document 31735062221068, Box 39, Folders 5–6, Wilfrid S. Sellars Papers, 1899–1990, ASP.1991.01, Archives of Scientific Philosophy, Archives & Special Collections, University of Pittsburgh Library System.]

(1) If there is free will, there are freely chosen actions.
(2) If there are freely chosen actions, there are actions not predetermined, i.e. there are, *in the strict sense*, actions.
(3) If determinism is true, then all 'actions' are predetermined i.e. not *in the strict sense* actions.
(4) Hence, if there is free will, determinism is false.

To find this argument is to appreciate Donagan's point, the consequences of which I shall shortly examine, that "incompatibility [with determinism] is built into its [free will's] definition" by the sophisticated libertarian.

IV

[28] Donagan next turns his attention to C. D. Broad, whose grasp of the metaphysical issues involved in the free-will problem is an order of magnitude greater than that of Sidgwick—though their philosophical temperaments are remarkably alike. He begins (p. 73-4) by endorsing Broad's claim that most of "those who profess to believe in Free Will" have a concept of free will according to which "volition satisfies two conditions, a negative and a positive. The negative condition is that it is not causally pre-determined." Before turning to an examination of Donagan's analysis and critique of Broad's well known argument, the crux of which concerns the concept of 'agent causation', I pause to stress the fact that Donagan unhesitatingly identifies the concept which 'most of those who profess to believe in Free Will' have (i.e. which certain *philosophers* have [W.S.]) with "the common concept of free will." (p. 74.) Donagan thus implies that the ordinary man, when he speaks of doing something of his own free will, is using concepts of causality and explanation which have been freed from their tie to the paradigm of the common sense explanation of behavior, and has thus transcended the domain of the practical concepts of 'circumstance', 'action', 'desire', 'impulse', 'habitual action', 'predetermined', 'caused to do', 'able to do', 'prevented from doing', in terms of which non-philosophers normally assess the responsibility of persons for what they do. Unfortunately, the fact that certain distinguished *philosophers* have built the falsity of scientific determinism into their concept of free will would confirm the idea that this falsity is intrinsic to the *plain man's* concept of 'action of one's own free will', only if there is reason to think that these philosophers have appreciated the distinction between these different types of explanatory framework. The concluding portion of Donagan's essay rests on the idea that "the common concept of free will" (i.e. the concept of free will *common to libertarian philosophers*) is the correct explication of 'the common concept of free will' in the sense of the plain man's concept of 'action of one's own free will'.

[29] Donagan praises Broad as unique among determinists for recognizing that sophisticated libertarians reject the idea (advanced, for example, by Clifford) that

the negative condition entails that human action involves "something wholly capricious or arbitrary, belonging to the moment only,"[6] and for recognizing that these libertarians would defend this rejection by insisting that the idea that volitions are not *predetermined* does not mean that they have no *cause*. The causation involved is, however, unique, for volitions are caused

> *by the self or agent*, considered as a substance or continuant, and not by a total cause which contains as factors events *in* and dispositions *of* the agent.
> (Broad [1], 214–215*)

Donagan summarizes Broad's account of the positive condition as follows:

> Acts of volition are events, but their causes are not prior events to which they are related according to laws of nature: they "originate from causal progenitors which are continuants and not events."
> (Donagan, pp. 74–5; the words in quotes are from Broad [1], 215)

To which he adds

> It is evident [!] that an act of volition caused by a continuant which could have caused a contrary act is not pre-determined.

Donagan then implies (but surely by oversight) that this astonishing claim is equivalent to the more technical formula:

> That an agent x caused a certain volition (say, the willing of A) at t, does not imply that there are laws of nature according to which x's willing A at t is deducible from x's existence at t. (p. 74)

Neglecting, for the moment, the obscurity of the notion of a volition being deducible (given certain laws of nature) from "x's existence at t," I note that the formula seems to be weaker than the original in that it is apparently compatible (as the latter is not) with the volition's being predetermined. One might think that the real point of the formula is to remind us that Broad approaches even this new and unique form of causation in terms of entailment. An agent's being the cause of his willing of A at t is to be construed as the entailment of the volition by the agent's "existence at t." But this theme plays no role in Donagan's critique of Broad, and, indeed, it obscures his argument. For if Broad were interpreting

---

[6] Clifford as quoted by Donagan (from Moore), p. 73.
* [Eds.—This and subsequent references to 'Broad [1]' are to C. D. Broad, *Ethics and the History of Philosophy* (London: Routledge & Kegan Paul, 1952). The quote is from p. 74 of Donagan.]

libertarianism as the claim that the cause of an act of free will is the agent's existence *at t*, it would be absurd for him to charge the libertarian, as he does, in a key passage quoted by Donagan, with construing the cause of a volition in such a way that it contains "no factor to which the notion of date has any application." (Broad [1], 215.)

[30] Yet Donagan's formula is not without reason, as emerges from the following considerations. In the course of pointing out (p. 75) that it is absurd to say that "the notion of date" has no application to, for example, Julius Caesar, who, the libertarian claims, was the cause of "his volition, at a certain moment *t* in 49 B.C. to cross the Rubicon," Donagan expostulates "do not his birth and death have well known dates?" But if the sense in which dates apply to Julius Caesar is derivative from the sense in which dates apply to events (his birth, death, etc.) pertaining to Julius Caesar, then one would expect that the sense in which dates apply to Julius Caesar *as a cause* is derivative from that in which dates apply to events pertaining to Julius Caesar *as causes*. And, given that the sense in which dates 'apply to' events is to be explicated in terms of dates occurring in event expressions (thus 'Caesar's crossing the Rubicon *in 49 B.C.*'), we would *seem* to be led back to the familiar idea that although it is as legitimate to speak of Julius Caesar as the cause of an event (in this case, supposedly, a volition), as it is to speak of a cow as the cause of the Chicago fire, this becomes, when unpacked, the idea that it is some (unspecified) event involving Julius Caesar which is, in a primary sense, the cause of the volition.

[31] One possible move, at this stage of the dialectic, is to grant that dates occur in the proper expression of the cause, in a primary sense, of a volition, but insist that the remainder of the expression involves not an *ordinary* event location (running, jumping, celebration, volition) but rather 'existence,' so that the full expression would have the unusual (but not outlandish) form

the existence of x at t.

Thus one might claim that it is the *existence* of Julius Caesar at a certain moment in 49 B.C., rather than any ordinary event involving him at that moment, which cause his volition to cross the Rubicon. And if we think of causation in terms of propositional entailment (however this be construed), is not this what the concept of the agent causation of volitions would amount to? Is this, perhaps, what Donagan had in mind?

[32] But to make *this* move is to be at a loss to explain how the *mere* fact of Caesar's existence at *t* could, as such, entail (with the assistance of relevant 'laws of nature'), or be an essential factor in that which entails,[7] the occurrence of any one

---

[7] Other than in the trivial sense that things which don't exist can't be causes.

volition rather than any other. And this consideration would lead us back to the idea that the cause of a volition must be a more 'determinate' event than 'the existence of x at t'.

[33] The truth of the matter, surely, is that if there is a legitimate sense in which a person (as continuant) is the 'cause' of his volition, it is absurd to construe this 'causation' on the entailment model. An effective reply to Broad must make this explicit. It is for this reason, and not as an exercise in plumbing Donagan's philosophical preconscious, that I have spent so much time on his reference to 'x's existence at t'.

[34] But is there 'a unique mode of causation' worthy of the name 'agent causation'? The answer to this question must be given in several stages. There is, in the first place, the truism that the mode of causation expressed by

Jones caused the book to burn

is 'agential' in that Jones *did* something (e.g. applied a lighted match to the book), and 'unique' in that the relevant concept of 'action', tied as it is to a cluster of concepts at the heart of which lies that of volition, does not apply, save metaphorically, to non-persons.

[35] Donagan, after quoting the epigraph to Chisholm's essay on 'Freedom and Action',[8] explicates it by pointing out that

> ...The ultimate movement in a series of movement is sometimes *not* the first cause in the series. We do not have: moving stone, caused by moving staff, caused by moving hand—*finis*; but rather: moving stone, caused by moving staff, caused by moving hand, *caused by man*. (p. 77)

But, why does Donagan feel impelled to write '*caused by man*' rather than '*caused by willing man*'? Surely when he took up his pen to continue, as he does, by writing,

> And further reflection on the first cause in this series shows that it involves causation of a different kind from that involved in the earlier stages. (p. 77)

it must have occurred to him that the distinctive feature of the "different kind of causation" with which the series ends is simply that it involves mental states and propensities which have in common an essential relation to the will, that is, as Donagan is prepared to grant, to volition. Aristotle himself, as has often been pointed out, does not offer a well-developed theory of the relation between

---

[8] "...a staff moves a stone and is moved by a hand, which is moved by a man." Aristotle, *Physics*, III, 256a.

thought and action, but, without going into exegetical niceties, would it be absurd to suggest that for Aristotle the series

> moving stone, moving staff, moving hand...

ends with *something like*

> desiring man?

Surely the role played in Aristotle's metaphysics by the concept of final causation escapes understanding if this move is not appropriate. It is sheer confusion to interpret the passage from Aristotle's *Physics* as an anticipation of contemporary concepts of non-occurrent causation.

[36] Donagan writes,

> If human agents are non-occurrent causes, then, as Chisholm has said, "We have a prerogative which some would attribute only to God: each of us, when we act, is a prime mover unmoved. In doing what we do, we cause certain events to happen, and nothing—or no one—causes us to cause those events to happen (Chisholm [1], 23*)."[9]

But *Aristotle's* prime movers are not, *in the usual sense*, agents. They do not engage in *actions*—though they are, of course, pure *act*. They are causes by being the objects of love or desire. For Aristotle the series

> (moving) stone, (moving) staff, (moving) hand

ends with man, not because man is the "non-occurrent cause" of the hand's moving, but because the desire which is the occurrent cause of the hand's moving is aroused by 'form'.[10] The latter is, indeed, a 'non-occurrent cause' but not in the sense in which agents as continuants are 'non-occurrent', as contrasted with the events in which they participate, but in the quite different sense in which the 'intentional objects' of desire are 'non-occurrent'. And the latter are causes not as things or persons are causes, but rather in a sense which reminds us that for Aristotle, 'cause' is said in many ways. Would it be wrong to suggest that the thread which ties these many ways together is the theme of explanation?

---

* [Eds.—This and the subsequent reference to 'Chisholm [1]' are to R. M. Chisholm, "Freedom and Action," in *Freedom and Determinism*, ed. Keith Lehrer (New York, Random House, 1966), 11–44.]

[9] Donagan, page 78. The Chisholm quotation is from *FD*. 'Freedom and Action', p. 23.

[10] An elaboration of this point would require an account of those strands of Aristotle's philosophy of mind which developed into the scholastic theory of mental acts, a theory which, in one form or another, has been with us ever since, particularly in the work of Brentano and his successors.

[37] According to Chisholm

In doing what we do, we cause certain things to happen, and nothing—or no one—causes us to cause those events to happen. (Chisholm [1], 23)

But further reflection on Aristotle's treatment of causation should have suggested to Chisholm that the idea that

...no thing or person causes us to cause event E to happen

which is only, as we shall see, for the most part true, might be compatible with the idea that

There is (in principle) a cause—in the sense of a theoretical explanation—for the occurrence of every event (including volitions and actions).

V

[38] In 'Metaphysics and the Concept of the Person' I argued that to say of a person that he is the cause of a certain action (his A-ing), where the context is the metaphysics of action,[11] is to say no more and no less than that the person A'd. I now agree with Donagan that my rhetorical claim that "nobody would think of dancing a waltz as causing a waltz" obscured rather than clarified the issue. It ran together the obvious point that the relation between a dancing and a dance (or a waltz) is not a causal one, with the moot point that the relation between a person and his dancing is not a causal one. It is certainly true that if a causal relation is involved, it is unilluminating to assimilate it to the form

X, by Y-ing, caused a certain event E.

thus

X, by dancing, caused a dance.

for, we would surely expostulate, X's dancing doesn't *cause*, but *is* the dance. But the issue concerns the appropriateness, not of the above formula, but of

---

[11] *The Logical Way of Doing Things* (ed. by Karel Lambert) New Haven, 1969. I.e. the attempt to explicate the very concept of an action—as contrasted with the praxiology of blame, excuses and punishment. [Eds.—MP is Ch. 8 of this volume.]

S caused his dancing

and, since the *esse* of a dance is someone's dancing, it is not unreasonable to say that one causes a dance by causing one's dancing—even though the relation between the dance and the dancing is, so to speak, logical rather than causal.

[39] Thus the philosophical point I wanted to make is not that there is no defensible sense in which a dancer can be said to be the cause of the dancing, for there is at least one such, it is rather that all of the interesting senses in which a dancer causes his dancing are, in the last analysis, to be explicated in terms of occurrent causation, and that when the dust has settled it will turn out that 'agent causation' *as construed by libertarians* amounts to nothing more than an unilluminating reparsing of the fact that people will and act.

[40] I shall begin a fairly long story by noting that since I have defended the view that actions are, or can be, caused by volitions, it might be thought that I would accept as proper the locution

X, by willing to raise his arm, caused the raising of his arm[12]

The answer, of course, is No. As Donagan clearly sees, volitions, as I construe them, though they are mental acts, are not mental actions. And what belongs after 'by' in the above locution is an action expression, as in

X, by firing the gun, started the race.

On the other hand, the following would be proper

X's willing to raise his arm, caused a raising of his arm.

I have already[13] called attention to the fact that our ordinary causal talk about inanimate objects is largely built on frozen metaphors in which things are treated as simple-minded persons. Thus, although 'by', in the above contexts, has the root sense of 'by means of,' we are willing, in this metaphorical vein, to say such things as that

The staff, by moving, caused the stone to move.
The hand, by moving, caused the staff to move.

---

[12] An adequate theory of action must obviously explore the relation of 'a raising of his arm' to 'a rising of his arm'.

[13] Page 108 above. See also *Science, Perception and Reality* (London, 1963), Chapter I, pp. 10ff., hereinafter referred to as *SPR*. [Eds.—Sellars's first reference is unclear. As in note 5, the reference is to page 108 of the author's proof, which is page 150 of the published version. On that page we find the second half of §2 and most of §3. Sellars's second reference is to PSIM.]

These are equivalent to the non-metaphorical

> The staff's moving caused the stone to move.
> The hand's moving caused the staff to move.

On the other hand,

> The staff, by willing, caused itself to move

is absurd, not because it is anthropomorphic, but because it is a category mistake, for at the level of non-metaphorical person talk,

> Jones, by willing to raise his arm, caused the raising of his arm

involves the mistake of treating volitions as though they were actions.[14] Thus in this case we are limited to the second alternative, i.e.

> Jones' willing to raise his arm caused a raising of his arm.

[41] Now, surely, if it is legitimate to say that

> *The cow* caused the Chicago fire

because we can say that

> *The cow's kicking the lantern* caused the Chicago fire

it is not unreasonable to say that

> *Jones* caused the raising of his hand

on the ground that

> *Jones' willing to raise his hand* caused the raising of his hand.

In traditional terms, the first pair of statements would concern 'transeunt causation,' the second 'immanent causation'.

[42] Well, then, if persons can be construed to be the cause of their actions, are they also cause of their volitions? And, if so, does a person cause his volition to do

---

[14] This is disguised, in some formulations, by using the term 'undertakes' as a primitive in action theory, for in *one* of its senses an 'undertaking' *is* an action—indeed an illocutionary performance.

A in any more interesting sense than that he so wills? The answer depends once again on the extent to which the term 'cause' is freed from the paradigm

X, by Y-ing, caused z to W.

and its connection with the more generic notion of an explanation of why a certain event took place is stressed. We can, in many cases, explain the occurrence of volitions by referring to such things as desires, deliberations, impulses, moral beliefs, etc.[15] On the other hand, the idea that the common sense framework contains the actual conceptual resources[16] for a deterministic theory in terms of which the occurrence of any volition could 'in principle' be explained, is a snare and a delusion. As I stressed above, it is vulgar determinism which blends the abstract pragmatic axiom, characteristic of the scientific outlook, that all events can be explained with reference to other events, with the fact that we explain human behavior in terms of such concepts as 'habit', 'desire', 'emotion', 'character', 'choice', etc., to form the bastard notion that, without going beneath the level of these conceptual forms, a complete explanation of what people do could, in principle, be obtained. The cash of determinism, if true, can only be found in the 'Scientific Image of Man-in-the World'.

[43] I shall now answer the question: are persons the cause of their volitions? in the affirmative, subject to the following considerations. Roughly, persons are the cause of their volitions in the sense in which any continuant is the cause of those of its states which are not, to any relevant extent, explained by what is going on outside them. I pointed out above that in the case of 'transeunt causation,' where

X, by Y-ing caused z to W

we can speak not only of x's Y-ing as 'the cause' of z's W-ing, but of x as 'the cause' of z's W-ing. I added that I see no objection to making the same move in the case of 'immanent causation'. Given that

x's Y-ing at t caused x to W^* at $t + dt$

---

[15] The structure of such explanation is an intricate topic which must be left to another occasion, along with the question as to the sense in which this explanation is 'causal'. I have discussed this topic in 'Actions and Events', *Noûs* 7 (1973) pp. 179–202, hereinafter referred to as *AAE*. [Eds.—Sellars uses the abbreviation 'AE,' but in accordance with contemporary convention, we use the abbreviation 'AAE' here and throughout the essay.]

[16] The sense in which it can contain these resources in the form of promissory notes will be explored below.

* [Eds.—Correction of "Z" in published version. In the typescript, Sellars has marked out "Z" and written "W" in the margin. The error remains in the author's proof, and Sellars does not correct it there (although he has marked a number of other corrections—mostly page number references to Donagan's article). The relevant typescript is document 31735062221084, Box 39, Folders 5–6, Wilfrid S. Sellars Papers, 1899–1990, ASP.1991.01, Archives of Scientific Philosophy, Archives & Special Collections, University of Pittsburgh Library System.

we *could* say that x is 'the cause' of its own W-ing. But we probably wouldn't, unless we were rebutting the claim that it was the action of something other than x which was, in a relevant sense, the explanation of x's W-ing.

[44] Thus I have no a priori objection to speaking of a person as 'the cause' of his volitions, provided that it is recognized that such a concept would be built on that of occurrent causation. The previous paragraph suggests that the point of speaking in this way would lie in its contrast with speaking of something or someone other than Jones as 'the cause' of one of his volitions.

[45] I pointed out that in the case of actions, we are quite willing to speak of persons as being caused to act in certain ways. We do so in cases where the relevant explanation of why a certain person did what he did lies in what was done by some other person or, perhaps, by an inanimate object. Would we be willing to say that one person's volition was caused by another person or thing? Not, of course, in so many words, for 'volition' is a technical concept involved in the rational reconstruction of how such varied states as desires, emotions, attitudes, deliberations, impulses, etc., relate to action. On the other hand, we are surely willing to speak of desires, emotions, etc., as externally aroused, and, on occasion, to pick out another person or external object as, in a relevant sense, 'the cause' of the desire or impulse with reference to which a given action is to be explained. Presumably, therefore, one who finds the concept of volition useful would be willing to speak of certain volitions as 'caused from without,' thus granting the contrast which would give point to saying, on occasion, that *Jones himself* was the cause of one of his volitions. Once again, however, the claim that on occasion it makes sense to say that someone (or something) other than Jones was the cause of one of his volitions would not be an entering wedge for scientific determinism, for the latter is certainly not the thesis that in *this* sense of 'cause' persons are caused to will whatever they will to do.

[46] It might be worth pausing to note that philosophers in the Stoic tradition have often thought of 'inclinations' as caused from without, and are, as such, to be contrasted with the 'inner' motive of reason or the sense of duty. I suspect that many of those who reject scientific determinism think of 'inclinations' as propensities to will which are grounded in bodily states (taking into account the effects of prior choices), whereas 'sense of duty' or 'sense of what is reasonable' refers to propensities to will which are not so grounded. From this point of view, to accept the 'identity theory' is to assimilate rational motives to inclinations, actions to passions. But, of course, the identity theory doesn't deny the distinctive character of reasoning and rational motivation, it simply argues* with Spinoza that things

---

* [Eds.—In the typescript, Sellars has marked out "argues" and written in "agrees." As was the case in §43 above, this change was not reflected in the author's proof.]

and processes which can be described in nonintentional terms can perform the functions which are implied by the use of intentional terms. But the topic of what it is to characterize a thing or process in intentional terms is one on which it is impossible to say anything illuminating in a few words, and I shall not attempt to do so now.[17]

[47] Let me return to Donagan's elaboration of Chisholm's use of Aristotelian terminology by asking

When Jones causes a book to burn is he a 'first cause'?

Not necessarily, if this means that in the *ordinary* sense of the phrase Jones was not caused to do that which caused the book to burn. For he might have been caused to do it by the order and power of the court. That people are in this sense caused on occasion to do what they do is, of course, no entering wedge for scientific determinism. In this sense, agents may or may not be the 'first cause' of what they bring about. The relevant distinctions are context dependent but generally concern the task of assessing responsibility. Scientific determinism, it must be remembered, does not claim that persons are caused to act (and will) as they do, but only that, in principle, every action, adequately described in the appropriate theoretical vocabulary, is a state of affairs which is derivable from an antecedent state of affairs given the principles of an ideal (deterministic) theory of what persons ultimately are.

[48] But, it will be urged, even if there is *a* sense in which persons can be caused to do things, Aristotle's pithy remark concerns another sense of cause in which persons are invariably the 'first causes' of actions which can be imputed to them from a metaphysical point of view. To put the question bluntly: Is there a sense in which persons are the 'first causes' of even those actions which they are, in the above sense, caused to do? And is *this* sense of 'first cause' incompatible with scientific determinism?

[49] Now any contemporary peripatetic worth his salt would surely agree that 'cause' like 'being' is said in many ways. *Distinguendum est*. Might it not be true that a person is, in this sought for sense, the 'cause' (or 'principle') of his actions, even though all his actions are subject to the principle of scientific determinism, and hence in *still another* (reasonable) sense *caused*?

VI

[50] At this point it might pull things together a bit if I return to Donagan's critique of Broad. It will be remembered that he argued, *contra* Broad, that the

---

[17] For my own views on this topic the reader should consult *Science and Metaphysics*. Routledge and Kegan Paul, London, 1967, Ch. 3, hereinafter referred to as *SM*. Earlier formulations can be found in 'Notes on Intentionality', *The Journal of Philosophy* 61 (1964), 655–65; and 'A Semantical Solution to the Mind-Body Problem', *Methodos* 5 (1953), 45–82.

'notion of date' does, indeed, have application to the agent who, according to the libertarian, is the cause of his volition. Unfortunately, as we saw, Donagan's argument would be an *ignoratio elenchi* unless he can show not only that the 'notion of date' applies to the agent (which Broad can easily grant), but that it applies to the agent *as cause*. We saw that Donagan seems to be aware of this, and that he apparently seeks to avoid the *ignoratio* by introducing the 'agent's existence at t' to be the cause. However, we also saw that this idea is no sooner introduced, than it is abandoned without trace—though we are left with a sense of puzzlement as to how the agent's mere existence at t can be (though obviously a necessary condition) the essential causal factor in the occurrence of a specific volition at t. And, as we shall see, this puzzlement remains after the schema

X's existence at t causes volition

is replaced by the formula, treated as basic,

X at t causes volition.

It is in terms of the latter that Donagan sums up the positive results of his examination of Broad. He writes

> I conclude that Broad's analysis enables us to give a clear answer to Moore's question: In what sense do believers in free will assert that a free agent is able to will otherwise than, at a given time, he does will? They assert it in this sense: (i) that willing as he does at the time is not deducible, according to laws of nature, from the state of the universe at an earlier time (Broad's negative condition); and (ii) he himself, as non-occurrent cause, at that time, of a certain volition (Broad's positive condition) could, at that time, have been the non-occurrent cause of some alternative volition. The "could" in (ii) is absolute: That it is not analyzable into "would have, if..." is implied by (i). (pp. 75-6)

[51] As for the negative condition, I have already argued that the philosophical libertarian includes it in his definition of 'action of one's own free will' because he mistakenly thinks that scientific determinism is incompatible with the claim that the agent could have acted (or willed) otherwise. We shall see in a moment that Donagan is prepared to grant that this *is* a mistake, which implies that he has some other reason for thinking that the negative condition must be included in the definition, if it is to be an *analysis* and not an arbitrary stipulation. But what of the positive condition? It is illuminating to note that no sooner has Donagan offered this "clear answer to Moore's question," than he turns his attention to the charge that the libertarian gives no more content to

X, at t, causes his volition to A

than

S, at t, wills to A.

He argues against this by offering an analogy. Strictly speaking, he develops this analogy in connection with the parallel charge concerning 'causing an action' and 'acting,' but he clearly intends it to apply also to the case of volition, and I shall formulate it accordingly.

> So a male sibling is no more than a brother, but... just as by thinking of brothers as siblings we get clearer about what brothers are, so by thinking of [willing volitions] as causings of a certain kind, we get clearer about what [willing] is.
> (Adopted from p. 76)

Now in my previous remarks on the issues involved in 'agent causation' I granted that there is a perfectly good sense in which a person is the cause of his volitions. But, although the spirit of my remarks was conciliatory, I insisted that agent causation in this sense is a special case of the 'immanent' counterpart of 'transeunt' *continuant causation*. Calling attention to the close tie between 'cause' and 'because' or explanation, I argued that the concept of agent *causation* hinges on the idea that a person's volitions are, on occasion, explainable with reference to antecedent mental states of that person, and has its primary application to those cases. I also pointed out that to say that *Jones himself* was the cause of a certain volition serves the dialectical purpose of rebutting the charge that the best explanation of that volition lies in someone or something other than Jones.

[52] By implication, I have left open the possibility that there are volitions, the occurrence of which cannot (even in principle) be explained in terms of our ordinary categories of psychological explanation. Notice, for example, that the term 'impulse' functions as an escape valve. Sometimes it stands for one or other of a familiar kind of short-termed desire—in which case it belongs to the framework of ordinary psychological explanation; but it can also cover cases where ordinary explanation simply fails.

[53] The following thought experiment may be helpful. Consider the case of a person whose brain is probed and whose arm goes up—*not*, however, because the relevant part of the *motor center* has been touched, but because his *conceptual center* is led to reverberate with the thought 'Why not raise my arm?' We might call this an 'impulse', and, indeed, unlike the results of stimulating the motor center, it can be resisted in the sense in which 'inclinations' are resisted. But if this practical question was confronted by no alternative, can we not suppose it to develop into the corresponding volition? Would we, perhaps, deny that the

'volition' was a *genuine* volition? Or would we not, perhaps, grant its volitional status, *but deny that the person was its cause*? Compare the case in which neural activity, initiated by stomach contractions, stimulates the conceptual activity 'Why not eat?' Surely a relevant consideration is that stomachs are parts of persons, but electronic probes are not.

[54] However one reacts to this thought experiment, I submit that unless *some* explanation in terms of antecedent states *of the agent* is, however indefinitely, presupposed, there is no meaning to the claim that the agent was the cause of his volition, other than that he so willed.[18] In other words, on my account of agent causation it makes sense to say that x's willing to A is *a kind of causation*, as brother is *a kind of sibling*. I do not see that Donagan is entitled to this analogy.

[55] The second point I wish to make about the positive condition in Donagan's definition of free will concerns the fact that it requires not only that the agent be the "non-occurrent cause, at this time, of a certain volition" but also that the agent "could, at that time, have been the non-occurrent cause of some alternative volition," where "the 'could'... is absolute," in other words, "is not analyzable into 'would have, if...'." The point is simply that the idea that the agent could have willed otherwise, *where the 'could' does not mean 'would have, if...'* is equally central to my reconciliationist position. It is true that in the case of *action*, I defend that idea that

X could have done A'

is to be analyzed as

X would have done A', if he had so willed

and, hence, in terms of the schema

could = would have, if...

but it is *not* true that I make a parallel move in the case of volition, nor (I believe) does Donagan think that I do. Thus he clearly sees (p. 67–8) that my account of volition precludes me from construing

X would have willed to do A'

as

X would have willed to do A', if he had willed so to will.

---

[18] I shall qualify this shortly, but in a way which leaves it essentially unchanged.

And, which is more important, his careful reconstruction of my analysis of

Throughout P, x is able to will A

does not exhibit it as having the form

During P, x would have willed A, if...

Thus, I take Donagan to grant that the sense I give to 'could' in 'could have willed otherwise' is 'absolute', in the sense that "it is not analyzable into 'would have,...'."

[56] One final point about the positive condition. After claiming, not without reason, that I have "not...succeeded in providing an analysis of ability to will, according to which determinism is compatible with ability to will otherwise than one wills," Donagan indicates the general lines along which such an account might be given, expresses a "strong inclination" to believe that it would be successful, and, tentatively, concludes that

...ability to will otherwise (understood as the absence of conditions preventing it) is compatible with determinism. (p. 71)

In other words, Donagan admits that a reconciliationist is entitled to an 'absolute' sense of 'could have willed otherwise'.

[57] What, then, is the issue? One begins to suspect that when all is said and done, it turns out *not* to be: Is 'could have done (willed) otherwise' compatible with determinism? Nor even: Are agents the non-occurrent causes of their actions (volitions)? *Sometimes* the relevant question seems to be:

Can agents be, in any genuine sense, the *immanent* cause of their volitions, if scientific determinism is true?

where the operative word is, of course, 'genuine'. No survey of the protean controversy about Freedom of the Will would be complete which failed to take this question into account; and since it does transpose some of the issues I have been discussing into a new key, I shall give it a brief, and somewhat rhetorical, inning.

[58] I have argued that agents are *non-occurrent* causes of their actions (volitions) only where they are the *immanent causes* of these actions (volitions)— where 'immanent causation' is to be understood in terms of explanation in terms of antecedent states of the agent. I have stressed the dialectical theme, according to which one says that *Jones himself* was the cause of his action (volition) in order to rebut the claim that the 'best explanation' of the action or volition is to be found in the activity of some person or thing other than the agent. At this point it might be

suggested that to say that *Jones himself* was the cause of his action (volition) is simply to *deny* that the explanation or cause of his action (volition) is, in this sense, external. This would yield *another* sense of 'agent causation' in which

X caused his action (volition)

would not simply be another way of parsing

X acted (willed)

for, even if only *negatively*, it would contain a reference to causation. Let me call this the purely negative sense of 'agent causation.' Notice that agent causation, in this sense, of an action (volition) would be compatible with the idea that the action (volition) in question *had no explanation at all*.

[59] Why should one think that agent causation in this purely negative sense is a useful concept for the explication of human freedom and dignity? After all, is it not enough that there is agent causation in the positive sense? But, it will be said, in those cases in which the best explanation of a person's action (volition) is to be found 'outside' him, he is not a genuinely free and autonomous agent. To *this* the reply, surely, is that these cases can be summed up under the heading 'actions which we are caused to do', and that the existence of such actions[19] would be philosophically interesting only if one could show that *all* our actions (volitions) are *really* caused 'from without'; i.e. that we are always *caused* to act and will as we do. But, it will be said, this is just what determinism implies. For according to determinism all our actions (volitions) are *caused* by—explainable (in principle) in terms of—events that happened long before we came into being. And what is more 'outside' us than the distant past? Only if there are actions (volitions) which are not *caused*, can there be actions (volitions) which we are not *caused to do* (*will*). Either determinism is false, and there are volitions which are 'agent caused' in the purely negative sense, *or* with John Wisdom[20] we must courageously face the prospect of having existed from all eternity.

[60] One can also see how a similar dialectic might lead to the claim that unless agents are the 'first causes' of their volitions, their volitions are merely 'their' volitions, indeed, merely 'their volitions'. In other words, just as Sidgwick thought that an 'action', the occurrence of which, could, in principle, be validly inferred from antecedent events by the use of an ideally true theory would be only an 'action' so-called, so the libertarian might be tempted to think that an ideally predictable volition would be only a 'volition' so-called.

---

[19] Notice that I deliberately avoid highlighting the special case of *compulsion*.
[20] *Problems of Mind and Matter*, Cambridge, 1934, Chapter 8.

[61] Finally, to match metaphor with metaphor, if the libertarian is tempted to say that if determinism is true, then the remote past *requires* our biographies, the determinist is certain to reply that the rest of the history of the world must fit around our lives as we fit into it. In this abstract sense, at least, we are autonomous. Whether we are in any more interesting sense autonomous, and to what extent, hinges not on abstract considerations concerning the 'causal principle,' but on the specific causal powers which characterize us as *rational* beings.

[62] I shall return to this final point in a moment, after pausing to remark that my aim in these polemical remarks is to challenge Donagan to say just *where* in *his* opinion the issue lies.

[63] Sophisticated libertarians can be expected to reject the charge that they are guilty of the above confusions, as they have rejected the charge that they confuse 'causation' with 'compulsion'. But what *is* the alternative? What *is* the issue? My deepest conviction, hinted at above, is that what *really* is at stake is the old issue of reasons and causes. If explanation of action in terms of *reasons* is a *special case of* explanation in terms of (occurrent) *causes*, then the concept of agent causation can be given a positive analysis in terms of immanent causation along the lines I have suggested. If *not* then 'action having a reason' becomes logically distinct from 'action having a cause', and, if these concepts are taken to be not only *distinct*, but *incompatible*, agent causation reduces to what I have called the purely negative sense. Alas! the topic of reasons and causes is long, and the remaining life of this paper short,[21] so I move on to my concluding remarks.

VII

[64] If any one theme has been central to my argument it is that reflection on the ordinary practical concepts in terms of which we assess responsibility and justify praise or blame provides no reason for supposing that actions (and volitions) which admit (in principle) of a causal explanation would be merely 'action' (and 'volition') so-called. To suppose that it does, I have argued, rests largely on a confusion of the various ways in which 'cause' is said, and, in particular, on the idea that 'cause' in the sense of scientific explanation is more closely connected than it is with 'cause' in the sense in which, by being 'caused to do something', a person may be less responsible than usual for what he does.[22]

---

[21] I have discussed this topic in *AAE*. [Eds.—Ch. 9 of this volume.]

[22] Much freer from confusion are such theological issues as whether God (or, perhaps, Nature) so controls the strength of our desires (and other motives) that He (or She) is the true cause of everything we do. (Compare my remarks on John Wisdom's well-known student opinion poll, *FD*, p. 161 [Eds.—§50].) It should not be forgotten that until the birth of modern science the problem of free will was largely—though not exclusively—a topic for theologians and theologically oriented philosophers; a

[65] Reviewing this theme will serve to bring me to the concluding paragraphs of Donagan's essay, in which he explores the relation between my two 'images' of man and my critique of libertarianism. Donagan begins by noting that although it is clearly possible to give a (stipulative) definition of 'action of one's own free will' according to which this phrase would not apply to actions which admit (in principle) of a scientific explanation, and that although "some distinguished philosophers have believed that we have free will in this sense,"

> It would be of interest to [Sellars] only if free will in that sense were implicit in the "manifest image" of man in the world. (p. 78)

Donagan explains that "a cardinal point in Sellars' distinction between the manifest and the scientific images of man in the world is that the latter alone makes use of scientific techniques of theory construction." Thus he quotes me as saying

> There is one type of scientific reasoning which [the manifest image], by stipulation, does *not* include, namely that which involves the postulation of imperceptible entities, and principles pertaining to them, to explain the behavior of perceptible things. (*SPR*, p. 7)

He then comes to the point by continuing,

> With good reason, Sellars regards the principle of determinism as a principle pertaining to postulated imperceptible entities: It was in fact introduced in connection with atomism. It follows that free-will, as Sidgwick, Clifford, and Broad understand it, cannot belong to the manifest image because it is defined in terms of the principle of determinism.

Unfortunately, while this passage contains truth, it does so in a distorted way, as I shall try to make clear.

[66] In the first place it is essential to distinguish between levels of conceptual structure. My contrast between the two images was *primarily* a contrast between two *first order* pictures of the world. This is not to say that in the essay to which Donagan refers I did not discuss the contrast between two conceptions of scientific method and two paradigms of scientific explanation. But my primary concern was the impact of *specific* postulational theories on our conception of man, and the new sense of urgency these theories have given to the venerable clash between

stablemate of the problem of evil. Perhaps the best way to clear one's head about free will is to read Pascal's *Lettres Provençales* (?) and then plunge into the clear cold waters of Plantinga's philosophical theology.

realist and instrumentalist interpretations of science. The distinction between conceptual levels I have in mind can be illustrated by the fact that a thinker of philosophical bent might live in the 'manifest image,' as I define it, and yet be either

(a) One who takes as his paradigm of scientific method, inductive generalization and deductive systematization; and who, when he turns to human behavior limits himself to the familiar praxiological categories in terms of which we explain why people did what they did and assess their responsibility.
(b) One who takes as his paradigm of scientific method atomic theories which (in principle) "save the appearances" by showing why perceptible things obey, to the extent that they do, and within the limits of experimental error, established inductive generalizations; and who, when he turns to human behavior, contrasts explanation in terms of familiar praxiological categories with an ideal explanation, which he glimpses through a glass darkly, and which would conform to his paradigm.
(c) One who takes as his paradigm of disciplined understanding, explanation in terms of final causes, and who postulates not only Cartesian human minds but an additional realm of super-wise, super-good and super-powerful beings (in 'analogical' senses of these adjectives, which have (perhaps inscrutable) super-purposes, by reference to which he makes sense of 'the way things are'.

Donagan correctly points out that my 'scientific image' is an *ideal* image in the sense that it would exist *in concreto* only "when all the facts are in." (p. 78.) He also recognizes that the 'manifest image' is, in another sense 'ideal', an 'ideal type' as Max Weber uses the term, and that the distinction between the images is a "theoretical one, in terms of which the nature of certain philosophical issues can be explained." (p. 79.) Unfortunately after these insightful remarks, he proceeds to muddy the waters by describing the manifest image as "the image of man implicit in the thinking in accordance with which he conducts his life in the world—personal, social, political," and used *this* description to argue that

> ...it would be wrong to follow Sellars in describing this image as corresponding to the world as we know it to be in ordinary experience, supplemented by certain inductive procedures, as though ordinary experience were its source. On the contrary, what a man's ordinary experience is depends in some measure on what manifest image underlies his thinking. (p. 79)

Now I certainly did not intend to identify *my* 'ideal type' with the "image of man implicit in his thinking according to which he conducts his life in the world—perceptual, social and political," for the 'ideal-ness' of my image consists not in its *implicitness* but—though it *is* implicit—in the *restrictions* I place upon it. I quite agree that interestingly different conceptual structures can be "implicit" in the thinking in terms of which different peoples and peoples in different cultures conduct their lives. My manifest image is, however, designed to be an ideal type *common core* shared by all these ways of thinking. It is, frankly, a version of the familiar notion of a 'groundfloor observation language' which, however, has been extended to include the fundamental categories of intentionality and—if you please—agent causation. As such it is a version of a highly controversial notion, and its use is to be justified[23] by the light it throws on basic philosophical controversies.

[67] But my aim in this section is not to defend the use I have made of these two images, but to correct misunderstanding. For it is the misunderstanding to which I have just called attention which underlies Donagan's culminating argument. He begins by writing,

> ...a man's religion if he has one, is part of the manifest image in terms in which he thinks about himself and other men. No religion is arrived at by simple observation and induction: many religions, in fact, postulate imperceptible entities, e.g. immaterial gods, immaterial souls. It follows that there may be many manifest images of man, although different manifest images may have much in common.

He illustrates his point by an appeal to the difference between the thinking of a cultivated Hindu, that of a cultivated Christian or Jew, and finally, that of an (uncultivated) Dayak headhunter, and brings his argument to a head by pointing out that

> ...in his ordinary life in the world, as well as in his scientific thinking, man postulates the existence of entities he does not see or touch, and for which he has no direct inductive evidence.

Thus Donagan seems to think that because such entities are not posited by *scientific* thinking, they must belong in the *manifest* image of the person who postulates them. To which the obvious reply is that given the point of *my* distinction, they belong in *neither*.[24] Donagan compounds confusion by asking:

---

[23] As is the use of a distinction between its 'Rylean' and 'post-Rylean' phases. For this use of Ryle as a means of clarifying issues in the philosophy of mind, see *SPR*, chapter 5, 'Empiricism and the Philosophy of Mind', also *SM*, Chapters 3 and 6.

[24] One might be tempted to say that the postulation of religious entities (gods, daimons, etc.), like the postulation of departed spirits is 'scientific' by virtue of being a, perhaps systematic, attempt to explain phenomena, and hence can belong to "a person's" scientific image. But my scientific image is, of course, a normative notion, that of the *truth* which is the formal, final and efficient cause of the scientific enterprise. And the problems I use it to explore arise because some philosophers seem to

Why, if 'a man's manifest image' can include religious entities, can't it include scientifically postulated entities? But once we appreciate the point he is trying to make, we see that all this iconoclasm has been a detour. It is contained in the following question and answer,

> What could be more natural than that a man whose image of himself is orthodox Christian—an immaterial soul informing a living body—should examine the implications of that image with respect to a deterministic conception of the physical world? Sidgwick, whose image of man was Christian, although not his theology, was doing that when he inquired whether, in deliberately choosing between an unattractive rational action and an attractive irrational one, he could conceive his choice as causally determined.   (p. 79-80)

The key to this passage is Donagan's earlier claim that according to my analysis,

> ... free-will, as Sidgwick, Clifford and Broad understand it, cannot belong to the manifest image, because it [free-will] is defined in terms of the principle of determinism.   (p. 78)

The truth of the matter is that 'free-will', thus defined, belongs *neither* to the manifest image *nor* to the scientific image, for it is a *higher order* principle concerning the limits of the derivability of events from prior events. If there is a connection of free-will, thus defined, with the scientific image, it lies in the *fact* that only the confusions of the vulgar determinist could lend plausibility to the idea that the conceptual resources of the (first level) manifest image are rich enough to generate (even in principle) a universal derivability of events, including human actions, from antecedent events.

[68] Thus, instead of demanding that libertarians show that free will, as they define it, is part of the manifest image, and making the issue turn on the relative merits of the manifest and (a supposedly deterministic) scientific image, I simply require the libertarian to show, using any conceptual resources he requires, that it is part and parcel of what we *ordinarily mean* by 'free and responsible action' that it is uncaused in a sense of occurrent causation which, though it belongs to the family of causation concepts, the elder generation of which includes those in terms of which a person is absolved from responsibility for an action or excused for doing what he did, is that junior member of the family which has grown up with modern theoretical explanation. This I submit he has failed to do.

---

believe that the general outline of the truth (stimulations of C-fibers!) is before our eyes. For a more sober assessment of how close we are to the scientific image, see my 'Science, Sense Impressions and Sensa, A Reply to Cornman', *Review of Metaphysics* 24 (1971).

13
On Knowing the Better and Doing the Worse*

I

1. The title of this chapter describes an experience common to all of us, whether we be saints, sinners, or run of the mill members of the moral community. One might think that such a common experience would be quite unproblematic, raising no problems except *per accidens*, as when a person makes a foolish mistake about what is in front of his nose. What could be more obvious than that people often do what they know perfectly well they ought not to do? And if the *fact* be obvious, why does it not lie quietly in the philosopher's collection of specimens, while he turns his attention to puzzles which, so to speak, jump out at him like nightmares in the dark?

2. The answer is a familiar story. Just as the heart of tragedy lies in the fact that death and desolation can result from a clash between parties, each of which, in no superficial sense, has right on his side, so in philosophy the most disturbing problems arise when obvious truths begin to twist and turn and fight among themselves.

3. But what obvious truth or truths conflict with the all too human phenomenon echoed by my title? Surely, if the history of philosophy is a reliable guide,

(A) To know that course *A* is better than course *B* is to have reason for following *A* rather than *B*;

and

(B) If a person has reason for following course *A* rather than course *B* he will follow *A* rather than *B*.

For, together, these imply

(C) To know that course *A* is better than course *B* is to follow *A* rather than *B*

which logically conflicts with the idea that there is such a thing as knowing the better and doing the worse.

---

* This is the revised text of the 1969 Suarez Philosophy Lecture delivered at Fordham University.

4. But, it will be said, the second truth (*B*) is obvious only if it is qualified. It should read

(B₁) If a person has reason for following course *A* rather than course *B* he will do *A* rather than *B*—unless he is overcome by impulse.

Since impulsive action is as common as blackberries, the paradox, it will be said, disappears; for the qualification, itself obvious, reconciles our new principles with the obviousness with which we began.

5. It does, however, only if *all* cases in which a person who, knowing the better, does the worse are cases of action "on impulse." But is this true? Surely there are cases in which, to use Bishop Butler's phrase, a person "sits down in a cool hour" and after careful deliberation resolves to do that which he nevertheless knows to be worse. This is what gives our problem its bite; for, man being what he is, the fact that impulse can lead him to fly in the face of reason is a sobering rather than a puzzling consideration.

6. This is not to say that there are *no* puzzles about the idea that impulse can lead men to act "against their better judgement." Like other general truths about behavior it needs to be fitted into a coherent philosophy of mind, along with, for example, the fact that men on occasion do act in accordance with their better judgement. Aristotle's account of the incontinent man can be viewed as just such an attempt. But does it touch our problem?

7. For our problem is posed by the fact—at least I shall assume it to be a fact—that we are confronted by an "inconsistent triad," i.e. by three propositions which separately command assent, but which cannot live together in the reflective mind:

(1) People know the better yet deliberately do the worse.
(2) To know that course *A* is better than course *B* is to have reason for following *A* rather than *B*.
(3) To have reason for following *A* rather than *B* is (impulse aside) to follow *A* rather than *B*.

II

8. But I probably have not yet persuaded you that these principles have that *prima facie* obviousness which makes it so difficult to lay them aside. Or, to put it differently, I may have concealed their claims by clumsy formulation. Let me try again by making them more explicit. Consider

(A₁) To know that course *A* is, *all things considered*, better than course *B* is to have a *conclusive* reason for following *A* rather than *B*.

for, obviously, one thing may seem to be better than another with respect to certain considerations, but not seem to be so when a larger context is taken into account.

9. To make our first principle thus explicit calls for a corresponding revision in the second, which becomes

(B_2) If a person has a *conclusive* reason for following course A rather than course B, he will (impulse aside) follow A rather than B.

Combined, these revised principles entail, as before, that, impulse aside, there is no such thing as knowing the better but doing the worse.

III

10. You will not have failed to notice that I have drawn heavily on the powers of that little word 'know'—one of the few four letter words which is not as "in" as it used to be. Is there such a thing as *knowing*—in a genuinely cognitive sense—that one thing or course of action is better than another? To convince the skeptic—and I don't mean the professional skeptic who would die rather than admit that he knows anything of substance, but rather one who has found grounds to question the possibility of such knowledge—would require that larger dialogue which, if Santayana is to be believed, goes on endlessly in Limbo—but, fortunately, not in the lecture hall. I shall, therefore, content myself with the reflection that the possibility of such knowledge—the knowledge that one thing is, all things considered, better than another—is really one of the *prima facie* obviousnesses with which philosophers begin.

11. But once we grant this possibility, it is bound to occur to us that it involves a distinction which might resolve our puzzle. For 'knowledge' contrasts with '(mere) belief.' Indeed, while we are at it, we might note that 'all things considered' can mean 'all things in point of fact considered for what they are thought to be' or (ideally) 'all *relevant* things considered for *what they really are.*'

12. Perhaps, then, what is "obvious" is that

(A_2) To *know* (rather than merely believe) that course A is, all relevant things considered for what they really are, better than course B is to have a *conclusive* reason for following A rather than B.

which, together with

(B_2) If a person has a conclusive reason for following course A rather than course B he will (impulse aside) follow A rather than B.

would entail that, impulse aside, there is no such thing as *knowing* the better but doing the worse. This time, then, the *prima facie* existence of exceptions could, perhaps, be accounted for by saying that the 'knowledge' of these agents wasn't *really* knowledge, but rather 'knowledge—loosely speaking,' a dignified form of mere opinion.

IV

13. I have already brought us face to face with the Socratic thesis that virtue is knowledge. I propose to examine it; not, however, as an exercise in exegesis, but because, being a card-carrying member of the Platonic tradition, I subscribe to the view that Plato wrong is usually closer to the truth than other philosophers right. But before embarking on this task, I shall sound a more contemporary note by reminding you of the distinction, baptized but not discovered by David Falk, between 'externalist' and 'internalist' theories of the relation between 'ought' and motivation.[1]

14. Roughly, the 'externalist' holds that it is *logically* possible for a person to 'know'—in a reasonable sense of this term—that he ought to do a certain action A, and yet have no motive for doing A. This means that the idea that he ought to do A fails, as such, to attract him toward the doing of A. The 'externalist' grants that in point of fact a person might be attracted towards doing A by the knowledge that A is what he ought to do. Such people, he would say, have a 'desire' to do what they know to be right. But the existence of this desire in people who have this knowledge would be a *contingent* fact. People could know what was right and lack any tendency to be moved to act by this knowledge.

15. 'Internalism,' on the other hand, is the view that to know that a course of action A is one's duty is, *ipso facto*, to be moved toward the doing of A—is, *ipso facto*, to *have a reason* for doing A. For there is a perfectly legitimate and familiar sense in which to be moved toward doing an action by the idea that the action is of a certain character is to have its being of that character as a reason for doing it. The reason may be good or bad, but it is one's reason.

16. Notice that internalism was defined above as the view that to know that A is one's duty is, *ipso facto*, to have *a* reason for doing A. This leaves open the possibility that even if one knows that one ought to do A, one might have other reasons which point in other directions, say to the doing of B. Thus internalism, thus defined, is compatible with the view that one can know that one ought to do A (the better) and yet be moved to do B (the worse). Indeed, the internalist need not limit such occasions to impulsive action. A person can know that he ought to

---

[1] "'Ought' and Motivation," *Proceedings of the Aristotelian Society* 48 (1947–48); reprinted in *Readings in Ethical Theory* (ed. by Wilfrid Sellars and John Hospers), New York, 1952. [Eds.—OMR is Ch. 2 of this volume.]

do *A* (the better), the internalist might hold, and yet *deliberately* do *B* (the worse). All we have committed him to is the view that if a person knows that he ought to do *A*, then he, *ipso facto*, as a matter of *logical* necessity, has *a* reason for doing *A*.

17. But once he goes this far, can the internalist avoid the more radical view that if a person knows that he ought to do *A* he has a *conclusive* reason for doing *A*, where this means that he has a reason for doing *A* which must 'overpower'—so to speak—all the reasons which incline him in other directions?

18. For, as William Frankena has reminded us,[2] we think that the fact that a person *ought* to do *A* is a *conclusive* reason for him to do *A*, and hence, that to know that one ought to do *A* is to *have* (i.e. be in mental possession of) *a conclusive reason* for doing *A*.

19. The connection between radical internalism and the topics with which I began is obvious. For if radical internalism is correct, then, if a person knows that course of action *A* is the *best* available alternative, the one he *ought* to pursue, then he has a *conclusive* reason for *A*, and hence a prevailing motive for this course of action, and will necessarily follow it.

V

20. Now the standard criticism of internalism, formulated most acutely by Frankena, is that it confuses two senses of 'having a reason for doing *A*':

(1) having (by virtue of certain facts) a *justification* for doing *A*
(2) having a *motive* for doing *A*.

This confusion, the critic contends, leads internalists to move mistakenly from the idea that a person would (in certain respects) be *justified* in doing *A* to the idea that he *has a motive* for doing *A*, indeed, to think that being justified in doing *A* is *ipso facto* having a motive for doing *A*.

21. Now the distinction to which Frankena calls attention is a proper one, but far from supporting the idea that the phrase 'having a reason for doing *A*' is ambiguous, it points in the opposite direction. For surely

S has (by virtue of certain facts) a justification for doing *A*

is equivalent, *not* to a sense of

S has a reason for doing *A*

---

[2] "Obligation and Motivation," in *Essays in Moral Philosophy* (ed. by A. Melden), University of Washington Press, Seattle, 1958.

but rather to

> S has (by virtue of certain facts) a *good* reason for doing A.

Thus the difference between (1) and (2) is to be accounted for, *not* by different senses of 'having a reason,' but by the difference between 'having a reason' and 'having a good reason,' the sense of 'having a reason' being the same. And if so, then it follows from the critic's own remarks that *in this sense* to have a reason *is* to have a motive.

22. Now there is a perfectly obvious sense in which one can 'have a motive' without being moved. Thus, to say, for example, of Jones that he has a motive for killing his aunt is not to imply that Jones is being moved to kill his aunt, nor even that the idea of killing his aunt is tugging at his will. The statement commits itself only to the existence of a certain hypothetical fact—roughly—that:

> If Jones knew such and such facts (e.g. she has made a will in his favor but is about to change it), then he would have a motive—in the occurrent sense—for killing his aunt.

23. Thus, if to be justified in doing A is to have a good reason for doing A, then, building as before on the critic's remarks, to say that Jones has a good reason for doing A is to affirm the existence of a hypothetical fact, this time to the effect—roughly—that

> If Jones knew such and such facts then he would have a *good* motive—in the occurrent sense—for doing A.

24. But if this is correct, then, taking account of the fact that to be *justified* in doing A is not merely to have *a* good reason but to have a *conclusive* reason, i.e. a good reason all things considered, for doing A, the 'conclusiveness' is seen to concern the *goodness* of the reason, and not its 'strength.' Thus

> S is justified in doing A

would have the sense of

> If S knew all relevant facts, S would have a *conclusively good* motive—in the occurrent sense—for doing A.

25. Thus we see that implicit in the critic's remarks is a valid point, *not* however against internalism, but against *extreme* internalism. For the latter is indeed confused; *not*, as the critic contends, by confusing two senses of 'having a reason,' but rather two senses of 'having a *conclusive* reason':

(1) having a conclusively *good* reason
(2) having a necessarily *prevailing* reason

26. For it is because of this confusion that the extreme internalist moves from

S knows that he ought to do A

to

S knows a conclusive reason for doing A

to

S has—in the occurrent sense—a prevailing motive for doing A

to

S does A.

VI

27. The upshot of the preceding remarks is that internalism, the view that knowing that one ought to do A entails being moved toward doing A, remains a viable position, even after Frankena's criticism has been taken into account. We have seen the proper target of the criticism to be *extreme* internalism, but if the latter has lost one of its supports—a confusion between 'conclusively *good*' and '*conclusively powerful*'—it is not without recourse. For it is open to the extreme internalist to argue that while these concepts are *different*, they are connected in such a way that if a reason is conclusively *good*, then, when known, it is, of necessity, conclusively *powerful*.

28. This brings me back to the Socratic thesis that Virtue is Knowledge. This thesis sums up a complex train of thought in which the following subordinate themes can be discerned:

(1) Virtue is, in the first instance (Virtue$_1$), the propensity to do right actions.
(2) Virtue is, in the second instance (Virtue$_2$), the state of the soul which ensures the presence of Virtue$_1$.

Clearly, when Virtue is said to be Knowledge, it is not meant that the propensity to do right actions *is* knowledge, but rather that the state of the soul which ensures the presence of this propensity is knowledge. The propensity to do right actions can exist in the absence of knowledge, for example, as the result of training by stick and carrot, given that the agent has true belief concerning what actions are in point of fact right. But, in the absence of the relevant *knowledge*, the propensity would have a precarious existence, and be at the mercy of the honeyed words of orators and poets.

29. If the true ground of Virtue is Knowledge—Knowledge of *what*? In the first instance, as one would expect, of the principles of right action. If, and to the extent that, one is mistaken about these, one's beliefs about what ought to be done would be false, and one's actions wrong. But the Knowledge which grounds Virtue includes not only knowledge of the principles of right action, but also knowledge of what makes for a satisfying life. Let me take these two modes of knowledge in order.

VII

30. So far as the principles of right action are concerned, Plato is, in a suitably broad sense, a utilitarian. By this I mean that he takes for granted that in each circumstance one ought to do that action which is for the good of the relevant community, which he tends to equate with the City (πόλις). As I have argued elsewhere,[3] conventions and positive law do not, as the Sophists tended to think, *constitute* principles of right action. They merely provide special circumstances which, like any circumstances (though more important than most, partly because they simplify many decisions), are relevant to determining what ought to be done, as elements in the total circumstance in which one must do it. Principles of right action are, for Plato as for Socrates, a special case of the principles of a craft. Indeed, they are the principles of the craft of shaping and maintaining a City which lives well. The principles of any craft have the form:

To make and maintain E, one *ought*: if in C_1, to do A_1
 if in C_2, to do A_2
 ....

and if the 'product' of the craft has any complexity, the principles will be correspondingly numerous and varied, for they must take account of all foreseeable contingencies.

---

[3] 'Reason and the Art of Living in Plato', presented in a conference on 'Greece: The Critical Spirit, 450–350 B.C.,' held at Ohio State University, April 5 and 6, 1968. A discussion of closely related issues is to be found in my essay "The Soul as Craftsman," in *Philosophical Perspectives*, Thomas, Springfield, Ill., 1967. [Eds.—RAL is Ch. 5 of this volume.]

31. The situation is exactly parallel in the case of the art of the citizen ; the form of a principle of right action is:

To promote the welfare of the City, one ought: if in C_1, to do A_1
　　　　　　　　　　　　　　　　　　　　　　if in C_2, to do A_2
　　　　　　　　　　　　　　　　　　　　　　................

Thus the practical necessity of doing A_i if C_i is a necessity which is relative to promoting the welfare of the City. Abstracted from this context, the formulae

One ought:　　　　　　　　　　　　　　　if in C_1, to do A_1
　　　　　　　　　　　　　　　　　　　　　if in C_2, to do A_2
　　　　　　　　　　　　　　　　　　　　　................

lose their intelligibility, and though they can be embedded in training and tradition, they can no longer be the objects of knowledge nor the purposes of informed action.

32. Thus one can *know* what one ought to do only by *knowing* that by doing it in the circumstance in which one finds oneself, one will be promoting the welfare of the City—or, to use a Socratic turn of phrase, that one will be effectively pursuing the citizen's craft.

33. The foregoing has been an explication of Plato's conception of justice in the sense of right action, i.e. justice as an attribute of actions. The latter must not be confused with justice as a virtue of the individual, nor with justice as a virtue of the City. As a virtue of the City, justice is that character which ensures that the City has the propensity to *act* justly. Plato, as is well known, conceives this character to consist in the agreement of all free men that the wise are to rule.

34. The City being the individual writ large, justice as an individual virtue would, accordingly, be the agreement of all 'parts' of the soul that reason is to rule.

35. But justice thus conceived as *one* virtue among *many* is not yet the true Virtue for which Plato is looking. For Virtue, as we saw, is that which guarantees right action, and hence which guarantees that the soul is, in the above sense, just, i.e. that all 'parts' of the soul agree that reason is to rule. Where is such a guarantee to be found?

36. Plato's answer, of course, is that Virtue in this ultimate sense is Knowledge—Knowledge, he tells us, of the Good. To many this has seemed to be the uninformative formula 'the Good is knowledge of the Good,' and has been ridiculed as such. But Plato, of course, meant that Virtue is Knowledge of what constitutes a satisfying way of life. Thus the 'Good for man' is a 'satisfying human life,' that which Aristotle called *eudaimonia* or, as this term is usually rendered, 'happiness.'[4]

---

[4] For an interpretation of Plato's theory of the nature and role of the Idea of the Good, see the chapter on 'The Soul as Craftsman,' in my *Philosophical Perspectives* (note 3).

37. But how does knowledge—even of the good for man—relate to action—let alone right action? Another premise is required, and again it is familiar: Each man 'wills' his own good. In other words, each man seeks to live a satisfying life. Each man sketches, more or less clearly, a life plan, an overarching end-in-view, for which particular appetites, inclinations, desires, and aversions are the raw materials which are to be shaped into a coherent and satisfying whole. When Plato says, then, that Virtue is Knowledge, he means that the frame of mind which guarantees right action consists in knowing the nature of, and hence striving to realize, a truly satisfying life.

38. Thus the art of living takes its place at the peak of the Platonic edifice. For although, as we shall see, the art of living essentially involves the art of the citizen (the statesman's craft), the prime mover of all craftsmanship is the individual's search for happiness as defined by his plan of life.

39. But if this is the reality of Virtue when the veils of appearance have been stripped away, how does it guarantee right action?

40. Clearly, if Plato could show that a truly satisfying life is one which has as its primary end-in-view the welfare of the City, he would have proved his point. But, as we have seen, a major premise of his argument is that each person's ultimate end-in-view is his own happiness, a continuing sequence of satisfying states of mind. What kind of necessary connection would there be between such a goal and the welfare of the City?

41. One might point out that the wise man's satisfactions are noncompetitive; that his living is a practice of dying; that the penalty of abstaining from the statesman's craft is to be ruled by knaves and fools. But none of these considerations does more than prepare the way for Plato's positive account of the incorporation of the welfare of the City into the truly satisfying life.

42. The ultimate irony of Plato's expulsion of the poets from the ideal City is that it is the contemplation of Beauty which constitutes the *sine qua non* of its existence. Among the raw materials of human life is the love of harmony and proportion. Indeed, the wise man's satisfactions primarily consist of those in which 'pure' or 'unmixed' pleasure colors the contemplation of intelligible order, not only in the world of Forms, but also in the world of Becoming. And it is clear that for Plato the complex harmony of a happy City is particularly pleasant to contemplate, and the contemplation of the disorders of timocratic, oligarchic, democratic, and tyrannized cities increasingly unpleasant as we go down the scale.

43. Must we not say, then, that the cash value of the Platonic thesis that Virtue is Knowledge is the claim that the wise man will do right actions because that to which right action is the means, namely the welfare of the City, is his end—not *directly* (for it is the direct end of the statesman's craft rather than of the art of living), but as *that the contemplation of which*—a most satisfying contemplation—is a necessary constituent* of a well-crafted life.

---

* [Eds.—Correction of "constitutent" in original printing.]

VIII

44. The Platonic doctrine is, it is clear, a form of 'extreme internalism,' the view that

> to know, all things considered for what they really are, that course of action A is what ought to be done, is to have a conclusively *powerful* reason for following it.

45. But if, in the last analysis, Plato's attempt to prove, by an appeal to an intellectual aesthetics, that to know the good for man and to know what actions are right is to have a conclusively *powerful* reason (motive) for doing what is right must be counted a failure, has he, perhaps, prepared the way for a more satisfying solution?

46. The answer is, on the whole, "yes," for he has called attention to the fact that unless we can in some sense take the welfare of the City as our end, there will be no logical connection between that which we aim at, all things considered, and doing in each circumstance the action which is conducive to the general welfare. Furthermore, he has given the problem its clearest, its most (so to speak) *undiluted* formulation by relating the two questions:

(1) What ought one to do, *all things considered as they really are*?
(2) What would we be moved to do, *all things considered as they really are*?

47. But whereas the art of the citizen (which is concerned to discover the principles of right action) views the welfare of the City from an impersonal point of view—that of a *craftsman qua* craftsman, Plato assumes that an account of what a person would be moved to do, all things considered as they really are, essentially involves a *personal point of view*. For the ultimate end-in-view is the agent's own well-being or 'happiness.'

48. Nevertheless, there is a sense in which this personal point of view becomes, in the sage, 'impersonal,' in that the state of affairs which he enjoys contemplating and the enjoyment of the contemplation of which is a constituent of his well-being, is defined in impersonal terms. When the sage enjoys contemplating a happy city he does so from the statesman's point of view, and the well-being of those who are to benefit by his actions is not dependent on their being persons who are for example, *familiar* to him, or who *resemble him in their tastes or inclinations*. It is not a matter of their being the *particular* persons they are, any more than the carpenter's choice of which piece of wood to place where is a function of its being the particular piece of wood it is. The choice is regulated by the general principles of the craft.

49. Thus, the art of the citizen defines right action in the spirit of the utilitarian maxim 'each person to count for one.' The tastes and inclinations of the citizens

who constitute the raw material of the city are relevant, not as the tastes and inclinations of particular people who stand in contingent relations to the craftsman, but as tastes and inclinations the coherent satisfaction of which is to constitute the well-being of the city.

50. All this is according to the letter—if not the spirit—of the golden rule and the categorical imperative. But when it comes to the carrying out of this program, the motive is not *that the welfare of the city be promoted*, but *that I enjoy contemplating the promoted welfare*. Thus, though in one sense the formula of the end-in-view is the promotion of the general welfare, when its full character is made explicit, the motive is personal in its point of view, the search for one's own happiness.

IX

51. But what is the alternative? It is to find in the members of the moral community a *mode of motivation* which is not impersonal in the Platonic sense—a subordinate impersonal moment in a personal satisfaction sought for as such—but is, rather, *directly* impersonal, or, better, *inter-personal*, as directly oriented toward the welfare of the community. This new mode of motivation would be that in which the individual views himself and the world from the standpoint of 'one of the community' or, as I have elsewhere put it, from the standpoint of 'one of us.'

52. This alternative would open the possibility that even after 'all things have been considered as they really are,' there would be two coherent motives:

(1) the welfare of our community viewed as related to the actions of each of us (inter-personal benevolence)
(2) one's own happiness or well-being, viewed from a personal point of view *as* one's own happiness or well-being—in traditional terms, self-love.

These would constitute over-arching motives in their own dimensions or points of view, but would be *incomparable*, and not only *capable* of conflict but typically conflicting, though often to an undramatic degree.

53. Obviously, there is a sense in which these over-arching motives could, and would, overlap. Thus the satisfaction of the inter-personal motive would be a personal satisfaction, and personal satisfaction would be a relevant element in the general welfare which is the object of the inter-personal aim. But these dialectical points are familiar to students of Bishop Butler's thought.

X

54. The position I have been sketching would be a form of 'internalism,' but not of that 'extreme internalism' which equates 'conclusively *good* reason' with 'conclusively *powerful* reason.' To know that one ought to do A—i.e. to know that it is conducive to the welfare of the community that in *these* circumstances one does A—would be to have a conclusively *good* reason for doing A; but not, necessarily, alas, a conclusively *powerful* reason (i.e. motive).

55. What might it mean to say that the reason (motive) is conclusively good? The true answer to this question would obviously be the keystone of a successful moral philosophy, indeed the philosopher's stone itself. I have wrestled with this problem at length elsewhere.[5] I shall limit myself at present to an abstract, and hence inevitably disappointing, statement of my conclusions.

56. First, two remarks which indicate the general strategy:

(1) If the ultimate answer is to satisfy the intellect it must follow from the meanings of the terms involved, for otherwise it would simply lead us on to new problems without end.
(2) The goodness of a *reason* is always, in the last analysis as the term 'reason' implies, a *logical* goodness.

57. Applied to our problem, the strategy involves pointing out that to think of oneself as a member of a community is to think of oneself as one of a many who view each other from what I have called the interpersonal point of view and who, therefore, share the mode of motivation described above. It is, therefore, a conceptual truth that to will that each of us does that which promotes our general welfare is to have that reason for acting the having of which constitutes being one of *us*.

58. But enough of promissory notes! I must devote the remaining moments to rounding off with pennies the payments I have been making on the promissory notes with which I began.

59. The bite of the traditional problem with which I have been concerned lies exactly in the fact that a conclusively *good* reason (i.e. a conclusively good motive) need not be a conclusively *powerful* reason (i.e. a conclusively powerful motive). One *can* know the better and do the worse; not just from *impulse*, but from self-love, all things considered for what they really are. It is for this reason that genuine moral conflict is imaginatively pictured as a conflict between two persons—one representing inter-personal commitment to one's community, the other, personal

---

[5] *Form and Content in Ethical Theory*, the 1967 Lindley Lecture delivered at the University of Kansas, and available from the Philosophy Department; also *Science and Metaphysics*, Humanities Press, New York, 1968, Chapter 7. [Eds.—The latter work—OIM—appears as Ch. 6 of this volume.]

commitment to one's own happiness on the whole. At the moment of decision, one or the other of these candidates for an orientation of the self-in-action—each in its own way over-arching—predominates. The choice is, in an important sense, between incommensurables. Which choice one makes is a revelation of what one, at that moment, *is*. It is often surprising, sometimes exhilarating, or disconcerting, even devastating—but always a revelation.

PART 4
DEONTIC LOGIC, PRACTICAL REASON, AND THE LOGIC OF INTENTIONS

14
Imperatives, Intentions, and the Logic of "Ought"

Introduction

[1] My purpose in this paper[1] is to explore the logic of "ought," with a view to determining the relations which obtain between it and certain other key terms of practical discourse. In particular, I shall be concerned with the relation between "I ought to do X" and "I shall do X"; "You ought to do X" and "Do X!"; "He ought to do X" and "He shall do X"; and between "I ought to do X" and "He ought to do X." I shall also be concerned with the relation between "Everybody ought to do A, if in C" and "Would that everybody were happy!" on the one hand, and "Would that I were happy!" on the other.

[2] Put in more traditional terms, this paper is about the relation between "*thinking oneself* under an obligation to do something" and "*(ceteris paribus)* deciding to do it for the reason that one ought to do it," and between "*being* under an obligation to do something" and "having a reason for doing it, namely, the reason that one ought to do it." Insofar as I have a thesis to defend it is the twofold one that to know that there are certain things that one ought to do *is* to have a sense of duty, and that obligation, by its very nature, is intersubjective. And if, thus baldly stated, neither component of this thesis is new (for the first smacks of emotivism and the second of intuitionism), some interest may attach to the way in which this joint thesis is developed, and the consequent clarification of the relation between the sense of duty on the one hand, and the impartial love of humanity on the other.

[3] If one were to ask a convinced student of *The Right and the Good*,[2]

Could a person "apprehend a principle of prima-facie obligation" to the effect that one ought, for example, to keep promises—that is, *Anglice*, could one know that, other things being equal, one ought to keep one's promises—and yet have no tendency to be moved to act on specific occasions by the thought that one ought to do *this* as being the keeping of a promise?

---

[1] This paper is a revised version of a paper which appeared in *Methodos*, VIII (1956), 227–268.
[2] W. D. Ross, *The Right and the Good* (Oxford: Clarendon Press, 1930).

—would he not answer (though I must qualify this in a moment) that there is no contradiction in the idea of such a person, or (if he should think that tending to be so moved is a defining trait of a *person*[3]) at least in the idea of such an intelligent animal? But if he finds no contradiction in this idea, would he be content to say that it is a contingent *empirical* fact about human nature that people who know what they ought to do tend to be moved to act by the thought that they ought so to act? Or would he not be more likely to subsume this fact under the heading of the "synthetic a priori"?

[4] It must be admitted, and this is the qualification mentioned above, that some intuitionists, notably H. A. Prichard, seem to think that it is not a merely empirical mistake but, rather, an absurdity to suppose that one might apprehend what he ought to do, yet have no tendency whatever to be moved to act by the thought that he ought to do it. Thus, when Prichard writes, "To feel that I ought to pay my bills is to be moved towards paying them,"[4] the context makes it clear that he is not thinking of the feeling that I ought to pay my bills as something distinguishable from (but built upon) the apprehension that I ought to pay them, but rather as being this apprehension itself. In comparing the apprehension of obligation to the apprehension of mathematical truths, Prichard writes that "in both [cases] insight into the nature of the subject leads me to recognize its possession of the predicate,"[5] but he nevertheless insists that the apprehension of an obligation is different from the apprehension of a mathematical truth.

My difficulty with Prichard on this point (as with the many philosophers who have insisted that moral thinking qua thinking is "conative," no "mere blend" of thinking and "emotion") is that he offers not even the beginning of a satisfactory analysis of this phenomenological insight, an analysis which would account for the fact that moral thinking differs from, but resembles, other forms of thinking, by relating both to the fundamental categories of an adequate philosophy of mind. Prichard's grasp of the distinctive traits of moral thinking exhibits the combination of thinness and acuteness which is characteristic of his philosophy. It is because Sir William David Ross has turned thin truth into quick error by forcing Prichard's insights into the procrustean bed of neo-Aristotelian theory, that we could picture, as we did, the response of the student of *The Right and the Good* to our question about ought and motivation.

[5] If, now, we turn to a convinced student of *Language, Truth and Logic*[6] and ask,

---

[3] For an interesting discussion of a parallel point, see Professor C. D. Broad's animadversions on the concept of a "rational being" in "Some Reflections on Moral Sense Theories in Ethics," *Proceedings of the Aristotelian Society*, Vol. XLV (1944–45), pp. 131–166.
[4] "Does Moral Philosophy Rest on a Mistake?" (1912), in *Readings in Ethical Theory*, ed. W. S. Sellars and J. Hospers (New York: Appleton-Century-Crofts, 1952), p. 154.
[5] *Ibid.*, p. 155.   [6] A. J. Ayer, *Language, Truth and Logic* (London: Victor Gollancz, 1936).

IMPERATIVES, INTENTIONS, AND THE LOGIC OF "OUGHT" 369

Can a person know that he ought to do *this* action without being moved to do it?

I think it reasonably clear that his answer would take the form of a commentary on the question. The upshot would be some such statement as the following: "The so-called thought that one ought to do A here and now is not, strictly speaking, a thought at all, but rather a specific way of being moved to do A. With this qualification the answer to your question is no, for the simple reason that to 'know' that one ought to do A here and now is to be moved to do it." If we press him to say just how the specifically moral character of the "being moved" is to be understood, if it is not a matter of being moved by the *thought* that one ought to do A, it is unlikely that we would get a satisfactory answer. For in its early stages emotivism, naïve or sophisticated, views as *analytic* the connection between "thinking that one ought" and "having a motive" which classical intuitionism, with the exception we have noted, takes to be either *empirical* or *synthetic a priori*. On the other hand, as is well known, it tends to view *thinking* that one ought as "*thinking*" that one ought.

[6] It was the signal merit of intuitionism, particularly of the deontological variety, to have insisted on the uniqueness of prescriptive discourse, as over and against traditional naturalism's attempts at reduction, and on the truly propositional character of prescriptive statements, as over and against the emotivist contention that ethical concepts are "pseudo-concepts" and the logic of moral discourse a "pseudo-logic." But the epistemological and metaphysical commitments of ethical intuitionism, which precluded it from understanding the logical connection between "thinking that one ought" and "being moved to do," thus forced it to make a mystery both of the conduct-guiding role of moral discourse, and of the uniqueness of prescriptive discourse which it had so happily emphasized.

[7] The situation seems clearly to call for a theory which, without denying that ought-statements stand, as such, in logical relation to one another, makes the connection between moral thinking and doing *analytic*, a matter of strict logic. That attempts along these general lines are in the air is clear. One of these, the neo-imperativist approach of R. M. Hare,[7] is, in my opinion, sufficiently close to the truth to be a useful point of departure for the ideas I wish to develop. While I think that something *like* his account of the concept of ought is true, I do not think that it will do as it stands. Indeed, I think that its very closeness to the truth has enabled it to obscure essential points about the concept of obligation.[8]

---

[7] *The Language of Morals* (Oxford: Clarendon Press, 1952). My understanding (to the extent that it is not misunderstanding) of Hare's view has been enhanced by an exchange of ideas in correspondence and personal conversation for which I am grateful. [Eds.—Sellars's correspondence with Hare is Ch. 20 of this volume.]

[8] May I take this occasion to acknowledge my indebtedness to my friend and former student, Dr. Hector-Neri Castañeda, whose dissertations for the M.A. and Ph.D. degrees from the University of Minnesota contain important and original contributions to the imperativists' approach to practical

Universality and the Logic of Imperatives

1

[8] A person who says, "X ought (morally) to do *this*," commits himself to supporting this statement with a statement of the form, "Doing this, in these circumstances, is doing A in circumstances C, and anyone ought always (*ceteris paribus*) to do A in C."[9] This fact is sometimes put by saying that singular ought-statements imply universal ought-statements. This is true, however, only in a special sense of "imply." Nor will it quite do to speak of "presupposing," for though one who makes a singular ought-statement is committed to support it with a universal ought-statement, it is not necessary that he have the latter "up his sleeve." If a wise man tells Jones that he ought to do a certain action, he has a reason to think that he ought to do it, and that the action could be subsumed under a moral principle, even though he is not in a position to do so. It is for this and related reasons that I have elsewhere[10] characterized this sense of implication as dialectical. Yet, though it is a "looser" relation than presupposing, let alone ordinary implication, it is, like the latter, a logical, as opposed to psychological, relation.[11]

[9] Now even if there is no plausibility at all to the suggestion that "You ought to do B" is simply the imperative "Do B!" with or without psychological embellishments, the claim that the ought-statement is equivalent to a singular imperative which is implicitly universal in the above sense is something to be reckoned with. This claim can be construed as the idea that "You ought to do B" is equivalent to "Do B!*" where the asterisk is a signal of a dialectical commitment to support it with an "argument" of the form,

---

discourse. I have also had the benefit of several lengthy discussions with him in the early spring of 1956. The present paper contains many traces of his influence, though I do not know how much of its detail he would find acceptable. [Eds.—Sellars's correspondence with Castañeda is Ch. 22 of this volume.]

[9] I am concerned in this section with the "implicit universality" of the moral ought. I do not wish, therefore, to be taken to deny that there might be varieties of ought which have a lesser scope than *all persons at all times*. An ought, however, which simply reflected one person's intentions here and now would be no ought at all.

Even the sense in which the moral ought applies to all persons requires careful analysis. It should not be assumed that the "everybody" in a moral principle has the force of "all human beings" in a purely descriptive, so to speak biological, sense of this phrase. It means, roughly, *all of us*, where *we* are those who accept each other as relevant participants in a discussion of what ought or ought not to be done, rather than simply belonging to the stage-setting of conduct. Today, *we* are men generally.

[10] "Presupposing," *Philosophical Review*, LXII (1953), p. 214, n. 9.

[11] It is, perhaps, worth noting that singular cause-statements are also, in this same sense, "implicitly universal." Thus a person who says, "Doing *this* to *that* in *these* circumstances caused it to behave *thusly*," commits himself to support his remark with a statement of the form, "*This* is an X, and doing *that* to an X is Y-ing it, and *these* circumstances are of kind C, and behaving *thusly* is Z-ing, and Y-ing an X in C causes it to Z. Singular cause-statements, then, like singular ought-statements, are not *merely* singular. Both are, so to speak, singular "after their own kind." Notice also that one can claim with reason that *this* caused *that* in *these* circumstances even though one does not have a causal universal "up one's sleeve" to cover one's claim. One can have reason to believe that the circumstances are such, and *this* and *that* of such kinds, that "there is" a causal universal under which they could be subsumed.

Let everyone universally do A in C!
Doing B is doing A in C
So, do B!

Thus, the claim is that in "You ought to do that," the ought plays the dual role of (1) giving the infinitive ("to do") which follows it the force of a verb in the imperative mood ("Do!"), and (2) embodying a commitment to support this singular imperative in the manner indicated above.

[10] Now this claim (which is, of course, only a rough approximation to more sophisticated analyses of the imperativist type) is open to many objections, some of which, in my opinion, are sufficiently compelling to call, at the very least, for a substantial revision. It will be useful to begin our exploration of the logic of ought by raising one of these objections, the full force of which will not emerge until a later stage of our argument. This objection is that the "ought" in the universal ought-statement "Everybody ought always to do A in C" does not seem to be redundant. Yet it cannot be accounted for in terms of the two roles of ought specified above. For the latter, (2), that of signaling a dialectical commitment to back up the sentence in which it appears with a sentence having the logical form of universality, is on the face of it irrelevant, in the case of the first principles of obligation, while the purpose of the former, (1), can easily be achieved by using the imperative mood to start with, that is, by simply saying, "Let everyone always do A in C!"

[11] The answer of one imperativist to this objection is to be found in the concluding pages of *The Language of Morals*. There Hare argues that in addition to playing roles which are essentially the same as those indicated above, the ought also gives the imperative it signalizes a truly universal force. He points out that in actual usage, "Let everybody always do A in C!" means "Let everybody *from now on* do A in C!" (it being silly to say, for example, "Let everybody wear blue suits yesterday!"). "Everybody ought always to do A in C" has, as Hare sees it, an imperative force which is suggested by the absurdity of "Let everyone do A in C throughout the past as well as the future!" in actual usage.

2

[12] To evaluate Hare's reply, we must begin by considering certain features of the logic of commands.

[13] The issuing of commands (i.e., commands only, not sentences in the imperative mood generally) is not a promiscuous activity. Not everyone on every occasion can properly command another to do a certain action. There must be something about one person's relationship with another which authorizes him to issue the command; and a relationship which authorizes one person to command another to do something may not authorize him to command

something else. I referred above to the issuing of commands as a *performance*, and this is, of course, the heart of the matter. The parallel with promising is instructive. As Austin has pointed out,[12] making a promise is a performance which creates a presumptive prima-facie obligation to do A on the part of the person who says, "I promise to do A." It "creates" this obligation by virtue of the moral principle which can, for our purposes, be formulated as follows:

If X appropriately says "I promise to do A" to Y, then X owes it to Y to do A.

[14] Now, whereas promising is a performance which binds the speaker, issuing a command binds the person to whom it is issued. Thus, issuing a command within the limits of one's authority "creates" a presumptive prima-facie obligation to do the action commanded on the part of the person to whom it is addressed. And this performance "creates" an obligation, *binds*, only because, like promising, it rests on a principle, in this case:

If X appropriately says to Y "I command you to do A!" then Y owes it to X to do A.

Thus the claim which commands have on our obedience is but a special case of the claim which our obligations have upon us. Obeying a command, like keeping a promise, is a special case of doing one's duty—though to characterize any particular obeying or promise-keeping as a doing of one's duty is, of course, a defeasible matter.[13]

[15] There is another, if closely related, respect in which the logic of commands resembles the logic of promises, and it is this respect which is directly relevant to our argument. Consider the sentence:

I promise to call you, if it rains.

There is no such reasoning as

I promise to call you tomorrow, if it rains tomorrow
It will rain tomorrow
So, I promise to call you tomorrow

or, in general,

---

[12] John Austin, "Other Minds," *Proceedings of the Aristotelian Society*, Suppl. Vol. XX (1946), pp. 169–174.
[13] For an explication of the concept of defeasibility, see H. L. A. Hart, "The Ascription of Rights and Duties," *Proceedings of the Aristotelian Society*, Vol. XLIX (1948–49), pp. 171–194.

I promise to do A in *dt*, if *p*
p
So, I promise to do A in *dt*.

It is, for reasons which will be developed in a moment, nonsense to suppose that one performance of promising can, as performance, be a conclusion from another. A person who believes that *p* and intends to do A, if *p*, may promise to do A, or, more cautiously, to do A, if *p*. His reasoning *in foro interno* as far as his intentions are concerned may perhaps be represented by the schema:

I shall do A in *dt*, if *p*
p
So, I shall do A in *dt*.

But while there would be an absurdity in saying "*p and* I shall do A, if *p but* I shall not do A," there seems to be no such absurdity in the saying "*p; and* I promise to do A, if *p; but* I do not promise to do A." (NB: "do not promise" must not be confused with "have not just promised.") It would, however, for reasons pertaining to the relation between promising and intending, be absurd to say "*p; and* I promise to do A, if *p; but* I promise not to do A."

3

[16] The opening remarks of the preceding section make it clear (if it was not already clear) that there would be a logical howler in any attempt to "reduce" ought-statements to commands. It might seem equally clear that to show this is not to show that ought-statements cannot be "reduced" to imperatives. For although commands, like promises, presuppose principles of obligation, surely, it will be said, simple imperatives do not. Telling someone to do something does not as such appear to create an obligation on his part to do it. On the other hand, the fact that you told him to do it (as contrasted with the possibility that he might merely have overheard you "intend out loud" that he do it, or even that you might have told him of your intention that he do it) is relevant in a special way to his deliberations on his rights and duties, particularly vis-à-vis you, and on whether he has good reasons for doing what he proposes to do. Intending out loud, telling *of* your intentions, and telling someone *to* do something are all of them pieces of conduct. They must, however, be carefully distinguished from one another, for they enter in different ways into the web of prescriptions and norms which govern our relations with our fellow men. Indeed, while it may be literally true that the fact that you tell someone to do something does not create an obligation on his part to do it, it may well

presuppose a context of obligations for its significance as *telling*. While simply telling someone of your intention to do something does not create an obligation on your part to do it—at least in that simple way which characterizes the institution of The Promise, nevertheless it would be misleading to say that telling one's intentions to somebody is logically prior to or independent of practical principles. Again, if X stands in certain relations to Y, the fact that X tells Y to do A generates a claim on Y to do A. It can even be argued that in the case of the highwayman who, brandishing a pistol, says, "Give me your money!" the ought of prudence is being mobilized, and that, in general, there are no proper imperatives without some connection with practical principles, or, at least, that in such cases telling degenerates into merely making manifest one's desires and intentions.

[17] I have contrasted "intending out loud" that X do A with telling someone (perhaps X himself) of one's intention that X do A. Both of these seem to be covered by the ambiguous phrase "expressing one's intention," though I think it is properly limited to the latter, or "telling of," case. A similar danger of confusion is to be found in the case of the "expression of belief." Here too we must draw a threefold distinction between "thinking out loud that p" (thinking out loud being the basic form of all thought), "telling someone of one's belief that p" (i.e., expressing one's belief that p), and "telling someone that p." For our purposes, the crucial distinction in each case is that between *telling of* (or expressing) one's intention or belief on the one hand, and *telling to* or *telling that* on the other. Telling of one's beliefs or intentions, as we are using this phrase, is not to be confused with describing oneself as having these intentions. It should not be overlooked, however, that the self-description "I intend that X do A" (though not its cognates in other persons, tenses, and moods) has the force of an expression of intention in addition to its descriptive role, just as "I think that p" has the force of an expression of "the thought that p" in addition to its autobiographical role.

[18] Before continuing with the argument, there are two terminological conventions I should like to adopt in this paper. The first, a simple matter of convenience, is that whether the subject of a sentence of the form

X shall do A

is "I" or "you" or "Jones," it always expresses the speaker's intention or resolve that X do A. Although this stipulation does minor violence to correct English usage, the awkwardness is more than offset by the gain in simplicity of formulation. Correspondingly, sentences of the form

X will do A

even in the first person are to be understood as expressions of the speaker's belief that the person referred to by "X" will do A.

[19] My second stipulation is that an utterance which not only expresses the speaker's intention that the person referred to by "X" do A, but plays the *telling to* role as well, is to be represented by the form

X shall do A!

where the "!" signalizes this role. Thus, in terms of this convention, the utterance

X shall do A

simply expresses the speaker's intention that the person referred to by "X" do A. It may be overheard by this person, but it is not, as overheard, a telling him to do A. It might appear that the form

You shall do A (as contrasted with "You shall do A!")

must be ruled out on the ground that utterances in the second person are not overheard by the person addressed as "you." That this is not the case will become clear from what follows.

[20] The concept of telling someone to do something is to be distinguished from that of telling someone one's intention that someone (perhaps the same person) do something. Thus, to say "I shall do A" to X is to tell X *of* one's intention to do A, but is not to tell anybody, even oneself, *to do* A. Correspondingly, to say to X "You shall do A," while it is at least a telling X of one's intention that he do A, need not have the force of "You shall do A!" i.e., the force of telling X to do A. Again, while

Tom shall do A

simply expresses the speaker's intention that Tom do A,

Tom shall do A!

said to Tom tells him to do A, and said to Dick, will, according to the conventions of this paper, have the force of the *imperative*, "Let Tom do A!" which not only tells Dick of one's intention that Tom do A, but tells Dick *to do* something, roughly what he reasonably can to ensure that Tom does A, and is, therefore, the equivalent, in terms of our convention, of

You (Dick) shall do what you reasonably can to ensure that Tom does A!

Furthermore, imperatives of the form

> Let it be the case that *p*!

will be represented in terms of our convention as

> It shall be the case that *p*!

which, as *tellings to*, would differ from both

> It shall be the case that *p*

as addressed to certain persons and advising them of one's intention that it be the case that *p*, and

> It shall be the case that *p*

as a simple expression of one's intention that it be the case that *p*.

> A parallel convention will enable us to distinguish
>
> S is P!

as telling someone that S is P, from "S is P" as a *telling of* (or expressing of) one's belief that S is P, and, a fortiori, from an utterance of "S is P" as a mere thinking out loud that S is P.

[21] We are now in a position to clarify our intuitive feeling that there is no such reasoning as

> I promise to do A in dt, if *p*
> *p*
> So, I promise to do A in dt.

This clarification will also make manifest that there is no such reasoning as

> Do A in dt, if *p*!
> *p*
> So, do A in dt!

i.e., in terms of our convention,

> You shall do A in dt, if *p*!
> *p*
> So, you shall do A in dt!

Also that there is no such reasoning (in terms of our "telling that" convention) as

q if *p*!
p!
So, *q*!

Though there are, of course, the reasonings

X shall do A in *dt*, if *p*
p
So, X shall do A in *dt*

and

q if *p*
p
So, *q*.

The point is a simple one about the concept of reasoning. Promising, telling to, telling that, and telling of are all public performances which require an audience. Reasoning is something which can go on *in foro interno*; and if it goes on out loud, it is the sort of thing which is overheard. It can also be expressed in a sense which parallels the expressing or telling of one's beliefs and intentions.

[22] Is there anything which stands to reasoning and to the expression of reasoning as "telling that" stands to "thinking that" and to "expressing the thought that," and as "telling to" stands to "intending" and to "expressing one's intention"? A plausible candidate is "arguing." But before we ask whether there are imperative arguings, let us note that not only are there no imperative reasonings *in foro interno* (which is obvious), there are also no expressions of reasonings which have imperatives as premise or conclusion. Only a confusion between a "telling to" and a "telling of" (or expressing) one's intention that X do A could lead to the contrary conviction. (The current practice of speaking of imperatives and resolutives as though they were coordinate from a logical point of view or even related as genus to species—"to resolve" being to tell *oneself* to do something—involves this confusion). It makes sense to suppose that an expressed reasoning could have occurred without being expressed; and if so, there cannot be such things as expressed reasonings the premises or conclusions of which are promisings, tellings to, or tellings that. In particular, there is no such thing as imperative inference.

[23] Is there, perhaps, such a thing as imperative *argument*? An argument is a performance in which a conclusion is defended by offering reasons which give it logical support or purport to do so. Is there, perhaps, such an argument as:

> You shall do A!
> because you shall do A and B!

Is there, perhaps, an argument of the form

> I promise to do A
> because I promise to do A and B

There are, of course, the arguments

> I told you to do A
> because I told you to do A and B

and

> I promised to do A
> because I promised to do A and B

but, of course, in the latter there is no telling to or promising. Again, there are the supported performances

> I promise to do A
> because you have been so kind

and

> You shall do A!
> because you have been naughty

but these are obviously not arguments of which the promising and the telling to are the conclusions. Rather they point to practical reasonings which have as their conclusions

> I shall promise to do A

and

> I shall tell X to do A

[24] It is tempting to suppose that since an argument is a performance analogous in certain respects to a telling that or a telling to, its conclusion can be a telling that or a telling to. That this is not the case becomes clear when we reflect that what is defended by the argument

q
because *p* and (*p* implies *q*)

is not the *telling someone that q* (for while there is a sense in which logic provides a reason for telling people that *q* when we have told them that *p* and that [*p* implies *q*], it does so via practical principles about "telling that" which compete with other practical principles about "telling that"), but rather the *thought* (*expressed or unexpressed*) *that q*. And once we see that not even the performance of telling someone that *q* is defended by the argument

q
because *p* and (*p* implies *q*)

so that there is no such thing as the argument

q!
because p and (*p* implies *q*)!

it becomes equally clear that there simply are no such things as the arguments

I promise to do A
because I promise to do A and B

and

You shall do A!
because you shall do A and B!

[25] Let me try to make my point in terms of Hare's example, which runs,

Take all the boxes to the station!
This is one of the boxes.
So, take this box to the station!

I do not wish to deny that, as Hare[14] has stressed, these three sentences are so related that a person who candidly said to Jones

Take all the boxes to the station! By the way, this is one of the boxes.

---

[14] *Op. cit.*, pp. 24ff.

and yet, though insisting that he had not changed his mind, refused to tell Jones to take *this* box to the station, would have convincingly shown that he did not understand either one or the other of these sentences. (This point is not unrelated to one made above about the logical absurdity of "*p and* I promise to do A, if *p but* I promise not to do A.")

4

[26] We have been arguing that the "telling to" signal, "!," like "I promise," does not belong within the context

—, so . . .

and that the only tellings which are appropriate to this context are tellings of. The fact that it does not make sense to speak of imperative inference ("telling to" inference) has been almost as potent a factor in leading people to suppose that there cannot really be such a thing as practical inference, as the fact that expressions of intention are neither true nor false.

[27] Let me begin a more detailed examination of the logic of practical reasoning by proposing the following analysis of the example of the boxes. The analysis breaks the reasoning down into the following moments:

M(1)   This is one of the boxes
So, (Jones will shortly take all the boxes to the station) implies (Jones will shortly take this box to the station)

M(2)   So, (Shall [Jones's shortly taking all the boxes to the station]) implies (Shall [Jones's shortly taking this box to the station])

M(3)   Shall [Jones's shortly taking all the boxes to the station]
So, Shall [Jones's shortly taking this box to the station]

These moments are to be explained as follows. M(1), when made more explicit, turns out to be the second moment of the sequence:

M(1-1)   (Jones will shortly take all the boxes to the station *and* This is one of the boxes) implies (Jones will shortly take this box to the station)
So, (This is one of the boxes) implies ([Jones will shortly take all the boxes to the station] implies [Jones will shortly take this box to the station])

M(1-2)   This is one of the boxes
So, (Jones will shortly take all the boxes to the station) implies (Jones will shortly take this box to the station)

IMPERATIVES, INTENTIONS, AND THE LOGIC OF "OUGHT" 381

Two remarks are necessary: (1) "Implies" means that relation between propositions which authorizes inference.[15] It will be assumed without argument that implication in this sense includes physical or natural implication as well as logical implication in the narrower sense. Nothing in this paper hinges on the treatment of inductive generalizations as principles of inference. The reader may, if he prefers, press the analysis to a "deeper" level in which laws are introduced as premises. (2) A distinction must be drawn between "independent" and "dependent" implication. Thus, in the conclusion of M(1-1), the first occurrence of "implies" is as independent implication, while the second occurrence is as dependent implication. A dependent implication is one which presupposes a state of affairs to obtain which is not explicitly asserted by the implication statement itself.

P dependently implies Q

presupposes that there is an R such that

P and R independently imply Q

Thus M(1-1), by a correctly interpreted use of the principle of exportation, as it applies to implication proper (as contrasted with "material" implication), takes us from one logical truth to another, where the second logical truth has as its consequent the dependent implication which, by virtue of the next moment to be considered, becomes the principle in accordance with which M(3) proceeds.

[28] M(2) has the form

(P) implies (Q)
So, (Shall [P]) implies (Shall [Q])

a move which holds where P and Q have a content appropriate to practical reasoning. Leaving aside for the moment considerations of tense and the question whether P and Q admit of analytic or self-contradictory values in the context "Shall [—]," we can lay down as a formation rule for shall-statements that one moves from an indicative statement to a shall-statement by turning the indicative statement into a gerund and prefixing it with the shall-operator. Thus, for example, we would go from

Tom will shortly cross the road

---

[15] Since we are concerned with modal contexts, it is important not to suppose that if P strictly implies Q, then (Shall [P]) implies (Shall [Q]). Stronger requirements are necessary to avoid paradox. As far as I can see, something like A. R. Anderson's reconstruction of "entails" is necessary.

to

> Shall [Tom's shortly crossing the road].

Notice that the latter does not imply

> Tom will shortly cross the road.

We can, in effect, note a parallel in this respect between the shall-statement and the modal statement

> Possible [Tom's shortly crossing the road].

On the other hand, it seems proper to stipulate that

> Shall [*my* shortly crossing the road]

implies

> I will shortly cross the road

i.e., that it contains the prediction, just as

> Necessary [Tom's shortly crossing the road]

contains

> Tom will shortly cross the road.

[29] It is important to note that according to the proposed formation rule, a shall-operator operates on only one verbal noun. Thus the conjunctive statement[16]

> Tom will shortly cross the road *and* Dick will shortly sit down

gives rise to

> Shall [*its being the case that* Tom will shortly cross the road and Dick will shortly sit down].

---

[16] It will be noticed that I am referring to statements of intention as statements. This seems to be in accordance with ordinary usage, although logicians have tended to restrict the term to items which are either true or false.

This means that for simplicity of representation we can leave the job of turning indicative statements into verbal nouns to the brackets and write the shall-statements corresponding to a given indicative as

Shall [(indicative)]

[30] Since we are representing shall-statements as a matter of an operator operating on a gerund, it might seem appropriate to follow Hare by interpreting indicative statements as a matter of an operator operating on a gerund also. This, however, is not only unnecessary, but seriously mistaken. Let us consider the indicative counterpart of the practical reasoning about boxes dissected above.

    $M'(1)$ This is one of the boxes
                So, (Jones will shortly take all the boxes to the station) dependently implies (Jones will shortly take this box to the station)
    $M'(2)$ Jones will shortly take all the boxes to the station
                So, Jones will shortly take this box to the station.

The important thing to note is that the "implies" of $M'(1)$ is a relation word which takes singular terms for its arguments. In the present context we are using it to take verbal nouns for its arguments. In other, but related, uses "implies" takes that-clauses or quoted expressions for its arguments. These singular terms are derivative from the corresponding indicative statements. One operates on an indicative statement to get the corresponding singular term. Thus in

(S is P) implies (S is Q)

the indicative statements "S is P" and "S is Q" have been turned into the singular terms "(S is P)" and "(S is Q)." Thus an inference in accordance with this license is to be understood not as

S being P, yes
So, S being Q, yes

which *adds* a yes-operator to a "phrastic," but rather as simply

S is P
So, S is Q

which *subtracts* the singular term operator which "suspends" "S is P" and "S is Q" in the inference ticket. Correspondingly, M'(2) is not to be "reconstructed" as

(Jones's being about to take all the boxes to the station) yes
So, (Jones's being about to take this box to the station) yes

for it is "perspicuous" as it stands.

[31] I have chosen my examples and oriented my discussion so as to imply that "shall" inference tickets are always of the form

(Shall [—]) implies (shall [...])

and rest on a corresponding indicative inference of the form

(—) implies (...)

Whether or not this is always true will be discussed at a later stage in the argument.

5

[32] To sum up the argument of the past few sections:

(1) There is no such thing as imperative inference, i.e., inference involving tellings to as tellings to. There is, however, practical reasoning, and there is argument involving *tellings of intentions*.

(2) We have emphasized that the only sense in which there is a special logic of imperatives is that exhibited by the reasoning

X tells Y (to do A if p)
p
So, X tells Y (to do A)

which is the counterpart of

X tells Y (that q if p)
p
So, X tells Y that q.

That these arguments are valid (with some requirement as to the ascertainability of p) is analytic of the concept of *telling* as a performance. Note that while

X tells Y to do A
Doing A entails doing B
So, X tells Y to do B

and

X tells Y that p
That p entails that q
So, X tells Y that q

are valid arguments, the same is not true if a less restricted use of "implies" is substituted for "entails." Indeed, it can be argued that this is the locus of the difference between what statements *entail* and what they *imply* without *entailing*. A related point concerns the validity of the arguments

X intends Y to do A
Doing A *entails* doing B
So, X intends Y to do B

and

X believes that p
That p entails that q
So, X believes that q

But to follow up the point would take us too far afield.
(3) We have suggested that "shall" inference tickets have the form

(Shall [—]) implies (shall [...])

where the shall-operator appears in both antecedent and consequent, and that they are parasitical upon indicative inference tickets of the form

(—) implies (...)

where the square brackets of the "shall-" tickets are understood to make participial expressions of the statements mentioned by the indicative inference ticket. It is important to note, though the full significance of the fact lies outside the scope of this essay, that although in the context "(—) implies (...)" gerund expressions are to be construed as singular terms, in the simple context "shall [—]" they are not. In other words, shall-statements, unlike implication statements, are in the object-language. In this respect "shall" resembles truth-functional connectives.

Universality and the Logic of Intentions

6

[33] It will be useful to conclude these animadversions on the logic of imperatives and resolutives with some remarks on the hypothetical imperative.[17] My main point is that to say "If you want A, do B!" is not a special case of telling someone to do something. Here, again, we find the imperative mood serving as the vehicle of a performance, but the performance is that of giving advice, rather than telling someone to do something.[18] The "want" of "If you want A, do B!" like the "want" of "What does he want me to do?" is roughly equivalent to "intend."[19]

[34] It might seem plausible to interpret the hypothetical imperative

If you want the red one, take *that!*

uttered by Jones to Smith, as having the force of

(Since *that* is the red one and you (Smith) want the red one).
"You (Smith) take the one you want!" implies "You (Smith) take *that!*"

and hence as the principle of the argument

You (Smith) take the one you want!
The one you want is the red one
That one is the red one
So, you (Smith) take it.

But, as we have already pointed out, the hypothetical imperative belongs to the category of advice, and in advice the imperative mood is used in answer to the question,

---

[17] Hypothetical imperatives, represented by the form "If you want A, do B!" are, of course, not to be confused with the conditional imperatives we were discussing a moment ago. The latter have the form "Do B, if *p*!" where *p* is any relevant statement of fact. Hare has made it clear that "if you want A" is not a descriptive-psychological condition serving as a special case of *p*, but rather specifies a resolutive premise which is thought to be (possibly) operating in the practical reasoning of the person to whom the hypothetical imperative is addressed.

[18] Hare, of course, construes "imperative" so inclusively that it covers "I shall do A" as well as "Do A!" Yet, since he construes all imperatives as *tellings to*, he construes "I shall do A" as telling oneself to do A, which it clearly is not; though, of course, there is such a thing as "telling oneself to do A."

[19] There are, of course, differences. It makes sense to say of a person that he intended to do or bring about something which he did not *want* to do or bring about. If one does B in spite of the fact that it brings about A, then one does not want to bring about A, although one intends to do so. It should also be clear that one may intend and, indeed, *want* that X do A although one does not *desire* that X do A. We do not use the word "desire" (or its cognates) in the case of action on principle.

What shall I (Smith) do?

It is, therefore, concerned with the *questioner's* intentions, whereas the *telling to* use of imperatives answers the question,

What do you want me to do?

and expresses the intention of the person who uses the imperative. When Jones advises Smith by saying "Do A!" in answer to the question "What shall I do?" Smith accepts this advice by forming the intention expressed by "I shall do A." It is as though Smith handed to Jones the incomplete sentence,

I (Smith) shall do...

and Jones had added "A" to complete it.

[35] In the case of the hypothetical imperative, "If you want the red one, take *that!*" Jones is telling Smith that *that* is the red one. He is, however, giving this information in a way which reflects the deliberative role it would play in Smith's thinking if, indeed, he does intend to take the red one. This role can be represented by

(1) *That* is the red one
So (I take the red one) implies (I take *that*)
So, (Shall [I take the red one]) implies (Shall [I take *that*])
(2) Shall [I take the red one]
So, shall [I take *that*]

Thus, to advise Smith with the hypothetical imperative in question is to answer, by anticipation, the question

I (Smith) shall take the red one, *so which* shall I take?

The answer, however, though verbally similar to the *telling to* "You (Smith) take *that!*" conveys the information that *that* is the red one for use as a premise in Smith's reasoning as outlined above.

7

[36] Let us now look at the implications of the above considerations for the analysis of ought-statements. At the end of Section 4 we were preparing to examine the idea that ought-statements are truly universal imperatives; that they have a force which it takes what is, from the standpoint of actual usage, the absurdity "Everybody do A in

C throughout all past and future time!" to represent. We are now in a position to understand this absurdity and to see that it just won't do to suppose that by a simple extension (for analytic purposes) of the ordinary imperative mood, we can represent ought-statements as truly universal imperatives. Reflection on the fact that imperative utterances are practical performances to which appeal can be made in justifying or excusing our conduct, makes it clear that they presuppose *publication* to those who are to do what the imperatives tell them to do. It is no accidental feature of imperatives that one can only tell people to do things in the future. And it is no accidental feature of imperatives that they are formulated by the use of tensed verbs in which the tense has its full and ordinary force. There can be no counterpart here of the "tenseless" *is* which philosophers use to formulate truly universal matters of fact. Only God at the time of creating Adam could have sensibly used the imperative "Everybody at all times and places do A in C!" for only then was all relevant time all future time.

[37] But if we cannot *tell* past people to do A in C, we can *wish* that they had done so. If moral principles cannot be interpreted as truly universal imperatives, may they not be the expression of truly universal wishes? "Everybody ought to do A in C," then, would have the force of "Would that everybody had done A in C, and did A in C from now on"—a wish which we may abbreviate to

Would that everybody *universally* did A in C!

This suggestion has the advantage (over the imperativist account) that

Would that everybody universally did A in C!
X is (was, will be) in C
So, would that X did (had done) A!

has the feel of deliberative reasoning. And though there are fairly obvious reasons to mistrust this suggestion, let us refuse, for the moment, to entertain them, for it will be useful to let it grow before it is modified or abandoned.

[38] Let us suppose, then, as a working hypothesis, that

Everybody ought to do A in C
X doing B in these circumstances is X doing A in C
So, X ought to do B

has the force of

Would that everybody universally did A in C!
X doing B in these circumstances is X doing A in C
So, would that X did B!

and let us suppose, again as a working hypothesis, that

> Would that I did B

has the force of

> I shall do B

and

> Would that X did B!

the force of

> X shall do B

where the shall-sentences are used in accordance with the stipulations of Section 3. Now let us add the logical point, which derives from the analysis of what it is to have an intention, that, other things being equal, a person who candidly says

> I shall do B

and is not a victim of self-deception, and is not mistaken about the circumstances, and does not change his mind, *will do* B; and that, with similar qualification, one who candidly says

> Tom shall do B

will do that which he believes would bring about Tom's doing of B. If we add this logical point, can we not claim that the above is at least a first approximation to an analysis of what it is to *have* a moral principle and act on it?

8

[39] But if this account has the merit of freeing ought-statements from "telling to," while preserving the connection with "intending" which was the sound core of the imperativist analysis, it won't do as it stands. Much more remains to be said about the universality represented, in this account, by "Would that everybody universally did A in C!" Then, when and if this hurdle has been crossed, the account must be freed from its stress on sentences having the special force of the form "Would that X did A!" Of these tasks, the former will prove decisive.

[40] Consider the case of someone who has a universal wish in a more ordinary and restricted sense of "universal." Suppose that Jones wishes that "everybody" do a certain kind of action, where the scope of "everybody" is, say, the people who are with him on a particular occasion. We who reflect on Jones's intention may ask ourselves

Why (for what reason) does Jones wish that everybody do A?

and we may arrive at an answer of one of the following types:

(a) Because if everybody does A, this would have as its *joint* result the state of affairs S (which he wishes to exist for its own sake).
(b) Because each doing of A has a consequence of a certain kind K (which he wishes to exist for its own sake), and if everybody does A, this would bring about the maximum number of K states of affairs.
(c) Because if everybody does A, everybody does A (i.e., *everybody doing A* is a state of affairs which he wishes to exist for its own sake; he is interested in single doings of A only as logically necessary conditions of everybody doing A.
(d) Because if everybody does A, there are that many individual doings of A. (He would wish any A-doing to exist for its own sake).

I do not wish to imply that this list exhausts the possible types of answer to the above question. There is also the answer

(e) Because they ought (as he thinks) to do A.

This answer, however, only poses all over again the puzzles we are seeking to solve.

[41] Answers of type (a) and (b) would seem to be clearly irrelevant to the analysis of action *on principle*, and I shall just assume, for the time being, that there is no sense in thinking that having the principle *Everybody ought to do A in C* is a matter of wishing that everybody did A in C *for the sake of the consequence of such action*. Answers (c) and (d) are useful points of departure for the solution of our first problem, that concerning the universality of ought-statements. Let us consider them in reverse order.

[42] The first thing to note is that while (d) grants that Jones wishes that everybody did A, it emphasizes that it is individual cases of A-doing in which he is interested; his wish that a given case of A-doing exist is not a wish that it exist *in order that* a set of A-doings exist. Rather, his wish that everybody do A sums up, so to speak, his wishes that this, that, and the other person do A. He "just likes" individual cases of A-doing to exist, the more the merrier. He does not deliberate

Would that "everybody" did A!
So, would that Tom did A!

If anything, he deliberates

Would that Tom, Dick, Harry, indeed that "everybody" did A!

Case (c), on the other hand, provides us with an example of

Would that everybody did A!
So, would that Tom did A!

Yet it clearly does not give us what we are looking for, as it specifies that Jones is interested in Tom's A-doing only as a necessary condition of the state of affairs *everybody doing A*, that is to say, as one component in the state of affairs

Tom doing A and Dick doing A and....

But action on principle is not *silly*, as it would be if it were a matter of wishing that I keep this promise as a logically necessary condition of a world-long and world-wide keeping of promises.

[43] If only we could combine that feature of (c) which is expressed by

Would that "everybody" did A!
So, would that Tom did A!

with that feature of (d) which is expressed by

Whether or not the others do A, would that Tom did A!

[44] Now the moral of the above example is that to understand action on principle, it is not enough to invoke *separately* the ideas of *universality* and *not as a means*. The universality of the intention of action on principle *is* the manner in which the action is not intended as a means. To understand the universality of the intention in action on principle is to understand the sense in which a particular action, done on principle, is done for the sake of the action itself.

[45] The point at which I am driving is, perhaps, best brought out by making a somewhat parallel point in another context, though to make it in such brief compass I must skate hurriedly over thin ice. To acknowledge that

All M's are *universally* N's

is to be prepared candidly to say such things as

> This is an M, *therefore* it is an N
> That is an N *because* it is an M
> If this *were* an M, it *would be* an N
> If this *had been* an M, it *would have been* an N
> If *anything* were an M, it would be an N.

The point of the parallel is that

> Would that everybody *universally* did A in C!

is the expression of commitment to a *principle*, only if it expresses a readiness to such reasonings as

> Would that Tom did A, *for* he is a person in C
> I am a person in C, *so* would that I did A!
> *Since* Dick was a person in C, would that he had done A!

[46] Once again, let us permit the suggestion to grow before submitting it to a closer scrutiny. If it is sound, then to represent the deliberation which culminates in "I ought to do this" by the form

> Would that everybody universally did A in C!
> I am in C
> So, would that I did A!

would be to make the mistake of treating an expression of the principle *in accordance with which* one reasons about particular cases as though it were the major *premise* of such reasonings. The corresponding mistake in the case of theoretical (as contrasted with practical reasoning) is represented by the form

> All M is *necessarily* N
> This is M
> So, it is N

[47] We shall come back to this point in a moment. In the meantime we can see why, if the suggestion is sound, approving *on principle* of a doing of A in C is not the same thing at all as favoring it simply because one recognizes it to be a doing of

A in C. To say of Jones that he favors an item simply because he thinks of it as being of a certain description is to say that it is the fact that Jones thinks of the item as being of that sort which explains why he favors it. We can represent this by the reasoning

> Jones thinks that x is f
> So, Jones approves of x

and the inference ticket which authorizes this reasoning as

> Whenever Jones thinks that an item is f, he approves of it.

But the fact that *we* reason about Jones's approval of x along these lines must not be confused with the idea that *Jones's* approval of x is a *reasoned* approval. That is, we must avoid the assumption that because *we* can correctly argue as above, Jones must have reasoned

> x is f
> So, would that x were defended, etc.

It is simply not true that if Jones's thought that x is f is the *explanation* of the approval, then his approval must be a *reasoned* approval. It *may* be, or it may not. And if it is a reasoned approval, then the explanation of his approval of x is, strictly speaking, not

> Jones approves of x because he thinks that it is f

but rather,

> Jones approves of x because he thinks that x is f *and* accepts the practical principle "If anything is f, would that it be defended, etc."

To represent Jones as thinking

> Would that x, which is f, were defended, etc.

is not the same thing at all as representing him as reasoning

> x is f
> So, would that x were defended, etc.

even though we add to the former the information that *whenever* Jones thinks of an item as f, he thinks (*ceteris paribus*)

Would that it were defended, etc.

[48] As a parallel it may be pointed out that (as Prichard has emphasized)

(1) Jones thought that it would thunder *because he thought* that lightning had just occurred

is authorized by "Whenever *Jones thinks* that lightning has occurred, *he thinks* that it will thunder," and can be a mere matter of the "association of ideas," whereas

(2) Jones thought that it would thunder because lightning had just occurred (Jones thought "It will thunder because lightning has just occurred")

cannot. A psychological commentary on Jones's thinking in the latter case would have to mention Jones's acceptance of the principle "One may infer the occurrence of thunder from that of lightning" (Jones thinks "Whenever lightning occurs it will thunder"). Notice that (2) endorses the idea that lightning has just occurred. If the speaker does not wish to endorse Jones's thought that lightning has just occurred, he would say

(3) Jones thought that it would thunder because (he thought) lightning had just occurred.

This parenthetical use of "he thought" must not be confused with the "he thought" of "*because he thought* that lightning had just occurred."

[49] Thus, we see, it is essential not to confuse

Smith did B because he thought his doing B would be doing A in C

with

Smith did B *because*, he thought, *his doing B would be doing A in C.*

The difference in punctuation highlights the difference between asserting that the occurrence of thoughts of the form "my doing B would be a case of doing A in C" constitutes a (partial) explanation of the occurrence which was Smith's doing of B, and asserting that it was practical thinking of the form "I shall do B because my doing B would be a case of doing A in C" which accounts for Smith's doing of

B. In the second case, the "he thought" is a parenthetical comment by the speaker on Smith's reason for doing as he did. It must, of course, be granted that reasons are causes, i.e., that *in general* we can move from statements of the second form to statements of the first, and vice versa. But these moves are not without their dangers. For, as is well known, in causal explanations we are content to single out one aspect of the total relevant situation within which the explanandum occurs, dub it the cause, and relegate the presupposed remainder to the category of *condition*. On the other hand, we have not given a person's reason for acting as he did, unless we have given the whole reason in its proper form. Thus, in attempting to indicate that Smith has acted on principle, we may begin by saying, in the order of causes

Smith did B because he thought that to do B in his circumstances would be to do (an action of kind) A in (circumstances of kind) C.

This, however, leaves it open whether, in our statement of Smith's *reason* for acting as he did, we should say

(A)   Smith did B because, he thought, doing B in his circumstances would be doing A in C

or

(B)   Smith did B because, he thought, doing B in his circumstances would be a case of *anybody* doing A when in C.

It is only (B) which represents Smith as reasoning (roughly),

(B′) Would that I did A, if I am in C
      (In the case of anybody, would that he did A when in C)
      To do B in these circumstances is to do A in C
      So, would that I did A.

On the other hand, (A) is satisfied if Smith's decision is of the form,

(A′) Would that I did A, if I am in C
      To do B in these circumstances is to do A in C
      So, would that I did B

provided only that if Smith were to think of *any* action of *any* person as a doing of A in C, he would wish it done for its own sake, and hence reason *in each case*

(A″) Would that Y did A, if Y is in C
To do B in Y's circumstances is to do A in C
So, would that Y did A

Even with this proviso, however, (A) does not acquire the force of (B). To reason *in each case* as in (A″) is not the same thing as to reason in each case *in terms of a principle applicable to each case*. Yet we will not have clarified the difference, in the case of practical reasoning, until we understand the status of the bracketed move in reasoning (B) above.

[50] Notice, also, that if this proviso is not added, and if, for example, the doing of A in C by other people would not be approved by Smith, then we would have to revise the statement of Smith's reason for doing what he did to read, correspondingly,

(A‴) Smith did B because, he thought, doing B in his circumstances would be a doing of A in C by Smith

and the original causal statement to read

Smith did B because he thought doing B in his circumstances would be a case of Smith doing A in C.

[51] Approving *on principle* is not the same as being disposed to "just like" each item which one comes to think of as being of a certain kind.[20] This is not, for the moment at least, to be construed as a denial that people *might* arrive at the espousal of a principle of doing A when in C by a process which began with "just liking" (however this might come about) individual cases of people doing A in C; nor that, regardless of how we come to espouse it, the principle, when challenged, *might* be "justified" by the fact that when all the chips are down and all the information in, we find that we "just like" any case of doing A in C, in a sense of "just like" which is not the espousal of the principle all over again.

---

[20] For an earlier statement of this point, see my "Obligation and Motivation," *Philosophical Studies*, II (1951), 21–25. [Eds.—OMR is Ch. 2 of this volume.] In the Introduction to the second edition of his *Language, Truth and Logic*, Ayer criticizes his earlier formulation of the emotive theory as follows: "...I fail to bring out the point that the common objects of moral approval or disapproval are not particular actions so much as classes of actions; by which I mean that if an action is labeled right or wrong, or good or bad, as the case may be, it is because it is thought to be an action of a certain type." Ayer is here on the point of recognizing the existence of practical reasoning as a genuine form of reasoning. But by failing to draw the above distinctions, he remains within the limits of his earlier formulation.

9

[52] Let us now return to the topic of universality. We had arrived at the point of suggesting that "Would that everybody *universally* did A in C!" expresses the espousal of a principle of conduct, as expressing a readiness to reason in accordance with the form

X is (was, will be) a person in C
So, would that X did (had done) A

where X is a variable which ranges over persons, that is to say, *us*.[21] But before we proceed, we must, as already noted, free our account from its overly close connection with *wishing*, which stems, it will be remembered, from its genesis in a critique of the imperativist analysis. But instead of examining the logic of "to wish" and showing how "would that..." is related to other forms of practical discourse in order to show how wishes can embody the same principles as other practical "attitudes," I shall limit myself to pointing out that while neither "X should have done A" nor "It should have been the case that p" can be said to express intentions, any more than "X did A" or "It was the case that p" can be said to express expectations; nevertheless, intending may have its past tense (and subjunctive) counterparts, as expecting has its counterpart in historical thinking. A person who thinks at 10:00 A.M.:

Shall [X doing A ten minutes from now]

can be said to intend that X do A in ten minutes. Is there no practical thought that he can think about X doing A at 10:20, assuming that he has not changed his mind? It is surely plausible to interpret

Should [X doing A ten minutes ago]

as a differently tensed counterpart of the former. But what role might such thoughts play? It is worth noting that "X should have done A" is much closer to "X ought to have done A" than are simple "shalls" to "oughts." If we throw more

---

[21] If we suppose that this principle can be put in the form
   If anybody were in C, would that he did A!
we notice that if this is confused with
   Would it were the case that (if anybody were in C, he did A)!
one arrives at the Kantian formulation,
   Would that it were a law of nature that people in C did A!

398 THE METAPHYSICS OF PRACTICE

light on the relation of "ought" to "shall," we may then be in a position to appreciate practical discourse in the historical mode. But first let us continue with our attempt to build "shall" into "ought" without letting that problem distract us.

[53] At the end of Section 4 we argued that reasoned decisions involving "shall" were ultimately of the form

Shall [—]
So, shall [...]

where the implication authorizing this inference, namely,

(Shall [—]) implies (shall [...])

rests on an implication between the indicative statements "—" and " ... " which, by being bracketed, i.e., turned into participial expressions, serve as operands which the shall-operator turns into shall-statements. A not too complex example of practical reasoning of this kind would be

I shall do A, if I have the money
I have the money
So, I shall do A

which, on the above analysis, breaks down as follows:

(1) Shall [my doing A, if I have the money]
(2) (I have the money) implies ([I will do A, if I have the money] implies [I will do A])
(3) I have the money
(4) So, (my doing A, if I have the money) implies (my doing A)
(5) (Shall [my doing A, if I have the money]) implies (Shall [my doing A])
(6) So, Shall [my doing A]

In this "breakdown" of the original inference, the antecedents and consequents of implication statements (2), (4), and (5) are either *both* indicatives or *both* resolutives. In other words, whereas the original formulation suggests that the reasoning proceeds in accordance with the principle

(I have the money) implies (Shall [my doing A])

or, perhaps,

"(If I have the money, then shall [my doing A]) *and* I have the money)" implies (Shall [my doing A])

in neither of which is the antecedent a shall-statement, the proposed breakdown separates the reasoning into separate stages which are either pervasively indicative or pervasively resolutive.

[54] Against this background what are we to make of the reasoning, characteristic of action on principle,

Jones is a person in C
So, Jones shall do A

Our first attempt may well be to construe this reasoning as authorized by the general inference ticket

(X is a person in C) implies (X shall do A)

But as this ticket has a shall in its consequent, but no shall in its antecedent, we may be tempted to think of it as a *derivative* inference ticket, one which must be explicated in terms of an inference ticket moving from shall to shall, and which, in its turn, rests on an inference ticket which moves from indicative to indicative. Thus, we might be tempted to reconstruct the argument as follows:

(1) Shall [(X) (X doing A, if X is in C)]
(2) "(X) (X does A, if X is in C)" implies (Jones does A, if Jones is in C)
(3) "Shall [(X) (X doing A, if X is in C)]" implies (Shall [Jones doing A, if Jones is in C])
(4) Shall [Jones doing A, if Jones is in C]
(5) (Jones is in C) implies ([Jones doing A, if Jones is in C] implies [Jones doing A])
(6) Jones is in C
(7) (Jones doing A, if Jones is in C) implies (Jones doing A)
(8) (Shall [Jones doing A, if Jones is in C]) implies (Shall [Jones doing A])
(9) Shall [Jones doing A]

But this suggestion, according to which moral principles are universal resolutives of the form

Shall [(X) X doing A, if X is a person in C]

runs up against the objection that it would be silly to espouse such resolutives knowing full well that in a great many cases people who are in C simply have not done, nor will they do, A.

[55] A more plausible approach, which has the advantage of interpreting the universality of moral principles in terms of *each* case rather than the totality of cases, draws on the concept of an *axiom schema*. According to it, instead of saying that

Shall [(X) (X doing A, if X is a person in C)]

is an axiom, we should rather say that every statement derived from the schema

Shall [X doing A, if X is a person in C]

by replacing X with the name of a person is an axiom or first principle of moral reasoning. According to this approach, the first three steps of the above breakdown are to be replaced by the characterization of (4) as an axiom conforming to the above axiom schema.

[56] But what is the difference between the following two conceptions of espousing a moral principle pertaining to people doing A in C?

(A) to espouse such a moral principle is to accept as a first principle of practical reasoning any resolutive conforming to the schema
Shall [X doing A, if X is in C]
(B) to espouse such a moral principle is to accept the general inference ticket, (X is a person in C) implies (Shall [X doing A])

To choose between these interpretations requires a closer look at conditional intentions, i.e., at the logical form of "X shall do A, if p" and its relation to the inference

X shall do A, if p
p
So, X shall do A.

[57] It has often been argued that the closest that ordinary language comes to exhibiting the truth-functional connective of *material implication* in its pure form is in the expression of conditional intentions. Or, to put the point the other way around, that whereas most ordinary uses of "if..., then—" give expression to basic or derivative relations of inferability, the "if..., then—" of conditional intention

has nothing to do with inferability, but rather is material implication pure and simple. But this way of putting the point is too strong; for if a person says

I shall do A, if p

and we subsequently find that in spite of becoming convinced that p, he does not do A, we shall infer either that he has changed his mind, or that he was mistaken about his frame of mind, or that he was deceiving us. Thus there is a logical connection between "I shall do A" and "p" stronger than material implication, and it would be incorrect to say that the force of "I shall do A, if p" has *nothing* to do with inferability. On the other hand, the inferability seems clearly to relate to the force of "shall" as governing the entire conditional, and not only to be compatible with the absence of an *independent* intentional connection between p and the doing of A but also to require that there be none. The inferability is exhibited by the following schema, in which (and hereafter in this essay) "*if...*, *then*—" stands for material implication.

X candidly says (thinks) "Shall [*if p, then* my doing A]"
X candidly says (thinks) "p"
So, X will do A

If so, then it is a mistake to interpret the "if..., then—" of conditional intention as anything more than material implication, even though one must grant that a relation stronger than material implication obtains between the corresponding biographical statements concerning intentions, beliefs, and actions.

[58] These considerations throw light on the difference between interpretations (A) and (B) above of what it is to espouse a moral principle. For it enables us to dispel the feeling that these proposals are *equivalent*. This feeling rested on the rough equivalence between accepting the *inference ticket*

(x is f) implies (x is g)

and accepting the *schema*

If x is f, then x is g

as defining a class of *axioms* (i.e., unconditionally assertable statements). Thus, if to espouse a moral principle *were* to accept the schema

If X is in C, then X shall do A

as defining a set of axioms, one might well conclude that to speak instead of accepting the inference ticket

(X is in C) implies (X shall do A)

would be to say essentially the same thing in other words. But if, as we have argued, it is a mistake to interpret expressions of conditional intention as having the form

If p, then X shall do A

and if they must, instead, be attributed the form

(Shall [if p, then X doing A]), i.e., (Shall [*if p, then* X doing A])

as must be done to bring the condition within the intention, the parallel disappears. Thus, (B) must be rejected, and (A) so interpreted as not to confuse

X accepts as a first principle of practical reasoning any resolutive conforming to the schema: (Shall [*if* X is in C, *then* X doing A])

which is (in first approximation) the correct account, with

X accepts as a first principle of practical reasoning any resolutive conforming to the schema (*if* X is in C, *then* shall [X doing A])

which is not.

[59] This account of espousing a principle has the additional merit of making clear *why* it won't do to interpret such espousal as a matter of having a *general* intention, thus:

X accepts as a first principle of practical reasoning the universal resolutive, "Shall [(X) (*if* X is in C, *then* X doing A)]."

For to intend *in this sense* that everybody do A in C, knowing, as one does, that "(X) (*if* X is in C, *then* X *does* A)" is false, would be, if not (as it seems to be) logically impossible, at least silly.

[60] Let me now suggest as the next step in the analysis of ought-statements that

X (as being a person in C) ought to do A

has the force of

Shall [X doing A] *because* X is in C and shall* [*if* X is in C, *then* X doing A]

where the asterisk attached to the second "shall" is a *signal* that the speaker recognizes resolutives of the form

Shall [*if* X is in C, *then* X doing A]

as first principles of practical reasoning. Needless to say, this answer is oversimplified in a number of respects, not the least of which is its presupposition that the A and C of the ought-statement are the action and circumstance categories of a principle at hand. For the relation between ought-statements and principles is more flexible than indicated above. To make an ought-statement one need not, as we saw in Section 4, have a principle up one's sleeve; rather, one commits oneself to the idea that "there is" an explanation having the form of the above because-statement, X's circumstances being of kind C and the action in question of kind A.

[61] A more radical defect in the above "analytical model," as we shall see, is its neglect of that dimension of moral principles which is the fact that they are *our* principles (not merely *my* principles) though it does justice to the fact that they are principles *about* us.

10

[62] There is a consideration pertaining to intentions and their expression which, though not strictly a part of the argument of this paper, indicates how it might fit into the broader framework of an empiricist philosophy of mind.[22] It is that to *intend* that person P do A is to *think* "P shall do A," i.e., to be disposed to have *thoughts* of the kind "P shall do A" where these thoughts are inner episodes construed on the model of the overt utterances which, in candid discourse, are *initiated by* these inner episodes, and in this sense, express them. (To *believe* that *x* is f is, correspondingly, to *think* "*x* is f," i.e., to be disposed to have thoughts of the kind "*x* is f," where these thoughts are inner episodes construed on the model of the overt utterances which, in candid discourse, are initiated by these inner episodes, and would be said to express this belief.) And if we must add that in a certain sense one can think "P shall do A" without really intending that P do A,

---

[22] For an elaboration of such a framework, see my "Empiricism and the Philosophy of Mind," in *Minnesota Studies in the Philosophy of Science*, Vol. I (Minneapolis: University of Minnesota Press, 1956), pp. 253–328. See also "Some Reflections on Language Games," *Philosophy of Science*, XXI (1954), 204–228.

this is not because intending that P do A is thinking "P shall do A" *plus* something else, but because that which appears to introspection as the thought "P shall do A" is only *presumptively* this thought. Thus, if someone candidly assures us "I shall do A," and it turns out at the appropriate time that, although he assures us that he has not changed his mind, the thought of doing A has no power to move him to act, then it would be proper to deny not only that he had really intended to do A, but also that the presumptive thought "I shall do A," which he had introspected, really was such.

[63] Notice that I am not saying that *intending*, for example, to do B in order to bring about A, is identical with the *power* of the thought "My doing B would bring about A" to move one to act. I am, however, insisting that the power, in the causal order, of thoughts of the form "My doing B would bring about A" to move one to act is a presupposition of the language of "shall" and the order of reasons—indeed, that "I shall do B in order to bring about A" embodies this presupposition.[23]

[64] It follows from the above conception of the status of intentions and beliefs, together with the interpretation of ought defended in this essay, that to *believe* "P ought to do A" is, in part, to *intend* "P shall do A."

11

[65] We must now face up to the fact that "shall" and its kindred express the intentions of the *speaker*. Thus, and the point is an obvious one,

Jones shall do A

differs from

Jones intends to do A

in that whereas the speaker uses the latter to ascribe to Jones the intention to do A, the former expresses *the speaker's intention that Jones do A*. Thus, if I say to Jones

---

[23] To appreciate at least the general force of this point, one has only to reflect that one has not learned to use "shall" unless, *ceteris paribus*, candid utterances of "I shall do A" are followed by the actual doing of A. "I shall do A" is, so to speak, "My doing of A in the future" as signalizing a forthcoming doing of A. Furthermore, the forthcoming doing of A which it signalizes is not a *blind* doing of A, and this in two respects: (1) the doing is, in a sense, brought about by the idea of doing A; (2) the bringing about itself is a *self-conscious* fact, and not a mere triggering of the action by the idea. This self-consciousness consists in the fact that the thought responsible for the action is "I shall do A," and can be traced to the fact that one hasn't learned the use of "shall" unless "I shall do A" is not only the signal of a forthcoming doing of A, but is understood to be such a signal.

These and other points concerning the interrelationships of the order of reasons and the order of causes will be developed in a separate paper which began as a section of an early draft of the present paper.

You shall do A

I have no logical right to expect him to concur by saying

Yes, I shall do A.

And if he should reply

No, I shall not do A

the logic of "shall" makes no demand that one or other of us change our mind by abandoning our intention—though logic does assure us that these intentions are incompatible in that they cannot both be realized. Consequently, if my statement

You (Jones) ought to do A

were simply

You (Jones) shall* do A

where the asterisk signals the presupposition of practical reasoning of the form

Shall [*if* Jones is in C, *then* Jones doing A]
So, Jones being in C, shall [Jones doing A]

in which the major premise is an axiom of the type discussed in Section 9, there would be no logical reason to expect Jones, given that he agrees that he is indeed a person in C, to meet *my*

You (Jones) ought to do A

with

Yes, I (Jones) ought to do A.

My point is that the language of morals differs from the language which simply expresses the speaker's intentions, not only by expressing or implying reasoning of the kind we have been exploring, but also by presupposing (in one sense of this much abused expression) that all disagreements of the form

A: Jones ought to do one thing
B: No! He ought to do another

are "in principle" reducible to disagreement *about matters of fact* and not to disagreement *in intention*.

[66] How is this presupposition to be understood? The explanation centers around a simple fact about the grammar of the word "ought": that *ought, unlike shall, has a proper negative*. Whereas shall is characterized by the two forms

Shall [X doing A]
Shall [X not doing A]

ought enjoys the full complement

Ought [X doing A]
Ought [X not doing A]
Not-ought [X doing A]
Not-ought [X not doing A]

In short, one person can *contradict* another person's ought, whereas shalls *conflict* but do not *contradict*.

[67] Let us introduce the concept of the *biographical counterpart* of a shall-statement. Thus, corresponding to Tom's shall-statement

Shall [X doing A]

there is the biographical counterpart

Tom intends that X do A

which, given that Tom speaks candidly and without self-deception, will be true. Using this concept we can pair off the following shall-statements and biographical counterparts:

(1*a*)   Tom intends that X do A
(1*b*)   Tom: Shall [X doing A]
(2*a*)   Tom intends that X not do A
(2*b*)   Tom: Shall [X not doing A]
(3*a*)   Tom intends that X do A or not do A as X pleases
(3*b*)   Tom: Shall [X doing A, if X so wishes *and* X not doing A, if X so wishes]
(4*a*)   Tom has formed no intention with respect to X doing A
(4*b*)   Tom: Shall [X doing A]?[24]

---

[24] I am assuming, of course, that the possibility of X doing A has occurred to Tom, and that he has been deliberating about it.

It is clear that these relationships do not require the form

Not-shall [X doing A]

because the one case which might seem to call for it, namely (3a), simply gives us another example of a shall-statement. But what of biographical statements of the form "Tom does *not* intend that X do A"? Do we not have

(5a) Tom does not intend that X do A
(5b) Tom: Not-shall [X doing A]

and is not (5b) equivalent to

(5c) Tom: May [X not doing A]

The answer is that (5a) is compatible with (4a), whereas (5c) clearly expresses the outcome of a deliberation, and is, indeed, the expression of an intention. In fact, it would not be implausible to regard (5c) as a variant form of (3b).

[68] Against the equation of (5c) with (3b), however, there are important considerations pertaining to the role of "may" in *telling to* discourse. It is, I believe, illuminating to regard the fundamental role of "may" as that of *withdrawing a telling to*. We have already called attention to the difference between expressing the intention that X do A, and telling X to do A, a difference which is represented in our symbolism by the difference between "Shall [X doing A]" and "Shall [X doing A]!" If, now we pair off *tellings to* with *their* biographical counterparts, we have, for example,

(6a) Tom tells X to do A
(6b) Tom: Shall [X doing A]!

Here the fact emerges that if Tom has told X to do A, he may subsequently (subject, of course, to certain conventions) withdraw this performance by saying "May [X not doing A]!" This direct withdrawal is not to be confused with the "implicit" withdrawal which is performed by "contramanding,"[25] i.e., presenting X with a new telling to, one which *conflicts* with the old, as,

---

[25] I am coining this expression because "countermanding" as ordinarily used appears to cover both simple withdrawal and what I am calling "contramanding."

Tom: Shall [X doing A]!
Tom (subsequently): Shall [X doing B]!

where doing B entails not doing A; or, in a weaker form,

Tom: Shall [X doing A]!
Tom (subsequently): Shall [X not doing A, if p]!

[69] Withdrawing a telling to is the practical counterpart of withdrawing a telling that. Therefore, it is important to distinguish between *withdrawing* a telling that, and *contradicting* a telling that. The difference is illustrated by the dialog,

Tom: S is P
Tom (subsequently): S is not P
Dick (chiming in): S is not P

Tom has both contradicted and by implication withdrawn his earlier telling that. Dick obviously cannot withdraw Tom's telling that; but he can, and does, contradict it. Notice that Tom might have withdrawn his earlier telling that by saying "S may not be P after all." This use of "may" is not to be confused with notions pertaining to possibility or probability in those uses which do have proper contradictories.

[70] The fallacy I am attempting to expose is exhibited by the following sequence of statements:

(1) *Countermanding* is the counterpart of *contradicting*
(2) To contradict is to assert the negative of what was asserted
(3) "May [X not doing A]!" countermands "Shall [X doing A]!"
(4) "May [X not doing A]!" = "Not-shall [X doing A]!"

The fallacy lies in the third step. "May [X not doing A]!" countermands "Shall [X doing A]!" in a sense which *is* the counterpart of contradiction, only if it is interpreted, roughly, as saying "Shall [X doing A, if X so wishes *and* X not doing A, if X so wishes]!"; in which case it is not a "not-shall" statement (whatever that might be) but simply another shall-statement which implicitly *withdraws* the original telling to. If, on the other hand, "May [X not doing A]" is taken to play the direct withdrawal role, then it is not the counterpart of a contradiction, and the argument also breaks down.

Universality and Intention: A Second Mode

12

[71] I pointed out above that whereas one person can *contradict* another person's ought, shalls *conflict* but do not *contradict*. But to make it intelligible how ought can "at bottom" be a shall, and yet have this radical intersubjectivity, we must bite a bit deeper. Consider the following exchange:

D(1)   Tom: S is P
       Dick: S is not P

Dick has contradicted Tom; and supposing candor on all sides, we can correlate with this dialog the following biographical counterparts:

BD(1) Tom thinks that S is P
       Dick thinks that S is not P

Consider, next, the dialog,

D(2)   Tom: I (Tom) shall do A
       Dick: You (Tom) shall not do A

This time the biographical counterparts are

BD(2) Tom intends that Tom do A
       Dick intends that Tom not do A.

If we reflect on these two pairs, we notice a point of resemblance and a point of difference. The point of resemblance is that in each of the dialogs what each speaker says expresses *his* frame of mind—in the one case the thought that S is (or is not) P, in the other the intention that Tom do (or not do) A. The difference consists in the already noted fact that whereas in the first dialog Dick has contradicted Tom, in the second he has simply expressed an intention which is not co-realizable with Tom's intention.

[72] Consider, next, the two dialogs,

D(3)   Tom: I (Tom) ought to do A
       Dick: You (Tom) ought *not to do* A
D(4)   Tom: I (Tom) ought to do A
       Dick: *It is not the case* that you (Tom) ought to do A.

Our analysis suggests the following biographical counterparts for the first of these dialogs,

> BD(3) Tom intends that Tom *do A* because he has such and such an "axiomatic" intention and such and such factual beliefs
> Dick intends that Tom *not do A* because he (Dick) has such and such an "axiomatic" intention (about Tom) and such and such factual beliefs.

But it leaves us puzzled as to just what to offer as the counterpart of D(4). For if our aim is to reconcile the idea that in D(4) Dick is contradicting Tom with the idea that the ought is a special case of shall, we can scarcely be satisfied with

> BD(4) *Tom* intends that Tom do A
> It is not the case that *Dick* intends that Tom do A.

For whereas in the biographical counterpart of D(1) the contradictory statements "S is P" and "S is not P" *reappear in the guise of that-clauses*; in BD(4) the supposedly contradictory statements have simply disappeared. On the other hand, if we simply represent the biographical counterpart of D(4) as

> BD(4′) Tom thinks that Tom ought to do A
> Dick thinks that not-(Tom ought to do A)

we say what is true, but lose contact with the "analysis" of ought in terms of shall.

[73] I suggest that (to put it in a radically oversimplified manner) the *autobiographical* counterpart of an ought-statement is not simply

> I intend that X do A because I have such and such an "axiomatic" intention with respect to X, and such and such factual beliefs

but rather

> *We* intend that X do A....

Thus, corresponding to the statements,

> D(5) Tom: I (Tom) ought to do A as being a person in C
> Dick: You (Tom) ought to do A as being a person in C
> Harry: He (Tom) ought to do A as being a person in C

we have as counterparts *not*

BD(5)   Tom "axiomatically intends" that Tom do A as being a person in C
Dick "axiomatically intends" that Tom do A as being a person in C
Harry "axiomatically intends" that Tom do A as being a person in C

but, rather, the autobiographical counterparts,

ABD(5)   Tom: *We* "axiomatically intend" that Tom do A...
Dick: *We* "axiomatically intend" that Tom do A...
Harry: *We* "axiomatically intend" that Tom do A....

And if, with this in mind, we form the autobiographical counterpart of D(4), we have something like,

ABD(4)   Tom: *We* "axiomatically intend" that Tom do A...
Dick: *We* do *not* "axiomatically intend" that Tom do A....

What is the force of such phrases as "*we* intend..." and "*we* are committed to the intention..."? Here we touch on the "institutional" aspect of morality. For "We intend..." is clearly not the logical sum, so to speak of "Tom intends...," "Dick intends...," "Harry intends...," etc. Nor does

Tom (who is one of *us*) does *not* intend that X do A

contradict

We intend that X do A

any more than

Tom (who is one of *us*) doesn't mind women smoking

contradicts

We disapprove of women smoking.

[74] Nor (I need scarcely add) does the fact that this is so involve the existence of a "group mind," capable of having beliefs and intentions, in a sense incompatible with empiricist principles. Empiricism has properly stressed the logical dependence of concepts pertaining to the beliefs and attitudes of groups on the corresponding concepts pertaining to individuals. This dependence, however, as the above examples make clear, involves a certain flexibility. Nevertheless, the fewer

the people in the group who believe that *p* or intend that X do A, the less defensible becomes the statement that the group believes that *p* or intends that X do A. These are familiar considerations. I wish to emphasize that when the concept of a group is "internalized" as the concept of *us, it becomes a form of consciousness* and, in particular, a form of *intending.*

[75] We saw above that "We intend that X do A" does not entail "Tom (who is one of us) intends that X do A." On the other hand, it is clear that a person who shares none of the intentions of the group could scarcely be said to be one of *us.* There is a particularly close logical connection between "We intend..." and "I intend...." This does not mean that it can never be proper to say "We intend..., though I, for myself, do not." On the contrary, this makes perfectly good sense. Yet there is clearly a tension between them. If to intend that X do A is, as I have suggested, to think "X shall do A," then we must distinguish between two shalls, one corresponding to "We intend..." and one to "I, for myself, intend...." Let us represent them, respectively, as "shall*w*" and "shall*I*." *I suggest that ought, as an expression of intention, is a special case of shallw.* There are, in this case, two dimensions to the universality of moral principles as universal intentions: (1) the formal universality, or universality of application which can be represented by the formula, "All of us shall do A in C"; (2) *the universality of the intending itself*, which can be represented by modifying the above formula to read, "All of us shall*w* do A in C."

Let me now bring all these considerations together. I suggest that the fact that ought-statements, unlike ordinary shall-statements, have a proper negation is built on the shared intending expressed by "ought." In other words, the *syntactical* intersubjectivity of ought-statements which permits Dick to contradict Tom as in D(4) above, and which *consists in* the existence of the form "not-ought [X doing A]" in addition to the form "ought [X *not* doing A]" rests on the intersubjectivity of the intention expressed by ought-statements.

[76] Notice that I am not saying merely that the existence of shared formally universal intentions is a sociological condition of the existence of intersubjective ought-talk. I am saying that intersubjective ought-talk *contains* within itself the "symbolic form" which is the very existence of *intending-as-one-of-us.* (Just as "I shall do A," in its candid, un-self-deceived use, is the very existence of a personal intending.) For this reason, a person who said "People ought to do A in C" but denied "We intend that people do A in C" would be like a person who said "I shall do A" but denied "I intend to do A." The truth of "X intends to do A" is a necessary condition of the "genuineness" (candor and absence of self-deception) of X's "I shall do A," much as the truth of "X believes that S is P" is a necessary condition of the "genuineness" of X's "S is P." Similarly, the truth of "Group

G intends that people do A in C" is a necessary condition of the "genuineness" of "People ought to do A in C" said by a member of the group. Here, however, "genuineness" is a more complicated matter than the candor and absence of self-deception of an individual. One can know that *he* intends that people do A in C, and yet be deceived about the group's intention. The group has shared intentions by virtue of the fact that its members intend in the mode "shall*w*." But that the members intend in this mode does not guarantee that in point of fact there are shared intentions. Intending in the mode "shall*w*" is a "form of life," a conceptual framework within which moral discourse exists and without which it is impossible. Yet the actual existence of shared universal intentions is no more an antecedent condition of participating in moral discourse than actual agreement on matters of fact is an antecedent condition of participating in factual discourse. In each case the forms of discourse set this agreement as a *task*. To abandon the idea that disagreement on moral matters is even in principle capable of resolution is not to retreat to a moral solipsism; it is to abandon the moral framework itself, and to retreat to the language or "form of life" of purely personal intention.

13

[77] We have argued that moral consciousness is a special form of *we*-consciousness, and, in effect, that one who does not intend in the *we*-mode, i.e., has no "sense of belonging to the group," cannot be said to have more than a "truncated" understanding of ought. The reader may be prepared to grant that something like a Darwinian natural selection of primitive cultures might bring it about that in the cultures which survive the internal and external dangers which beset them, people decide certain matters of conduct, *ceteris paribus*, on principles of the form

Shall*w* [*if* X is (was, will be) a person[26] in C, *then* X (not) doing (having done) A]

where these principles are *unexamined*, and the fact that people acknowledge them a matter of "social inheritance." But what of *examined* morality? How can we combine the conception of moral action as action on principle, with the idea that the principles in question are *reasonable* principles? Why "Everybody ought to do A in C" rather than "... A′ in C" or "... A″ in C"? And if we have a reason, and if this reason is a state of affairs, does one not therefore act in order to realize this state of affairs, and no longer on principle?

---

[26] See note 8 for an interpretation of "person" as "one of us."

[78] Now one line of thought is that to justify a set of principles is to find that, all things considered, one wishes doings of A in C, A' in C', etc., *as such* to exist. But, as we saw in Section 8, this might have either of two meanings. The first is that to speak of such wishes is a misleading way of referring to the acknowledgment of these very principles themselves, in which case the "justification" amounts to the *fact* that we still espouse them after the factual heights and depths of the world have been explored. The bearing of "all things considered" on the continued espousal of the principles is left completely in the dark. The second is that "One wishes doings of A in C, etc., *as such* to exist" is intended to refer not to an approval of such doings on principle, but rather to a liking of these ways of doing things which, though general, is not on principle, and can be compared to other naturalistic (or, in Kant's sense, pathological) likes and dislikes, in which case the suggestion is most implausible. Is our favoring of promise-keeping *as such* a naturalistic one?

[79] A more plausible line of thought is that which finds the reason for *these* principles rather than *those* in a relation they have to the general welfare. But if we have regard for the general welfare, and find it to be such a reason, does this not mean that we now act in order to promote the general welfare, and envisage doings of A in C, A' in C', etc., as means to this end? And does this not, in turn, mean that we are no longer acting *on principle*? Can a person have a reason for his principles, and yet, without having to forget this reason, act *on* these principles? Indeed, can there be such a thing as having principles *and* having a reason for them at all?

[80] Now once the question is posed in these general terms, the source of the puzzle becomes clear. It lies in a failure to distinguish two senses in which a person may, at the time of acting, be said to *have a certain intention*. In the first place, there is the intention of the action, i.e., what he intends to do *as doing that particular action*. Then there are the purposes and intentions which, though he has them in mind, in an appropriate sense, at the time of acting, and though they may be closely relevant to that action, cannot correctly be said to be part of what he intends to do as doing that particular act. Plans, purposes, policies and the like do not have to be consciously entertained in order to be "in mind" and not forgotten. What I want to emphasize, however, is that even when they are consciously entertained, and as intimately related as they can be, after their own manner, to the intention of the action, they need not, for that reason, be part of the intention of the action.

[81] I shall first develop this point in a way which oversimplifies the logical relations involved. Suppose that Jones, however he may have come to do so, loves his neighbor as his brother, and his brother as himself. "Would," he says, "that men, generally, were happy!" A study of the hearts of men and the ways of the world convinces him that an essential condition of the general welfare is that people generally do A in C, A' in C', etc. It also convinces him that for this to be

the case, it is necessary that people, generally, act *on* the corresponding principles. (It may also convince him that general action *on* principle, in addition to being an indirect condition of the general welfare, is a direct condition, even, in some sense, a component, of it.)

[82] Now it cannot be true that Jones intends that *everybody* act *on* these principles, unless it is also true that Jones intends that he himself act *on* these principles.

Would that everybody acted *on* $P_1, P_2, \ldots P_n$!
So, would that I acted *on* $P_1, P_2, \ldots P_n$!

But his decision to acknowledge these principles is the decision to acquire (or, if already acquired, to reinforce and maintain) the character trait of arriving at decisions on matters of conduct by reasoning which, for our present purposes, can be represented by the form

Doing *this* would be a case of a person's doing A in C (or A′ in C′, etc.)
So, I shall do it

and while his efforts to acquire (and maintain) these dispositions have the *purpose* of doing that which is conducive to the well-being of men generally, these traits, once acquired, manifest themselves in doings of A in C, A′ in C′, etc., of which, in an important sense, the *complete* intention has the form represented immediately above. Or, to put it in the language of ought,

Doing this would be a case of a person's doing A in C
So, I ought to do it.

In other words, these dispositions manifest themselves in actions of which, in an important sense, the motive is *not* the love of one's fellow men, but the sense of duty.

[83] Yet if, in an important sense, Jones does A because it is what he ought to do rather than because it will further the well-being of his fellow men, there is still a sense in which he can be said to have both intentions in doing this action. They are not, however, cooperating intentions on the same level. We must say, rather, that each particular case of conscientious action on the part of Jones is supported by his abiding intention to develop and maintain in himself the dispositions to act *on* the principles, i.e., to espouse them; and this intention, in turn, is part and parcel of his abiding intention that these traits of character be a common possession of men generally, which, in turn, is a consequence (given his beliefs about the hearts of men and the ways of things) of his intention that men generally be happy, a state of affairs which he wishes to exist for its own sake.

[84] Let us take a closer look at the move from "Would that men generally were happy" to "Would that I espoused such and such principles of conduct." The logical bridge between these statements can be schematically represented (in a way which obviously oversimplifies the empirical dimension of the reasoning) as follows:

Would that men generally were happy!
(Men generally being happy) implies (men generally doing A^i in C^i)
So, would that men generally did A^i in C^i
(Men generally doing A^i in C^i) implies (men generally espousing P^i)
So, would that men generally espoused P^i
(Men generally espousing P^i) implies (my espousing P^i)
So, would that I espoused P^i

Two objections can be raised against this reasoning. The first is that if we interpret "men generally" as "everybody," the argument founders on the fact that we know that not everybody will do A^i in C^i and also that not everybody will espouse P^i. The justification of moral principles is not soft-headed sentimentality. While if we interpret "men generally" as "most people," the conclusion simply does not follow.

[85] This objection is too strong as it stands, for it can be countered by taking the second horn and pointing out that from "Most A is B" to "(probably) this A is B" *valet consequentia*—given, of course, that we have no reason to suppose that this A is one of the exceptions. Yet the objection does prepare the way for a more penetrating objection. This objection is that the empirical facts do not discriminate between "most men" and "most men with the exception of myself," and, in particular, between "most people espousing P^i" and "most people (with the exception of myself) espousing P^i." The way seems open for a compromise between benevolence and self-love which undercuts the above reasoning. One who raises this objection will grant that a person fraught with benevolence but lacking in self-love would, on sitting down in a cool hour, be in a position to reason as above. But, it is argued, surely one who combines a modicum of self-interest with even a substantial amount of benevolence would find a loophole for a compromise. That this compromise would itself be the espousal of a general policy or plan of life is no answer, for it would not be the espousal of universal principles impartially applicable to all.

[86] To rebut this objection we must take a closer look at the concept of benevolence. For, as might be expected, the bridge between benevolence and the life of principle requires a sense of "benevolence" which logically precludes the above compromise. Is there such a sense? Once again the answer lies in reflection on the force of "we" and its relation to "I." For the sense of "benevolence" that is

required is not the impartial love of everybody, which is, as Kant saw, the espousal of a principle of conduct (roughly that one ought to help other people realize their ends), but the simple recognition of people generally as *we*. We have already seen that moral principles involve the consciousness of *us*. In fact, we have found it to play a dual role in principles, as can be brought out by representing them by the form "We shall*w* do A if in C." We can now add a third role to our list, the role which relates to the cool hour in which we rise above the level of conscientiousness as the unreflective fruit of "good upbringing." By now the direction of my argument should be obvious. For if we replace "*most people* but not I" by "*we* but not I" in the formulation of the objection, we move from consistency to incoherence. There is no *logical* place for a compromise between benevolence and self-love, where "benevolence" is understood as the consciousness of oneself and one's fellow men as *we*.

[87] It is particularly important to distinguish the "loyalty" to people generally, the recognition of each man everywhere as one of *us*, from the impartial love of one's fellow men which is itself a matter of principle. For if one confuses these two, one will suspect that to defend principles in terms of impartial love is to reason in a circle. The recognition of each man everywhere as one of *us* was the extension of tribal loyalty which exploded it into something new. It has a precarious toehold in the world, and *we* are usually a far smaller group. Kant's conception of each *rational being* everywhere as one of us is a still more breath-taking point of view which may yet become a live option.

14

[88] We have seen that, and how, the idea that the prime mover of reflective moral consciousness is benevolence can be reconciled with the idea that moral action is action *on principle*. It must be admitted that the character trait of acting on principle can exist without loyalty, as the fruit of training, precariously reinforced by praise and blame, and, on a larger scale, as a factor making for the selective survival of social groups and communities. Nevertheless, a conscience of this "chilly" kind must be threatened by every "cool hour" of critical reflection. For while self-love can find reasons for doing the things which good men do, it is unlikely to find reasons for maintaining the dispositions to act on moral principles which make good men good.

[89] Self-love could, indeed, support the effort to acquire and maintain the disposition to arrive at a decision on certain matters of conduct by reasonings which are ultimately of a form represented by the schema

Shall [*if* I am in C at t, *then* my doing A]

that is to say, by reasoning which is built on an *ego-centric* intention, universal only with respect to time. Self-love could support such self-discipline on the ground that it is by being disposed to act *on* these principles that I shall be most likely to achieve my happiness.

[90] But even the prudential ought is not to be confused with such egocentric rulishness. For ought, as we have seen, signalizes the presupposition of agreement. And the distinctive feature of the prudential ought is not its restriction in *scope*, but rather the fact that it is reflectively acknowledged that the reason for being prudentially conscientious is the fact that it is a means to one's own happiness. The prudential ought encompasses individual differences by bringing them into the content of its legislation, and, in this way, adds realism to its presupposition of intersubjectivity.

[91] If this is correct, we should not expect the distinction between moral and prudential principles to have been made until men were on the threshold of reflective morality and had seriously begun to sit down in cool hours and raise the familiar groping questions which gave rise to moral philosophy. This does not mean, of course, that to have arrived at a reasonably clear conception of a certain class of principles as justified by self-love, and, hence, to have set these apart as "principles of prudence," one must have arrived at an equally clear conception of moral principles as justified by benevolence.

[92] I have emphasized in the foregoing that[27] the only frame of mind which can provide direct support for moral commitment is what Royce called Loyalty, and what Christians call Love of Neighbor (*caritas*). This is a commitment deeper than any commitment to abstract principles. It is a precious thing, the foundation for which is laid in earliest childhood, though it can arise, in adult years, by a phenomenon known, in other contexts, as conversion. Recent psychological studies make clear what has always, in a sense, been known, that the ability to love others for their own sakes is as essential to a full life as the need to feel ourselves loved and appreciated for our own sakes, unconditionally, and not as something turned on or off depending on what we do. Thus, in a deeper sense, really intelligent and informed self-love supports, and can be an incentive to forming, the love of neighbor which, nevertheless, alone gives *direct* support to the moral point of view when we are alone in that cool hour.

---

[27] These concluding remarks were taken from an unpublished paper, "Ethics and Philosophy," which was read to the Phoebe Griffin Noyes Library Association, Old Lyme, Connecticut, on January 26, 1960. [Eds.—This paper became SE, which is Ch. 4 of this volume.]

Appendix

[93] Since submitting this paper to the editors of *Methodos* I had an opportunity to read, in mimeograph, Chapter IV of Professor Castañeda's forthcoming important book on the logic of prescriptive discourse. While I disagree with certain aspects of his argument, and, in particular, with his defense of the concept of imperative inference, I do agree that the manifold of practical discourse is illuminated by viewing it against the model of a single mode of practical discourse variously enriched. Indeed, it is largely to him that I owe my possession of this insight, around which have clustered such additional insights as I have accumulated since I began my attempt to reconcile Prichardian intuitionism with naturalism some twenty years ago.

[94] Until I read this chapter it had not occurred to me that *promising* and *commanding* ("I command...") admit of being viewed as specific enrichments of basic practical sentence forms. Thus, while I would have explained the fact that there are no such reasonings as

(1) I promise to do A, if p
    p
    So, I promise to do A

or

(2) I command you to do A, if p
    p
    So, I command you to do A

as opposed to

(1a) I promised to do A, if p
    p
    So, I promised to do A

and

(2a) I commanded you to do A, if p
    p
    So, I commanded you to do A

by saying that the *signals* "I promise" and "I command" do not belong in the scope of "—, so...," this claim, sound in essence though it is, would have been scarcely more than the report of an isolated "logical intuition."

[95] In the terminology of this paper, "I promise to do A, if p" differs from "I shall do A, if p" (and, similarly, "I command you to do A, if p" from "You shall do A, if p!") in that they are not only *tellings* but tellings which, by virtue of the presence of the phrases "I promise" and "I command" are (if appropriately performed) subsumed under specific moral principles, as explained in Section 2. "I promise to do A, if p" has, therefore, the form "I shall do A, if p^*," and "I command you to do A, if p" has the form "You shall do A, if p^{**}," where "*"

and "**" represent, respectively, the promise-making and the command-issuing signals. Like the telling-to signal "!", these signals are not, as such, ingredients in practical reasoning. But if there are no such practical reasonings as (A) and (B) above, there is the reasoning

First step:	p
	So, (its being the case that *if p, then* X does A) implies (X doing A)
Second step:	So, (Shall [its being the case that *if p, then* X does A]) implies (Shall [X doing A])
Third step:	Shall (its being the case that *if p, then* X does A)
	So, Shall (X doing A).

[96] I also wish to take this opportunity to thank Dr. Karl Potter, whose helpful criticism of the previous version of this paper led me to substitute the convention according to which "X shall do A" is the sheer *expression* of an intention, whereas "X shall do A!" is a *telling to* as well, for a considerably less perspicuous representation of this distinction.

15
Reflections on Contrary-to-Duty Imperatives*

I

[1] In his paper on "Contrary-to-Duty Imperatives and Deontic Logic"[1] Roderick Chisholm argues, correctly in my opinion, that "a logic of conduct, or 'deontic logic,' which is to be of use for people who are not morally perfect, should be able to deal with 'contrary-to-duty imperatives'." (p. 33) The latter concept is explained by the form: You ought to do a, but if you don't do a, you must, by all means, do b. Chisholm then advances the thesis that "most of the deontic logics, which have been developed in recent years, cannot be applied to situations in which we wish to assert such imperatives."[2]

[2] Chisholm begins his argument by distinguishing between what he takes to be two senses in which a statement of obligation may be conditional. These are represented, respectively, by the forms

F_1: O(if a then b)
F_2: if a then O(b).

He claims that whether 'a' and 'b' stand for actions, propositions or states of affairs, "the locution 'O(if a then b)' as it is interpreted in these logics is *not* adequate for the expression of 'contrary-to-duty' imperatives". For example, "if the letters 'a' and 'b' are taken to stand for actions, then 'O(if a then b)' is interpreted in such a way that it is equivalent to 'it is obligatory that one refrain from doing that joint act which consists in doing a and not doing b'... Hence, if a is an act one

---

* I have, I hope, profited from comments made by Hector-Neri Castañeda and Louis Goble on an earlier draft of this paper written in the fall of 1965.
[1] *Analysis*, XXIV (1963): 33–36
[2] He tentatively, but rightly, in my opinion, makes an exception in the case of H-N. Castañeda's system. Castañeda's system distinguishes between imperative and propositional variables, so that Chisholm's paradoxical statements can be symbolized as follows, where capital letters stand for imperatives, excepting 'O', which stands for 'It is obligatory that,' and small letters stand for propositions: (1) O(A); (2) O(a ⊃ B); (3) ~a ⊃ O(~B); (4) ~a. From these the rules of the system do not allow the derivation of a contradiction. See his "The Logic of Obligation," *Philosophical Studies*, X (1959): 12–23. Professor John Robison in an independent discussion has also made what I take to be an essential move. See his "Further Difficulties for Conditional Permission," *Philosophical Studies*, XVIII (1967).

ought not to perform, then, no matter what b may be, one may affirm 'it is obligatory that if a then b'." (p. 34)

[3] The underlying thought is clearly that *refraining* from doing that joint act which consists in doing a and not doing b is necessarily equivalent to *doing* that act which one performs if and only if one either refrains from doing a or does b. And, indeed, if 'a' and 'b' are construed as 's does a' and 's does b', respectively, and an appropriate tie is made between 'refraining' and negation, familiar principles of propositional logic would authorize the implication

$$\sim a \rightarrow \sim a \vee b$$

and the equivalence

$$\sim a \vee b \leftrightarrow a \rightarrow b$$

and hence, reading 'a → b' as 'if a then b,' and appealing to some such principle as

$$P_O: \text{if x logically implies y, then Ox implies Oy}$$

it would follow that for any value of 'b'

$$O(\sim a) \text{ implies } O(a \rightarrow b)$$

Returning, now, to a reading 'in terms of actions' we would have the apparently paradoxical thesis, formulated above, that "...if a is an act one ought not to perform, then, no matter what act b may be, we may affirm 'it is obligatory that if a then b.'"

[4] To illustrate his point, Chisholm asks us to "suppose that we wish to remind a potential thief of the duty to restore stolen property. The locution of the obligatory conditional—'It is obligatory that if you steal you return the money'—is not adequate for what we want to say. For, if stealing is wrong, then this locution 'O(if a, then b)' interpreted in the way thus described, also allows us to say 'It is obligatory that if you steal, then you do *not* return the money' and, indeed, 'It is obligatory that if you steal, you steal again and lead a life of sin henceforth.'"

[5] What exactly is the paradox? The initial answer is that we seem to be entitled by the above argument to assert both

$$O(\text{if you steal, then make restitution})$$

(on the basis of a specific moral principle) and

O(if you steal, then do *not* make restitution)

(on the basis of finagling with material implication).
[6] But there is a deeper answer. It is clearly assumed that the move from

O(if a, then b)

together with the factual premise 'a' to the conclusion

O(b)

is valid, so that from the first of the above assertions we may detach

You ought to make restitution

and from the second

You ought *not* to make restitution

which are in direct conflict.
[7] Chisholm, however, does not explicitly raise the question of the validity of the schema

O(if a, then b)
a
Therefore, O(b)

as contrasted with the schema

a → O(b)
a
Therefore, O(b).

Instead, he moves on to a second paradox. The moral he draws from the first paradox is that in order to express contrary to duty imperatives, we need, in addition to

F_1: O(if a then b)

the form,

F_2: If a then O(b)

It is not clear, however, how the addition of this second form will help, unless something is done about the first. For as long as the argument schema

O(if a, then b)
a
Therefore, O(b)

(Together with the resources of material implication and something like principle P_O) is allowed, we can apparently conclude both that the thief ought to make restitution, on the specific ground that thieves ought to return their booty, and that he ought not to make restitution on the odd ground that he has done something which he ought not to have done.

[8] The most drastic move would be to eliminate the schema

O(if a, then b)
a
Therefore, O(b).

A less drastic step would be to keep it, but subject it, if possible, to restrictions which exclude paradoxical cases, perhaps by requiring that it not be the case that O(~a). Another possible move would be to disallow 'O (if a, then b)' where O(~a). Perhaps this is what 'not using "O(if a, then b)" to express contrary-to-duty imperatives' amounts to. Still another alternative would be to place restrictions on P_O to exclude the move from

~a logically implies a → b

to

O(~a) implies O(a → b).

[9] Before taking a closer look at these alternatives, let us continue with Chisholm. He argues that if statements of form F_2 are introduced, then "their use, to express such [contrary-to-duty] imperatives, gives rise to contradiction." (p. 34) He finds that "among the principles common to these logics are the following: (I) If it ought to be the case that a occur and if it ought to be the case that if a occur then b occur, then it ought to be the case that b occur; and (II) It is not true to say, of any a, both that a ought to occur and that a ought not to occur." He then continues with an example designed to show that if these principles are combined with the acceptance of F_2, a contradiction can be constructed.

[10] "Let us suppose: (1) it ought to be that a certain man go to the assistance of his neighbor; (2) it ought to be that if he does go, he tell them he is coming; but (3) if he does not go, then he ought not to tell them he is coming; and (4) he does not go.

[11] "By applying the first of two principles above to (1) and (2), we may deduce that the man ought to tell his neighbors that he is coming. By applying the rule of detachment to (3) and (4) we may deduce that he ought not to tell them that he is coming. But the two conclusions, when combined, are inconsistent with the second of the two principles above."

[12] Symbolized in the familiar manner, the argument looks as follows:

(1): $O(g)$ premise
(2): $O(g \to t)$ premise
(3): $\sim g \to O(\sim t)$ premise
(4): $\sim g$ premise
(5): $O(t)$ (1) (2), I
(6): $O(\sim t)$ (3) (4) MP
(7): $O(t) \cdot O(\sim t)$ Conj. Int.
(8): $\sim[O(t) \cdot O(\sim t)]$ II

Since (7) and (8) are mutually contradictory, something must give. Either the premises are inconsistent or one of the steps is invalid. The initial target of suspicion is likely to be principle I. But before we examine its credentials, some distinctions are in order. For above all, there is the possibility, emphasized by Chisholm, that the traditional symbolism is unperspicuous, obscuring important distinctions and permitting ambiguity to take its usual toll. That this is more than a possibility is suggested by the fact that the puzzles and paradoxes of deontic logic have not been put to rest by its use.

II

[13] We are all familiar with the distinction between the *primary* use of logical connectives, which is to build statement expressions into compound statement expressions, and such *derivative* uses as that of forming compound predicates (e.g. 'red and square', 'if red, then square') or compound expressions for kinds of event (e.g. 'raining and blowing'). The use of logical connectives to form compound expressions for action kinds is at the heart of our problem. It will be remembered that Chisholm speaks of "refraining from doing that joint act which consists in doing a and not doing b" (p. 34). He characterizes this "joint act" as "the act one performs if and only if one does a and does not do b." The concept of a joint action in this sense is important, but it is in the neighborhood

of other concepts from which it must be carefully distinguished, under penalty of serious confusion.

[14] Before we can be clear about expressions for compound or "joint" actions, we must take a closer look at expressions for kinds of action. They come, of course, in families. A paradigm example is the family consisting of the verb 'to stab' and its cognates 'a stab' 'stabbing' etc. Another family is made up of 'to run' 'run' 'running' etc. From a logical point of view action kind expressions, in the strict sense illustrated by these paradigms, 'contain' implicit variables (a) for an agent (in the case of joint actions, agents), (b) for temporal (and, perhaps, spatial) location, and (c), in some cases, for a direct object (e.g. 'stabs') or even (d), an indirect object (e.g. 'gives'). In what follows I shall neglect as an unnecessary complication the spatial dimension (e.g. 'in the heart'). Thus the expressions,

x stabs (to stab, stabbing...) y at t
x stabs (........................) Caesar at t
x stabs (........................) Caesar at t_1

(where t_1 is the appropriate time on the Ides of March in the appropriate year B.C.) constitute a series of specifications of the basic action kind, and are themselves 'expressions for action kinds' only in that extended sense which amounts to the presence of at least one variable which remains to be pinned down.[3] Consider now the compound action kind expression

stab and curse.

Normally one would unfold this (and, for reasons which will shortly emerge, I highlight the infinitive form) as

x to stab-and-curse y at t

but, in a mildly extended sense, there can also be the action kind

x to stab-y-and-curse-z at t

and even

x to stab-y-at-t-and-curse-z-at-t.

---

[3] Compare the sense in which 'x is taller than Abraham Lincoln' can be said to 'stand for a characteristic'. Some philosophers are squeamish about saying that '(x is) larger than Chicago' stands for a universal, others are not. The point, of course, is that not the terminology, but using it coherently and effectively, and, above all, not being misled by it, is the important thing.

But, leaving this refinement aside, consider the series,

x to stab-and-curse y at t

.

.

.

x to stab-and-curse Jones at t_2
Tom to stab-and-curse Jones at t_2

The point I wish to emphasize is that while there is a sense in which the last expression in the series 'expresses an action,' it would be as much a mistake to call it an 'action expression' as to call

Tom is tall

an 'attribute expression' (i.e. predicate). Or, to put the matter differently there is an important sense in which

stab and curse

is an action expression, but

Jones to stab and kill

is not, though the latter might be called a 'propositional action expression' while preserving the spirit of the distinction.

[15] The next point to note is that

Jones [A and B]s

is equivalent to

Jones As and Jones Bs.

Indeed, we can conceive of a language in which, in general, there is a form

$x[acB]α^*$
$x [a \ c \ B]α$

---

* [Eds.—This seems to be an inadvertent duplication of the formula in the printed version. In Sellars's typescript, the formula only appears once (as written the second time, with spaces between 'a', 'c', and 'B'). The relevant typescript is document 31735062221019, Box 39, Folders 1–3, Wilfrid S. Sellars Papers, 1899–1990, ASP.1991.01, Archives of Scientific Philosophy, Archives & Special Collections, University of Pittsburgh Library System.

which is equivalent to

$$x \, A\alpha \, c \, x \, B\alpha$$

where 'c' represents a connective and 'α' indicates a grammatical modification. But ordinary English is clumsy with respect to locutions pertaining to compound actions. Thus a danger arises which will be illustrated shortly.

[16] The primary danger, however, which arises from a failure to clarify adequately the concept of an action expression is that a symbolism will be used which is unperspicuous in that it fails to warn against interpretations which move from one sense to another of 'its action expressions,' even within the same context. Thus the expressions

a and b
a or b
if a, then b

where these occur in the context 'O(...),' may sometimes be interpreted as compound action expressions proper, sometimes as a combination of an action expression proper with a propositional action expression, sometimes as a compound propositional action expression.

[17] To develop this theme, let us consider four examples:

(1) If it is raining, Jones ought to come inside
(2) If he is smoking, Jones ought to use the ashtray
(3) Jones ought to either refrain from smoking or use the ashtray
(4) Jones ought, if he smokes, to use the ashtray.

The first two examples have the form 'If p, then x ought to do A' or, making an appropriate use of 'O',

$$F_3: \text{if p, then } O(x \text{ to do } A).$$

It would not, however be improper to represent them both by the form

$$F_4: O(\text{if p, then } x \text{ to do } A)$$

and the special case where, as in (2), the antecedent concerns an action of the agent, by

$$F_{4.1}: O(\text{if } x \text{ does } A, \text{ then } x \text{ to do } B),$$

thus representing more adequately the fact that the obligation itself is conditional. By construing the context 'O(...)' as transparent to the *indicative* propositional expression 'p'—e.g. 'it is raining,' 'he (Jones) is smoking'—and permitting the argument schema

O(if p, then x to do A)
p
Therefore, O(x to do A)

one would achieve the result otherwise achieved by the use of F_3 together with *modus ponens*.

[18] Notice that in both

O(if it is raining, then Jones to come inside)

and

O(if he is smoking, then Jones to use the ashtray)

the 'then-' clause is a propositional action expression and *not* an action expression proper (an 'action kind' expression in the extended sense). It is also the expression on which the 'O' operates 'directly' (though 'conditionally') in the sense that the only obligation which can be directly detached from this premise by the use of a factual minor is the obligation for x to do A.[4]

[19] Notice also that although in both the above examples the 'then-' clause is a propositional expression, it is not an indicative propositional expression. Thus we should not assume that

O(if p, then x to do A)

entails

O(if x not to do A, then not-p)

For no meaning has, as yet, been given to 'O' other than as bearing on action expressions proper in the infinitive, nor to 'if-' clauses, in this context, which are non-indicative propositional action expressions. The related use of 'O(x,p)' to represent 'x to make it the case that p', and of 'O' to represent 'it ought to be the case that...' will be explored subsequently.

---

[4] The use of normative minors to detach obligations will be explored shortly.

[20] It is clear that of our examples (2) has the same general form as (1) and differs only in that the indicative 'if-' clause concerns an action of the agent who is asserted to have a conditional obligation. The third example, on the other hand, involves a compound action expression proper. It has a form which can be represented, in the first instance, as

$$F_5: O(x \text{ to } [\sim A \vee B])$$

where '$[\sim A \vee B]$' stands for a compound action expression proper. Since this expression is equivalent to '$[A \to B]$' we can also represent (3) by the form

$$F_6: O(x \text{ to do } [A \to B])$$

Thus

$$O(\text{Jones to } [\text{smoke} \to \text{use ashtray}]).$$

The logical powers of ought statements concerning 'implicative' actions will be one of our chief concerns.

[21] Although the use of disjunctive action expressions is relatively common, we do not often find statements such as

(3′) Jones ought to if-smoke-then-use-ashtray.

This is, however, an accidental feature partly accounted for by the danger of confusing (3′) with (4). Thus, since in the latter a reference to the agent occurs before the 'if', it might be thought that the pronominal reference to the agent after the 'if' and before the 'smokes' is merely a making explicit of an agent variable which is only *implicitly* present before the 'smoke' in (3′). Nothing could be further from the truth. The *only* agent expression which belongs with the 'smoke' of (3′) and its disjunctive counterpart (3), is the *explicit* expression 'Jones', for in (3′) 'smoke' is simply a part of one single action expression 'if-smoke-then-use-the-ashtray', as in (3) it is a part of 'either-not-smoke-or-use-the-ashtray.' Thus (4) is simply another way of expressing that which is expressed by (2) and, from the standpoint of a 'rational reconstruction,' is simply another example of F_4.

[22] It is my conviction that failure to distinguish between these various ways in which complexes pertaining to action can properly be brought within the scope of a single 'ought' operator makes it easy to confuse these complexes with superficially similar complexes with which this cannot properly be done. This point will be elaborated in the following section.

[23] One further point in this connection. It will be noted that in (3) and (3′) we find 'smoke', while in (4) we find 'smokes'. The presence of 'smokes' in the latter is

indicative of the transparency of the context to the propositional expression pertaining to smoking, i.e. 'he (Jones) smokes,' and hence the validity of the argument schema,

O(Jones, if he smokes, to use the ashtray)
he (Jones) smokes
Therefore, O(Jones to use the ashtray).

On the other hand, the 'smoke' in (3) and (3′) is indicative of the fact that 'O' bears directly on the whole compound action of which smoking is simply one constituent.

[24] It was pointed out above that ordinary English contains no provision for a systematic use of compound action expressions such as might be represented by the contrived

Jones [if smoke, then use ashtray]s

or

Jones [use ashtray, if smoke]s

as contrasted with

Jones uses the ashtray, if he smokes.

In the case of conjunctive action expressions, where there is ostensibly less danger of confusion,

Jones to stand up and shout

becomes, in the indicative mood,

Jones stands up and shouts

rather than

Jones [stands up and shout]s

even here, though, a notorious danger lurks in the neighborhood. Consider the well-worn example,

Jones ought to put on his parachute and jump.

The safe way to formulate the content of this assertion is, roughly,

O(x to put on his parachute) • O(if x has put on his parachute, then x to jump)

If we telescope this conjunction into a single ought statement (postponing for a moment the question of the presuppositions of such telescoping) it becomes something like

O(Jones to put on his parachute now and if Jones puts on his parachute now, Jones to jump).

The form involved would seem to be

F_7: O(x to A • (x does A → x to B))

which must not be confused with the closely related form

F_8: O(x to [A • (A → B)])

designed to express obligations to perform compound actions of a certain complicated type.

[25] It is obvious that we are in trouble if we construe the parachute-jump obligation as having the form

F_9: O(x to [A • B]).

Intuition tells us that we would not be much better off with F_8.

[26] Notice that in F_7 the 'O' operates on *two* infinitive expressions, 'x to A' and 'x to B'. It is interesting to note that in the 'ordinary English' formulation of the parachute-jump example, there is only one 'to' which governs both put and jump. This suggests that in addition to compound action expressions formed from expressions for action kinds only, thus

O(x to [A → B])

we recognize action expressions which embody propositions. For example we might have

x to [p → A].

If we make this move, we can reformulate F_7 as

O(x to [A • (x does A → B)])

or, using the 'turnstile' to make the relevant proposition out of an action expression,

$$O(x \text{ to } [A \bullet (\vdash A \rightarrow B)]).$$

Let us call action expressions of the form

$$\text{to } (p \rightarrow A)$$

'conditional' action expressions, as contrasted with the 'implicative' action kinds previously introduced. This manoeuver enables us to specify that the scope of 'O' is to contain only one infinitive. Notice, of course, that

$$O(x \text{ to } [p \rightarrow A])$$

is equivalent to

$$O(p \rightarrow x \text{ to } A).$$

The upshot of these remarks is that

$$O(x \text{ to } [A \bullet (A \rightarrow B)])$$

must be carefully distinguished from

$$O(x \text{ to } [A \bullet (\vdash A \rightarrow B)])$$

Both forms have their usefulness, but it is the latter rather than the former which captures the logic of the parachute jump.

III

[27] Instead of making an elaborate use of compound action expressions, ordinary English makes distinctions corresponding to that between

$$F_6: O(x \text{ to } [A \rightarrow B])$$

on the one hand and

$$F_{4.1}: O(x \text{ does } A \rightarrow x \text{ to } B)$$

and

$$F_{4.2}: O(x \text{ to } [B, \text{ if } x \text{ does } A])$$

on the other, by representing the latter as

x ought to do B, if he does A

and F_6 by some such locution as

F_{10}: x ought to bring it about that if he does A, he does B.

The awareness of this locution and the desire to have a uniform method of symbolizing obligation statements of whatever kind, have combined to generate a new temptation to confusion. For F_{10} is clearly a special case of

F_{11}: x ought to bring it about that if p, then he does B

where 'p' is no longer restricted to propositions pertaining to the actions of x, and might be, for example, 'it is raining.' F_{11}, in its turn, is a special case of

F_{12}: x ought to bring it about that if p, then q,

where 'q' also is freed from this restriction. Thus an example of F_{12} might be

Jones ought to bring it about that if it is raining, then the car is in the garage.

The temptation easily arises to represent both

Jones ought to either refrain from smoking or use the ashtray

and

Jones ought to use the ashtray, if he smokes

as

Jones ought to bring it about that if he smokes, he uses the ashtray

and conceive of both as instances of F_{10}, F_{11} and F_{12}.

[28] A closer examination of the rubric 'x ought to bring it about that...' reminds the more sensitive ear that there is available, even within this rubric, a

way of drawing the distinction we have been highlighting. Thus, consider the two statements

> Jones ought to bring it about that if he smokes he use the ashtray

and

> Jones ought to bring it about that either he refrains from smoking or he uses the ashtray.

Notice that in the subordinate clause of the former we have the verb forms 'smokes' and 'use,' while in the latter we find 'refrains (from smoking)' and 'uses'. The differentiation in the former case enables the statement to make *using the ashtray* the direct target of the obligation. What is expressed is a conditional obligation equivalent to

> If Jones smokes, then he ought to use the ashtray.

In the former case, then, the rubric is transparent to 'he (Jones) smokes' so that

> Jones ought to bring it about that if he smokes then he use the ashtray

is equivalent to

> If Jones smokes, then he ought to bring it about that he use the ashtray.

[29] In the second statement on the other hand, the lack of difference in form between the two verbs in the subordinate clause fits the statement to express the case in which not *using the ashtray* but rather the compound action of *either-refraining-from-smoking-or-using-the-ashtray* is the direct target of the obligation.

[30] This device, if extended to the case where the connective is 'if..., then...' would enable a distinction between

> Jones ought to bring it about that if he smokes, then he use the ashtray

and

> Jones ought to bring it about that if he smokes, then he uses the ashtray

The former being equivalent to

$$O(\text{Jones smokes} \rightarrow \text{he use the ashtray})$$

and the latter to

$$O(\text{Jones to [smoke} \rightarrow \text{use the ashtray]})$$

In the latter we would have an example of a new way of forming a compound action expression, thus

x to bring it about that [if he smokes, then he uses the ashtray]

as contrasted with

x bring it about that [if he smokes, then he use the ashtray].

We can represent the distinction between the two cases by accenting the propositional expression which is the direct target of the obligation. Thus we would get the two forms

F_{13}: x ought to bring it about that (a → b')
F_{14}: x ought to bring it about that (a → b)'

where 'a' and 'b' represent propositional expressions pertaining to an action. The former, but not the latter, would be equivalent to

F_{15}: a → x ought to bring it about that b'.

[31] Notice that, as the phrase '*the* target', used above, implies, an obligation has only one direct target, though that target may be a compound one. Thus, only one accented expression belongs in the scope of 'x ought to bring it about that...'. This corresponds to the fact that, according to our previous analysis, only one action expression proper, though it may be a compound one, belongs in the context 'O(x to...)'.

[32] In the more general cases where the propositional expressions are not restricted to x's actions, we would have the additional pairs

F_{16}: x ought to bring it about that (p → a')
F_{17}: x ought to bring it about that (p → a)'
F_{18}: x ought to bring it about that (p → q')
F_{19}: x ought to bring it about that (p → q)'

If we now use 'O' to mean 'ought to bring it about that', our pairs become

$F_{13.1}$ $O(x, (a \to b'))$ = .a → $O(x,b')$
$F_{14.1}$ $O(x,(a \to b)')$
$F_{16.1}$ $O(x,(p \to a'))$ = .p → $O(x,a')$
$F_{17.1}$ $O(x,(p \to a)')$
$F_{18.1}$ $O(x,(p \to q'))$ = .p → $O(x,q')$
$F_{19.1}$ $O(x,(p \to q)')$

Similar distinctions must be drawn when we move to the rarified atmosphere of the rubric

it ought to be the case that...

Thus, if we use 'O' to represent this rubric, we must distinguish (and I move directly to the most general case) between,

F_{19}: $O(p \to q')$ = .p → $O(q')$
F_{20}: $O(p \to q)'$.

IV

[33] With these distinctions under our belt, let us return to the second paradox pertaining to contrary-to-duty imperatives, represented by the argument schematized on p. 307 [Eds.—§12] above. We are now in a position to see that, if our argument to date is correct, Chisholm's principle I is ambiguous. Depending on how it is interpreted, I becomes either

Ia: if $O(a)^5$ and $O(a \to b')$ then $O(b)$

or

Ib: if $O(a)$ and $O(a \to b)'$ then $O(b)$.

The questions arise, which of these principles is true? Is neither true? Are they, perhaps, both true? Again, how are we to represent the second premise?

(2.1) $O(g \to t')$?
(2.2) $O(g \to t)'$?

---

[5] The accent can be omitted where a single propositional expression falls within the scope of 'O.'

If we take the former course, the relevant principle is Ia and the argument becomes

(1) $O(g)$
(2.1) $O(g \to t')$
(3) $\sim g \to O(\sim t)$
(4) $\sim g$
(5) $O(t)$ (1),(2.1),Ia
(6) $O(\sim t)$ (3),(4),MP

The result, as before, is a contradiction.

[34] Suppose we take the second course. This time the relevant principle is Ib and the argument becomes

(1) $O(g)$
(2.2) $O(g \to t)'$
(3) $\sim g \to O(\sim t)$*
(4) $\sim g$
(5) $O(t)$ (1),(2.2)†,Ib
(6) $O(\sim t)$ (3),(4),MP

Again a contradiction!

[35] How have our distinctions helped? Let us begin by taking a closer look at the two principles Ia and Ib. If the line taken in the preceding section is correct, we can see right away that something is wrong. For if, as was claimed, 'g' occurs transparently in

$$O(g \to t')$$

So that

$$O(g \to t') = g \to O(t)$$

then the premise which is required to detach 'O(t)' would seem to be 'g' rather than 'O(g)', and we would have a straightforward case of modus ponens. And if we supply this premise, we would end up with a contradiction simply because our premises contained a contradiction.

[36] By permitting the premise 'O(g)' the principle gains in power, though its plausibility may rest on confusion with modus ponens. The fact that the principle is used in a paradoxical argument would seem enough to condemn it, unless the

---

* [Eds.—Correction of:
    $\sim g \to O(t)$
in original printing.]
† [Eds.—Correction of '(2)' in original printing.]

trouble can be located elsewhere. On the other hand, the principle is not completely lacking in intuitive support, and there may be a principle distinct from any we have so far considered which is sufficiently like it to account for its 'positive instances.' This will indeed turn out to be the case.

[37] But what of the second reconstruction which uses (2.2) and Ib? This time things are not quite so easy. A finer grained analysis is called for. If we make use of the distinctions we have developed, we see that in turning our attention from

$$O(a \to b')$$

to

$$O(a \to b)'$$

we are turning our attention from

$$O(x \text{ does } A \to x \text{ to do } B) \text{ i.e. } O(x \text{ to } [\vdash A \to B])$$

to

$$O(x \text{ to } [A \to B])$$

Thus, Ib becomes

Ib': if $O(x \text{ to do } A)$ and $O(x \text{ to do } [A \to B])$ then $O(x \text{ to do } B)$,

the appropriate form of the second premise becomes

$$(2') \ O(x \text{ to}[go \to tell])$$

and the argument becomes

(1') $O(s \text{ to go})$
(2') $O(s \text{ to } [go \to tell])$
(3') s does not go $\to O(s \text{ not to tell})$
(4') s does not go
(5') $O(s \text{ to tell})$ (1'),(2'),Ib'
(6') $O(s \text{ not to tell})$ (3'),(4'),MP
(7') $O(s \text{ to tell}) \cdot O(s \text{ not to tell})$ (5'),(6'),Conj.Int
(8') $\sim[O(s \text{ to tell}) \cdot O(s \text{ not to tell})]$ II'

where II' is the appropriate reformulation of II. The puzzle clearly remains.

V

[38] As our next move, instead of focusing our attention on principle Ib′, let us take a closer look at the premises. Indeed, let us raise the question 'whence the premises?' For it is only if we appreciate the logical form of the *source* of the premises that we will appreciate the importance of the distinctions we have been drawing for resolving Chisholm's puzzles.

[39] Whence 'O (s to go)'? Whence 'O(s goes → s to tell)' and 'O(s to [go → tell])'? And which of the latter do we want? The answer in each case is, of course, "from specific principles of obligation." What is the form of such principles? It is in the answer to this question that the solution of our problem lies. And since our aim is to clear away Chisholm's puzzles 'in principle,' it will suffice if we give an account 'in principle' of principles, i.e. a schematized account which clarifies the logic of the situation without pretending to represent the 'open-textured', 'working basis' character of the principles we actually employ or their 'major-them-with-riders' structure.

[40] I shall use the letters 'f_1,' 'f_2'...'f_n' to stand for what might be called 'normatively relevant circumstance factors.' And I shall use the form 's is f_1' to express the idea that s (a person) is in a circumstance which includes the factor f_1. As examples to make the symbolism somewhat intuitive, one may think of such things as *having made a promise* and *being in a position to prevent suffering*. These are obviously very 'generic' notions, and it is clear that situation factors fall into families, the members of which are differentiated by value of the item promised, the amount of suffering, etc. The *relevance* of a normatively relevant circumstance factor with respect to a certain sphere of action is simply a matter of its occurrence in antecedents of the normative principles which pertain to this domain. I shall assume that the principles are in 'first principle' form, i.e. that abstraction has been made from the determinate empirical characteristics and the empirical generalizations which enable the derivation of intermediate principles and ultimately the application of the principles. I shall also assume that situations and actions are described in a manner which permits the direct application of such principles. Let me call such descriptions 'normatively essential descriptions' or 'essential descriptions' for short.

[41] A 'normatively relevant circumstance', or briefly, a 'circumstance,' can be intuitively characterized as a maximum set of compatible circumstance factors. We can think of it as specified by a conjunction of expressions referring to circumstance factors or their negations.

$f_1 \cdot f_2 \cdot \ldots f_n$
$f_1 \cdot f_2 \cdot \ldots \sim f_n$
...
$\sim f_1 \cdot \sim f_2 \cdot \ldots \sim f_n$

Circumstances, as contrasted with circumstance factors, will be represented by expressions of the form 'C_i' and actions by expressions of the form 'A_i'. Thus, a set of principles would look something like the following:

PO$_1$:   if x is C_1 at t, then x ought to do A_1 at t$'$
PO$_2$:   if x is C_2 at t, then x ought to do A_2 at t$'$

.
.
.

PO$_n$*:   if x is C_n at t, then x ought to do A_n at t$'$

where 'x is C_i' expresses what we would normally put by saying 'x is in C_i'; A_i may or may not be identical with A_j as may t with t$'$. In accordance with the above terminology, 'C_j'† can be called a total essential description.

[42] In building a bridge from the above to our problems, the first thing to note is that it would be at least as appropriate to represent first principles by the form

P$_i$:   O(x is C_i at t → x to do A_i at t$'$)

where the presence of 'O' at the beginning expresses the fact that the obligation is a conditional obligation, and that the involvement of the condition in the obligation is not external or *per accidens*.

[43] I developed this 'in principle' approach to normative principles in the late 1940's to clarify the problem of the 'conflict of duties' and the concept of a *prima facie* duty. According to this approach a *prima facie* principle of obligation would have the form

In the absence of over-riding factors, O(s‡ is f_1 at t → x to do A_j at t$'$).

The concept has both intensional and extensional aspects. The former concerns the existence of principles in which the concept of the circumstance, C_k, includes the concept of the circumstance factor f_i, where some of the principles specify an obligation to do A_j, while others specify an obligation to do something other than A_j. The extensional aspects concern the relative frequency of the *cases* of f_i to which the latter, 'over-riding,' principles apply.[6]

---

* [Eds.—Correction of 'PO$_m$' in original printing.]
† [Eds.—In Sellars's typescript, this is 'C_i'.]
‡ [Eds.—In the typescript, this variable is 'x' rather than 's'. Consistent with earlier principles such as P$_i$, we suspect that Sellars intended for this to be 'x' rather than 's'.]
[6] For an independent development of related distinctions see Nicholas Rescher's "Semantic Foundations for Conditional Permission," *Philosophical Studies,* forthcoming.

[44] For our present purposes, however, the above is not enough. Certain additional features of normative principles must be stressed which have not always been taken into account. The most obvious of these is (a) that the circumstances in which an action of a certain kind is to be done (according to a certain principle) at a certain time by a certain agent, do not include either the doing or the refraining from doing by the agent of *that action*. The point is a delicate one for, (b), the circumstances in which an action of a certain kind is to be done (according to the certain principle) often include as a circumstance factor the fact that the agent has performed an action of a certain (perhaps the same) kind—indeed, that he is performing an action of a certain (perhaps the same) kind—and the obligation may be to repeat the action in question, in which case there is a sense in which both the *circumstance* and the *what is to be done* may involve the 'same' action. But these subtleties are mentioned only to clear the way for the use of simpler paradigms to which they are not relevant. Thus, we shall be concerned with cases in which the agent's obligation to do something, B, at t′ rests, in part, on the circumstance factor that he has done something else, A, at t.

[45] The next thing to note is, (c) that expressions for circumstance factors and expressions for actions as things to be done have fundamentally different grammars, even in those cases where a circumstance factor consists in an action's having been performed. This latter point is simply a restatement of the main theme of the opening section of this paper. Notice finally, (d), that principles are designed to authorize practical arguments of the form

s is C_i
Therefore, s ought to do A_i

(where, for simplicity, the time variable has been absorbed into the expressions for circumstance and action). Thus, if we represent the principle as

$O(x$ is $C_i \rightarrow x$ to do $A_i)$,

the argument schema, made fully explicit becomes

$O(s$ is $C_i \rightarrow s$ to do $A_i)$
s is C_i
Therefore $O(s$ to do $A_i)$.

I have commented above on both the appropriateness of putting the 'O' at the beginning of a statement of conditional obligation, and the pressure to do so which results from the search for embracing rubrics (e.g. x ought to bring it about that...; it ought to be the case that...) by the use of which a large variety of obligation statements can be represented. The present point is simply that whatever *other* arguments normative principles may function in—and there are *others*—their primary purpose is to permit the detachment of a normative conclusion when a factual premise is supplied. It is, as was pointed out above, the transparency of 'O' with respect to the indicative antecedent 'x is C_i' which makes the form of this argument essentially a matter of *modus ponens*, as in the alternative, but philosophically less illuminating, rubric

x is $C_i \rightarrow$ O(x to do A_j)
x is C_i
Therefore O(x to do A_j).

[46] One final point before we come to grips once again with our paradoxes. It is well said that probability is always relative to the evidence.[7] A similar feature holds of obligation. It is always relative to its grounds. Again, probability involves a principle of total evidence. Commitment to the statement that h has probability p because of evidence e involves commitment not only to the idea that e obtains but also that it is the total evidence at hand. Analogous points hold of obligation. Thus

O(x to do A_j), *because* s is in such and such a circumstance

implies that the circumstance *is* such-and-such, and that *being such-and-such* is an empirical specification of a 'normatively relevant circumstance' in the sense defined.

Let us embody these points in our symbolism by representing

x ought to do A_j *because* x is C_i

as

O(x to do A)/x is C_i

where the principle which is being applied is

O(x is $C_i \rightarrow$ x to do A_j).

VI

[47] The fact that obligations are relative to circumstance specifications is the key to the solution of our puzzles. To show this, let me postulate the following three principles of obligation:

---

[7] That categorical statements of probability may nevertheless in a legitimate sense be detached, I have argued in "Induction As Vindication," *Philosophy of Science,* XXXI (1964):197–231.

PO-1: $O(x \text{ is } C_1 \to x \text{ to } [go \bullet (go \to tell)])$
PO-2: $O(x \text{ is } \{C_1 \bullet goes\} \to x \text{ to tell})$
PO-3: $O(x \text{ is } \{C_1 \bullet \text{ does not go}\} \to x \text{ not to tell})$

where '$\{C_1 \bullet goes\}$' or, more abstractly, '$\{C_1 \bullet \vdash g\}$' represents (roughly) that complete circumstance which differs from C_1 in that whereas C_1 includes neither a *going* by x nor a *refraining from going* by x *at the time when* (by the application of the principle) *going is to be done*, $\{C_1 \bullet goes\}$ includes a circumstance factor which *is* a going by x at the time when, relative to C_1, going was to be done. Clearly the concept requires polishing, but it will do for our purposes.

[48] To these principles of obligation, let me add a higher order principle

PPO-1:   If doing A logically implies doing B, then '$O(x \text{ is } C_i \to x \text{ to do A})$' implies '$O(x \text{ is } C_i \to x \text{ to do B})$'

PPO-1 is, in view of what we have just said, a special case of our original P_O, which was to the effect that if doing one thing logically implies doing another, the obligation to do the former implies the obligation to do the latter.

[49] This new higher order principle, PPO-1, enables us to derive from PO-1 the three consequent-partial, dependent principles.

DPO-1.1 $O(x \text{ is } C_1 \to x \text{ to go})$
DPO-1.2 $O(x \text{ is } C_1 \to x \text{ to } [go \to tell])$
DPO-1.3 $O(x \text{ is } C_1 \to x \text{ to tell})$

[50] The question might be raised, Do we need the converse higher order rules

PPO-2   if Oa and Ob, then $O(a \bullet b)$
PPO-3   if $O(x \text{ is } C_i \to x \text{ to do } A_i)$ and $O(x \text{ is } C_i \to x \text{ to do } A_j)$ then $O(x \text{ is } C_i \to x \text{ to do } [A_i \bullet A_j])$?

The answer is as I see it, that properly understood, such principles do no harm, but, at the level of first principles, the purported conclusion must actually be prior to the premises. Thus, in the case of PPO-2, it is proper to conjoin 'Oa' and 'Ob' without explicitly relativizing them to circumstances, only where the *same* circumstance is understood. And from 'Oa/$C_i \bullet$ Ob/C_j' ($C_i \neq C_j$) no conclusion of the form 'O (a $\bullet$ b) /C_k' can be drawn. On the other hand where the circumstance is the same, the ultimate principle in which they are grounded must also be the same. Indeed, this principle must be such that from it, together with factual information, a conclusion of the form roughly represented by 'O(a $\bullet$ b)' can be directly derived without going through PPO-2.

[51] With these principles in mind, let us take another look at the go-tell paradox as it was formulated on p. 321 above. This formulation, it will be remembered, made use of the principle:

Ib′: if $O(x$ to do $A)$ and $O(x$ to do$[A \to B])$, then $O(x$ to do $B)$.

It will also be remembered that from the premises

(1′) $O(s$ to go$)$
(2′) $O(s$ to $[\text{go} \to \text{tell}])$

we derived

(5′) $O(s$ to tell$)$ (1′),(2′),Ib′

while from the premises

(3′) s does not go $\to O(s$ not to tell$)$
(4′) s does not go

we derived, by *modus ponens*

(6′) $O(s$ not to tell$)$.

[52] We are now in a position to see where the trouble lies. For, when the argument is made fully explicit, we see that the second premise, (2′), must rest on

DPO-1.2 $O(x$ is $C_1 \to x$ to $[\text{go} \to \text{tell}])$

for only if it does can the circumstances presupposed by '$O(x$ to go$)$' and '$O(x$ to $[\text{go} \to \text{tell}])$' be the same, namely C_1. There is, of course, in the neighborhood, the obligation expressed by

$$O(x \text{ to } [\vdash\text{go} \to \text{tell}])$$

but this, being equivalent to

$$O(x \text{ goes} \to x \text{ to tell})$$

points to a principle which we might initially formulate as

$$O(x \text{ is } C_1 \to (x \text{ goes} \to x \text{ to tell}))$$

but which, when put in standard form, turns out to be

PO-2 $O(x \text{ is } \{C_1 \bullet \text{goes}\} \to x \text{ to tell})$.

This principle however cannot be mobilized without contradicting the presupposition of the first premise, i.e. that the circumstances are C_1. Thus step (5') can be reached only in the form

(5'a)   O(x to tell)/s is C_1.*

As for step (6'), it involves an appeal to the principle

PO-3:   O(x is $\{C_1 \bullet$ does not go$\} \to$ x not to tell)

and consequently can be reached only in the form

(6'a)   O(x not to tell)/s is $\{C_1 \bullet$ does not go$\}$.

[53] As we have now reconstructed it, therefore, step (5) of the original argument involves the premise that the circumstance is C_1, whereas step (6) involves the premise that the circumstance is *not* C_1 but rather $\{C_1 \bullet$ does not go$\}$.[8] Thus the original argument, as modified to fit Ib', can derive contradictory conclusions from seemingly compatible premises only because, when made explicit, the premises are actually incompatible. The argument becomes

(0)	s is C_1	Premise
(1)	O(s to go)	(0),DPO-1.1
(2)	O(s to[go $\to$ tell])	(0),DPO-1.2
(3)	O(s is $\{C_1 \bullet$ does not go$\} \to$ s not to tell)	PO-3
(3')	s is $\{C_1 \bullet$ does not go$\} \to$ O(s not to tell)	Alternative form of (3)
(4)	s does not go	Premise
(4')	s is $\{C_1 \bullet$ does not go$\}$	(0),(4),Def. of '[$C_1 \bullet$ does not go]'
(5)	O(s to tell)	(1),(2),Ib'
(6)	O(s not to tell)	(3'),(4'),MP.

---

* [Eds—It is unclear in 5'a (and in 6'a, which follows shortly) if Sellars meant for both variables to read 'x' or 's'.]

[8] It is important to bear in mind that although there is a sense in which '$\{C_1 \bullet$ does not go$\}$' involves 'C_1', there is an equally important sense in which it does not. For although, by the convention in terms of which it was introduced, it mentions the circumstance factors involved in C_1, it does not specify them as the total set of relevant factors, as does 'C_1' *simpliciter*. The parallel with a possible convention according to which '$\{E \bullet e_j\}$' refers to new total evidence which involves the previous total evidence E is clear.

The inconsistent premises are (0) and (4′). The conclusions (5) and (6) are inconsistent not only by virtue of their explicit form, but because they have incompatible presuppositions by virtue of having, *implicitly*, the forms

(5′) $O(s \text{ to tell})/s$ is C_1

and

(6′) $O(s \text{ not to tell})/s$ is $\{C_1 \bullet \text{does not go}\}$.

[54] Notice that instead of appealing to DPO-1.1 and DPO-1.2 and using Ib′ in the form

Ib″: If $O(x \text{ to } A)/x$ is C_i and $O(x \text{ to } [A \rightarrow B])/x$ is C_i then $O(x \text{ to } B)/x$ is C_i,

we could have appealed directly to DPO-1.3, deriving (5) as follows

(0) s is C_1
(5) $O(s \text{ to tell})$ (0),DPO-1.3.

In this case, the only specifically deontic second level principle we would have used would have been that which enabled us to derive DPO-1.3 from PO-1, namely PPO-1.

VII

[55] We are now in a position to assess the intuitive claims of principle Ia according to which

$$O(a) \bullet O(a \rightarrow b') \rightarrow O(b).$$

Interpreted as

Ia-1 $O(a)/C_i \bullet O(a \rightarrow b')/C_i \rightarrow O(b)/C_i$

it is unsound. But consider

Ia-2 $O(a)/C_i \bullet O(a \rightarrow b')/C_i \rightarrow O(b)/\{C_i \bullet \vdash a\}$.

This is a valid principle, but close inspection reveals that it rests on the principle that

$$O(a \to b')/C_i$$

entails and is entailed by

$$O(b)/\{C_i \bullet \vdash a\}$$

Thus, if one ought to do b, if a is the case, as determined by a principle which specifies the circumstances as C_i then one ought to do b as determined by a principle which specifies the circumstances as $\{C_i \bullet \vdash a\}$. If one ought to tell if one goes because the circumstances are C_j, then one ought to tell if the circumstances are $\{C_i \bullet \text{goes}\}$. Reflection shows that the categorical assertion of 'O(b)' requires the assertion of 'a' and the use of modus ponens. Since the circumstances of a particular action cannot be both C_i and $\{C_i \bullet \vdash a\}$—save in the trivial case where the doing of a is morally irrelevant—the acceptance of Ia-2 does not generate the go-tell paradox, and amounts to no more than the propriety of locating 'conditions' of action either in the obligation statement itself or in the presupposed circumstance, with corresponding changes in the formulation of the relevant principles.

VIII

[56] Let us now return to Chisholm's first paradox and see if our distinctions help us here as well. It will be remembered that the argument went

(1) $O(\sim s)$ Premise
(2) s Premise
(3) $\sim s \to \bullet \sim s \lor b$*   Add.
(4) $\sim s \to \bullet s \to b$ (3), Def '$\to$'
(5) $O(s \to b)$ (1),(4),P_O

where P_O is

P_O: If x logically implies y, then $O(x)$ implies $O(y)$

How is (5) to be understood? In terms of our distinctions is it

(5.1) $O(s \to b')$ $= s \to O(b')$

---

* [Eds.—Correction of
$\sim s \to \bullet s \lor b$
in original printing.]

or

(5.2) $O(s \to b)'$?

If we move immediately to the finer grained level of analysis, is it

(5.1′) O(Jones steals → Jones to A)

or

(5.2′) O(Jones to [steal → A])?

where 'A' stands for any action kind one we like, say 'make no restitution.'
[57] Now, if our argument to date is correct, the principle which must be operating at this level of analysis is

PPO-1′: If doing A logically implies doing B, then 'O(x does A)/s is C_i' implies 'O(x does B)/x is C_i'

for this is where we are led if we follow PPO-1. But this tells us that at the finer grained level, assuming a relevant principle (PO-4) to the effect that stealing is wrong, the argument becomes

(0) Jones is C_2 Premise
(1′) O(Jones not to steal) i.e.
     O(Jones not to steal)/Jones is C_2 (0),PO-4
(3′) Not stealing logically implies
     either not stealing or A   Add.
(4′) Not stealing logically implies
     [stealing → A]   Def. '→'
(5′) O(Jones[steal → A]) i.e.
     O(Jones to[steal → A])/
     Jones is C_2 (1′),(4′),PPO-1′

Can we now use premise (2) in its fine grained form, i.e.

(2′) Jones has stolen

to make the step

(6′) O(Jones to A)?

i.e. to conclude that Jones ought to make no restitution? To do this we need the principle:

PPO-4   If x does A and if O(x to do[A → B]) then O(x to do B).

It will not, however, have escaped the reader's notice that if we treat (6′) as we did (1′) and (5′) by construing it as

$$O(\text{Jones to do A})/\text{Jones is } C_2$$

then it would not follow that

$$O(\text{Jones to A})/\text{Jones has stolen.}$$

We must surely think of having stolen as a morally relevant factor, for we realize that the paradox arises because in the background is a *prima facie* obligation to make restitution *if one has stolen*.

[58] Thus we know that

$$\text{Jones is } C_2$$

is incompatible with

$$\text{Jones is } \{C_2 \bullet \text{ has stolen}\}$$

where the stealing is the stealing he ought not to have done.

[59] The obvious move is to restrict PPO-4 to those cases where the ground of the obligation to do [A → B] is a circumstance (not a mere circumstance factor) which is compatible[9] with, in the sense that it can include, a doing of A by x at the relevant time. This restriction excludes the paradoxical case. That is, as long as he has not yet stolen, the obligation not to steal entails the obligation to not-steal-or-whatever, and hence the obligation to-if-steal-then whatever. But once he has stolen, the obligation not to do that particular stealing no longer applies, but moves into the past tense (Jones ought not to have stolen), and the *prima facie* obligation to make restitution takes over (if we can assume it not to be overridden by unusual circumstance factors). And the key circumstance factor relevant to this *prima facie* obligation is the fact of having stolen.

---

[9] One is reminded of Goodman's puzzle about cotenability and the lines along which it is to be resolved. See my "Counterfactuals, Dispositions and the Causal Modalities," *Minnesota Studies in the Philosophy of Science*, II, eds. Herbert Feigl, Michael Scriven and Grover Maxwell (Minneapolis, 1957).

[60] If we move from the finer grained analysis to the level at which we use the rubric 'it ought to be the case that...', we now see that step (5) is to be interpreted as having the form

(5.2) $O(s \to b)'$

rather than

(5.1) $O(s \to b')$

which latter is equivalent to '$s \to O(b)'$.' The paradox proceeds as before if we permit ourselves to use the factual premise

(2) s

to generate

(6) $O(b)$ (5.2),(2),PPO-4'

where PPO-4' is an unrestricted principle to the effect that

> PPO-4': If p and $O(p \to q)'$ be cotenable[10] in the sense that 'p' is compatible with the circumstance on which the ought-to-be ness of the conditional is grounded.

IX

[61] We are now in a position to see that if we extend P_O, in that form which explicitly concerns the ought-to-be of states of affairs, i.e.

P_1: If p logically implies q then $O(p)'$ implies $O(q)'$,

to cover cases of implication relative to an asserted condition or, as it might be called, an assumption, then PPO-4' is no longer needed as a special principle.

[62] The concept of implication relative to an assumption can be given the following informal explanation. Where

$p \cdot r$ logically implies q

---

[10] See note 9.

we can also say

$$p \text{ would imply, if r were the case, } q$$

which we may present by the schema

$$p \models^r q.$$

This amounts to the idea that if r were the case then the inference

$$p$$
$$\text{Therefore } q$$

would be justified. If, now, we add to the above the assumption that r is actually the case, we have

$$p \text{ implies } q, \textit{ because } r \text{ is the case}$$

which tells us that the inference

$$p$$
$$\text{Therefore } q$$

is justified, because r is the case. This we may represent by the schema

$$p \models^{/r} q$$

Where the / before 'r' indicates that r is asserted to be the case.

[63] If, now, we so use 'implies' that it covers the case of implication relative to an assumption, then from the tautological character of

$$p \bullet p \to q : \to q$$

we can derive first

$$p \to q \models^p q$$

and hence, by a suitable form of our putative generalized form of P_1,

$$O (p \to q)' \models^p O(q)',$$

which might be read

$$O(p \to q)' \text{ would imply } O(q)', \text{ if p were the case}$$

and, secondly, where the assumption that p is made,

$$p \to q \, \llcorner^{/p} q$$

which, given a principle to the effect that

$$\text{if } \alpha \, \llcorner^{/\gamma} \beta \quad \text{then } O(\alpha)' \, \llcorner^{/\gamma} O(\beta)' \, *$$

(where 'α', 'β' and 'γ' represent prepositional expressions), generates

$$O(p \to q)' \, \llcorner^{/p} O(q)'.$$

If, now, we extend the term 'implies' to cover such cases our generalized principle becomes

$$P_2: \text{if } \alpha \text{ implies } \beta \text{ then } O(\alpha)' \text{ implies } O(\beta)'.$$

The requirement that the assumption on which the implication rests be normatively cotenable with the ground of $O(\alpha)'$ must, of course, be retained, if paradox is to be avoided. But if this is done, and if suitable requirements pertaining to causal cotenability are forthcoming, there is hope that we can extend P_2 to cover causal as well as logical implication, i.e. so interpret 'implies' that it covers (as it actually does in ordinary usage) any relation which authorizes inference.

[64] But while our treatment of ought-to-do arguments was reasonably intuitive, the situation with respect to ought-to-be arguments is not so clear. Our generalized form of P_O raises difficulties which cannot, it seems, be met even by requiring a 'normative cotenability' of factual premises with the grounds of the normative premises—whatever this might mean when spelled out in greater detail.

---

* [Eds.—Correction of
$A(\alpha)' \, \llcorner^{/\gamma} O(\beta)'$
in original printing.]

(1) $O(g \bullet (g \to t))'$ premise
(2) $O(\sim g \to (\sim t)')$
     $= \sim g \to O(\sim t)'$ premise
(3) $\sim g$ premise
(4) $g \bullet (g \to t)$ implies t logical truth
(5) $O(g \bullet (g \to t))'$ implies $O(t)'$ (4),P_2
(6) $O(t)'$ (1),(5),MP
(7) $O(\sim t)'$ (2),(3),MP

If, now the go-tell paradox is reformulated so as to bring out the grounds on which the normative premises rest by transposing the relevant ought-to-do principles in to ought-to-bes OB-1 and OB-2, the argument begins somewhat as follows

(0) D_1 premise
(00) $D_1 \to O(g \bullet (g \to t))'$ application of OB-1
(1) $O(g \bullet (g \to t))'$ /D_1 (0),(00),MP
(2) $D_1 \bullet \sim g: \to O(\sim t)'$ application of OB-2
(3) $D_1 \bullet \sim g$ premise

If we now take a line like the one we took before we would say that premise (3), now necessary to derive $O(\sim t)'$, is inconsistent with the idea that D_1 is the total essential description of the situation on which, given the ought-be principle OB-1, $O(g \bullet (g \to t))'$ is grounded.

[65] But since we are no longer talking about what ought to be done at a given time in the circumstances which then obtain, but, rather, about what ought to be the case given that certain states of affairs are the case, *regardless* of time, it is not so intuitive that a total essential description which grounds

$$O(g \bullet (g \to t))'$$

can't include $\sim g$. Surely, it might be said, the fact that the world doesn't include the state of affairs which is Jones' going is perfectly compatible with the ought-to-be of that going. The objection, however, is an *ignoratio*. For one can grant *this* compatibility, as indeed one must, while insisting that the grounds of the ought-to-be of a state of affairs cannot include the *is* (or the *is not*) of that state of affairs. The principle thus recommends itself that since ought-to-bes are relative to an assumed total essential description adequate to mobilize a principle, no premise be added in the course of an argument which could not be included in this description. Since the descriptions of which we are speaking are in rarified 'first principle' terms, the spelling out of this requirement involves a discussion of the ways in which more "concrete" descriptions can cause trouble by implying essential descriptions which violate this requirement.

[66] If the total essential description on which the ought-to-be of $(g \bullet (g \to t))'$ rests cannot include either g or not-g, we can have both

$$O(g \bullet g \to t)' \qquad /D_1$$

and hence

$$O(t)' \qquad /D_1$$

and

$$O(\sim t)' \qquad /D_2$$

where D_2 includes not-g.

[67] It might be asked, how can both

$$O(t)' \qquad /D_1$$

and

$$O(\sim t)' \qquad /D_2$$

be true? for they include incompatible commitments, the one to D_1, the other to D_2, as the total relevant description. The answer to this challenge would seem to be that the property of being a total relevant description is relative to the complete set of principles. And since one of these principles concerns the ought-to-be of (a going and a telling, if going), given a danger, the corresponding description cannot include, in addition to the danger, *that* going or *that* telling, if going. Hence the assertion of this description does not conflict with the assertion of a description which enables the application of a principle concerning the ought-to-be of a not-telling, given a not-going.

[68] Needless to say, in actual argument we do not give anything that looks even remotely like a total essential description, let alone a total specific description, of a situation with respect to which the question

$$O(p)'?$$

has arisen. Nor do we actually spell out the ought-to-be principles which would realize the demands we have placed on principles "in principle." But the above "in principle" considerations do function in our arguments, in that we stipulate that certain facts are "all that is relevant" and hence that nothing over-rides the *prima facie* ought-to-be which rests on them. Thus when any factual premise is introduced in the course of the argument, the question "is it relevant to the original question

$$O(p)'?"$$

arises, and if the answer is yes, then the argument must begin anew, rather than simply continue.

X

[69] Another notorious difficulty confronts our permissive principle, P_2. Consider the argument

(1) It ought to be that Tom's cut be bandaged [$O(b)'$]
(2) Tom's cut is bandaged implies Tom has a cut [b implies c]
(3) It ought to be that Tom have a cut [$O(c)'$].

This argument, spelled out in our formalism, becomes

(1) $O(b)'$ premise
(2) b implies c   premise
(3) $O(b)'$ implies $O(c)'$ (2),P_2
(4) $O(c)'$ (1),(3),MP

The finger of suspicion points directly at P_2. Can it be exonerated? Notice, to begin with, that the logical form of the first premise is not obvious. How exactly does Tom's cut get into the ought-to-be? In what sense, if any, is it part of the 'target'? Clearly in some sense (1) implies that Tom has a cut, but not that it is bandaged; and the target seems to be the bandaging but not the existence of the cut. This suggests that it has the form

$$O(c \cdot b'), [=c \cdot O(b)']$$

where 'b' has been reformulated to omit any reference to a cut and this reference is separately made by 'c'. Consider, now

It ought to be that Tom's hand, which has been cut, be bandaged.

This premise would have the form in question, and would not generate the *original* paradoxical conclusion—though it would generate a puzzle of its own. Thus we would have

(1) $O(c \cdot b')$ premise
(2) $c \cdot O(b)'$ (1) rewritten
(3) $O(b)'$ (2) Simp.
(4) b implies Tom has a hand [h]   conceptual truth
(5) $O(b)'$ implies $O(h)'$ (4),P_2
(6) $O(h)'$ (5),(3),MP.

The conclusion tells us that it ought to be that Tom have a hand.

[70] In order to pry more deeply into this situation, let us, as on a previous occasion, consider the ground and principle on which the cut-bandage ought-to-be rests. The first thing to note is that when put in first principle form these ought-to-bes have the form

$$O(\alpha)' \quad /D_i \quad OB_i$$

where α does not imply that D_i is the case, although there is a sense in which $O(\alpha)'$ implies something of the sort. Let me explain in terms of the ought-to-be of repaying of a loan. We can describe the repaying as a repaying, which logically implies a borrowing, or we can describe it as a transferring of a sum of money, which does not. But though the existence of a transferring of money does not imply the existence of a borrowing, the *ought-to-be* of the transfer implies a disjunction of ground-descriptions in some of which a reference to borrowing will occur. Thus the requirement that the description be in first principle terms insures that the structures of the premises will be such that where the application of the first principle gives us

$$O(D_i \to \alpha') \;[=D_i \to O(\alpha)']$$

and this is combined with the assertion of the ground D_i, yielding

$$O(D_i) \cdot O(D_i \to \alpha')^*$$

or, which is equivalent to it,

---

* [Eds—Correction of
   $O(D_i \cdot O(D_i \to \alpha')$
in original printing.]

$$O(D_i \bullet (D_i \to \alpha'))$$

and hence, by P_2 and simplification, both

$$O(\alpha)' \qquad /D_i$$

and

$$O(D_i \bullet \alpha') \quad /D_i.$$

[71] There will nevertheless be no implication of the 'good samaritan' type

$$\alpha \to \beta$$

to generate a *paradoxical*

$$O(\beta)'$$

We would, indeed, have

$$O(\alpha) \text{ implies } D_i \vee \ldots D_j$$

(for an ought-to-be must have a total ground), but this does not permit a move to

$$O(D_i \vee \ldots D_j)'$$

though independent principles, i.e. principles other than that mobilized by the original premise, might well tell us, for example, that

$$O(D_i)'$$

or (for that matter)

$$O(\sim D_i)'$$

The moral of this is that in formulating an ought-to-be we must beware of combining with the essential description of the state of affairs which ought-to-be any proposition which implies the obtaining of a state of affairs p which is an element of the total ground of the ought-to-be (or an empirical specification of such an element). Schematically, we must avoid the move from

$O(p \bullet q \bullet r \ldots a')$ $\qquad$ $p \bullet q \bullet r \ldots = D_i$

to

$O(q \bullet r \ldots (p \bullet a)')$.

[72] At this point the more general objection might be raised, what about the fact given your P_2 it follows from

O (dollars be transferred) $\qquad$ /D_1

that

O(there be such things as dollars) $\qquad$ /D_1.

This is indeed, not as paradoxical as a conclusion to the effect that

O(there be a borrowing)

as in an earlier example, but it is, none the less, a puzzle. Surely, however, the puzzle, such as it is, arises from the fact that dollars are specific bearers of economic value. If we move to 'first principle' level, there seems to be no puzzle about the existence of contractual obligations implying that there are ways of fullfilling them.

[73] What about the following?

O(Tom receives $10.00) $\qquad$ /D_i
Therefore, O(there be such a person as Tom) /D_i.

One way of coping with this is to argue that the total essential description D_i doesn't imply that the logical subject of the ought-to-be exists or exists at the relevant time. Hence the ought-to-be mobilized by D_i contains a *hypothetical* reference to the subject of the ought-to-be. Thus, we might conceive of the principle as yielding something like

if D_i, and if Tom is still around, then it ought to be that he receive $10.00

or, schematically,

$\qquad$ $D_i \bullet$ Tom exists $\to$ O(Tom receive $10.00) where the criteria of the referring expression 'Tom' are put in normatively essential terms. It seems wise to put this by saying that

$$O(S \text{ be } P) \; [=O(S \text{ is } P)']$$

like

$$S \text{ is } P$$

implies (presupposes, in something like Strawson's sense) that there is something which satisfies the relevant criteria for being referred to as S.

[74] Can we not, indeed, say that it is properly

$$O(S \text{ be } P)$$

or, in our symbolism,

$$O(S \text{ is } P)'$$

rather than S be P—a possible reading of (S is P)'—*by itself* which implies (or presupposes) that S exists? If so then our permissive principle P_2 would pass this test as well.

[75] But we are not yet at the end of our troubles. For we have permitted causal as well as logical implications to evoke P_2. Thus consider the argument schema

(1) $O(\alpha)'$ /D_i OB_i
(2) α causally implies β
(3) $O(\alpha)'$ implies $O(\beta)'$ P_2
(4) $O(\beta)'$ (1),(3),MP

The conclusion appears paradoxical where we are inclined to say that β ought not to be the case.

[76] But with respect to what principle? For if, as seems reasonable, in deciding that, all things considered, a certain state of affairs ought to be the case, the causal as well as the logical implications of that state of affairs are to be taken into account, then the fact that α causally implies β will be relevant to the question whether or not α ought to be. Thus, if α ought to be, it ought to be *in spite of* the fact that α causally implies β; i.e. the fact that β *prima facie* ought not to be is overridden by the *prima facie* ought-to-be of α. Thus what is primarily implied by D_i, on the assumption that it is the total relevant description, will be, at least,

$$O(\alpha \bullet \beta)'$$

and the above argument simply makes explicit the fact that, on the assumption that D_i is the total relevant description, the three propositions

$O(\alpha)$	/D_i	OB_i
$\sim O(\beta)$	/D_i	OB_i
α causally implies β		

constitute an inconsistent triad.

XI

[77] We have not yet exploited the full permissiveness of P_2, for we have not yet considered an example of 'implication relative to an assumption.' Let us so formulate Chisholm's first paradox that it provides such an example.

(1)	$O(\sim s)$	premise
(2)	s	premise
(3)	$\sim s$ implies $\sim s \vee b$	Add.
(4)	$\sim s$ implies $s \rightarrow b$	(3), Def. '$\rightarrow$'
(5)	$O(\sim s)'$ implies $O(s \rightarrow b)'$*	(4), P_2
(6)	$O(s \rightarrow b)'$	(1),(5), MP†
(7)	$s \bullet (s \rightarrow b)$ implies b	Theorem
(8)	$s \rightarrow b \,\llcorner^s b$	(7), Def. '$\llcorner$'
(9)	$s \rightarrow b \,\llcorner^{/s} b$	(2), (8), Def. '$\llcorner^{/}$'
(10)	$s \rightarrow b$ implies b	(9), Def. 'implies'
(11)	$O(s \rightarrow b)'$ implies $O(b)'$	(10), P_2
(12)	$O(b)'$	(6), (11), MP.

[78] We seem to have derived a conclusion to the effect that any state of affairs we please ought to be, from premises which are consistent. Our finer grained analysis of this paradox has given us a shrewd idea of what the trouble is. Clearly we want *some* principle connecting an inferential tie between α and β with an inferential tie

---

* [Eds.—Correction of
$O(\sim s)'$ implies $O(x \rightarrow b)'$
in original printing.]
† [Eds.—Correction of
(5), MP
in original printing.]

between either the corresponding ought-to-be statements. What restrictions are to be imposed on the tie between α and β and what is to be their rationale? Once again the restrictions must concern the fact that oughts have grounds i.e. that

$$O(\alpha)'$$

has the form

$$O(\alpha)' \text{ because } D_i \text{ and } PFOB_i$$

or in our symbolism,

$$O(\alpha)' \quad /D_i \quad PFOB_i$$

where 'D_i'* asserts that conditions obtain such that the *prima facie* ought-to-be principle $PFOB_i$ applies and is not overridden. We must therefore rule out arguments which would take us from

$$O(\alpha)' \quad /D_i$$

to

$$O(\beta)' \quad / D_i,$$

by the use of assumptions which are inconsistent with the idea that D_i is such as to mobilize an overriding ought-to-be principle.

[79] This objective can be achieved by keeping our principle P_2 and adding the proviso:

> provided that the implication of β by α has no assumption which either implies that α obtains or does not obtain, or, which when added to the assumption D_i on which $O(\alpha)'$ is grounded, would mobilize an overriding normative principle.

From this vantage point the paradox is undermined, as before, by spelling out the argument in such a way as to make all assumptions explicit, thus by placing them on the right hand side after '/'. The argument begins, straight-forwardly enough, as follows

---

* [Eds.—Original printing here reads 'D_1' instead of 'D_i'. However, Sellars's typescript reads 'D_i', and it seems that is what Sellars meant here.]

(0)	D_i		premise
(1)	$O(\sim s)'$	$/D_1$	(0), $PFOB_1$
(3)	$\sim s$ implies $\sim s \vee b$		Add. $\sim$
(4)	$(\sim s)$ implies $s \to b$		(3), Def. '$\to$'
(5)	$O(\sim s)$ implies $O(s \to b)'$		(4), P_2
(6)	$O(s \to b)'$		(1), (5), MP*
(7)	$s \bullet s \to b$ implies b		Theorem
(8)	$s \to b \mathrel{\llcorner}^s b$		(7), Def. '$\llcorner$'

Can we now mobilize premise (2) in such a way as to proceed

(2)	s		premise
(9)	$s \to b \mathrel{\llcorner}'^s b$	$/s$	(8), Def. '$\llcorner'$'
(10)	$s \to b$ implies $b^\dagger$	$/s$	(9), Def. 'implies'
(11)	$O(s \to b)'$ implies $O(b)'$	$/s$	(10), P_2
(12)	$O(b)'$	$/s$	(6), (11), MP

which concludes with the idea that on the assumption that s is the case, any state of affairs you please ought to be the case. But the original assumption D_1 on which $O(\sim s)'$ is grounded must be carried down, so that by the time we get to (9) the assumption is $D_1 \bullet s$. And, indeed, although held in abeyance, this assumption was confronted, in its role as premise, with D_1 from the very beginning. In other cases the assumption on which a conditional implication rests may be introduced covertly, i.e., without being laid down as an explicit premise. In any event, the argument violates the restriction we have placed on P_2, for s cannot be part of the ground of the ought-to-be of $\sim s$.

[80] An apparently more serious objection to the original formulation of our unrestricted principle, P_2, is that by using it one can prove that anything which *is* the case, *ought to be* the case. Thus consider the following argument

(1)	$O(p)'$	premise
(2)	q	premise
(3)	$p \bullet q$ logically implies $p \bullet q$	Theorem
(4)	$p \mathrel{\llcorner}^q p \bullet q$	(3) Def. '$\llcorner$'

---

* [Eds.—Correction of
   (2), (5), MP
in original printing.]
† [Eds.—Correction of
   $s \to b$ implies
in original printing.]

(5) $p \mathrel{\llcorner}^{/q} p \bullet q$ (2),(4) Def. '$\mathrel{\llcorner}$'
(6) p implies $p \bullet q$ (5), Def. 'implies'
(7) $O(p)'$ implies $O(p \bullet q)'$ (6), P_2
(8) $O(p \bullet q)'$ (1), (7), MP
(9) $p \bullet q$ logically implies q Theorem
(10) $O(p \bullet q)'$ implies $O(q)'$ P_2
(11) $O(q)'$ (8), (10), MP.

where q, being anything, might be, for example, the dropping of the first atomic bomb. When made explicit, however, the argument becomes,

(0) D_i premise
(1) $O(p)'$ /D_i (1), OB_i
(2) q premise
(3) $p \bullet q$ logically implies $p \bullet q$ Theorem
(4) $p \mathrel{\llcorner}^q p \bullet q$
(5) $p \mathrel{\llcorner}^{/q} p \bullet q$*   /q
(6) p implies $p \bullet q$ /q   (5), Def. 'implies'[†]

and the argument can continue only if D_i and q are cotenable, i.e., if q satisfies the restriction we have placed on P_2. If it does, then the conclusion is harmless, and nothing is involved but the need to regard everything which *is* the case as a potential disrupter of the claim that something else *ought to be* the case.

---

* [Eds.—Correction of
$p \mathrel{\llcorner}^{/q}$
in original printing. The justification lines for premises (4) and (5) are blank in the original printing; presumably if filled they would be identical to the justification lines for (4) and (5) in the directly preceding argument.]
† [Eds.—Correction of
Def. 'implies'
in original printing.]

16
On Reasoning about Values

I

1. In spite of strong currents to the contrary, perceptual metaphors—intuition, contemplation, insight—continue to dominate our conception of logical and mathematical knowledge. Knowing is knowing *that*, and to know that is to *see*. Even when metaphors from the language of practice are allowed a place in the sun, as when we speak of *constructing* numbers, propositions and proofs, the elements are seen to fit and the outcome is a structure to be, if not *seen*, at least *grasped*.

2. Obviously there is good sense in these metaphors. Logical thinking not only *inquires* but, on occasion, *achieves*. There are, as James put it, perchings as well as flights. Contemplation in the ordinary sense may not be the pure, unchanging act of the perennial philosophy, but it is at least a perceptual consummation and is fitted for its metaphorical role.

3. One *sees* that contradictory propositions cannot both be true. And, in particular cases, this and other *insights* guide our thinking. Is this because we have a, perhaps innate, perhaps instilled, dislike for the illogical? Is it a contingent matter of fact that we prefer "*p* or not-*p*" to "*p* and not-*p*"? Or is it, perhaps, a synthetic necessary truth that the awareness of inconsistency arouses disbelief and stills desires?

4. However the fact is to be understood, it seems clear that there is a real connection between knowing logical truths and being disposed *positively* to believe the implications of our beliefs and, *negatively* not to think logically incoherent thoughts.

5. Of course, any such connection must be a matter of "other things being equal" propensities, for many different factors enter into the explanation of a course of thought. But if the awareness of logical truth did not, as such, exert pressure on the mind and contribute to shaping thought, it would be only *per accidens* that we were rational.

6. These considerations can be expanded to include another dimension—one which, I believe, provides a vantage point from which to get an over-view of our problem. For what is involved is not only the awareness of logical truths, but the having of logical concepts and the understanding of logical words. These, too, imply the above propensities. Bluntly put, to understand such words as

"and," "or," "not," "if," "then," "all," and "some" is to be disposed to conform (*ceteris paribus*, of course) to the simpler principles of elementary logic.

7. It is obviously true that the meaning of a logical word is a function of its contribution to the implications of sentences in which it occurs. That this is true, at least in part, of the meaning of *every* word may be less obvious, but is certainly of equal importance.

8. Most words contribute specific implications pertaining to specific subject matters. Thus the word "bachelor" in

Jones is a bachelor

brings it about that this sentence implies

Jones is unmarried.

And the attributive "large" in

Mickey is a large mouse

brings it about that this sentence implies

Mickey is large for a mouse.

9. There are however certain words which, like logical words, contribute *general* kinds of implication to the sentences in which they occur. Thus, consider the present tense copula in

There *is* thunder.

It brings it about that the sentence implies

There *will have been* thunder.

To "understand the meaning" of these words is to "see" these implications, and to have the corresponding propensities pertaining to inference and belief.

10. To "see" that

'P' implies 'Q'

is, *ceteris paribus*, to have the propensity to believe 'Q' if one believes 'P.' But since, if 'P' implies 'Q,' "not-Q" implies "not-P", it is equally to have the tendency to believe "not-P" if one believes "not-Q."

11. Thus to "see" that 'P' implies 'Q' is, in part, to have the propensity not to believe both 'P' and "not-Q"—which leaves open the following combinations of belief in 'P' or belief in "not-P," with belief in 'Q' or belief in "not-Q"

believing 'P' and believing 'Q'
believing "not-P" and believing 'Q'
believing "not-P" and believing "not-Q."

Which of these combinations is realized is not, of course, determined by "seeing" the implication.[1]

12. For example

"X is made of lead" implies "X is heavy for its size,"

so that "seeing" this implication, I will have a propensity *not to believe* with respect to a certain object, O, that

O is made of lead and O is not heavy for its size.

which leaves open for belief,

1. O is made of lead and O is heavy for its size
2. O is not made of lead and O is heavy for its size
3. O is not made of lead and O is not heavy for its size.

Which of these beliefs I arrive at will be a function of other factors, e.g.

A. I scratch O and it looks like lead. I will tend to believe in the *first* alternative.
B. I heft O and it doesn't feel heavy for its size.
   I will tend to believe in the *third* alternative.
C. I scratch O and it looks like lead;
   I heft O and it doesn't feel heavy for its size.
   I will tend to believe in the *second* alternative.[2]

---

[1] If we also take into account the fact that to "see" that 'P' implies 'Q' is also, in part, to have the propensity to believe 'Q' if one believes 'P' and to believe "not-P" if one believes "not-Q" then we must also take into account the combinations in which there is an *absence of belief* with respect to either 'P' or "not-P" or an *absence of belief* with respect to either 'Q' or "not-Q." Of these 12 possible combinations only two conflict with the propensities in question, namely, (a), "*believing 'P' and not-believing 'Q,'*" and (b), "*not-believing 'not-P' and believing 'not-Q.'*" Which of the remaining combinations is realized is, again, not determined by "seeing" the implication.

[2] Of course, if I scratch O and it looks like lead and heft O but it doesn't feel heavy for its size, I just *might* be on the road to a revolutionary disconfirmation of the implication itself.

13. On the other hand, I may have no encounter with O, and no evidence pertaining to its composition or specific gravity. In this case if I have any belief about O connected with "seeing" the above implication, it will be that

O is not both made of lead and not heavy for its size.

II

14. The examples I have chosen so far have come from discourse directed toward what *is* the case, as contrasted with what ought to *be* the case—discourse about *facts* as contrasted with *values*. In this connection we have considered

   (a) subject-matter independent implications which accrue to sentences from logical words.
   (b) subject-matter pervasive implications which accrue to sentences from words pertaining to spatial and temporal location.
   (c) implications which are tied to specific subject matters, as in the example just discussed.

15. This classification, highly informal, makes no claim to be either tidy or complete. Indeed the second category was introduced to prepare the way for a further category of subject-matter pervasive implications—implications which accrue to sentences by virtue of the fact that they contain expressions of a kind to which I have not yet directed attention, but which will be at the center of the stage for the remainder of this essay.

16. Consider the word "would" as it occurs in

Would that Jones were here!

It is a word which has a very general function. Sentences involving it, as we say, *express a wish*. In using it, one isn't *describing* an object. Rather, one is, in a suitably broad sense, *expressing an attitude* towards some conceivable object or state of affairs.

17. What are the logical or, should I say, conceptual implications of this word? What implications does it contribute to sentences in which it occurs?

18. In the first place, a person who candidly or sincerely says

Would that Jones were here!

can be expected, other things being equal, to try to bring it about that Jones is here. Thus, if a person comes to think it *possible* to bring it about that Jones is here they[3] will—other things being equal—attempt to do so.

---

[3] In this essay, to avoid the awkward 'he/she' I shall use the somewhat idiosyncratic but by no means non-existent construction 'a person...they' and 'one...they.'

19. Thus one who sincerely says

> Would that Jones were here!

and believes that by doing A, Jones's presence can be secured, will, other things being equal, do (or try to do) A.

20. This, of course, raises the question, What are the 'other things' which must be 'equal'? In a sense this question is *the* topic of the argument to follow.

21. Let us try the following ideas on for size:

(a) The person must believe that there is a real possibility that Jones will be present.
(b) The person must believe that by doing A they will be doing something which contributes to Jones's presence.
(c) The person must have no desire which overrides their wish that Jones were here.

22. The *first* is connected with the difference between a wish and a desire.

The *second* is connected with the difference between a *desire* for a state of affairs and the *intention* to do an action which might bring it about.

The *third* is connected with the difference between what one wishes, *some* things considered, and what one wishes *more* things considered.

Let us take up the latter two in order.

23. We began our discussion of practical implications with *wishes*, which, as such, are conceptually remote from action—even though they have a conceptual tie with action. As we saw, other things being equal, "x wishes that-p" implies "x tries to bring it about that-p." Let us now turn our attention to purposes which are very close to action, thus

> I will take the 4PM flight to Houston today.

where this expresses an *intention*, and is not a mere prediction. Compare

> Jones will take the 4PM flight to Houston today.

24. In the former context "will" is a cousin of "would that." Its implicative tie with action is to be found in the fact that, *ceteris paribus*,

> Jones candidly says "I will do A in 10 minutes"

implies

> Jones does A in 10 minutes

which involves the idea that, *ceteris paribus*,

> Jones candidly says "I will do *A right now*"

implies

> Jones does *A right now*.

Here "*ceteris paribus*" guards against the possibility that, for example, Jones is paralyzed or about to be struck dead, and presumes that *A* is an action which Jones is in a position to do.

25. Thus we can lay down the principle

> *Ceteris paribus*, people carry out their here-now intentions

which is a special case of

> *Ceteris paribus*, people do what they intend to do

and this, in turn, of

> *Ceteris paribus*, people realize their purposes.

III

26. A bit of linguistic regimentation is in order. The above use of "will"—the use in which it expresses a *purpose* or *intention*—is limited in Standard English to first person action contexts, thus

> I will do *A*.

But we can, of course, have intentions which pertain to the obtaining of states of affairs other than our own actions.

27. Thus it can be my purpose that my children have a good education. Obviously I can *wish* it:

> Would that my children have a good education.

But if I think it *possible* that this state of affairs might obtain, I can *desire* it. Interestingly enough the Standard English way of expressing *this* desire is by the use of the auxiliary "shall," thus

My children shall have a good education

where this, as before, is no mere prediction, but expresses the intention or purpose that this be the case. To achieve a uniformity of representation, i.e. to avoid a constant shuffle between "will" and "shall," I shall use the auxiliary "shall" in all my examples to represent the expression of an intention. After all, it is so used in connection with most of the kinds of intention in which I shall be interested; and, furthermore, "will" in Standard English serves for the most part to form the future indicative.

28. Thus, instead of

I *will* do A

I shall use

I *shall* do A

to bring it in line with

It *shall* be the case that my children have a good education.

29. Furthermore, since I am not particularly concerned with *mere* wishes (i.e. with cases in which one is "favorably disposed toward a state of affairs" but doesn't think that it can be realized, I shall concern myself with the logic of *intentions*, and hence with *the logic of my regimented "shall."*

30. The most fundamental principle of this logic is a reformulation of an earlier point about "will." It is to the effect that

Jones candidly says "I shall do A *here and now*"

implies, *ceteris paribus*,

Jones *does* A here and now

Put more abstractly, the principle affirms a connection between

having intentions to do A here and now

and

doings of A.

31. The next logical feature to be noted concerns the connection between the statements

> My children *shall* have a good education
> My children *will* have a good education only if I put aside money

and

> I *shall* put money aside.

32. Before examining the *logic* of this sequence in depth, let me make an obvious, but nevertheless crucially important, point about intentions. It is essential to distinguish between the autobiographical *factual* statement

> I intend to do *A*

which *ascribes* an intention to me, as

> Jones intends to do *A*

ascribes an intention to Jones, and, on the other hand,

> I *shall* do *A*

which (in our regimented idiolect) *expresses* that intention.

33. Notice, however, that in the first person case the functions of the two sentences overlap. Thus

> I intend to do *A*

not merely *ascribes* an intention to me, but also, for reasons familiar to students of Moore's Paradox[4] serves to *express* it. In the third person case, thus

> He, Jones, intends to do *A*

the statement obviously does not express Jones's intention to do *A*. *I* can express an intention *about Jones doing A* by saying

> Jones *shall* do *A*

---

[4] I.e. The logical oddity of "It is raining, but I don't believe it."

which would express my intention that Jones does *A*, and is equivalent to

It *shall* be the case that Jones does *A*.

34. It is therefore essential to distinguish between what is implied by an *intention* and what is implied by the fact that a person *has* the intention—just as it is essential to distinguish between what is implied by a *belief* (i.e. the proposition believed) and what is implied by the fact that a person *has the belief* (believes the proposition).

35. Let us equate for present purposes

Jones believes that-*p*, e.g. that it is raining

with

Jones, if in a candid frame of mind, would assent to "It is raining" (or its counterpart in Jones's idiolect)

and correspondingly

Jones intends that-*p* be the case, e.g. that his children get a good education

with

Jones, if in a candid frame of mind, would assent to "My children *shall* get a good education."

36. Thus we can distinguish between the implications of the sentence

It is raining

e.g.

The streets are getting wet

and the implications of the sentence

Jones believes that it is raining

e.g.

Jones expects to get wet, if he ventures outside

and, correspondingly, between the implications of the sentence

My children *shall* get a good education

e.g.

My children *shall* go to college

and the implications of the sentence

Jones intends that his children get a good education

e.g.

Jones believes that his children are docile.

37. Notice that if one proposition 'P' implies another proposition, 'Q,' it doesn't follow that a person who believes 'P' also believes 'Q,' but only that they are *subject to criticism* on logical grounds if they believe 'P' and either don't believe 'Q' or believe "not-Q."

38. Similarly if one intention implies another intention it doesn't follow that a person who has the former also has the latter, but only that they are subject to criticism on logical grounds if they have the one and don't have the other or have the contradictory intention.[5]

39. Thus, the intention expressed by

"I shall eat a healthy diet"

implies (by virtue of the principles of nutrition)

"I shall eat complete proteins"

but a person may very well have the former intention without having the latter.

40. This example calls attention to the fact that just as one proposition may imply another without a person realizing that it does, so one intention may imply another without a person realizing that it does.

41. Of course, when it comes to actual cases of *reasoning*, the only implications that enter the psychological picture are the implications which the reasoner takes

---

[5] Notice that in most contexts in which I refer to intentions, the latter are to be construed as *intention candidates* or *intendibles*. The context should make it clear whether I am discussing a *had* intention or a mere *intendible*. Roughly, intentions stand to intendings as propositions to believings.

into account. But from the standpoint of logical criticism and evaluation, the implications are what they are whether or not the reasoner takes them into account.

IV

42. With the above distinctions in mind, let us return to the main line of the argument.

43. We were interested in the special implications which attach to the word "shall." Of these the most basic was that which relates the intention expressed by "I shall do *A* here and now" to action. We can now see that this implication relates the *having* of such an intention, to *action*. Thus

> Jones *has* the intention to do *A* here and now

implies, *ceteris paribus*,[6]

> Jones does *A* here and now.

Also

> Jones intends to do *A* in 10 minutes

implies, *ceteris paribus*,

> Jones will do *A* in 10 minutes

(if, e.g. he doesn't change his mind).

44. From these implications we must distinguish those other implications relating to "shall" which concern *the intentions themselves* and not the fact that someone *has them*.

45. Thus, consider

> My children *shall* get a good education

or, in general,

> It *shall* be the case that-*p*.

---

[6] The qualification is obviously necessary to take into account, for example, the possibility that the actual circumstances prevent Jones from doing *A*, or that he unwittingly becomes paralyzed.

Intuitively, this implies

> I shall (*ceteris paribus*) do that which contributes to bringing it about that my children get a good education.

The "*ceteris paribus*" is clearly necessary, although its exact role remains to be discussed. The crucial point, however, which it helps to highlight, is that there is a conceptual tie between

> It *shall be the case that*...

and

> I *shall do*...

Abstractly put, intentions that something be the case imply intentions to do.[7]

V

46. With one exception to be noted in a moment, and one possible exception to be considered near the end of the argument, these are the implications which pertain directly to "shall" and specify what might be called its conceptual grammar. Expressions of intention have other kinds of implications, but, as we shall see, they are grounded in implications between indicatives.

47. The fundamental principle connecting indicative implications with the logic of "shall" is

> S-Imp.: if 'P' implies 'Q,' then "It shall be the case that-P" implies "It shall be the case that-Q".[8]

It is because of this dimension that the logic of purposes (and values) is largely derivative from the logic of facts.

48. The fundamental simplicity of this encompassing principle enables me to cover a substantial amount of ground by means of a few regimented

---

[7] It will shortly become clear that the distinctive feature of such implication lies in the connection between 'It shall be the case that I do A' and 'I shall do A.' The remaining features of the above example, including the *ceteris paribus* clause, reflect the implicative pressures which relate one 'shall be the case' to another, i.e. which transcend the distinction between 'shall be' and 'shall do.'

[8] This principle can be formulated as a biconditional, but I forbear to do so lest I open the door to misunderstandings, based on other things I have written, which there would be no time to alleviate.

examples. But first a word or two about the nature and scope of the principle are in order.

49. In the first place, implication is to be understood as a relation which authorizes inference and, more generally, serves as a criterion for the compatibility of beliefs and, correspondingly, of intentions, along the lines discussed in the opening sections. We noted there, without attempting a complete classification, that implications may be logical in the narrower sense—subject matter independent—or they may arise from categorial features of the concepts involved, or, as in the case of causal connections, they may be tied to specific subject matters. The latter clearly play a central role in practical reasoning.

50. In the last case it is important to distinguish between causal implications which are explicitly general and can be formulated as lawlike statements, and causal implications, which, while presupposing the truth of *some* lawlike statement, do not specify these statements—which may not even be at hand. Thus we may *know* that *in circumstances like these*, 'P' causally implies 'Q' without knowing exactly what it is about *these* circumstances by virtue of which the implication obtains.

51. The task of botanizing implications and the ways in which they depend on other items for their existence and their knowability is, as I have implied, a difficult one. Indeed, it is, to a surprising extent, unfinished business. Fortunately, it will be sufficient for my purposes to rely on our intuitive sense of which matter-of-factual propositions imply which other matter-of-factual propositions, and concentrate on the relation of such matter-of-factual implications to practical reasoning.

VI

52. Another framework point remains to be made which is fundamental to all that follows. It is a point which has seemed to many whose judgement I respect[9] to fly in the face of reason. The implications between intentions which arise from implications pertaining to matters of fact concern only the *content* of intentions and not their status *as intentions*.

53. This thesis is the upshot of the distinctions which were drawn in sections III and IV above. It is reflected in the fact that, as I shall argue, negation, for example, enters into the expression of an intention only as part of what is governed by the "shall" rubric.

---

[9] I have particularly in mind Bruce Aune and Hector Castañeda, who have repeatedly taken me to task on this matter.

54. Thus, in our idiolect, we have

I shall do A   It shall be the case that-p
I shall *not* do A   It shall *not* be the case that-p[10]

but *not*

I *not*-shall do A
It *not*-shall be the case that-p

e.g.

My children not-shall have a good education.

55. If we regiment

I shall do A

as

Shall [I do A]

and

It shall be the case that-p[11]

as

Shall be [p]

then we would have negations

Shall [I not do A]

and

Shall be [not-p]

---

[10] For our purposes, "It shall *not* be the case that-p" is equivalent to "It shall be the case that *not-p*." Problems which concern the relation between "It is true that *not-p*" and "It is not true that-p" which arise in connection with the distinction between the Principle of Bi-Valence and the Principle of Excluded Middle have no bearing on the problem to be discussed concerning a possible double occurrence of negation in expressions of intention.

[11] Note that the construction "It shall be the case that-p" takes advantage of the logical equivalence of 'p' and "It is the case that-p" to permit "shall" to exhibit its role of auxiliary verb, which "Shall [p]" does not do.

but not

Not-shall [I do A]

nor

Not shall be [p].

56. To generalize this claim, before submitting it to closer scrutiny, logical operators do not occur outside expressions of intention, or, to put it in other words, expressions of intention do not occur within the scope of logical constants and quantifiers. Thus we do not have

Shall be [p] *or* shall be [q]

as contrasted with

Shall be [p or q]

nor

For all x, shall be [if x is a future danger, then I will escape x]

as contrasted with

Shall be [*for all x*, if x is a future danger, then I will escape x].

57. This conceptual point is *not* a consequence of the fact that expressions of intention are neither true nor false for, as I pointed out in "Thought and Action,"[12] they do have the semantical values, *realized* and *not-realized* depending on whether the correlated expression of belief is true or false. The fact, however, that they have these semantical values does *nothing* to counter the idea that an expression of intention *as an expression of intention* can only be negative by virtue of having a negative *content*. "Not-shall [I do A]" is false in the radical sense of conceptually incoherent. The fact, when it is a fact, that my intention to do A is not *realized* does not make the (nonsensical) 'not-shall [I do A]' true.[13]

58. It is time, now, to take into account a fact which *seems* to make nonsense of the above claim. I have in mind the obvious fact that expressions of intention can

---

[12] In Keith Lehrer, ed., *Freedom and Determinism*, New York, 1966. [Eds.—TA is Ch. 7 of this volume.]
[13] We shall see, towards the end of the argument, that there is a place for another pair of values for expressions of intention, namely *reasonable* and *unreasonable*, but this neither requires nor permits an external negation.

occur in a text along with other expressions of intention and, indeed, with declarative sentences which are expressions of belief.

59. Again, is it not a fact that

I intend to do *A* and I intend to do *B*

makes perfectly good sense? If so, should not

Shall [I do *A*] and shall [I do *B*]

also make good sense. But the former makes sense *qua* conjunction of "I intend to do *A*" and "I intend to do *B*" in their intention *ascribing* roles (see paragraph 33 above). It by no means follows that the same is true when they are replaced by primary expressions of intention.

60. Another possible source of confusion is the fact that the punctuated *text*

My children *shall* have a good education.
I have already begun to put money aside,

can easily be confused with the conjunctive statement

My children *shall* have a good education *and* I have already begun to put money aside.

The latter would be a *prima facie* counter-example to the thesis I have been advancing.

61. Can it seriously be maintained that the only sound conjunctive expression in the neighborhood has the form

Shall be [*p* and *q*]?

62. To see why the answer is Yes, it is necessary to reflect on a feature of ordinary logic which is so familiar that it is treated with contempt: Conjunction Introduction (CI).

63. I called attention above to the distinction between a text and a conjunction. An example of a text would be

The weather was clear. The temperature was low.

Here there is *punctuation* but no *logical connective*, no "and." We have *two* sentences rather than *one conjunctive* sentence. CI tells us that '*p*' and '*q*' together imply '*p* and *q*.'

It is a principle of implication which takes one from separate sentences to a single conjunctive sentence.
64. Thus the above *text* implies the conjunction

The weather was clear *and* the temperature was low.

65. In the opening paragraphs of this essay I commented on the connection of logical concepts and implications with propensities to believe and not to believe, and on the pressures they exert in the direction of coherence and the absence of inconsistency. In CI we find a related pressure, this time one which constrains us to bring together statements and beliefs which, though they *coexist*, are not confronting one another, and combine them into a functional unity in which they rub shoulders; into a single statement or belief whose implications can be drawn in accordance with logical principles.[14]
66. Before discussing the bearing of CI on practical reasoning, on reasoning about purposes and values, one more principle which concerns an implication tied directly to "shall" (in my idiolect) remains to be introduced.

So-Be-It: "Shall be [φ]" and '*p*' imply "Shall be [φ and *p*]" where 'φ' is a formula which may or may not be logically complex.

Implications conforming to this principle push in the direction of getting relevant beliefs into the scope of our purposes and intentions, and hence into the scope of practical reasoning.[15]
67. Notice that So-be-it requires that

Shall be [I will do *A*]

where "will" is the Standard "shall," not have the same sense as

Shall [I do *A*].

---

[14] There are also the pressures and constraints of relevance, about which much would have to be said to get significantly above the intuitive level. If I engage in hand-waving in introducing a pressure of relevance, I am at least in good company

[15] It is important not to confuse the concept of *intention* with that of *desire* or *motive*. A state of affairs can be a constituent of an intention without being an object of desire or a source of motivation. For an examination of key topics pertaining to the relations between the concepts *desire*, *intention*, and *satisfaction*, see my "Thought and Action" in Lehrer (ed.), *Freedom and Determinism*, New York 1966. See particularly Section III. [Eds.—TA is Ch. 7 of this volume.]

My doing A in the future can enter into an intention either as a *target*[16] of an intention or, *via* So Be It, as something which I believe will happen, as when, confronted by a highwayman, I believe, fatalistically, that I will hand over my money. A similar distinction might be drawn between

Shall be [my lawn will be mowed]

and

Shall be [my lawn be mowed]

where the infinitive indicates that this content is not present in the intention by virtue of So-be-it. But these niceties would not contribute to the solution of the problems with which I am concerned.

68. These considerations support the principle

Shall-Be: "Shall [I do A]" implies "Shall be [I do A]."

Note that this infinitive phrase "I do A" presents the action as up to one, and not, like "Shall be [I will do A]," *sub specie* So-Be-It. Thus, the converse of Shall-Be as formulated above is also true, which it would not be if the implicate were "Shall be [I will do A]." It is Shall-Be which, together with S-IMP underwrites the intuition expressed in paragraph 45 above.

69. It might be thought that the distinction between what I *intend* to do and what I *believe I will do* is "merely psychological." This is of a piece with claiming that *in general* the distinction between believing and intending is "merely psychological." It is the "merely," of course, which is out of place. Is the difference between *expecting* ("It *will* rain") and *retrospecting* ("It *did* rain") "merely psychological"—or are there *conceptual* points to be made about tenses? Clearly the latter, and this is the parallel on which I have insisted.

70. As for CI, in practical contexts, it is simply a consequence of the above basic principle, where this has been generalized to cover the implications of two or more sentences, thus

If 'P_1,' 'P_2,' ... 'P_n' together imply 'Q,' then "Shall be [P_1]," "Shall be [P_2]," ... "Shall be [P_n]" together imply "Shall be [Q]"

In the case of CI we would have

---

[16] Roughly speaking, the target of an intention is that which is being viewed *sub specie* "up to me." For an elaboration of this distinction see "Some Reflections on Contrary to Duty Imperatives," *Nous* 1, 1967, pp. 315 ff. For its application to an argument of Castañeda's, see "Volitions Re-affirmed," *Action Theory*, ed. by Myles Brand and Douglas Walton (Dordrecht, 1976), p. 62. For a *caveat* on degrees of up-to-me-ness, see paragraph 82 below. [Eds.—CDI is Ch. 15 of this volume, and VR is Ch. 10.]

'P_1,' 'P_2' ... 'P_n' together imply 'P_1 and P_2 and ... and P_n'

hence

"Shall be [P_1]," "Shall be [P_2] ," ... "Shall be [P_n]" together imply "Shall be [P_1 and P_2 ... and P_n]"

VII

71. The fact that So-be-it involves the introduction of beliefs into the contents of intentions calls for a review of our regimented formulation of intendibles.

72. One must distinguish between those constituents of a complex intendible which are there merely as, so to speak, factual connective tissue, i.e. items which one who adopts the intention believes to be the case, and those constituents which constitute the *target* of the intention, i.e. the presence of which makes it an intention.

73. One might think that the distinction in question coincides with that between items which are present as sources of motivation, either positive or negative, and items which are motivationally neutral. But that would be a mistake.

74. In the first place, a constituent of a scenario can be something that is believed to be the case and yet be directly relevant to a preference between that scenario and its alternatives, thus

Shall be [... Jones has insulted me *and* if I see him, I frown ...]

and

Shall be [... Jones has insulted me *and* if I see him, I smile ...]

75. And in the second place, one wants to allow for the possibility that one and the same intention can be carried out for different motives. This requires a way of representing intentions which abstract as far as possible from the distinction between motivating and non-motivating factors.

76. We must distinguish between questions concerning the nature and logic of intentions, and questions concerning the explanation of why a person adopts a certain intention or prefers one course of events to another.

77. Of course, the representation of an intention can be combined with a representation of motivational structure by the use of such words and phrases as "in order to," "in spite of" and "because"—thus,

Shall be [I do A in order to bring about X, in spite of the fact that X would also bring about Y, because X would enable me to do B].

78. What we are looking for is a way of representing complex intentions which abstract from the structure introduced by such words and phrases.

79. From this point of view, the *basic* distinction between intention-factors is that between those which are viewed *sub specie* "up-to-me," and those which are viewed as *given*, i.e. those items which are there by virtue of So-be-it. And this distinction can be represented grammatically by using verbs in the infinitive for the former, and statement-making sentential forms for the latter, thus

Shall be [I do A][17]

as contrasted with

Shall be [... and I *will do A*]

and

Shall be [my lawn *be* mowed]

as contrasted with

Shall be [... and my lawn *will be* mowed].

80. Notice that in each case the So-be-it item is introduced by " ... *and*." This is because every intention must have at least one "up-to-me" constituent.

81. The "up-to-me"-ness of intendible constituents can be made explicit by prefixing them with the conditional "if it is up to me," thus

Shall be [if it is up to me, I do A]
Shall be [if it is up to me, my lawn be mowed].

This antecedent would get affirmed by virtue of So-be-it.

82. Problems concerning the criteria for determining what is up to an agent and, perhaps, to what degree or extent are notoriously difficult. Fortunately (like issues pertaining to probability) they do not bear on the central topics of this paper—so I simply look them in the face and move on.

---

[17] Notice that the entire conditional
 If I do A, I will be punished
is a statement-making form, and hence is appropriately changed into an intention by So-be-it, thus
 Shall be [... If I do A, I will be punished].

VIII

83. We are now off and running. With the principles already presented (along with constraints of relevance) we have a *logical* pressure to bring our *separate* intentions together with our *separate* beliefs into one picture or scenario. Thus consider the text,

> I *shall* go downtown tomorrow, if the weather is clear. The weather will be clear. If the weather is clear, the streets will be crowded. If the streets are crowded, I will be miserable.

This text implies, by virtue of Shall-Be, So-be-it and CI, the *conjunctive* intention

> Shall be [I go downtown tomorrow, if the weather is clear *and* the weather will be clear *and* if the weather is clear, the streets will be crowded *and* if the streets are crowded, I be miserable].

84. Notice that of the contents of this intention, "If the weather is clear tomorrow, I go downtown" is present as an *intendible* derived by CI from the conditional intention at the beginning of the text, whereas "if the weather is clear, the streets will be crowded" is a propositional constituent *via* So-be-it. Notice also that while "if the streets are crowded, I will be miserable" is introduced as a whole *via* So-be-it, its consequent is represented as an *intendible* state of affairs as being "up to me."

85. The above conjunctive intention, in turn, implies, by three subordinate uses of Modus Ponens, the intention

> Shall be [I go downtown tomorrow and be miserable].

I ask myself if I accept this intention. If I reject it, I am logically committed to rejecting either

> Shall be [I go downtown tomorrow]

or

> Shall be [I be miserable tomorrow].

Presumably I will reject the former.

86. Notice that I can also ask myself

> Is it really true that if the streets are crowded and I am there, I will be miserable?

and decide, on reflection, No; in which case that conjunct drops out and I am left with

> Shall be [I go downtown tomorrow if the weather is clear *and* the weather will be clear *and* if the weather is clear, the streets will be crowded]

which implies

> Shall be [I go downtown tomorrow *and* the streets will be crowded]

which, in turn implies, by simplification,

> Shall be [I go downtown tomorrow]

and, finally, since "shall be" is no longer serving to embrace So-be-it factors,

> Shall [I go downtown tomorrow]

which, if I accept it, is the intention to go downtown tomorrow.

87. Notice that it might occur to me as relevant that when my friend Jones is with me I am happy, even though the circumstances are otherwise unpleasant. Thus, even if I retain my belief that if the streets are crowded and I am there I will be unhappy in the *weaker* form

> If the streets are crowded, and I am there, then, *other things being as expected*, I will be unhappy.

I now see that other things are *not* equal in that

> If the streets are crowded and Jones is with me, I will not be unhappy.

88. At this point I may wish and, indeed, if the situation can be realized, intend that Jones be with me tomorrow. Furthermore, I may believe that Jones will be with me if and only if I invite him. So-be-it takes me to

> Shall be [Jones be with me *and* Jones will be with me if and only if I invite him]

I am confronted by the choice

> Shall be [I invite Jones *and* he be with me]?
> Shall be [I not invite Jones *and* he not be with me]?

If I opt for the former, simplification takes me to

Shall be [I invite Jones]

and, hence, by Shall-be (converse), to

Shall [I invite Jones].

89. The *fact that I intend* to invite him implies, by virtue of the basic principle pertaining to "shall" (paragraph 43), that *ceteris paribus* I will in point of fact invite him. Believing that other things are in fact equal, I can be expected to believe that I will invite him, and, hence, to believe that if I go downtown, Jones will be with me. So-be-it inserts this into the intention matrix as follows,

Shall be [If the weather is clear, I go downtown tomorrow *and* the weather will be clear *and* if the weather is clear, the streets will be crowded *and* if I go downtown, Jones will be with me *and* if the streets are crowded and Jones is with me, I be happy]

which implies

Shall be [I go downtown tomorrow *and* be happy]

which in turn implies

Shall [I go downtown tomorrow].

90. Of course, if I learn that Jones will not be able to accompany me, the question

Shall [I go downtown tomorrow]?

will be reopened—unless I am bored by the whole business.

91. The example we have been considering should remind us that an essential feature of practical reasoning is the fact that it constantly involves an appeal to preference.[18] This occurs when one is confronted by alternatives, thus

Shall I do *A*?
Shall I do *B*?

---

[18] For a more detailed account of preference, see "Thought and Action" in Keith Lehrer (ed.), *Freedom and Determinism*, especially pp. 113 ff. and pp. 131 ff. The role of CI was smuggled in under the name "the summative phrase." I there emphasize—which I do not here—that the summative phrase constructs alternatives each of which includes the implications of not choosing the others. [Eds.—TA is Ch. 7 of this volume.]

e.g.

> Shall I eat the yogurt?
> Shall I eat the ice cream sundae?

92. The following relevant considerations occur to me

> The yogurt is plain. Plain yogurt is blah.
> The yogurt has less calories.
> The ice cream sundae is very fattening.
> The ice cream sundae is very tasty.

CI and So-be-it expand the content of the above alternatives, thus

> Shall be [I eat the plain blah yogurt with few calories]?
> Shall be [I eat the tasty ice cream sundae which is very fattening]?

93. Confronted by these alternatives I may opt for one or the other, in which case that is my preference on the occasion. Or I may remain in a state of indecision, casting about for other alternatives or additional relevant considerations pertaining to the alternatives at hand. Thus it may occur to me that I have to work in the garden tomorrow, and so can stand a few more calories. The above alternative becomes

> Shall be [I eat the plain blah yogurt with few calories which I shall more than use up in the garden tomorrow]?
> Shall be [I eat the tasty ice cream sundae which, though very fattening *in general*, will not fatten me since I will use the calories up tomorrow working in the garden]?

The choice of the ice cream sundae is now humanly predictable. I opt for the latter alternative, which implies

> Shall be [I eat the ice cream sundae]

and, hence,

> Shall [I eat the ice cream sundae].

94. Thus CI together with So-be-it, takes our separate purposes and relevant beliefs and puts them together into encompassing alternatives:

1. Shall be [I do A at t, which means that...]?
2. Shall be [I do B at t, which means that...]?
3. Shall be [I do C at t, which means that...]?

The successive steps are

(a) elaboration by CI and So-be-it, and the drawing of implications
(b) choice, e.g. (2), or, continuing indecision
(c) simplification. Shall be [I do B at t]
(d) intention to act. Shall [I do B at t]

which, when time t comes (and I do not change my mind), generates a doing (or an attempt to do) B.

95. This picture is one according to which practical reasoning is essentially the process of elaborating alternative scenarios for a choice.

96. The *elaboration* is "rational." What about the choice? Is there any sense in which the choice can be "rational" over and above that in which it is so by virtue of being a choice between *rationally elaborated alternatives*, i.e. in which relevant considerations and relevant implications have been taken into account? Let me postpone this question until I have explored another line of thought.

IX

97. We have been considering implications between purposes or intentions

I_1 implies I_2

where I_1 is, for example, "Shall be [I go downtown tomorrow, if the weather is clear, and the weather will be clear]" and I_2, "Shall be [I go downtown tomorrow]." The implication tells us that the combination

Accepting I_1 and not accepting I_2 (or accepting the contradictory)

is unreasonable. Thus the combination

accepting "Shall be [I go downtown tomorrow, if it is clear *and* it will be clear]" and not accepting "Shall be [I go downtown tomorrow]" (or accepting "Shall be [I not go downtown tomorrow]")

is subject to logical criticism.

98. But, of course, the fact that the implication tells us that this combination is unreasonable tells me nothing about the reasonableness or unreasonableness of accepting I_1 or of accepting I_2.

99. The implication, however, can be interpreted as telling us that accepting

"Shall [I go downtown tomorrow]"

is reasonable *relative to* accepting

"Shall be [I go downtown tomorrow, if it is clear *and* it will be clear]."

Relative reasonableness, however, is not what we were looking for when asking our postponed question. What we had in mind was rather a reasonableness which is not in the above way relative—and which we might be tempted to characterize either as "absolute" or as "intrinsic."[19] Can we find it ? Let us follow Hume's example and beat about in the neighboring fields.

100. What is the relation between

I *shall* do A

and

I *ought* to do A (or I *should* do A)?

The answer to this question must surely run somewhat as follows: The latter makes a positive assessment of the intention expressed by the former.

101. Since to make a "positive assessment" of something amounts to characterizing it as in some sense *good*, and since there is clearly some sort of conceptual tie between "good" and "ought" (or "should"), as illustrated by the truistic feel of "one ought (or should) choose the good," the first fruit of our beating would seem to be that *if* we can get a grip on "ought" or "should," we might get a grip on "good," and, perhaps, on our "absolute" or "intrinsic" reasonableness as well.

102. Consider the statement

If Jones wants X, he should (ought to) do A

Clearly the underlying theme is that given Jones's circumstances, C, and a proper spelling out of just what it is that Jones wants,

"Jones gets X" implies "Jones does A"

---

[19] These two tags are, of course, provisional, for until we clarify the concept of relative reasonableness, it remains unclear what it is to be contrasted with.

or, equivalently,

"Jones's getting X" implies "Jones's doing A, if Jones is in C"

because, for example, a person's doing A is causally necessary for their getting X, if they are in C.

103. Suppose that Jones does want X, i.e. his purpose or intention is to get X; can we reason

If Jones wants X, he should (ought to) do A, since he is in C
Jones wants X
So, Jones should (or ought to) do A?

If so, we would have arrived at a positive *evaluation* of Jones's doing A from a *factual* premise (Jones "wants X") together with a premise the gist of which is a causal connection between an outcome and an action. In other words we would ostensibly have derived a *value* from matters of *fact*, an *ought* from *ises*.

104. But, of course, this is an illusion. We have simply run into another case of relative reasonableness. The hypothetical proposition

If Jones wants X, he ought to do A, if in C

which is based on, but not identical with, the causal implication in question, tells us that

"Shall [I, Jones, get X]" implies "Shall [I, Jones, do A if in C]"

i.e. that the intention

"Shall [I, Jones, do A, if in C]"

is reasonable relative to the intention

"Shall [I, Jones, get X]"

by virtue of the implication

a person's getting X implies their doing A if in C.

105. Thus, given that Jones wants X, i.e. intends "Shall [I get X]" all we are entitled to conclude is that

"Shall [I, Jones, do A]"

is implied by and hence reasonable relative to an intention which Jones actually has. But, again, this is not what we were looking for—though it may be all we can get. Nothing is implied about a "non-relative" reasonableness of getting X. In spite of the "oughts" and "shoulds" there is not the ghost of a hint as to how the intention to get X might be "non-relatively" reasonable.

106. Some light is, indeed, thrown on the goodness of objects and instrumentalities by the concept of relative reasonableness. Thus *part* of the conceptual tie between "good" and "should be chosen" is captured by so-called "hypothetical imperatives," i.e. statements of the form we have been considering. Clearly there is an intuitive connection between 'juicy apples are good" and "if a person wants enjoyable apples, they should choose juicy ones."

107. Yet, after all, we distinguish "goods" from "necessities (relative to a purpose)." Thus, *strictly speaking*, the core of

If Jones want S, he ought to do A

is

If Jones wants X he *must* do A

for that is the proper force of the implication on which it is grounded, which tells us that Jones doing A is a necessary condition of Jones getting X.

108. And the same is true of

If Jones wants an X which is φ, he should choose one which is ψ.

The "must" can be weakened by a *ceteris paribus* clause to allow for optional alternatives, but this root idea remains that of a necessary condition.

109. And, after all, there is an air of paradox about

If Jones wants to shoot people quietly, he should (ought to) use a silencer.

We would feel more comfortable with

If Jones wants to shoot people quietly, he must (would have to) use a silencer.

110. Reflection on this fact suggests that when either "ought" or "should" is used in the phrasing, the implication is that the "want" clause refers to a purpose which is in *some* way connected to an intrinsic good.

111. Thus we are willing to say that

If Jones wants to be healthy he should (ought to) eat a balanced diet where we think of eating a balanced diet as a good by virtue of its relation to health. More, however, seems to be involved than that the intention to eat a balanced diet is reasonable *relative to* the intention to be healthy, for the goodness of eating a balanced diet seems to be grounded in the *goodness* of health. Is health, in turn, a good by virtue of its relation to something else? Is not our search for a non-relative reasonableness equivalent to a search for an intrinsic good?

112. And, indeed, we do think of instrumentalities as *good* because we think of the intention to have them available as reasonable *relative to* an intrinsically good purpose. But what might such a purpose be?

113. And is the intrinsic goodness of a purpose (i.e. a *purposed—intended— state of affairs*) a matter of a *non-relative reasonableness* of the *purposing— intending*?

X

114. Consider the intention expressed by

Would that I lived a satisfying life all things considered.

It has long been argued[20] that *what* pattern of life would satisfy a given person is a question of *fact*—difficult to be sure, but *in principle* capable of being given an objective or, in a non-pejorative sense, scientific answer.

115. It has also been argued, for an equally long time, that *of necessity* a person does seek his own happiness. The *oddness* of the intention

Would that I did *not* lead a satisfying life, all things considered

has been construed as a matter of a *psychological* impossibility of having this intention.

116. Indeed there has been a tendency to think that as a matter of psychological necessity, all deliberate or reflective (as contrasted with *impulsive*) action is grounded in an intention of which

Would that I led a satisfying life, all things considered

---

[20] Since the time of the Platonic Socrates. For a more detailed analysis of the issues about to be raised, see "Reason and the Art of Living in Plato," in Dale Riepe (ed.), *Phenomenology and Natural Existence: Essays in Honor of Marvin Farber* (Albany), 1973 [reprinted as Chapter 1 in *Essays in Philosophy and Its History*] and "On Knowing the Better and Doing the Worse," *International Philosophical Quarterly*, vol. 10, 1970 [reprinted as Chapter 2 in EPH], and also Chapter 7 of *Science and Metaphysics*. [Eds.—RAL appears as Ch. 5 of this volume; KBDW appears as Ch. 13; OIM appears as Ch. 6 of this volume.]

is the over-riding constituent in the sense—explicated in terms of the distinctions I have been drawing—that in particular circumstances the rationally elaborated alternatives in which the idea of leading a satisfying life, all things considered, occurs, are *very* schematically,

(α) Shall be [I lead a satisfying life, all things considered, which means p *and* not-q and... *and* that I do A and that I do not do B]?
(β) Shall be [I do B which means that I not do A and q and not-p and... and that I not lead a satisfying life all things considered]

of which only the former can, as a matter of psychological necessity, be accepted.

117. Of the mistakes which spoil the insight contained in this tradition, the most obvious is that which posits that the intention

Shall be [I lead a satisfying life, all things considered]

is a constituent in all rationally elaborated alternatives (i.e. in all non-impulsive action).

118. Notice that the phrase "satisfying life all things considered" represents what the scholastics called a *formal* end. As such it has only such force in particular practical reasonings as a "namely rider" would provide. Thus the text of the above intention with respect to a particular occasion should read, schematically,

Shall be [I lead a satisfying life, all things—namely: $p, q, r, \ldots$—considered].

119. Yet there is a more basic mistake, as is shown by the appeal to psychological necessity. The reader will remember my *caveat*, in paragraph 69 above, against supposing that the difference between intending and believing is "merely psychological." A related point needs to be made here.

120. Is the oddness of accepting alternative (β) above a "mere" matter of psychological impossibility? Is one simply appealing to the principle "ought implies can" in the form "what can't be, can't be reasonable" to conclude that alternative (β) can't be reasonable? After all, it might be said, an intention can't be reasonable unless it can be had!

121. But, of course, it wouldn't follow from the non-reasonableness of (β) that (α) was reasonable.

122. And, indeed, in what sense could (α) be a *reasonable* intention? Perhaps because of the phrase "all things considered." For we have seen that the principle of taking all relevant facts and purposes into consideration is built into the *logic* of practical reasoning.

123. Thus it would seem that intentions which are arrived at by taking all relevant considerations into account are, in so far forth, reasonable.[21]

124. If, however, the formal intention

Shall [I promote my own happiness, all things considered]

were *intrinsically* reasonable, then the intentions which are implied by it would also be *reasonable, period*. This is to say, they would not merely be reasonable *on the hypothesis* that something else is reasonable, but reasonable *because that something else is reasonable*. We must distinguish between *categorical* reasonableness (of which intrinsic reasonableness is the prime mover) and *relative* (or *hypothetical*) reasonableness. Reasonableness (like theoremhood) can be simultaneously *categorical* and *derivative*.

125. And if all this is correct, then the idea that the intention that one lead a satisfying life is a psychologically necessary intention can be traced to a misconstrual of the connection, pointed out in the opening paragraphs of this essay, between "seeing" implications and having *ceteris paribus* propensities to exhibit uniformities in one's modes of thought.

126. Thus it is *not* psychologically impossible to opt for alternative (β). All we need say is that the "pressure of reason" is against it. And the source of this pressure lies *not* in the *formal end* "satisfying life all things considered," but in the conceptual pressure to include in the elaboration of *this* intention on *this* occasion all relevant *specific* considerations, i.e. to enrich the "namely" rider.

127. The "specific" considerations deemed relevant on any particular occasion will inevitably be, to a greater or lesser extent, fragmentary and generic. But this humanly unavoidable fact would be a flaw only in the practical reasoning of an angel.

XI

128. That it is not psychologically impossible to fly in the face of intentions having the formal structure "would that I led a satisfying life all things considered," is important, not only because it is true, but because it opens the door for a class of intentions which have logical features not yet considered, and which provide the framework for an understanding of the moral point of view.

---

[21] I leave to other occasions the problem of mobilizing such distinctions as those between *known* relevant considerations, *available* relevant considerations, *potentially available* relevant considerations, and between objective reasonableness, subjective reasonableness, etc. The point is to get reasonableness into the picture.

129. And, indeed, if one places the conceptual considerations advanced in the preceding section in the context of classical moral philosophy, it is immediately apparent that they constitute a sophisticated form of what has come to be called Rational Egoism according to which the fundamental intrinsic value is one's own happiness, all things considered.

130. Rational Egoism, of course—except in its most extreme form—acknowledges the existence of sympathy and benevolence, and even grants that sympathetic and benevolent purposes can be wide in scope and intense in feeling. Yet it denies that they can generate a mode of reasonableness which is other than the relative reasonableness of such hypothetical imperatives as

If one wants to help widows and orphans, one should, for example, support laws against fraud and embezzlement.

Intrinsic reasonableness, the Egoist argues, requires an over-arching purpose which can find a place for both self-oriented and other-oriented "particular" purposes—and this, it is argued, can only be provided by the pursuit of one's own happiness, all things considered.

131. Yet we saw that the "can" is suspect. Is it a matter of psychological possibility? That is, is Self Love the only over-arching purpose one *can* have? Or is Self Love the only over-arching purpose that can generate an intrinsic reasonableness? One suspects that by granting the existence of "particular" sympathetic and benevolent intentions, the Egoist has weakened the traditional argument from the supposed psychological impossibility of "cool hour" altruism. What, then, about reasonableness?

132. That informed self-interest and the moral point of view do, on occasion, conflict is a fact which is built into the human situation. To understand the nature and possibility of this conflict, we must take into account a further *dimension* of practical reasonableness—one which, indeed, is closely tied to the very nature of reasonableness itself.

133. The challenge we face is, in essence, the following: Can we preserve the general strategy of the argument to date, and yet take distinctively moral values into account? I think so, and I will begin to sketch a line of thought which, I believe, adds the necessary dimension to the logic of purposes and intentions.

134. Consider the wish,

Would that I were happy.

This wish is obviously I-centered. How exactly is this I-centeredness to be understood? What feature of the expression of the wish embodies it?

135. To begin with, there is the obvious fact that the subject matter of the wish is formulated by means of the context dependent referring expression "I." The belief expressed by

I am in Houston

is in the same way I-centered.

136. If Jones also says

I am in Houston

there is a sense in which he is saying the "same thing" I did and a sense in which he is saying something different. As Strawson would put it, he is using the same sentence to make a different statement. To this we could add that he is ascribing the same property, *being now in Houston*, to *himself* that I ascribed to *myself*.

137. Let us put this by saying that the wish and the belief are referentially I-centered.

138. Thus, if King Jones thinks

Shall be [I possess Paris]

and King Smith thinks

Shall be [I possess Paris]

they have, in a sense, the same intention, and, in a sense, different intentions. This fact makes possible a familiar witticism. Each can truthfully say: that which *he* wants, *I* want also.

139. From this perspective, the intention expressed by

Shall be [the nations remain at peace]

would not be referentially I-centered.[22] Yet if the argument of the early sections of this essay is correct, there is a way in which this expression of intention is *covertly* subject matter I-centered. For we found it to be a conceptual truth that, given that its being the case that-*p* implies my doing *A*,

It shall be the case that-*p*

implies, *ceteris paribus*,

---

[22] Of course the expression is *implicitly* I-centered in that it directly or indirectly involves the use of indicator words ("indexicals"). But tokens of spatial indexicals (e.g. "here") and temporal indexicals (e.g. "now") can have the same reference when used by different persons, whereas, truistically, "I" cannot. And the *important* way in which expressions of intention can be covertly I-centered, is tied to this latter fact.

I shall do A.

140. In other words, even though the manifest content of 'p' is not referentially I-centered, expressions of intention of the form

Shall be [p]

have, by virtue of the conceptual grammar of "shall," a conceptual tie to expressions of intention of the form

Shall [I do A]

which latter *is* referentially I-centered.

141. After all, it is a conceptual point about the universe of *intentions* that its *point d'appui* lies in intentions *to do* and, in the last analysis in the I-here-now intentions to do which are volitions, and, paralysis aside, culminate in action.

142. We might put this by saying that all intentions are explicitly or implicitly action I-referential.

143. To put it in this way, however, obscures the fact that although "in the last analysis" all action is action by individuals, and although all volition has "in the last analysis" the form

Shall [I do A here and now]

there is an important sense in which even such intentions can transcend I-centeredness.

144. The key point lies in the fact that one can think of oneself as a member of a group. This obvious truth is tied to certain features of the conceptual grammar of reference to groups.

145. I can refer to myself either verbally or *in foro interno* as Wilfrid Sellars, as the author of "Empiricism and the Philosophy of Mind," or as *I*.

146. Similarly I can refer to a group as the Society for the Prevention of Cruelty to Animals, as the organization which won the Pittsburgh Civic Medal last year, or I can refer to it as *we*. Which group is, on any occasion, referred to as *we* can be made explicit by a modifier, thus *we Texans, we members of the American Philosophical Association*, etc.

147. But before we can put these familiar points to good use, they must first be elaborated. We must take into account certain other features of the logical grammar of "we."

148. In the first place, there is the obvious fact that *we* includes *I*.

149. Then there is the related fact that actions can be ascribed to individuals not only where they are picked out by singular terms, e.g.

Socrates ran. The president ran

but also where they are referred to by using the apparatus of quantification, thus

Everybody ran

or, more interestingly,

Each of *us* ran.

150. Consider, therefore, the intention

Shall be [each of us will run a hard race].

Notice, in the first place, that this intention is *intersubjective* (with respect to *us*) in the sense that any of *us* can have *this* intention, where, *qua* state of affairs *intended* it is, in a strong sense, the *same*. In this respect it resembles

Shall be [the nations remain at peace]

151. But it has already been suggested that the latter is action I-centered. Thus, consider the dialogue

Jones: Shall be [the nations remain at peace]
Smith: Shall be [the nations remain at peace].

Although Jones and Smith are expressing a shareable state-of-affairs intention, the former, as expressed by Jones, implies, given certain relevant considerations,

Shall [I, Jones, do *A*]

and the latter

Shall [I, Smith, do *B*].[23]

152. We can put this by saying that a shareable state-of-affairs intention (where this amounts to more than a shareable *wish*) implies, for each person by whom it can be shared, referentially I-centered action intentions.
    153. Consider, next

---

[23] Remember that what is implied by Jones's (or Smith's) intention is implied by that intention whether or not Jones (or Smith) comes to have the implied intention.

(α) Shall be [each of us have a new car].

This subject-matter shareable (among *us*) intention obviously implies every intention the expression of which results from replacing "each of us" by a designation of a member of us, e.g. Tom, thus

(β) Shall be [Tom have a new car].

Thus, each person who has shareable intention (α) has an intention which implies intention (β), which is also a subject-matter shareable intention.

154. On the other hand, each person (e.g. Dick) who has intention (α) has an intention which implies for him an intention of the form, (γ)

(γ) Shall be [I, Dick, have a new car]

which, of course, is not a subject matter shareable intention.

155. We might be tempted to call it a referentially I-centered intention; and, indeed, to do so would be in accordance with our usage up to now. Yet if we consider it in relation to (α) which implies it, the phrase "I-centered" strikes us as inappropriate. For in *practical* contexts, the phrase "ego-centered" has an implication with respect to motivation which is inconsistent with the idea that Dick has reasoned

Shall be [each of *us* have a new car]
So, Shall be [*I*, Dick, will have a new car].

156. In his reasoning, so to speak, Dick has come into the picture as "one of us." We might, therefore, reformulate his intention as

Shall be [I, Dick, *because* I am one of us, have a new car].

Notice that here we are taking into account features of the content of intentions from which we have hitherto made abstraction. (See paragraphs 77-8.) It is important to realize that *because* is just as much a part of the *content* of the above intention as it is a part of the belief content expressed by

The Pirates should win *because* they are the better team

and has the same rationale.

157. Notice, next, that although (α) is a *state-of-affairs* shareable intention, it does not seem to be an *action shareable* intention, for as far as anything we have brought into the picture so far is concerned, its connection with action is *via* the fact that as a state of affairs intention it implies for each person who can share it,

e.g. Dick, given that Dick's promoting the state of affairs each *member of the group having a new car* implies *Dick's* doing *A*, e.g. contributing to a fund,

(δ)   Shall [I, Dick, contribute to the car fund][24]

158. We can put this by saying that an intention can be we-referential *qua state-of-affairs* intention, and yet be *action* I-centered.

159. This would be a special case of the idea that an intention can be shareable in its manifest content, thus

Shall be [the nations remain at peace],

and yet be action I-centered in the sense that all its implications with respect to intentions to do are of the form

Shall [I, S, do A]

XII

160. We have seen (paragraph 141-2 above) that in a sense all intentions are explicitly or implicitly action I-referential. We are now in a position to ask the framework question: Is there any way in which an intention can be not only *we*-referential, but *action* we-referential?

161. To answer this question, we must retrace our steps and remember that way back before the concept of *we*-intentions was introduced, it was noted that a person can envisage one of their actions *sub specie* So-be-it, as when, for example, I represent myself as handing over money to a highwayman, thus

Shall be [... *and* I will hand over the money]
So-be-it

which contrasts with the *sub specie* "up-to-me" intention

Shall [I keep my cool].

162. A scenario which contains the latter is *explicitly* action I-referential, for it contains my doing *A* as an intention *to do* rather than as (*via* So-be-it) a factual constituent of an intention.

---

[24] Given the facts of the matter, of course, it might imply that Harry *instead of contributing to the fund*, butters up his friend the automobile dealer.

163. Thus consider the difference between

    Shall be [... and most of us *will not resist temptation*]
                                                          So-be-it

and

    Shall [each of us *resist* temptation].

In the former, the action of resisting temptation enters into the intention as a constituent of a belief rather than as something intended.

164. Whereas in the latter, resisting comes in as something to be done. Thus the latter is surely the we-intention counterpart of the explicitly I-referential action intention

    Shall [I keep my cool].

165. Schematically, the difference is that between

    Shall be [... and each of us *will do A*, if in *C*]
                                                      So-be-it

and

    Shall [each of us *do A*, if in *C*].

166. The following is a perfectly coherent intention

    Shall be [each of us *do A and* most of us *will not do A*].[25]

167. It is essential to note that the intention

    Shall [*any* of us do *A*, if in *C*]

must not be confused with the intention

    Shall [*everyone* of us do *A*, if in *C*].

---

[25] The reader should reflect on the intention

    Shall [each of us *not take* the short cut this week unless more than ten of us will take it]

See my comment on the "generalization argument" in *Science and Metaphysics*, Chap. VII, sec. xiii. [Eds.—OIM, §§81–5, Ch. 6 of this volume.]

The latter is an intention which is realized *only if* everyone of us who is in C does A. The former is realized *even if* only a single one of us who is in C does A.[26]

168. It must also be carefully borne in mind that although the concept of a group intention and a group action is a perfectly legitimate one, the action we-referential intentions we are considering are intentions had *by individuals*. It is *individuals* who intend

Shall [each of *us* do A, if in C].

169. We have seen that the intendible constituents of an intention (as contrasted with the So-be-it constituents) are there *sub specie* "up to me." One might therefore be tempted to expostulate: "What *others* do is not up to *me*. How, then, can 'Shall [each of us do A]' express a proper intention, since 'each' refers to others than oneself?"

170. A superficial answer would point out that on occasion what another does is, at least to some extent up to me. That we can influence people is as relevant to practical reasoning as that we can influence sticks and stones.

171. The answer which meets the question, however, involves the fact (noted in paragraph 81) that to say that the intendible constituents of an intention are those which are present *sub specie* "up to me" is equivalent to accompanying them with the conditional "if it is up to me," thus

Shall be [if it is up to me, I do A].

172. Now "up to me" is the first person form of "up to X." Obviously other referring expressions can replace "X." Thus the correct answer to the above challenge consists in calling attention to the fact that the "up to the agent"ness of action we-referential intention is to be formulated as follows,

Shall [each of us, if it is up to *them*, do A]

and *this* in no way requires that what others do be up to *me*.

173. Notice, finally, that the circumstances in which each person is to act may include (*via* So-be-it) a reference to what it is believed that others will in point of fact do, thus

Shall [each of us pick up the torch, if the one of us to the right of them drops it]

---

[26] Thus, for

Shall [any of us do A, if in C]

to be a proper intendible, it need not be practically possible that everybody does A, if in C.

taken together with "My neighbor to the right has dropped the torch" implies, *via* Shall-be and So-be-it,

> Shall be [each of us pick up the torch if the one of us to the right of them drops it *and* my neighbor to the right has dropped it]

and hence, *via* the instantiation move from "each of us" to "I," Modus Ponens and Shall-be,

> Shall [I pick up the torch].

XIII

174. We are almost through with the necessary hair-splitting. As a matter of fact all that remains to be done is to combine the above distinctions with those which were drawn in the first part of this essay and apply them to some intuitively relevant cases.

175. Thus, consider the intention

> Shall be [whooping cranes survive].

This is a shareable intention available for members of the Whooping Crane Society, as is

> Shall be [each of us WCS members do what he can, *ceteris paribus*, to promote the survival of whooping cranes].

176. And consider the general hypothetical imperative,

> If a member of the WCS wants to promote the survival of the whooping crane, he should pay his dues and obey the by-laws.

This tells us that

> "Shall [each of us members of the WCS pay his dues and obey the by-laws]"

is reasonable relative to

> "Shall [each of us members of the WCS promote the survival of whooping cranes]."

177. We have an implication which relates one we-referential action intention to another.

178. We-referential action intentions imply intentions to act on the part of individuals, not simply by virtue of the general principle which relates "Shall be" to "Shall I do," but *directly* by virtue of the relation between "Shall *anybody* do" and "Shall *I* do."

179. If the reasonableness of an available intention of the form

Shall [I do A]

is a matter of its reasonableness relative to (i.e. its being implied by) an intention of the form

Shall [any of us do ...]

this might be indicated by flagging the "shall" of the former intention with a subscript "we," thus

Shall$_{we}$ [I do A].

Thus understood, the latter is equivalent to the schema

Shall [I do A, *because* shall any of us do ...]

At this point paragraph 156 should be reviewed.

180. Correspondingly, if a person *has* the intention

Shall [I do A]

and has it *because* it is implied by the intentions

Shall [any of us do A]

which he also *has*, we can say that Jones intends to do A *sub specie* "one of us," and flag our representation of his intention with a subscript "we," thus,

Jones intends "Shall$_{we}$ [I do A]"

181. If I have the intention

Shall be [whooping cranes survive]

I may infer, first

Shall be [the Whooping Crane Society survive]

and, then, by virtue of the connection between state-of-affairs intentions and intentions to do (together with relevant considerations)

Shall [I pay my dues].

In this case, my intention, though it *concerns* the WCS, of which I am a member, is not from the point of view of a member of the WCS.[27]

182. Thus which of the implication structures I 'pick up' in my deliberations about paying my dues determines whether the point of view from which I am reasoning is "private" or that of a member of the group.

183. Notice finally, that a shareable state-of-affairs intention will, in general, have implications with respect to intentions to do of both the I-referential and the we-referential kind. (Since the latter, in turn, imply I-referential action intention, we might distinguish *we-derivative* from *primary* I-referential action intentions.) The facts by virtue of which these implications obtain may well overlap, though they cannot coincide.

XIV

184. But the facts that we-referential intentions can be *shared* and that an *action* intention can be we-referential are logical points which establish at best a *necessary* condition for the possibility of a distinctively moral point of view. What can be added to turn this necessary condition into a *sufficient* condition?

185. The dialectics of our elaboration of Rational Egoism suggests that what we are looking for is a *non-relative* reasonableness pertaining to *we-referential* action intentions. Is there such a thing?

186. That there is, is suggested by the fact that the purpose or intention expressed by

Shall [each of us WCS members promote the survival of whooping cranes]

---

[27] Notice that the WCS can be said to have a point of view *as an organization*, just as it can be said to act *as an organization*. The concept of groups' purposes, intentions and actions is an important and highly relevant one which, however, I am skirting on the present occasion.

is reasonable *for members of the WCS*, because it is by virtue of that shareable intention that there is such a thing as the WCS.

187. This intention defines what might be called "the WCS member's point of view." It is the prime mover intention of this point of view,[28] and generates, given matters of factual implications and premises, subordinate intentions, the relative reasonableness of which is grounded in its intrinsic and non-relative reasonableness as constituting the WCS point of view.

188. Of course, any member of the WCS can, and indeed often will, work out in his practical reasoning not only the implications of the WCS point of view for people who are in their particular circumstances, but also the implications of these circumstances for the personal point of view, or, in more traditional terminology, that of Self Love, i.e.

Shall [I promote my happiness].

189. Is there, then, an intention which defines the moral point of view? Is there an intrinsically reasonable we-referential action intention which stands to a moral community as the intention that "we" promote the survival of whooping cranes stands to members of the Whooping Crane Society?

190. Notice that while the intention that we members of the WCS promote the survival of whooping cranes is intrinsically reasonable for members of the WCS, the bare intention that whooping cranes survive, if reasonable, does not have this same kind of reasonableness. The point becomes obvious if we change the example to that of the Society for the Preservation of Architectural Landmarks.

191. In discussing Rational Egoism I distinguished between the *formal* intention

Shall [I do that which promotes my happiness, all relevant things considered]

and the specific *contentual* intentions which, in particular circumstances, "spell out" this "regulative principle" with namely riders.

192. I pointed out, in paragraph 124 above, that if the above formal intention is *intrinsically* reasonable, then the intentions which are implied by it are also *reasonable, period.* That is to say, they are not merely reasonable *on the hypothesis* that something else is reasonable, but reasonable *because that something else is reasonable.* Thus we distinguish between *categorical* reasonableness (of which

---

[28] Notice that there is a sense in which this intention can be construed as grounded in the intention

Would that whooping cranes survive!

which is a shareable intention, one, however, which abstracts from the distinction between we-referential and non-we-referential action intentions.

intrinsic reasonableness is the prime mover) and *relative* (or *hypothetical*) reasonableness. Reasonableness, we saw, can be both *categorical* and *derivative*.

193. Our question thus becomes, Is there an intrinsically (and hence categorically) reasonable formal intention which is the regulative principle of the moral point of view?

194. Analogy would suggest the following:

> Shall [each of *us* do that which, in the circumstances, promotes the happiness of each and every one of *us*, all relevant things considered].

195. [Notice that this is a shareable we-referential action intention. Furthermore, it is one which, unlike the intentions characteristic of associations formed to pursue what might be called 'limited' or 'external' goals,[29] e.g. the survival of whooping cranes, the preservation of architectural landmarks, the formal intention we are]*... [c]onsidering has as its state of affairs intention core

> Shall be [each and every one of us leads a satisfying life, all relevant things considered]

which is the formal specification of an intrinsic and encompassing good.

196. Shareable by whom? Who are *we*? Though these questions are, in a sense, the same, let me begin with the second. Who are *we*? Not, it should be clear, the members of a corporate group, a group having corporate intentions and doing corporate deeds. The conceptual framework with which we are concerned is *presupposed* rather than constituted by "shoulds" and "oughts" which pertain to groups considered collectively.

197. This calls attention to the fact that a key feature of the above formal intention is the absence of an *explicit* membership rider for the "us"—as contrasted with the "us members of the WCS" of the shareable intention we have just been exploring, and the "us Texans" mentioned earlier.

198. Is there, perhaps, an "implicit" and indeterminate membership rider, one which is left to be specified by the context on particular occasions?

199. Notice that what a person who is deliberating in the framework of this formal intention *thinks* their circumstances are is (obviously) not specified by the

---

[29] Notice that an association can have a goal which though not 'external' is 'limited,' e.g., the University of Pittsburgh Credit Union.

* [Eds.—This bracketed text—including footnote 29—was present in an earlier typescript, but was (apparently inadvertently) dropped in the process of copying, and ultimately omitted from the published version of ORAV and replaced with an ellipsis. The relevant typescript is document 31735062220433, Box 36, Folders 2–5, Wilfrid S. Sellars Papers, 1899–1990, ASP.1991.01, Archives of Scientific Philosophy, Archives & Special Collections, University of Pittsburgh Library System. §195 can be viewed on pp. 46–7 of the typescript. We are grateful to Lionel Shapiro for alerting us to the missing passages and directing us to the relevant typescript.]

intention. The *reasonableness* on particular occasions of thinking that the circumstances are such and such is not to be equated with their being in fact thought to be such and such.

200. Can we similarly distinguish between what a person who is deliberating in the framework of this formal intention *thinks of as us*, and what it is *reasonable* for the deliberator to think of as *us, all relevant things considered*?

201. Of course, the formal intention does not specify what all these relevant things are, any more than the principle of Self Love tells one in particular circumstances the actual cash value of promoting one's happiness on the whole, all relevant things considered, in just *these* circumstances.

202. Thus, the absence of an explicit membership rider for the "us" does not mean that there is an "implicit" namely rider which is filled, in any given context, by a reference to whatever group a deliberator happens to "identify with" or think of as *us* (e.g. we WASPs).

203. The mere fact that a person identifies with WASPS no more entails that it is *reasonable* for him to identify with WASPs, than the fact that one believes oneself to be on *terra firma* entails that it is *reasonable* for one to believe this.

204. It is in the logical pressures generated by the principles which govern practical reasoning, and which find their expression in "all relevant things considered" that we find the point of the distinction between the moral community and those with whom we identify.

205. It will be remembered that I asked not only "who are *we*?" but "shareable by *whom*?" Do the above considerations throw any light on the latter question?

206. Surely once we have distinguished between the moral community and those with whom one who deliberates in the moral point of view happens to identify, we cannot stop short of identifying the moral community with that group with which it is reasonable for us, all relevant things considered, to identify. And, in the context of the formal intention

> Shall [each of us do that which in the circumstances promotes the well-being of each and every one of us, all relevant beings considered].

Who can that be, but rational beings generally?

207. Notice that I am *not* saying that everybody *shares* this shareable intention. I am simply saying that it defines the moral point of view, as contrasted with, say the WASP point of view. The intention

> Shall [each of us WASPs do that which, in the circumstances promotes our common good, all relevant things considered]

is a shareable (by WASPs) we-referential action intention which is *logically* respectable. It simply does not constitute the moral point of view.

208. The question is it egoistically reasonable to acquire or maintain a propensity to intend *sub specie* "one of us" is a perfectly meaningful one. (Why should I be moral?) The fact that it is so in no way brings into jeopardy the autonomy of the moral point of view.

209. Finally the reader should bear in mind that this essay has been concerned with what a Kantian would call the formal structure of the moral point of view. In other words, I have been concerned with such issues as the intersubjectivity, universalizability, and reasonableness of categorical imperatives. For an exploration of how a utilitarian content fits into this Kantian form, the reader should consult the concluding sections (pp. 218–29) of *Science and Metaphysics*.[30]

Note: This paper was initially presented as the first of three Tsanoff lectures at Rice University in September of 1978. It was expanded and revised in response to conceptual pressures from Kurt Baier, Gerald Massey, and Don Morrison. I am grateful for the care with which they read and commented on the text. As a result a number of mistakes have been corrected and some topics brought to a sharper focus. That the main line of argument remains essentially unchanged may, of course, be due to pig-headedness.

---

[30] London and New York, 1968. [Eds.—OIM appears as Ch. 6 of this volume. Sellars is referring to sections XVII–XXI (§§119–154).]

17
Conditional Promises and Conditional Intentions
(Including a Reply to Castañeda)*

I

1. Some years ago in a busy paper on practical reasoning[1] I laid down the thesis that

   I promise to do A and B, *therefore* I promise to do A

is ill-formed. Promisings are not conclusions of arguments.

2. If this isn't intuitively obvious as it stands, try the equivalent formulation

   I *hereby* promise to do A and B, therefore I *hereby* promise to do A.

3. Yet there *are* arguments pertaining to promisings which are sufficiently close to non-starters like the above to generate the illusion that

   'I promise to do A and B' entails 'I promise to do A'

An examination of these arguments will serve to introduce the fundamental ideas in terms of which I hope to clarify some controversial issues pertaining to the logic of practical reasoning.

4. But before looking at the particular arguments I have in mind, it is important to acknowledge that there are indeed cases in which 'I promise to do A' is properly preceded by 'therefore'.

5. Thus, consider

---

* [Eds.—Sections I–II of this chapter also appear in Sellars's letter of 6 June 1979 to Judith Jarvis Thomson. Their correspondence is located in Box 162, Folder 16 of Wilfrid S. Sellars Papers, 1899–1990, ASP.1991.01, Archives of Scientific Philosophy, Archives & Special Collections, University of Pittsburgh Library System.]

[1] "Imperatives, Intentions and the Logic of 'Ought,' *Methodos* 7, 1956 [reprinted with revisions in H. N. Castañeda and G. Nakhnikian (eds.), *Morality and the Language of Conduct*, Detroit, 1963. The reference is to p. 171 of the latter.] [Eds.—IIOR, Ch. 14 this volume.]

I want to put your mind at ease, *therefore* I promise to get you (Smith) to the airport by 9:00 A.M.

6. Notice, however, that in this case the relevant entailment does not have the form

'...' entails 'I promise to do A'

for it consists in the fact that, in the circumstances, my promising to get him to the airport by 9:00 A.M. is a necessary condition of Smith's enjoying peace of mind.

7. The entailment is, in essence,

'I will put Smith's mind at ease' entails 'I will promise Smith to get him to the airport by 9:00 A.M.'

8. The case is similar to one in which I say to Smith

I want you to feel secure, *therefore* I will put a lock on your door.

9. The difference lies in the fact that whereas uttering the words 'I will put a lock on your door' is not the action which will result in Smith's feeling secure, uttering the words 'I promise to get you to the airport by 9:00 A.M.' can simultaneously be the *action* which will result in Smith's mind being at ease and the *proposition* that a certain state of affairs will obtain, i.e. my having promised to get Smith to the airport by 9:00 A.M. It is in the latter respect that the entailment between Smith's peace of mind and my promising obtains. And it is in this respect that the entailment resembles that between Smith's feeling secure and my putting a lock on his door.

10. Consider the following scenarios:

Scenario I:
    Jones: I want you to feel secure, *therefore* (because this entails my having put a lock on your door), I will put a lock on your door.
    (*Puts a lock on the door.*)

Scenario II:
    Jones: I want to put you at ease, *therefore* (because this entails my having promised you to get you to the airport by 9 A.M.), I will promise to get you to the airport by 9 A.M.
    (*Promises Smith to get him to the airport by 9 A.M.*)

11. Notice that the second scenario could have ended not with a stage direction, but with the additional piece of dialogue

> ...I promise to get you to the airport by 9 A.M.

which would give us Scenario IIa.
    12. Finally, Scenario III:

> Jones: I want to put your mind at ease, *therefore* (because this entails my having promised you to get you to the airport by 9 A.M.), I promise to get you to the airport by 9 A.M.

13. I suggest that we view Scenario III as an ellipsis for Scenario IIa.
14. I return from this digression to the original example. One who says

> I promise to do A and B

has, *ceteris paribus*, promised to do A and B, and, in so doing, has promised to do A *and* promised to do B.
    15. Thus, the following entailments obtain by virtue of the conceptual structure of the promise practice:

> (α) "x (at t) says 'I promise to do A and B'" entails
>   "x (at t) promises to do A and B."
> (β) "x (at t) promises to do A and B" entails
>   "x (at t) promises to do A"

16. Of these, (β) is a special case of a more general principle, namely,

> (γ) "x (at t) promises to do X" and "Doing X entails doing Y" together entail "x (at t) promises to do Y."

17. Thus, in spite of the fact that there is no such entailment as

> "I promise to do A and B" entails "I promise to do A"

there *is* the entailment

> "I have promised (at t) to do A and B" entails
> "I have promised (at t) to do A."

18. If the narrative present is used in phrasing this, it becomes

> "I promise (at t) to do A and B" entails "I promise (at t) to do A"

which, as a first person form of (β), looks like, but *only* looks like, the pseudo-entailment with which I began.

19. It is perhaps worth adding to the above the following footnote. One who says

> I promise to do A and B.
> *There!* I have promised to do A

would be speaking quite correctly. The utterance of the first sentence would, by virtue of (α), be a promising to do A and B, and the second utterance would be true by virtue of (β) and the fact that the first utterance took place. The argument in the background is

> I have promised to do A and B
> *Therefore*, I have promised to do A.

II

20. I turn now to the initial topic of this paper, the conditional promise. Here, again, the first point to be made is that there is no reasoning of the form

> I promise to do A, if p
> p
> *Therefore*, I promise to do A

21. On the other hand, we clearly need something more than (γ)—see paragraph 16 above—to get us from

> x promised (at t) to do A, if p

to

> x promised (at t) to do A

22. The proposition 'p' is clearly needed as a premise. But *how* does it relate to the major premise? I suggest that what is needed is a cousin of (α).

23. I have called this cousin 'the principle of the conditional promise.' It can be formulated in two parts as follows:

> (δ) "x (at t) says 'I promise to do A, if p'" entails "x promises (at t) to do A on condition that p."

(ε) "x promises (at t) to do A on condition that p" and "p" together entail "x promises (at t) to do A."

(The '(at t)' in the consequent of (ε) calls for comment, which I shall make later.)
24. In accordance with this principle, the following argument is valid,

Jones promised (at t) to do A, if p
p
Therefore, Jones promised (at t) to do A

as is its first person counterpart.
25. In other words, although "I promise to do A, if p" and "p" do *not* together entail "I promise to do A," the following entailment does obtain

"I have promised to do A, if p" and "p" entail
"I have promised to do A."

26. The point which was made in paragraph 18 applies with equal force to this entailment. Once again some part of the plausibility of a pseudo-entailment is accounted for.
27. And notice that, in a parallel with the conjunctive case, one who says

I promise to do A, if p
p
There! I have promised to do A

would be speaking quite correctly.
28. Indeed, in this case the speaker could appropriately have used "therefore," rather than "There!" because he has given one of the premises—namely 'p'—of the argument which is in the background. Notice also, however, that his first utterance is not a premise of *that* argument, which is, of course,

I have promised to do A, on condition that p
p
Therefore, I have promised to do A

And, of course, what makes the major premise of *this* argument true is the performance which is the first sentence occurring in what the speaker actually said. This performance 'gives' the other premise of the background argument and reinforces the appropriateness of the 'therefore.'
29. One final remark to round off this section. It may seem puzzling that one who says at t

I promise to come in if it rains

has, given that it rains at t + δt, promised *at t* to come in. Clearly the speaker promised *at t* to come in *if it rains*. But the speaker didn't say 'I promise to come in' *simpliciter*. How, then, can the speaker have made an unconditional promise at t? The answer seems to be that the *performance* which, after all, did take place at t became a promise to come in *simpliciter* at t + δt. Some Cambridge changes are fraught with moral significance.

III

30. In his penetrating analysis of, and commentary on, my successive attempts to formulate the logic of intentions, Hector-Neri Castañeda criticizes the view that my intention operator 'shall' can do the work I want it to do, if construed as operating on future indicatives to generate corresponding expressions of intention.

31. So construed, 'shall' would operate on 'I will do A' to generate a formula 'shall[I will do A]' which is to be the regimented counterpart of

I shall do A[2]

32. The problem he poses concerns the analysis of conditional intentions.

33. He begins by pointing out that in my regimented notation, 'shall' never appears in the scope of logical connectives or quantifiers.[3] Thus, the following are ill-formed:

not (shall[I will do A])
shall[I will do A] or shall[I will do B]
(x) (shall[x will do A])

as contrasted with

Shall[I will not do A]
Shall[I will do A or I will do B]
Shall[(x) x will do A]

---

[2] Which, in turn, is my regimented counterpart of *anglice* 'I will do A.' Here the point of the regimentation is to make 'shall' uniformly the *intention* auxiliary and 'will' uniformly the *future* auxiliary in all persons of the verb which is modified. I shall write in this idiolect in what follows.

[3] For a recent elaboration and defense of this position see my "On Reasoning About Values," *American Philosophical Quarterly* 17, 1980. See particularly Section VI. [Eds.—ORAV, Ch. 16 this volume.]

34. That this regimentation does not mirror the surface grammar of ordinary English is clear. But this, of course, is no decisive consideration when it comes to evaluating the soundness of the reconstruction.

35. A successful theory of the conceptual structure of the language of intentions must, indeed, enable us to account for its surface grammar. But the explanation, appealing as it must to a variety of considerations which relate the expression of intentions to language as a whole, can be expected to trace no simple route from depth to surface.

36. Thus, consider the case of conjunction. Is it not clear that

I shall do A and I shall do B

expresses a conjunctive intention? Nothing would seem to be less problematic.

37. Yet when we reflect that a conjunctive intention should be a *single* intention, albeit *conjunctive* in form, we begin to feel uneasy.

38. It is important to distinguish between a punctuated *text* and a conjunctive statement; between

Tom is tall. Mary is wise.

and

Tom is tall *and* Mary is wise.

39. Both 'Tom is tall' and 'Mary is wise' can serve as expressions of belief. Conjunction introduction operates on these sentences to transform them into a single sentence which also can serve as the expression of a belief—a single belief which includes the beliefs expressed by the conjuncts.

40. If the notion of an intention operator makes sense at all—a point which I am not arguing on the present occasion—would we not expect conjunction introduction in the context of expressions of intention to move from the punctuated text

I shall do A. I shall do B.

to the sentence which would express the conjunctive intention to A *and* B, i.e.

I shall do A and B

or, in regimented discourse, from

Shall[I will do A]. Shall[I will do B].

to

Shall[I will do A *and* I will do B]

41. That a transformation of the latter to the surface form

Shall[I will do A] *and* shall[I will do B]

could be permitted and, hence, the surface grammar in my idiolect of

I shall do A and I shall do B

mirrored—is not at issue. What is at issue is philosophical perspicuousness.

42. I have long argued that similar considerations apply to conditional intentions. A conditional intention is *one* intention, *conditional* in form, thus

I shall *do A, if p*

i.e.

Shall[I will do A, if p].

43. That a transformation[4] of the latter to the surface form

If p, shall[I will do A]

could be permitted, and hence the surface grammar in my idiolect of

If p, I shall do A

mirrored—is also not at issue.

44. What is at issue is the logical structure of practical reasoning.

IV

45. Notice in this connection a certain parallel between conditional intentions and conditional promises. Thus, compare

---

[4] The rationale of this transformation will be explored in depth in the concluding sections of this essay.

I promise to do A, if p

with

If p, I promise to do A.

Each of these sentences can be used to make a promise to *do A on the condition that p*.

46. In both cases, the 'if p' is to be understood as part of the performance governed by the promise rubric. In this respect, the first of the two sentences is more perspicuous.

47. We can account, in part, for the existence of the second sentence, by pointing out that while principles $(\gamma)^5$ and $(\varepsilon)^5$ are both relevant to reasonings about conditional promises, it is usually (ε) which is involved. And *this* requires the use of 'p' as an independent premise outside the context provided by the verb 'to promise.'

48. Since, by virtue of the very nature of a conditional promise

x has promised to do A, if p

and

if p, x has promised to do A

are strongly equivalent, there is a temptation to view the logic of conditional promises as simply a matter of *modus ponens*.

49. But while

If p, x has promised to do A
p
Therefore, x has promised to do A

is, indeed, a simple case of *modus ponens*, its major premise is, in the envisaged situation, true *because* x has promised *to do A if p*, where the italics highlight the fact that, in the performance, 'if p' as well as 'do A' was in the scope of 'I promise.'

V

50. Let us return to the examination of conditional intentions. This time, however, let us take as our point of departure the fact that occurrent intendings like occurrent believings *are not performances*.

---

[5] For (γ) see paragraph 16; for (ε) see paragraph 23.

51. One intends as one believes, *in foro interno*.

52. An utterance which expresses a belief may, if the circumstances are of a certain sort, take on the character of being a *statement*. It may be the illocutionary act or performance of making a statement.

53. Similarly, an utterance which expresses an intention may, if the circumstances are of a certain sort, take on the character of being a *commitment*. It may be the illocutionary act or performance of committing oneself to do something.

54. To commit myself to doing A, or to doing A, if p, I need not use the promise rubric. It may be sufficient to say

I shall do A

or

I shall do A, if p.

55. I want, therefore, to emphasize that in developing a logic of intentions, indeed a logic of practical reasoning, I have expressly abstracted from those logical features which are common to expressions of intention *qua* commitments and to promises.

56. Conditional *intentions* are not conditional *commitments* and their logic is not akin to that of conditional promises.

57. The fundamental principle of the logic of intentions is

FP: If 'P' implies 'Q,' then 'Shall[P]' implies 'Shall[Q]'

where 'implies' stands generically for any logical relation which authorizes inference: logical or nomological; unconditional, or relative to an hypothesis.

58. Notice, in particular, that no principles of the logic of intentions spell out the requirements of illocutionary success—for the obvious reason that there are none. Thus, while FP above is the counterpart of $(\gamma)^6$, there are no counterparts of $(\alpha)^6$, $(\delta)^6$, and $(\varepsilon)^6$.

VI

59. We are now in a position to examine and evaluate that argument which, among the many Castañeda directs against my logic of intentions, he believes to be decisive.[7]

---

[6] For (γ) see paragraph 16; for (α) see paragraph 15; for (δ) and (ε), paragraph 23.

[7] See his essay "Some Reflections on Wilfrid Sellars' Theory of Intention," in H. N. Castañeda (ed.) *Action, Knowledge and Reality* (Indianapolis, 1975). The argument in question occurs on pp. 34–5.

Consider my conditional shall-intention:[8]

(1) If I (will) finish this essay at time t, I shall visit Bruce Aune at time t'.

Evidently, the if-clause is a future-tense first-person sentence that expresses the proposition *I will finish this essay*, *not* the intention *I shall finish this essay*. Now—given Sellars' view that 'shall' is never in the scope of a connective, and... in accordance with the view that 'shall' operates on future-tense first-person sentences, Sellars would be committed to analyzing (1) as

(2) Shall [if I (will) finish this essay at time t, I will visit Bruce Aune at time t'].

Now, correctly on my view, Sellars insists that "The 'if..., then' [of conditional intentions] is not 'implies' but the '→' of truth functional logic."[9]

Thus we can write (2) more perspicuously as

(2a) Shall[I will finish this essay at time t → I will visit Bruce Aune at t']

Patently, (2a) is not even equivalent to (1). The different practical roles played by my finishing the essay and visiting Aune in (1) are lost in (2a). In (1) my finishing the paper is a condition and my visiting Aune an intention. In (2a) neither future-tense first-person proposition plays either role. Indeed, (2a) is equivalent to the disjunctive intention

(2b) Shall[I won't finish this essay at time t or I will visit Bruce Aune at time t']

60. Now the first thing to notice about this argument is that if HNC had *expressed* his conditional intention to someone concerned about his whereabouts at time t', and if HNC was aware of that concern, then HNC would, in expressing this intention, have made a *commitment* to visit Aune at t' on condition that he finishes the essay. And it is, indeed, obvious that a conditional commitment by HNC to visit Aune at t', if he has finished his essay at t is quite other than a conditional commitment by HNC not to finish his essay at t, if he does not visit Aune at t'.

61. The point stands out clearly if we move to the more institutionalized case of conditional commitment which is the conditional promise. Consider the following two conditional promises, which I deliberately formulate in a very abstract manner, so that subordinate features do not obscure the logic of the situation:

---

[8] For purposes of reflecting certain distinctions which are not directly germane to this paper, Castañeda italicizes the 'shall' operator throughout, thus 'SHALL'. I have taken the liberty of reformulating his argument in my own terminology.

[9] The reference is to *Science and Metaphysics*, p. 181. [Eds.—OIM §14(g); Ch. 6 this volume.].

I. HNC: I promise that q, if p
II. HNC: I promise that not p, if not q

Notice that by virtue of principles (α) and (γ), which pertain to promising generally, these two promises have logically equivalent contents.[10] In each case HNC has committed himself to its not being the case that p and not q.

62. Indeed, as far as principles (α) and (γ) are concerned, the following promises have logically equivalent contents:

(a) I promise that q, if p
(b) I promise that not p, if not q
(c) I promise that not both p and not q
(d) I promise that either not p or q.

63. But to say that they have logically equivalent contents is not to say that they are equivalent with respect to all their logical powers. We must also take into account the logical powers stemming from the principles which define the institution of the *conditional* promise; namely (δ) and (ε).

64. And it is here that a disparity breaks out. Of the four promises, the latter two, (c) and (d) do not even fall under (δ) and (ε). They are simply not conditional promises.

65. On the other hand, (a) and (b) *are* conditional promises. But while they are equivalent in *content*, they are specifically different in their character as conditional promises.

66. Thus (a) is the conditional promise that q *on the condition that* p; while (b) is the conditional promise that not p *on the condition that* not q.

67. Now this suggests that when Castañeda writes

> The different practical roles played by my finishing the essay and visiting Aune in (1) are lost in (2a). In (1) my finishing the paper is a condition and my visiting Aune an intention. In (2a) neither future-tense first-person proposition plays either role.

he is, indeed, guided by sound intuitions. It also suggests that this *intuition* concerns not the logic of intentions as such, but the logic (in a suitably broad sense) of conditional *commitments*.

68. The fact, on which Castañeda lays such stress, that finishing the paper is the *condition* of the visiting would, on the above diagnosis, stem not directly from the if-then-ishness of the *content*[11] of the promise, but rather from the fact that the

---

[10] The content of a promise can be characterized as the content of the intention implied by the promise, i.e., the content of the intention which the promisor has, if the commitment is sincere.

[11] See footnote 10 above.

occurrence of the illocutionary act to which Castañeda without noticing it, has transferred his attention, entails, by virtue of principle (ε) that

If Castañeda finishes his paper at t, he has committed himself to visit Aune at t'.

VII

69. It would be tempting to stop at this point and construe Castañeda's argument against my account of conditional intentions as an *ignoratio elenchi* arising from a confusion between expressions of intention as such and expressions of intention *qua* illocutionary acts. But this would be a mistake. And while, as I see it, the preceding section does throw some light on why Castañeda finds his critique so convincing, its primary virtue is that it brings to the fore the idea that there need be no simple connection between the *conditionality* of a conditional intention and the if-then-ishness of the *content* of the intention.

70. That there is more to Castañeda's critique than can be accounted for by the above confusion will be seen by anyone who happens to have read an earlier comment of mine on a related criticism by Castañeda.

71. In "Volitions Re-Affirmed"[12] I wrote

Castañeda has argued that according to my original analysis, the following sentences
   I. If I don't press button B, I shall press button A
   II. If I don't press button A, I shall press button B
express logically equivalent intentions, although it is clear after a moment's reflection that they don't. He is right. In my original account they both transform into
   Shall [either I will press B or I will press A]

to which I added

On the present account, the first expression (I) treats my not pressing B as something which is decided to be the case; my pressing button A, on the other hand, as something to be decided to do—the reverse holding in the case of (II).

72. The addendum might be thought to amount to a concession on my part of Castañeda's claim that my account of the logic of conditional intentions cannot be correct because, as he puts it,

---

[12] In *Action Theory*, edited by Myles Brand and Douglas Walton (Dordrecht, Holland: Reidel, 1976). [Eds.—VR, Ch. 10 this volume.]

the different practical roles played by my finishing the essay and visiting Aune in (1)[13] are lost in (2a).[14] In (1) my finishing the paper is a condition and my visiting Aune an intention. In (2a) neither future-tense, first-person proposition plays either role. Indeed (2a) is equivalent to the disjunctive intention

(2b) Shall [I won't finish this essay at t or I will visit Bruce Aune at t']

73. But everything hinges on Castañeda's move from the idea that finishing the essay and visiting Aune *play different practical roles* in the conditional intention expressed by (1) to

In (1) my finishing the paper is a condition and my visiting Aune an intention.

74. One can grant the difference in the practical roles of the two states of affairs in the conditional intention without concluding that the latter's status as an intention consists in its having an *intention proper* as a consequent and an antecedent which is a proposition *rather than* an intention.

75. Once again, the issue concerns not surface grammar, but the depth grammar of expressions of intention.

76. An intention can be viewed as a scenario for possible action on the part of an agent. As such, it has, in addition to the action, two radically different types of constituent: (a) the circumstances[15] in which the action is to be performed; (b) that which is to be brought about by the action. The former concern what is believed by the agent to be the case as the relevant context of the envisaged action; the latter the expected impact of the action on this context.

77. Constituents of the first type get into the scope of the intention *via* what I have called the So-be-it principle,[16] according to which a state of affairs, p, properly belongs in an agent's scenario if he or she believes it to be the case (and to be relevant). It governs the conceptual move from having a scenario

Shall be [α]

to having the scenario

Shall be [α *and* p]

78. It might be thought proper to represent this move as the inference

---

[13] I.e., "If I finish the essay at t, I shall visit Aune at t'."
[14] I.e., "Shall [I will finish the essay at t → I will visit Aune at t']."
[15] The reader should note that instead of the word 'circumstances' I might well have written 'conditions'. This hints at another way in which the term 'conditional' might be relevant to intentions.
[16] For discussions in depth of this principle see the essays referred to in notes 3 [Eds.—ORAV] and 12 [Eds.—VR; published version mistakenly references note 14] above.

Shall be [α]
p
So, Shall be [α and p]

79. But I submit that while an inferential move is, indeed, involved; instead of representing it as an inference from a combination of a *resolutive* premise and an *indicative* premise, it is more perspicuous to represent it as a direct inference from the resolutive

Shall be [α]

to the *resolutive*

Shall be [α and p]

and to connect the role of the premise 'p' to the justification of the rule of inference which governs this transition.

80. Let me explain this. In paragraph 57 I formulated the fundamental principle of the logic of intentions as follows:

FP: If 'P' implies 'Q', then 'Shall [P]' implies 'Shall [Q]'

and added that "'implies' stands generically for any logical relation which authorizes inference: logical or nomological; absolute, or relative to an hypothesis." The second of these contrasts is directly relevant to the topic now being considered.

81. It is, for example, an 'absolute' logical truth that

'p' and 'p → q' implies 'q'

This rests on the tautological character of the formula

(p • p → q) → q

82. Notice, however, that it makes sense to say

On the hypothesis that-p, 'p → q' implies 'q'

where this means

Given that-p, *one may infer* 'q' from 'p → q'

83. The reasoning

If p, one may infer 'q' from 'p → q'
p
Therefore, one may infer 'q' from 'p → q'

involves a detaching of

...one may infer 'q' from 'p → q'

But this detaching does not involve a commitment to the *unconditionality* of this permissible inference.

84. That is to say, it does not involve a commitment to

'p → q' logically implies 'q'

85. Obviously

(p → q) → q

does not hold in all possible worlds involving p and q.

86. It would be an obvious howler to argue

If p, then, necessarily, (p → q) → q
p
Therefore, *it is necessary that* (p → q) → q

The major premise is true; the conclusion, however, false.

87. On the other hand

(p → q) → q

does hold in all possible worlds *in which p holds*.[17]

88. Compare

If p, it is permissible to interrupt
p
Therefore, it is permissible to interrupt

This inference involves a detaching of the conclusion

---

[17] It is worth reflecting that the fundamental intuitions involved in the concept of implication relative to an hypothesis are captured by the role of subordinate proofs in systems of natural deduction (e.g., that of Fitch).

...it is permissible to interrupt

But it does not involve a commitment to

It is unconditionally permissible to interrupt.

89. Compare, also,

   If one has promised to do A, one is under an obligation to do A
   Jones has promised to do A
   Therefore, Jones is under an obligation to do A

Obligations are essentially tied to grounds; but this does not mean that obligation statements have to contain their grounds.
   90. Thus

   Jones is under an obligation to do A

is, in an important sense, a complete statement.
   91. Yet it is, by virtue of the conceptual grammar of obligation talk, defeasible. It raises the question 'Why?'
   92. Appropriate replies are

   Because he promised to do A
   Aune said he ought to, so there must be some reason.
   On reflection, I see that I was mistaken. There is no reason why Jones is under an obligation to do A. I withdraw the assertion.

93. Similarly,

   One may infer 'q' from 'p $\to$ q'

is complete, but defeasible. In particular, one can reply to the question 'Why?'

   Because: p; and in all possible worlds in which p is the case, q is the case, if p $\to$ q is the case.

94. Of course, the statement

   One is logically entitled to infer 'q' from 'p $\to$ q'

where this means

528   THE METAPHYSICS OF PRACTICE

One is, *as a mere matter of logic*, entitled to infer 'q' from 'p → q'

is false. But only by confusion can one conclude that

One is entitled to infer 'q' from 'p → q'

is false.

95. If, for some true (or obtaining) H, 'P' implies-relative-to-H 'Q' let us say that

'P' R-implies 'Q'

96. We can bring all this to a focus, then, by pointing out that a special case of the fundamental principle (FP) is

If 'P' R-implies 'Q', then 'Shall [P]' R-implies 'Shall [Q]'

97. Since

'p → q' implies-relative-to-p 'q'

we have

'Shall [p → q]' implies-relative-to-p 'Shall [q]'

and since

'α' implies-relative-to-p 'α and p'

we have

'Shall [α]' implies-relative-to-p 'Shall [α and p]'

98. The first of these derivative principles covers the case of conditional intentions; the second that of So-be-it.

99. What is the point of all this? Why is it important to construe the logic of conditional intentions in terms of

Shall [p → q]
Therefore, Shall [q]   (because 'p → q' R-implies 'q')

rather than

p → Shall [q]
p
Therefore, Shall [q]

and the logic of So-be-it in terms of

Shall [α]
Therefore, Shall [α and p]   (because 'α' R-implies 'α and p')

rather than

Shall [α]
p
Shall [α and p]?

100. The fundamental answer to this question stands out most clearly in the case of conditional intentions. For the above approach enables us to make sense of the idea that a conditional intention is an *intention*, albeit a *conditional* one.[18]

101. In other words, it takes seriously the idea that an agent's scenarios contain both those states of affairs he believes to be the case independently of what he proposes to bring about by a certain action, and those states of affairs which he is considering *sub specie* 'up to me.'

102. Finally, it enables us to construe the *inferential* logic of intentions as completely derivative from the logic of propositions; and to tie this logic to a philosophically perspicuous depth grammar *in which logical connectives occur only in propositional contexts.*

VIII

103. The last paragraph explains why, in discussing the logic of intentions, I have emphasized the propositional character of the items in the scope of my 'Shall' operator, thus

Shall [p and q]

and suggested the reading 'Shall be (the case that)' for 'shall,' where what is at stake is simply the inferential relationships of scenarios, thus

Shall be [α and if it rains, I will stay home]

---

[18] See paragraphs 42 and 74 above.

The latter is, from the standpoint of inferential connections, logically equivalent to

Shall be [α and either it does not rain or I will stay home]

104. But carefully to be distinguished from the *logic* of intentions are certain *conceptual* truths about intentions which can, indeed, be said to belong to the logic of intentions, but only in that extended sense of 'logic' which has muddied so many waters.

105. The logic, *strictu sensu*, of intentions concerns relationships of compatibility or incompatibility between the contents of scenarios.

106. It is, however, as I have already noted, a conceptual truth about scenarios that they involve a contrast between states of affairs which belong in their content by virtue of being believed to be the case or about to be the case, and states of affairs which are considered by the agent to be 'up to me.' In the written expression of an intention, those constituents of the scenario which belong in the first category might be underlined, and those which belong in the latter category might be marked with an asterisk. Or the former might be formulated as sentences in the indicative mood, the latter as infinitive or gerundive phrases—although this latter device would, as we have seen, obscure, for philosophically oriented onlookers, the fact that with respect to the logical connections between scenarios the two types of constituent are on a par.

107. A particularly interesting case is provided by examples in which an agent *believes* he will do a certain action, because he knows that he has decided to do it, and that the time is ripe and the circumstances propitious.

108. Strictly speaking, of course, it is still up to him whether or not he does the action in question. Yet his being about to do it is already functioning *in his thinking* as part of the context in which other actions might be done.

109. In this sense, then, it comes into other scenarios *sub specie* So-be-it rather than *sub specie* 'up to me.'

110. With this in mind, let us return to Castañeda's button-pressing example.[19] Thus consider the two scenarios

Shall be [I will not press B → I will press A]
Shall be [I will not press A → I will press B]

From the standpoint of the logic, *strictu sensu*, of intentions, these scenarios are logically equivalent to one another and to the scenario

Shall be [either I will press A or I will press B]

---

[19] Paragraph 71 above.

111. Now, consider the inferential sequence, consisting entirely of expressions of intention,

> Shall be [I will press A or I will press B]
> Shall be [I will not press A]
> So, Shall be [I will press B]

The validity of this reasoning can be exhibited in depth as follows:

1. Shall be [I will press A or I will press B]	premise
2. Shall be [I will not press A]	premise
3. 'I will press A or I will press B' and 'I will not press A' together imply '(I will press A or I will press B) and I will not press A'	Conj. Int.
4. 'Shall be [I will press A or I will press B]' and 'Shall be [I will not press A]' together imply 'Shall be [(I will press A or I will press B) and I will not press A]'	3, FP
5. Shall be [(I will press A or I will press B) and I will not press A]	1,2,4, M.P.
6. '(I will press A or I will press B) and I will not press A' implies 'I will press B'	Logic
7. 'Shall be [(I will press A or I will press B) and I will not press A]' implies 'Shall be [I will press B]'	6, FP
8. Shall be [I will press B]	5,7, M.P.

112. In a similar way, the reasoning, also consisting entirely of expressions of intention,

> Shall be [I will not press A → I will press B]
> Shall be [I will not press A]
> So, Shall be [I will press B]

can be shown to be valid in accordance with my rational reconstruction of the logic of intentions.

113. Now, however, let us turn our attention to cases of mixed reasoning. Consider

> Shall be [I will press A or I will press B]
> I will not press A
> So, Shall be [I will press B]

Here the first premise is the expression of a disjunctive intention, while the second premise is an expression of belief.

114. The validity of this reasoning can be exhibited in depth as follows:

1. Shall be [I will press A or I will press B]	premise
2. I will not press A	premise
3. If I will not press A, 'I will press A or I will press B' R-implies 'I will press B'	Logic, Def. 'R-implies'
4. 'I will press A or I will press B' R-implies (and hence implies) 'I will press B'	2,3, M.P.
5. 'Shall be [I will press A or I will press B]' R-implies (and hence implies) 'Shall be [I will press B]'	4, FP
6. Shall be [I will press B]	1,5, M.P.

115. Notice that in this reasoning the second premise serves as a premise in a step (4) which is not, *as such*, a piece of practical reasoning. It is rather a premise in a meta-logical sub-argument which establishes the existence of a propositional implication to which FP can be applied.

116. The implications which govern all the steps which are expressions of intention are of the form

'Shall be [P]' implies 'Shall be [Q]'

and are derived (by FP) from propositional implications.

117. In a similar way, the reasoning

Shall be [I will press A → I will press B]
I will press A
So, Shall be [I will press B]

can be shown to be valid in accordance with my conception of the logic of intentions.

118. What, then, is the logical relevance of the difference, highlighted by Castañeda, between the *propositional* character of the antecedent and the *resolutive* character of the consequent in the following expression of the conditional intention,

If p, I shall do A?

119. Does it require that 'p' be a proposition *rather than* a constituent of the intention? Surely not. To think so is to be taken in by grammatical surface. What it does highlight is the fact that p is a constituent of the intention *via* So-be-it. In the mode of representation suggested above it becomes

(a) Shall be [p → (I will do A)*]

and is to be contrasted with the alternatives

(b) Shall be [p* → (I will do A)*]
(c) Shall be [p* → I will do A]
(d) Shall be [p → I will do A]

120. Thus, we are now in a position to see exactly why

If I will not press A, I shall press B

and

If I will not press B, I shall press A

do represent different intentions; and to appreciate exactly what these intentions have in common. They are, respectively, the intentions represented by

Shall be [*I will not press A* → (I will press B)*]

and

Shall be [*I will not press B* → (I will press A)*]

121. These intentions have the same *content,* a content which can be neutrally represented as

Shall be [either I will press A or I will press B]

but though they have the same content, they point to different reasonings. The former points to a reasoning in which 'I will not press A', entering into the intention *via* So-be-it, serves to establish an implication. The conclusion of this reasoning would be an intention to press B. The latter points to a reasoning in which 'I will not press B', entering into the intention *via* So-be-it, serves to establish an implication. The conclusion of this reasoning would be an intention to press A.

122. Yet the fundamental principles governing these reasonings are the principles of propositional logic and the 'Shall'-implications they generate by virtue of FP. That p and *my doing A* play different roles in the surface form

If p, I shall do A

doesn't mean that the fundamental logical form of the content of the intention is not the material implication

p → I will do A

123. Furthermore, it doesn't mean that 'p' is a proposition *rather than* part of the intention, nor that 'I shall do A' is an intention *rather than* a proposition.

124. It does, however, mean that the manners in which they belong to the content of the intention are different. And while this difference in manner points to different reasonings, these reasonings all hinge on the logical form of the content of the intention being the material implication in question, as is made clear by the analysis in depth of paragraphs 111–117 above.

125. Suppose Jones believes that he will in point of fact not press button B. As long as this remains his belief, the scope of his practical deliberations is limited to scenarios which would contain as a factor in the *conditions* of envisaged action (So-be-it!), his not pressing button B, thus

Shall be [α and *I will not press B*]

126. Thus, given that he has an intention with the content

Shall be [I will not press B → I will press button A]

there is available to him a valid piece of practical reasoning which reaches the conclusion

Shall be [I will press A]

127. If he does not believe that he will in point of fact *not* press button B, his logical route to that conclusion would involve having the intention

Shall be [α and (I will not press B)*]

in which pressing button B enters the content not *via* So-be-it but *sub specie* 'up-to-me.'

128. Thus the content of an intention can be conditional in form, without the intention being *in a full sense* a conditional intention; i.e. the intention expressed by a sentence of the surface form

If p, I shall do A

129. We can now understand how the content of an intention can be *hypothetical* in form without the intention being in the full sense a *conditional* intention, i.e. an intention properly expressed by a sentence of the surface form

If p, I shall do A

This fact is the valid core of Castañeda's objection to my original analysis.

PART 5
MANUSCRIPTS AND CORRESPONDENCE

18
Practical Reasoning*

III. Self-Love

[1] Against the background of these distinctions, let us explore some familiar topics pertaining to ends and means in human conduct. And let us begin with some remarks on the concept of Self-Love. To clarify this concept we must remind ourselves of a distinction drawn above between desires as conceptual needs and needs other than desires.[1] The first thing to note is that it is not a necessary truth that all desires have as their *objective* the satisfaction of the agent's needs. If this *were* true, then psychological egoism would be true in a very radical sense. This idea, however, involves a confusion between the fact that what would 'fill' that desire *qua need* is, like all need-fillers, a state of the needer, with the false idea that what *realizes* the objective of a desire is always a state of the agent. It also involves a misconstruction of the role that the filling of needs plays in shaping our desires as a matter of the filling of the agent's needs being the objective of desire.[2]

[2] It is sometimes thought that all primary desires are desires for the satisfaction of personal needs other than desires, of which the most prominent are bodily hungers everything else being desired-as-a-means. This idea springs from a confusion of this false idea with the truth that the satisfaction of personal needs plays a key role in shaping our acquiring and losing of desires and the *falsehood* that all primary desires are desires for these satisfactions. We can, of course, and constantly do, desire the filling of personal needs, but nothing in the notion of primary desire requires that this always be the case. Again, the idea that the objective of a desire is always personal pleasure may arise from a confusion of the pleasure which results from the satisfaction of a desire *qua need to believe that the objective is realized*, with the objective itself, which is realized only if the belief in question is true.

[3] I shall assume, then, that what might be called first level desires include not only desires for the fulfillment of our own needs, but also desires which, though

---

* [Eds.—This is an unpublished manuscript fragment housed among the Wilfrid S. Sellars Papers at the University of Pittsburgh Library. It is document 31735062214733, Box 16, Folder 8, Wilfrid S. Sellars Papers, 1899–1990, ASP.1991.01, Archives of Scientific Philosophy, Archives & Special Collections, University of Pittsburgh Library System. This folder also contains handwritten notes for a 1963 lecture, also titled "Practical Reason," delivered at DePauw University in Greencastle, Indiana.]

[1] The latter include not only non-conceptual needs but also certain conceptual needs which are not desires. Thus the need to exercise one's mind might be called a conceptual need in a broad sense, but not a desire.

[2] We can, of course, desire that a need be fulfilled. We can also have a higher order desire that a lower order desire (which is, in our interpretation a need) be satisfied.

they are *our* needs, have as their objectives states of affairs other than the fulfillment of personal needs, and in particular that some first level desires have as their objectives the fulfillment of the needs of others.

[4] Now desires, preferences, attitudes of approval, etc. form a complicated system, and much analysis (or phenomenology) needs to be done in order to grasp how inclinations, attitudes, feelings, emotions and desires of various degrees of specificity or inclusiveness may fit together in a human person. My strategy will be to free, where necessary, our intuitive understanding of these matters from confusions generated by philosophical mistake and bad phenomenology, and to press on to the rarified level of abstraction where the battleground of which I spoke at the beginning of this lecture is found.

[5] A central theme in classical moral philosophy has been the concept of self-love, which can be characterized in first approximation as the long-range desire to bring about the maximum satisfaction of (a) our non-conceptual needs, (b) our conceptual needs other than desires and (c) our desires other than self-love—which latter will include "other regarding desires" unless *radical* psychological egoism is being defended.[3] Notice that this formulation, by including particular desires (which we have analyzed as special cases of conceptual needs) among the needs which self-love takes into account, makes the latter a higher order desire than the desires the satisfaction of which is involved in its objective.

[6] Now the concept of self-love was used to formulate a thesis shared by philosophers as different as Plato, the Sophists, Spinoza and Hobbes to the effect that

> In deliberate action or, to put it somewhat more strongly, action in which one attempts to take everything into account, a person is always motivated by self-love.

In other words the claim is that in the practical reasoning which culminates in the intention to do a certain action, the decisive role is played by a premise which characterizes this action as more conducive to personal satisfaction than any available alternative.

[7] Notice furthermore that in its Platonic form, at least, is a "life plan" desire for the possession by one's future experience of this maximum satisfactoriness. How this property is to be understood is best left at an intuitive level. The important thing to note is that the "life plan" in question is not to be confused with the intention one might have at a certain time if one were taking a "total view" and envisaged as many obtainable future situations as possible, i.e. envisaged all courses of action which might be initiated *now*, $a_1 \ldots a_n$ and, summing

---

[3] The achieving of this maximum satisfaction would involve, where appropriate and feasible, replacing some needs and desires by others.

the results of these actions in accordance with our schema, let one's preferences[4] express themselves in the decision, thus

Shall $[\Sigma_1 \bullet \sim\Sigma_2 \ldots \sim\Sigma_n]$
Shall $[\Sigma_1]$
Therefore shall $[A_1]$

For essential to Plato's argument is the idea that self-love has as its objective a satisfactoriness on the whole which is definable independently of one's preferences at the moment. One's desires and intentions are often out of harmony with the course of action which would bring one satisfaction on the whole. A person could achieve all his first order objectives and yet gain only the fleeting satisfaction of believing them to be realized. A life which realizes one's first order desires need not be a satisfactory life.

[8] According to the doctrine of self-love, furthermore, the primary or underivative intention in all life-plan action would be the same. People would differ only (a) in the *circumstances* of their action—including, of course, the needs to be selectively satisfied—and (b) the *beliefs* they have about themselves, the world and their fellow men.

[9] It is also easy to see why, in a certain sense, this position is a deterministic one. For it implies that in deliberate action, in this stringent sense, it could not be the case, relative to one's beliefs, that one do anything other than what one actually does.

[10] Now Plato's aim in the *Republic* was to show, by an analysis of human nature and the nature of reality, that although life-plan action was motivated in this sense, by self-love, nevertheless *informed* self-love would result in essentially the same actions as are prescribed by familiar moral rules. Thus, although the latter make no *reference to* the agent's self-interest, the actions they prescribe would *coincide* with true self-interest. Let us see how this idea looks in the framework we have been developing.

[11] The intentions we have been considering thus far have been *singular* intentions; at least we have left to tacit understanding the ways in which intentions can be general. Furthermore, these intentions have had a relatively simple logical form. To advance the argument, we must now take a closer look at what we have called *conditional intentions*, i.e. intentions of the form expressed by

I shall do A, if p
Shall [I will do A, if p]

We saw above that relatively to the assumption that-p

---

[4] The assumption would be, of course that in this deliberation only satisfaction and frustrations would count.

Shall [I will do A, if p]

implies

Shall [I will do A]

We might represent this by the schema

Shall [I will do A, if p] ⊦^{P} Shall [I will do A]

We can speak of this as a derivative practical implication, or a practical implication relative to the assumption that-p. In more classical terminology it would be called a derivative hypothetical imperative.

[12] Let us now* introduce the concept of a *derivative intention*. Where one intention implies another intention, whether logically or causally, and whether underivatively or derivatively, thus

Shall [P] implies Shall [Q]

we shall say that on the assumption that the antecedent intention obtains the consequent expresses a derivable intention, a derivable intention relative to the assumption 'Shall [P]'.† To illustrate, suppose that avoiding a cold today (physically) implies coming in, if it rains. From this it follows that

Shall [I will avoid a cold today] implies Shall [I will come in if it rains]

Relative to the assumption of the categorical intention expressed by the antecedent, the hypothetical intention expressed by the consequent is a derivable intention. It might be represented as follows

| Shall [I will avoid a cold today]

Shall [I will come in if it rains]

If, now, we take into account the fact that a conditional intention can be general in that it concerns many possible occasions, thus

Shall [I will do A, whenever I am in C]

---

* [Eds.—Correction of "not" in the original.]
† [Eds.—Handwritten in the margin at this point is "Change derivable to derivative?"]

and that general conditional intentions can be derivative, we are in a position to clarify the concept of a policy. Thus, to generalize our preceding example, suppose that

Avoiding a cold (physically) implies always coming in when it rains.

This generates the practical implication

Shall [I will avoid colds] implies Shall [I will always come in, when it rains]

or, schematically,

Shall [I will bring about E] → Shall [I will always do A, when in C]

and, assuming the antecedent intention to obtain

| Shall [I will bring about E]

Shall [I will always do A when in C]

Let us call a derivable general conditional intention a *policy* for realizing the goal or end in view, E.

19
Practical Reasoning Again*
Notes for a Revision of "Thought and Action"

VI. Practical Reasoning Again

[1] The preceding sentences on the nature of desire, and its relation to intention and enjoyment have, perhaps, served to suggest some of the requirements which the formal machinery sketched in the opening section of this essay must satisfy in order to provide a reasonably realistic reconstruction of the logic of practical reasoning. To come directly to the point, what interesting implications of the form

Shall[P] implies shall[Q]

can be generated from the higher order principle

P implies Q implies (and is implied by) shall[P] implies shall[Q]?

[2] Although my recognition of the fact was only implicit in the original version of this essay,[1] we need to recognize a principle of Conjunction Introduction for practical reasoning. This principle can be derived by the above higher order principle from Conjunction Introduction as it pertains to ordinary propositional logic, i.e.

'P' and 'Q' imply 'p and q'

where the first 'and' occurs in the meta-language and connects meta-linguistic *referring* expressions, while the second 'and' is an autonomous mention of 'and' as a *sentential* connective in the language to which 'P' and 'Q' belong. The corresponding practical principle is

---

* [Eds.—This manuscript, titled "Notes for a Revision of 'Thought and Action'," is document 31735062222140, Box 43, Folders 1–3, Wilfrid S. Sellars Papers, 1899–1990, ASP.1991.01, Archives of Scientific Philosophy, Archives & Special Collections, University of Pittsburgh Library System.]

[1] In my discussion of what I called the 'summative stage' of the practical syllogism.

'Shall[P]' and 'shall[Q]' imply 'shall[P and Q]'[2]

This must not be confused with

'Shall[P]' and 'shall[Q]' imply 'shall[P] and shall[Q]'

of which the consequent is as senseless as 'not-shall[P]'.
[3] Equally fundamental is the principle that

'shall[P and Q]' implies 'shall[P]'

which corresponds to

'P and Q' implies 'P.'

[4] Now without in the least impugning the validity of these principles, it must be admitted that in the absence of a more detailed account of how ordinary expressions of intention are to be transcribed into the formalism, they are threatened by ostensible counter-examples of devastating force. The first step in this more detailed account consists in pointing out that I have so far treated 'I shall do A' (regimented into 'shall[I will do A]') as though it were simply a special case of 'it shall be the case that-P.' My aim was to emphasize from the beginning that the content of intentions is not limited to the agent's doings, and that it can, and, indeed, must include states of affairs which are not only *not* actions, but which are even such that whether or not they come to be realized is not up to the agent. After all, when one decides to do A because one prefers the state of affairs which would result from doing A to that which would result from some alternative action, the state of affairs in question will necessarily include elements which, though not up to the agent, are nevertheless relevant to his decision and which he must take into account. Thus, when the questions arise

Shall[— and r]?   Shall[— and not-r]?

(where r is something which the agent believes to be up to him), the scope of '—' might include, for example, that the theatre is showing *Gone With the Wind*.
[5] Of course, when we make a conjecture as to the 'intention' with which a certain action is done, we focus our attention on the agent's preferences with respect to what he takes to be within his power. But these preferences will essentially involves states of affairs which he knows (or at least believes) *not* to

---

[2] In the original version I explicitly rejected this principle for a very bad reason.

be up to him, though this may be disguised by including a reference to the latter in the description of what he *does* believe to be up to him, thus, 'seeing the theatre's offering of *Gone With the Wind*.'

[6] The upshot of these considerations is that any realistic reconstruction of practical reasoning which uses the formula

Shall[P]

whether this be construed as 'It shall be the case that-P' or 'I shall bring it about that-P', must give a central place to the distinction between those constituents of P, the state of affairs intended, which the agent believes up to him, and those which he believes to be independent of his will. Using 'U' to represent states of affairs which are 'up to me' and 'N' for those which are not, we get the schema

Shall[N and U].

To this it should be added, by way of anticipation, that where the *explicit* content is limited to what the agent believes not to be up to him, the relevant 'shall' is 'It shall be the case that —,' and the principle by virtue of which this content belongs there is one which I am about to introduce. This principle, however, must take into account the fact that there is always an *implicit* reference to what is 'up to me' in practical reasoning, in that 'It shall be the case that —' is conceptually tied to 'I shall bring it about that —'. Again, at the other end of the spectrum, i.e. where the *explicit* content is limited to what the agent believes to be up to him, 'I shall bring it about that-P' transforms into 'shall[I will do A],' where 'doing A' is the appropriate redescription of 'bringing it about that-P.'

[7] Since, however, there will obviously be states of affairs, Q, which are relevant to decision and action, but which the agent neither believes to be up to him, nor believes not to be up to him, the question arises as to how they are to be taken into account. The answer is that the question 'Is Q up to me?' like the question 'Is Q the case?' is a theoretical rather than a practical question, to be given such answers as the following: 'yes,' 'probably, yes,' 'it is probable to degree n that-Q'... 'probably, no,' 'no.' The role of probability arguments in practical reasoning is an intricate one, and the problems it poses will be ignored in this essay. If we leave them aside, what remains is the not uninteresting point that even before the above questions are answered by a simple 'yes' or 'no,' their substance can be taken into account in practical thinking by what might be called 'hypothetical evaluation.'

[8] It might be thought that hypothetical evaluation is captured, for example, by

If 'Q' were up to me, I would prefer '[N and U and Q]' to 'N and not-(U and Q)]', i.e. would answer affirmatively to

Shall[N and U and Q]?

as contrasted with

Shall[N and U and not-Q]?
Shall[N and not-U and Q]?
Shall[N and not-U and not-Q]?

But it seems clear, on reflection, that hypothetical predictions about how one would answer such questions presupposes a more basic form of practical thinking, which is the carrying on of thought experiments. This points to

If 'Q' were up to me, $\begin{cases} \text{shall[N and U and not-Q]?} \\ \text{shall[N and not-U and Q]?} \\ \text{shall[N and not-U and not-Q]?} \\ \text{shall[N and U and Q]?} \end{cases}$

and to the (hypothetical) decision, for example,

If 'Q' were up to me, shall[N and U and Q].

I stress this only to call attention to the fact that here we seem to place shall-expressions in the context of a logical operator. But to see that this is no counter example to the general thesis advanced above requires only an appreciation of the very special notion of nature of the contexts, and reflection on certain other uses of the conditional which do not lend themselves to *modus ponens*.[3] Unhypothetical assent to 'Shall[—]?' requires that the context be limited to (1) what the agent has decided to be the case; (2) what he conceives of as up to him. Otherwise the outcome

Shall[— and I will do A]

or

Shall[— and I will not do A]

might hinge on the agent's preference for a combination of doing A with some state of affairs which he has no reason to believe will be the case.

---

[3] Thus, the Austinian 'If you want biscuits, you will find them on the sideboard.' Notice that this hypothetical makes sense in the first person.

[9] We must ultimately relate the distinction between 'U' and 'N' to the concept of an action locution: locutions built upon verbs of the form 'to A,' 'to do A,' 'to bring it about that-p.' The last of these is particularly useful, since, though the point can be misunderstood, every action verb is equivalent to an expression having this form.[4] But it will be best to let the need for looking more closely into the content of 'U' and 'N' arise out of specific problems.

[10] I began this essay by stressing first person sentences of the form

Shall[I will do A at t]

of which a special case is

Shall[I will do A *now*]

(where the 'now' is the practical 'now' rather than the 'now' of 'that is the way it is'). Notice, however, that without making much ado about it, I have been stressing a sense of 'shall' in which it is equivalent to 'It shall be the case that —,' for I have been using the 'shall'-operator in such a way that states of affairs which the agent believes not to be up to him belong in the context

Shall[—].

Thus, taking seriously the form

Shall[N and U]

and the fact that on the principles I have laid down it is related by implication to

Shall[N]

commits me to the idea that the problems with which we are now dealing involve 'Shall[it be the case that —].' For not even the context 'Shall[I bring it

---

[4] Some philosophers, by construing

    person brings it about that-p

as

    person causes it to be the case that-p

infer that a metaphysics of action requires the concept of 'personal causation' or 'agent causation,' i.e. requires that persons cause actions in a sense irreducible to 'event causation.' I have discussed the concept of 'agent causation' in my "Reply to Donagan." In the present context I need only note that though in some cases persons cause it to be the case that-p by doing something else which causes it to be the case that-p, in other cases 'causing it to be the case that-p' is logically equivalent to 'p,' as when 'p' has the form 'x does A,' and that which makes it the case that-p is simply x's doing of A. [Eds.—RD, Ch. 12 of this volume.]

about that —],' which will turn out to mediate between 'Shall[it be the case that —]' and 'Shall[I will do —]' is appropriate to the context

Shall[N]

Thus even though I am right in claiming that the *ultimate* cash of 'shall' is to be found in

Shall[I will do A]

nevertheless all three senses of 'shall' are essential to the logic of practical reasoning.

[11] Now, presumably, what is up to me is that which I can bring about. This suggests that the schema

Shall[it be the case that(N and U)], i.e. shall[N and U]

is equivalent to

Shall[it be the case that(N and I bring about U)], i.e. shall[N and I bring about U]

[12] Can we say anything more about N? Indeed we can, and, in doing so, we shall be led to the heart of the problem of the logic of practical reasoning. We have granted that the content of intentions must include states of affairs which the agent believes *not* to be up to him. This suggests that we need a principle which gets such states of affairs into the context

Shall[—]

if they are believed to be the case *nolens volens*.

[13] Thus if I believe that whether I like it or not the theatre is going to show *Gone With the Wind*, the principle will take me from

The theatre will show GWTW

to

Shall[— *and* the theatre will show GWTW].

I call this the 'So-be-it' principle; it might also be called the reality principle. In effect, it authorizes the move

    p
    so, shall[— and p].

What is the status of this principle? Is it fundamentally new, or can it be derived from principles already accepted? The answer seems to be that So-be-it can be justified by our single higher order principle, making use of the fact that since, for any α

    'α and p' implies 'α and p'

it follows that

    'α' implies 'α and p' relatively to the assumption 'p,'

and hence that

    'shall[α]' implies 'shall[α and p]' relatively to the assumption 'p.'

This tells us that given the truth of 'p,' the latter is appropriately added to the content of one's intention, and, of course, that it would be inappropriate to add 'not-p.' Whether, all things considered, it is reasonable to add 'p' hinges on considerations of relevance. But such considerations play a role in any translation of implications into actual patterns of thought. More remains to be said about the relation of this derived principle to So-be-it, but this will do for the moment.

VII

[14] Before moving on to discuss the logic of conditional intentions, such as are expressed by sentences of the form

    If p, I shall do A

it will be helpful to discuss some formalized patterns which are related to, though by no means identical with, this logic. Thus, consider

    Shall[it rains at t → there will be thunder at t]
    It rains at t
    So, shall[there will be thunder at t]

Mobilizing the principles set forth so far, the reasoning, made more explicit, becomes

1. Shall[it rains at t → there will be thunder at t]   Premise
2. It rains at t   Premise
3. So, shall[it rains at t]   2, So-be-it
4. So, shall[it rains at t and (it rains at t → there will be   3, 1, C.I.
    thunder at t)]
5. Shall[there will be thunder at t]   4, M.P.

[15] Notice that in this reasoning, 'shall[it rains at t]' enters in by So-be-it, the proposition that it rains at t being accepted as true. Thus, perhaps t is *now* and one sees it to be raining or, although t is still future, one has conclusive reasons for believing that it will rain at t. Is So-be-it the only principle by virtue of which 'shall'–premises concerning what the agent believes *not* to be up to him enter practical reasoning? The answer is, fundamentally, yes. But this answer must be qualified to take account of the fact that practical reasoning, like the thinking of practical thoughts in general, can be 'bracketed' by hypotheses to which one is not committed. Thus we not only have

If 'Q' were up to me, shall[N and U and Q]

but

If it's raining or not at t were up to me,

  Shall[it rains at t]
  Shall[it rains at t → there will be thunder at t]
  So, shall[it rains at t and (it rains at t → there will be thunder at t)]
  So, shall[there will be thunder at t].

Here the reasoning itself becomes an experiment *in mente* bracketed by an 'hypothesis' about what is up to the agent.[5] In the case of the present example, to remove the bracketing the agent (except in the case of gods) need only take into account the fact that whether or not it rains is *not* up to me, in which case the only way in which the premise 'Shall[it rain at t]' can be preserved is by So-be-it, which involves accepting the proposition that it rains at t. On the other hand, in cases where it does turn out to be up to one whether Q, and one has opted for Q, the reasoning (assuming no change of mind) is simply unbracketed and one gets

---

[5] Of course, much practical reasoning occurs at the meta-level in which one reasons about *what* is implied by *what* at the object language level. Such meta-reasoning also suspends commitment to object language premises. But I think it helpful to look at the object language patterns themselves, and to use the above technique for representing suspension of commitment.

Since 'Q' is up to me,
    Shall[Q]   Premise
    Shall[Q → R]   Premise
    So, shall[Q and (Q → R)]   C.I.
    So, shall[R]   M.P.

[16] It should always be borne in mind that 'shall'-premises

Shall[P]

always have, implicitly, the form

Shall[α *and* P]

where 'α' represents those intention-elements N and U which are in the background, i.e. are not being called into question at the time of reasoning. To recognize this is simply to take seriously the principle of Conjunction Introduction. But questions *can* be reopened, and implications have their contrapositives.[6] Thus, the contrapositive of the implication which authorizes the final step in the previous reasoning, would authorize the second step in

If Q were up to me,
    1. Shall[not-R]   Premise
    2. So, Shall[not-(Q and (Q →R))]   T.T.
    3. Shall[Q → R]   Premise
    4. So, Shall[not-Q].   Logic

Of course, as a result of this experiment *in mente*, the background intentions represented by 'α' and implicit in these 'shall'-statements, may themselves be called into question, and the whole matter of arriving at preferences between alternatives reopened. This option can be represented by the schema

---

[6] It should be remembered that the contrapositive of
    'Shall[P]' implies 'Shall[Q]'
is
    'Shall[not-Q]' implies 'Shall[not-P]'
for the latter, like the former, is parasitical upon its indicative counterpart. I emphasize, once again, that 'shall'-statements are not subject to external negation.

If 'Q' were up to me,
$$\begin{cases} \text{Shall}[\alpha \text{ and } Q \text{ and } (Q \rightarrow R)]? \\ \text{Shall}[\alpha \text{ and not-}(Q \text{ and } (Q \rightarrow R))]? \\ \text{Shall}[\text{not-}\alpha \text{ and } Q \text{ and } (Q \rightarrow R)]? \\ \text{Shall}[\text{not-}\alpha \text{ and not-}(Q \text{ and } (Q \rightarrow R))]? \end{cases}$$

In any actual case, however, only a fragment of the background intention represented by 'α,' would be called into question.

VIII

[17] The next preliminary point concerns the fact that, construing 'shall' as 'it shall be the case that,' 'Shall[p → q]' and 'Shall[q → p]' are mutually consistent and are both compatible with 'p.' It has been argued in connection with the logic of 'imperatives' that to accept both the following patterns

I   !(α → β)   II   !(α → β)
     α   !(α)
So, !(β)   So, !(β)

involves an incoherence on the ground that it would justify the following pattern:

1. !(p → q)   Premise
2. !(q → p)   Premise
3. p   Premise
4. So, !(q)   1, 2, I
5. So, !(p)   2, 4, II

The charge of incoherence rests on the claim that '!(p)' is conceptually inconsistent with 'p.' Now if '!' is read 'Make it the case that —!' there is, indeed, a conceptual inconsistency between '!(p)' and 'p.' But, read in this way, the conceptual content of '!(p)' would not be the same as the conceptual content of 'p.' They would stand to one another as "Make it the case that the door is closed!" stands to 'The door is closed.' Suppose, on the other hand, that '!' is read 'Let it be that —!', then the conceptual inconsistency vanishes, for, obviously, 'Let it be that the door is closed!'[7] is quite consistent with 'The door is closed.'

[18] I have paused for this excursus into 'imperative logic' because a related point is essential to my argument. For not only do I hold that 'shall[p]' is consistent with 'p,' I have offered a principle to the effect that the latter *implies*

---

[7] Which, of course, must not be confused with 'Let it be that the door *remains* closed!'

the former. Thus, I accept as valid patterns of practical reasoning corresponding to both I and II above, thus

I' Shall[α → β]
α
So, Shall[β]

II' Shall[α → β]
Shall[α]
So, Shall[β]

But, it is important to remember, I have explained the validity of pattern I', which involves mixed indicative and resolutive premises, in terms of a pattern which (like II') has only resolutive premises. According to this explanation, the role of the indicative proposition represented by 'α' is to be the premise in a meta-argument which establishes a derivative implication which introduces the So-be-it or realistic element into intentions,

p
So 'α' implies (relatively to p) 'α and p'
So 'Shall[α]' implies 'Shall[α and p]'

All (nonprobabilistic) practical reasoning was thus brought under a single higher order principle according to which implications between resolutives are based on implications between indicatives.

IX

[19] I deliberately chose as my first regimented example of resolutive reasoning involving 'if's a case where the states of affairs involved are obviously not up to the person who deliberates. The examples to which I now turn come closer to the topic of conditional intentions to act, although they still fall short of providing an adequate explication. Compare the following:

C. 1. Shall[it rains at t → I study at t]   Premise
   2. It rains at t   Premise
   3. So, shall[it rains at t]   2, So-be-it
   4. So, shall[it rains at t and (it rains at t → I study at t)]   1, 3, C.I.
   5. So, shall[I study at t]   4, M.P.

D. 1. Shall[I do not study at t → it does not rain at t]   Premise
   2. I do not study at t   Premise
   3. So, shall[I do not study at t]   2, So-be-it
   4. So, shall[I do not study at t and (I do not study at t → it does not rain at t)]   1, 3, C.I.
   5. So, shall[it does not rain at t]   4, M.P.

We notice at once that whereas the third step in C is, I hope, unproblematic, the same is by no means true in the case of D. One is tempted to expostulate that the use of So-be-it presupposes that the state of affairs to which it is applied is not up to the agent, whereas studying and not studying are just the sort of thing that it is up to people to do. The answer is, in part, that the phrase 'So-be-it' has overtones which (though discountable) are, as such, inappropriate to the use to which I am putting it. It implies a 'fatalistic' attitude. Using it, however, will enable me to force a clarification of the way in which the state of affairs to which it is applied enters into the content of intentions.

[20] The propositions to which So-be-it is applied enter into intentions by virtue of being accepted as true. Now in the case of states of affairs which are *not* up to us, credibility is independent* of our intentions. On the other hand, in the case of states of affairs which *are* up to us, this is not so; indeed our ground for believing that they will obtain is our very intention that they obtain.[8] With this in mind, let us take another look at the structure of D. The first thing to note is that the state of affairs involved in the conclusion is not up to the agent. This suggests that, as we've been putting it, the argument is an experiment *in mente* on the hypothesis that the weather is 'up to me.' After all, reasoning does play a role in establishing our preferences in abstraction from a commitment to do anything about them.

[21] What of step D-1? It might come in through So-be-it. The agent might know that

It rains at t and I do not study at t

is ruled out, for example, by parental authority. This would involve prefacing D-1 by two antecedent steps, thus,

O.	Not-(r and not-s)	Premise
O'.	So, shall[not-(r and not-s)]	So-be-it
D-1.	So, Shall[not-s → not-r].	Logic

This interpretation requires that though the reasoning is bracketed by the hypothesis of the weather's being up to me, studying is taken *not* to be up to me, *if it rains*.[9] Perhaps, then, we can construe the reasoning to be bracketed by the more complex rubric,

---

* [Eds.—This is typed "dependent" in original document. However, it seems Sellars means "independent" here; and Sellars wrote "independent" in an earlier version of this manuscript. The earlier typescript is document 31735062222132, Box 43, Folders 1–3, Wilfrid S. Sellars Papers, 1899–1990, ASP.1991.01, Archives of Scientific Philosophy, Archives & Special Collections, University of Pittsburgh Library System.]

[8] Needless to say we may well be mistaken in our belief that something is up to us; and even where this belief is correct, our intentions may change, and our original expectations turn out, for this reason, to be mistaken. But these considerations do not affect the logic of the reasoning involved.

[9] The moral to which I am pointing is, obviously, that a study must be made of the logic of 'up to me' with respect to complex states of affairs and their constituents.

Although if it rains, it is not up to me whether I study,

Thus, 1.	Not-(r and not-s)	Premise
2.	So, shall[not-s → not-r]	So-be-it

if it is up to me whether I study, if it doesn't rain

3.	Not-r	Premise
4a.	Shall[not-r and not-s]? Shall[not-r and s]?	?
4b.	Shall[not-r and not-s]	Premise
5.	Shall[not-r]	4b, Simpl
6.	Shall[not-s]	4b, Simpl

Here there seems to be an *embarras de richesses* with respect to deriving 'Shall [not-r].' We can derive it from 3 *via* So-be-it. We can derive it as above from the preference formulated by 4b. We can, ostensibly, derive it from 2 or 6 *via modus ponens*. Of these, however, the hypothesis which governs steps 3 ff. would point to the use of So-be-it, for the alternatives considered in the preferential questions are limited by the assumption that it doesn't rain.

[22] On the other hand, D-1 might come in as a simple expression of preference. In this case, since the relevant alternatives are 'r and s,' 'r and not-s,' 'not-r and s,' and 'not-r and not-s,' the reasoning would involve a commitment to a certain answer to the bracketed family of questions:

If r and s were both up to me,
   shall[r and s]?
   shall[r and not-s]?
   shall[not-r and s]?
   shall[not-r and not-s]?

and, since these questions are respectively equivalent to

Shall[(r and not-s) or (not-r and s) or (not-r and not-s)]?
Shall[(r and s) or (not-r and s) or (not-r and not-s)]?
Shall[(r and s) or (r and not-s) or (not-r and not-s)]?
Shall[(r and s) or (r and not-s) or (not-r and s) or (not-r and s)*]?

D-1, on this interpretation, would amount to an affirmative answer to the second question, by virtue of its equivalence to

---

* [Eds.—In the original, the third and fourth disjuncts are identical; it seems that the fourth disjunct should instead read "not-r and not-s".]

Shall[not-(r and not-s)]?

and hence to

Shall[not-s → not-r]?

[23] But what are we to make of step D-3 on this new interpretation? This question brings us face to face with what is puzzling about the whole pattern. Surely, we are tempted to argue, if to study or not to study is up to the agent, his ground for asserting that he will not study must be his intention not to study. If that is so, however, step D-2 is otiose, D-3 being directly available. Indeed, the whole point of D-1 would seem to disappear, since we can rest at the preferential question 'Shall[not-r and not-s]?' and obtain

1. Shall[not-r and not-s]		Premise
2. So, Shall[not-s]		1, Simpl.
3. So, Shall[not-r]		1, Simpl.

[24] On neither of the above interpretations of D is there a real place for the use of So-be-it to derive D-3. One might be tempted to conclude from the above that *in general* there is no place for the use of So-be-it in connection with states of affairs which are up to the agent. This, however, would be a mistake. Consider a case which involves two states of affairs, each of which is, in some preanalytic sense, up to the agent. (Let 'P' abbreviate 'I will go to Paris next summer' and 'L,' 'I will visit the Louvre next summer'.)

E.	1. Shall[P → L]*	Premise
	2. P	Premise
	3. So, Shall[P]	2, So-be-it
	4. So, Shall[P and (P → L)]	1, 3, C.I.
	5. So, Shall[L]	4, M.P.

How does this reasoning, with its use of So-be-it, differ from

F.	1. Shall[P → L]	Premise
	2. Shall[P]	Premise
	3. So, Shall[P and (P → L)]	1, 2, C.I.
	4. So, Shall[L]	3, M.P.

---

* [Eds.—Correction of 'Shall[P → L)]' in original manuscript.]

which does not use So-be-it, but simply introduces 'Shall[I will go to Paris*]' as a premise? Notice that F is equivalent to

F'. 1. Shall[(P and L) or (not-P and L) or (not-P and not-L)]   Premise
    2. Shall[(P and L) or (P and not-L)]   Premise
    3. Shall[not-(P and not-L)]   1, Logic
    4. Shall[P and L]   2, 3, T.P.

The answer is to be found by noticing that just as we can hypothesize that states of affairs are up to us which we know *not* to be in our power, so we can consider our own possible actions 'objectively' i.e. as states of affairs which obtain or do not obtain, rather than as actions to be done or not done.

[25] What is clearly needed is a formalism which gives expression to this intuitively grasped distinction between viewing our possible actions as constituents of alternative states of affairs with respect to which we engaged in establishing our preferences, and viewing them directly as answers to the question 'What shall I do?' Actually the means of drawing this distinction have already been presented—though not yet adequately exploited. I have in mind in first instance, the distinction between

    Shall[It be the case that —], abbreviated as SB[—]

and

    Shall[I bring it about that—]

or, as I shall now represent it (to give it a distinctive abbreviation,

    Shall[I make it that —], abbreviated as SM[—]

In both cases, the content represented by '—,' consists of straightforward indicative expressions for states of affairs e.g. 'The theatre will show GWTW,' 'I will go to Paris next summer,' 'If it rains at t then it will thunder at t.' The distinctive feature of the second rubric is that it involves the action locution 'I make it that,' which governs the whole content, and represents the fact that this entire content is being considered *sub specie actionis*.[10] The same states of affairs belong in both contexts, 'SB[—]' and 'SM[—],' but the former abstracts from the agent's agency,

---

* [Eds.— Correction of 'the Louvre' in original manuscript.]

[10] Notice that the action verb 'make,' which is what is directly governed by 'Shall,' is an infinitive and lacks assertive force. The same is true of the 'be' of 'Shall[it be the case, that —]'. From this point of view, 'Shall' plays a role akin to Hare's neustic 'please' though purged of the latter's performative

with respect to the content considered, and is suitable for reasonings where one is working out the implications of preferences with respect to complex states of affairs which include our own possible actions without viewing the latter as possible answers to the question 'what shall I do?'

[26] Yet, since a tie to the question 'What shall I do?' is central to the concept of intent, this means that a commitment to an intention of the form

SB[—]

dialectically implies a commitment to intent of the form

SM*[—]

I have attempted to capture this intent by saying that 'It shall be the case that-P' is equal to 'I shall do what is in my power to bring it about that-P.' Usually, that which is in our power to do is something not included in, but causally related to, the state of affairs which we intend to be the case. But in the limiting case it may be included in it as an action of mine *qua* state of affairs. In which case, given that by doing the action, I can realize the complex state of affairs which includes my doing it,

SB[N and I will do A]

collapses into

SM[N and I will do A]

It should be borne in mind, however, that intentions of both kinds can be bracketed by hypotheses concerning what is up to the agent, along the lines discussed in previous sections.

[27] The introduction of this distinction carries with it other requirements. Thus 'SM[P and Q]' will imply 'SM[P]' only where 'P' is up to the agent. Otherwise, what is implied is the weaker 'SB[P].' Again 'SM[P and Q]' presupposes that at least one of the two states of affairs 'P' and 'Q' is taken to be up to the agent. If one of them, say 'P,' is not so taken, at least by a bracketing hypothesis, it must enter into the content of the intention by way of So-be-it.

---

overtones. No nominalizations ('My bringing it about that —,' 'It's being the case that —')—Hare's phrastics—are involved in the above reconstruction, nor is there any hint that a 'yes' operator is called for to account for the assertiveness of declarative utterances.

* [Eds.—Correction of "SB" in original manuscript. Sellars has written this correctly (as "SM") in the earlier version of this typescript previously cited; the passage in question is handwritten on the back of page 23.]

[28] Again, this distinction between actions as states of affairs and actions as to do's enables us to take into account the fact that what is up to me at one time may no longer (though still future) be up to me at another. Obviously the past is no longer up to me, and when I have performed an action it is no longer up to me to perform *that* action, though it may be up to me to perform another action of the same kind. Thus, when I have gone to Paris at t, going to Paris at t is no longer up to me, though it may be up to me to go there on another occasion. Thus we have room for the hypothesis,

If going to Paris next summer, were no longer up to me because I will have gone there;

1. $SM[P \rightarrow L]$ Premise
2. P Premise
3. $SB[P]$ 2, So-be-it
4. $SM[P \bullet (P \rightarrow L)]$*   1, 3, C.I.
5. $SM[L]$ 4, M.P.

[29] This distinction brings out the merit of construing So-be-it as derivative from the fact that

'α' implies 'α and p' relatively to the assumption that-p.

For this enables us to distinguish

So-be-it$_{SB}$: '$SB[\alpha]$' implies '$SB[\alpha$ and $p]$' relatively to the assumption that-p

from

So-be-it$_{SM}$: '$SM[\alpha]$' implies '$SM[\alpha$ and $p]$' relatively to the assumption that-p

The use of So-be-it$_{SM}$ presupposes that 'α' is up to the agent.

[30] Let us examine the logic of this difference with respect to So-be-it. For this purpose, let us return to example C. With this new rubric, it becomes

C′. 1. $SM[$it will rain $\rightarrow$ I will study$]$ Premise
     2. It will rain   Premise
     3. $SM[$It will rain and (it will rain $\rightarrow$ I will study)$]$ So-be-it$_{SM}$
     4. $SM[$I will study$]$ 3, M.P.

---

* [Eds.—The conjunction symbol (•) is missing from the original manuscript. However, it is present in the version of the proof from the earlier typescript cited previously. The proof is handwritten on the back of page 24.]

This reasoning culminates in the decision to bring it about that I will study, i.e. the decision to study.

[31] Again, we see that in example D, on that interpretation which introduces step D-1 by So-be-it, the first two steps must be

1. not-s → not-r	Premise
2. SB[not-s → not-r]	1, So-be-it$_{SB}$

of which the following would be a valid continuation,

3. SB[not-s]	Premise
4. SB[not-s and (not-s → not-r)]	2, 3, C.I.
5. SB[not-r]	4, M.P.

[32] Let us now review example E in the light of these considerations. If this pattern is to culminate in a decision to visit the Louvre, it must be reconstructed as follows

E'.	1. SM[P → L]	Premise
	2. P	Premise
	3. SM[P and (P → L)]	1, 2, So-be-it$_{SM}$
	4. SM[L]	M.P.
	5. Shall[I visit the Louvre this summer]	?

As such it would contrast with the original argument in which 'shall' was interpreted as 'it shall be the case that,' which becomes

E''.	1. SB[P → L]	Premise
	2. P	Premise
	3. SB[P and (P → L)]	1, 2, So-be-it$_{SB}$
	4. SB[L]	3, M.P.

[33] Notice that the final step in E' consists in the move from

Shall[I make it that I will visit the Louvre this summer]

to

Shall[I visit the Louvre this summer]

This involves what might be called the 'reduction' of the pleonastic action verb 'to make it the case that I visit' to the action verb 'to visit.' This principle might be called Action Reduction (A.R.).

[34] Notice that the symbolism I have been using stresses that 'shall' operates on the whole of the expression which follows it in brackets. This wholistic theme is also expressed by the verbs 'to be the case that —' and 'to make it the case that —.' These verbs can be said to be the targets of the 'shall'-operator. It is natural to put the target verbs in the infinitive, as above. For a verb which expresses intention functions (in English) as an auxiliary verb which takes the infinitive. Yet once one sees that nominalizations are not needed, (Hare's 'phrastics'), there seems to be no reason not to use the simple indicative, thus

Shall[it will be the case that —]
Shall[I will bring it about that —]
Shall[I will visit Paris this summer]

[35] But what, it may be said, is the point of straining at Hare's nominalizations, if you are content with the 'that'-clauses in

A. Shall[it will be the case that —]

and

B. Shall[I will bring it about that —]?

The answer is that once we see that the target of 'shall' in A is the compound proposition represented by '—,' we also see that we can simply replace A, without loss, by

A'. Shall[—]

In the case of B, however, the story is more complicated. There is in ordinary language no standard way of constructing single action verbs out of actions and states of affairs which are not actions which verbs are equivalent to 'to bring it about that —' but without the use of propositional nominalization.* It is, however, clear from particular cases that this can be done, and this is all that is necessary to quiet the nominalistic anxieties aroused by B.

---

* [Eds.—This sentence is a bit difficult to follow. In the earlier version of PRA cited in a previous editorial note, the sentence reads as follows:

> There is in ordinary language no standard way of constructing single action verbs which knit together actions and states of affairs which are not actions which yields the equivalent of "to bring it about that —" without the use of propositional nominalization.

The sentence in question is handwritten on the back of p. 27.]

X

[36] We can now understand the difference in feeling between

    C. 1. Shall[it will rain → I will study]   Premise
       2. It will rain   Premise
       3. Shall[it will rain and (it will rain → I will study)]   1, 2, So-be-it
       4. Shall[I will study]   3, M.P.

and

    D. 1. Shall[not-s → not-r]   Premise
       2. Not-s   Premise
       3. Shall[not-s and (not-s → not-r)]   1, 2, So-be-it
       4. Shall[not-r].   3, M.P.

Although C and D are on a par, construed as SB patterns, C has an SM counterpart with which it might be confused, whereas D does not. Despite the fact that we can *begin* to construct an SM counterpart of D, thus,

    D″. 1. SM[not-s → not-r]
        2. Not-s
        3. SM[not-s and (not-s → not-r)]   So-be-it$_{SM}$

the conclusion, 'SM[not-r]' would be out of place, unless the entire reasoning were bracketed by "if the weather were up to me."

[37] Notice that both

SM[r → s]

and

SM[not-s → not-r]

are well formed, because, although the weather is not up to the agent, regardless of what the weather turns out to be, it is up to the agent to realize the intention. Thus, if it rains he does so by studying. If it does not rain, he realizes it whether he studies or doesn't study. We may be tempted to say "*it is realized* regardless of whether he studies or doesn't study," but since the context is one of *intentions* being realized, rather than merely of states of *affairs* being realized, the former locution is not out of place when explicating the up-to-one-ness of a complex state of affairs.

[38] Let us turn our attention, once again, to the pattern

G. 1. Shall[r → s]
    2. Shall[r]
    3. So, Shall[r and (r → s)]
    4. So, Shall[s]

According to considerations advanced above, this is equivalent to

If such and such were up to me, then
  1. SM[r → s]
  2. ....
  3. So, SM[r and (r → s)]
  4. So, SM[s]

But what is the scope of 'such and such'? Study? At least. But perhaps also the weather. If both, then the following is correct

If study and the weather were up to me,
  1. SM[r → s]   Premise
  2. SM[r]   Premise
  3. So, SM[r and (r → s)]   C.I.
  4. So, SM[s]   M.P.

we would have an explicated instance of pattern II' (§18 above*):

Shall[α → β]
Shall[α]
So, Shall[β]

[39] If, on the other hand, the scope of 'such and such' is limited to study, then the above would not be correct, but rather the following:

If study were up to me
  1. SM[r → s]   Premise
  2. r   Premise
  3. So, SM[r and (r → s)]   1, 2, So-be-it$_{SM}$
  4. So, SM[s].   3, M.P.

---

* [Eds.—Original reference was to p. 12 of the manuscript.]

We would have an explicated instance of Pattern I' (§18 above*).

[40] The point at which I am driving is that if the conclusion of a pattern of practical reasoning is to be (if only hypothetically) a decision to act, a state of affairs not up to the agent can enter the reasoning only by So-be-it$_{SM}$. It can not enter simply by virtue of being a constituent of a preferred state of affairs which abstracts from what is up to the agent.

[41] Now the distinctive feature of G is the fact that it was presumably up to the agent whether or not to study. What of the case where one is exploring *in mente* one's preferences concerning items that are not up to one? The above considerations suggest that

> Shall[r → t]
> Shall[r]
> Shall[r and (r → t)]
> Shall[t]

has the form

> If rain and thunder were up to me,
> > SM[r → t]　　　　　　　　　　Premise
> > SM[r]　　　　　　　　　　　　Premise
> > So, SM[r and (r → t)]　　　　　C.I.
> > So, SM[t]　　　　　　　　　　M.P.

and the restriction imposed above on detachment, namely that given that 'P' implies 'Q,' 'SM[P]' implies 'SM[Q]' (as contrasted with 'SB[Q]'), only where Q is up to the agent, would be justified by the fact that although the bracketing imposed by '*If* such and such is up to me' is *directly* removed by '*Since* such and such is up to me,' to the extent that 'such and such' includes items which are recalcitrantly *not* up to one, the latter can be removed from the bracketing only *via* the So-be-it principle, i.e. by being accepted as factually true.

[42] From this point of view,

> SB[r → s]
> SB[r]
> So, SB[r and (r → s)]
> So, SB[s]

---

* [Eds.—Original reference was to p. 12 of the manuscript.]

is equivalent to the bracketed

> If weather and study be up to me,
> SM[r → s]
> SM[r]
> So, SM[r and (r → s)]
> So, SM[s]

and the two stages in its unbracketing would involve two alternative intermediate steps,

> If weather be up to me, and since study is up to me,
> SM[r → s]
> SM[r]
> So, SM[r and (r → s)]
> So, SM[s]

> If study be up to me, and since the weather is not, and it will rain,
> SM[r → s]
> r
> So, SM[r and (r → s)]   So-be-it$_{SM}$
> So, SM[s]

but the same unbracketed reasoning,

> Since study is up to me and the weather is not but it will rain,
> SM[r → s]
> r
> So, SM[r and (r → s)]
> So, SM[s]

XI

[43] Against this background, how are we to understand the conditional intention to act expressed by

> If p, I shall A?

Clearly it expresses a readiness to reason

> p
> .
> .
> .
> .
> .
> So, Shall[I will do A]

But this is not all. It presupposes that this reasoning would be sound or valid. Thus it will not do simply to say that to have the conditional intention amounts to accepting the inference ticket

'p' implies 'shall[I will do A].'

A look at what might be called conditional beliefs will illuminate the situation. Consider

If p, q.

This, as has often been noted, is not the ordinary language counterpart of 'material implication,' though the locution can be given a technical sense in which this is what it stands for. Rather it expresses a readiness to reason

p
.
.
.
.
.
So, q

But more than this, it presupposes that when this reasoning is fleshed out, it would turn out to be sound. In other words it presupposes that one has defensible premises $(r_1, \ldots r_n)$ up ones sleeve which, combined with p, logically imply q, thus

p
$(r_1, \ldots r_n)$
So, q

[44] If this is correct, we cannot interpret

if p, I shall do A

as creating, so to speak by stipulation, an implication which would take one from 'p' to 'I shall do A,' but rather must view it as implying that there are available premises, not explicitly stated, such that combined with 'p' they would generate a valid argument. Now it seems to me obvious that the argument hinted at by the conditional intention will involve (1) a premise of intention, (2) a use of So-be-it. Let us see what we can make of

If it rains, I shall study

To be sure, this is not to be identified with

shall be[r → s]

for it tells us, which the latter does not, (1) that whether or not it rains is not up to the agent[11] and comes into the reasoning via So-be-it; (2) that the situation 'not-(r and not-s)' is up to the agent. Furthermore, it implies that given the relevant facts, the agent prefers [the facts and not-(r and not-s)] to [the facts and (r and not-s)]. Thus it amounts to a preparedness to reason in accordance with the pattern

1. SM[facts and (r → s)]	Premise
2. r	Premise
3. So, SM[facts and r and (r → s)]	1, 2, So-be-it$_{SM}$
4. So, SM[s]	3, M.P.

upon obtaining the premise r. This reasoning is valid in terms of the principles explored in the preceding sections.

[45] It might be thought that since the condition which qualifies the intention is 'it will rain,' the alternatives considered at the preferential level need only be

Shall[— and r and s]?   Shall[— and r and not-s]?

In which case the reasoning to which one is committed could be the simpler

1. r	Premise
2. So, SB[— and r]	1, So-be-it
3. So, SB[— and r and s]	Premise of preference
4. So, SM[— and r and s]	s up to me
5. So, SM[s]	

But the question 'What shall I do if it rains?' is naturally paired with 'What shall I do if it doesn't rain?' When this is done the dialectical situation makes relevant the four alternatives,

---

[11] This interpretation can be extended to the case
If I go to Paris, I shall visit the Louvre
By noting as we did above that once I have gone to Paris, *going to Paris* is no longer up to me.

> Shall[— and r and s]?
> Shall[— and r and not-s]?
> Shall[— not r and s]?
> Shall[— not r and not s]?

On the other hand, since to be in a position to say

> If it rains, I shall study

is not necessarily to be in a position to answer the alternative question (other than, perhaps, by thinking 'if it doesn't rain, I don't know what I shall do'), it is not unreasonable to expect the preferential premise to take the form of a negative answer to the second alternative, thus,

> Shall[not-(r and not-s)]

which, given r, carries a commitment to

> shall[r and s]

via So-be-it, as in the preceding reconstruction.

[46] The conditional intention

> If it doesn't rain, I shall not study

would be built on the same basic alternatives, but involve a commitment to

> Shall[— and not-(not-r and s)]

and to the reasoning

> Shall[— and not-(not-r and s)]
> Not-r
> So, shall[— and not-r and not (not r and s)]
> So, shall[not-s]

[47] What is the relationship between reasonings which are bracketed by the rubric 'if such and such were up to me,' and the reasonings which exist in suspended animation when commitment is made to a conditional intention? The answer is that rehearsal of the former is a way of making explicit the implications of one's preferences, in abstraction from what is up to one. Conditional intentions, however, involve a commitment with respect to what is

up to me, but not to what the facts are. They are, therefore, rehearsals of reasoning culminating in decisions to act.

[48] We can now understand why, although

If p, I shall do A

and

If p, I shall not do A

are *incompatible* intentions, their logic is to be understood in terms of the logic of

Shall[p → q]

and

Shall[p → not-q]

which are compatible intentions, amounting together to

Shall[not-p].

[49] Again, we see why, although

Shall[p → q]

is equivalent to

Shall[not-q → not-p]

the conditional intention

if p, I shall do A

is not equivalent to

if I do not do A, shall[not-p].

[50] An important terminological point. It might be thought that since the core of Kant's concept of a 'hypothetical imperative' concerns intentions rather than imperatives, one should speak of 'hypothetical intentions.' But this would be to confuse what is expressed by

> If I want X, I ought to do A

namely

> 'Shall[I will get X]' implies 'Shall[I will do A]'

with

> if I want X, I shall do A

The former expresses a relation of implication between intentions. The latter considers my wanting X (or not) *sub specie* objective matter of fact, entering into reasoning *via* So-be-it, and implies a conditional commitment to the reasoning

> I want X
> .
> .
> .
> .
> .
> So, shall[I will do A]

20
The Hare–Sellars Correspondence, 1953–1980

H1. Hare to Sellars, 5 July 1953

Dear Professor Sellars,

It was very kind of you to send me offprints of your two articles. By a coincidence they reached here the same day as the July number of *Mind*, with your article on 'Inference and Meaning'. I shall read them all with great interest. The one on 'Particulars' deals with a subject about which, after reading the Lukasiewicz-Anscombe-Popper symposium in the current Aristotelian Society Supplementary volume, I am very desirous of becoming clearer.[*] The other two touch on a question which I have for some time thought to be absolutely central to the subject which most interests me, Ethics.[†] As it happens, I had a graduate class here [Eds.—at Balliol College, Oxford] last term, in which we discussed the very questions which you discuss, with particular reference to moral reasoning, and Toulmin and Herbst[‡], who both came, maintained positions which—from a very cursory glance at your papers—seem to me not unlike yours, or at any rate such as you would view with sympathy. Also Baier[§], whom you may have met when he was over your side, has tried to convince me of the validity of a similar line of reasoning. None of these people have yet convinced me; perhaps you papers will when I have had time to read them properly. In the mean time very many thanks for sending them; I am sadly in need of some expert assistance in sorting out this troublesome but fundamental problem.

Yours sincerely,
R. M. Hare.

---

[*] [Eds.—Jan Lukasiewicz, Elizabeth Anscombe, and Karl Popper, "Symposium: The Principle of Individuation," *Proceedings of the Aristotelian Society, Supplementary Volumes* 27, Berkeley and Modern Problems (1953): 69–120.]

[†] [Eds.—Sellars may be referring to OMR, and either to LRB or MMB. However, Hare refers to "offprints" of "articles," and both OMR and LRB appeared in edited volumes.]

[‡] [Eds.—Steven Toulmin and Peter Herbst.]   [§] [Eds.—Kurt Baier.]

S2. Sellars to Hare, 22 July 1953*

[*Editorial note—In a journal entry dated 29 August 1953†, Sellars has copied out the "substantive" (numbered) paragraphs of this letter (through paragraph 8), and has added "remarks... by way of clarification and amplification." After each paragraph, we have added his journal remarks in italics. Phrases struck through or underlined appear as such in the journal.*]

Dear Mr. Hare:

I was delighted to receive your friendly letter. I quite agree that the topics discussed in the off-prints are of central importance for Ethics (I only wish the papers themselves lived up to the topics). However, I have been increasingly struck by the fact that certain topics discussed in Ethics are of central importance for these epistemological topics in return. How much more needs to be said (and said carefully) about the whole notion of 'rules of language' and about rules generally!—particularly if one is going to defend a thesis like mine. I have therefore been devoting more and more time to brooding about the language of rules. It is in this frame of mind that I have been reading your really excellent book.‡ As a matter of fact I was moved to send you the off-prints by reading your remarks on Carnap's P-rules.§ And I was mentally working up some comments on your account of the relation of ought-statements to imperatives when your letter arrived. It has encouraged me to develop them in the form of a letter to the author. I am in such complete sympathy with your approach, and with the general lines of your conclusions, that I am led to hope that I can communicate to you my difficulties with some of the things you say.

1. You rightly insist that ought-statements, in their primary or evaluative use, have a necessary relation to the guiding and control of conduct. In traditional terms, there is a necessary connexion between obligation and motivation.

The important point to notice here is that <u>he ought to do X in C doesn't entail he is moved (to some extent) to do X in C</u>. On the other hand 'I ought to do X in C' does seem to entail 'I am moved (to some extent) to do X in C' and 'he thinks he ought to do X in C' does seem to entail 'he is moved (to some extent) to do X in C.' [The motivation in question is not of the doing-it-because-he-wants-it-or-a-result-of-it

---

* [Eds.—In the upper-right corner of the page, there is the following handwritten note: "W: I hope to learn more about this! H." It seems likely to be from the hand of Hector-Neri Castañeda.]

† [Eds.—"Dated Philosophical Journals, 1949–1956," Volume 2, pp. 88–87. The journal is document 31735062216746, Box 25, Folders 1–2, Wilfrid S. Sellars Papers, 1899–1990, ASP.1991.01, Archives of Scientific Philosophy, Archives & Special Collections, University of Pittsburgh Library System. We are indebted to Lionel Shapiro for directing us to this journal entry, as well as for his transcription of the entry.]

‡ [Eds.—R. M. Hare, *The Language of Morals* (Oxford: Clarendon Press, 1952).]

§ [Eds.—*The Language of Morals*, §§1.7 and 3.5.]

sort — see Hagerström*]. Of course, the point is that my <u>statement</u> "I ought to do X in C" pragmatically implies my assenting to (my <u>thinking</u>) "I ought to do X in C" and in general 'X thinks he ought to do A in C' entails 'X is moved (to some extent) to do A in C.'

2. If an intuitionist is asked, "Could a person apprehend a set of prima-facie obligations, and yet have no tendency to be moved to act by thoughts of the form 'I ought to do X'?" he must surely reply either (a) "It is a contingent empirical fact that people are motivated (to some degree) by such thoughts," which is implausible, or (b) "It is a synthetic necessary (a priori) truth that people are so motivated" which is disturbing.

Here the key point is that since the intuitionist assimilates thinking 'I ought to do X in C' to thinking 'I am six feet tall' or '2 + 2 = 4' he doesn't see how 'thinking one ought to do A in C' could <u>logically</u> entail 'being moved to do A in C.' Hence he seems forced to hold that this relation must be a law of human nature learned by observation + generalization or else that it is a matter of <u>a priori</u> insight into a synthetic necessity.

The truth of the matter is that 'thinking one ought to do A in C' includes a motivational aspect. [Moral philosophers have often been tempted to say that one apprehends moral truths by means of moral emotions]. How this can be becomes clear when put in "linguistic terms."

3. The emotivist or—as he might better be called—motivationist, on the other hand, makes the relation *analytic* by claiming that to "think" one ought to do X *is* to be motivated to do X. (This is, of course, a radical over-simplification; but the point would still stand after the necessary qualifications had been made). The emotivist, in other words, claims that to learn to use the word 'ought' is to acquire a tendency to do A when one hears 'You ought to do A' or says to himself 'I ought to do A'. (Also an over-simplification).

It should be added here that the emotivist, when careful, distinguishes ethical motivation from 'doing actions because one likes doing the action for its own sake or wants some result which the action brings about.' Saying to someone 'you ought to do X' is not the same sort of thing as saying 'by doing X you will get Y (which you want).' or anymore than obeying a command is doing the commanded action in order to secure promotion or please the sergeant.

4. Now the emotivist account is open to the objection that even if it is part of the business of 'ought' to serve as a motivational trigger, this by no means exhausts its function in ethical discourse. 'Ought' has a complex logical grammar by virtue of which it has *conceptual* status, and is more than a prick or goad. In particular, 'I ought to do X in C' entails 'Anybody ought to do X in C.' (Again an over-simplification—but you see what I mean). The intuitionist, relying on traditional

---

* [Eds.—Presumably Axel Hägerström.]

accounts of conceptual meaning, infers that ought-sentences are tailored to fit antecedent apprehensions of ethical facts.

The point at which I am driving is that ethical discourse is not a combination of fact stating discourse ~~plus~~ with a set of prick or goad noises, nor is it a ~~special~~ mode of discourse for stating a special kind of fact – it is rational <u>qua</u> ethical even though not fact stating <u>qua</u> ethical – or if in a broad sense it can be said to be "fact stating <u>qua</u> ethical," since it makes sense to reply to "One ought to keep promises" with "That's a fact," or to say "It is a fact that one ought to keep promises," the point is that the agreement with another person which leads one to say 'yes it's a fact that one ought to keep promises' is an agreement in <u>motivation</u>, and this motivation is a <u>rational</u> motivation, in that it is "syllogistic."

5. You correctly point out that the emotivist, in effect, is confusing singular ought-statements with singular imperatives.* On the other hand, you recognize that imperatives admittedly have the power to shape and guide conduct which is essential to ought-statements in their evaluative use.† Indeed, you appear to claim that *only* imperatives have the *job* of shaping and guiding conduct (I say 'job' because almost any sentence will on some occasions serve to bring about conduct, e.g. "There's a car coming on the right.") so that if any statement not an imperative has this job‡, it must have it *indirectly* by virtue of entailing an imperative.§

6. But, perhaps, instead of making a substantive claim about imperatives, you are proposing rather to use the word 'imperative' in such a way that any form of sentence which conventionally serves the purpose of evoking (or tending to evoke) conduct is an imperative, *whether or not it is in the imperative mood*. You might then be claiming that 'I ought to do A' *is* an imperative, but preferring to say that it *entails* an imperative, since it has so many other facets ('meanings'). The verbal bridge which would make this line plausible is: x entails y if y is part of the meaning of x; being an imperative is part of the meaning of 'I ought to do A;' therefore 'I ought to do A' entails an imperative. (Note that I am not attributing this line of thought to you).

The sentence beginning "The verbal fudge…" should be deleted as the verbal fudge is so "unsafe" that it adds nothing to the point made in the first two sentences.

7. But if one were to ask "*What* imperative (in the above broad sense) does it entail?" the answer would seem to be "I ought to do A." To give any other answer is to imply that the form of words 'I ought to do A' has motivational force only by virtue of its relation to some other form of words having motivational force.

---

* [Eds.—See, e.g., *The Language of Morals*, §§10.3 and 11.5.]
† [Eds.—*The Language of Morals*, ch. 11.]
‡ [Eds.—In the original letter, this reads "power" instead of "job." But when Sellars transcribes the letter into the journal, he substitutes "job," and writes in brackets, "letter has 'power' but should be changed." Aside from that, Sellars provides no commentary on this paragraph.]
§ [*The Language of Morals*, ch. 11.]

8. Now, it is my conviction that ethical discourse has motivational force which is not borrowed from non-ethical discourse. In other words, if I were to adopt the use of 'imperative' suggested in 6 above, I would say that 'I ought to do A' *is* an imperative. I prefer, however, to distinguish between a broad category of statement forms the learning to use which involves acquiring dispositions to act in manners referred to in the statements, and a narrower category of statements in the imperative mood. This, however, is a verbal point. Let me say again, however, that if 'imperative' is used for the broader category, I would claim that 'I ought to do A' *is* (rather than *entails*) an imperative.

[In this connection let me make the point I was making to Bob* up at Coon Lake last weekend. Since the differentiating feature of ethical discourse from other discourse having the motivating rôle lies in the fact that E (Jones doing A in C) rests on E (anybody doing A in C) where 'E' represents the "ethical" component of the statement, ethical discourse might well be of imperative mood with this difference that the ethical sentences in the imperative mood would contain an intention that this relationship was involved. For example a typical ethical sentence might be "Thou shalt do A in C" where the difference between "Thou shalt do A in C" and "Do A in C" (both said to a certain individual) would entail the fact that behind the latter stands (or might be) "Everyman, do A in C."

As a matter of fact, one might well say that 'Jones, you ought to do A in C' has the force of 'Jones, do A in C! as a case of Everybody do A in C!' To put it somewhat differently 'ought' is an object-language indicator of the ~~relation between its~~ fact that it is only correct to say 'Jones, do A in C' provided one is prepared to say 'Smith, do A in C' 'Roberts, do A in C' etc. for all men. This theme that 'ought' is an object language indicator of the fact that ~~it is correct to say~~ in committing oneself to the particular directive one is committing oneself to the corresponding general directive is being developed by Castañeda in his PhD dissertation. [in different language, 'ought' symbolizes a presupposition of specific ethical directives.]

But to say this is not to say that ought sentences are "really" sentences <u>in the imperative mood</u> plus an indicator of presupposition of a general imperative. They are, in the broad sense, imperatives and the word 'ought' does have a grammar by virtue of which to say 'Jones ought to do A in C, but not everybody ought to do A in C,' (all ethically relevant respects being summed up in C) is to show that one doesn't understand ought sentences – just as to say "it is possible for the released object not to fall, but all released objects necessarily fall" (all physically relevant respects being included in 'released') shows that one doesn't understand necessity sentences.

Yet it can be helpful to say that singular ought sentences are "in effect" singular imperatives salted with an indicator that the singular command is correctly made

---

* [Eds.—Presumably Robert Binkley.]

only where the commander is prepared to offer the corresponding general *command.]**

9. Now, as I understand your argument, you deny that 'I ought to do A' *is* an imperative (i.e. you do not take the line suggested in 6), but claim that Jones isn't using 'I ought to do A' evaluatively unless he would *assent* to the imperative 'Jones, do A!' (You make this explicative of 'evaluative use'.)† You then argue that since failure to *assent* to 'Jones, do A!' upon *assenting* to 'Jones ought to do A' (used evaluatively) is conclusive evidence that Jones has failed to understand 'Jones ought to do A' (used evaluatively), we can say that 'Jones ought to do A' (in its evaluative use) entails 'Jones, do A!'‡

10. But what can be meant by 'assenting to an imperative'? To serve the purpose of your argument, 'assenting to an imperative' should concern the conduct-guiding aspect of imperatives. But surely the proper way to refer to this is by such terms as 'obeying' or 'tending to obey' in speaking of the person, and 'evoking' or 'tending to evoke' in speaking of the imperative.

11. When we do use the phrase 'assenting to an imperative' we have in mind such situations as a father assenting to his wife's command to their child. If he assents, *he joins with her in commanding*. Thus, in the special case where I assent to a command given *me* by Jones, I join with Jones in commanding myself to do the action.

12. Thus, you would seem to be claiming that assenting to 'Sellars ought to do A' (in its evaluative use) involves being prepared to join others in commanding myself to do A. But surely it would be more plausible to claim that assenting to 'Sellars ought to do A' (in its evaluative use) involves being prepared to issue to myself the imperative§ 'Do A!' (omitting the reference to others). This, however, abandons the word 'assent' and makes it no longer plausible to say that ought-statements *entail* imperatives. We can now say, at most, that assenting to 'Sellars ought to do A' entails (*not* the command 'do A!' but) *a readiness to command* 'do A!'

13. But why should we suppose even this? Surely it is plausible only if one starts out by assuming that sentences in the imperative mood have a 'legal monopoly' on the business of evoking conduct specified by the evoking sentences (other sentences bootlegging or borrowing this power). For if one abandons this assumption, one sees that it is quite possible that a person might have a decided tendency to respond to 'I ought to do A' by doing A, and yet such a distaste for the imperative

---

* [Eds.—Sellars clearly intended to write more—his journal entry for 23 December 1953 (p. 104) begins, "Remember to continue with letter to Hare (pp 88ff)"—but there are no further entries concerning this letter.]

† [Eds.—See, for example, *The Language of Morals*, §§11.2 and 11.3.]

‡ [Eds.—See, for example, *The Language of Morals*, §11.3]

§ [Eds.—In the margin, there is a handwritten note indexed to this occurrence of 'imperative', which reads "to do A yourself?" It is either Sellars's or Castañeda's handiwork.]

mood, that in spite of understanding it as a grammarian might, he not only has no tendency to obey, but has a positive tendency to disobey.

14. The sum and substance of my remarks is that just as one has not learned imperative language unless one tends to respond to 'Do A!' by doing A, so one has not learned normative language unless one tends to respond to 'I ought to do A' by doing A.

++++++++++++++++++++++++++++++++

I am afraid that the above remarks show the effects of hasty composition; but I hope that they are not so slap-dash as to be unintelligible. In case you would be interested in a considered (but condensed, not to say opaque) statement of my present views on these matters, I have published a discussion of "Obligation and Motivation" in *Readings in Ethical Theory* (W. Sellars and J. Hospers, eds., N. Y. Appleton Century Crofts, 1952). The paper published under this title in *Philosophical Studies* is only the first and less interesting part of the paper as it stands in the *Readings*.

Sincerely yours,
Wilfrid Sellars

H3. Hare to Sellars, 28 September 1953

Dear Professor Sellars,

I am very sorry to have been so long in answering your letter. I scribbled some notes on it when I received it, but thought it better to wait till I had time to write something more carefully. In the interval I have had to compose some rather detailed lectures on part of Aristotle's *Ethics*, and this took me longer than I had expected.

I will assume that you have kept a copy of your letter, as I have of this, and will comment on your paragraphs one by one:

1. I would not object to 'guiding'; but I am doubtful about 'control', and do not like 'motivation', any more than I do 'motivational trigger', 'prick or goad', 'shape', 'bring about', 'this power', 'evoking', and other such phrases (paras. 4, 5, 6). I think that in much writing on this subject there has been a radical confusion between two quite different things: (1) the effects which a remark has or may have or may be intended to have; and (2) what the speaker is saying.* This confusion is clearest in the case of simple imperatives. To know what an imperative means† is to know that the speaker is telling me (not necessarily seeking to cause me, which is something quite different) to do something, and to know further *what* he is telling me to do. It is to know that it is the sort of remark which can be obeyed or disobeyed (and not, for example, one that can be believed or disbelieved), and to know what action would obey it, or would constitute obedience to it. Thus the meaning of imperatives can be explained without the use of causal or psychological terms. I think, therefore, that the commonly-made distinction between descriptive and pragmatic meaning can be very misleading. The distinction between the meanings of indicatives and imperatives is not between what a sentence is used to say and what effects the speaker intends to produce; it is a distinction between two sorts of things that sentences are used to say (telling *that* and telling *to*—see further, what I have said in my book pp. 12–16).‡ I hope you will forgive me if, in the effort to get to the vital point, I emend certain phrases in what you have written in order to exclude these psychological, causal words, since I think that the point, which is a logical one, can be put more clearly without them.

2. If what the intuitionist asks is put in the form in which you put it, I should say that it is indeed, or may be, a contingent empirical fact that people are motivated by such thoughts. For 'motivate' is a term of empirical psychology;

---

* [Eds.—This remark suggests Hare's sympathy with the views of J. L. Austin, whose *How to Do Things with Words* (1962) is based on lectures delivered at Oxford from 1951 to 1954 and at Harvard in 1955. In particular, Hare's distinction above maps onto Austin's distinction between the illocutionary force and perlocutionary force.]

† [Eds.—We have underlined phrases that are, in the Archive's copy of this letter, underlined in pen or pencil, though it is not clear whether that is Sellars's or Hare's underlining. When the underlining is from the typewriter, we will italicize (as is our usual practice) rather than underline.]

‡ [Eds.—*The Language of Morals*.]

we should find out what motivated a person to do a particular action by observing him (including, if you belong to the right school of psychologists, what he says about his 'private' experiences) and trying to find some circumstance (some thought for example) which was always or generally followed by acts of the same type. But of course it is only possible to take this line if we interpret the expression 'X has the thought that he ought to do A' as the description of a particular circumstance (compare the sentence 'The thought crossed his mind that he ought to do A, and he did A'. We may on the other hand mean by 'X has the thought' something which would be more naturally expressed by 'X really thinks'. And we may interpret the word 'really' in such a way as to make analytic the statement 'if X really thinks that he ought to do A, he will do A'. We do this by making his doing of A, at the appropriate time, a necessary condition for saying that he really thinks that he ought. If he doesn't do A, we don't admit that he really thinks he ought. This is a logical point, and no talk of motivation need enter. I confess that I do not see the need for admitting a synthetic necessary truth. The statement 'If he really thinks that he ought to do A, he will be *motivated* to do A' only appears to be synthetic because an expression of empirical psychology, 'motivated', has been grafted on to the already analytic statement 'If he really thinks that he ought to do A, he will (unless of course he changes his mind in the interval) do A'.

(*Note*: It might be said, on the other hand, that 'motivate' is *not* an expression of empirical psychology; but on this view, what *is* its status? Its Aristotelian equivalent is, so it seems to me, an expression of *metaphysical* psychology; that is to say, it is sometimes used to make remarks, in the material mode of speech, about logic, and on the other hand it is sometimes used to do what it always *looks* as if it were doing, make remarks which are genuinely empirical. But this is too long a story; I think that since it is always extremely hard to tell whether a sentence containing the word 'motivate' has the one or the other of these functions, the word is better avoided; for the logical statements can be made in 'language-language', and the empirical statements in less dubious terms.)

3. From the above, you will see that I agree with the emotivist's position in substance, but object to his language. To do A is not indeed a *sufficient* condition for being said to think that one ought to do A, but it is a *necessary* condition, if 'think' is interpreted as 'really think' in the sense explained above. Other necessary conditions are, perhaps, his disposition to act in a similar way on other occasions, to rebuke others if they do not, commend them if they do, and so on. So I would exclude the word 'motivate' from the statement of the emotivist's position. Similarly I would alter the words 'to acquire a tendency to do'. 'Tendency' is a word from the vocabulary of causal explanation and prediction. To learn to use the word 'ought', or any other word, is not to acquire, necessarily, any tendency; it is to acquire an ability (when we have learnt something, we have become *able* to do something, though perhaps no one will be able to predict what we will or will

not actually do. On the other hand, if someone has a *tendency*, we are able to predict that on most or many occasions he will act in a certain manner. This is what 'having a tendency' means). So to learn to use 'ought' is to acquire the ability known as 'understanding the use of "ought"'. It is not to acquire a tendency to do anything, but to learn that when another person uses this expression, he is telling us, or saying to us, a certain kind of thing, *agreement with which would involve*, among other things, a tendency to do something.* I have to agree (i.q. sincerely assent) before I do it on each occasion. It is as if someone said 'To learn to ride a bicycle is to acquire a tendency to go journeys on a bicycle' (the word 'learn' really *is* used in somewhat this way in the sentence 'You'll learn better manners when you get in the Army'). But as a matter of fact, when I learnt to ride a bicycle, I at the same time acquired such a distaste for the machine that now, although I *have* learnt, and *can* ride, I always walk rather than ride. Actually, learning the use of a word is more complicated than learning to ride a bicycle. If I have learnt (and know) the use of a word, there is one thing I cannot help doing, and that is understanding its use in typical cases (if I don't understand its use, I am said not to know or not to have learnt). But however much I understand the use of 'ought', I don't have to *act* in any way; I may understand what the man is saying but *always* do the opposite because I like frustrating my fellow-men. When the word 'ought' (or for that matter the imperative) was invented, no new *power* of man over man was thereby instituted (though of course commands *coupled with* threats or with various drills or conditionings-to-obey *do* have such a power, the threats or the conditionings introducing a quite new factor; note also that we can threaten without using anything but indicatives, and can condition people to act on indicatives, without them thereby becoming imperatives; in the British Gunners when the Number Three says 'Unhooked' the Driver drives away, but 'Unhooked' is not an order.)

4. I think, therefore, that it is possible to state the 'emotivist' position in such a way as to meet your objection—though of course the name 'emotivist' becomes thereby quite inappropriate. The dichotomy 'conceptual' *vs.* 'prick or goad' is utterly misleading. There are two quite different distinctions which have got confused in the current terminology (1) Utterances which affect or usually affect or are intended to affect or have the 'job' of affecting people's behaviour *vs.* Utterances, if any, which do not; and (2) Imperative and other prescriptive kinds of sentence *vs.* Indicative and other descriptive kinds of sentence. The first distinction is between effects of utterances, the second between meanings of sentences (what they are used to say or tell someone).† Now the emotivist account

---

* [Eds.—In the margin, and in Sellars's hand, we read:
    Of course I have to agree with "You ought to do A" said by Jones. The question is does not my thinking that I ought to do A entail that I have a tendency to do A!]

† [Eds.—Again, J. L. Austin comes to mind. In his terminology, we can say that the first distinction is between perlocutionary acts and nonperlocutionary acts; the second, between types of illocutionary acts. See *How to Do Things with Words*.]

can be reconstituted as follows: 'Sentences containing the word "ought" are prescriptive; and this means that to understand them is to realise that agreement with them involves *doing* something in certain circumstances (which may or may not arise).' If we put it this way, we see that it is no longer being maintained that 'ought'- sentences are pricks or goads or motivational triggers, but rather that they are used to tell us something different from what ordinary indicatives are used to tell us—something which is naturally put in the same *genus* as what imperatives (simple) are used to tell us (telling *to*, not telling *that*). Though of course the *species* are very different. Of course, then, 'ought' 'has a complex logical grammar in virtue of which it has a *conceptual* status'*, and so have simple imperatives. I need to know just as many concepts in order to understand what a man is saying when he says 'Shut the door' (tells me to shut the door) as I do in order to understand what he is saying when he says 'You will (future indicative) shut the door' (tells me that I am going to shut the door). And 'ought' is more complex than these, being, as you imply, covertly universal—but none of this is inconsistent with its being prescriptive.

5. Having said that imperatives and 'ought'-sentences are both in the *genus* 'prescriptive', it is obviously necessary to say what is the *differentia* between them; and I think that it lies in the covertly universal character of 'ought'-sentences.† Since to be universal is to stand in a certain relation (of conditional entailment) to a certain class of singular sentences, I am bound to say that 'ought'-sentences entail *some* class of singular sentences. This class of singular sentences cannot be the class of apparently singular 'ought'-sentences, for I have said that these are not really singular. Singular imperatives seem to be the obvious candidate; and some credibility is lent to this choice by the fact that proper universals cannot be formed in the imperative (see my book, pp. 177–9).‡ Thus imperatives and 'ought's have each a gap in their logical grammar which the other neatly fills. The situation is certainly much more complicated than that of singular and universal indicatives; the quasi-singular 'I ought now to do A' and the quasi-universal 'Never tell lies' require accounting for; but I think I can do this (pp. 175-6).§ Now empiricists used to say—and there was much in it—that the more complex kinds of statement, such as universal statements, had, in order to be shown to be significant, to be reduced to some sort of logical combinations or *relata* of singular ones. My programme is not dissimilar. I want to bring out the significance of 'ought'-sentences, which are certainly complex, by exhibiting them as related to singular *imperatives* in the same general sort of way (whatever that is—and it is certainly obscure) as universal *indicatives* are related to singular ones. If once we admit that all

---

* [Eds.—Here, Hare is quoting Sellars's earlier letter (S2, §4)].

† [Eds.—In addition to *The Language of Morals* (§§10.2-10.3) Hare develops this strand of his thought in "Universalizability," in *Proceedings of the Aristotelian Society* 55 (1955): 295–312, reprinted in *Essays on the Moral Concepts* (London: Macmillan, 1972): 13–28.]

‡ [Eds.—*The Language of Morals*.] § [Eds.—*The Language of Morals*.]

'ought'-sentences, including superficially singular and simple sentences like 'You ought to go', are logically complex (and I do not see how this can be denied) we are *bound* to look for a class of sentence which really is singular and simple, yet has the prescriptive character which is obviously required. The simple imperative is such a sentence.

6. I do not wish (though I may have slipped up inadvertently in my book) to use the word 'imperative' in any other way than it is used by grammarians. I try to use the word 'prescriptive' on the other hand as a general term to cover both (1) ordinary imperatives and (2) 'ought'-sentences and other value-sentences. In maintaining that there is a logical relation between (1) and (2), I am not saying that sentences of the other class are really imperatives, or seeking to extend the meaning of 'imperative' (if I say that men are related to apes and that both are anthropoids,* I am not saying that men are really apes). Suppose that we had a word for singular indicatives, or for a sub-class of them, or for a class of indicatives which included them but did not include universal indicatives (it does not matter which). Let us call them 'basic sentences'. Then, suppose that we tried, as some have, to show that universal sentences in the indicative are related to basic sentences by the relation of conditional entailment. To do this would not be to try to show that universal sentences are really basic sentences, nor to try to extend the meaning of the term 'basic sentences'. And in the same way, in trying to show that 'ought'-sentences are related to simple imperatives by the relation of conditional—or in some cases unconditional—entailment, I am not seeking to show that they are really imperatives, nor trying to extend the meaning of the word 'imperative'. (Perhaps I ought to apologise for the term 'conditional entailment'. P entails Q conditionally when it entails it in conjunction with a further premiss; thus 'All men are mortal' conditionally entails 'Socrates is mortal'. 'Ought'-sentences of the form 'One ought always to...' conditionally entail 'ought'-sentences of the form 'X ought now to...' (X has to be in the appropriate circumstances); and these latter unconditionally entail imperatives of the form 'Let X...'. So the first kind of sentence conditionally entails the third.)

7. Though I agree that 'I ought to do A' does entail 'I ought to do A', this will not fulfil my purpose of showing how the complex sentence 'I ought to do A' is related to simpler forms of sentence (see above).

8. If we were to omit the words 'motivational force' and substitute logical terms for this and other psychological ones, I could agree with a position very like the one you advocate. I try to use the word 'prescriptive' for your 'broad category', except that instead of 'acquiring dispositions to act' I would say 'Understanding that sincere assent to sentences of this category involves doing something' (really 'conditionally involves'; for of course I do not have to do anything if, for example,

---

* [Eds.—Hare's own footnote here reads: "I am not sure if this the right term; but we could invent one."]

the 'ought'-sentence is 'Women ought to use make-up' and I am a man). It seems to me that to say that 'ought'-sentences conditionally entail imperatives, and to say that sincere assent to them conditionally involves doing something, come to much the same thing. For to do something is to carry out a command (not in the sense in which one can only carry out a command which has actually been given, but in the sense in which, for any act which has been done, a command to do it can be framed *ex post facto*. I can see no objection to this sort of talk which would not apply equally to the quite common way of speaking whereby we say that an event constitutes a verification of a proposition whether or not the proposition has actually been uttered). If, therefore, you will allow me to say that in this sense anything that is done is the carrying out of a command, then may not I say that if sincere assent to an 'ought'-sentence involves doing something, then the sentence itself entails the imperative (or some imperative) which is carried out in doing that something? Suppose X says 'I ought to go now'. If he does not go, we say he does not really think what he has just said (in the sense of 'really think' explained above). Is not this because if he had really thought it, he must have understood that it entailed 'Let me go' (in the sense of an imperative addressed to himself); but if he understood this, and accepted it, he would have gone; but he did not go, therefore... therefore he cannot have really thought he ought to go?

9. This is a fair summary of what I think.

10. I try to distinguish in my book between 'assent' and 'sincerely assent'.* To assent is simply to say 'yes' or 'aye aye sir' or repeat the remark with the pronouns changed as necessary. To assent sincerely is to say this, and further to do those things which are tests of sincerity. The test of sincerity of assent to a prescription is, performing some action (or rather this is one of the tests). The test of sincerity of assent to a descriptive statement is, believing it (whatever that consists in). That is to say, assent, as I use the term, is a verbal performance. In your example (para. 11) the father assents to his wife's command by *saying* 'Yes, give him it back'; if he really intends his son to give it back, he is being sincere; if, on the other hand, he intends his son to disobey, in order that he may have an excuse for punishing him, he is being insincere.

11. I agree with this.

12. I think it involves both. But this is not to abandon the word 'assent'. For in issuing to myself the command 'Do A', I am assenting to this command as given by another. I am therefore doing one thing that I must do, if I assent to 'You ought to do A'. (One thing, because the fact that P entails Q does not mean that Q is as strong logically as P). 'Ought'-sentences entail imperatives because, if someone else says 'You ought to do A', and I say 'Yes I ought' (assent to 'ought'-sentence) but, when the other man says 'Then do A', reply 'No I won't' (dissent from

---

* [Eds.—*The Language of Morals*, §2.2.]

imperative) I show that I have misunderstood his 'ought'-sentence, by not understanding it evaluatively.

'Entailment' I use as a relation between sentences (one ought, I suppose, to say 'statements'; only unfortunately there is no general word to cover both statements and commands, unless we say 'judgements'; and I have been rebuked for saying this). Therefore I would not say that 'assenting to "…" entails a readiness to command "—"'. I would rather say that because '…' entails '—', assenting to '…' involves assenting to '—' (in the sense that refusal to do so lands one in a contradiction).

13. I have given my reasons above, such as they are, for saying that 'ought'-sentences entail imperatives. This does not seem to me to be a question of bootlegging or monopoly. Would you say that, if universal sentences (indicative) are shown to entail conditionally singular ones, therefore the latter have a legal monopoly of statement-making, the universal sentences bootlegging or borrowing this power?

I think that in your example, if one abandons the 'tendency' phraseology, the example does not count against my position. For I am only speaking of 'understanding' (whether as a grammarian might or as anyone else might; it comes to the same thing). Understanding is not having a tendency. Therefore, although it may well be that for some reason I act on 'ought's but not on commands, I may perfectly well and in the fullest sense understand both of them. Suppose I think (as you perhaps suggest) that it is rude to utter singular imperatives outside the Army, and that therefore I never obey them. The fact that I never obey them does not mean that I do not understand them. Indeed, I wouldn't be offended unless I did understand them. And since what sentences entail what, is a question of their meaning (i.e. of what I understand when I understand them), all I need to show is that you cannot understand the 'ought' without realising that assent to it involves assent to the imperative; I am not bound to show that you cannot have a tendency to act on the 'ought' without having a tendency to act on the imperative.

14. I would agree, if you rephrased as follows: Just as one has not learnt imperative language unless one realises that sincere assent to 'Do A' involves doing A, so one has not learnt normative language unless one realises that sincere assent to 'I ought to do A' involves doing A. And I would add, that this is because 'I ought to do A', understood normatively, entails 'Let me do A', and so sincere assent to the first entails sincere assent to the second, and sincere assent to the second involves doing A.

I wish my remarks were as coherent as yours. I hope that you will reply to this, because I am very conscious that I have not really been answering your objections, but only restating my own position rather dogmatically, and, what is worse, restating yours in my own terminology, which may be to beg the whole question. So I have done nothing but try to clear the decks; the real argument will have to follow.

I have not had time to more than glance at the two papers you sent me, but I have now read the one in *Mind*.* To my great surprise, it has for the moment completely convinced me that there are material rules of inference in ordinary language—I never thought that after resisting all Toulmin's blandishments I should succumb to someone else. But I am not at all sure what it is I am convinced of.

I cannot follow the concluding part of your argument. It is the step from your position (2) to your position (1) that I still resist. Surely we must allow for the place of observation in establishing material rules of inference, if there are such. And if so, they cannot be established only by reference to the meanings of words (but perhaps this is not what you are maintaining). I think it possible, however, that we have to distinguish two classes of rule: (1) e.g. 'From "It is raining" you may infer "The streets will be wet"'; and (2) 'From statements of the form "Something (*A*) is happening which has always in the past been succeeded by something else (*B*)" you may infer "*B* will happen"'. I certainly think that (2) is not established by observation. (1), on the other hand, is established by observation, assuming (2). Therefore, let us confine ourselves to the question of the status of (2). It seems to me that it is synthetic. Is it *a priori*? Well, the word is so ambiguous. We, most of us believe (2). But we are not unconditionally bound to believe it, as we are to believe an analytic statement. It is, in any case, not a statement, but a permissive (and, I agree, can be reduced to a prescriptive). And in a sense *all* prescriptives are *a priori*. They are not empirically established. But surely the synthetic-*a-priori*-mongers wanted more than this? They wanted *statements* which were not empirically established, but which we were unconditionally bound to accept. And you yourself do not claim anything so powerful.

To sum up, *a priori* seems to be used in two quite different ways: (1) In the sense in which analytic statements are *a priori*, it means 'not established by observation, universally true, cannot be denied'. (2) In the sense in which the ultimate principles of morals and science are *a priori* (though synthetic), it means 'not established by observation' only. Analytic sentences (indicative) express *statements* (though vacuous). Synthetic '*a priori*' sentences express not statements but rules or regulative principles—so of course they cannot be established by observation, and on the other hand of course they cannot be called universally *true* (though we may adhere to them as of universal application); and we cannot say of them that they cannot be *denied* (we don't *deny* rules, though we may either adhere or not adhere to them).

Please excuse the length, obscurity and spikiness of this letter. I hope I shall hear from you again.

Yours sincerely,
[R. M. Hare]

* [Eds.—IM.]

S4. Sellars to Hare, 23 November 1953

Dear Mr. Hare:

Before I get down to commenting in detail on your letter, I must tell you what a pleasure it has been to work through your fresh and persuasive argument. It was exceedingly generous of you to reply at such length to my original remarks. Please feel under no obligation whatever to reply to this reply to your reply. (This could go on forever!) But now to the business at hand.

1.1 I quite agree that "there has been a radical confusion between ... (1) the effects which a remark has or may have or may be intended to have; and (2) what the speaker is saying," and that this confusion has infected many treatments of imperatives. I also agree that there is a sense in which "the meaning of imperatives can be explained without the use of causal or psychological terms." For one can explain the meaning of a particular imperative by *translating* it into another imperative.

Jones: What does 'Fetch the volume!' mean?
Smith: It means *Bring the book*.

If Smith is confident that Jones' question arises from his lack of familiarity not with such words as "fetch" or "volume," but with a particular imperative idiom, he will give a reply which, though different, still has the general character of a translation.

Jones: What does 'Book, please' mean?
Smith: It means you are to bring the book.
     or
It (the form '----, please') means you are *to do* something, in this case bring the book.

Compare,

Jones: What does 'Some tables instantiate triangularity' mean?
Smith: It means they are triangular.
     or
It means they have the property in question.

Now it is clear that to explain in *this* sense the meaning of an imperative is not to discuss the causes or effects of imperative utterances, since such explanation consists in using *more* imperative discourse, though in the context "It means ... " Notice that in the same sense of "explaining the meaning of ... " one can explain the meaning of an observation sentence without the use of causal or psychological terms.

Jones: What did the umpire mean by 'Fault!'?
Smith: He meant *Outside*!

1.2 On the other hand, there is *another* sense of "explaining the meaning of imperatives" in which it is not so clear to me that one can do this without using causal or psychological terms. After all, if we 'identify' (in *some* sense) the meaning of an expression with its *use*, we must distinguish between two ways of 'giving the use,' (1) by *using* an equivalent expression, in which case one often introduces the equivalent expression by the rubric 'It means ...' (2) by *mentioning* the use. And one can agree that giving the use by using an equivalent does not involve causal psychological talk about the expression, and yet insist that (in the case of observation and prescriptive terms) giving the use by mentioning the use *does* involve causal psychological talk. Mentioning the use even of such terms will, of course, also involve *rule* talk (which is not causal-psychological).

1.3 Certainly, to know what an imperative is, is to "know that it is the sort of remark which can be obeyed or disobeyed (and not, for example, one that can be believed or disbelieved)." But can the meaning of 'obeying a command' be explicated without using causal or psychological terms? Surely *obeying* a command is to be distinguished from doing that which in point of fact fulfills a command even though one is completely unaware that a command has been given. But more of this later.

1.4 I also agree that "the distinction between descriptive and pragmatic meaning can be very misleading," and that "the distinction between the meanings of indicatives and imperatives is not between what a sentence is used to say and what effects the speaker intends to produce; it is a distinction between two sorts of things that sentences are used to say ... " Indicatives and imperatives do indeed have different (though related) logical grammars, and it would be incorrect to say either

'Jones, do *A*!' means Jones does *A*
or
'Jones does *A*'* means Jones is to do *A*

On the other hand, might it not be part of the use of the imperative form that 'Let me do *A*!' cause me to do *A*? Put thus bluntly, of course, the situation is radically oversimplified. We surround imperatives with all sorts of considerations as to who ought to be obeyed; and we often dislike doing what we are properly commanded

---

* [Eds.—The typescript has this sentence as follows: "'Jones does A! means Jones is to do A." We have replaced the '!' with an single quotation mark for the following reasons: (i) Sellars is discussing the logical grammars of indicatives and imperatives; and (ii) "does" in the second sentence suggests the sentence is an indicative; (iii) this brings the sentence pair in line with the schema: "'----' means ...."]

to do so much that we just don't do it—we often choose not to obey a command. But if, for these reasons, we cannot say simply that it is part of the use of imperatives that they cause the addressee to perform the actions they enjoin, can we not say that it is part of their use that *other springs of conduct aside* they have this effect? And can we not put this by saying that a tendency to bring about the action they enjoin is part of their use? Can we not say that it is part of the use of observation words that they be evoked by situations of the kind they are correctly said to mean? Certainly, this aspect of their use will not be *mentioned* in a sentence in which we "explain their meaning" by giving synonyms.

Jones: What does 'chrome' mean?
Smith: 'Chrome' means yellow.

But can we explain the use of observation words in the sense of mentioning their use without using 'causal or psychological terms'?

2.1 My use of the term 'thought' in the second paragraph of my letter was, indeed, unfortunate. I would call attention, however, to the fact that the question I ask the intuitionist begins with "Could a person *apprehend* a set of prima facie obligations..." which is typical intuitionist jargon for "Could a person *know* that he ought to...." In short, I was asking, "Could a person know that he ought to do action A in circumstances C, and know that the circumstances were C, and yet have no tendency to do A?" I suggested that the intuitionist (given his general philosophical commitments) must choose between saying (a) "It is a contingent empirical fact that people are moved to do what they know they ought to do" and (b) "It is a synthetic necessary truth that people are so moved." I am quite happy, however, to phrase my question in terms of "really think." It must, however, be remembered that for the intuitionist, knowing that one ought to do A in C is analogous to knowing that 2+2=4. He speaks of both in terms of 'intuiting' or 'apprehending' a 'truth.' Thus, for the intuitionist, as far as what is analytically contained in *knowing a moral truth* is concerned, one could know that one ought to do A in C without ever doing or being to any degree moved to do A in C. If you were to say to him, "But surely we refuse to say that a person *really thinks* he ought to do A in C unless (roughly) he does A in C!" he would reply, "If so, that can only be because we make a queer use of 'thinks' in ethical contexts."

2.2 Now, you and I are agreed that something is wrong here, and I *think* we agree that the source of the trouble lies in the intuitionist's account of knowing that one ought to do A in C (and, for that matter, his account of knowing that $2 + 2 = 4$). Certainly we agree that a person doesn't really think he ought to do A in C unless (roughly) he does A in C. But it seems to me that at this point you reason as follows:

It would be incorrect to put a phrase mentioning motivation in the blank space of "'Jones ought to do *A* in *C*' means Jones ---------*A* in *C*," therefore it would be incorrect to say that playing a role in the motivation of conduct is part of the use of 'ought.'

I hope to have convinced you that while the premise of this argument is sound, the conclusion does not follow.

2.3 You write, "... we may interpret the word 'really' in such a way as to make analytic the statement 'If *X* really thinks that he ought to do *A*, he will do *A*'... a necessary condition for saying that he really thinks that he ought." Suppose, however, that Jones always does *A* in *C*, but from selfish motives, would we say that he really thinks that he ought to do *A*? Well, you might reply, if he does *A* in *C* for selfish motives, then it is only in an accidental sense that he 'always does *A* in *C*', for if doing *A* in *C* were in the next case not conducive to selfish interests he might not do *A*. In short, you would be pointing out that it is only if he does *A* in *C* "without ulterior motive" that he can be said always to do *A* in *C*. But, surely, to say this is to grant my point, for to say that Jones does not do *A* in *C* from ulterior motives is to characterize his motivation. It is to characterize it as doing *A* in *C* in some sense 'just because it is doing *A* in *C*,' a notion by no means easy to analyse, but which, to be relevant to our problem must be distinguished from merely having the "blind" habit of responding to *C* with *A*. In short, Jones must have the general notion of doing *A* in *C*, and if his action is not to be doing *A* in *C* "just because he likes doing it".... But you see where I am going. Again, suppose that Jones is strongly inclined to do *A* in *C* as being his duty, but is moved by selfish considerations to do something else instead; would we not admit that he might really think that he ought to do *A*? Don't we feel that some account of what brings Jones to do, or to fail to do, *A* in *C* must be given before we decide that he does or does not really think that he ought to do *A* in *C*?

3.1 I quite agree that to learn to ride a bicycle is not to acquire a tendency to go for bicycle rides. But does not learning to ride a bicycle involve acquiring *other* tendencies? Acquiring the *ability* to use imperative discourse involves acquiring *some* tendencies, and *might*, therefore, in spite of the initial plausibility of your analogies, involve acquiring a tendency to respond to "Let me do *A*!" by doing *A*.

3.2 You point out correctly that "however much I understand the use of 'ought' I don't have to act in any way; I may understand what the man is saying, but always do the opposite because I like frustrating my fellow men." But (a) it is part of the use of 'ought' that only those 'ought-'sentences of the form 'I ought to do *A* in *C*' to which there correspond *universal* 'ought-'sentences ('Anyone ought to do *A* in *C*') *which I accept as my moral framework* have the power to move me (given that I believe that the circumstances are *C*); and (b) to say that such sentences have the *tendency* to move me (given that I have learned the use of 'ought') is *compatible* with supposing that having learned this use in the course of acquiring a particular moral framework (which I may later modify by creative decisions of the kind you so admirably describe), I thereafter *never* ('conflict of motives') do what I really think I ought to do, though this is, of course, most unlikely.

4.1 We agree that both 'ought-'sentences and imperatives have their characteristic logical grammars. We agree that

"Jones, do *A*!" says that Jones *is to do A*.

We also agree that 'ought-'sentences and imperatives are species of the genus (adopting your terminology) *prescriptive sentence*. I am not, however, completely happy about saying that 'ought-'sentences tell us *to* rather than *that*. In the first place, it is surely correct (if unexciting) to say

"Sellars ought to do *A*" tells me *that* I am under an obligation to do *A*.

But, you reply, your very example counts against you, because "*to do A*" occurs in the statement of what I am being told; and, after all, instead of saying

"Jones, do *A*!" tells Jones *to do A*

one can say

"Jones, do *A*!" tells Jones *that* he is *to do A*

which also involves a 'that' as well as a 'to.' But, then, it should be noticed that whereas we can put the imperative example both as

..... tells Jones *that* he is *to*

and

..... tells Jones *to*

It is not obvious that it is strictly correct to say

"Sellars ought to do *A*" tells me *to do A*.

4.2 In the second place, if it were strictly correct to make the latter statement, would not this imply that "Sellars ought to do *A*" is *itself* an imperative? For is not the basic rationale of the form "'_____' says........" that '........' be (perhaps a partial or schematic) *translation* of '_____'?

4.3 Before going any farther, it might be well to point out that for my money the essential difference between 'ought-'discourse and ordinary imperatives lies in the fact that singular 'ought-'sentences presuppose universal 'ought-'sentences.

Suppose, however, we used as our language of morals *archaic* imperative forms, thus

Jones, do thou A in C!

where the archaic 'do thou!' was a conventional *signal* that acceptance of the singular imperative presupposed acceptance of the universal imperative

Everyman, do thou A in C!

Would not such imperative discourse have the force (but not the indicative character) of our 'ought-' language? If we can answer this question in the affirmative, we can understand why we find it illuminating to say that 'ought-' language is a species of imperative language, that an 'ought-'sentence is an imperative the indicative "clothing" of which *signalizes* an implicit universality.

4.4 Notice that we would feel uncomfortable about saying that

'Jones, do thou A in C!' means Jones is to do A in C

just as we feel uncomfortable about saying that

'Jones, you ought to do A in C' means Jones is to do A in C.

In the former case, we would give as the reason for our discomfort not that 'Jones, do thou A!' is not an imperative, but that it is an imperative *and something more*, and that this something more is neglected by the right hand side. We would point out that since this something more is a *signal of* (*not* an *assertion of*) a presupposition, the only way we can capture it on the right hand side of a "'....' means _____" statement is by using a form of words on the right hand side which *signalizes* the same presupposition.

4.5 *Parallel*: We feel uncomfortable about saying

'All A is B' means $A \subset B$

because 'All A is B' signalizes the presupposition 'There are A's'. It would be incorrect to say

'All A is B' means $A \subset B$ and there are A's

for this implies that 'All A is B' translates into '$A \subset B$ and there are A's'. We could say

'All A is B' means $A^+ \subset B$

and stipulate that '+' signalizes the presupposition that there are A's.
4.6 Could we not, then, say

'Jones do thou A in C!' means Jones do$^+$ A in C

and stipulate that '+' signalizes the presupposition 'Everyman do A in C!'?
4.7 This line of thought tempts me to say that

"Jones, you ought to do A in C" means Jones, do$^+$ A in C,

where it is stipulated that '+' signalizes the presupposition 'Everybody, do A in C!'*
4.8 But, illuminating though this might be, I am still inclined to say that (a) 'ought-'discourse is not a species of imperative discourse, though it is a species of prescriptive discourse; (b) 'ought-'discourse and imperative discourse have in common the fact that it is part of the use of singular sentences in these two modes of discourse that they tend to bring about the conduct they mention in the persons to whom they are addressed and to whom they apply—though, in the case of 'ought-'discourse, only if this person accepts the relevant universal 'ought-'sentence; (c) singular 'ought-'sentences signalize the presupposition of the universal 'ought-'sentence; and (d) it is a metaphorical extension of "tell us *to*" to say that 'ought-'sentences tell us *to*.

5.1 I am just not convinced by any of this. Surely we can agree that it is part of the grammar of 'ought' that 'Jones ought to do A in C' presupposes 'Everybody ought to do A in C' without concluding that 'Jones ought to do A in C' is not "really singular."? To say that 'I ought to do A in C' or (given the circumstances) 'I ought to do A' is *quasi*-singular is surely only to say that it *is* singular but presupposes the corresponding universal. To be *quasi*-singular is to be singular and something more, it is not to be not-singular. I just do not find the gap in the grammar of 'ought' which is essential to your thesis (in some of its formulations). I am convinced that you would not have said that universal 'ought-'sentences are related to singular imperatives as universal indicatives are related to singular indicatives unless you had already convinced yourself on other grounds that 'ought-'sentences entail imperatives. Since I shall be discussing your arguments for the latter contention in a moment, let me limit myself here to pointing out that if you indeed wish to say that universal 'ought-'sentences are related to singular imperatives as universal indicatives are related to singular indicatives, you are committed to the thesis that the entailment between universal 'ought-'sentences

---

* [Eds.—The "...in C" has been added by hand in the margin.]

and singular imperatives is of that literal and intimate kind which involves that a person couldn't make correct use of 'ought-'discourse unless he also used (and made correct use of) imperative language.

6.1 I have no quarrel with this paragraph. I certainly did not intend to charge you with any of the confusions you mention. Let me again express my conviction that even if you were prepared to admit that singular 'ought-'sentences stand to universal 'ought-'sentences as singular indicatives stand to universal indicatives, you would still be moved to insist that 'ought-'sentences entail imperatives, and, in particular, that 'I ought now to do A' entails 'Let me do A!' Moreover, and this is the heart of the matter, it is my conviction that at the back of your mind is the notion that only imperatives are *in a primary sense* prescriptive, sentences other than imperatives being prescriptive by virtue of entailing imperatives. Needless to say, to charge you with this notion is *not* to charge you with holding that the sentences which you believe to entail imperatives (and hence to be in derivative sense prescriptive) are themselves "really imperatives." My own conviction is that 'ought-'sentences are prescriptive in their own right, i.e. not by virtue of entailing imperatives.

6.2 At the end of paragraph 6, you *do* seem to abandon the claim that universal 'ought-'sentences entail singular imperatives as universal indicatives entail singular indicatives. For on the account you now give, whereas 'All men are mortal' conditionally entails 'Socrates is mortal,' 'Everyone ought to do A in C' conditionally entails *in the first place* 'Socrates ought to do A.' And it is only because you believe yourself in a position to add that 'Socrates ought to do A' *in turn* entails 'Let Socrates do A!' that (appealing to the transitivity of entailment) you are moved to say that 'Everybody ought to do A in C' "conditionally entails" 'Let Socrates do A!' But clearly, in this context, 'x conditionally entails y' can no longer have the force of 'x entails y *as the universal indicative entails the singular indicative*,' for the universal indicative directly (if conditionally) entails the singular.

7. No comment.

8.1 First a comment on the word 'sincere.' As I see it, we use this term in rebutting the charge (actual, or looming on the horizon) that a certain piece of conduct is *feigned*. Thus, a *sincere* smile is not a special kind of smile, it is a smile which is not feigned, i.e. it is not a piece of conduct which merely looks (and is intended to look) like a smile. Thus, *sincere assent* should be *not* assent *plus*, but something which is really a case of assent instead of a piece of conduct which looks (and is intended to look) like assent. (Similar considerations arise in connection with "really thinks".) But this is a verbal point. What ever be the best way of putting it, what you have in mind, I take it, is the difference between 'thinking something' in the 'thin' sense of 'entertaining the idea,' 'having it before the mind', and the 'thinking something' which is a 'commitment to the idea,' an 'affirmation' or, you suggest, 'judgment.' Now, I want to say that it is part of the use of 'ought-

'statements and imperatives that the *affirming* use (it may be *concurring*, when someone else is speaking) of such sentences, when they apply "to oneself, now" involves *doing*. And I would be happy about the qualifications "*really* affirming" or "*sincerely* affirming" only if they were being used *not* to imply that there can be an affirming use which does not involve doing, but to distinguish *affirming* from, say, *entertaining*. I would add, of course, that the manner in which affirming use involves doing requires causal talk for its clarification.

8.2 To come now to the heart of your paragraph 8, you write that "to say that 'ought-'sentences entail imperatives, and to say that sincere assent to them conditionally involves doing something, comes to much the same thing." You reason as follows (my paraphrase):

'x sincerely assents to "I ought to do A now"' entails 'x does A'.
'x does A' entails 'x fulfills (in your terminology, *carries out*) the command "Let me do A!"'
Therefore, 'x sincerely assents to "I ought to do A now"' entails 'x fulfills the command "Let me do A!"'

You are thus, in effect, proposing a convention according to which

'I ought to do A now' entails 'Let me do A!'	$=_{Df}$	'x sincerely assents to "I ought to do A now"' entails 'x fulfills the command "Let me do A!"'

You point out that a command may be fulfilled (carried out) in the sense relevant to this argument even though no one actually frames the command.

8.3 Well, if this were the sum and substance of the contention that 'ought-'sentences entail imperatives, I would be the last to disagree, provided that it were made clear that this *is* what "'ought-'statements entail imperatives" is being used to mean. But I am not convinced that this is the sum and substance of your contention. For, on the above account, my 'ought-'statements would entail imperatives even though neither I myself nor my community knew how to use imperative discourse. In other words, 'ought-'discourse would entail imperative discourse in the above sense even though the users of 'ought-'discourse were in no sense familiar with or able to use imperative discourse. But surely in a more usual sense of entails, where '......' entails '-----' it is because the inferrability of '----' from '....' is part of the *use* of '....'. And surely you often imply that 'ought-'statements imply imperatives in the more usual sense.

8.4 That you yourself are not satisfied with the sense you have just given to "'ought-'sentences entail imperatives" emerges at the end of paragraph 8, where you write (apparently under the impression that you are recapitulating the above argument), "If he does not go, we say that he does not really think what he has just said... Is not this because if he had really thought it, he must have understood that it entailed 'Let me go!'..." But on the above account, all we are entitled to say is that if he had really thought it, he must have gone and hence *fulfilled* (carried out) 'Let me go!'—which command need not occur to him—so that his really thinking it involved fulfilling the command, though not in any sense which requires that he "must have understood that it entailed" the command. It is only if 'I ought to do A now' entails 'Let me do $A!$' in the direct "syntactical" sense in which 'if p then q' entails 'if not-q then not-p' (which you seemed about to establish when you claimed that universal 'ought-'sentences entail singular imperatives as universal indicatives entail singular indicatives) that you would be entitled to say "...if he had really thought it, he must have understood that it entailed 'Let me go!'..."

8.5 In other words, at the end of the paragraph you are arguing that sincere assent to 'I ought now to do A' involves doing A *because* 'I ought to do A now' entails 'Let me do $A!$' and sincere assent to 'I ought to do A now' involves doing A. Here the entailment between the 'ought' and the imperative is a *premise* whereas at the beginning of the paragraph it was the conclusion. And in this new argument, the ground for saying that 'I ought to do A now' entails 'Let me do $A!$' can no longer be that sincere assent to the 'ought-'sentence involves doing A and hence fulfilling the imperative, for *that* sincere assent to the 'ought-'sentence involves doing A is exactly what this new argument purports to establish.

9, 10, 11 No comment.

12 In 12 you offer still another argument for the thesis that 'ought-'sentences entail imperatives. I am not convinced. It seems to me clear that I can *dissent from* the imperative 'Sellars, do $A!$'—as voiced, say, by Jones—*and yet do A,* thus *fulfilling* (in your terminology, carrying out) the imperative. Consider such statements (by no means uncommon) as 'I'll do it, but I'll do it because I ought to, and not because you told me to!'

13 You write "...all I need to show is that you cannot understand the 'ought' without realizing that assent to it involves assent to the imperative." I can crystallize my unhappiness by asking "Do you mean by 'assent to the imperative' *carrying out* the imperative or do you mean *concurring* in the imperative (or giving oneself a command, and hence doing what *would be* a concurring if the command were issued by another)?" We are agreed that one doesn't understand the 'ought' unless one realizes that assent to it involves doing A. We agree that doing A is *fulfilling* the imperative. But surely one can realize that assent to the 'ought' involves *doing A* without realizing that assent to the 'ought' involves fulfilling the imperative. Parallel: Scott is the author of *Waverly*, but I can know that that man is Scott without knowing that that man is the author of *Waverly*. To escape from this, you must show that the relation between 'ought-'discourse and imperative discourse is so "intimate" that a person couldn't use 'ought-'discourse correctly without making correct use of ordinary imperative discourse (the

syntactical thesis), rather than a relation which obtains merely *via* the fulfilment relation. But this you have not done.

13. No comment.

14.1 This paragraph is, to my mind, an exceptionally clear example of the ambivalence I pointed out in 8 above. You argue that "sincere assent to 'I ought to do A' involves doing A" because "'I ought to do A' understood normatively entails 'Let me do $A!$' and so sincere assent to the first entails sincere assent to the second, and sincere assent to the second involves doing A." The focus of interest in this argument is, of course, the premise "'I ought to do A' understood normatively entails 'Let me do $A!$'" It is obvious that if this premise rests on the idea that sincere assent to 'I ought to do A' involves *fulfilling* the imperative 'Let me do $A!$' then the above argument is circular. But then the premise in question must rest on the idea that there is a "syntactical" connection between "I ought to do A" understood normatively (i.e. not understood as 'I feel obligated to do A') and "Let me do $A!$" But perhaps you have in mind a "pragmatic" or psychological sense of entails; something like

'Ought-'statements entail imperatives	$=_{Df}$	given the purposes which lead people to use ought statements, people who use them are often ready to use the corresponding ordinary imperatives.

I mention this only for the sake of completeness, since I am certain that it is not what you have in mind.

14.2 Let me conclude this part of my letter with the suggestion that what you are driving at might better be put *not* as the claim that 'ought-'statements entail imperatives, but as the claim that singular 'ought-'statements are themselves "really" imperatives which signalize universal imperatives as their presuppositions (see 4 above), where to say that this is what they "really" are is to point up (a) the similarities between the uses of imperatives and 'ought-'statements, (b) the fact that singular 'ought-'statements signalize universal 'ought-'sentences as their presupposition.

++++++++++++++++++++++++++++++

I was planning to add some rather lengthy remarks on your comments on my *Mind* paper.* Since the above is already fantastically long, and I am anxious to put it in your hands without further delay, I shall limit myself to the following brief points.

1. I quite agree that "we must allow for the place of observation in establishing material rules of inference" and that "if so they cannot be established only by

---

* [Eds.—IM.]

reference to the meanings of words..." But I would argue that to "establish" universal propositions of the kind used in explanation (that is to say, which we would be willing to formulate as subjunctive conditionals) is to justify the choice of a framework of meaning—but see 7, 8 below—or symbols governed by material rules of inference, with which to enrich or modify our actual usage. And exactly because the rules are *material* rules (in my sense), there *is* a choice, a choice which cannot be made by merely contemplating meanings.

2. But from the fact that 'All A is B' containing the concepts 'A' and 'B' (with the material rule: 'x is B' is derivable from 'x is A') cannot be justified merely by considering the meanings of 'A' and 'B' it does not follow that "All A is B" (thus used) cannot be correctly said to be 'true *ex vi terminorum*.' For if I say

'All A is B' (used in a certain way) is true

I am, in effect, endorsing, indicating a willingness to assert on my own behalf, either 'All A is B' (thus used) or a translation of 'All A is B' (thus used). In short, I can correctly say

'All A is B' is true

only if I myself make the same use of 'All A is B' (or translation thereof) as that on which I am commenting. And if what I wish to convey is that my assertion of 'All A is B' (or its translation) is unconditionally authorized by a rule (material or formal) of language, I shall say

'All A is B' (in this usage) is *necessarily* true

If I wished to use "true-false" language to deny that in my usage 'A' and 'B' (or their translations) are governed by the rule "'x is B' is derivable from 'x is A'," I should say

'All A is B' is not necessarily true,

going on, perhaps, to add that as a matter of fact

'All A is B' is false.

If, on the other hand, my purpose were to question the wisdom of using 'A' and 'B' in accordance with* certain rules at a certain place in the logical space of our language, it would be incorrect for me to say

---

* [Eds.—The word "with" is missing in the original letter.]

'All A is B' (thus used) is *false*

For the latter implies that

'Some A is not B' (used in this way) is *true*

which far from challenging the use, presupposes it. And it would be equally incorrect for me to say

'All A is B' is not necessarily true

for this is correctly used to challenge not the idea of using 'A' and 'B' in accordance with such a rule, but the idea that they are in point of fact so used.

3. I quite agree that my synthetic propositions a priori which hold by virtue of material rules of inference (and can be said, with the above cautions, to be true *ex vi terminorum*) would not be regarded by traditional proponents of the synthetic a priori as specimens of this animal—for the reasons that (a) my 'synthetic a priori propositions' have genuine alternatives (which do not, however, *contradict* them); (b) our adoption of *this* framework of 'synthetic necessary propositions' rather than *that* rests on experience.

4. There is no such thing as shaping a conceptual framework to fit a *given* which presents itself as instances of qualities and relations. "Experiences" do not classify themselves. To classify, in however rudimentary a form, is to apply a symbol which plays a role in a "symbol game" analogous to that played by *predicates* in the sophisticated "language games" with which we are familiar.

5. What, in effect, I am arguing is that the meaning of a classificatory symbol is constituted by its *moves* (cf. 'the bishop's moves') in the game to which it belongs. I am also arguing that there is no way of justifying the adoption of a "symbol game" from a vantage point outside all "symbol games". In particular, observation is always observation 'in terms of' 'observation sentences' in a symbol game.

6. Primitive man acquired concepts not by inventing symbol games to fit his "observations" but by a kind of 'natural selection' of his 'mutant' responses to his environment, nature playing the role of 'animal trainer,' with carrot and whip.

7. On the other hand, we can deliberately choose to modify and expand our language game. This is made possible by the fact that we have learned to play "meta-language games" (are self-conscious). But though we can deliberately modify (usually enrich) our language 'in order better to explain our observations,' this is not because we find in observation a *pou sto* or vantage point 'beyond the strife of systems.' The giving of reasons is always a move *within a language game*, and giving a reason for adopting new pieces (or new moves for old pieces) into our language, is a move in the meta-linguistic wing of our linguistic wing of our linguistic house. And if the reason is of the form "... because there is a red circle

over there," this merely exhibits the fact that the metalanguage game in which scientific justification occurs contains as a proper part the language game in which the observation is made.

8. To be sure, the scientist may deliberately modify his observation language, but only *in part* at any one stage. For the reasons he gives involve using *other* observation terms. The analogy which comes to mind is 'repairing an aeroplane in flight.'

Cordially,
[W.S.]

S5. Sellars to Hare, 15 September 1956

Dear Hare:

I am taking the liberty of enclosing a copy of my latest attempt to think through the logic of 'ought,'* on the off chance that you might be able to fit a glance at it into your schedule before term begins. It is the only part of the latest stage of a 'continuous' (but not, I hope, 'dense') series of rewritings of my (much too hastily prepared) Oxford talk which has some semblance of publishability.† The remainder, which I have had to lay aside for the moment because of other commitments, concerns the analysis of such terms as 'shall,' 'intends,' 'in order to,' 'reason,' 'motive,' etc. along the lines barely hinted at in footnote 40.‡

It occurs to me that a remark or two on my use of the term 'motive' might not be out of place. It may be that to your ear I make an unorthodox, or even incorrect, use of this term. I believe that I am following Prichard in distinguishing between 'saying what a person's motive was for a certain piece of conduct' in the sense, *roughly,*—see comment (b) below—of saying what his *reason* was; and 'saying what a person's motive was, etc.' in the sense of giving a *causal explanation* of his conduct *as a piece of conduct* (i.e. an explanation which, though causal, is not behavioristic nor physiological). In the pair of exchanges,

(1) Tom: What was Harry's motive?
Dick: His motive was *to make her happy.*
(2) Tom: What was Harry's motive?
Dick: His motive was *the desire to make her happy.*

I don't think that Dick's first answer is elliptical for his second.

Comments: (a) 'Motive' in the first sense is a cousin of 'reason.' (See next comment.) *Roughly*, a person's motive in this sense is that part of the envisaged scenario of his action the thought of which moves him to act. It is, so to speak, the *effective* part of the *intention*, more accurately, of the set of things he would admit to having brought about intentionally. One species of *motive*, in this sense, is *purpose*. But, as Prichard has emphasized, not all motives, in this sense, are purposes, thus

(1′) Tom: What was Harry's motive?
Dick: ... to do his duty.

---

* [Eds.—It is most likely that Sellars is referring to IIO.]
† [Eds.—The "Oxford talk" Sellars references may be "Some Remarks on the Logic of 'Ought'." The archive copy has a note at the top of the first page indicating it was read at Oxford and in London in March 1956. See document 31735062219387, Box 31, Folders 3–6, Wilfrid S. Sellars Papers, 1899–1990, ASP.1991.01, Archives of Scientific Philosophy, Archives & Special Collections, University of Pittsburgh Library System.]
‡ [Eds.—Neither IIO nor IIOR contains a footnote 40; but IIO was Sellars's only substantial engagements with the logic of 'ought' up until 1956, so the reference here is unclear.]

to which there corresponds, in the second sense of 'motive,'

(2′) Tom: What was Harry's motive?
Dick: The feeling that he ought to do it.

(b) I said that 'motive' in the first sense is a cousin of 'reason'. My reason for saying this is that—and I am illustrating my point—we say *not* "Harry's reason was to make her happy," but, for example, "Harry's reason was that she was lonely." In other words, in speaking of Harry's reasons we refer to the factual premises which Harry used in his practical reasoning.

(c) We are all aware (as Prichard was not) that explanation in terms of desire is analogous to explanation in terms of short term dispositions.

(d) Perhaps the most striking and familiar use of *motive* is as in

(3) Tom: What was Harry's motive?
Dick: Love.

It is clear that 'love' sums up a complex family of hypotheticals and mongrels among the members of which are to be found desires. Other motives, in this sense, are Hate, Envy, etc.

But I won't bore you with these familiar tangles. I just wanted to make clear that when I have written of the relation of *ought* to "motivation" I have not meant to bring in such contexts as

(4) Tom: What motivated Harry?
Dick: The sound *you-ought-to-do-A* impinging on his ears
initiated a chain of stimulus-response connections which resulted in a rapid to-and-fro motion of his right index finger.

Please give my greetings to Mrs Hare. May I say that the day I spent with you was one of the high points in my all-too-brief stay in England. I look forward to seeing you both again during the course of your American visit.

Sincerely yours,

P.S. Robert Binkley, who will shortly be in Oxford for a year of study as a Fulbright scholar, is one of the ablest students I have ever had. I would not hesitate to compare him to Castañeda. He is completing a PhD thesis on *good reasons*. I have suggested that he get in touch with you. He is wonderfully quick and agile in his thinking, but penetrating as well, and endowed with a "robust sense of reality."

W.S.

H6. Hare to Sellars, 3 December 1956

Dear Professor Sellars,

You must be thinking me very discourteous for not thanking you earlier for sending me your paper on 'Imperatives'. I received it in time to read it through once before term began; but I found it so difficult that I put it aside in order to read it again before replying; and inevitably once term began the reply got postponed. I think I can truly say that it is the most difficult paper that I have ever read twice; some passages I have had to read a good many times more than that, but it has been worth it. I have also discussed it with Binkley; he came to lunch with me the other day, besides himself reading a very able and clear paper to Nowell-Smith's and my class on 'The Bearing of Ethics on Morality'. I think he is extremely good. I have also, concurrently, been discussing the same sort of subject with Frankena, who has been here. As a result of all this I have myself become a good deal clearer, I think, about these matters; and what I am going to write to you may turn out to be more about my own thoughts than about your paper. I have put my remarks on separate sheets.

We are now more or less fixed to come up to the States in early August, and shall make some sort of a journey round the country before settling down at Princeton in September.

Yours sincerely,
Richard Hare

P.S. It occurs to me that Castañeda might be interested in this correspondence. If you think so, perhaps you would pass my notes on to him. You have no doubt let him see your paper. I have kept a copy of my notes; and I should be grateful if I might hang on to the paper for the time being; but do not hesitate to ask for it back if you are short of copies.

H6+. "Remarks on Sellars, [IIO]"*

It seemed to me that the most important difference between your views and mine is now that where I use *imperatives* for the purpose of analyzing moral judgments, you use *resolutives*. I have a tendency to conjugate the imperative verb 'Let me run', 'Run', 'Let him run', etc.; you conjugate the 'resolutive' verb 'I shall run', 'You shall run', 'He shall run', etc. I have had in the past some tendency to regard the first persons of these two verbs as rough equivalents; and indeed to regard the two verbs as a whole as equivalents. This would obviously be inexact, though I also think that there is a very close affinity (should we say even a common element of meaning) between the two verbs.

In the past I have also been tempted to say, in face of attacks such as you made in your paper at Oxford, that the 'brick' I require for my analysis is not the ordinary imperative as found in language; this always has, as actually used, extraneous elements (such as the necessity for the user to have authority to command) which may not be present in those statements (e.g. moral statements) which we wish to analyze in terms of it. This has prompted me to say, on occasion, that what I really want is not the ordinary imperative but something rather like the 'basic sentence' of the atomists; an artificial creation not found in its pure form in ordinary language, but somehow having its meaning explained in terms of the nearest approaches to it in ordinary language. This would be, as it were, a 'basic prescriptive'; its *only* logical feature would be that sincere assent to it involved action here and now, just as the basic sentence of the atomists was supposed only to record a here-and-now sensation.

My recent thought on this subject has been much influenced by consideration of what has occurred to the atomists' basic sentences (I have been reading Urmson and, lately, Ayer's really excellent new Penguin). It now seems to me that in order to analyse (new style) material-object sentences we do not require *basic sentences*; we only require to know what *experiences* are relevant to their truth, and in what way. That is to say, analysis is not a logical construction of houses out of simple linguistic bricks; it is an understanding of the relation of the language we use to experience itself. Carnap and Co. erred through thinking that they had to produce a *linguistic* atom; since language does not give us any such atom, nor even the means of explaining its meaning if we invent one, this programme inevitably failed. All this, of course, has been common talk for some time. What has now occurred to me (it must have occurred to many people, perhaps also to yourself, before this) is that we can get rid of these troublesome imperatives in the same sort

---

* [Eds.—We are unable to locate in the archives a typescript of IIO that matches the pagination referred to by Hare. When Hare refers to a particular page number, we will refer in brackets to the page number (in the *Methodos* edition) and the paragraph number (in the Sicha edition) to which he seems to be referring.]

of way, by going back to Aristotle and saying that the conclusion of the practical syllogism is an *action*. We then no longer have to say such unpopular things as that moral judgments entail imperatives (or resolutives); we have merely to say that *actions* are in appropriate cases the tests of whether a person has accepted, or has even understood, a moral judgment. I have long been accustomed, in talking to my pupils about the meaning of the word δεῖ in Aristotle, to say that it is a pure evaluative; its meaning is simply *what makes the practical syllogism valid*. We understand the meaning of δεῖ if we understand that the person who professes to assent to παντὸς γλυκέος γεύεσθαι δεῖ and to τουτὶ γλυκύ, and yet does not, though not prevented, taste, *must* (logically) have either misunderstood or been insincere.*

This way of giving an account of the meaning of evaluative words seems to me to have two main advantages. The first is that to which I have already alluded: it means that we need not, if we do not want to, talk about imperatives (or resolutives) at all. If we do talk about them, we can talk about them in their own right, or even use them as simpler *illustrations* of features which the more complicated prescriptives, i.e. moral judgments etc., also have; we do not need to say that moral judgments are *analysable in terms of* imperatives (or resolutives) or even that they are analysable partly in terms of them, as you still seem to wish to do. Still less do we have to do what I myself have never done—though I have been accused of doing it—treat moral judgments as *equivalent* to (ordinary) imperatives. This at least prevents us from giving the sort of offence to our fellow-philosophers which prevents them understanding the important part of what we have to say.

The second advantage is this: on the way of doing things that I followed in my book moral judgments are related to actions in two steps, and *each* of these steps can cause one to stumble. There is the step from moral judgment to imperative, which can be challenged by the person who says that one can accept the moral judgment without accepting the corresponding imperative. And there is the step from imperative to action, which can be challenged by the person who says that one can accept the imperative and still not do the action. Thus *akrasia*-troubles arise at two points; on my new procedure they can only arise at one point. This of course does not make them any easier to cope with; but it considerably simplifies the question. We then may use the relation between imperatives or resolutives and actions as *illustrations* of the relations between prescriptives generally and actions,

---

* [Eds.—These Greek phrases seem to be from the *Nicomachean Ethics* 1147a28: "Everything sweet ought to be tasted" and "this is sweet." "δεῖ" (dei) is the root of the English word "deontology;" it connotes "ought," "must," or "it is fitting." Aristotle says *hos dei* frequently in the *NE* in unpacking his notion of "the mean": The person of practical wisdom acts *in the **right** way, at the **right** time, toward the **right** person, for the **right** reasons*. Those instances of "right" are all instances of "dei." We are grateful to Nancy Sherman for providing us with commentary on the Greek. Sellars himself cites this passage in OMR (§11, n. 2).]

and try to give a satisfactory account of *akrasia* in these simple cases; and this may to some extent help us to give an account of it in the more complicated moral case; but we do not have to get the different cases mixed up.

I do not know whether this suggestion will commend itself to you. Binkley did not seem to like it at first impression; but I did not fully understand his misgivings. If you do like the suggestion, I think that, by abandoning both imperatives and resolutives as analytical 'bricks' we could contrive to agree upon an account of the matter which would express the important content of your latest paper (with which I am in substantial agreement). We shall then have (1) Universal moral judgments related directly to actions in the way outlined above; (2) Singular moral judgments ('I ought to do this') related to actions in the same way, but without the need of a minor premise; and differentiated from both resolutives and imperatives by the implicit appeal to a universal moral judgment; (3) imperatives and resolutives of ordinary language similarly related to actions, but without the appeal to any universal judgment. The differences between imperatives and resolutives I will not now discuss.

The difficulties which this sort of suggestion encounters seem to me to be only the difficulties with which we are familiar; and they seem to arise in a somewhat simpler and clearer form. There is, for example, the difficulty of saying what 'implicit appeal' means in the above account. You seem to me to have said something important about this on your p. 37 [pp. 256–7/§50]. I have been having a correspondence about the whole question of mixed sentences (containing both imperative and indicative neustics) with Duncan-Jones, about which I must tell you when we meet. I think that there are sentences of ordinary language which have mixed neustics (e.g. 'There is a book on the table; give it to me') and that the same sort of problem will arise in giving an account of the way in which a singular moral judgment, though prescriptive, also implies that there *is* a principle from which it is derived. I hope I am not mistaken in thinking that at the point referred to you are troubled by this problem, which arises acutely in connection with p. 191 of *The Language of Morals*.

With regard to your covering letter, I do not any longer attribute to you the errors which I wrongly suspected lay concealed in the letter which you first wrote me when our original correspondence began. I do, however, detect a trace of the cloven hoof at the bottom of page 28 [p. 249/§35] of your paper. It seems to me that I might candidly say 'Tom shall do X' and still not do *whatever* I believed would *bring about* Tom's doing of X. For example I might stick at the use of the thumbscrew. I would prefer to say that one who candidly says 'Tom shall do X' implies that in so far as Tom has explicitly or implicitly delegated to the speaker the authority to decide for him whether he shall do X or not, the decision is that he shall do X. But there are also other contexts in which this locution can be used; perhaps thumbscrews can occur in some of them.

About the general question of motives *vs.* reasons I am still very much in the dark. Frankena and I have been discussing this inconclusively. I find what you say in your letter and your paper distinctly helpful.

It has occurred to me that some of the inferences on your page 12 [p. 234/§15] (and perhaps some that I have in the past allowed) are open to the objection that they cannot be contraposed. Thus there is no inference from

He did not promise to call me

and

It is raining

to

It is not the case that he promised to call me if it rained.

At least I do not think so. And I also feel unhappy about the words 'becomes an unconditional promise' at the bottom of that page [p. 235/§15].

On your page 36 [p. 256/§§48–9], I felt just the *same* sort of uneasiness with regard to expressions of intention about the past as most people (myself included) do about imperatives about the past. 'Jones should have done *A*' is not an expression of an intention about the past; at the most it is the indication that we had, in the past, an intention; or it may be the expression of a *wish* about the past, or, better, of our *finding amiss* what actually was done in the past. In a way it seems to me more like a command trying to attach itself to a past possible action than like an intention trying to do this.

Your page 40 [p. 259/§§54–6] makes me have typical doubts about the use of the word 'cause' in connection with thoughts, desires, etc. I think I understand this when the word is used in one of its Aristotelian senses; but it seems to me to be incongruous with the modern sense of the word to say that desires cause me to act (at least, if there is this sense, as perhaps there is, what is said here is utterly different from what is said if we say 'The billiard ball hitting the other billiard ball caused it to go into the pocket').

P. 43, lines 1–5 [pp. 260-1/§57]. Isn't there?* Surely if Tom were the commander of C company and the colonel, the adjutant, the brigadier etc. were discussing the arrangements for the battle, they might all agree, 'Tom shall attack hill 503'. I do not see that to make Tom a party to the conference, so that he can say 'I shall' and they can say 'You shall' or 'He shall' makes a difference. But I may have misunderstood your stipulations about 'shall'.

---

* [Eds.—The passage Hare seems to be querying reads, "Consequently, if my statement 'You (Tom) ought to do A' were simply 'You (Tom) shall do A' as expressing the following practical reasoning

Tom is a person in C
So Tom shall do A

there would be no logical reason to expect Tom, factual agreement aside, to meet my 'You ought to do A' with 'Yes, I ought to do it'" (IIO pp. 260-1/§57).]

H7. Hare to Sellars, 3 January 1958

Dear Sellars,

Thank you very much for your Christmas card. Before I go back (on the 9th) I should like to say how sorry I was to miss you at the Cambridge meeting. I had hoped to come to your symposium, but arrived too late by about an hour, having had to stop in Princeton to pack up our house there. I was the more sorry not to be at your meeting in that I hear that you were the object of an ill-natured assault, and I should have liked to have been there to support you.* But I had the satisfaction of silencing the same gentleman at my symposium.

I wrote a thing about you for the Guggenheim people at their request.

I was invited to Minnesota next summer to a conference on the philosophy of religion sponsored by the Danforth Foundation. I think they thought I would still be in the U.S. then, and hardly suppose they were wanting to bring me over specially from England. From their silence I assume that my conjecture was right. So it looks as if we shall not now meet—at which I am sorry.

Yrs. Sincerely,
Richard Hare

---

* [Eds.—Here, Hare refers to a vertically written marginalium, which reads "Though I heard many comments afterward which indicated that you did not require any, since the meeting was on your side."]

H8. Hare to Sellars, 13 January 1959

Dear Sellars,

Thank you for your letter. I shall be interested to see the latest version of your paper on 'Ought', and will try to send you some comments on it—but that may take some time. May I send you in return a duplicated copy of a thing I wrote in Princeton and have been revising called 'The bearing of Ethics on moral decisions'? This will form part of the new book I am writing*, and since it is rather a central part I want to get all the snags pointed out to me before rather than after I build on it. The new book is a sequel to the first; I have been moderately gratified how little all the criticism I have had has caused me to change my views; and now I feel I can go on and, on the basis of what I have said in *The Language of Morals*, carry the subject a little further and in a more obviously practical direction.

I am sorry, by the way, that you should have been told that my first book is out of print. I have verified that it is still in print. 10,000 copies were printed, of which I don't think more than about 6,000 have yet sold. Possibly a new batch was binding when you asked (they didn't bind them all at the time of printing); or possibly your bookshop didn't make the right enquiries. In any case the Oxford Press Depot in the High St. here has plenty of bound copies. If sales go on as at present I hope to bring out a new edition in about five years time; it won't have any substantial alterations but may have a new preface.

Yours sincerely,
R.M. Hare.

---

* [Eds.—Hare is likely referring to *Freedom and Reason* (Oxford: Clarendon Press, 1963).]

H9. Hare to Sellars, 29 January 1959

Dear Sellars,

Thank you very much for sending me your paper about 'Ought'. I have read the latest version with interest and, I hope, profit. I am in sympathy with your main intention, which is, as I understand it, to produce a logic of moral discourse which brings out its 'practical' or 'prescriptive' character without assimilating it too much to other kinds of practical discourse (in particular imperatives). When I wrote my book I was impressed by the resemblances between imperatives and moral judgments, but was quite aware that there were also important differences between imperatives in natural languages and moral judgments, some of which differences I noted. In spite of this, I thought that the best way to approach the analysis of moral judgments was to take the ordinary imperative and show what had to be taken away from its logical character and what added in order to make it a tolerable imitation of a moral judgment. Briefly, I thought, one had to take away the particular associations of particular uses of the imperative mood (e.g. in commanding in the narrow sense, sc. with authority; and in entreating) so as to leave a kind of basic singular prescriptive. I thought, and still think, that if this is done to imperatives, the difference between first-person resolutives and imperatives in the other persons gets very tenuous, and indeed that between resolutives and imperatives generally. I am therefore much in sympathy with your attempt (if I describe it right) to approach moral judgments *via* resolutives; such an approach might well reach the same point in the end as my own approach. After the imperative had been purified in this way of irrelevant associations, I thought that it could be turned into a passable imitation of moral judgment by the addition of universalisability. I am grateful to you for your very subtle discussion of the various things which this might mean; the paper which I sent you will show you that in my new book I am going to place a great deal of weight on universalisability, and shall therefore have to explain very carefully in what sense I am using this term. I hope that I shall not have to make the logical character of moral judgments quite so rich as you do at the end of my paper, in order to reach my conclusions; that is to say, I want if I can to do the trick with fewer cards.

I have two main criticisms to make of your paper, which, though they are on matters of detail, may have a good deal of bearing on your argument. The first is about your inferences on p. 7, etc., of the form

> He promised to call me, if it rained
> It is raining
> So, he promised to call me.

This inference, and the others like it, seems to me to be, intuitively, invalid. For with a valid inference, if the premisses are true, one can do the inference and affirm the conclusion, and forget about the premises. But with this inference, one cannot do this. For it just isn't the case that, even given that the premises are true, the man promised to call you, period. He promised to call you, *if* it rained, and that is all that he promised. It is quite true that the promise has become one which cannot be fulfilled now unless he calls you, in view of the fact that it is raining; but it has not been turned, by the fact that it is raining, from a conditional into an unconditional promise. To put the matter another way, it would be most misleading for someone who had ascertained the truth of the premises

Jones promised to come if the plane wasn't cancelled

and

The plane wasn't cancelled

to make your sort of inference and pass on the information

Jones promised to come;

for then someone who heard the information might very justly blame Jones for his improvidence in making the (unconditional) promise to come, when he ought to have known that there was a typhoon approaching and the planes would almost certainly be cancelled.

The other point is similar to one I made before. On p. 10 you seem to be making the sentence 'Let Tom do A' equivalent to 'Cause Tom to do A', which, it seems to me, it is not. I wanted to make a similar point about what I thought was your interpretation of 'intending Tom to do A'; but I cannot now find the passage to which I wished to take exception.

I am, as I said, very grateful to you for letting me see this latest revision; and I hope that we shall keep in touch. Here there seems to be a growing tendency towards obscurantism in moral philosophy; but I am heartened by the appointment of Ayer as Professor of Logic.*

Yours sincerely,
R.M. Hare

---

* [Eds.—Ayer was appointed Wykeham Professor of Logic, Oxford, in 1959, which he occupied until his retirement in 1978.]

*S10.** Sellars to Hare, 14 February 1959

Dear Hare:

Many thanks for the paper. I have found it very exciting. The connection it draws between inclination and obligation via formal universality is persuasive in the types of case you consider, and I look forward eagerly to the chapter in which you will develop and apply the *fascinating* suggestion of the last few pages. There are some things you say about being in the moral framework and using the language of obligation which I want to think about. If I get anywhere, I will drop you a line.

Your comment on the argument, 'Jones promised to call Smith, if it rained/ It is raining/ So, Jones promised to call Smith' hit home, but did not completely convince. It was the latest in a long line of comments to this general effect; but it was the first that really disturbed me. My colleague Terrell, on reading the original draft, claimed that the only argument in this neighborhood that was good was 'Jones promised to call Smith, if it rained/ It is raining/ So, Jones ought to call Smith' and others have reacted in the same way. Would you give me your reaction to the following, which I am debating inserting in the text:

[On page 7 delete the last 10 lines of the text, beginning with "On the other hand..."; and on page 8, delete everything up to the beginning of section VII]
[Replace with

VI

On the other hand it does seem to me, though nothing in my argument hinges upon it, that the fact that Jones said 'I promise to call you, if it rains' authorizes the reasoning

Jones promised to call Smith, if it rained
It is raining
So, Jones promised to call Smith

This reasoning clearly involves a non-performatory use of the verb 'to promise,' and its principle would be

P-2. If x says to y 'I promise to do A, if p'
then, if p, x has promised y to do A

The performance 'I promise to do A, if p' would thus be a performance which, if p, takes on the character of a promise to do A. The step from being a *conditional* promise, a promise *to do A, if (condition)*, to being a *conditioned* promise *to do*

---

* [Eds.—Letters *S10* and *H11* are from R. M. Hare's Papers and Manuscripts at the Archives of Balliol College, Oxford. We thank the Archivist, Ms. Anna Sander, for answering Kyle's queries and alerting him to their existence. We also thank Mr. James Stockton for sharing with Kyle his high-resolution images of *S10* and *H11*. Copies are also available in Box 30, Folders 3–6, Wilfrid S. Sellars Papers, 1899–1990, ASP1991.01, Archives of Scientific Philosophy, Archives & Special Collections, University of Pittsburgh Library System.

A (*simpliciter*) is, as I see it, part of the conceptual framework of promising. In other words I reject the assumption that because what Jones *said* was 'I promise to do A, if p' it cannot be correct, on learning that-p, to say that Jones promised to do A.[13a]

13a If we reject this assumption, we must, of course, reject the inference from 'Jones promised to do A' to 'Jones said "I promise to do A"' (or its equivalent). The correct inference would have to be '*either* Jones said "I promise to do A" *or* there is a state of affairs, p, such that p is known to be realized, and Jones said "I promise to do A, if p."'

This rejection entails a reshaping of the principles which govern the promise along roughly the following lines,

P-3a If x says to y 'I promise to do [—]'
       he has promised to do [—].
P-3b If x has promised y to do [A, if p],
       then, if p, he has promised y to do A
P-3c If x has promised y to do A, x owes it
       to y to do A.

The alternative is to supplement the principle formulated on page 6 (bottom), which we may now call P-1, with

P-1c If x says to y 'I promise to do A, if p'
       then, if p, x owes it to y to do A.

This new principle would authorize the reasoning

Jones promised to call Smith, if it rained
It is raining
So, Jones ought to call Smith

To accept this account of the matter is to imply that it would be incorrect to answer the question 'Why ought Jones to call Smith?' by a simple 'Because he promised to.'

Similar problems and alternatives arise in connection with the interpretation of conditional commands.]*

ϵ   ϵ   ϵ

Well, I'm very uneasy about all this. I can see that I may very well have talked myself into a bottle to twist one of W--n's† metaphors. I need some therapy. Would you give it a try?

Yours sincerely,
Wilfrid Sellars

---

* [Eds.—For Sellars's final expression of his thinking on these problems, see CPCI, Ch. 17 of this volume.]
† [Eds.—Ludwig Wittgenstein.]

H11. Hare to Sellars, 17 February 1959

Dear Sellars,

Thank you very much for your letter. I will report progress in my own argument, if I make any.

I think that your proposed amendment to your own paper is an improvement; but I am still not convinced. Indeed, it seems to me that the consideration referred to in your new footnote 13a is an additional objection. I also have the impression (though I have not had time to read through your paper again) that some of your later arguments depend on the validity of inferences of the type under dispute. I certainly thought so at the time when I read the paper.

The question of the status of inferences of the form:

Jones promised to call Smith, if it rained,
It is raining,
So, Jones ought to call Smith,

is very puzzling. I don't myself feel inclined to say that the principle of this inference is analytic; not only because there are cases where we ought *not* to do what we have promised (these cases could perhaps be taken care of by a *ceteris paribus* or stronger clause), but because it seems to me to be a moral principle of substance that we ought to keep our promises. Yet it doesn't seem to me either, that we just *happen* to have a moral principle that promises ought to be kept. The source of my disinclination to say the latter is that, if we didn't have such a principle, we shouldn't have a use for the word 'promise'. So ought we perhaps to say that this is a case where an expression *e* could not have a use unless some proposition *p*, containing the expression *e*, were true; but in which, nevertheless, the proposition *p* is not analytic of *p*, nor indeed analytic at all. Another example, perhaps would be, that, although we should not have a use for the word 'cause' unless there were regularities in nature (whatever that means) the proposition that there are regularities in nature is not analytic. To make the parallel complete, we should have to formulate the proposition so as to include the word 'cause', which might be done: 'There are some things which cause other things to happen in accordance with a natural law'. One might argue that, similarly, unless we believed that one ought, in general, to keep one's promises, the words 'I promise' would go out of use. But I am not entirely happy about this parallel. A closer one would perhaps be this: unless, more often than not, people were disposed to do what they are asked to do, or unless at any rate they were sometimes so disposed *because* asked, there would be no point in having a formula for requests. I.e. if requesting made no difference to action (N.B. *not* by *causing* actions), then we should not make requests.

Yours sincerely,
R.M. Hare.

H12. Hare to Sellars, 1 August 1980

Dear Professor Sellars,

I should have thanked you before for sending me your paper. But I have been very much preoccupied with finishing my own book on moral thinking.* I have got about half way through your paper and am in much sympathy with it, but have now to depart for the east by car. I shall be back in a month's time, but don't know when I shall be able to read the rest of your paper—perhaps on the journey. One thing I liked very much was the para. near the beginning about the meanings of *all* words being at least partly determined by their logical properties; this was an almost identical thought to one I had just been expressing in my own book, but more neatly put by you. If I may, I will quote it in a footnote.

Yours sincerely,
R.M. Hare

---

* [Eds.—*Moral Thinking: Its Levels, Method and Point* (Oxford: Clarendon Press, 1981).]

21
The Binkley–Sellars Correspondence, 1956–1959

B1. Binkley to Sellars, 3 December 1956

Dear Wilfrid,

I was very glad to get your letter. Oberlin sounds like the best of all possible possibilities to actualize. I await news eagerly.

I had something of a success last week. I read a paper to Hare and Nowell-Smith's class on the bearing of ethics on morality. I criticized some of the things Hare had been saying the previous week about the principle of universalizability. He regards it as a logical principle belonging to ethics which, given the right non-moral desires or inclinations, determines bits of moral content, and thus shows one bearing of ethics on morality. I pointed out that what determined moral content was his principle that Oughts entailed imperatives, and that, while this was all right, it only worked for the step from "Jones has not the slightest inclination to do A" (Doesn't assent to 'Do A!' in the slightest degree) to "Jones doesn't think he ought to do A." I granted that this could be used to prove to Jones that in the interests of consistency he must retract his statement that he ought to do A. Once this was done, the principle of universalizability would require retracting similar moral judgments made in similar cases. Hare seems to think there is a little more to it, that it captures this sort of moral reasoning; "Should I keep my promise to him? Well, what would I think if it were a matter of his keeping a promise to me? I wouldn't like that, so I'd better keep my promise." We finally reached a cloudy sort of agreement on this, but I'm still not sure that we understand each other. I then presented something like the argument of the last part of your paper showing a connection between adopting moral principles and the impartial love of mankind, suitably adapted to the new environment. Roughly, that given a preference for the good society and the belief that including a certain principle in the moral code is a necessary condition for that, and also given no stronger competing desires, it would be unreasonable of a man to not subscribe to that principle. Hare and Nowell-Smith seemed to accept this at first, but it may just be part of their pedagogical technique. Grice and Pears were there, though, and as far as I can see, utterly refuted the argument in the form I presented it. Their main objection was that even though having society adopt the principle as part of its code might be a necessary condition for the good society, *my* subscribing to the principle might not conduce to society's subscribing to it. If it is a matter of everybody's subscribing to it then, since some people won't, the necessary condition is unfulfillable no matter what I do. If it is a matter of just *most* members of the society subscribing to it, then the good society could be realized even though I didn't accept the principle. Further, my subscribing to the principle might have no effect on people's generally subscribing to it, or it might even have a negative effect, if I were extremely unpopular. I had presented this as an instance of ethical principles combining with desires and factual beliefs to determine moral content. It didn't work because everything depended on the logical principle that who wills the end wills the means (plus a certain conception of what morality is). That permitted the critics to bring in a lot of extraneous matters about the actual effectiveness of the means. I don't think it will work unless the man has already taken up some kind of a moral standpoint. Taking up this standpoint might amount to reasoning as though he were legislating for all mankind (even though, of course, he is not) or imagining the argument directed not to a single man but to the society as a whole. And I don't see how it could be shown to be unreasonable to refuse to take up the moral standpoint. As far as I can see, these objections also apply to the argument as you develop it in your paper (middle of page 29 of mimeo version, for copy of which thanks).*

Anyhow, Hare was quite pleased with the paper; he asked me out to lunch (at luxurious Golden Cross) and we had a long philosophical talk. He is puzzled by some things in your paper, and is working up a letter to you. While we were talking, he came up with an idea that he has been toying with. It was suggested, he said, by something Ayer says about the connection between experiences and material object sentences, which Hare interprets as the claim that object sentences are entailed not by sentences describing experiences but somehow by experiences themselves. Similarly, it might be possible to say that oughts entail actions directly, and there would be no need for the imperatives in between. It is only the possibly false idea that only linguistic things can be entailed that requires imperatives in the analysis of ought. He is not committed to these ideas, or anything like it; perhaps I shouldn't even be telling you about it. But, in a way, it looks like a sort of halfway house to Sellarsianism.

The Chisholm correspondence was interesting. I have stamped it TOP SECRET and keep it hidden under the floorboards.

I am still spilling ink in a thesis-like way. (How I hate it now, though.) I still hope to drop the damn thing in the post box on Christmas Eve.

---

* [Eds.—As with *H6+* in the Hare-Sellars correspondence, we were unable to locate a typescript that exactly matches the pagination referred to by Binkley. Binkley seems to be referring to §§63–5 of IIO (pp. 264–5 of the *Methodos* version).]

I have met Prof. Frankena, who is here with apparently nothing very definite to do. He read a paper too, arguing among other things that you couldn't decide about the bearing of ethics on morality until you settled whether naturalistic definitions of 'ought' were possible. And since the naturalistic fallacy wasn't really a *fallacy*, this question was still open.

We enjoy England and Oxford immensely. If I had the money, I think I'd just settle here for the rest of my life. Petrol rationing or no petrol rationing.

Cheerio (or however they spell it.)
Bob

S2. Sellars to Binkley, 7 December 1956

Dear Bob:

I couldn't sympathize more on the matter of the thesis, but I take it that it is still a good idea to have it under the graduate school's belt when applying for a job. Unless you have changed your mind in this respect, I look forward to receiving it early in the new year.

You write: "I then presented something like the argument of the last part of your paper... Roughly that given a preference for the good society and the belief that including a certain principle in a moral code is a necessary condition for that, and also given no stronger competing desires, it would be unreasonable of a man not to subscribe to that principle." I think, however, that if you read page 29 of my paper carefully you will see that this is just *not* my argument.* The above is an argument we agreed in rejecting way last summer. My argument differs from the above by specifying the belief that everybody's *subscribing* to the principle is a necessary condition of the 'good society.' Given this belief it follows that wishing the 'good society' he wishes that he himself subscribe. I said nothing about the reasonableness of this belief. And I would be the first to admit that *thus formulated* this belief is false and unreasonable. I do think that something *like it* is true and reasonable. And the crucial point is that even if it were of the form "Most people's subscribing to p_i is a necessary condition of the general welfare" there is good sense to the argument

> Jones believes that most people's subscribing etc.
> Jones wishes the general welfare
> *So* Jones wishes that he himself subscribe.

"Most people subscribing" is not the same thing as "Either (*A* subscribes and *B* subscribes.... and *N* does not subscribe) or (*A* subscribes and *B* does not subscribe.... and *N* does subscribe) or...." Thus, though it is indeed true that "If it is a matter of just *most* members of the society subscribing to it, then the good society could be realized even though I didn't accept the principle," this fact does not militate against the argument immediately above, nor, therefore, against the point I wish to make. (I grant that more would have to be said to bring out the argument's "good sense.")

I must break off, now, and go back to my office. (I am using the typewriter near the ditto machine). I am enclosing a revised section VII and VIII together with an appendix for the paper. The appendix specifies the location and amount of

---

* [Eds.—Again, the reference seems to be to §§63–5 of IIO (pp. 264–5 of the *Methodos* version).]

revision that is made by these changes. Please pass it on to Hare, once you have had a chance to look it over.

I will write again soon.

As you say, Cheerio,
[Wilfrid Sellars]

Encl: Revised Section VII, VIII
     and appendix for the paper.

B3. Binkley to Sellars, 13 February 1957

Dear Wilfrid,

I am sending the first few chapters of the thesis. I have been saving them until I could send the whole thing but I have now decided that half a loaf is better than none. This is not as much as I had planned to have done, nor indeed as much as I *said* I would have done, and I feel properly contrite. I am continuing to inch my way through it which means that if it is to be of finite length I shall eventually reach the end of it.

About the job situation. Oberlin is out, I take it, since Hector tells me that Buck* is going there. Wayne is out, Nakhnikian tells me in the pleasantest letter of this kind I have ever received because Hector is going there and he doesn't want two Minnesotans. I am very hopeful about Pomona College. Jones† had a Professor Muhlhauser of their English department who is in London this year on a Guggenheim, come up and interview me. He has completely sold me on the place. I hope to hear from Jones in a week or two, and I'll probably accept any reasonable offer if it is made. I am also applying at Duke, but I can't work up the enthusiasm for a southern university that I can for a western liberal arts college.

Hector sent me the fourth chapter of his book, and asked for comments. I think that 'permissive commands' are a problem for him. (I say to my son, "You may play outside now.") Grammatically it is a normative, but in other respects it is like an imperative. Universalizability doesn't apply, for example. And it has all sorts of similarities to commands. I like Austin's method here. "You may..." stands to "I permit you to..." as "Do A!" to "I command you to do A." And then you can go on to consider the nature of the conventions that make commands and permissions possible. I suppose this is the line you would take. While you 'reduce' imperatives to resolutives you are not committed to this line. The uttering of an imperative or a command to do A could be a performance based on the resolutive "You shall do A". But it could also, and this is more likely in the case of commands, be a deliberate action based on the resolutive "I shall tell you to do A." Similarly, the resolutive "I shall give you permission..." could lead me to say "You may..." But I don't think there is a resolutive of which "You may..." could be an 'expression' in the same way that "Shut the door" is an 'expression' of "You shall shut the door." You, of course, don't *have* to find such a resolutive. But Hector does have to find a corresponding imperative. If he doesn't regard it as a normative, that is. "Do A or not A" won't do because it is analytic, and there is some *point* to granting permission. "Do A if you want to" is better. But this is a funny kind of imperative. I wouldn't regard my permission as 'unfulfilled' if you wanted to do A but still didn't do it (on account of some independent obligation, say.) And if 'want' is stretched to make this impossible, then "Do A if you want" is funnier still, and I think it becomes analytic.

* [Eds.—Roger C. Buck.] † [Eds.—W.T. Jones.]

In your last letter you charge me with misrepresenting your view about the relation between the impartial love of mankind and adopting moral principles, and adopting a position we rejected last summer. I plead innocent, though I grant that what I said in my letter was vague enough to permit this interpretation. It is the reasoning from "If people generally did A in C on principle it would be a good thing" to "I shall adopt the principle 'Do A in C'." The premise is ambiguous as between everybody doing A in C and most people doing A in C. On the first interpretation the argument seems to be valid, because my adopting the principle is a logically necessary condition of everybody's doing so. But, as you agree, the premise on this interpretation is not likely to be true in the relevant sense, ie, one which would require that everybody's doing A in C is a significantly better state of affairs than everybody but me doing it. Further, everybody's doing A in C is an unattainable state of affairs (practically).

If "generally" is interpreted as "most people do A in C" it is not unreasonable to suppose that people generally doing A in C is a necessary condition of social welfare. But my doing A in C is not a necessary condition of this. You say there is some kind of sense to the argument from "Most people's doing A in C (on principle) is a necessary condition of human welfare" to "I shall adopt the principle." But I don't think either of us has been able to say in what this good sense consists. I am now inclined to think that it rests on a meta-moral principle, which can be represented as just this inference principle, some cousin of which one must accept to be called a moral agent. But I'm not very happy about this. Surely there were moral agents before it occurred to anyone to question moral principles and so to devise a meta-principle.

B. A. O. Williams and I are thrashing around with this, but neither of us has any very clear ideas about it. I'm hearing Austin's lectures on performatives and attending his class, and I am enormously impressed with him. Dummett, Anscombe, and Hao Wang have a class on Wittgenstein's philosophy of math. Very entertaining, Anscombe treating the text* with almost religious awe, Dummett doing his best to make sense of it and Hao Wang trying not to give offense with too much formalism.

Bob

---

* [Eds.—Correction of "test" in original manuscript.]

S4. Sellars to Binkley, 14 May 1958

Dear Bob:

A word or two about this 'noddable nodder' business. Under the stimulus of your final chapter*, I have sat down and tried to spell out to myself just what I was up to.†

1. I reject—and have never accepted—the neustic-phrastic account of indicative inference. The fact that we can formulate inference tickets in the form

S being f implies *S being g*

in which the sentences 'S is f' and 'S is g' are turned into singular terms by turning the 'is' into a participle, by no means supports the idea that the corresponding inferences have the form

S being f, yes
So, S being g, yes

This comes out even more clearly if we formulate the inference ticket as

That S is f implies *that S is g*

The inferences authorized by this ticket do not have the form

That S is f, yes
So, that S is g, yes

In both cases the inferences are simply of the form

S is f
So, S is g.

Once one has Church's arguments under control, it is best to regard the inference ticket as having the form

'S is f' implies 'S is g.'

---

* [Eds.—Robert Williams Binkley, "Moral Reasoning," PhD Thesis, University of Minnesota, 1958. Chapter VIII at pp. 245–84.]
† [Eds.—In IIO.]

2. What I was most concerned to do was to suggest that, as a first approximation, it is helpful to split up a shall-sentence into an 'operator' and a participial clause, the latter being the form taken by an 'is'-sentence when it is being fitted for use in non-truth-functional contexts; thus,

    I shall do A

into

    Shall /my doing A/

This approach, it seemed to me, throws some light on the logic of means-end deliberation. Consider, to begin with, the reasoning,

I shall do A		Shall /my doing A/
	i.e.	
So, I shall do B		So, shall /my doing B/

The inference ticket supporting this inference simply concerns the 'causal relation' between the doing of A and the doing of B, and has, as such, nothing to do with 'shall'-sentences. One is tempted to say that to "know how to use 'shall'" is to be prepared, if one accepts the inference ticket

    My doing A implies my doing B

to reason, either

I shall do A		Shall /my doing A/
	i.e.	
So, I shall do B		So, shall /my doing B/

or

I shall not do B		Shall /my not doing B/
	i.e.	
So, I shall not do A		So, shall /my not doing A/

3. I certainly did not intend to commit myself to the neustic-phrastic model when I proposed the above analysis of a means-end reasoning. For, to repeat, I do *not* analyze the inference

    It is day,
    So, the sun is shining

as

It being day, yes
So, the sun being shining, yes

4. As I now view the matter, I made too much of a concession to the neustic-phrastic mode of analyzing deliberative inference; certainly in the terminology I used. As I now view the matter, I am quite prepared to say that the means-end reasoning

I shall do A
So, I shall do B

is *directly* related to the license

'I shall do A' implies 'I shall do B'

which, in turn, is derived from the license

'I am about to do A' implies 'I am about to do B'

in accordance with the commitments bound up with the use of 'shall.' But this needs to be supplemented by an analysis of the relation of 'I shall do A' to 'I am about to do A', if the fact that 'shall'-sentences are, so to speak, built from 'is'-sentences is not to be obscured.

5. If I had it to do over, then, I would not make even the concession to Hare's terminology of speaking of 'shall' as a nod. I would simply say that means-end reasoning is from 'shall'-sentence to 'shall'-sentence where the implication between the 'shall'-sentences is derived, given the role of 'shall', from implication between 'is'-sentences. Thus,

First step:
    (α) 'I am going to do A' implies 'I am going to do B'
    (β)* So, 'Shall /my going to do A/' implies 'Shall /my going to do B/'
Second step:
    Shall /my going to do A/
    So, shall /my going to do B/

---

* [Eds.—The *alpha* and *beta* are added in Sellars's copy of this letter.]

or, to take an example from reasonings which are not means-end, but are still not at the level of action on principle,

First step:
  'p' implies '"I am about to do A if p" implies "I am about to do A"'
  p
  So, 'I am about to do A if p' implies 'I am about to do A'
Second step:
  So, 'Shall /my being about to do A if p/' implies 'Shall /my being about to do A/'
Third step:
  Shall /my being about to do A if p/
  So, shall /my being about to do A/

6. From this standpoint, the distinctive feature of 'ought' is that the inference ticket in which it appears is not, so to speak, the 'shall'-ing up of a counterpart inference ticket which is related to it as (α) to (β) in the first example of the preceding section. In other words (but see section 8 below)

  I am in C
  So, I ought to do A

would have the form

  I am in C
  So, I shall do A

where the inference ticket has the form

  'P is a person in C' implies 'Shall /P doing A/'

7. If, in this spirit, we do away with the whole nodding-noddable terminology, we can put the view recommended in IILO more simply by saying that the difference between (the moral) 'ought' and 'shall' is that the former is associated with a commitment to "primitive" inference tickets of which the consequent is of the form 'Shall /P doing A/', while the antecedent is of the form 'P is a person in C.'

8. Having made this step, I am now in two minds about analysing moral principles into such inference tickets, for it is open to me to hold that they can be treated in a way which is parallel to the treatment of conditional intentions as in the second example of section 5 above, thus

First step:
>'*P* is a person in *C*' implies "'*P* does *A* if *P* is a person in *C*' implies '*P* does *A*'"
>So, '*P* is a person in *C*' implies "'Shall /*P* doing *A* if *P* is a person in *C*/' implies 'Shall /*P* doing *A*/'"

Second step:
>I am in *C*
>So, 'Shall /my doing *A* if I am in *C*/' implies 'Shall /my doing *A*/'

Third step:
>Axiom............Shall /(*P*) *P* doing *A*, if *P* is a person in *C*/*
>So, Shall /my doing *A*, if I am in *C*/

Fourth step:
>So, Shall /my doing *A*/

9. But I would like to reflect some more about the advantages and disadvantages of these two analyses. That they are in a sense equivalent does not mean that one of them may not be more illuminating.† Thus, once we appreciate the force of lawlike universal statements, we see that they are equivalent to inference tickets, but I find the latter form the more illuminating. I am inclined to think that the analysis of moral principles as primitive inference tickets is more illuminating because it doesn't require that there be such a thing as intending that everybody keep promises, knowing that in many cases people don't. See my treatment of a parallel problem relating to causal inference in sections 89ff of "Counterfactuals, Dispositions and the Causal Modalities" [Eds.—CDCM] in the second Center volume.

10. The above discussion applies, mutatis mutandis to the prudential 'ought'.

11. I have left out of the picture, of course, the 'intersubjectivity' aspect of principles, moral or prudential.

Well, Bob, I am afraid the above is hasty and ill-considered, but it may give you some feeling for how I would respond to the critical comments on IILO which you so sensibly make in your last chapter.

As ever,
[Wilfrid Sellars]

---

* [Eds.—Sellars has written in the margin of his copy of this letter, "replace *axiom schema* Shall [*P* doing *A*, if *P* is in *C*]."]

† [Eds.—In his copy of the letter, Sellars has written the following annotation at this point:

Of course, what is equivalent to the inference ticket

>'*x* is in *C*' implies '*x* shall do *A*'

is

>(*x*) *x* is in *C* implies *x* shall do *A*.]

B5. Binkley to Sellars, 5 September 1958

Dear Wilfrid,

I have been pondering the question whether moral principles are to be construed as rules of inference or universal intentions. Something in the nature of a third possibility occurred to me. What you need in object language as counterpart to inference rule is not

(1) $S(p) \, Cp \supset Ap$ (S = shall)

but   (C = circumstances)

(2) $(p) \, Cp \supset SAp$ (A = action)

                                                                                                     (P = person)

which, on standard views, is not well formed because, (1) involves applying S operator to propositional function, not proposition [and] (2) involves applying S operator to only a part of a complex prop[osition].

But, couldn't we say that this is allright and, in fact, is just what converts a "shall" in to an "ought"? This would be an alternative to the 'noddable nodder' interpretation. Thus,

$(p) \, Cp \supset SAp$

would represent

"everyone ought to do A in C."

We could even keep this for particular "ought"-statements, by this method;

$(\exists p) \, SAp$ – "There is someone who ought to do A"
[not: "$S(\exists p)Ap$", which means "Someone shall do A"]
$(\exists p) \, SAp \cdot p =$ Jones – "Jones ought to do A."

To preserve universalizability add a rule something like:

"$(\exists p) \, SAp$" implies "$(\exists C)(p)Cp \supset Sax$"

This looks odd, but I may, even so, try to work it up into a note for *Phil. Studies*.

With regard to justification of morality, I think that we can be reconciled—Accepting the added principle (analogous to principle of induction) which *I* think is needed may be (part of) what *you* mean when you say that the desire for welfare of all men must be treated as *supreme* desire. I am now patching up my paper on ultimate justification of ethics for Hector, and I am trying to work this out.

I survived the summer school here* somehow—My introductory course even turned out rather well, thought the tough-minded-tender-minded theme rather got lost in the problem of universals—which is what I might have expected, using Plato, Hobbes, Russell. But I am now about to be swamped by the new semester with only about half of my summer projects completed.

How do you like Yale—[you are bound to be there when you get this letter]. I got a copy of Nick Karalis's funny article on acts of thought[†], which reminded me that he will now be again a part of your intellectual environment. I wish you luck in the long discussions with him that I foresee for you.

We meet soon with the U.N.C. people (Stover[‡] is there this year, by the way) to decide on our guest speakers. I am going to push your name, and I have also heard talk about Rulon Wells.

Bob

PS. I trust Rigo[§] got through with his Ph.D. in time.

---

* [Eds.—Duke University, Durham, North Carolina.]
† [Eds.—Nicholas Karalis, "Knowledge of Other Minds," in *Review of Metaphysics* 9 (June, 1956): 565–8.]
‡ [Eds.—Presumably Robert Stover.]   § [Eds.—Rigoberto Juárez-Paz.]

B6. Binkley to Sellars, 26 September 1958

Dear Wilfrid,

Here is a copy of your letter. I checked it through once for misprints, but there may still be some. (probably lots in this one too. I have borrowed our logic typewriter [∃, ∈, ⊃, =, ≡] and it doesn't have at all the same feel as mine.)

Don't take the ideas of my letter of a few weeks ago too seriously. It was scribbled off in a fit of midnight madness, and I have been having second thoughts, scattered only, in odd moments. They seem to be along these lines.

1. What is needed is a rational explanation of practical discourse, the sort of thing that Hector is doing, only more 'natural'.

2. The following seem to be some of the requirements that it should meet.
   a. It should work in with the rational explanation business in my thesis.
   b. Practical discourse should be parasitic on descriptive discourse.
   c. Action on principle should be marked off from other actions by a difference in the logical form of the practical reasoning involved.
   d. In line with (b), practical discourse is to be built on to descriptive discourse by adding an operator to the language which, applied to a descriptive sentence, turns it into a sentence expressing the intention that the original sentence be true. (The original sentence expresses the belief that it is true)
   e. In line with (a), logical connections must be set up connecting sentences expressing beliefs and intentions and the descriptive sentences describing people as having those beliefs and intentions.

3. Let us use '$' for the new operator. (Thus, perhaps, making analytic what Europeans are always saying about us Americans.) Let 'p', 'q', etc. be descriptive sentences. Thus 'p' might be 'It is raining', in which case '$\$p$' would be 'It shall rain'.

4. Part of incorporating '$' into one's language would be picking up the motivational aspect of it.

5. One should have in the descriptive part of the language two operators, 'I' and 'B' which, applied to a sentence and the name of a person yield sentences to the effect that the person intends that the sentence be true, or believes that it is. (They apply only to descriptive sentences.) Thus, 'B,Jones,p' would say that Jones believes that it is raining, and 'I,Jones,p' would say that he intends that it does. (This is a Geach type maneuver that needs some working out, but let that pass)

6. In line with (2e), we should have the following: (or something like it)
   i. x can sincerely use 'p' if and only if B,x,p.
   ii. x can sincerely use '$\$p$' if and only if I,$x$,$p$.

7. Concerning inference, at least the following would seem to hold.
   iii. If 'q' follows from 'p', then $(x)(B,x,p \supset B,x,q)$ [and converse]
   iv. If '$\$q$' follows from '$\$p$', then $(x)(I,x,p \supset I,x,q)$ [and converse]

[These would have to be modified to allow for logical neighborhood business]

8. Perhaps we could make $-inference parasitic on descriptive inference by saying

v. $(x)[(B,x,p \supset B,x,q) \equiv (I,x,p \supset I,x,q)]$

(This won't quite do, but let it go for a bit)

9. (v) plus (iii) and (iv) will take us back and forth between "q' follows from 'p'" and "$\$q$' follows from '$\$p$'". With this, (we hope) a person who knows descriptive inference and learns his '$\$$' will be able to do $-inference even though

10. $-sentences are not allowed to enter into molecular complexes, nor to yield sentential functions. This is to prevent our parasitism from turning into symbiosis. It fits in with the moves you make in and around section (5) of your letter.

11. Now, about practical principles. The key notion is that somehow you reason from a belief about your circumstances to an intention to act. Perhaps we can get at it by saying that for Jones to hold a practical principle, it must be true of him that [B, Jones,p implies I,Jones,q], or something on that order. Thus, for Jones to hold as a practical principle that when in water he should swim, it must be true of him that

vi*. B,Jones, Jones in water $\supset$ I,Jones, Jones swims

(The '$\supset$' probably isn't right, but let that go.)

12. Perhaps, along these lines, we can even use the following as an analysis of "Jones believes, as a matter of personal principle, that he ought to do an A-action when in C-circumstances."

vii. B,Jones, Jones is in $C \supset$ I, Jones, Jones does A

13. Similarly, for "Jones believes that everyone ought to do A when in C", we would have

viii. (x)B,Jones, x is in $C \supset$ I, Jones, x does A†

("Analysis" is perhaps a bit strong.)

14. The problem of 'ought' and moral reasoning is then to see how such things as (vii) and (viii) can be (or come to be) true of a person. Let us work with the simple case,

ix. B,Jones,$p \supset$ I,Jones,q.

15. Part of what is involved must be that when Jones comes to be in a state of mind expressible by 'p', he then/also comes to be in a state of mind expressible by '$\$q$'. This is further supposed to be a matter of reasoning, and so, by analogy with (7) above, we should have

x. '$\$q$' follows from '$p$' for Jones $\equiv$ [B,Jones,$p \supset$ I,Jones,q]

---

* [Eds.—Starting here, Binkley has misnumbered several of these lines. We have renumbered them, and also corrected his in-text references to these lines.]

† [Eds.—Written in the margin at this point, in Sellars's hand, is "The intention that x do A never is a syllogistic one."]

16. Thus, if (ix) is true of Jones, he is in position to reason

    xi. p, so $\$q$

17. If we let '*' be a signal which, added to an $-sentence indicates that it is derived by reasoning of the form xi, then '$p*$' might be a first approximation to 'It ought to be the case that p'.

18. Notice that we haven't yet violated (10) above, since we have not yet resorted to anything like '$p \supset \$q$', which so far is still nonsense.

19. But won't we be forced to introduce something like this? Ordinarily, one would think, whenever there is the reasoning..., so ___, there is also the statement (or whatever)... $\supset$ ___. That is, how are we to account for the major premisses in such reasonings as

    xii. If p, then q ought to be the case
        $\underline{p}$
        q ought to be the case

and, more plausibly

    xiii. Anyone in C ought to do A
        $\underline{\text{I am in } C}$
        I ought to do A

20. One's first inclination would be to treat them as

    xii'. $p \supset \$q$
       $\underline{p}$
       $\$q*$

and

    xiii'. $(x)Cx \supset \$Ax$
        $\underline{C(\text{me})}$
        $\$A(\text{me})*$

The major premises here clearly violate (10).

21. Before thinking what to do about this, consider such examples as

    If you ought to do A, I ought to do B.
    More people ought to keep their promises than do keep them.
    etc. (examples of 'ought' that don't seem to be directly involved in the principle application context.)

These examples suggest that 'ought', unlike '$', must be allowed the full range of descriptive grammar.

22. Following out this line would lead us to say that a new operator, 'O', is required which converts a sentence into a sentence saying that the first ought to be the case. Thus, xiii' would become

$$\text{xiii''. } (x)\ Cx \supset OAx$$
$$\frac{C(\text{me})}{OA(\text{me})}$$

from which a rule to the effect that Op entails $\$p$ would enable us to pass to '$A(\text{me})$'. The trouble with this approach is that it is unclear how far we would be fulfilling requirement (2c) above.

22. In section 8 of your letter, I take it, you suggest that perhaps the major premise of xiii could be construed as

$$\text{xiv. } \$(x)(Cx \supset Ax),$$

the argument then being reconstructed in a way that avoids violating the demands of (10) above. But as you point out, it does seem implausible to identify a universal ought statement with expression of a universal intention.

23. You suggest that this is an equivalent to the view that treats universal oughts as inference principles, but that it may be more illuminating. Problem: if they are equivalent, and if this one is implausible, doesn't it follow that the other is implausible too?

24. But, they aren't equivalent. Applying ii (from [6] above) to [xiv]* would yield

$$\text{xv. I,me,}(x)(Cx \supset Ax)$$

But, according to viii [from (13) above], which in view of iii, iv and v, is a sort of direct application of the rule of inference idea, we should have gotten

$$\text{xvi. } (x)(B,\text{me},Cx \supset I,\text{me},Ax)$$

25. For comparison, take

$$\text{xv'. B,Jones,}(x)(Cx \supset Ax)$$

---

* [Eds.—Reference to premise xiv missing in original manuscript.]

and

xvi′. $(x)(B,\text{Jones},Cx \supset B,\text{Jones},Ax)$

It seems to me that xvi′ could be true and xv′ false. Might it not be the case that there is no one concerning whom Jones will not reason that he does A if he believes him to be in C (xvi′) and yet Jones believes that there is a person in C who does not do A (denial of xv′)?

Suppose that by mere association of ideas, Jones will believe that a person is F if he comes to believe that he is in C, and that every person who is F and is in C will do A. This would make xvi′ true. (or would it?) But he still might believe that some people in C are not F (though he would never believe that he had found an instance of it), and if so, xv′ would be false.

The same should apply to xv and xvi.

26. Second thought on (24) and (25). Not too convincing. Perhaps it can be cleared up by tightening up the meaning of '$\supset$' in xvi and xvi′.

27. This is enough, or rather, too much, for one letter. But it will give you an idea of how my thoughts are running on these topics these days. Fairly chaotic on the whole, as you see.

We are supposed to be having a hurricane* today. I am looking forward to it, but there are no signs of it yet other than clouds.

I showed your Yale lectures paper to Bo Clark†, who was quite impressed with it on first reading, and may use it in his Analysis seminar. I am trying to get it back now so that *I* can start pondering it.

Bob

---

* [Eds.—Hurricane Helene (1958).]   † [Eds.—Romane "Bo" L. Clark.]

B7. Binkley to Sellars, 22 January 1959

Dear Wilfrid,

I received your letter and the revised version of the ought paper at about the same time, and so your hope that I would already have discovered the misprints was frustrated. I read the paper yesterday (and didn't notice any further misprints that made any difference) and my first reactions are as follows.

The main overall impression is that the various complaints I've made (in my thesis, etc.) no longer apply. Thus, the 'noddable nodder' has gone, progress has been made in the elaboration of the logic of shall (withdrawing, countermanding, permission, etc.) and the "we" business seems to get round my objections to the derivation of principles from the love of mankind. I haven't yet fully grasped what's going on in the latter part of section XIII* (rule of inference vs. axiom scheme) but I think it fits in with and clarifies the remarks and puzzles in my letter to you this fall [viz. B5].

In section XVII, I think you state clearly the problem and solution that I was trying unsuccessfully to state clearly last summer. Where you bring 'Us' into the picture, I was talking vaguely about needing an additional principle or something that would express one's decision to adopt the moral point of view, or join the human race or society, etc. I still think there is a comparison to be made here with the principle of induction, but I don't see it very clearly yet.

An area of the logic of 'shall', ought, etc. about which I am especially puzzled at the moment is the problem of 'ought implies can' and/or the reasoning (if it is reasoning) through which one gives up an intention on discovering the impossibility of fulfilling it. There is surely something irrational about trying to do something that one knows is impossible, and one would expect the irrationality to be traceable to a violation of the logic of practical reasoning, but it is hard to see how this is to be done, especially in view of your discussion of 'may' and withdrawing. Perhaps it depends on the logic of the prudential 'ought' which might also include a 'we', that is, 'we sensible fellows', though this doesn't look too promising.

I was planning to write you anyhow when I got your letter and paper. I have been reading a paper by Reginald Jackson, "Practical Reason", in *Philosophy*, 17 (1942) pp. 351-367. It strikes me as being some sort of a minor classic, and I wonder that I have never seen it discussed anywhere. I wanted to ask what you thought about it.

- - - - - -

Dashes indicate interruption during which I went off to Chapel Hill to hear Austin on performatives. I'd heard it all before in Oxford, but it was still a good talk. He didn't say anything not in keeping with what I said he would say in the report I gave on his lectures last year. Tonight he speaks to us on "What I mean to do".

---

* [Eds.—In this paragraph and the next, Binkley is referring to IIO, not IIOR. Section XIII is pp. 255-8 (§§48-53) of the *Methodos* version; Section XVII is pp. 265-6 (§§66-69).]

We had Norman Malcolm down last week to read two papers. First, there was a strange one on the ontological argument, in which he seemed to say that the argument was essentially sound, that is, (I interpret) within the frame of religious discourse, 'god exists' is a necessary truth. I raised the question of how one was to sensibly reject this framework, and the issues at once became hopelessly confused. He seemed to want to say both that of course you couldn't 'prove religion' with this argument and also that a person who didn't accept religion couldn't really understand what religion was. Tried to draw analogy with practical implications involved in using moral language. His other paper, on dreams, took the line that all there is to dreams is the fact that people sometimes wake up under the impression that certain things had happened when they really hadn't. To say of a sleeping man that he is dreaming amounts to predicting his dream-telling. The argument seemed to be essentially that it makes no sense to talk of mental processes going on during sleep because such mental processes would be necessarily inexpressible—If you can express thoughts, you are awake to some extent. Argument similar to Wittgenstein's 'no private language' argument. Confronted with cases of people correlating eye movements during sleep with dream content, he said that to say that the dream is actually going on at the time of the eye movements would be to distort the concept of dreaming. I suggested that our actual concept of dreaming was essentially this 'distorted' one, and he replied maybe so—we are awfully vague in ordinary talk—but *his* account indicates what a really *clear* dream concept would be. This move I hadn't expected.

Otherwise, it goes fairly well with me here. I give a graduate course for the first time next semester—seminar in contemporary ethical theories. Also I do my Philosophy of Religion, and freshman ethics. I did an advanced undergraduate course in epistemology last semester, using Reichenbach and Ayer ("Problem of Knowledge").

Best regards,
Bob

22
The Castañeda–Sellars Correspondence, 1956–1967

C1. Castañeda to Sellars, 29 October 1956

Dear Wilfrid,

Thank you very much for the additional copies of your paper "Imperatives, Intentions, and the Logic of 'Ought'." I have made them available to the other members of the Department, and one is to be left in the seminar room for the graduate students.

I thank you very much for your kind mention in footnote 6 [p. 230/§7]*. I really think that it is exceedingly generous. I am glad to see that you have gone into a much greater detail to expound what I insist on calling "Sellars's pragmatic theses about normative languages." I agree with the substance of your views in that part of your essay. For that reason I want to refer to your discussion of imperatives.

1. I certainly agree with you in distinguishing between commands and imperatives in general. But I notice that you want to make of imperatives *simpliciter* the linguistic units which are employed in *telling to*; whereas I prefer to distinguish several varieties of prescriptive discourse (among which I include commanding, advising, recommending, entreating, requesting) and say that imperatives are the incomplete sentences common to all varieties.

2. What you call *command* seems to correspond to what I call *Justified command*, and in view of my semantical thesis and the presence of the Austin-operators in ordinary language, I agree with you that "the claim which commands have on our obedience is but a special case of the claim which our obligations [i.e., norms] have upon us." (p. 7 [p. 234/§14])

3. Now, I think that you have failed to establish that there are no arguments like

---

* [Eds.—We are unable to locate in the archives a typescript of IIO that matches the pagination referred to by Castañeda throughout this letter. When Castañeda refers to a particular page number, we will refer in brackets to the page number (in the *Methodos* edition) and the paragraph number (in the Sicha edition) to which he is referring.]

I promise to call you, if it rains
It is raining
So I promise to call you.

Your reason is that "it is obvious logical nonsense to suppose that a *performance of promising* can be the conclusion of an inference." (p. 7, my italics [p. 234/§15].) This seems to be a non sequitur, even though your last assertion is true. (i) It seems to me that in that schema nobody wants to claim that a performance of promising is a conclusion or a premise; what is supposed to be the conclusion is the *promise* itself or the sentence which formulates the promise, and it is quite immaterial whether the promise is formulated by means of Austin-operators. (ii) It is the *uttering* of "I promise...", not this sentence,* which is a performance. (iii) I can conceive of circumstances in which a reasoning like the above may be used, e.g., because the speaker is very pedantic or enjoys teasing his listener; so that the above inference does not offer a greater difficulty than the inference from "Jones will call me" to "Either Jones will call me or Jones will call you."

4. For that reason I also think that you have not established that there are no command or imperative or *resolutive*† inferences. Indeed, your grounds for such denial remain the same: "'Do *A*!' and 'I will do *A*,' then, while they are not obligation creating performances, are *practical* performances. And in this respect their logic resembles that of promises and commands." (p. 9 [p. 237/§19]) Once more I think that "Do *A*!' and "I will do *A*" are not performances, but sentences which when uttered express an imperative of some kind and a decision. In general, the fact that an imperative has or has not an Austin operator cannot be a ground to infer that it cannot be a premise or conclusion.

5. It seems to me that you do not establish that

(A) Take all the boxes to the station
     This is one of the boxes
     So take this to the station

is not a legitimate inference. It seems to me that your acknowledgment that "a person who candidly said to Jones

Take all the boxes to the station! By the way, this is one of the boxes in question

---

  * [Eds.—Sellars's MS annotation: "isn't the sentence an utterance (token)[?]"]
  † [Eds.—This word is underlined by hand in the letter (instead of by typewriter, as are the other words we have italicized).]

and yet, though insisting that he had not changed his mind, refused to tell Jones to take *this* box to the station, would have convincingly shown that he did not understand one or the other of these sentences" weakens your assertion.* For one thing, you seem to acknowledge that (A) can be used in some situation to preface the imperative "so, take *this*, too." For instance, if there is in the room or storehouse a box which is the only one with a different wrapping or of an obviously different size or kind in general, and the person who is taking the boxes to the station has left it behind or aside, we may issue a reasoned order by uttering (A).

I have gone into the detail of some situation in which (A) could be employed to issue a reasoned command, for this is what you after all deny, even though you prefer to speak of "a reasoned decision," phrase which I prefer to use in connection with first-person sentences. It seems to me that you are denying that (A) is not so used *in ordinary language*; if your meaning is different I have utterly failed to understand you. If I understand you rightly, then by constructing a case in which (A) can be used to make a reasoned "decision" in your sense, I have a counter-example which falsifies your assertion.

6. Your discussion of "the proper form of a reasoned decision which might, as addressed to Jones, be the *telling* him *to* take *this* box to the station" (p. 11 [p. 241/§24]) is extremely difficult; I do not understand it. You offer two formulations, and your idea seems to be to present the inference which one may mistakenly think (A) to be. But one may insist that (A) is what it purports to be, and it is that better than any substitute. Moreover, your substitutes contain, besides descriptive sentences, the sentences "Jones shall take all the boxes to the station" and "Jones shall take this to the station"; but these sentences—you said on p. 9 [p. 236/§18]—"merely express the speaker's intention that someone...do A". So your substitutes cannot really replace (A), i.e., they cannot really be the proper form of a reasoned decision in which *telling to* rather than merely expressing one's intention is involved.

7. In fact, if there is to be a reasoned *telling to*† someone to do A, then it is just not true that "it is a mistake to suppose that telling someone to do something can be, as telling, the conclusion of an inference." (p. 10 [p. 239/§21]) I really do not see why the language for telling-to should be one incapable of allowing for inferences.

8. Your distinction between "the indicative mood as the vehicle for *telling that*, and the indicative mood as the sheer expression of thoughts and reasonings" (p. 12 [p. 242/§26]) is not very clear to me. One obvious way of interpreting it reminds me of what I called argument II against imperative logic in "A Note on

---

* [Eds.—In the margin, Sellars has written, "? where," although it is not clear whether this query is appended to the sentence preceding or following this note.]

† [Eds.—Sellars's MS annotation: "there isn't."]

Imperative Logic," *Philosophical Studies*, 1955. And thus the dispute concerning imperative inferences is verbal, for it amounts to restricting or not the use of 'inference' in connection with truth-values. The only thing that I could say would be: let us compare accounts of imperative and normative discourse in which imperative inference is accepted with accounts of the same degree of completeness in which imperative inference is denied, not to choose which is better, but to gain more insight into imperative and normative discourse through two different reconstructions.

Of course, we may accept the difference provided it is restricted to *descriptive* thoughts and reasonings, so that we may proceed to make a parallel distinction between two roles of the other moods. That is to say, we could complete your assertion by saying that the logic of *telling that* is parallel to the logic of *telling to*, not the latter to general indicative logic, but general imperative logic is indeed parallel to general indicative logic.

I take the liberty of referring to my own work, for which I apologize. With regard to point 8 above I should say that my system N* is one in which there is no room for imperative inference; but my new system M*, informally outlined in the chapter you have received does accept imperative and resolutive inferences.

Your discussion of commands has increased my interest in having your comments on my old semantical thesis about normatives, whose later formulation is found on pp. 25-27 of the chapter above mentioned. I also hope you will find that my discussion of the pragmatics of prescriptive discourse is not too unworthy of being prefaced by the phrase "Sellars's pragmatic thesis."

I leave my comments on the second part of your paper for another occasion. So, I want to finish with my request for you to greet everybody there on my name. My colleagues here* have all asked me to send their best regards.

As ever,
Hector-Neri Castañeda

---

* [Eds.—Department of Philosophy, Duke University, Durham, North Carolina.]

S2. Sellars to Castañeda, 7 December 1956

Dear Hector,

Many thanks for your letter, which I have not answered because it has given me so much food for thought.

I shall not take up everything you advance because I have rewritten sections VII and VIII to remove possible sources of misunderstanding and am enclosing a copy of the new material. Please return it when you have had a chance to look at it, as it is my only copy.

I grant, of course, that it's not a sentence or the uttering of a sentence which is the performance. My trouble, and I may just be being obtuse, is that I see no other use for the *utterance* "I promise to do *A*" than that of making the promise. On the other hand, I do recognize that "I promis*ed* to do *A*" fits into the context (*of utterances*)........*so*, I promised to do *A*. But I try to spell this out in the enclosed.

Again, I do not deny—indeed insist—that there is *resolutive* "inference". What I have denied and continue to deny is that there is *imperative* inference. (I put the word "inference" after "resolutive" in quotes only to emphasize that of course there is resolutive *reasoning*, but that we tend to limit the word "inference" to reasonings concerning what is the case.) *Let me repeat.* There are such reasonings—real, genuine Kosher reasonings as

 I shall go down town
 Going down town implies taking the bus
 So I shall take the bus

I thought you might be interested in some correspondence I have been having with Chisholm of Brown on intentionality. I had a limited number of copies made for local discussion. Don't give it too wide a distribution, but I would like some reactions.

I hope this finds you and your family well. Give my best to the Duke and N. C. department.

P.S. I read your chapter IV with great interest: I admire the clarity with which you have succeeded in formulating your present views, with which I am, with exceptions elsewhere noted, in substantial agreement.

Cordially,
Wilfrid

C3. Castañeda to Sellars, 15 December 1956

Dear Wilfrid,

Thank you for your last letter and the enclosed papers. I have read your corrections to your paper with great interest. Once more, thank you, very very much for your kind mention in the appendix.

I am delighted with the second half of your paper. Your discussion of normatives in terms of optatives is very, very illuminating. Your discussion of benevolence and universality are very satisfactory to my taste, even though I still want to include universality only in moral 'ought's, not in others. But this, of course, does not appear in your paper.

On the other hand, I remain unconvinced by your arguments that there are no imperative inferences at all, and that there are no "decision" inferences except in a distorted sense. (I did not use the word 'resolutive' because in the way I use it there are only first-person resolutives, so that our meanings are different.)

It seems to me that in your paper the arguments against imperative inferences are three: (1) the performative character of the phrases 'I order...', 'I command...', 'I am telling you to...', etc.; (2) the fact that you conceive of *tellings to* as built up on *expressions of intention*; (3) your claim that there is "a distinction between the indicative mood as the vehicle for *telling that*, and the indicative mood as the sheer expression of thoughts and reasonings." (p. 12 [p. 242/§26]).

1. In my previous letter I referred to (1). You reply: "I see no other use for the *utterance* 'I promise to do A' than that of making the promise." (Your last letter) But is it incompatible for an utterance to constitute the making of a promise and at the same time to function as an assertion and be a premise or conclusion in an inference? I would say that at least this incompatibility is not obvious. Since in your paper you mention Austin, I would add that he has pointed out quite successfully the difference between 'I promise' and 'I promised', on the one hand, and between 'I promise' and 'you promise' on the other; but this difference lies in a feature possessed by 'I promise' which is lacked by the other expressions, not in a feature which 'I promise' lacks and is possessed by the others.

Now, it seems to me that a more complicated analysis of 'I promise to do A' is needed, for other reasons. One which since 1953 was agreeable to me is briefly as follows: (i) 'I promise...' is an assertion in the meta-language of prescriptive discourse which talks about the "acceptance" by the speaker of a set or system of normative sentences, namely, that which formulates the content of the promise and those which are entailed by it, e.g., "I ought to do A," "If it is the case that if I can do A I ought to do B, then I ought to B." (ii) Because of (i) we can infer by means of a general normative logic in the normative system thus accepted; so that we can assert "X (the promiser) ought to do A," and any sentence entailed by this.

The performative character of 'I promise...' is analyzed by (i) and (iii) the utterance of 'I promise...' *is* the acceptance of that normative system.

On this view, 'I promise...' differs from 'I promised...' and 'You promise...', etc. in that 'I promise...' alone has (iii), whereas all involve (i) and (ii).

Furthermore, in the last weeks I have tentatively thought that it may be convenient to distinguish between (a) an *active* and (b) a *dormant* performative role of an utterance. If this can be accepted, there are uses of 'I promise...', 'I command...', 'I order...', 'I advise...', 'I suggest...', 'I entreat...', etc. in which they are performative in the sense that they are prefixed to clausal sentences to make them instances of promises, commands, orders, pieces of advice, suggestions, entreaties, etc., but they are not fully performative in the sense that these promises, commands, etc. are "asserted" or "affirmed". If this is granted, we may say that the Austin-operators (the above expressions) are employed, e.g., to use imperatives in the antecedents of conditionals, as when we say "If I order you to do A, then do A," which is analytic, or "If I ask you to do A, call Peter."

If the preceding view is accepted, then the obvious restriction of imperatives to consequents does not constitute a *logical* lack of parallelism to ordinary indicatives, but only a purely grammatical one.

2. I agree with you that Hare's definition of entailment (*LoM*, p. 25) is *not* a satisfactory analysis of entailment, so that the fact that failure to understand one of two sentences once assent is given to first but not to the second, does not establish that the first sentence entails the second, in the ordinary sense of entailment. But I think that you exaggerate when you say about

(A) Take all the boxes to the station!
     This is one of the boxes
     So take this to the station!

that "to form this sequence of expressions is simply to misuse ordinary language. There is no such reasoning." (p. 7 of your Corrections [p. 240/§23].) I can very well conceive of many situations in which that sequence of sentences can be used. Would the use of (A) in any circumstance whatever be the utterance of nonsense? Indeed, I find that often when I can use (B) below I can employ (A) instead:

(B) I told you to take all the boxes to the station!
     This is one of the boxes.
     So I told you to take this!

Indeed, the more I consider (B) the more I am persuaded that the expression 'I told...' is in (B) a performative prefix, if we take the exclamation signs seriously. In fact, the use of (A) may very often carry the implication of a scolding in addition to a reiteration of the order or command; i.e., (A) suggests that the universal order was given before and was not fully obeyed, a suggestion which is more explicit in (B), and we may even say that (B) makes it explicit while retaining the reiteration of the order to take *all* boxes to the station.

(B) seems to me a typical case in which a performative role is combined with other functions, as indicated in 1 above.

3. I think that I have been unable to understand your argument based on the distinction between *telling* and *expressing intention*. Page 2 of your Corrections makes it very clear that every case of telling is a case of expressing one's intention. This seems to me very good. But then I would have thought that at least there are imperative inferences in so far as there are "resolutive" inferences (in your sense of resolutive). Moreover, if every case of *telling*, i.e., every use of a *telling* imperative, is also a case of expressing one's intentions, the argument whether imperatives are not premises or conclusions, but that only the expressions of intentions contained in them are such (in some sense) seems to me to be purely academic. This sort of distinction can be useful, of course, in a different context. If you are concerned with cataloguing or systematizing the formal rules of inference which govern both imperative and "resolutive" reasonings, then that distinction may be construed as the suggestion that we only need a basic set of rules which govern "resolutive" inference and the rules which relate to the *telling* or imperative operator we apply to "resolutives" to obtain the latter. But obviously your purpose is quite different.

I confess that I am completely blind to the point or aim of your argument. I find that in practical life we do use the inferential words 'so', 'for', 'since', 'therefore', 'because', to connect an imperative with another sentence (imperative or indicative). "Bring the chair, *for* we needed it here"; "open the window, *because* he needs some fresh air"; "He is very sick, *so* call a doctor."*

You do not want to deny the above fact about imperatives. Do you not feel that a simple analysis is to say that those words are also used inferentially in those cases? I fail to detect a difference in category between the meaning of 'for', 'since', 'because', etc. as employed in those cases and the meaning these words have in the cases in which they are used to connect indicatives only— "He is sick, for his X-ray shows it"; "he is sick, because he ate poisonous mushrooms."

I really do not see why there could not be reasoned *tellings*, orders, recommendations, entreaties, petitions, requests, etc. Just the opposite, I remember that in many of my requests, applications, petitions, entreaties, I have offered reasons for them. And on a few occasions when I have been in a position to order I have also given reasons. On reflection, I feel that if reasons can be offered to express decisions that I or somebody else do something, orders, commands,

---

* [Eds.—At the end of this paragraph (and directly above the word "imperatives" in the next sentence) Sellars has written the word "enthymemes."]

recommendations, etc. require backing reasons more than mere expressions of *my* intentions. The latter do not involve in the same strong way a *moving* the person to do the action in question, whereas the former by aiming at influencing the listener's behavior are the stronger if they have a fund of reasons to which resort if challenged. This seems to be of the very essence of the rationality of prescriptive discourse in general, as I have learned from you.

4. Your third argument is to a very large extent* irrefutable. In your letter it is adumbrated in your saying that "we tend to limit the word 'inference' to reasonings concerning what is the case." It is true that the meaning of the word 'inference' has been made very precise in the field of indicative sentences, particularly those which assert what is the case. An inference is valid, we say, quite rigorously, if the conclusion cannot be *false* once the premises are regarded as *true*. So, we may have come to use the word 'inference' exclusively in connection with truth-values (*Cf.* what I called argument II in my note in *Phil Studies*). And if you decide to use the word in this restricted sense you are right—there are no imperative inferences, and there are no resolutive inferences (in your sense of 'resolutive').

But, can you say that there are normative inferences if you want to limit the use of 'inference' to what *is* the case? Of course you want to insist on a normative being an indicative sentence, but if you have excluded 'shall'-sentences from the class which can genuinely be items in inferences, how is it that 'ought'-sentences embody an additional inferential role for 'shall'-sentences? (P. 23 of your paper [p. 257/§51]). Perhaps you only wanted to say that there are "inferences" of normative sentences, i.e., 'ought'-sentences.

On the contrary, *I* want to say that there is imperative and resolutive inference if and only if there is a fruitful generalization of the notion of truth-values so that we could speak of similar imperative values. I mean this in a general sense so as to allow the possibility of three or more values for imperatives. (Well, you know my chapter 4.)

5. Your analysis of (apparently) inferential uses of "resolutives" seems to be a consistent alternative. (It is the sort of thing I was committed to in the case of imperative inferences when I wrote my M.A. thesis and "A Note on Imperative Logic.") I do not understand why you cannot apply to imperatives generally and preserve the use of 'inference' for indicatives and accept the obvious inferential character of the examples given in section 3 above. Indeed, since, e.g., in "Since he is very sick, call a doctor quickly" the (apparent) premise is an indicative your case can be made more easily.

---

* [Eds.—This passage has a single line drawn through it in the original letter. It is not clear whether this was drawn by Sellars or by Castañeda; Castañeda generally marked out typos and even longer deletions by covering them with typewritten 'x's.]

Yet, I think that your analysis is too complicated to be preferred to other alternatives (if available). To avoid additional disagreement I will consider only your resolutive reasonings—(not inferences). But of course I believe that what follows applies to imperatives point by point.

On p. 24 [p. 258/§53] you mention the case of a person who says: "If p, I shall do A," and later on (we may assume that very shortly after so that this assertion can get together with the following so as to be possible for them to constitute a reasoning or inference) the same person asserts that *p*, and finally he says "so, I shall do A." I understand that you do not deny that the following sequence of sentences *can* be meaningfully employed in some occasions:

(C) I shall do A, if p.
     p.
     ―――――――――
     So, I shall do A.

Why should it not be a legitimate inference? This would seem to be an obvious course, and the reasoning could be accounted for as a valid inference by a simple appeal to *modus ponens*. You deny this and propose the following de-composition of (C):

(D) p
     ―――――――――――――――――――――――
     So my doing A if p *implies* my doing A
     I shall do A if p
     ―――――――――――――――――――――――
     So I shall do A.

I am not sure what is the gain. I gather that your 'implies' is not just a conditional, but an inferential connection. I do not understand the difference between 'so' and 'implies' in (D). One naively tends to think that in (D) "I shall do A" is functioning as an ordinary conclusion, or otherwise the sense of the second 'So' is difficult to appreciate. One also feels tempted to ask: Is not the difference between (C) and (D) that an indicative conditional or an indicative inference is interposed between the two premises of (C)? But in any case "I shall do A in P" seems to continue to be a premise and "I shall do A" seems to continue to be a conclusion. Should we say then that a resolutive inference is valid if, in the case of *modus ponens*, we add an inferential premise or step like "So my doing A if p *implies* my doing A"? To be sure one can complicate the rules of inference for any kind of sentences; but if this complication is to be applied systematically it will be a wholly unnecessary complication.

I gather that what you want to say is that (C) could be taken as a valid inference because it can be validated by analyzing it as in (D), and that as (D) would show the essential step is one which concerns indicatives alone. This is the interpretation I assumed in the preceding paragraph. Now something like this may be said to be true—namely, that (C) is validated by a principle of inference which applies to the most basic logic: *modus ponens*. We speak of the "most basic logic" in the sense that any type of logic (ie., the logic of any type of discourse) will include the ordinary propositional and functional logic. And this logic is the logic which, when taken exclusively, defines or is general indicative logic. This seems to me to be the truth contained in your discussion of 'shall'-sentences. But this of course does not prove that (D) is correct whereas (C) isn't; on the contrary, it proves only that (D) is correct because (D) is just a redundant complication of (C).

(Jørgensen suggested that there was no proper imperative inference, that all inferences are indicative, so when we have something which looks like an imperative inference what we have to do is to replace the imperative pseudo-premises by indicatives, apply ordinary logic, and at the end put imperative conclusions instead of indicatives. My objection to procedures of this kind is that the first and the last replacements must be justified by proper rules with adequate restrictions, so that we have after all imperative inference. Once this is recognized, the systematization of the rules of inference may be carried along different lines, including this one in which imperatives (or resolutives) appear on both ends only.)

6. If the above arguments are correct or it is true that 'shall'-sentences are legitimate conclusions or inferences (regardless of whether this is true of imperatives or not), one of your theses concerning 'ought'-sentences is incorrect—namely, that "'p *ought* to do A' is ... to be construed as 'p shall do A' as embodying this *additional* role. In other words, 'ought'-statements are to be understood as the expression of reasoned intentions" (p. 23 [p. 257/§51]).

Now this thesis seems to be somewhat wrong in another respect. It seems to me that 'ought'-statements do not have to involve a reference (implicit or explicit) to *reasonings*. (My view has been that an 'ought'-statement says in the object language the same as "The imperative (-resolutive) "...." is Justified or *reasonable*.")

So, I think that this view should be emended in any case. And when you eliminate the reference to reasonings there will be no reason to oppose inferential reasonings of either imperatives or resolutives.

C4. Castañeda to Sellars, 4 October 1959

Dear Wilfrid:

I have not heard from you for quite a long time now. I hope that absence of news means happy completion of all changes that were due and full devotion to your research. My very best regards to your wife. Please extend my greetings to Alan.

The Spanish volume should be ready sometime in January or February. You had said nothing about the paper; I would be unhappy if no paper of yours appears in it. You must have something in ethics which we can use.

The English volume with George should be going to the Press toward the end of this month; at the latest in early December.*

Now, I have read the whole of your paper for the latter volume, and I do find that many changes have made your argument clearer.† There are many new points. Somehow, however, you make use of rather technical devices which make the reading of the paper a bit hard. But this is a matter of style which anybody seriously interested in moral philosophy must overcome. The topic on which I find your position unaltered is, of course, one of the things that have divided us for some time: imperative inference. You use strong language "it doesn't make sense to speak of imperative inference (telling to inference)" (p. 15 [p. 173/§26]). Yet your arguments are not convincing. You do not offer a single argument presented in one piece, with all its premises clearly formulated.

As far as I can see the only argument you have runs something like this:

Imperatives are used performatively, and their performative character is signaled by the imperative mood. The imperative mood can be eliminated in favor of performative prefixes like 'I command', 'I order', 'I am telling you to', etc. Imperatives are used to realize a performance of telling-to. (Imperatives in the imperative mood or in the indicative with a performative prefix are like statements of the form 'I promise....', which is Austin's paradigm of performative sentence. "It is logical nonsense to suppose that one performance of promising can, as performance, be a conclusion from another." (p. 8, top [p. 165–6/§15]). Likewise, imperatives cannot formulate conclusions, for they would be formulating a performance as a conclusion from another performance.‡

---

* [Eds.—*Morality and the Language of Conduct*, edited by Hector-Neri Castañeda and George Nakhnikian. Detroit: Wayne State University Press, 1963.]

† [Eds.—Castañeda is providing critical commentary on a typescript version of IIOR. The version of the typescript he seems to be commenting on can be found among the Wilfrid S. Sellars Papers at the University of Pittsburgh; all the page references Castañeda makes match up. The relevant typescript is document 31735062219336, Box 31, Folders 3–6, Wilfrid S. Sellars Papers, 1899–1990, ASP.1991.01, Archives of Scientific Philosophy, Archives & Special Collections, University of Pittsburgh Library System. When Castañeda refers to a particular page number, we will refer in brackets to the page number (in the original print edition edition) and the paragraph number (in the Sicha edition) to which he is referring.]

‡ [Eds.—In the original, there is no closing parenthesis to complement the opening parenthesis appearing before "Imperatives."]

This argument assumes that if a sentence is used to make a practical performance it cannot be* a conclusion or a premise. This, however, you never argue for, but merely assume. Yet this premise is far from obvious. It begs the question. For one thing, it is not clear what 'performative' or 'Performatory' means. To utter "It is raining" is also to perform—an act of telling-that; in normal contexts it presupposes the conventions of ordinary communication and creates for me a presumptive commitment to back it up if challenged as well as the *prima facie* obligation to abide by its implications (Your characterization, p. 7 [pp. 164-5/§13-14]).† The notion of a performative utterance, as Austin introduced it, does not put the emphasis on the creation of presumptive obligations. It is of importance to note that the whole notion of *performative utterances* between pure and impure performatives, but has indeed been discussing a large classification of linguistic acts, in which the notion of performative has almost disappeared.

Performative or not, it makes good sense to say that "I promise to do both A and B" entails "I promise to do A", so that the reasoning "I promise to do both A and B, *so* I promise to do A" is valid.‡ It may be true that actual conditions for use are such that we never are in the position to offer the argument (in your distinction between 'reasoning' and 'argument').

Likewise, performative or not, it makes good sense to say that "This is a box and take all the boxes to the station" entails "Take this, too". Indeed, it seems that the circumstances for making the argument:

(1) "Take all the boxes to the station;
     This is a box,
     so, take this to the station, too"§

are quite easy to imagine. If the person is one who is looking for an opportunity to do less than he is ordered to, that chain of sentences is quite appropriate. You say on page 15 [p. 173/§26]: "We have been arguing that the *telling to* signal, '!',

---

* [Eds.—Sellars has inserted here by hand "as performance".]

† [Eds.—In the margin next to this sentence and the next, Sellars has written, "see p. 9." This seems to be a reference to IIOR [pp. 166-7/§ 16]. In the opposite margin, by the sentence beginning "The notion of a performative utterance...", Sellars has written, "ok".]

‡ [Eds.—In the margin next to this sentence, Sellars has drawn a question mark. At the top of the page, he has written:

I promised to do A • B
So I promised to do A.

Compare Sellars's discussion in CPCI, where he argues that while there are no valid arguments involving expressions of promises, there are valid arguments involving reports or ascriptions of promises—something we discuss in the CPCI chapter summary in the introduction to this volume.]

§ [Eds.—In the margin, Sellars has written, "There might be a *use* for this, but we are *reconstructing*".]

like "I promise", does not belong within the context —, *so*...". Well, (1) is a counter-example. If the conclusion of your argument is false, then either your argument is invalid or at least one of your premises is false. The false premise is "A performative utterance cannot be the utterance of a premise or a conclusion".*

In your discussion of (1) preceding page 15 [p. 173/§26], where, according to the phrase just quoted we should find part of your argument for that quotation, you say nothing that really counts. On page 13 [pp. 172-3/§25] you accept that it would be a sign of misunderstanding to utter the two sentences preceding the 'so' of (1) and refuse to utter the sentence following that 'so'. On page 14† you just restate your contention twice. First you say but we have no argument "Do A, if p; p; *so*, do A". Then you explain why statements of intention can appear in arguments, but the whole thing is just a repetition of the claim. If (1) is a performance of the arguing kind, here you have a case where the major premise and conclusion are performances of the telling-to kind.‡ It is only because you have begged the question by defining arguments in terms of telling-that that you can say that (1) is not a performance of the arguing kind.

Now, on page 15 [p. 173/§27], you explain the logic of the reasoning (1). Your analysis is tremendously complex, and many questions come to my mind: (i) it seems doubtful that the logic of (1) requires the logic of modality or entails, or the use of a metalanguage, if 'implies' is a metalinguistic term; (ii) you need not speak of a dependent-implication; your analysis loses nothing if you replace this by material implication; (iii) in ordinary language (1) does not seem more complex than "Peter will take all the boxes to the station; this is a box, *so*, he will take this, too".

In any case, you do not deny that (1) is a legitimate argument; just the opposite, you go on to explain the several steps which are telescoped in it.§ Yet your whole argument has been intended to prove that there are no imperative arguments or reasonings. Indeed, on page 12 [pp. 165-6/§15], you explicitly say that even though there are arguments involving statements of intention, there are no arguments involving statements of intention which *also* discharge a telling-to-function. Thus, one would expect you to say that (1) is not an argument or reasoning *at all*.

---

* [Eds.—In the margin, Sellars has written, "in one sense yes in another no."]

† [Eds.—The materials from p. 14 of the typescript do not make it into the published version of IIOR, although in §15 of IIOR Sellars does touch on some of the same issues (e.g., that there are no valid arguments involving expressions of promises).]

‡ [Eds.—In the margin, Sellars has written, "1. An argument is a performance which doesn't contain performances."]

§ [Eds.—Next to this sentence, Sellars has written in the left margin "do I", and in the right margin:
   I deny it
   see top of previous page

The reference seems to be to the previous page of the typescript (i.e., page 14, the contents of which did not make it into the published version of IIOR), not to the previous page of the letter.]

However, you could have said that though (1) is not a reasoning at all, it somehow monkeys a reasoning, namely,*

(2) "You shall take all the boxes to the station
This is a box;
so, you shall take this to the station, too."

And then offer your analysis of (2). However, it is a perplexing feature of your view that even though imperatives cannot be part of the context '—, *so* ...', they monkey such contexts, and ordinary imperative language does involve the possibility of such monkeying in a great scale.

Your formal rules can be easily made to cover cases like (1); all you need is a provision for the manipulation of '!'. But your performative assumption prevents you from doing that consistently. Given that assumption the only course open to you is the one you have taken on page 12 [pp. 165-6/§15].

These remarks cover pp. 7-19 [pp. 165-178/§§14-32]. To emphasize, your basic assumption is false as a matter of ordinary use. There is no misuse of language in the following situation. A boss orders his secretary at 10: "If Mr. X comes, turn that switch". At 10:02, the inter-com rings and he says to his secretary: "Mr. X is just coming, *so* turn that switch". In this case as in (1) above it is correct to say that a *reasoned* order has been issued.† It is a purely verbal matter whether one calls the issuing of reasoned commands, orders, requests, *reasonings* (inferences, etc.) or not. But it is false to deny that imperatives do not belong to the context '——, *so* (hence, therefore) ...' or to deny that they stand in entailment-relationships. (Well, that's what it seems to me.)

I would like to hear your countercomments. I am enclosing a short thing on which I am anxious to receive your criticisms.

With my gratitude and
affection unchanged,
Hector

---

* [Eds.—In the margin, Sellars has written, "does (1) exist?"]
† [Eds.—Sellars has drawn a line next to the previous three sentences and written in the margin: analyse—
   p, so do A!
   ———
   yes
   but
   ———
   do A if p!
   p
   ———
   So do A!   no.]

C5. Castañeda to Sellars, 1 June 1967

Dear Wilfrid,

Your "Form and Content in Ethical Theory" is very impressive.* I have read it twice and it seemed even better on the second reading. You are right: this paper does bring us much closer than ever before.

I have only a few remarks which express my lack of understanding rather than my criticism.

1. I am delighted at your posing the problem with the distinction between the act of intending and the intended content. This immediately leads to the distinction between a property of the act and the semantical values of the content. And once we allow for the intended contents to have entailment relationships we are immediately led to distinguish between the semantical values of the content and the validity or invalidity of the purported inferences involving those contents. Thus, we have three distinctions: (A) the reasonableness and unreasonableness of the intendings, to use your terminology on page 4 [FCET §12/OIM §87]; (B) the semantical values of intentions, let us call them Justifiedness and Non-justifiedness, as I did in *Morality and the Language of Conduct*, "Imperative Reasonings," *et. al.*; (C) the validity and invalidity of reasonings (or arguments) involving intentions, since at bottom (as is indicated in "Imperative Reasonings") it is really a verbal issue whether one uses the words 'logic of imperatives (or intentions)', 'valid' or 'implication', etc. for what seems to be "valid imperative (or resolutive) entailments."

But I am somewhat confused by the several applications of the term 'reasonableness' that you make in your paper. I am sure that you can straighten me out of my confusion. (i) On page 4 [FCET §§11-12/OIM §§18 and 87] you seem to me to use the term as above, to refer to a property (shall we call it "pragmatical?") of cognitive acts, whether purely cognitive as believing or practico-cognitive as intending. (ii) On page 6 [FCET §19/OIM §91] you speak of relative reasonableness, and this seems to be an altogether different animal, namely, being an intention implied by another intention. (iii) On page 6, footnote 5[†], reasonableness seems to be a property of actions or acts. (iv) On page 7 [FCET §20/OIM §92] you claim that truth is a special case of reasonableness, thus making reasonableness a semantical value. In other words, it *seems* that you use the word to refer to either something which belongs in (A) or (B) or (C).

---

* [Eds.—The Philosophy Department at the University of Kansas published FCET as a stand-alone volume in 1967. It was reprinted in a collection of the Lindley Lectures, *Freedom and Morality*, Humanistic Studies, 46, edited by John Bricke (Lawrence: University of Kansas Press, 1976), 71-91. Most of FCET was reproduced in OIM.]

† [Eds.—Castañeda may mean to refer to footnote 6. Footnotes 5 and 6 from FCET are, respectively, notes 14 and 15 (§90) of OIM.]

2. That reasonableness in the sense of (A) is wholly different from reasonableness in the sense of (B) is clear. It may sometimes be reasonable to believe a falsehood, or to intend a Non-justified intention (or mandate). That reasonableness in the sense of (B) is different from reasonableness in the sense of (C) is also clear. A Non-justified (non-reasonable) intention may be implied by another intention (i.e., may be reasonable relative to the latter).

Thus, I am unable to apprehend the problem you are raising on page 12 [FCET §33/OIM §99] with your question

> But how can the content* of an intention be involved in its reasonableness, without turning the latter into a disguised form of the relative reasonableness asserted by a hypothetical imperative?

This question *seems* to imply that the analogies drawn between intention and proposition, truth and reasonableness, and reasonable relative to intention I and implied by proposition P_I (where the function relating I and P_I is still unspecified) are to be modified. But the direction of the modification is not clear; at least I cannot find it.

3. I am very much interested in the principle of the logic of intentions you formulate on page 4 [FCET §10/OIM §13]. I think that under some natural interpretations it is true. For instance, [it seems to me to be true,]† if your variables 'P' and 'Q' range over pure states of affairs, or propositions, i.e., propositions that have no intentions or imperatives (mandates) or deontic propositions as components. But this is really a general remark to the effect that I do not fully understand your principle because I do not know the rules of formation or transformation of your operator 'Shall'. A trivial example to illustrate. *If* your 'Shall' can be prefixed to molecular compounds of the form "P&Q," where 'Q' stands for, say, "Shall(R)," then an instance of your principle is

"Shall (P&Shall(R))" implies "Shall(P&R)",
if and only if "P&Shall(R)" implies "P&R".

Yet I am inclined to believe that if "Shall (P&Shall(R))" is well-formed it implies "Shall(P&R)"; but clearly "P&Shall(R)" does not, in general, imply "P&R."

In my old calculus M* ("The Logic of Obligation,"‡ "Outline...") as well as in the calculus D* ("Acts, the Logic of Obligation, and Deontic Calculi")§, it seems to

---

* [Eds.—In the published versions of FCET/OIM, this reads "specific subject matter," not "content." Sellars seems to have changed the wording in response to Castañeda's criticism. See S5, Ad 2, from this correspondence.]

† [Eds.—This qualification is added in Castañeda's manuscript on the bottom of the page.]

‡ [Eds.—Hector-Neri Castañeda, "The Logic of Obligation," in *Philosophical Studies* 10, no. 2 (1959): 17–23.]

§ [Eds.—Hector-Neri Castañeda, "Acts, the Logic of Obligation, and Deontic Calculi," in *Philosophical Studies*, vol. 19, no(s). 1/2 (Jan.–Feb., 1968): 13–26; originally published in *Critica* 1, no. 1 (1967): 77–99.]

me the hard core of your principle is represented by the principle that if in a sentence or formula expressing a propositional truth-table tautology, or a quantificational logical truth, a propositional variable or a predicate variable is replaced throughout with an imperative-resolutive variable or an imperative-resolutive predicate variable with the same arguments, the result is a sentence or formula expressing a logically valid (Justified) imperative-resolutive. Thus, you see I am very much in favor of your principle, so much indeed that I am anxious to see the formation rules that give it logical shape.

4. But my sympathy with your principle makes me unhappy with what you do on page 5 [FCET §10/OIM §14]. You now use the word 'implies' in a different sense from the one one naturally takes you to be using when you say "the *logic* of intentions is... parasitical..." [FCET §10] (my italics). One property of implication, logical or causal, not "material implication," is that the principle of exportation* does not hold in general. From "P and Q imply R" it does not follow "If P, then Q implies R" or "Since P, hence Q implies R." Yet, this *seems* to be what you are doing on page 5.

It seems to me that when my doing an action A in circumstances C brings about, or causes, my bringing about some situation E, it is not the case that "I, Castañeda, brought about E" implies, causally or logically, "I, Castañeda, did A." Hence, by your principle of the logic of intentions, it is not the case that "I, Castañeda, shall bring about E" implies "I, Castañeda, shall do A."

You next move to introduce the new technical expression 'implies (for S)' [FCET §15]. But if it is only another way of formulating, (as it seems to be), the implication from "I, S, shall—" to "I, S, shall...," we still have to account for what appears to be a violation of your fundamental principle of the logic of intentions.

In section 16 you immediately explain the role of the qualifier '(for S)' in a way that seems to involve an appeal to a false principle of exportation. This, again, raises a question about your fundamental principle of the logic of intentions, for the 'implies' relating P and Q is not governed by exportation.

5. On page 9 [FCET §25/OIM §51] you move from

(1) "x bring about E_k" implies "x does A_i if in C_j"

to

(2) "I shall bring about E_k" implies "I shall do A_i, if in C_j."

This, however, looks like a violation of your fundamental principle of the logic of intention. According to it, you should move from (1) to

---

* [Eds.—Exportation (Exp) is a replacement rule, according to which $((p \cdot q) \supset r) \equiv (p \supset (q \supset r))$.]

(3) "I shall bring about E_k" implies "I shall (I do A_i, if in C_j)."

Since obviously the pronoun 'I' occurs in the formula represented by 'C_j', such a formula and 'I do A_i' express or formulate propositions (states of affairs) about the speaker (or thinker). Clearly, one's intention whose content is the disjunction that one do A_i or one not be in circumstances C_j does not imply the conditional that if one is in C_j one is to do A_i.

This is a very interesting juncture. It seems to me that here what you need is a distinction, in the terminology of "Acts, the Logic of Obligation, and Deontic Calculi," between acts prescriptively considered and acts considered as circumstances, i.e., the difference between actional (imperative-resolutive) sentential variables and propositional sentential variables, which has been characteristic of my deontic calculi all along. Your 'Shall' operator will have to behave, and here you want it to behave, in the way my 'K' or 'Ought'-operator behaves in my calculi. Briefly, what you need here is the analogue for your 'Shall' of my axiom

$$O(p \supset \underline{q}) \supset (p \supset O(\underline{q})),$$

where the underlining indicates that the variable is imperative-resolutive.

This is interesting. Indeed, this analogy between your 'Shall' and my 'Ought' may be evidence that you have been right all along in suggesting that 'Ought' is analyzable in terms of resolutives or intentions. It is also interesting because it shows how close we have come. But there is an important difference and a further similarity. Your 'Shall' is an operator mapping propositions into intentions and what you need here is, therefore, a distinction logically prior to the introduction of this operator. My distinction between acts prescriptively considered and acts considered as circumstances (represented by the two kinds of sentential variables) *is*, in part, the distinction between propositions and intentions. But if I were to adopt your fundamental principle of the logic of intentions I would have to introduce a further distinction. And I don't know what it would be like. In "Imperative Reasonings" I appealed to a different principle in order to handle the case of hypothetical-imperative inferences.

6. The preceding discussion of your move from (1) to (3) above seems to suggest that, *perhaps*, your principle on page 11 [FCET §30/OIM §96] that intentions can only be derived from intentions is not without difficulties. Indeed, a general discussion of the logic of intentions may have to allow for implications of the form "P implies that if not-P, then Shall(Q)." These are, doubtless, not counterexamples to what you have in mind on page 11, but seem to point out for the case of intentions to difficulties in formulating the principle in question precisely, which difficulties are analogous to the well-known difficulties of putting Hume's or Poincare's principle in precise formulation.

7. What you say in section 13 [OIM §88] is absolutely to my liking. If you make the additional claim that there is no analysis of 'ought', and 'reasonableness' is the name of the semantical value of intentions analogous to truth, i.e., what I have called Justifiedness, then your claim in section 31 [OIM §97] is part of what I have referred to as the semantical thesis about ought. See "Outline...", *Morality and the Language of Conduct*, pp. 281f., etc. This seems to me a strong point of contact between our views.

8. Practical reasonings involving hypothetical "imperatives" are sometimes valid. Thus, there are semantical values of intentions analogous to truth which, if present in the intentions which are premises, are preserved in the intentions which are the corresponding conclusions. This has nothing to do with morality or moral reasoning. Thus, the semantical values of intentions have nothing to do with morality. If categorical reasonableness is involved with moral considerations it cannot be, in general, the counterpart of truth for *practical* inference. It is *at most* the counterpart of truth for moral reasoning.

If, as you claim on p. 9 [FCET §26/OIM §52],

(4) "I shall bring about E_k" implies "I shall do A_i if in C_{jW},"

where I have a 'W' for your diamond, then there is a semantical value analogous to truth, which if the premise has it the conclusion has it, too. This value has nothing to do with your relative reasonableness, which is merely an implicational, not a semantical-value, concept. Since these intentions have nothing to do with we-intentions, the semantical values relevant to the implication that (4) claims to exist are different from the semantical values involved in inferences containing we-intentions.

It seems to me that here again we are very close. As you have probably noted, in "Outline...," in *Morality and the Language of Conduct*, and, especially in "Imperative Reasonings," I claimed that there are many Justifiednesses of imperatives and resolutives. I tried to give a general analysis of "Justified-in-content-C," which has some similarity to your "reasonable relative to I (for S)." I then went on to characterize what I called the absolute context and Justifiedness-in-the-absolute-context. The general ideas of those analyses are correct, it seems to me, but the details of my earlier proposals need a good deal of improvement. The main ideas are somewhat akin to yours. Your idea of we-intentions is, it seems to me, very closely related to my idea of an absolute context common to several persons. I think your idea of a community of persons sharing intentions is, however, superior. But there is one point in which it *seems* to me I still differ from you. The validity of practical reasoning requires that there be semantical values analogous to truth, but these values need not be related to morality. A community of agents can share, in my terminology, a consistent absolute context of ends, purposes, procedural conventions and decisions, so that their reasonings are logically valid and, hence, their intentions conclusions of arguments Justified without such intentions being in the least Morally Justified.

* * * *

These are, Wilfrid, the main points on which I need more instruction. Since you can see things as wholes better than I, I wouldn't be surprised if, as you suggested, we are even closer than I think.

If you come to Ann Arbor before August 5th, please give me a ring so that we can get together.

Cordially,
Hector

S6. Sellars to Castañeda, 7 June 1967

Dear Hector:

Many thanks for the letter. It is very helpful. I will take up the points in order.

Ad 1. I am not happy about a distinction between the reasonableness of intendings (acts) and the reasonableness of intentions (contents). As far as I can see for an intending (act) to be reasonable is a matter of its having a reasonable content. I grant that it can be reasonable to believe a false proposition. But surely this is a matter of the proposition (content) having that reasonableness which is probability relative to available evidence. The categorical reasonableness with which I am concerned is the practical counterpart of truth, which is an 'ideal' reasonableness. One is reminded of the distinction between 'objective rightness' and 'subjective rightness' as these terms were used by the intuitionists. I have simply neglected that reasonableness which is probability.

Ad 2. I should not have used the word 'content' in paragraph 33 (P. 12) [OIM §99], but rather the phrase 'specific subject-matter'*. If you re-read it with this in mind, you will see that the question is an echo of Kant's worry about how the 'matter' of maxims can be relevant to their validity without construing them as hypothetical imperatives. Thus the question has none of the implications you suggest.

Ad 3. I do not think that 'Shall(p · Shall(q))' is well formed. I agree that I have been cavalier about the formation rules for 'shall,' but see my discussion on p. 175 [IIOR §§28-9] of "Imperatives, Intentions and the Logic of 'Ought,'" where I specifically use verbal nouns to be the targets of 'shall.'

Ad 4. I do not use a principle of exportation. Rather I introduce the notion of implication relative to a presupposition. See p. 111 [TA §12] in Lehrer's *Freedom and Determinism*, which gives the necessary correction to the analysis on p. 190 of "IIL'O'." [IIOR §53]

Ad My principle requires that doing A if in C be a necessary condition of getting E. Your Castañeda example is one of the sufficient condition type.

Ad 5. We are in accord.

Ad 6. Likewise.

Ad 7. I am inclined to think that the equivalence in paragraph 31 [OIM §97] amounts to an analysis of the categorical sense of 'ought.'

Ad 8. I agree that morality is but one part of the domain of the prescriptive, and that the concepts of reasonableness involved are special cases of concepts

---

* [Eds.—Sellars's edit is reflected in §33 on p. 12 of the published version of FCET. This means that Castañeda's references are to a pre-publication draft, perhaps the one from which Sellars delivered the Lindley Lecture.]

having more general applicability. Thus I am largely in agreement with what you have to say in this interesting paragraph.

I am studying your papers with care. I am sure that they will help me replace my intuitions with a more rigorous and systematic structure of ideas.

Cordially,
Wilfrid Sellars

P.S! I should have added in *Ad* 4. that the 'implies (for S)' has nothing to do with exportation, but comes in because of the fact that the implication involves the egocentric 'I'. Thus, the general hypothetical imperative has the form

For all s, 'Shall[I will get E]' implies (for S) 'Shall[I will do A]'

or, more explicitly,

For all values of 'I' and for all s, 'Shall[I will get E]' implies (for s) 'Shall[I will do A]'

23
The Aune–Sellars Correspondence, 1961–1979

S1. Sellars to Aune, 19 October 1961

Dear Bruce:

I have enjoyed reading your Free Will paper.* It is very well written, and I am in close sympathy with its general drift. I am a bit uneasy about some features of the argument, however, and feel that you may be misinterpreting what Taylor says—although on the central issue you are right and he is wrong.

Classically it was customary to distinguish between 'absolute' and 'hypothetical' and 'relative' modalities. (The terminology differed, but the distinctions, by and large, did not.) Thus $p \lor {\sim}p$ is absolutely necessary, while q is necessary on the hypothesis p and $(p \supset q)$. In the case of the physical or natural modalities, *if lightning then thunder* is absolutely necessary, but thunder is necessary on the hypothesis of lightning. As for the relative modalities, q will be said to be necessary relative to p, if q is necessary on the hypothesis that p and it is implied that the hypothesis is true. Let us use 'NP[p]' to say that p is necessary in the absolute physical sense, 'MP[p]' to say that p is possible in the absolute physical sense, 'NP[q]/p' to say that q is necessary (in the physical sense) on the hypothesis that p, and, correspondingly, 'MP[q]/p' for the case of hypothetical physical possibility. Finally let us express relative physical necessity and possibility by adding an exclamation mark to the two last forms, thus: 'NP[q]/p!' and 'MP[q]/p!'

You are of course right that from 'p and NP[if p then q]' we cannot conclude 'NP[q].' We can, however, conclude 'NP[q]/p!' And if we represent '(∃p) NP[q]/p!' by 'NPR[q]'—*Anglice* use 'q is relatively physically necessary' for 'There is a p such that p is the case' and 'if p then q is physically necessary in the basic or absolute sense'—we can move from 'NP[q]/p!' to 'NPR[q].'

So much for basic modal notions. To make the points about 'ability to do something' which I want to make, I must introduce some more terminology, the most important of which is the notion of a 'minimal action'. Abstracting from

---

* [Eds.—Most likely Bruce Aune, "Fatalism and Professor Taylor," *Philosophical Review* 71 (October 1962): 512–9. Aune's other early foray into the free will debate—in which Taylor merits only a brief mention—is "Abilities, Modalities, and Free Will," *Philosophy and Phenomenological Research* 23 (March 1963): 397–413.]

mental actions or doings, a minimal action can be roughly characterized as a bodily change which is under our voluntary control and is not brought about by bringing about some other change which is under our voluntary control. Roughly it is an action which does not have a 'smaller' action as its initial segment.

Let 'Am(x,t)' mean *x does minimal action Am at t*
Let 'Vam(x,t)' mean *x wills at t to do Am*
Let 't′' mean *the time just before t*
Let 'CAN[Am(x,t)]' mean *x is able to do Am at t*

Definition:

$$CAN[Am(x,t)] = NP[Vam(x,t) \supset Am(x,t)] = NP[Am(x,t)]/Vam(x,t)$$

Notice that

$$CAN[Am(x,t)]$$

entails

$$MP[Am(x,t)]$$

but not

(K) $MP[Am(x,t)]/K(x,t')$ where 'K' is a variable ranging over states of affairs

though, of course it does entail

$$MP[Am(x,t)]/Vam(x,t')$$

We can now introduce a more inclusive concept of action and a corresponding concept of ability to do.

Actions other than minimal, and circumstances of minimal actions, are represented by 'A' and 'C', respectively, and introduced in terms (roughly) of the schemas:·

$$A(x,t) = R(x,t) = (\exists C)(\exists Am) \, C(x,t) \cdot Am(x,t) \cdot NP[C(x,t) \cdot Am(x,t) \supset R]$$

where 'R' stands for the "result" and 'R(x,t)' has the sense of 'x at t′ brings about R'.

(It will be noticed that I have attempted to tie the notion of 'circumstance' to that of action in such a way that circumstances are what combine with minimal actions to bring about the existence of more inclusive actions. In the sense of circumstance I am attempting to characterize, being paralysed would not be a circumstance. But this is not essential to the points I want to make in this letter.)

We can now define 'x is able to do A' as follows:

$$CAN[A(x,t)] = (\exists Am)(\exists C) \, CAN[Am(x,t)] \cdot C(x,t) \cdot NP[C(x,t) \cdot Am(x,t) \supset A(x,t)]$$

The relation of determinism to ability can now be formulated as follows:
If determinism is true, then 'x did not do A at t' i.e. '$\sim A(x,t)$' entails

$$(\exists K) \, K(x,t') \cdot NP[K(x,t') \supset \sim A(x,t)]$$

Consider the case of minimal actions. From

$$K(x,t') \cdot NP[K(x,t') \supset \sim Am(x,t)]$$

it would, of course, be incorrect to infer

$$K^* \sim MP[Am(x,t)]$$

but quite correct to infer not only

$$\sim MP[K(x,t') \cdot Am(x,t)]$$

but

$$\sim MP[Am(x,t)]/K(x,t')!$$

and even

$$\sim MPR[Am(x,t)]$$

which, though it asserts the *relative* impossibility of a doing, turns out, when unpacked, to assert the impossibility of a complex state of affairs rather than that of a doing, as you well point out.

Now the crux of the matter is that

---

* [Eds.—In Sellars's letter, the letter "K" seems to be typed to the left of the logical statement. It is not clear why. Sellars wishes to deny we can infer "It is not possible for x to perform minimal action Am at t" from the above conjunct; it is not obvious what role K would play here.]

$\sim$MPR[Am(x,t)]

doesn't entail

$\sim$CAN[Am(x,t)]

The latter has, in accordance with our definitions, the sense of

$\sim$NP[Vam(x,t) ⊃ Am(x,t)]

Thus, although 'It was (relatively) P-impossible *that* x do Am' and 'It was impossible *for* x to do Am', i.e. 'x was unable to do A', look deceptively alike, the former has the form

$[\exists F]F(x,t') \cdot NP[F(x,t') \supset \sim Am(x,t)]$

whereas the latter has the form

$\sim NP[F(x,t') \supset Am(x,t)]$

The above applies to minimal actions. The extension of the point to non-minimal actions is straightforward. As in the case of minimal actions, '$\sim$MPR[A(x,t)]' is compatible with 'CAN[A(x,t)]'. The latter is falsified by any one of the following:

$\sim(\exists Am)(\exists C) \, CAN[Am(x,t) \cdot C(x,t) \cdot NP[Am(x,t) \supset A(x,t)]]$

I.e. there was no combination of a minimal action which x was able to do together with a circumstance which obtained which would bring about a doing of A

$(\exists Am)(\exists C) \, CAN[Am(x,t) \cdot NP[Am(x,t) \supset A(x,t)] \cdot \sim C(x,t)]$

I.e. there was a minimal action which x was able to do at t which would result in a doing of A if the circumstances had been of a certain kind which they weren't

$(\exists Am)(\exists C) \, C(x,t) \cdot NP[Am(x,t) \supset A(x,t)] \cdot \sim CAN[Am(x,t)]$

I.e. x was in a circumstance which if combined with a certain kind of minimal action would have brought about a doing of A, but x was not able to do the minimal action at the time in question.

Well, Bruce, I hope the above is not too incomprehensible, and if comprehensible a worthwhile comment on your stimulating paper. You will find a hint of these views in a footnote to the phenomenalism paper.*

As ever,
Wilfrid

---

* [Eds.—Wilfrid Sellars, "Phenomenalism," in *Science, Perception and Reality* (New York: Humanities Press, 1963), Ch. 3, written in 1959. It is the footnote to §43, on p. 78:

> It is perhaps relevant to note that the idea that determinism is incompatible with 'could have done otherwise' rests on a confusion between
>
> > It could not have been the case that x did A at t
>
> and
>
> > x was not able to do A at t.
>
> The former has the sense of
>
> > That x did A at t is physically impossible relative to the antecedent state of the universe.
>
> In the case of minimal actions (roughly, bodily actions under voluntary control) 'x was able to do A at t' means, roughly,
>
> > If x had willed at t to do A, then x would have done A
>
> and neither it nor its denial makes reference to the antecedent state of the universe.]

A2. Aune to Sellars, 23 October 1961

Dear Wilfrid,

Your letter came this morning, and it pleased me very much to get your comments and to hear that you found my paper interesting. You were the first, in fact the only, one to comment seriously on it—and for this, as well as for [the] excellence of your comments, I am deeply grateful.

Feigl was here last week to give a series of lectures, and we talked about the paper a little. He found it interesting—and my conclusions a little surprising—but he didn't have time to think the argument through, and hence didn't have much to say by way of comment on it. He did mention, however, that he thought it was worth publishing, and he said that if I could get it down to the equivalent of 16 pages of *Phil. Studies*, he would recommend it for publication in your journal. I have revised it since he left, however, and now I fear that it is too long. At any rate, in order to free myself from constant revision, I sent the revised version off to *Phil. Rev.* I sent it there because they make their decisions very promptly, and because *Mind* and *Phil. Quarterly* have papers of mine they have yet to print. (Perhaps sending it was premature, but then, thanks to your letter, I have additional ammunition for making replies.)

But now for some comments on your comments, and then some comments on your phenomenalism paper. First, I liked your idea of minimal actions. Actually, I had something like this in the back of my mind, but I didn't know quite how to put it. That was why I said so much for *trying*. I know it sounds awkward to speak of trying to move one's own finger, say; but I don't think it is nonsense. A paralyzed child may try to move his legs but fail; though we don't normally speak of trying if he succeeds*. But because there are cases where one can try to move a muscle, an analysis of trying—a just analysis, that is—must wrestle with the problems of thought and action, and this means handling the notion of minimal actions, both mental and physical. Because these problems are bound up with the now hotly debated notion of "the will," I tried to circumvent the whole tangle by fixing on the admittedly loaded concept of trying. Once this concept is unpacked, however, something like your view of thought and action (as expressed, e.g., in your Language Games paper†) will have to emerge, along with, of course, your comment on minimal actions.

I was very interested in your analysis of hypothetical and relative necessity, which was quite new to me. It is possible that Taylor had something like this in mind, though I am sure that he was too confused about physical necessity to envisage anything like the complex analysis you present. In fact I was moved to

---

* [Eds.—Sellars has underlined "trying" and "succeeds" and written in the margins, "succeed or fail → try".]

† [Eds.—SRLG.]

write about physical necessity as I did because I thought he, like many contemporary Oxbridgians, was led to plump for an anti-scientific view of man because, among other things, he was confused about the implications of the physical modalities.

Your own suggestions, especially about the logic of "x is able to do A," struck me as extremely thorough-going, making me realize that my analysis scarcely scratched the surface of a highly complex matter. I found one difficulty in your account, however. Your definition of "x is able to do A," namely

$$CAN[A(x,t)] = (\exists Am)(\exists C) : CAN[Am(x,t)] \cdot C(x,t) \cdot NP[Am(x,t) \supset A(x,t)],$$

seems to imply that one has a given ability only in circumstances favorable for its execution or exercise. But doesn't it make sense to say "I have the ability to read French novels, but because I am not in favorable circumstances, no such novels being in my office, I cannot presently exercise this ability"?

If, in accordance with this difficulty, you delete the "C(x,t)" as a main conjunct in your definition (and put it, perhaps, in the antecedent of "NP (Am(x,t) ⊃ A(x,t))," since it cannot be NP that A(x,t) follows from Am(x,t) in *any* circumstances), then, given that CAN(A(x,t)), for some x, the event of A(x,t) depends on two factors, viz. Vam(x,t) and C(x,t). This seems more in line with the ordinary notion of ability and it is also in line with your informal remarks, for it would be odd if one could gain and lose a number of abilities merely by undergoing the change in circumstances involved in walking round the block!

Again, in your formulae at the bottom of page 3 illustrating possible falsifications of "CAN(A(x,t))," I think you should include "C(x,t)" in the antecedent of "NP(Am(x,t) ⊃ A(x,t))," for in connection with the second one, viz.

$$(\exists Am)(\exists C) : CAN(Am(x,t)) \cdot NP(Am(x,t) \supset A(x,t)) \cdot \sim C(x,t),$$

it might happen that Vam(x,t) occurs (since it is consistent with C(x,t)), and this would mean, in view of CAN(Am(x,t))*, that A(x,t) must also occur—which would be very odd if ~CAN(A(x,t)) obtains.

Now, if you are willing to make the suggested change in the position of "C(x,t)," your analysis comes a lot closer to the one expressed in my paper. Certain differences, of course, remain, two of which are slight and another of which is more basic. The slight or trivial differences are these: (1) you speak of willing and minimal actions while I speak of trying, and (2) your definition contains the operator "NP." These differences are not basic, i.e. they indicate no serious disagreement, because (a) I am willing to admit that the analysis of trying must

---

* [Eds.—Here, Aune has inserted by hand "and, of course," and has drawn an arrow to "NP(Am(x,t)" in the above logical formula.]

mention willing and minimal actions (though willing, too, needs careful analysis), and (b) I use a complicated subjunctive conditional in my definition, and when this is analyzed symbolically it will probably require modal operators. Our basic difference, then, lies in my use of a bound variable, ranging over states or conditions of persons. (If one's abilities are not partly determined by one's present circumstances, "state" is perhaps a bad word: "condition" is probably much better in that it lacks some of the temporal connotations of the latter.)

How can we resolve our apparent disagreement about the bound variable? Well, perhaps there really is no disagreement here; perhaps the variable will appear when the notion of willing is analyzed. If willing is to involve the framework of thoughts, i.e., "self-directed commands," then, since thinking essentially involves frames of mind which are dispositional states, then a bound variable will probably have to be supplied. On the other hand, you might maintain that "CAN(A(x,t))" does not really involve more than a conjunction of hypotheticals, that abilities are really just "conjunctive-conditional properties." (For your definition, unpacked, is:

$$(\exists Am)(\exists C) : NP(Vam(x,t) \supset Am(x,t)) \cdot NP(C(x,t) \cdot Am(x,t) \supset A(x,t)),$$

where the above suggestion about changing the position of "C(x,t)" is carried out.) Now, if it is your view that abilities are iffy in this way, then I am inclined to disagree, though I have no strong arguments to offer. I mainly have a feeling, a strong one, that "x has the ability A" is to be unpacked along the lines of "x *is such that if*...," where the "is such that" requires symbolic treatment along the lines of "$(\exists \emptyset)(\emptyset x, now \cdot (y)(t')(\emptyset y, t' ...))$," the universal quantifiers being required in order to pin down, though indirectly, the condition in point. As I said, however, I have no strong arguments to offer for this interpretation, which also applies, though in a slightly different way, to dispositions.

A word, now, on your Phenomenalism paper. The earlier stages of your argument raise no special puzzles for me: having already pondered your views very carefully, I found it easygoing and elegantly done. But the later sections bothered me a bit. At first, when I thought about your points on sensations and logical subjects, I felt that the conclusions of my Feigl paper* were neatly wrecked. But now, after another week's thought, I think that my position there is still sound—though it is far less thorough-going than yours. Let me explain.

As I set up my solution to the problem of sensory consciousness, I am still within the framework of physical things, though I assume, to be sure, that it is still possible to speak of neurophysiological processes. I do of course look forward to a utopian stage of neurophysiological research, but the stage at which I handle the puzzle is still not as utopian as yours—that is, the stage I consider has not yet reached the point where the physical thing framework is

---

* [Eds.—Bruce Aune, "Feigl on the Mind-Body Problem," in G. Maxwell and P. Feyerabend, eds., *Matter, Mind and Method: Essays Presented to Herbert Feigl* (Minneapolis, 1966), pp. 17–39.]

dispensable for the biological sciences. I assume that the physiologist still speaks of animals and their nervous system, though he is capable of identifying highly intricate neural conditions and specifying them in terms of various functors. Having identified such conditions, however, he might discover that some of them are associated with characteristic patterns of observable behavior—behavior, that is, that we commonsensically term the effects or manifestations of certain raw feels. Allowing that our talk of a condition or state of a person is elastic enough to permit us to speak of a *person's* being in a certain Ø-state (instead of a part of his brain's being in such a state—cf. my remarks on pp. 28–29 of the Feigl paper), then, given that we can characterize raw feels in behavioral terms, i.e., by description (as *the* condition such that ...), and taking seriously the implied uniqueness condition (as discussed in my paper, p. 27), it is easy to prove, given the requisite progress in neurophysiology, that R = C, where "R" applies to a given raw feel and "C" applies to a brain state characterized in neurophysiological terms, i.e., in terms of spike potentials, etc., of certain groups of nerve fibers. (Wow, what a sentence!) And once we admit that introspective reports are legitimate, we must take seriously a person's ascription of phenomenal properties to his raw feels—which means, given that R is a raw feel and P is a phenomenal property truly ascribed to it, that a cortical state C also has that phenomenal property. Since C is specified in terms of physical-2 functors, it may be said that C has phenomenal as well as mathematical properties. Since C is a Ø-state of a person, more accurately a set of events in a person's cortex, it is C, not its phenomenal or mathematical properties themselves, that results *in* observable behavior and results *from* changes in his sense-organs or in his immediately perceptible environment. This means that though my position involves a sort of dualism (as so far developed), it is very different from either parallelism, interactionism, or the usual forms of epiphenomenalism.

Now I repeat that I do not disagree with your solution; in fact I am certain that something very like your position must be true. Still, I think that my view is sound as at least a partial resolution of a puzzle formulated *within* the frame of persons, their experiences, and states of *their* nervous system. As far as our differences are concerned, I am inclined to think that they stem from the stage of scientific progress with respect to which we formulate a solution of the raw feel–brain state problem.

Your reflections on the future framework of neurophysiology or physical science generally, while I am strongly inclined to agree with them (I feel that they *must* be sound), still take my breath away. For I wonder how, within this frame, we are to deal with the semantic matters of empirical significance, *public* confirmability, and the like. Must we always retain the physical-thing-person frame for these purposes? That is, can we have a pragmatic metalanguage without terms for persons, and can a philosophically comprehensive semantics be utterly separate from a pragmatics?

I hope that these fragmentary remarks don't strike you as too obtuse—but I enjoyed your letter and paper (which I am still thinking about!) and wanted to record my reaction, even though the amount I could say in a letter was necessarily minimal.

Perhaps when I see you in Denver this winter, we can carry the discussion forward!

Cordially,
Bruce

P.S.: I have discovered that p. 55 of your Phenomenalism paper is missing too. My copy had an extra page 54 (which I enclose because you might need it).

S3. Sellars to Aune, 11 November 1961

Dear Bruce:

Thanks for the careful letter. I enjoyed reading—studying it. Here are some comments and meta-comments.

1. You are, of course, quite correct in pointing out that '$Am(x,t)$' is not a sufficient condition of '$A(x,t)$', i.e. that '$NP[Am(x,t) \supset A(x,t)]$' presupposes the obtaining of a favorable condition. I was quite aware of this in giving my definition of '$CAN[A(x,t)]$'. In effect I was using '$NP[\ldots \supset \ldots]$' in the sense of the short arrow introduced at the top of p. 252 in my Vol. II essay.* This wasn't too ill-advised at that stage—compare the definition of '$Sol(x,t)$' as 'immersed$(x,t) \to$ disintegrates (x,t)', which will do for the occasion—but it messed things up in the subsequent discussion. It would have been better to conjoin '$C(x,t)$' with '$Am(x,t)$' in the antecedent of the NP clause right from the beginning, or, at least, to have used the concept of hypothetical necessity, thus,

$$NP[Am(x,t) \supset A(x,t)]/C(x,t)$$

and given the following definition,

$$CAN[A(x,t)] =_{Df} (\exists Am)(\exists C)\, CAN[Am(x,t)] \cdot C(x,t) \cdot NP[Am(x,t) \supset A(x,t)]/C(x,t)$$

2. I am inclined to distinguish between 'x can do A at t' and 'x is (at t) able to do A', e.g. between 'x can swim at t' and 'x is (at t) able to swim.' The concepts are obviously closely related. If we define 'Able-to-do-$A(x,t)$' as

$$(\exists Am)(\exists C)\, CAN[Am(x,t)] \cdot NP[Am(x,t) \supset A(x,t)]/C(x,t)$$

then we could define '$CAN[Am(x,t)]$' in terms of this predicate somewhat as follows,

$$CAN[A(x,t)] =_{Df} \text{Able-to-do-}A(x,t) \cdot C(x,t)$$

But there is no need to ring the changes on possible analysanda. It might, however, be worth noting that in the case of minimal actions

Able-to-do-$Am(x,t)$

---

* [Eds.—Sellars is referring to CDCM.]

would coincide with

$$\mathrm{CAN}[\mathrm{Am}(x,t)]$$

both having the sense of '$\mathrm{NP}[\mathrm{Vam}(x,t) \supset \mathrm{Am}(x,t)]$' though I grant that the concept of a minimal action needs careful exploration to determine whether it coincides with the notion of what can be done that circumstances cannot hinder.

3. As for the question whether dispositions and abilities are to be analyzed in terms of 'such that if...', this might or might not hold us up, depending on whether you conceive of the quantified variable as ranging over "micro-states" or as ranging over thing kinds (and circumstances). I think it important to distinguish between the *analysis of* a disposition and the *explanation of* the disposition. A failure to draw a distinction between these two interpretations of "such that" involves a danger of mixing levels of discourse (roughly observation language and theoretical language) and I suspect that your treatment of the sensory consciousness problem tacitly commits this error. But of this more later.

Notice that if we take the thing-kind cum circumstances approach, and use the special variable 'p' to express the categorial nature of *person* as contrasted with ordinary thing kinds, and recognize further the 'internal relation' between being a person and willing, we see that

$$\mathrm{CAN}[\mathrm{Am}(p,t)] =_{\mathrm{Df}}{}^* \mathrm{NP}[\mathrm{Vam}(p,t) \supset \mathrm{Am}(p,t)]$$

needs no supplementation by quantified variables or such thats—which is not, of course, to say that it is incapable of further analysis.

4. Notice also the difference between being *paralysed* and being *hindered*. This distinction is analytically related to that between minimal and non-minimal actions. Abbreviating 'x is paralysed at t with respect to Am' by '$\mathrm{ParAm}(x,t)$', we can define it as follows,

$$\mathrm{ParAm}(x,t) =_{\mathrm{Df}} \mathrm{NP}[\mathrm{Vam}(x,t) \supset {\sim}\mathrm{Am}(x,t)]$$

Once again, the *definition* of a paralysis must be distinguished from its explanation, whether molar or micro-. '$\mathrm{ParAm}(x,t)$' clearly entails '${\sim}\mathrm{CAN}[\mathrm{Am}(x,t)]$', i.e. '${\sim}\mathrm{NP}[\mathrm{Vam}(x,t) \supset \mathrm{Am}(x,t)]$'. Is the converse true? Does '${\sim}\mathrm{CAN}[\mathrm{Am}(x,t)]$' entail '$\mathrm{ParAm}(x,t)$'? It sounds as though it should, but it does not follow from our definitions *as they have so far been explicated* that this entailment obtains. For, schematically, '${\sim}\mathrm{NP}[fx \supset gx]$' obviously doesn't entail '$\mathrm{NP}[fx \supset gx]$'.

---

* [Eds.—This letter is typewritten (as is the majority of Sellars's correspondence), but Sellars has handwritten the logical symbols. In this case, Sellars omitted "$=_{\mathrm{Df}}$"; we have added it to the text.]

5. A closer examination of the situation is rewarding. Notice that whereas ordinarily the conjunction of singular statements

$$f(a,t_1) \cdot g(a,t_1')$$

merely authorizes the consequence

$$\text{Possible}[f(a,t_1) \cdot g(a,t_1')]$$

(from actuality to possibility the argument is good); in the case of volitions we can go from

$$\text{Vam}(\text{Tom},t_1) \cdot \text{Am}(\text{Tom},t_1')$$

to

$$\text{CAN}[\text{Am}(\text{Tom},t_1)]$$

which, in spite of the word 'CAN' expresses a statement of necessity, for it is equivalent to

$$\text{NP}[\text{Vam}(\text{Tom},t_1) \supset \text{Am}(\text{Tom},t_1')]$$

so that in this case from actuality to *necessity* the argument is good. To understand why this is so is to understand why we think that "we have a non-indicative insight into the causal nexus between volitions and minimal actions." Why is it so? The answer lies in the explication of the concept of a volition. Roughly we mean by a volition (pertaining to minimal actions) a thought which culminates in a minimal action unless one is paralysed. Thus we have not only

$$\text{Vam}(x,t) \cdot \text{CAN}[\text{Am}(x,t)]$$

entails

$$\text{Am}(x,t)$$

which on our definitions is analytic, but also

$$\text{Vam}(x,t) \cdot \sim\text{ParAm}(x,t)$$

entails

Am(x,t)

which, on the preceding definitions is not. To bring out the character of the second entailment, we must note that

Vam(x,t)

entails

CAN[Am(x,t)] ∨ ParAm(x,t)

ex vi terminorum. A person may not yet have acquired the ability to will to do Am, but if he has, then it is a necessary truth that if he does so, either he is paralysed or he performs Am. Further ramifications of this point might be spelled out on a subsequent occasion.

6. A minor point. Not all *doing* involves *trying to do*: but all *succeeding in doing* does. 'x succeeded' entails 'x tried.' An interesting question is 'Does it make sense to speak of trying to do a minimal action?' Certainly, one can (a) try to find out if one is able to do Am; (b) try to acquire the ability to do Am. But my suspicion is that 'x tried to do Am' is nonsense unless it is used to mean 'x tried to do A and for some people A is a minimal action.'

7. I want to take up the problem of sensory consciousness on a subsequent occasion, so I will limit myself to a few off the cuff remarks. As far as I get it, your solution is along naturalistic Aristotelian lines. One state of a person has both 'phenomenal' and 'physical-2' properties. The raw feel state and the neurophysiological state are identical. They are two only in the sense in which the author of *Waverly* and the author of *Ivanhoe* are two.

The state which has (phenomenal property) = the state which has (physical-2 property)

The attractiveness of this solution (which is essentially the same as the "double knowledge" solution developed by my father in his first book (*Critical Realism*) and subsequent publications) lies in avoiding (at least prima facie) both dualism of *things* and dualism of *episodes*, and, in particular, dualism of bodily states and *epiphenomena*. Instead it has a dualism (parallelism?) of attributes of single states. It is not too different from the classical double aspect theory, save that the latter tended to think of aspects not as properties or attributes, but as 'abstract particulars' (thus tending to revert to parallelism).

8. In spite of its plausibility I don't think it will work, unless it is tacitly reinterpreted along the lines of my solution. As I indicated in section 3, I think that your interpretation of dispositional statements has led you to a mixing of

conceptual frameworks. The mistake is analogous to that involved in saying, for example, that the elasticity of a rubber band *is identical with* a certain microproperty of the system of sub-atomic particles "of which it consists," or that the wetness of water is identical with a physical-2 property of H_2O. The crucial issue is "In what sense are glasses of water and their states *identical with* collections of particles and their states?" These are familiar points, but their application to concepts pertaining to persons may not be obvious until you ask yourself in what sense a network of neurons is "part of a person."

9. I am enclosing a copy of two lectures I gave last year at Pittsburgh.* It may help resolve the issue one way or the other.

10. By the way, I am still not certain what is going to happen to the phenomenalism paper. I sent it to *Kantstudien* two years ago and have as yet received no definite commitment on Gottfried Martin's part to print it. The objection is the length. Is there any chance that it would be acceptable for the Oberlin volume? I did read a substantial section there. Would you be willing to explore the matter with your colleagues?

11. It would be nice if we could narrow our differences (which in any case are on matters of detail, rather than broad principle) by correspondence. But a thorough exploration of the issues will have to wait until we can talk things over. I hope it will be soon.

As ever,
Wilfrid

---

* [Eds.—PSIM.]

A4: Aune to Sellars, 19 September 1969

Dear Wilfrid,

Can you take a minute to help me with your notion of dependent implication mentioned in Ch. 7 of SCIENCE & METAPHYSICS? I have been asked to review the book, and I am a bit hung up on the matter.

My problem is that I do not know how you propose to justify such practical arguments as the following, mentioned on p. 182*:

Shall (If p, q)
p
Therefore, Shall (q).

I realize that we're here concerned with dependent implication, which might be represented more perspicuously by

$$\left[\frac{S \text{ (if p, q)}}{Sq} \right] \text{ rel p}$$

But I cannot see how your third-level principle can justify such an argument, as you suggest on p. 182 of S & M and on p. 111 of the Lehrer volume[†].

On a straightforward approach it would appear that '((if p, q) implies q) rel p' is true iff '((if p, q) & p) implies q.' But on this approach '(S (if p, q) implies Sq) rel p' is true iff '(S (if p, q) & p) implies Sq.' Yet I do not see how this latter implication can be derived from your third-level principle, '(p implies q)' implies and is implied by 'Sp implies Sq.'

It seems to me that your shall-operator behaves like a modal operator for relative necessity. Thus if RNq means (Ep) (p & N (if p, q)), then the following is valid:

N (if p, q)
p
―――――
RNq

The practical argument that concerns me seems to have the same form; reconstructed it is as follows:

---

* [Eds.—The reference is to §14 of OIM, in particular to subsection (i), although Sellars also discusses dependent implication in subsection (h), which begins on p. 181 of the edition Aune is referencing. OIM appears as Chapter 6 of this volume.]

† [Eds.—The reference is to §12 of TA, which appears as Chapter 7 of this volume.]

$$\frac{S\ (\text{if } p,\ q)}{RSq}$$

I believe that you will need an additional modal principle to validate arguments of the latter kind; I can see no way of validating them merely by the use of your third-level principle.

If I am confused about this, please let me know—in fact, let me know even if I am not confused about it. If it is easiest for you to reply by telephone, call me at 413-xxx-xxxx.

I hope things are going well with you and that you enjoy a pleasant fall (season). I am plodding along as usual; my new book has been thoroughly revised and will appear in February under the title RATIONALISM, EMPIRICISM, AND PRAGMATISM: AN INTRODUCTION.

Cordial regards,
Bruce

A5. Aune to Sellars, 26 September 1969

Dear Wilfrid,

I read through your paper* in the Castañeda volume, and I think I can now put my finger on the weakness of your treatment of the practical syllogism: S(A if M), M; therefore, S(A).

On page 190 [§53] you expand this argument as follows:

1. S(A if M)
2. M implies ([A if M] implies A)
3. M
4. (A if M) implies A
5. S[(A if M) implies S(A)]
6. S(A).

The trouble with this argument is that premise (2) is false for any kind of *implication* I can think of. Though M & (A if M) implies A, we cannot use exportation to infer that M implies [(A if M) implies A]; the most we can infer is

7. M implies [(A if M) ⊃ A]

or perhaps

8. pm(M) implies [(A if M) implies A],

where 'pm' represents the kind of positive modality appropriate to the use of 'implies' in question. But (7) and (8) are not adequate to permit the derivation of (6) from (1) and (3).

I don't think it will be satisfactory to argue that you are simply using 'implies' so that exportation is valid for it. This alternative is ruled out (or seems to be ruled out) by your admission that nomologicals and at least Anderson implications are implications in your sense. Exportation does not, so far as I know, hold for these latter relations.

Note that on p. 173 [M(1-1)] [§27] of Castañeda you imply, and on p. 174 [§27] you say, that a principle of exportation holds for implication; you also use a premise analogous to (2) on pp. 190 and 191 [§§53 and 54].

Further reflection on your use of dependent implication has made me somewhat unhappy for other reasons. I now believe that, taken literally, the following claim is false:

---

* [Eds—IIOR, Ch. 14 of this volume. In this letter, we have inserted paragraph references in brackets wherever Aune makes a page number reference to this article.]

9. S(A if M) implies S(A) relative to M.

The trouble is that even if M is true, S(A) is not a reasonable inference from S(A if M). In order for the inference to be reasonable*, the subject of the Shall-statement (the agent) must *believe* that M is true. This point is, of course, implicit in your analysis, for the premises of the practical argument are to be understood as the agent's premises. But this feature of practical syllogisms (which is not possessed by theoretical syllogisms) is so special that it does not stand out when such syllogisms are represented in the form of a standard argument—or when the corresponding implication is given the form of (9). A more explicit rendering of the intent of (9)—i.e. your intent—would therefore have to be something like the following:

10. S(A if M) implies S(A)† relative to the agent's assumption M.

The point I am trying to make is not trivial, because you define dependent implication in the Castañeda volume in a way that does not take account of it. Thus, you define 'P dependently implies Q' as (ER) (R &. [P&R] implies Q)—and this latter formula merely tells us that *there is* a true statement R such that P&R implies Q; it does not tell us that such an R is *known to the agent* or believed true by him.

Well, if I am confused in all of this, please let me know; I shall in any case be eager to hear what you think.

Cordial regards,
Bruce

PS: I recently heard from Herbert Feigl. He tells me that his health is now much improved. He has been swimming this summer and it seems to have helped him.

---

* [Eds.—Sellars has underlined "reasonable" and written the following in the margin:

　　dist.
　　valid　　　}
　　good　　　}　　arg.
　　reasonable　}

It wouldn't be reasonable for Jones to argue
--
All mules are barren
Daisy is a mule
..
Daisy is barren
--
if he didn't accept one of the 'true' premises

"Dist." is clearly an abbreviation for "distinguish." Language very similar to the above appears in S6, Sellars's reply to A5.]

† [Eds.—At this point, Aune has inserted by hand, "(perhaps) *for an agent*."]

S6. Sellars to Aune, 3 October 1969

Dear Bruce:

I really appreciate your care in following up the question you raised about the adequacy of the principle

(p implies q) implies (Shall [p] implies Shall [q]).

I found your letter exactly to the point, and sat right down to reflect on an answer. Perhaps the following remarks will help orient further discussion.

I have never—not even on p. 190 [§53*] of the Castañeda volume—said that 'exportation holds for implication.' After all, I was brought up on Lewis and Langford[†] and learned almost at my mother's knee to avoid confusing

$p < (q < r)$[‡]

with

$p < (q \supset r)$.

What I have done is argue that there is a *generic* notion of implication which is such that (roughly)

'p' implies 'q' ≡ The (con)sequence 'p, q' is justified

In other words, if 'p' implies 'q' in this generic sense, then if 'p' belongs to one's corpus then the addition of 'q' is justified. This generic notion of implication leaves it open whether or not the justification is purely "formal" or "intra-conceptual," or whether it would appeal to matters of fact. (I will not distinguish "formal" from "intra-conceptual" in this letter, since my point can be made without exploring physical implication—though my treatment of the latter would, I believe, add grist to my mill.) What logicians have tried to do is systematize certain species of implication where the justification would appeal to purely formal considerations. I would certainly agree with your point that exportation does not hold with respect to the implications thus systematized.

---

* [Eds.—The only place in IIOR where Sellars mentions exportation is page 174/§27, which is the page Aune references in A5. Perhaps Sellars errs in referring to p. 190 instead of p. 174 in his rebuttal.]

† [Eds.—C.I. Lewis (1883–1964) and Cooper Harold Langford (1895–1964).]

‡ [Eds.—S6 is hand-written, and one must infer what Sellars intends by the "<" symbol, which Sellars seems to be using for strict or logical implication. In CIL (§2/p. 289), Sellars uses the curved symbol "<" to represent Lewis's notion of strict implication. It is possible that this is the symbol he intends here, but this is a substantive interpretive question, not an editorial one. See also CDCM §26, where he seems to use the '<' symbol to denote a sort of modal notion of implication. We are grateful to Lionel Shapiro for helpful correspondence on this issue.]

Clearly 'p ⊃ q' should not be read as "'p' implies 'q'." The latter means that the move from 'p' to 'q' is justified and, usually, that it is logically or conceptually justified. *On the other hand, given that 'p ⊃ q' is true, the sequence 'p, q' is justified, though not formally so.* The relevant formally true implication is, of course,

'p · p ⊃ q' implies 'q'

On the other hand, knowing this latter, and knowing that 'p ⊃ q' is true, I know that if I am entitled to add 'p' to my corpus, I am also entitled to add 'q.'

Similarly, if I know that 'p' is true, then I know that 'p ⊃ q : ⊃ q' is true, because

'p ⊃ [p ⊃ q : ⊃ q]'

is formally true. As a result, I know that the sequence '(p ⊃ q), q' is justified, though not formally so. (As you correctly point out

p < [p ⊃ q : ⊃ q]

does not entail

p < [p ⊃ q : < q].)

In other words, I know—though not on purely formal grounds—that I am entitled to add 'q' to my corpus if I am entitled to add 'p ⊃ q.' This means that in the *generic* sense of 'implies' I know that

'p ⊃ q' implies 'q'

It would, in my opinion, be a serious mistake to treat any of the standard theories of logical implication as an explication of the pre-analytic notion of implication which we constantly employ in practical *and theoretical* reasoning. If I gave the impression in the Castañeda volume that the term 'implies' as it occurs in the examples of practical reasoning which I gave has the sense of 'strictly implies' or 'logically implies' (i.e. <-implies)* this was carelessness on my part. I was well aware that the arguments are fallacious if 'implies' is taken in the usual sense given by logicians. Perhaps the above remarks will throw light on what I was

---

* [Eds.—As noted in a previous editorial note, S6 is handwritten, and this parenthetical is ambiguous. Andrew Chrucky transcribes it as "L-implies." We read it as "<-implies," which (in our view) makes more sense in the context. For Chrucky's transcription, see: <http://www.ditext.com/sellars/csa.html>.]

trying to do with the phrase 'relative implication' or 'implication relative to an assumption.'

As far as the new point you raise is concerned, I simply don't see it. We must, in the case of theoretical argument, distinguish not only between the validity of an argument and its goodness (i.e. its being valid and having true premises) but between these and the reasonableness of a given person offering it, thus

> All mules are barren
> Daisy (we shall suppose) is a mule
> So, Daisy is barren

is both valid and good. But if Jones believes either of the premises to be false, it would be, in a legitimate sense, unreasonable of him to offer it.

> It would be unreasonable of me to reason
>> Shall [I will do A, if p]
>> So, Shall [I will do A]

if I doubt that p. But this is because it would be unreasonable of me to believe

> 'I will do A, if p' implies 'I will do A'

if I do not accept p. The point in question is independent of the distinction between 'theoretical' and 'practical' reasoning.

I was delighted to learn that Herbert is better. I must drop him a line.

Cordially,
Wilfrid

A7. Aune to Sellars, 8 January 1970

Dear Wilfrid,

We are having our mid-term vacation here at UMass, and a cold, snowy morning is just the time to reply to your philosophical letter of October 3. I told you that I felt very uneasy with your specification of the generic sense of 'implies.' I now think I can put my finger on the point that bothers me.

In view of your admission on page 2 of your letter that "given that 'p ⊃ q' is true, the sequence 'p,q' is justified...," it follows that

(I) 'p' implies 'q' iff p ⊃ q

holds for all *statements* 'p' and 'q'—i.e., for items that are true or false. The proof of this seems straightforward. If 'p' implies 'q' then 'p & ~q' is false and 'p ⊃ q' is accordingly true. On the other hand, if p ⊃ q, then 'p ⊃ q' is true and the sequence 'p,q' is justified. Hence, if p ⊃ q, then 'p' implies 'q' and vice-versa.

The thesis (I) may, of course, be no surprise to you, but it seems to me that it is seriously at odds with your purposes in dealing with the logic of practical reasoning. On page 183* you say, for example, that if 'p' implies 'q' then it is *unreasonable* to believe that p without believing that q and also (given your principle concerning shall-statements) unreasonable to intend that p be the case without intending that q be the case. Yet these claims seem extremely implausible if (I) is granted.

Let E be the statement that Nixon will *not* end the war and let W be the statement that Nixon wants to end the war. Assume that E is true, though no one happens to know it. It is then an accidental and perhaps "vacuous" truth that

(1) W ⊃ E.

But if (1) is analytically equivalent to

(2) 'W' implies 'E'

then it would be unreasonable to believe that W without believing that E and also unreasonable to intend that W without intending that E. But this is surely too strong. And surely it is too strong to hold that if E is true, then if an ideally rational being believed that W he would have to believe that E and if he intended that W (as we all do) he would have to intend that E (as most of us do not). But this

---

* [Eds.—Of *Science and Metaphysics*. See OIM §18 (Ch. 6 of this volume). In this letter, we have inserted paragraph references in brackets wherever Aune makes a page number reference to OIM.]

latter claim would also seem to follow from what you say about an ideally rational being on page 183 of *Science and Metaphysics* [OIM §§15–19].

Note also that (I) is inconsistent with your claim on page 197 of *Science and Metaphysics* [OIM §57] that "'p' implies 'q'" presupposes the truth of 'p'. Even if 'p' and 'q' are false, it will be true that p&q ⊃ p and therefore, by (I), true that 'p&q' implies 'p'. This consequence will hold even if it is presupposed that 'p&q' is false. Your claim on page 197 (of *Science and Metaphysics*) also makes trouble for your principle that 'Shall(p)' implies 'Shall(q)' iff 'p' implies 'q'. Even if 'A&B' is true, it need not be true (or rationally acceptable) that Shall(A&B).

I just thought of another unwanted consequence of the principle (I). Suppose that ~(s does A) and that an agent makes the move 'Shall(s does A)' but would never even consider making the move 'Shall(s does B).' Since ~(s does A), we may infer that (s does A) ⊃ (s does B) and, by the principle (I), conclude that 's does A' implies 's does B'. Given your axiom concerning shall-statements, we may then infer that 'Shall(s does A)' implies 'Shall(s does B)'. Since, however, the agent has made the move 'Shall(s does A)' he is committed to the move 'Shall(s does B),' which he would regard as the most repugnant of all. This case is extremely serious because 'Shall(s does B)' can be any intention at all. This reasoning shows, in other words, that if a man intends to bring about a state of affairs that does not obtain, then he is committed to every intention whatever.

I am now inclined to believe that your original strategy in validating practical arguments such as

Shall (A if p)
p
Therefore, Shall (A)

by reference to the principle 'S(A)' implies 'S(B)' iff 'A' implies 'B' and the notion of dependent implication will not work out. Either the relevant notion of implication is too strong to be validated by the strategy outlined in your paper in *Methodos** or it is weak enough to be subject to counter-instances of the kind mentioned above. I do agree, of course, that one is entitled to reason as follows: "Since p, if I will do A if p, then I will do A." But, as I said in an earlier letter, I don't think this kind of reasoning can be reconstructed along the lines of: "'I will do A if p' implies 'I will do A' relative to the truth of 'p.'" If we are to speak of relative implication in this kind of case, we must understand the implication as relative to a premise *possessed by the agent* who reasons "So, I will....." (This is just another

---

* [Eds.—IIO, the precursor to IIOR.]

manifestation of the peculiar "subjectivity" that (as you yourself stress) is distinctive of practical arguments.)*

Tell me what you think of all this when you have time. It was good to see you in New York.

Cordial regards,
Bruce

---

* [Eds.—The parenthetical sentence is inserted by hand in Aune's handwriting.]

S8. Sellars to Aune, 28 January 1970*

Dear Bruce –

The paragraph at the bottom of page 2 of my letter is not a model of clarity.[†] Let me try again along somewhat different lines. My aim was to explicate the concept

α implies β relative to assumption δ

in a way which brings out its relation to the idea of one proposition implying another *simpliciter*.

The argument should have begun by pointing out that if, for example, 'p' implies 'q' *simpliciter*, then, *without knowing the truth values of 'p' and 'q'* we can reject the sequence[‡]

p

$\sim$q.

(We can also reject the sequence

$\sim$q

p ($= \sim\sim$p)

by virtue of the contrapositive: '$\sim$q' implies '$\sim$p.' For present purposes I can treat such pairs of sequences, which differ only in their order, as the same.)

Consider, now, the claim that 'p ⊃ q' implies 'q' relative to the assumption 'p.' [I change my example to fit the structure of reasoning involving conditional intentions—see the example analysed in George and Hector's book.[§]] To what extent can we analyse this case along similar lines? Thus, can we say that *given the truth of 'p'* we can reject the sequence

p ⊃ q

$\sim$q

---

* [Eds.—Aune had his secretary produce a typed copy of this letter, which he included in his 7 July 1970 reply to Sellars. Sellars added his own corrections and comments to that version, which we have noted throughout.]

† [Eds.—Sellars seems to be referring to S6. The paragraph at the bottom of page 2 of the original begins, "Clearly 'p ⊃ q' should not be read as "p' implies 'q'.'"]

‡ [Eds.—In the typewritten version of this letter, Sellars has written in the margin next to the first part of this sentence, "This consists in the fact that...." Presumably this is meant to replace or follow "then."]

§ [Eds.—*Morality and the Language of Conduct.*]

without knowing the truth values of 'p ⊃ q' and 'q'?

The following line of thought seems to support an affirmative answer: We know, to begin with, that the following implication *simpliciter* is logically true

'p · p ⊃ q' implies 'q'

Consequently we know that *without knowing the truth values of 'p', 'p ⊃ q', and 'q'* we can reject the sequence

p

p ⊃ q

~q

The above implication by itself, however, is compatible with accepting the sequence

p ⊃ q

~q

for it is compatible with accepting the sequence

~p

p ⊃ q

~q

of which it is a part. If, however, we now add the assumption that 'p' is true, the latter sequence becomes unacceptable, and hence both the sequence

p

p ⊃ q

~q

and

~p

p ⊃ q

~q

are unacceptable.

Let me call these sequences the 'p'-elaborations of the sequence

$p \supset q$

$\sim q$

and suppose that since both 'p'-elaborations of the latter sequence are unacceptable, the sequence itself is unacceptable. The principle here is that if a sequence is to be acceptable, then for any proposition α either the sequence which results by adding α or the sequence which results by adding $\sim\alpha$ must be acceptable, i.e. one or other of the α-elaborations of the sequence must be acceptable. (This can be put in terms of embedding the sequence in a model set or possible world.)

Thus, if we took only the logical implication

'$p \cdot p \supset q$' implies 'q'

into account, the sequence

$p \supset q$

$\sim q$

would not thereby be specified as unacceptable, for its 'p'-elaboration in terms of '$\sim p$' is acceptable, though that in terms of 'p' is not.

It might be objected that I am bringing in other grounds of acceptability than implication, for on the above account the unacceptability of

$\sim p$

$p \supset q$

$\sim q$

rests on the *truth* of 'p' and hence on the falsity of '$\sim p$' as a constituent of the sequence? So what?! The fact remains that in this case the unacceptability of the sequence

$p \supset q$

$\sim q$

can be known without knowing the truth values of its constituents, and this is what I am claiming to be the core notion of implication.

What of the example in my letter?

'p' implies 'q' *relative to the assumption* 'p ⊃ q'

The pattern is the same. We are entitled to rule out the sequence

p
~q

without knowing the truth value of 'p' and 'q.' Once again the logically true implication

'p · p ⊃ q' implies 'q'

enables us to rule out the sequence

p
p ⊃ q
~q

But it still permits the sequence

p
~q

for it permits

p
~(p ⊃ q)
~q

of which it is a proper part.

Now let us stipulate that 'p ⊃ q' is true. Both 'p ⊃ q'-elaborations of

p ⊃ q
~q*

---

* [Eds.—It seems that Sellars meant to write here "p, ~q" instead of "p ⊃ q, ~q". And indeed, in the typewritten version, Sellars has crossed out this sequence and written the following correction/clarification in the margin:

p		p ⊃ q	~(p ⊃ q)
	→	p	p
~q		~q	~q

The two sequences after the arrow have both been crossed out, presumably to signal that (as indicated in the letter) they are unacceptable elaborations of the sequence p, ~q.]

are now unacceptable, and, hence, the sequence itself is unacceptable, and *known to be so independently of knowing the truth values of 'p' and 'q'*—though, it does, of course, require knowledge of the truth value of 'p ⊃ q.'*

I think that some such general notion of implication throws light on a number of interesting uses of 'implies,' though to show this would require an elaboration and sophistication of the above account. Consider, for example,

'Nixon is wise' implies 'Nixon exists'

This rules out the sequence

Nixon is wise
Nixon does not exist

Notice, however, that the original implication is not equivalent to the contrapositive

'Nixon does not exist' implies 'Nixon is not wise'

This, however, is but the beginning of a larger story.
I hope this makes sufficient sense (and is legible enough) to be of help.

Cordially,
Wilfrid

---

* [Eds.—Sellars has written the following at the end of this sentence:
   and if one isn't in a position to make a stronger claim, this points to knowing the truth values of p and q.
Presumably the "stronger claim" would be that p → q is true (or, equivalently, that p generically implies q), not just that the material conditional p ⊃ q is true (or, equivalently, that p materially implies q). See Sellars's first marginal comment toward the beginning of *A9*.]

A9. Aune to Sellars, 7 July 1970

Dear Wilfrid,

This is a sadly delayed response to your last letter on implication, a partial copy of which I enclose. (I had my secretary type up the philosophical part of the original, but she forgot to include the date.)

Even though I have had plenty of time to study your letter, I do not, I am sorry to say, have any useful comments. The main trouble, I think, is that you do not really offer an analysis of the kind of generic implication you are concerned with; what you do offer is a necessary condition of the truth of "P implies Q":

> If P implies Q, then the sequence (P, ~Q) may be rejected without knowing the truth-values of P and Q.

But the condition stated here is also a necessary condition for the truth of "P materially implies Q." This is so, because "P & ~Q" must be false if "P ⊃ Q" is true.*

The notion of implication is, of course, metalinguistic, but the same is true of material implication: P materially implies Q iff either Q is false or P is true.† In other words, although "P ⊃ Q" should not be read "P materially implies Q," the notion of material implication is still a legitimate one and it must be distinguished from the notion of generic implication you are concerned with. Thus, if "P ⊃ Q" is true (in L), then it is true of L that "P" materially implies "Q." I mention this last point not because I think it is news to you, but because I want you to know that I agree with the point, made frequently by you, that we should not confuse a sentential connective with the predicate "implies."

Since you give only a necessary condition for "P generically implies Q" (which is also a necessary condition for "P materially implies Q"), your extension of the condition to relative implication does not distinguish relative generic implication from relative material implication. In my last letter I explained why, in my view, generic implication must be stronger than material implication. Since you agreed with this view, you must supplement your new account of generic implication. After reading your letter, I couldn't figure out how you might do this. So I am still in a state of uncertainty. If you have any further thoughts on generic implication, I would be very interested in hearing them. (I may have missed something in your letter.)

I have been extremely busy since your last letter arrived. As you probably know, I managed to get Vere Chappell to replace me here as department head and we

---

  * [Eds.—In the margin next to this paragraph, Sellars has written, "how about p → q iff the sequence p, ~q may be rejected without knowing the truth value of 'p' + 'q'".]

  † [Eds.—Aune has gotten these backward, and Sellars has written in the margin at this point, "either P is false or Q is true".]

also hired Bob Wolff. Although I shall be technically in charge of the department until January when Chappell arrives, Robison* will be doing most of the administrative work from now on. I am extremely glad to be through with administration. I look forward to doing something in philosophy if I can. (I hope I have not spent too much time withering on the vine.)

I hope you got the copy of my new book.[†] It is introductory, but the last chapters do represent an advance in my thinking about experimental reasoning. I shall be eager to hear your reaction on that chapter and, indeed, on the book as a whole. I have just finished my half of a book on logic for Freshman English[‡]; Martin Steinmann of the Minnesota English department is doing the other half. Its philosophical content is zero; I wrote my half strictly for the royalties.

I hope you are having a pleasant summer and that your work is going well. I am giving a course on your work in the fall, so if you have copies of new papers, I should be very glad to have them. —I have also been asked to write an essay on your views on epistemology, but I haven't the foggiest idea of what to say. I had better start rereading your papers; perhaps some idea will come to mind.

Best regards,
Bruce

PS: Was my review of your SCIENCE AND METAPHYSICS alright?[§] I see that I made one blunder in passing, but I hope the review will nevertheless be helpful to prospective readers of your book.

---

* [Eds.—John G. Robison.]

† [Eds.—Bruce Aune, *Rationalism, Empiricism, and Pragmatism: An Introduction* (McGraw-Hill, 1970).]

‡ [Eds.—We are unable to locate this title; it appears it was never completed, or completed but never published.]

§ [Eds.—Bruce Aune, "Review of *Science and Metaphysics*," *Journal of Philosophy* 67, no. 8 (April 1970): 251–6.]

S10. Sellars to Aune, 20 July 1970

Dear Bruce,

Thank you for the request for additional clarification. It was in order.

I certainly agree that

'p' materially implies 'q'

is to be distinguished from

p ⊃ q

I will even countenance the locution 'material implication', but would point out that I am attempting to characterize a generic concept of implication which does not include 'material implication.' This generic notion is intended to be the converse of 'is inferable from.' (Compare C.I. Lewis' discussion of the contrast between 'strict' and 'material' implication, though his discussion does not take into account the difference between connectives and metalinguistic predicates.)

Suppose we define material implication by the schema:

'p' materially implies 'q' $=_{df}$ 'p' is false or 'q' is true

(You have the definiens turned around in your letter.*) If we dispense with quotes, letting propositional expressions function as autonyms in metalinguistic contexts, then your claim is that

the sequence (P, ~Q) may be rejected without
knowing the truth values of P and Q

is a necessary condition of

P materially implies Q

so that when I lay it down as a necessary condition of

P implies Q

---

* [Eds.—See our second editorial note to A9.]

in my generic sense of 'implies', I have not distinguished my generic sense from material implication.*

But is this really so? Surely

(1) Knowing the truth values of P and Q is sufficient for knowing that P materially implies Q.†

hence

(2) We may know that P materially implies Q without being in a position to reject the sequence (P, ~Q) without knowing the truth values of P and Q—for‡ our knowledge that P materially implies Q will be grounded in our knowledge of the truth values of P and Q.

Of course

(3) Where our knowledge that P materially implies Q is grounded in our knowledge that P implies (in a stronger sense) Q, we will be in a position to reject the sequence (P, ~Q) without knowing the truth values of P and Q.

On the other hand

(4) Knowing the truth values of P and Q is neither necessary nor sufficient for knowing that P implies Q—in the sense of 'implies' that I am attempting to characterize.

It is this feature of this sense of 'implies' which stands behind my claim that

(5) To know that P implies Q is to be in a position to reject the sequence (P, ~Q) without knowing the truth values of P and Q.

Thus the counterpart of (2) does not hold in the case of implication proper, as contrasted with 'material implication.'

Perhaps the above will help, though I have not worked out its implications with respect to the proper formulation of the points I was attempting to make about 'dependent' implication in my letter. I think, however, that they can stand as they are.

---

* [Eds.—In the margin next to this long sentence, Sellars has written: "re my point is that the *epistemic* necessary condition raises a quest 'how do we know that P ⊃ Q?'"]

† [Eds.—In the margin, Sellars has written, "when it *does*".]

‡ [Eds.—Sellars has drawn a diagonal line across the word "for" and written in the margin, "in the case that".]

Congratulations on getting Chappell and Wolff. You are really well off, and should not grudge us Belnap. We have acquired Gerald Massey from Michigan State. He is our new chairman, and we are all delighted. Otherwise things are much as they were.

I was very pleased with your generous review of *SM*.* I know that I would have found it a difficult book to review, had it not been mine. I am awaiting critical reaction to get my motivation stoked up. I am sending under separate cover my reply to Cornman's paper in the *Review of Metaphysics*.† It is a 60 page effort which has occupied a good deal of my time these past few months.

As ever,
Wilfrid Sellars

---

* [Eds.—Bruce Aune, "Review of Sellars's *Science and Metaphysics*." *Journal of Philosophy* 67, no. 8 (April 1970): 251–6.]

† [Eds.—Wilfrid Sellars, "Science, Sense Impressions, and Sensa: A Reply to Cornman." *The Review of Metaphysics* 24, no. 3 (March 1971): 391–447.]

A11. Aune to Sellars, 3 September 1970

Dear Wilfrid,

Thanks for the letter of July 20. I was on vacation when it arrived, so I didn't get to it until recently. I wasn't convinced by your last remarks (see below) and I decided to write up a little paper putting all my doubts about your views on practical reasoning together. My thought was that I might produce a long study of you on practical reasoning for the planned Castañeda volume and I could include the material from this short paper as a section.* But I am not committed to the plan. The paper (which I enclose) is not intended for general circulation; I am mainly interested in your reaction. As you will see, my doubts about the *foundation* of your theory of practical reasoning are serious, but the further development of your theory is, I believe, unaffected by my criticisms.

Now about your letter. Your statement (5) is problematic. Surely if P implies Q, then it is false that P & ~Q. Hence, if I know that P implies Q, then I know that either P is false or Q is true. I do not, of course, know what the exact values of P and Q are (or at least I need not), but then the same may be true of my knowledge that P only materially implies Q.

Note that, strictly speaking, your (1) is false. If I know that P is true and Q is false, I know the truth-values of P and Q but I do *not* know that P materially implies Q since $\sim(P \supset Q)$. What you meant in laying down (1) was that if I know that P is false or Q is true, then I know that P materially implies Q. This claim is, of course, correct, but it doesn't cast doubt on anything I said in my last letter.

As I understand your letter, you are distinguishing your generic implication from material implication on the ground that while knowing that P is false or Q is true is sufficient for knowing that P materially implies Q, it is not sufficient for knowing that P generically implies Q. This strategy does, of course, distinguish the two kinds of implication in a weak sense, but it does not throw any light on the generic sense of implication which I knew full well would not be truth functional. The point of my last letter was that what you claimed to be necessary for P implies Q—namely, that one *could* reject the sequence P,~Q without knowing the exact truth-values of P and Q—is also necessary for P materially implies Q. The reason that this condition is necessary in both cases is that the knowledge of an implication, whether generic or only material, requires one to know that the sequence P,~Q is unacceptable.

Tell me what you think of the enclosed paper.

Best regards,
Bruce

P.S. I saw Herbert Feigl when I was in Minneapolis. His legs are bad, but he looks surprisingly good. We had a pleasant chat.

---

* [Eds.—Bruce Aune, "Sellars on Practical Reason," in *Action, Knowledge, and Reality: Critical Studies in Honor of Wilfrid Sellars*, ed. Hector-Neri Castañeda (Indianapolis: Bobbs-Merrill, 1975), 1–25.]

A12. Aune to Sellars, 28 April 1973*

Dear Wilfrid,

I told you some time ago that I would send you a copy of my chapter on the logic of practical reasoning, but I eventually ran into some snags, and now I think my strategy in that chapter was seriously wrong. I now have another chapter in my head, but I haven't had the time, energy, or perhaps courage to sit down and write it out. But this letter will give you some idea of what I now think about practical reasoning. I'd appreciate your reaction to it if you can spare the time.

1. Re your basic axiom

As you formulate it, the axiom merely allows the derivation of an S-conclusion from a single S-premiss. This follows from your claim that S-statements cannot be conjoined with other statements. Since you use 'implies' to mean the converse of 'is inferable from', we can reformulate the axiom as follows:

(A) S(C) is inferable from $S(P_1),\ldots,S(P_n)$ just in case C is inferable from $P_1,\ldots,P_n$

This reformulation does not in any way change the fundamental idea behind your axiom, for it still allows us to say that an inference from S-premisses to an S-conclusion is valid (or acceptable) just in case a corresponding inference from indicative premisses to an indicative conclusion is valid.

The question why we should accept this axiom still arises, however. It seems to me that we can answer this question by some obvious semantic considerations. These considerations show, incidentally, that the axiom need not be taken as a substantive logical principle: it may be derived as a meta-theorem.

To say, as you do, that an S-statement is neither true nor false is not to imply that such a statement has no semantic value. In fact, it would seem obvious that they do possess such a value. Since S-statements represent the content of intentions, and since we think of intentions as being realized or unrealized, we should be able to say that an S-statement has either the value R (for *realized*) or U (for *unrealized*). But these values have an obvious and systematic relation to the values T and F. In general:

       Val(S[P]) is R iff Val(P) is T
and Val(S[P]) is U iff Val(P) is F

---

* [Eds.—Bruce Aune has written the following at the top of the first page:
    I don't know if this letter was actually sent or not? Its first paragraph begins just the way my May 5, 1973 begins. So I doubt that I sent them both.—BA
We have included the 28 April letter, and not the 5 May letter, because the former (but not the latter) has a substantive elaboration of Aune's reasoning concerning Sellars's views.]

Now, what exactly can we mean by saying that an intention S(P) implies an intention S(Q)? We don't mean that if a man has the first intention he will have the second intention. What we do mean, I think, is that S(Q) will have the value R (ie be realized) whenever S(P) has the value R. Another, equivalent way of looking at the matter is this: S(P) implies S(Q) just in case anyone who intended S(P) would be inconsistent if he also intended S(~Q). More exactly:

(B) S(P) implies S(Q) iff the set [S(P),S(~Q)] is inconsistent.

Now, two intentions are inconsistent iff the states of affairs intended are inconsistent. That is,

(C) The set [S(P),S(~Q)] is inconsistent iff the set [P,~Q] is inconsistent.

Since the set [P,~Q] is inconsistent iff P implies Q, it follows from (B) & (C) that:

(D) S(P) implies S(Q) iff P implies Q.

Since the considerations I have just mentioned hold for implications with arbitrarily many premises, it follows that (A) is a meta-theorem, not a basic axiom.

We must now consider mixed inferences, those involving essentially both S-statements and indicatives. I think it is clear from the semantical treatment I have given your axiom that your talk of relative implication will not suffice to validate such inferences. The claim that S(P) implies S(Q) relative to R would then be equivalent to the claim that the set [P, ~Q] is inconsistent relative to R. But what can this latter claim mean, if not that the larger set [P, ~Q, R] is inconsistent? Yet this set is inconsistent just in case S(Q) is validly derivable from S(P) and R—and this last derivation is clearly not warranted by your axiom.

Suppose we accept your idea, which I have hitherto rejected, that "I *will* do A if P" has the form of "S(P ⊃ I shall do A)," where "shall" indicates mere futurity. It seems to me that the obvious strategy for validating the inference

S(P ⊃ I shall do A)
P
∴ S(I shall do A)

is to follow Hector and introduce a special "designated" value defined as follows:

$v(\emptyset) = 1$ iff either (a) $\emptyset$ is P & $v(P) = T$ or (b) $\emptyset$ is S(P) & $v[S(P)] = R$

We then modify the standard account of validity and say that an argument is valid in our mixed language iff any truth-value assignment (defined for the atomic statements of our language) that gives the premisses the value 1 also gives that value to the conclusion. This amounts to saying that an argument is valid just in case its conclusion is true-or-realized whenever its premisses are true-or-realized. It is obvious that this strategy validates the argument form given above: if the first premiss is true, then 'P ⊃ I shall do A' is true; and if P is true, it then follows that 'I shall do A' is true and 'S(I shall do A)' is realized.

This approach should be acceptable, formally speaking, if the approach I first suggested is acceptable. After all, the following is valid given your axiom:

S(P ⊃ I shall do A)
P
―――――――――
S(I shall do A)

But the second premiss here is realized just in case the indicative P is true. Hence, intuitively speaking, if the argument is valid, the corresponding argument with P in place of S(P) should also be valid.

A consequence of this approach, which I regarded as disastrous for some time, is that it validates the following inferences:

S(P)   P   S(P)
―――   ―――   P ⊃ Q
 P   S(P)   ―――
                         S(Q)

But these inferences now strike me as quite all right. The first one doesn't imply that every intention is true; it merely says that if an intention is realized, then the corresponding indicative (or belief) is true. The second is your so-be-it inference, which seems to me all right even when "P" affirms something within an agent's control. The key question to ask ourselves here is when, in general, an indicative would ever be inconsistent with an S-statement. If we think of S-statements as representing intentions and indicatives as representing beliefs, then such statements would be inconsistent (or a man would be inconsistent in affirming them) just in case the state of affairs he intends to obtain is inconsistent with what he believes to be true. Thus, if he intends that P be the case and yet believes that ~P, then he would be inconsistent. If this is right, however, then since the set [P,~P] is inconsistent, it follows that both [P, S(~P)] and [~P, S(P)] are inconsistent and thus S(P)/P and P/S(P) are valid. You yourself have said on many occasions that the intention to do A involves the belief that one will do A (see p. 175 of Hector's *Morality*... volume*), and when you remarked that the S-operator represents a "*manner* rather than a *content* of thought," you help make a case for both

---

* [Eds.—*Morality and the Language of Conduct.*]

inferences. If, however, you think that the so-be-it inference should be restricted to cases with* the corresponding indicative does not attribute to the agent some action within his power, it is worth considering how odd it would be to have the premiss that one would do something within one's power (ie think it is true) and yet actually intend that this *not* be the case. Yet if [P, S(~P)] is inconsistent for all P—and thus for ['I shall do A', 'I *won't* do A'], where the 'won't' is volitional—then we must accept P/S(P) is valid.

In my paper for the Sellars *Festschrift*† I claimed that it would be disastrous to allow as valid S(P), P ⊃ Q / S(Q) on the ground that an unfulfilled intention would commit an agent to all intentions and thus to incompatible intentions. But I was confused. If an agent has the premisses S(P) and P ⊃ Q, he should be entirely happy with the conclusion S(Q); and if he has S(P) and ~P, then, for the reasons I gave in the last paragraph, he would have inconsistent premisses and anything should quite properly follow. —Thus, from my present vantage point, all three of the problematic inferences I mentioned at the bottom of the previous page now seem quite all right.

If the three inferences I have just discussed are valid, then your axiom, whether in the original or the revised form, will not be adequate for all valid argument forms. But this should not be distressing, for (a) your axiom just drops out as a meta-theorem anyway, and (b) the idea behind your axiom holds good still—namely, the idea that an argument involving S-statements is valid just in case an argument in the logic of indicatives is valid. To find the appropriate argument in the logic of indicatives, just delete the S-operators from the argument being tested: the result is a purely indicative argument, and this argument is valid if and only if the original argument is valid. In other words, if this resulting argument is valid, then so is the original argument; if it is not valid, then the original argument isn't valid either. —Thus, we really don't need any *axiom* for practical inference; once we have an appropriate conception (or *definition*) of practical validity, we have everything we need for determining the validity of practical inferences: we can rely on ordinary logic.

But what about the objections I had in my *Festschrift* paper to your treatment of conditional intentions? The answer is that I don't think they are decisive. I still think "I *will* do A if P" is not synonymous with "S(P ⊃ I shall do A)", but they are close enough for logical purposes—in particular, they are as close as the English "If... then..." is to the technical "...⊃....." Thus, just as it is paradoxical (but harmless) to regard "P ⊃ Q" as true when P is false, so it is paradoxical (but harmless) to regard "I *will* do A if P" as realized when P is false. As for my

---

* [Eds.—Perhaps Aune intended to write "where" instead of "with"; this substitution makes the sentence more readable.]

† [Eds.—Bruce Aune, "Sellars on Practical Reason."]

transposition argument, I would now say that the intentions "I will do A if P" and "I won't do A if P" simply imply ~P—just as the intentions "I will do A if P" and "I will do A if ~P" imply "I will do A." These inferences go through without trouble on the semantical approach I recommend.

A13. Aune to Sellars, 9 June 1975

Dear Wilfrid,

Thanks for sending me a copy of your paper "Volitions Re-Affirmed."* It came just this morning, but I zipped through it and thought I would convey a couple of the thoughts it brought to mind.

Before trying to convey those thoughts, I want to say that the copying center here has just run off some copies of my new manuscript (book)† and that I'll put one in the mail for you today. On the whole, I am quite happy about it; I think it is far and away the best thing I have yet done in philosophy. (I hope I don't change my mind the day after tomorrow!) You will see that the book is pretty Sellarsian in all-over orientation; in particular, the theory of volition I propound and defend is pretty close to yours. I acknowledge my debt in footnotes, and I'll also say something in the preface. Actually, I haven't read your stuff on volition in a long time, but reading your new paper makes it obvious that I have internalized a lot of your thought on the subject. (Just so you don't misunderstand me, I might add that I always try to think things through for myself when I write and I don't like to have other philosophers' work too freshly in mind at the time of composition—unless, of course, I am writing about their work.) I hope you'll approve of what I say, at least in general outline.

Now about your new paper. I am happy with what you say about volition, but not too happy with the new stuff on practical reasoning: frankly, I like your earlier, simpler theory better. Here are some specific comments.

1. It seems to me that, for purposes of logical theory (which always involves a little regimentation), there is no need to distinguish intentions to do from intentions that p. On p. 13 you remark that "It shall be the case that p" is equivalent to "I shall do what I can to make it the case that p," but I find this equivalence doubtful. Consider the expression of intention "My son shall study this afternoon." It seems doubtful that this actually *entails* an assertion to the effect that I will *do* something (if...). And apart from this doubt, it is not clear exactly what the form of "I will do what I can to make it the case that p" is supposed to be. Surely, it is not "S[for all A, if I can do A and my doing A will bring it about that p, I shall do A." Obviously, I can anticipate alternative means of bringing it about that p, and I need not intend to realize all the alternatives.‡

If we think of "It shall be the case that John studies" as meaning merely "S(J will study)" and "I will do A" as meaning "S(I shall do A)," where the "S" operator

---

* [Eds.—VR, Ch. 10 of this volume. Aune's page-number references are to a prepublication draft. The Winnipeg Conference on Human Action, at which Sellars delivered VR, was held at Winnipeg, Manitoba, Canada, 9–11 May 1975.]

† [Eds.—Bruce Aune, *Reason and Action* (Dordrecht: Springer, 1977).]

‡ [Eds.—At the very end of this paragraph, at the bottom of the page, Sellars has written, "cf. relation of 'ought to be' to 'ought to do'."]

merely expresses a volitional attitude*, then the relation of "S(J will study)" to an intention concerning something I will do will depend on other practical premisses at my disposal. Thus, if I believe that J will study only if I (shall) do A†, then the premise "S(J will study)" will entitle me to conclude "S(I shall do A)." Thus, IF WE DON'T DISTINGUISH "SHALL DO" FROM "SHALL THAT," WE SHALL HAVE A SIMPLER, MORE NATURAL THEORY OF PRACTICAL INFERENCE. In other words, in our canonical system we have just one S-operator just as we have one sign of negation. In this way we can avoid the formula "Shall [I to do A at t]."

2. Re your remark at the top of p. 16.‡ Though I have argued in my book (& in my Sellars paper) that the S-operator is not really necessary, it is certainly OK as an explicit indicator that a formula expresses a volitional attitude. Thus, I myself don't think there is anything "crude" (as you put it) about the assimilation of "I shall do A" and "Shall be [I will do A]." But what about Hector's point that our "future actions" enter our reasonings sometimes as actions to be done and sometimes as actions it is hypothesized that I will do? The point is sound, but it has no implications (as far as I can see) about the *logic*—the formal logic—of practical reasoning. Even if, as I hold, "S(P)" is logically equivalent to "P," it doesn't follow that "S(P)" and "P" are not *different formulas* and that a person could not affirm one without actually affirming the other. As far as the "ethics of volition" (as one might call it) is concerned, my view of the semantics of volitional discourse simply stipulates that one is logically *entitled* to express a *volitional attitude* toward anything one believes will be the case; one is not actually *required* to do so, however. —But there is no need to elaborate this point; I took it up in my recent letter to Hector, a copy of which I sent you a couple days ago (or was it a week or so ago?).§

I guess my main general worry about the more complex system you now favor is that its semantical underpinnings are unclear. I am not always convinced that semantical considerations are crucial, but in practical inference the appropriate semantical values bear so heavily on the acceptability of various patterns of

---

* [Eds.—Sellars has underlined the passage "merely expresses a volitional attitude" and written the following in the margin:

    but the volitional attitude = thinking
        'Shall [I to do A now]'
        'Shall [I will do A now]'

Sellars also underlined "expresses a volitional attitude" and "volitional attitude" in the subsequent paragraph.]

† [Eds.—Sellars underlined the sentence up to this point, and wrote the following in the margin:

    Yes, but 'Shall be' involves some commitment to 'Shall do' even where we have no specific action in mind.]

‡ [Eds.—The reference seems to be to §38 of VR.]

§ [Eds.—Bruce Aune to Hector-Neri Castañeda, 31 May 1975; enclosure of Aune to Sellars, 2 June 1975. We have not included the 2 June letter as its contents are primarily social in nature, and Aune does not address philosophical issues in it.]

inference that we have to come to terms with them. Since your original system (its spirit if not its actual formulation) allows us to collapse everything into truth and truth preservation, it has a great deal to commend it even though it requires some regimenting of practical discourse. I hope the remarks in my revised MS are at least tempting.

All the best,
Bruce

PS: I saw a copy of the Sellars *Festschrift*, though my copy was never forwarded to me out here. It's a splendid volume, which I look forward to reading. I enjoyed your autobiographical remarks, which I did manage to look over.*

---

* [Eds.—AR.]

S14. Sellars to Aune, 23 June 1975

Dear Bruce:

Thanks for the two letters* and for the handsome manuscript which has just arrived. I had intended to wait until you had a chance to get re-settled in Amherst before I began bugging you, but I cannot refrain from sending a few disjointed comments to show how interested I am in getting a dialogue going.

I don't think I am as far away from my "earlier simpler theory" as you take me to be. I am just trying to fit it into a larger context which places less stress on inferences, and more on the place of practical reasoning in a theory of persons as agents. But you will be the best judge of that after I wrestle with a few of your probing questions.

Let me begin by noting that in your letter to Hector of May 31, 1975 you write (p. 3):

> ... let me emphasize again that, although I regard "I will do A" and "I shall do A" as semantically or formally indistinguishable, I do not think (or claim) that they are indistinguishable *tout court*. Their difference is logically unimportant but practically very important. Not only do utterances of "I will do A" express attitudes that are not expressed by utterances of "I shall do A," but thoughts of the form [sic] "I will do A" have important causal properties that thoughts of the form "I shall do A" do not have.

I put in the 'sic' to call attention to the conceptual tension involved in saying that formally indistinguishable utterances have different forms. You will reply, of course, that different senses of 'form' are involved in these two contexts. But would that not be to grant that there is more than a 'practical' and 'causal' difference between 'I will do A' and 'I shall do A'? I suspect that the old issue as to what is to count as a 'logical' principle is lurking in the underbrush. Is the difference between 'I will do A' and 'I shall do A' a difference in 'logical' form? When is a difference in form a 'logical' difference? Are all differences in 'conceptual' power differences in 'logical' powers? (Similar considerations relate to the term 'semantical.') To point up these tentative queries, I note that on p. 1 of your letter to Hector you say that 'P and Q' and 'P although Q' have the same logical form. I don't object to this. I share your taste for keeping the terms 'logic' and 'logical form' on a tight leash. I *would*, however, object if you went on to say that the difference between these two statements is merely 'practical' and 'causal,' i.e.

---

* [Eds.—Sellars is referencing—in addition to *A13*—a letter from Aune dated 2 June 1975. We have not included that letter as its contents are primarily social in nature, and Aune does not address philosophical issues in it.]

that there is no interesting sense of 'form' in which the difference is a formal one, or sense of 'logical' in which the difference is a logical one.

Perhaps, from a strictly *logical* point of view one captures the logic of 'Shall [I to do A]' by identifying it with 'Shall [I will do A]'[1]. From this point of view,

Shall [if I will do A, I not to do B]
So, shall [if I will do B, I not to do A]

coincides with (cannot be distinguished from)

Shall [if I will do A, I will not do B]
So, shall [if I will do B, I will not do A]

Another way of putting this might be to say that from a strictly logical point of view 'I to do A' occurs amid logical connectives only as a corrupt version of 'I will do A.'

Yet there might be a conceptual difference between the two expressions which is to be explicated along the lines suggested in "Volitions Re-Affirmed." The difference (relating to the role of the So-be-it principle) might be called 'dialectical' rather than 'logical.'

But enough of this background painting! Let me turn to specifics. On p. 2 of your letter to me [Eds.—A13 §2] you write:

> Though I have argued...that the S-operator is not really necessary, it is certainly OK as an explicit indicator that a formula expresses a volitional attitude.

I suspect that here is the crux. I think of a 'volitional attitude' in terms of tokening or having propensities to token expressions having a constituent with the conceptual powers of an S-operator. To be sure, these conceptual powers *include* the causal power of 'S [I to do A now],' but they are not exhausted by it. Thus from my point of view, to attempt to explain the S-operator in terms of an independently specifiable 'volitional attitude' is somewhat like trying to explain 'not' in terms of an independently specifiable 'attitude' of negation.

The above has a direct tie-in with your doubts about my emphasis on the distinction between intentions to do and intentions that something be the case. My views on the importance of this distinction developed from brooding about Kant's argument for the existence of God: (roughly)

---

[1] I am, of course, using my idiolect in which 'will' is simply the future declarative.

Virtue ought always to be rewarded. So, it can be the case that virtue is always rewarded. Only if God exists can it be the case that virtue is always rewarded. Therefore, God exists.

The fallacy is exposed by unpacking the first premise as 'If any agent(s) is (are) in a position to bring it about that virtue is always rewarded, he (they) ought to do so.' This unpacking of 'ought to be' in terms of 'ought to do' blocks Kant's simplistic use of the 'ought implies can' principle. But this unpacking surely requires a corresponding unpacking of 'shall be' in terms of 'shall do' (i.e. *anglice* 'will do'). This I have always believed, though I have never paid enough attention to spelling it out.

It is, undoubtedly, an oversimplification to say that 'It shall be the case that-p' is equivalent to 'I shall do what I can to make it the case that-p.' Yet this account is, I believe, on the right track, even though it hasn't gone very far. Is it an analysis? That would be too strong a claim; but the truth it contains must be grounded in an analysis of the relevant concepts—which I shall attempt to sketch below. For the moment I shall simply express my conviction that there is a very strong conceptual tie between intending that something be the case and intending to do something, i.e., that

> Jones intends that-p but has no intention to *do* anything (not 'anything *specific*,' '*anything*')

is conceptually incoherent.

Clearly the putative analysans must be construed as somehow involving a *ceteris paribus* clause. Yet this is the most trivial aspect of the problem, for it merely points up the fact that insofar as one is rational, one is prepared to take new information into account and even to allow for the possibility of simply changing one's mind. I quite agree that it would be irrational to intend to do *all* of a number of as yet unspecified actions *each* of which would *ensure* its being the case that-p.[2] Why keep a dog and bark yourself? So we don't want

> Shall be [p]

to imply (in the desired sense)

> Shall [(A)(t) I do A at t ensures p → I to do A at t].*

---

[2] As usual one abstracts from considerations of probability. I tried to develop a strategy for taking probability into account in the concluding section of "Induction as Vindication." [Eds.—IV.]

* [Eds.—Revised from "Shall [(A)(t) I do A at t ensures p → I to do A at A at t]".]

Well, why not

> Shall [(∃A)(∃t) I do A at t ensures p → I to do A at t]?

Suppose I accept 'It shall be the case that-p'. I discover that by doing A_1 (which I abhor) at t_1, I can ensure that-p. Unless I am really dedicated to its being the case that-p, I will ponder

> Shall be [α and p and I do A_1 at t_1]?
> Shall be [α and not-p and I not do A_1 at t_1]?

and choose

> Shall be [α and not-p and I not do A_1 at t_1]

Notice, however, that since it was not stipulated that my doing A_1 at t_1 was *necessary* to its being the case that-p (but only that it was *sufficient*), I can still intend that-p

> Shall be [α' and p]

where the background constituent represented by 'α'' now includes 'I do not do A_1 at t_1.' According to the putative analysis, we would have

> Shall [α' and ((∃A)(∃t) I do A at t ensures p → I do A at t)]

It is time to give a little more cash in support of the claim that we are on the trail of an *analysis*. Surely we need a distinction between those intention-constituents which get into a scenario through So-be-it, and those which are regarded by the agent as up to him and not yet decided. Remember that even if it has been decided that something will be the case—a fact—it still gets into a scenario—into the scope of an S-operator—by virtue of being relevant to a choice between alternative scenarios, thus

> Shall [α and p and I bring about X]?
> Shall [α and p and I bring about not-X]?

We would expect surface grammar to reflect these distinctions. When I stress the difference between

> Shall [I will do A]

and

   Shall [I to do A]

my concern is to capture the way in which the *surface* grammar of practical sentences reflects connections which are *conceptual*, though not in your sense *logical*.

It should be clear by now that from my point of view the fundamental unit of intending is the scenario. As a first (and crude) approximation I give it the form

   I shall* bring it about that [...]³

All 'shall be's and 'shall* do's are to be construed as abstractions from this matrix. And if we construe 'I shall* bring it about that [...]' as 'I shall* do what I can to bring it about that [...]', then, while

   Shall be [p]

is not *itself* to be analyzed as

   I shall* do what I can to bring it about that-p

it presupposes that 'p' is a constituent of the scenario having the form

   I shall* bring it about that [... and p ...]

Only if 'p' is up to the agent does the latter imply

   I shall* do what I can to bring it about that-p

Even if 'p' is not up to the agent, however, it implies the weaker

   Shall be [p].

Notice that it is because this cumbersome shall-operator

   I shall* bring it about that ...

---

³ From now on, 'shall' with an asterisk will represent the English 'will.'

takes declarative sentences (atomic, molecular, quantified) in its scope, that one is motivated to introduce indicators to reflect the surface grammar distinctions which appear in ordinary language pertaining to intentions. This explains why I wrestled with 'targets' in my paper on "Contrary-to-Duty Imperatives."

If all this is not completely misguided, I can withdraw my claim that 'It shall be the case that-p' is equivalent to 'I shall* do what I can to make it the case that-p,' while preserving the intuition which led me to make it. Perhaps the best thing to do is to stress the importance of the clause *'what I can.'* For if the agent believes that 'p' is not up to him *a fortiori* he believes that there is nothing he *can* do to make it the case that-p and the equivalence collapses. The general point that intentions differ from wishes ('shall' from 'would') by virtue of the fact that 'Jones intends that-p' implies 'Jones thinks it possible that-p' ('Jones does not think it impossible that-p'?) is a relevant consideration here.

But what, then, are we to say from the standpoint of the logic (in the strict, Aune, sense) of intentions about the suggested equivalence between

Shall [p]

and

Shall [($\exists$A)($\exists$t) I do A at t ensures p $\to$ I do A at t]

I see no reason to abandon it. It preserves at the hard core level the connection between intending that-p and intending to do what one can to ensure its being the case that-p, if that-p is up to one. Of course, if it turns out that that-p is up to one, say, by doing A_1, one may decide to pass up the opportunity. But, then, as you rightly stress in your letter to Hector, logic never forces us to take a volitional attitude towards any state of affairs, not even

Shall [p or not-p]   So-be-it!

As ever,
Wilfrid

A15. Aune to Sellars, 7 July 1975

Dear Wilfrid,

Thanks for the long, interesting letter. I have had the letter on my desk for a few days now, but I have not yet been sufficiently unwound from the long trip back to Amherst to do anything about it until today.

I am embarrassed by my careless use of 'form' in my letter to Hector. My thought was that statements having the *surface* form, or structure, of "I shall do A" and "I will do A" have the same *logical* form. In this respect pairs of such statements are analogous to the pair "A & B" and "A although B."

I am afraid that I was not sufficiently explicit when I said that "I will do A" expresses a volitional attitude not expressed by typical uses of 'I shall do A.' My view is that 'I will do A' and 'I shall do A' express the same propositional attitude but 'I will do A' expresses (or discloses) a propensity to make certain movements (if A is a minimal action) or to draw some conclusion that is, intuitively speaking, closer to action. This latter propensity (to move or, if necessary, infer) is what I had in mind in speaking of a volitional attitude.

If 'I will do A' and 'I shall do A' have the same logical powers (in the narrow sense), then they have the same logical form: that is, they are logically indistinguishable even though they express (disclose, give vent to) different propensities to act. My reasons for holding that 'I will do A' and 'I shall do A' have the same logical powers are indicated in my Sellars *Festschrift* paper and also in my manuscript: the key point is that 'S(p)' seems both to imply and be implied by 'p'. It seems to me that Hector has in no way cast serious doubt on the validity of this two-way implication.

I am still not convinced that we need a distinction between 'Shall be' and 'Shall do' for purposes of formal logic. If a person has a propensity to engage in practical reasoning, then if he has a premiss 'S(p)' that does not immediately move him to act, he will have the propensity to derive a statement that does move him to act if he has available a premise that relates 'p' to an appropriate action statement. Thus, if he has the premise 'p only if I shall do A,' he will naturally be moved to conclude 'S(I shall do A)' or 'I *will* do A.' Thus, the connection you see between 'shall be' and 'shall do' is not for me, a logical one but a consequence of a learned propensity.

I turn now to the equivalence you suggest between 'S(p)' and 'S($\exists$A)($\exists$t)(I do A at t ensures p only if I do A at t).' One reason for rejecting this equivalence as logically true is that, although *not* everyone is entitled to affirm 'S(p)' [for a given p], everyone is, in fact, entitled to assert or affirm the longer formula. The reason is that every person no doubt intends to do something or other at some time or other, and thus is entitled to the premise 'Shall [($\exists$A)($\exists$t)(I do A at t)].' But this premise *logically* implies 'Shall [($\exists$A)($\exists$t)(I do A at t ensures p only if I do A at t)].' This is shown by the fact that '($\exists$A)($\exists$t)(I do A at t)' implies '($\exists$A)($\exists$t)[I do A at t *or* not-(I do A at t ensures p)].'* I am, of course, assuming here that the dagger or 'only if' in your formula is a material conditional. You could dispute this point, but I think you will agree that we should try to get along with the material conditional if we can possibly do so.

A point worth emphasizing here is that we can account perfectly well for inferences from 'shall be' premises to 'shall do' conclusions without introducing any special axioms, definitions, or meaning postulates that relate 'shall be's to 'shall do's. As I see it, this is the principal advantage to my approach. Both of us can agree that the following sequences are unobjectionable:

S[p]   S[p]
p only if I do A   I do A only if p
S[I do A]   I do B only if p
               S[I do A] or S[I do B]?
               S[I do A]!

I would, of course, want to say that 'S[I do A]' is elliptical for 'S[I shall do A].' But if I can account for valid practical inferences with only one S-operator and with, in effect, only one axiom—namely, Sp iff p—then my approach has a lot to recommend it. This axiom is an obvious truth if, as I contend, the volitional 'It shall be the case that p' amounts to no more than '*It will be the case that p*,' where the italics indicate merely a volitional 'manner' of assertion that does not modify the 'content' of what is asserted.

Well, tell me what you think of this. I shall not try to comment on the Kantian argument you mentioned because it introduces complications about the logical form of 'ought' statements. My approach to these statements is given in the penultimate section of the manuscript I sent you. I will say, though, that I do not think the Kantian argument requires us to introduce an important distinction between 'shall be' and 'shall do.'

A final remark. The main thing that troubles me about your recent approach to the logic of S-statements is its complexity and the obscurity of its semantical foundations. If the 'shall be' is not *defined* by reference to the 'shall do,' then you will have *two* undefined S-operators in your system (this is my worry about complexity). The worry about semantical foundations is not trivial (or so I believe) because it seems to me that my basic controversy with Hector, Binkley, and you can be boiled down to a controversy about the appropriate semantical values of S-statements and about how these values are related to truth.

---

* [Eds.—We have made small revisions to these formulae, correcting bracket- and parenthesis-related errors in the original. On the back of page 1 of Aune's letter, Sellars has formally reconstructed the argument Aune is suggesting here. We have included this hand-written reconstruction as an appendix to this letter.]

It was only in writing the last version of my contribution* to the Sellars *Festschrift* that I became fully convinced of the crucial importance of the basic semantical issue, and this conviction has been strengthened a hundredfold in my discussions with Binkley and Hector.

Since returning to Amherst, I have had the opportunity to examine the Sellars *Festschrift*. Even though I am one of the contributors, I think it is a fine volume—a fitting tribute to you as a teacher and philosophical writer. I particularly enjoyed the autobiographical remarks you contributed.† For better or worse, we all become interested in the lives of the people we admire, and a great many people will no doubt be fascinated by the view you disclose of the man behind the complicated books and essays. (I must say, though, that I think the difficulty of your later writing is highly overrated: most of it strikes me as clear, straightforward, and remarkably elegant.)

All the best,
Bruce

---

* [Eds.—Bruce Aune, "Sellars on Practical Reason."]   † [Eds.—AR.]

A15+. Appendix to A15

[Eds.—Sellars wrote the following proofs on the back of page 1 of *A15*. As the proofs are too lengthy to place in a footnote, we have decided to include them as an appendix to *A15*.]

1. (∃A)(∃t) I do A at t   premise
2. (∃A)(∃t) I do A at t → (∃A)(∃t) I do A at t or not [I do A at t ensures p]   Log
3. (∃A)(∃t) I do A at t or not [I do A at t ensures p]   1, 2, MP
4. (∃A)(∃t) I do A at t ensures p → I do A at t   3, logic (def '→')
5. ⊢{(∃A)(∃t) I do A at t → [(∃A)(∃t) I do A at t ensures p → I do A at t]}   1-4, Condit.

'Shall [(∃A)(∃t) I do A at t]' implies 'Shall [(∃A)(∃t) I do A at t ensures p → I do A at t]'

Compare

cf   1. α   premise
       2. α ⊃ (α ∨ ~β)   Logic
       3. α ⊃ (β ⊃ α)   def '⊃'
       4. β ⊃ α   1, 3 MP
       5. ⊢[α ⊃ (β ⊃ α)]   1-4, conditionalization
       'α' implies 'β ⊃ α'
       'Shall [α]' implies 'Shall [β ⊃ α]'

S16. Sellars to Aune, 30 April 1979

Dear Bruce:

I hope that you understood my 'one page' remark. I did *not* say that I could refute your theory of practical reasoning in one page—rather that I could refute a certain criticism you made of *my* theory (in your Pitt volume essay)* in one page. It was only after you left and I was pondering the intensity of your reaction that I realized that you might have misinterpreted me.

+ + +

The point as I see it, is simple. You claim that my principle

P1.   'S(α)' implies 'S(β)' $\equiv$ 'α' implies 'β'

generates such relative implications as

$(p \supset q) \vdash^{S(p)} q$

Well, let's see!

The concept of relative implication is defined by the schema

Def. I F_i implies F_k relative to F_j $\equiv$ F_i and F_j imply F_k

(where the 'F's represent formulas which are either indicative or resolutive). Consider now,

P2.   'S(α)' and 'S(β)' imply 'S(γ)' $\equiv$ 'α' and 'β' imply 'γ'

which is the generalization of P1 for the case of two premises. How are we to connect this principle with relative implication? In the first place, the following (P3) is a consequence of P2 and Def. I.

P3.   'S(α)' implies 'S(γ)' relative to 'S(β)' $\equiv$ 'α' implies 'γ' relative to 'β'

---

* [Eds.—Bruce Aune, "Sellars on Practical Inference," in *The Philosophy of Wilfrid Sellars: Queries and Extensions*, ed. Joseph C. Pitt (Dordrecht: D. Reidel, 1978), 19–24. Sellars implies that Aune's criticism (discussed below) is from this volume; as Aune notes in A17, he actually makes this criticism of Sellars in Aune (1977). For why Aune thinks the below criticism raises difficulties for Sellars's account of practical reasoning, see our summary of the Aune-Sellars correspondence in the Introduction to this volume.]

But I clearly need something more than P3 to get my

$$S(p \supset q) \vdash^P S(q)$$

Furthermore, you need something more to get what you wish to hang on me, namely

$$p \supset q \vdash^{S(p)} q$$

In point of fact, what *you* need is

'S(α)' implies 'S(γ)' relative to 'S(β)' ≡ 'α' implies 'γ' relative to 'S(β)'

I take it, then, that you are attributing to me the following principle of relative implication

P4. 'S(α)' implies 'S(γ)' relative to F_i ≡ 'α' implies 'γ' relative to F_i

where the occurrences of F_i are either *both* indicative or *both* resolutive.
  But while I accept

P5. 'S(α)' implies 'S(γ)' relative to F_{IND} ≡ 'α' implies 'γ' relative to F_{IND}

I reject

P6. 'S(α)' implies 'S(γ)' relative to F_{RES} ≡ 'α' implies 'γ' relative to F_{RES}

And it is only if P6 is granted that the validity of

$S(p)$
$S(p \supset q)$
$\therefore S(q)$

generates

$$p \supset q \vdash^{S(p)} q$$

Of course, you can say that when I argued that relative implication is a *genuine form of implication* (i.e., one which authorizes inferences), after laying down the principle that

'S(P)' implies 'S(Q)' ≡ 'P' implies 'Q'

I was implicitly granting that

'S(P)' implies-relative-to-F_{RES} 'S(Q)' ≡ 'P' implies-relative-to-F_{RES} 'Q'

To this I can only reply that a generous interpretation of the text would have attributed to me the view that

'S(P)' implies-relative-to-F_{IND} 'S(Q)' ≡ 'P' implies-relative-to-F_{IND} 'Q'

for this was what I needed to make my point about hypothetical imperatives. To attribute the former was gratuitous. After all, whereas I hold that

'S(P)' implies 'S(Q)' ≡ 'P' implies 'Q'

in which indicatives and resolutives appear symmetrically, I also hold that

'S(P)' implies 'S(Q)' *because* 'P' implies 'Q'

in which they do not. It is the *explanatory primacy* of indicative implication which underlies my theory of practical reasoning.

As ever,
Wilfrid Sellars

A17. Aune to Sellars, 15 May 1979

Dear Wilfrid,

Thanks for your letter of April 30, which arrived just a few days ago. I didn't realize that my response to your remark was intense, but I was surprised by your remark and I did think that it concerned my theory of practical reasoning, not just one of the criticisms I made of your theory. I also thought, perhaps mistakenly, that your mood was unusually aggressive that evening, and I wondered if I had unwittingly said or written something that offended you. However that may be, I want you to know that you are one of the few people I genuinely like and admire, and my occasional disagreements with your views do not indicate disrespect. I have felt for some time that one of the worst things that can happen to a philosopher is to become convinced that some other philosopher has all the answers, for the only thing to do then is to close up shop and become either a historian or an expositor. Since I want to keep working at philosophy, I have to assume that you don't have all the answers, though I also have to admit that you have a good many of them.

But enough of this personal stuff. As far as the content of your remark is concerned, I can make two unshakeable counter-claims right away: the criticism of your theory that you attack in your letter did not occur in the Pitt volume, and your criticism took nearly four pages rather than one.

The criticism by me to which you refer occurred in a footnote in my *Reason and Action**—specifically, fn. 8 on page 194.† (It also occurred in a footnote in Hector's volume.‡) I think you can reasonably object to that criticism, but the strategy for eluding it given in your letter does not get you entirely out of the woods.

Let me begin by explaining the strategy of my criticism. I was attacking your claim that, given your original axiom, we may move from

(1) $p \supset q$ implies q (relative to p)

---

* [Eds.—Bruce Aune, *Reason and Action*, Philosophical Studies Series in Philosophy, Vol. 9 (Dordrecht, Holland: D. Reidel, 1977).]

† [Eds.—The note in question reads as follows:

The derivations for these forms follow the same strategy as Sellars's derivation. The derivations for I and II are based on the premiss that, since 'P' and 'P ⊃ Q' imply 'Q', then 'S(P)' and 'S(P ⊃ Q)' imply 'S(Q)'. We can therefore say that 'S(P ⊃ Q)' implies 'S(Q)' relative to 'S(P)'. From this we infer that 'P ⊃ Q' implies 'Q' relative to 'S(P)', which validates form I. To validate form II we use the premiss above to conclude that 'S(P)' implies 'S(Q)' relative to 'S(P ⊃ Q)' and then to conclude that 'P' implies 'Q' relative to 'S(P ⊃ Q)'. To validate form III we simply note that 'P' implies 'Q' relative to 'P ⊃ Q' and then infer that 'S(P)' implies 'S(Q)' relative to 'P ⊃ Q'.]

‡ [Eds.—Bruce Aune, "Sellars on Practical Reason," p. 15 n. 8. Note 8 is word-for-word identical to the footnote in *Reason and Action* just cited by Aune and reproduced in the previous editors' note.]

to

(2) S(p ⊃ q) implies S(q) (relative to p).

I assumed that you regarded this move as formally correct, and I supposed that you were tacitly employing a principle of Interchange of Equivalents. Since "p ⊃ q implies q" and "S(p ⊃ q) implies S(q)" are strongly equivalent according to your fundamental principle, (2) would follow from (1) by the application of the Interchange principle.* Also, since your fundamental principle is wholly symmetrical, (1) would also follow from (2) by an application of the principle. To deduce the consequences I obtained, I simply used the interchange principle to derive various formulas containing S-statements in the relative-clause. I think the supposition I made was entirely natural in the circumstances, and I don't think there was anything uncharitable about it. Of course, if you reject the supposition, you can reasonably reject the consequences I derived from it.

As I mentioned above, this means of avoiding the consequences I derived from your fundamental principle does not get you entirely out of the woods. The reason is that, if you do not employ the Interchange principle, you have to come up with a justification for the move from (1) to (2). It won't do to argue that the Interchange principle can be applied to contexts like (1) and (2) but not to contexts in which an S-statement occurs in the rel-clause. The fundamental reason for this (as I see it now) is simply that the Interchange Principle cannot validly be applied to the main formula in a relative implication statement. The difficulty is connected with the failure of exportation in implication-statements or in conditionals with modal connectives. As you point out, "p implies q (rel r)" just means that the conjunction of p and r implies q, and this latter assertion does not even contain "p implies q" as a sub-formula. As far as I can see, (2) is, in fact, not validly derivable from (1); I can think of no valid principle that could take one from (1) to (2). Thus, although I will concede that my attempt to derive what you regard as unacceptable consequences from a relative-implication statement that you accept is objectionable, I also think that the notion of relative implication provides no support for your theory of practical reasoning.

I reread my Pitt paper† in preparing this letter, and I can say that my remarks in that paper give a pretty good summary of my objections to your current account of practical reasoning, though they do not include the things I said about the consistency of "I will do A" and "I shall not do A" in Reason and Action. When I read the paper you recently sent me on practical reasoning, I couldn't see that

---

* [Eds.—Aune is inconsistent about how he capitalizes (or doesn't capitalize) "Interchange Principle" throughout his letter. We have left things as is and have not tried to impose consistency.]
† [Eds.—Bruce Aune, "Sellars on Practical Inference."]

you dealt with the objections I raised in my Pitt paper or in my *Reason and Action*. Essentially what you did, in the relevant parts of that paper, was to reformulate the general lines of your view and to add some remarks, directed at my position (not my objections), on the logical character of such operators as "It was the case that...." Thus, I really didn't have anything to say in reply. I will grant, for example, that "It was the case..." is a logical operator, a logical constant, but this doesn't commit me to anything, one way or the other, about the S-operator.

For what it is worth, I might add that I do not regard the objections I gave to your theory as clear-cut refutations of it. What I think I have done is to point to a number of difficulties with your theory and to offer an alternative account that lacks the difficulties and yet does justice to your claim that practical logic (to the extent there is such a thing) is entirely derivative from ordinary indicative logic. My nonsystem is internally consistent and has a clear-cut semantical interpretation. The obvious place to attack it is to attack the semantical interpretation. Hector has offered what he takes to be counter-instances to my theory, these being arguments that he would not acknowledge to be valid. But he has another semantical interpretation up his sleeve, one that I have given my objections to in my *Reason and Action*.

I guess I don't have anything more to say about practical inference. I have been reading your *Naturalism and Ontology* with a good deal of interest, and I will probably discuss it with Cynthia Freeland if she gets a copy. If any useful thoughts occur to me, I'll send them on to you.

It was a real pleasure seeing you in New Haven and in hearing your talk on Kant. I may be giving a seminar on the *Critique of Pure Reason* next year.

All the best,
Bruce

A18. Aune to Sellars, 9 June 1979

Dear Wilfrid,

In my last letter to you I claimed that a key principle you use in connection with your concept of dependent implication is, as I now see it, invalid, but I was too lazy to think up a counter-instance to that principle. Lying in bed this morning, I decided to think up a counter-instance, and the following occurred to me.

The objectionable principle is this: If p implies q rel to r and p implies q implies and is implied by (IIB) s implies t, then s implies t rel to r.

Here's a counter-example.

Let   r = x is a male (M)
        p = x is unmarried (U)
        q = x is a bachelor (B)
        s = x is unmarried (U)
        t = x is a spinster.

Given this interpretation, the following appears to be true, though both p implies q and s implies t are false:

(K): p implies q IIB s implies t.

But while it is true that p implies q rel r (i.e. p & r implies q), it is false that s implies t rel r (i.e. s & r implies t). QED.

The kicker here is the principle (K), according to which being unmarried implies being a bachelor iff being unmarried implies being a spinster. It seems to me that this principle is clearly true, though I have no way of proving it. The key to constructing a counter-example for *your* principle is, in any case, this: find interpretations of p implies q and s implies t according to which both formulas are false and yet imply one another, where the conjunction of p and r nevertheless implies q. I think that (K) does the trick, but here is another possibility if you are not convinced. Let x and y be positive integers. Then the following is true:

$x^2 = y$ and $y < 2$ implies $x^2 = 1$.

But for an arbitrary positive integer w, it seems true that

($y < 2$ implies $x^2 = 1$) implies & is implied by ($w < 2$ implies $x^2 = 1$).

Yet it is not true that

$x^2 = y$ & $w < 2$ implies $x^2 = 1$.

If neither of these counter-instances convinces you, I am sure that I can find others. There is something tricky about them, for we have to find two false formulas that imply one another, and the notion of implication is somewhat obscure. Nevertheless, to go back to my last example, it seems obvious that, for arbitrary x and y, we can assert and deny that $y < 2$ implies $x^2 = 1$ just when we can assert and deny that, for an arbitrary w, $w < 2$ implies $x^2 = 1$. The same for the kicker in my first example: we can assert and deny that being unmarried is sufficient for being a bachelor just when we can assert and deny that being unmarried is sufficient for being a spinster. So I think both of my counter-examples are OK.

Tell me what you think.

All the best,
Bruce

S19. Sellars to Aune, 3 July 1979

Dear Bruce:

Thank you for the friendly opening paragraph of your letter.* The episode at the Fogelins'† was, I believe, a case of misperception all around.[1] I was exhilarated by having my first lecture—always the most difficult—behind me. I can easily see why my mood seemed aggressive. It was certainly expansive—and the line between expansion and aggression is notoriously difficult to draw. Since one is at least as responsible for the appearance one presents as for the reality, my sincere apology.

You have long been one of the very few on whom I can count for understanding criticism. You are at home—if not always comfortably—in the dialectic, and can quickly spot questionable moves. This is why, in the few cases in which you have not convinced me, I keep on trying to convince you.

The current exchange is a case in point. I don't think I am flogging a dead horse, if I attempt at least a partial rebuttal. Thus I most certainly did not "tacitly" appeal to "a principle of Interchange of Equivalents" in order to get from

(1) $p \supset q$ implies q (relative to p)

to

(2) $S(p \supset q)$ implies $S(q)$ (relative to p).

I quite agree that the following argument is invalid,

$p \supset q$ implies q (relative to p)
[$p \supset q$ implies q] implies and is implied by (IIB) [$l \supset m$ implies m]
therefore, $l \supset m$ implies m (relative to p)

What I actually did was set up what you refer to as the 'fundamental principle'

P implies Q IIB S(P) implies S(Q)

and interpret the two occurrences of 'implies' as a *generic* term for relations which authorize inference. I claimed that 'logical implication,' 'nomological implication' and 'implication on an hypothesis' are *species* of this relation. (A check on what I wrote in "Thought and Action" and *Science and Metaphysics* will confirm this.)

Thus, as I saw it,

---

* [Eds.—The references in this letter (including the below reference to "a principle of Interchange of Equivalents") seem to be to *A17*.]

† [Eds.—Robert and Florence Fogelin.]

$p \supset q$ *implies-relative-to-p* q IIB $S(p \supset q)$ *implies-relative-to-p* $S(q)$

is simply a special *case* of the fundamental principle rather than something to be established by a combination of the fundamental principle and "a principle of Interchange of Equivalents." There may be—indeed undoubtedly are—problems about the moves I made. But they are not open to your counter-example.

What, then, of the idea that *implies-relative-to-p* is an inference authorizing relation? Obviously,

$$(p \supset q) \supset q$$

does not hold in all possible worlds involving p and q. It would be an obvious howler to argue

If p, then, *necessarily*, $(p \supset q) \supset q$
p
Therefore, *it is necessary that* $(p \supset q) \supset q$

The major premise is true; the conclusion, however, false.

On the other hand,

$$(p \supset q) \supset q$$

does hold in all possible worlds *in which p holds*.[1] Does it not make sense to say

Given that-p (or on the hypothesis that-p), $p \supset q$ implies q

where this means

Given that-p, *one may infer* q from $p \supset q$?

The reasoning

If p, one may infer q from $p \supset q$
p
Therefore, one may infer q from $p \supset q$

involves, indeed, a detaching of

---

[1] It is worth reflecting that the fundamental intuitions involved in the concept of implication relative to an hypothesis are captured by the role of subordinate proofs in systems of natural deduction (e.g. Fitch). [Eds.—Original reads "...implication relation to an hypothesis...."]

...one may infer q from p ⊃ q

But this detaching does not involve a commitment to the *unconditionality* of this permissible inference. That is to say, it does not involve a commitment to

p ⊃ q logically implies q

Compare,

If p, it is permissible to interrupt
p
Therefore, it is permissible to interrupt

This also involves a detaching of the conclusion

...it is permissible to interrupt

but it does not involve a commitment to

It is unconditionally permissible to interrupt

Compare, also,

If one has promised to do A, one is under an obligation to do A
Jones has promised to do A
Therefore, Jones is under an obligation to do A

Obligations are essentially tied to grounds, but this does not mean that obligation statements have to specify their grounds.

Jones is under an obligation to do A

is, in an important sense, a complete statement. Yet it is, by virtue of the conceptual grammar of obligation talk, *defeasible*. It raises the question 'Why?' Appropriate replies are

Because he promised to do A.
Aune said he ought to, so there must be some reason.
On reflection, I see that I was mistaken. There is no reason why Jones is under an obligation to do A. I withdraw the assertion.

Similarly,

> One may infer q from p ⊃ q

is complete, but defeasible. In particular, one can reply to the question 'Why?'

> Because: p and in all possible worlds in which p is the case, q is the case if p ⊃ q is the case.

Of course, the statement

> One is logically entitled to infer q from p ⊃ q

where this means

> One is, *as a mere matter of logic*, entitled to infer q from p ⊃ q

is false. But only by confusion can one conclude that

> One is entitled to infer q from p ⊃ q

is false.

* * *

I should, perhaps, have made it more explicit that

> α *implies-relative-to-*γ β

has the same sense as

> If γ, then α *would* imply β

i.e., to put it in terms of inference,

> If γ, then one *would* be entitled to infer β from α.

It is this which underlies the reasoning

> p ⊃ q implies-relative-to-p q
> p
> Therefore, p ⊃ q implies q

Once again, the conclusion of this argument does not have the sense of p ⊃ q logically implies q

i.e.,

□[(p ⊃ q) ⊃ q]

and the argument does not commit the fallacy of exportation.

* * *

To turn to the bearing of the preceding on the logic of conditional intentions, consider the following sequence

1. p   Hyp.
2. S(p ⊃ q)   Hyp.
3. p · p ⊃ q implies q   Logic
4. p ⊃ q implies-relative-to-p q   Rel. Imp.
5. p ⊃ q implies q   1, 4, Rel. Imp. → Imp.
6. S(p ⊃ q) implies S(q)   5, Fund. Prin.
7. S(q)   2, 6, M.P.

Compare it with

1. p   Hyp.
2. S(p ⊃ q)   Hyp.
3. S(p)   1, So-be-it
4. S[p · (p ⊃ q)]   2, 3, C.I. [Shall]
5. p · (p ⊃ q) implies q   Logic
6. S[p(p ⊃ q)] implies S(q)   Fund. Prin.
7. S(q)   4, 6, M.P.

As far as I can see, these arguments are conceptually equivalent. In each case one is led to consider possible worlds in which p obtains, and, therefore, possible scenarios (intention structures) in the content of which p is a conjunct. And this is done in terms of a conceptual grammar of beliefs and intentions which brings them together without admitting

p *and* Shall(p ⊃ q)

into the depth grammar, i.e., without doing violence to the scope-ishness of the shall operator.

* * *

The reference to the scope-ishness of the shall operator reminds me of your comment on my animadversions on tense logic in "On Reasoning About Values." You write,

> ... what you did ... was to reformulate the general lines of your view and to add some remarks directed at my position (not my objections), on the logical character of such operators as "It was the case that..." Thus I really didn't have anything to say in reply. I will grant, for example, that "It was the case that..." is a logical operator, a logical constant, but this doesn't commit me to anything, one way or the other, about the S-operator.

But my point wasn't that tense locutions are logical operators or logical constants (they aren't!). It was rather that tense locutions have a "logic" or "conceptual grammar" which is not reducible to principles of the propositional and functional calculi. This conceptual grammar can be presented in terms of a system of implications. Thus I was comparing the implications involved in the meaning of 'shall' to the implications involved in the meaning of tense locutions, e.g.

'S is P (at t)' implies 'It will always be the case that S was P (at t)'

Thus, in the passage to which you referred I wasn't attacking your position, at least directly, but, rather, highlighting what I regard as one of the strengths of my own position, i.e., the fact that it does have something specific to say about the *conceptual role* of 'shall'/'will'. I have always stressed that just as the characteristic expressions of language entry transitions involve both world→word connections and intra-linguistic word→word connections (inference patterns), so the characteristic expression of language departure transitions involves both word→world connections and inference patterns.

There is, I take it, no disagreement in principle between us that the role of 'shall' and its cousins can be described in causal terms. Furthermore, I would not regard it as incorrect to emphasize, as you do, that the *distinctive* feature of intentions is their causal role in bringing about actions. But I would immediately want to add, as you do not, that the causal role of expressions of intention is not limited to this word→world role—(a) they are causally involved in specific inference patterns; (b) these specific inference patterns are *distinctive* moments in the distinctiveness of the framework of intentions.

But perhaps I have misunderstood you. In any event, I hope that my pressing of this point will help us clear away a persistent source of polemical exchanges on what must surely be, in the last analysis, peripheral issues.

You write,

What I think I have done is to point to a number of difficulties in your theory and to offer an alternative account that lacks the difficulties and yet does justice to your claim that practical logic (to the extent that there is such a thing) is entirely derivative from ordinary indicative logic. My nonsystem [own system?] is internally consistent and has a clear-cut semantical interpretation. The obvious place to attack it is to attack the semantical interpretation...

I hope that the opening paragraphs of this letter have clarified my strategy for dealing with the difficulties you have raised with my theory. Furthermore, since we agree that "practical logic (to the extent that there is such a thing) is entirely derivative from ordinary indicative logic," I would expect to find no disagreement with respect to the semantical interpretation of valid argument forms relating scenarios to scenarios. If the general thrust of this letter is correct, such differences as there are between us concern not 'practical logic' in this narrow sense, with respect to which semantical interpretation is decisive, but rather the conceptual grammar of resolutive locutions. From my point of view, practical logic in the narrow sense is *embedded* in this conceptual grammar, and its formulations, to be philosophically perspicuous, must reflect the depth grammar of resolutives, and, in particular, the scope-ishness with respect to which you and Hector have lined up against me from the start.

Have, as they say, a good summer,
Wilfrid

P.S. I enclose a Xerox of my previous letter in which typos in the arrow formulae have been corrected.

A20. Aune to Sellars, 18 July 1979

Dear Wilfrid,

Many thanks for your letter of July 3. I am a little slow to answer because my mind has been focused on the new book I am writing, on metaphysics,* and it has been hard for me to think seriously about another matter. Also, as Russell in effect said once, basic philosophical problems are so difficult that one is doing very well if one can manage to think hard about one of them for even a few moments each year. Thinking *hard* about practical reasoning is not something I can manage to do every day.

Your last letter clarifies your position very well. I was aware that you thought of the "implies" in your FP as a generic one, but I thought it had enough of a modal force to fall prey to the counterexample I constructed (or some formally analogous one). I now have no difficulty with your use of relative implications—as I say, your recent letter was very helpful—but I think that your use of it still raises problems for your general theory, for it allows one to validate argument forms that you probably wouldn't want to accept as valid.

Consider the following argument; call it Argument A:†

1. P implies-rel-to-(P ⊃ Q) Q.
2. S(P) implies-rel-to-(P ⊃ Q) S(Q).   1, FP
3. Therefore, S(P) and (P ⊃ Q) jointly imply S(Q).   2, Def I (Apr 30 letter)

Now consider Argument B:

1. P and (P ⊃ Q) together imply Q
2. S(P) and S(P ⊃ Q) together imply S(Q)   1, FP as generalized in your [ORAV,] p. 21

Now consider Argument C:

1. S(P)   Ass.
2. ~P   Ass.
3. S(~P)   So-Be-It
4. S(P & ~P)   1, 3, C.I. (Shall)
5. Therefore, S(P) implies P.   Reductio, 1, 2.

---

* [Eds.—Bruce Aune, *Metaphysics: The Elements* (Minneapolis: University of Minnesota Press, 1985).]

† [Eds.—In the original letter, no instance of "P ⊃ Q" in Argument A is enclosed in parentheses. For greater clarity, we have enclosed all three instances.]

Since 4 here is the practical counterpart to a contradiction, we must, I think, regard 1 and 2 as inconsistent, which means that 1 implies 2. It seems to me that this argument for the principle of resignation, to use Binkley's term, is every bit as good as the So-Be-It principle*, for the latter involves the same idea.†

If Argument C is valid, so is the argument D:

P and S(P ⊃ Q) jointly imply Q.   in *Reason and Action*‡

In fact, all the argument forms I declared to be valid on your principle turn out to be valid even though no use is made of the principle of implication relative to an S-statement. But if all these argument forms are valid, there is, as I claimed in my book, no logical or formal difference between S(P) and P and the S-operator is mere decoration, logically. (It may, of course, have a very significant nonlogical role to play.)

An extra point: Note that the inference from S(P) to P should be held to be valid on the ground that S(P & ~P) implies any S-statement at all.§

There is another matter I want to say something about, DSTs.¶ I have been writing about propositions during the past week, and I have had to come to terms with the problems that arise for the strategy (at least the general strategy) that you and I both favor. It just occurred to me that a problem that Gettier raised when we were at Pittsburgh has a pretty obvious solution. I had, in effect, advanced the claim that P is a true statement just when anyone who says that p would speak truly. He countered by focusing attention on a special case of my claim, roughly:

> "There are statements" is true iff anyone who says that there are statements speaks truly.

His objection was that although the LHS of the equivalence is clearly contingent, the RHS is necessary, which undermines the special case and therefore the more general position. Although it didn't occur to me at the time, there is an obvious strategy to counter his objection—roughly, an appeal to a type distinction. To avoid paradox while accepting standard logical principles, we must avoid explicit self-reference at least in cases where truth or falsity is being affirmed. Consequently, a given statement can affirm something only of lower-order

---

  * [Eds.—In the margin next to this paragraph, Sellars has written, "as the argument for the So-be-it principle?" He seems to be suggesting a correction to Aune's "as the So-Be-It principle".]
  † [Eds.—Here, Aune has written in the margin, "ie, the inconsistency of P and S(~P) or ~P and S(P)".]
  ‡ [Eds.—Bruce Aune, *Reason and Action*.]
  § [Eds.—At the end of this paragraph, Sellars has written in the margin, "remember—I don't explain the soundness of So-be-it in terms of preservation of semantic value."]
  ¶ [Eds.—A DST (distributive singular term) is a term that applies to or is true of all tokens or individuals in a class. For example, "The lion is tawny," has the surface grammar of a sentence about a single lion, but the subject term ("the lion") is a DST; hence, the statement is really making a claim about all lions.]

statements. To make appropriate sense of Ed's example, we should then have to formulate it somewhat as follows:

> "There are statements$_1$,"$_2$ is true iff anyone who says$_2$ that there are statements$_1$ speaks truly$_2$ (ie makes a true second-order remark).

Since the speaker's statement is a second-order statement about first-order statements, the fact that he makes the second-order statement does not imply that his statement is true. If there were no first-order statements (ie tokens) then his second-order assertion would be false.

I realize, of course, that the basic claim you want to make—namely,

> The •PROP• is true $=_{df}$ all •PROPS•s are true

does not actually imply the special case Ed criticized, though you might want to defend a version of it on other grounds, e.g. in distinguishing statements from beliefs. But it is good to note that Ed's objection is no good at all.

Here is another matter. I have been reading over your letter to Loux (April 6). On p. 207 you lay down a principle to deal with the problem of (roughly) nonexistent tokens. (I keep saying "roughly" because I don't want to make all the necessary qualifications.) The principle is:

> The s_i is (normatively) the same as [the?] s_j iff s_i and s_j are pure rule-bound sortals and every rule matrix which holds of s_i holds of s_j* and vice versa.

The difficulty I have with your strategy here is that I cannot see how it avoids the crucial problem. To take the example you give on p. 208, suppose that there are no •rapid•s or •quick•s but also no •slow•s. Let M be a variable for rule matrices. As far as I can see, the following is true:

> $(x)(y)(M)(x$ is a •quick• and y is a •slow• $\supset (M)(M$ holds of x iff M holds of $y))$

Given that there are no •quick•s and no •slow•s, the assertion is vacuously satisfied. How do you avoid this difficulty?

I have been thinking about the problem of nonexistent tokens along different lines. I am strongly inclined to say that eg

> the •snow is white• is true $=_{df}$ (t)(if t were a •snow is white•, t would be true)

---

* [Eds.—Aune has underlined "s_i holds of s_j" and written in the margin:
   ?
   or s_i's and s_j's]

This kind of analysis (or suggestion) is more promising than it may appear. For some years now philosophers and logicians have written as if subjunctive conditionals always have some lawlike force, but this is clearly wrong. If a friend were standing in front of me right now, I could truly say "If you were to turn your head around 180° and look straight ahead, you would, in point of fact, see a bookshelf." The idea is that, given the actual state of the person's environment, if he did turn around, then he would, as a matter of fact, see a bookshelf. It is possible, empirically, that turning his head around would cause him to go blind, but this possibility will not, in fact, be actualized. So my counterfactual assertion is contingently true.

I am very strongly tempted to say the following:

1. (t)(if t were a •snow is white•, t would (in point of fact) be true).
2. (t)(if t were a •2+2 = 4•, then t would (of mathematical necessity) be true).

I realize that, to avoid logical nonsense, one must be very careful about the range of the relevant variables here. If "•grass is green•" were a meaningful substituend for 't,' we should probably have nonsense:

If •grass is green• were a •snow is white•, ...

On the other hand, if we quantified over mere inscriptions or noises, we could avoid this kind of problem.

I say I am "tempted" to say the above because I am not sure that I want to say it. I am not clear enough about the relevant logic. The horseshoe strikes me as too weak to deal satisfactorily with the relevant contexts, but modal conditionals strike me as too strong. Do you think (*if* you have trouble dealing with the matter I brought up at the end of my last page) that the metaphysical considerations favoring extensional logic may be ill-served by the material conditional?

Let me know what you think. I have been writing a lot of stuff, but I am not sure whether it is any good. Still, writing keeps the demons of boredom & depression at arm's reach, at least.

All the best,
Bruce

24

Sellars to Solomon, 28 June 1976*

Dear David:

Here are some considerations which may dispel some of the more puzzling features of my views on logically sharable intentions and the moral point of view.

1. Distinguish, of course, between

'We shall do A'

and

'We intend to do A'

2. Take into account the familiar (but much neglected) distinctions between, on the one hand,

A_1: predicates which ascribe 'mental states' to groups (e.g. Russia fears China)

and

A_2: predicates which ascribe mental states to individuals;

and, on the other hand, between

B_1: group actions

and

---

* [Eds.—W. David Solomon. This letter is most likely Sellars's response to an early draft of Solomon's "Ethical Theory," in *The Synoptic Vision: Essays on the Philosophy of Wilfrid Sellars*, eds. C. F. Delaney, Michael J. Loux, Gary Gutting, and W. David Solomon (Notre Dame: University of Notre Dame Press, 1977), 149–88. See also Solomon's "Sellars' Defense of Altruism," in *The Philosophy of Wilfrid Sellars: Queries and Extensions*, ed. Joseph C. Pitt (Dordrecht: D. Reidel, 1978), 25–39. The latter volume derives from a workshop on the philosophy of Wilfrid Sellars held at Virginia Polytechnic Institute and State University in November 1976.]

B_2: individual actions.

3. Thus,

'We intend to do A'

doesn't (because of these possible ambiguities) formally entail

'I intend to do A.'

4. And, by virtue of the A-distinction,

'We (as a group) intend that Jones fly a kite'

doesn't entail

'I intend that Jones fly a kite.'

5. While, by virtue of the B-distinction,

'We intend to disperse'

doesn't entail

'I intend to disperse.'

6. Again, also by virtue of the B-distinction

'We shall do A'

doesn't formally entail

'I shall do A.'

Thus,

'We shall disperse'

doesn't entail

'I shall disperse.'

7. On the other hand

> 'We shall disperse'

will have *some* implications (*which* will depend on the circumstances) of the form

> 'I shall do A.'

Thus, at the very minimum, it implies

> 'I shall not impede the dispersal.'

8. I am now in a position to make the first positive point, which is that

> 'We shall do A'

has the logical *intersubjectivity* which you correctly point out I was looking for. It *permits* different people to have, in a strong sense, the *same* intention.

9. Notice that

> 'We shall do A'

need not, as some critics have supposed, be 'chorused.' It is a form of practical thought which can go on *in foro interno*. *I* can think in terms of *we*. In this sense it is a 'form of life.'

10. Obviously people need not agree in their logically intersubjective intentions. The point is that they *can* literally agree.

11. Coming closer to the target, we must distinguish between

> 'We shall (as a group) do A (e.g. disperse)'

and

> 'We shall (each of us, individually) do A (e.g. fly a kite).'

12. Clearing away one last possibility of confusion,

> 'Shall [any of us do A, if C]'

is not, as such, the expression of a *logically intersubjective* intention. It can still represent the 'personal point of view'—even though it contains a reference to *any of us*. Consider

'Shall [any of us scratch my back, if it itches].'

13. Notice, however, that the latter does, according to my theory of practical reasoning, entail

'Shall [I scratch my back, if it itches].'

14. Now to hit the target. The moral point of view involves the form

'*We* shall any of *us* do A, if C,'

which entails

'I shall do A, if C.'

To flag its *origin* (or *ground*) in a logically intersubjective intention, I represent the latter as

'Shall$_{we}$ [I do A, if C].'

15. The fundamental intention characterizing the moral point of view has the form

'*We* shall any of *us* do that which (in his/her circumstances) promotes (maximizes) *our* common good.'

16. I have argued that such an intention can be construed as 'categorically valid' because sharing such an intention defines what it is to be members of a community.

17. Obviously there can be a 'nesting' of communities. The community involved in a '*moral* point of view' is what I have called the 'embracing community,'* i.e. that which is taken by those involved in a moral dialogue to be the inclusive *we* to which an intersubjective intention of the above (15) pertains.

---

* [Eds.—Sellars uses this language in §39 of OMP and §112 of PSIM.]

18. Accordingly, the case of conflict between the moral point of view and the personal point of view which I describe in "this I, he or it (the thing) which thinks..."* involves the alternatives of affirming *either*

'Shall$_{we}$ [I do A] (because the circumstances are C)'

as derived from the categorically valid† intersubjective intention

'We shall any of us do that which (in his or her circumstances) maximizes our general welfare (common good)'

with the addition of factual premises believed true;

or

'Shall$_I$ [I do B] (because the circumstances are C),'

as derived from

'Shall$_I$ [I do that which promotes my happiness]'

where the I-flagging indicates that this intention is not, in turn, derived from a logically intersubjective intention.

- - - - -

This is all tersely put and certainly leaves a lot of ground uncovered. But it will, I hope, clarify what I have been up to in wrestling with moral philosophy. You have done an excellent job of tracing the dialectical structure of my thinking on these topics. You have been particularly successful in grasping what I was up to in 'IILO.'‡ My only *caveat* is that that paper stems from the 50's, and that more of its weaknesses than you seem to allow were corrected (I believe) in the less involuted papers which followed.

Cordially,
Wilfrid Sellars

---

* [Eds.—I: Wilfrid Sellars, "...this I or he or it (the thing) which thinks...," in *Proceedings and Addresses of the American Philosophical Association* 44 (1970-71): 5-31. Sellars delivered this paper as his presidential address at the meeting of the Eastern Division of the American Philosophical Association in Philadelphia on December 28, 1970.]

† [Eds.—The word "valid" is missing in the original.]   ‡ [Eds.—IIOR, Ch. 14 of this volume.]

Index

ability to do 316
aboutness 61, 70, 241
action reduction principle 559
actions
    agents and 33
    causation and 237
    circumstance and 660-61
    contrary-to-duty imperatives and 422
    in Davidson 258
    events and 263
    group 503
    intentions as scenario for 524
    knowledge and 360
    minimal 29, 194, 238-40, 273, 309, 659-60, 662, 664, 669, 671
    moral obligations and 149
    moral principles and 115
    in Taylor 239
    volitions and 140, 193, 240, 272
    volitions vs. 32, 140
    voluntary 306-7
"Actions and Events" (Sellars) 29-30, 248-69
"Actions, Reasons, and Causes" (Davidson) 258
adverbial theory 231-32
adverbial theory of objects of sensation 231-32
agency 25-31
    causation and 242
    indicatives and 556-57
    non- 320
    rational 41
agent causation 342, 345
Aikin, Scott F. 2-3
akrasia 31-36
altruism 16
andness 226
Anscombe, G. E. M. 621
anthropology 97, 99
arguing 377-78
Aristotelianism 220-22, 368
Aristotle 118, 134, 221, 240, 271-72, 333-35, 340
artifacts 122
ascription 42, 55, 83-84, 93, 108, 147-48, 179-80, 281, 667
association, inference vs. 29, 254
assumption, implication relative to 43. *See also* relative implication

atomism 347
attitudes, emotions vs. 111
Aune, Bruce 7, 19, 43, 521, 659-731
Aune-Sellars correspondence 51-54
Austin, John 255, 285, 319, 577, 621, 634, 636, 647-48
"Autobiographical Reflections" (Sellars) 66
autobiographical reports 36, 76, 147, 209, 281, 374, 410-11, 472
autonomy 131, 510
axiom schema 400
Ayer, A. J. 6, 17, 36, 110-12, 604, 616

Baier, Kurt ix, 510, 570
becoming 118
behaviorism 13, 64-65, 70-71, 255, 257, 262
beliefs 144-45, 207-10
    conclusions and 287
    conditional 565
    in declarative sentences 479-80
    intentions and 26-27
    knowledge vs. 353
    occurrent 271
    self-love and 539
    what is implied by belief vs. what is implied by having belief 473
benevolence 22, 24, 38, 168, 172, 181, 183, 186, 416-17
Bergmann, Gustav 222, 225
Binkley, Robert 345-47, 634-35
Binkley-Sellars correspondence 48-49, 615-35
Blanshard, Brand 248, 249, 251, 260, 262
Brandom, Robert 1-2
Bratman, Michael 6
Broad, C. D. 32-33, 186, 330-32, 340-41
Butler, Joseph 96, 115, 222

Castañeda, Hector-Neri ix, 31, 42-43, 275-76, 278-79, 286, 345, 347, 369, 419, 516, 520-24, 530, 532, 620, 629, 636-58, 676, 678
Castañeda-Sellars correspondence 49-51
categorical imperatives 8, 20, 163, 186-87
    as derivative general conditional intentions 9, 21-22, 163
categorical reasonableness 23, 169, 171-73, 175, 177-78, 495, 507-8, 655, 657

causal implications 477
causality. *See also* scientific determinism
    agent 342, 345
    in Aristotle 333–34, 340
    change and 253
    compulsion and 33, 306–7
    free will and 293
    interventionist 236, 253–54
    normativity and 46
    in Pepper 293
    predictability and 294
    volition and 338, 344, 346
causal reducibility 12–14
causation, compulsion and 33
charity 10, 96, 115
Chisholm, Roderick 38, 334–35, 339–40, 421–22, 424–25, 439, 461, 616, 640
circumstance factors 440, 442
citizenship 17–18
Clark, Romane 267–68, 633
coherence 90–92, 95, 468, 551
collectivism 54–55
Collingwood, R. G. 293
commands 371–73, 419, 636
community 3, 13, 25–26, 35, 93–94, 109–10, 735
compatibilism 31
compulsion 33, 306–7, 319, 321
"Concepts as Involving Laws and Inconceivable without Them" (Sellars) 481
conditional belief 565
conditional intention 41–43, 171, 286, 513, 518–21, 523–24, 528–29, 539–41, 548, 564–65, 567–68
conditional obligation 39–40, 43
conditional promise 514, 518–19, 521–22, 611
"Conditional Promises and Conditional Intentions" (Sellars) ix, 41–43, 511–34
conjunction introduction 44, 480–83, 485, 488–89, 550
conjunctive intention 485, 517
consciousness 75–76, 78, 97, 411–13, 666–67, 672
consequentialism 37
contents, of intentions
    belief 145
    beliefs in 483
    implying other contents of intentions 276
    inferential relations among 19
    as intendables 485
    intensions vs. 651
    logically equivalent 43
    logic of 42
contrary-to-duty imperatives
    actions and 422

convention 122–23, 127, 129–30
copying errors xi–xii
corrections, to text xi
correspondence ix, 45–55, 570–736
"Counterfactuals, Dispositions, and the Causal Modalities" (Sellars) 11, 248, 626
craft 18, 121–22, 126–27, 130–31, 133
craftsmanship 122, 126, 135
criteriological ethics 100
Critique of Practical Reason, The (Kant) 186
culture
    moral consciousness of 97
    moral principles and 98–99

Dach, Stephanie 4, 36–37, 41
Davidson, Donald 258–60
decision procedure 9
decisions, volitions vs. 140
deontic detachment 39
deontic logic 36–43, 142–43, 421, 424
derivable intention 43, 540
derivative general conditional intentions. *See* categorical imperatives
derivative intention 149, 173, 540
descriptive properties 108–9
desire 200–204, 470, 537, 542
detachment, factual vs. deontic 39
determinism. *See* causality; scientific determinism
"Determinism and Freedom: Sellars and the Reconciliationist Theory" (Donagan) 32
deVries, Willem 1–2, 15
distributive singular term (DST) 226–27
doing, enjoying and 204–7
Donagan, Alan 10, 32–34, 319, 322, 324–25, 327–33, 335–36, 340–41, 343–44, 347, 349–50
DST. *See* distributive singular term (DST)
dualism 13, 27, 71, 220–21. *See also* Mind-Body Dualism; Mind-Body problem
Ducasse, Curt John 70
duty 186

egocentricity 19–20, 23, 41, 150, 155, 174–76, 276, 418, 537. *See also* intention(s), as egocentric
egoism, rational 21–22, 40, 496, 506–7
emotions
    attitudes vs. 111
    feelings vs. 111
emotivism 6, 14, 110–11, 572–73, 578–80
empiricism 17, 103–5, 142–43, 411–12
"Empiricism and the Philosophy of Mind" (Sellars) ix, 299

enjoying 204–7
entailment 30, 46, 241, 248, 251–52, 256–57, 331–32, 512, 515, 580–81, 583, 642
enthymemes 63
epiphenomenalism 71
epistemic predictability and determinism 294
errors xi–xii
ethical naturalism 63, 65
events
  actions and 263
  defined 263
  as species of proposition 30
existence 61
exportation, principle of 381, 653, 657–58, 676, 678, 717, 725
expressivism 16–17
extensionalism 71–72
externalism 354

factual detachment 39
"Fatalism and Determinism" (Sellars) 10, 31–32, 66, 293–318
feelings, emotions vs. 111
Feigl, Herbert 113, 664
formalism 22, 456, 543, 556, 621
formal logic 119
"Form and Content in Ethical Theory" (Sellars) ix
form of life 3, 413, 734
Forms 117–20, 135–37
  Form of 136
founding intentions 25–26
Frankena, William 353, 357, 617
Fraught with Ought: Writings from Wilfrid Sellars on Mind, Meaning, and Metaphysics (O'Shea, Ranaee, and Seiberth, eds.) 1
free will 31–36, 52, 293, 329–30, 343, 350
Fundamental Principles of the Metaphysics of Morals (Kant) 186

Geach, Peter 299, 629
generalization principle 167
Gentle Murder Paradox 38
genuineness of intention-expressions 412–13. *See also* sincerity
Gödel, Kurt 294
good
  community and 109–10
  in emotivism 110
  Forms and 119–20, 136–37
  intentions and 55
  necessity vs. 492
  "ought" and 490
  in Plato 17
  as property 107–8, 110

Gorgias 133
Grapes of Wrath, The (Steinbeck) 3
Grice, Paul 615
"group mind," 411–12

habit 33, 67–69, 134, 325–27, 338
Hampton, Jean 40
Hare, John 45–48, 153, 192, 369, 371, 383, 615–16, 642
Hare, R. M. 36
Hare-Sellars correspondence 45–48, 570–614
Hegel, Georg Friedrich Wilhelm 11, 25–26, 119
historical law 300, 322–23
Hobbes, Thomas 88, 538
"-hood," 226
Hume, David 18, 31, 293–95, 319, 654
hypothetical imperatives 155, 166–67, 169–70, 172–74, 183, 386–87, 568, 655
hypothetical intentions 568
hypothetical necessity 664–65
hypotheticodeductive method 98

identity 222, 225
impartiality 75
imperative inference 63, 286, 638–41
imperatives
  argument 377
  assenting to 575
  categorical 8, 20, 163, 186–87
  contrary-to-duty 421–64
  defined 192
  force of 375
  in Hare 47
  hypothetical 155, 166–67, 169–70, 172–74, 183, 386–87, 568, 655
  logic of 370–85, 551
  meaning of, knowing 577
  moral principles as universal 388
  "ought" and 371, 373, 574, 581–83
  "oughts" as 340, 591–93
  "oughts" entailing 338–40, 593
  "oughts" vs. 124, 589–90
  performative use of 647
  in practical reasoning 192
  as prescriptives 46, 579–81
  resolutives vs. 604
  universality and 370–85
"Imperatives, Intentions, and the Logic of 'Ought'" (Sellars) 36–38, 44–45, 47–48, 50, 55, 66, 367–420, 625, 676
"In Any Event: Davidson's Analysis of the Logical Form of Action Sentences" (Clark) 267
inclination 611
incoherence 551

indicative mood 638–39
indifference 199, 281
individualism 54
"Induction as Vindication" (Sellars) 18, 248
inference 63, 286, 340, 343, 381, 398–99, 477, 526, 624–25, 627, 632, 637–41
  among intentions 6, 19
  association vs. 29, 254
  deontic 38
  empiricism and 142–43
  intentional 51
  moral judgments and 5
  "ought" and 44–45
  practical 11–12
"Inference and Meaning" (Sellars) 46, 570
inferential role semantics 3
instrumentalism 347–48
instrumentalities 18, 122, 126, 134, 492
intelligibility 18, 119–22, 135–36, 294, 298
intending-as-one-of-us 412–13
  so-be-it$_{SB}$ vs. so-be-it$_{SM}$ 558–59
intending out loud 374
intention(s)
  belief and 26–27, 207–10
  categorically valid 735
  categorical reasonableness and 23
  conditional 41–43, 171, 286, 513, 518–21, 523–24, 529, 539–41, 548, 564–65, 567–68, 625, 698–99, 725
  conjunction introduction and 550
  conjunctive 485, 517
  derivable 43, 540
  derivative 149, 173, 540
  desire and 202
  as egocentric 19–20, 23, 41, 150, 155, 174–76, 180–81, 276
  expression of vs. ascription of oneself to 54–55, 179–80, 209
  expressions of 270–71
  formalism and 543
  founding 25–26
  group 503
  having intention vs. 473
  hypothetical 568
  "I" and 276
  intersubjectivity and 178, 184–86
  intrinsically reasonable 8–10, 21, 24–26, 40, 43–44, 173, 495–96, 507
  in Kant 186
  logically intersubjective 735
  logic of 7, 36–43, 51–52, 141, 195–97, 279–80, 386–408, 476–77, 516, 520, 529–30, 542, 652–54, 708, 725
  moral judgment and 4, 19, 22, 36, 66, 148, 196

  moral principles and 627
  motivation and 46
  "ought" and 113, 170, 654
  in practical reason 36–44, 141–43, 216, 279, 547
  preference and 543–44
  proposition vs. 524
  reasonableness of 168–70, 172–73
  reasoning among 40, 49 (See also intention(s), logic of)
  representation of 483
  same 149–50
  as scenario for action 524
  "shall" and 142–43, 149, 153, 191–92, 194, 261, 270, 277, 373–75, 521
  singular 539
  so-be-it principle 31, 39, 42, 44, 283, 471, 481, 483–84, 516, 524, 547
  state-of-affairs 500–501
  as states vs. intention-contents 144, 651
  targets of 483
  telling of 286, 375, 384
  telling vs. expression 63
  that someone else do something 145
  that something be the case 23, 145, 174
  in "Thought and Action," 191–97
  universality and 409–18
  validity and 159, 170
  volition and 27–29, 141
  volitions as 276–77
  we-referential action 505–6, 508–10
intentional inference 51
intentionalism 6
intentionality 61
Interchange of Equivalents principle 54, 717, 721–22
internalism 35, 353–54, 356–57, 361, 363, 411–12
intersubjectivity 7–9, 18–26, 61, 139, 151, 175, 178, 184–86, 412–13
  objectivity and 24
  "ought" and 19–20, 22, 24
  practical reasoning and 23
In the Space of Reasons (Scharp and Brandom, eds.) 1–3
intuitionism 6, 103, 368–69, 572, 577–78, 587–88
"is," "ought" and 62
I "...this I or he or it...," ix, 24–25, 275n8, 736
"-ity," 226

Jackson, Reginald 634
Jørgensen, Andrew 646
justice, in Plato 359

justification
  of moral principles 114
  motivation vs. 46
justified command 636

Kant, Immanuel 10–11, 18, 22, 24–28, 70,
    120–21, 168–69, 173, 182–83, 185–87, 220,
    236, 243–47, 296, 416–17, 568
knowledge
  actions and 360
  belief vs. 116, 353, 359
  double 672
  externalism and 354
  "I" and 245
  as instrumentality 134
  internalism and 35
  language and 68
  moral "ought" and 92
  moral principles and scientific 80
  in Plato 126–27, 134–36, 357–60
  "representing mind as substance," 244–45
  self- 139, 301–2
  values and 103
  virtue as 357–58
Korsgaard, Christine 40

Language of Morals, The (Hare) 44–45, 47, 371
"Language, Rules, and Behavior" (Sellars) ix, 29
Language, Truth and Logic (Ayer) 6, 110
law-like statements 142–43, 156, 626
letters, ix. *See also* correspondence
libertarianism 33, 293, 320–21, 327, 329, 341,
    346–47, 350
life plan 538–39
logical notation x
logical predictability 294
logical reducibility 12
logic of imperatives 370–85, 551
logic of intentions 36–43, 52, 386–408, 516,
    529–30, 654
logic of practical reason 511, 547
love 10, 16, 96, 115, 621. *See also* self-love
loyalty 10, 96, 115

Mackie, J. L. 14
Malcolm, Norman 635
manifest image 33, 246, 296–98, 348–50
marginalia x
Massey, Gerald 510
material implication 285, 400–401
materialism 61
McDowell, John 17, 30–31
meaning-talk 11
Melden, Abraham 241, 259–60

mentalistic discourse 69
Metaphysical Elements of Ethics (Kant) 185–86
"Metaphysics and the Concept of a Person"
    (Sellars) 27–29, 220–47, 335
microparticles 28
Mill, John Stuart 31, 293–95, 319
"Mind, Meaning, and Behavior" (Sellars) 12–15,
    61–72
Mind-Body Dualism 64–65. *See also* dualism
Mind-Body problem 12–13, 62–63, 65–66
monism 61
Moore, G. E. 17, 105–10, 203, 319
Moore's paradox 472, 717, 721–22
moral consciousness 75–76, 78, 97, 413, 417
moral "form of life," 3
moral judgment(s)
  actions and 8, 347–48
  as cognitive 5
  decision procedure for 9
  imperatives and 47, 604–5, 609
  as intentions 4–5, 7, 30
  intersubjectivity and 7
  in intuitionism 6
  justification of 100
  meaning and 14
  nominalism and 14–15
  in "Obligation and Motivation," 14–15
  positive concern in 17
  vindicatory explanation and 17
moral point of view 12–26
moral principles 15–16, 49
  as abstractions 81
  anthropology and 97
  competing 101
  consequences and 168
  culture and 98–99
  inference and 627
  intentions and 627
  justification of 114
  language and 101
  logic and 100
  love of mankind and 621
  as objective 82
  prudential principles vs. 418
  scientific knowledge and 80–96, 100
  standard account of 80–81
  as universal imperatives 388
  in utilitarianism 168
moral psychology 26–31
Morrison, Don 510
motivation
  empirical psychology and 578
  goodness of 363
  impartiality and 75

motivation (*cont.*)
  intention and 46
  internalism and 356
  intuitionism and 577–78
  justification *vs.* 46
  obligation and 571
  "ought" and 77, 345, 368
  prescriptives and 45
  reasoning and 35, 344

Nagel, Ernest 29, 248, 249, 251–53, 260, 262
naturalism 63, 65, 236, 369, 414, 419, 672
nature 122, 127, 247, 296
necessity(ies)
  causation and 248, 319
  goods *vs.* 492
  hypothetical 664–65
  inference and 251
  physical 664–65
  psychological 493–94
  relative 308, 664–65
neo-Aristotelianism 368
"-ness," 226
neutral monism 61
nominalism 11, 14–15, 18
non-cognitivism 110
non-descriptive properties 108–9
normative ethics 99, 113
normative inference 63
normative principles 440, 442
normative vocabularies 13–14
Nowell-Smith, Patrick 346, 615

objectivity 18–26, 61, 131, 182
  intersubjectivity and 24
  of moral principles 82
"Objectivity, Intersubjectivity and the Moral
  Point of View" (Sellars) ix, 10–11, 17–26,
  68–69, 138–87
obligation
  actions and 149
  conditional 39–40, 43
  grounds and 527
  inclination and 611
  intuitionism and 587
  motivation and 571
  "ought" and 78–79, 367
  political 130
  prima-facie 367
  universality and 611
"Obligation and Motivation" (Sellars) 14–15, 19,
  22, 36–37, 43–44, 46, 49, 73–79, 655
"Obligation, Intersubjectivity and the Moral
  Point of View" (Sellars) ix

"On Accepting First Principles" (Sellars) 18
"On Knowing Better and Doing the Worse"
  (Sellars) 35–36, 43–44, 70, 351–64
"On Reasoning about Values" (Sellars) xi–xii,
  20–21, 23, 25, 40–41, 44, 54, 66–67, 465–510
O'Shea, James 1
"ought," 66
  action and 45
  of coherence 16, 90–91
  commands and 373
  conduct and 571
  contradiction of 409
  egoism and 22
  emotivism and 579–80
  entailing imperatives 338–40, 593
  everybody 15
  expressivism and 17
  good and 490
  hypothetical imperative and 166–67
  I 15
  as imperative 340, 591–93
  imperatives and 371, 373, 574, 581–83
  imperatives *vs.* 124, 589–90
  inference and 44–45, 632
  intention and 113, 171, 389, 654
  intersubjectivity and 19–20, 24, 151, 412–13
  "is" and 13, 62
  I *vs.* everybody 76–77
  logic of 367–420, 634
  moral judgments and 15
  moral principles and 15–16
  motivation and 77, 345, 368
  negation of 406, 412
  obligation and 78–79, 367
  as prescriptive sentence 579–81, 591
  "shall" and 19, 22, 36, 66
  "shall" *vs.* 148, 196
  singular 46
  to-be 453
  to-do 453
  truth and falsity of 150
  values and 87
  "want" *vs.* 73
"'Ought' and Moral Principles" (Sellars) 15–17,
  43–44, 80–96

Paradox of the Gentle Murder 38
paragraph referencing x
"Paralogisms of Pure Reason" (Kant) 220
Peano's postulates 144
Pears, David 615
Peirce, Charles S. 25–26, 139
Pepper, Stephen C. 293
performance of promising 637

personhood 27–29
"Phenomenalism" (Sellars) 28
Philebus (Plato) 133–34
philosophical behaviorism 13, 64–65, 71
"Philosophy and the Scientific Image of Man" (Sellars) 31
placement problems 11
Plato 17–18, 22, 25–26, 35, 88–90, 116–37, 164–65, 357–60, 538–39
pleasure 134–35
PMese 13, 64–65, 71, 223
Poincaré, Henri 654
political obligation 130
practical reason 2–3
  conjunction introduction and 481
  defined 191
  hypothetical imperatives and 655
  imperatives in 192
  intention in 30, 36–44, 141–43, 216, 279, 547
  intersubjectivity and 8, 23, 139
  logic of 511, 547
  nomologicals and 19
  Plato and 17–18
  practice and 139
  as reason 147
  self-love and 35, 537–41
  "shall" and 210, 285
  values and 138
  volitions and 139–40, 299
  we-intentions and 10
"Practical Reason" (Jackson) 634
"Practical Reasoning" (Sellars) 43–44, 537–69
"Practical Reasoning Again" (Sellars) 42, 44–45, 542–69
practical syllogism 210–19
predetermination 327
predictability 294, 296, 298, 328
preference 197–200, 543–44, 554
prescriptives 579–81, 591
  motivation *vs.* 45
  primary 46
presupposing 370
Prichard, Harold Arthur 6, 70, 164, 368
Principia Ethica (Moore) 203
Principia Mathematica (Whitehead and Russell) 64, 223
principle of conditional promise 514
principle of exportation. *See* exportation, principle of
principles, acting on 37. *See also* moral principles
promising 372, 377, 419, 514, 521–22, 611, 637
propositional logic 52, 422, 533
Protagoras 131–33

psychology
  empirical 577–78
  moral 26–31
  philosophical 3–4
  rational 245
punctuation x

"queerness objection," 14
quotation marks x

Ranaee, Mahdi 1
rational discipline 17
rational egoism 21–22, 40, 496, 506–7
rationalism 17
rationality 10
rational psychology 245
reasonableness 8–9, 21–24, 51–52, 168–75, 177–78, 490–96, 505–10, 651–52, 657
"Reason and the Art of Living in Plato" (Sellars) xi, 17–18, 35, 116–37
reasoning. *See also* practical reason; theoretical reason
  among intentions 40, 49
  instrumentalities and 18
  motivation and 344
  in Plato 116–37
  promising and 377
  resolutive 63, 552, 640, 645
  values and 40–41
  we 16
reasons
  justifying 35
  motivating 35
  motivation and 344
reconciliationist compatibilism 31
reducibility 12–14, 61, 63, 66
"Reflections on Contrary-to-Duty Imperatives" (Sellars) xi, 38–40, 421–64
relative implication 53–54, 680, 682, 689, 696, 713–14, 717, 728
relative necessity 308, 664–65
"Reply to Alan Donagan" (Sellars) 10, 32–34, 319–50
reporting 47, 113. *See also* autobiographical reports; self-ascriptions
Republic (Plato) 116, 119, 132–34, 137, 539
resolutive inference 63, 637
resolutive reason 63, 552, 640, 645
resolutives 347, 609
Right and the Good, The (Ross) 367–68
Ross, W. D. 36, 66, 367–68
Royce, Josiah 10, 96

sameness 222
Scharp, Kevin 1–2

744 INDEX

Science, Perception, and Reality (Sellars) 347
"Science and Ethics" (Sellars) 10, 16–17, 97–115
Science and Metaphysics: Variations on Kantian Themes (Sellars) 1–2, 19, 138, 681
scientific behaviorism 13, 16–17, 65, 67–68, 70–71
scientific determinism 295–96, 321–22, 325–26
scientific knowledge, moral principles and 80–96, 100
second nature 297
Seiberth, Luz Christopher 1
self-ascriptions 84, 147
self-interest 16, 88, 93, 115
self-love 35, 43–44, 115, 417, 496, 509, 537–41
"Semantical Solution of the Mind-Body Problem" (Sellars) 13–14
sense identity 12
"shall"
  about to *vs.* 624
  conflicting 409
  conjunction introduction and 44
  egocentricity of 150
  external negation of 148
  implications of 475, 533
  indicatives and 381
  intention and 4, 36, 65, 142–43, 153, 192, 521
  linguistic role of 26–27
  logic of 634
  negation of 406
  "ought" and 19, 22, 36, 66
  "ought" *vs.* 148, 196
  in practical reasoning 210, 285
  preference and 197
  statement requirements 22
  truth or falsity with 149
  "will" *vs.* 471
  "would" into 163
"shall be," 4, 23, 31, 486, 505
Sicha, Jeffrey x
Sidgwick, Henry 325, 327–29
S-Imp 66
sincerity 582
Singer, Marcus 167
Smart, J. J. C. ix
so-be-it principle 524, 543–44, 547–49, 553, 556
social practice 3
Solomon, David 54–55
Solomon, W. David 732–36
Sophists 122–23, 131–32, 538
"Sovereign Reason" (Nagel) 248
Spinoza, Baruch 339–40, 538
Steinbeck, John 3
Stevenson, C. L. 274
Structure of Morality, The (Castañeda) 49–50

sub specie 184, 482, 484, 501, 503, 510, 529–30, 534, 569
  actionis 556
  communitatis 11, 218
  individualitatis 218
swarms 28
symbol game 343
systematicity 62

Taylor, Charles 664–65
Taylor, Richard 32, 236–37, 240–41
"that," 226
"that" clauses 30
theoretical reason
  deductive logic and 138
  goodness of arguments in 170
  implication and 679
  intersubjectivity and 175
  validity in 170
thinking-out-loud 299–302, 305
Thomson, Judith Jarvis ix, 41–42
"Thought and Action" (Sellars) 11, 26–27, 43, 191–219
thought expression 302
Timaeus (Plato) 126
time 222–25
transitions, language 29
tryings 140, 271, 303
typesetting errors xi–xii

universality 370–418, 611
universalizability 627
universalization 48–49, 615
utilitarianism 168, 358

values
  facts *vs.* 468
  in "On Reasoning About Values," 465–510
  practical reason and 138
  reasoning and 40–41
valuings 16, 82–85, 88–89, 91–95, 161–63, 178–80
verbal behaviorism 255, 257, 262
vindicatory explanation 17
virtue, knowledge and 357–59
volitions 6, 241, 299–305
  actions and 140, 193, 240, 272
  causation and 338, 344–46
  decisions *vs.* 140
  deducibility of 331–32
  as intentions 276–77
  intentions and 27–29, 141
  practical reason and 139–40, 299
  as thoughts 299
  tryings *vs.* 271, 303

"Volitions Re-Affirmed" (Sellars) 26, 30–31, 44, 270–89, 523
voluntary action 306–7

Wang, Hao 621
"want," "ought" vs. 73
we-consciousness 413
we-intentions 7–8, 10
we-reasoning 16

Wiggins, David 17
Wilfrid Sellars (deVries) 2
Wilfrid Sellars: Naturalism with a Normative Turn (O'Shea) 1
Williams, Bernard 621
willing to do 316
Wisdom, John 307
Wittgenstein, Ludwig 255, 621
"would," 160–61, 163